REVISION SYMBOLS

ab	Faulty abbreviation	27b
adj	Adjective forms	8c
adv	Adverb forms	9d
agr	Agreement	10
amb	Ambiguous reference	11a, 11c
awk (k)	Awkward sentence	15
ca	Case	8b, 11a
cap	Capitals	27a
coh	Coherence	5c
coord	Coordination	12d
cs	Comma splice	17a
d	Diction	29b, 30
dm	Dangling modifier	20e
doc	Documentation	41
emp	Emphasis misplaced	12c
frag	Fragment	16
fs	Fused (run-on) sentence	17b
gl/gr	Glossary of Grammatical Terms	p.G-21
gl/u	Glossary of Common Usage	p.G-1
gr	Obvious grammatical error	10, 11, 16–20
inc	Incomplete construction	18b, 18c
ital	Italics	26d
jarg	Jargon	30d
lc	Lowercase	27a
log	Logic	34, 35, 37
mixed	Mixed construction	19
mm	Misplaced modifier	20
ms	Manuscript form	47
n	Numbers	27c
om	Omitted words	18b
p	Obvious punctuation error	21–26
pass	Passive voice ineffective	12e

pl	Pronoun	8b, 11
pron	Pronoun	8b, 11
ref	Pronoun reference	11
rep	Repetition	15b
rev	Revision needed	4b
sexist	Sexist language	30e
shift	Needless shift	18a
sing	Singular needed	8a, 8b
sl	Slang	30c
sp	Spelling	28
st	Sentence structure	7, 12–15
str	Stringy sentence	17c
sub	Subordination	12c, 15a
t	Tense	9a, 18a
trans	Transition	5c
unity	Unity	3d, 5c
var	Variety in sentence structure	13
vb	Verb form	9a, 9b
w	Wordiness	15
ww	Wrong word	28b, pp.G-1–G-20
ˇ	Apostrophe	24
︰	Colon	23b
⌃	Comma	22
. . .	Ellipsis	26c
!	Exclamation point	21b
- — ( ) [ ] /	Hyphen, Dash, Parentheses, Brackets, Slash	25
⊙	Period	21b
" "	Quotation marks	26b
⌃	Semicolon	23a
¶	Paragraph needed	5a
No ¶	No Paragraph	
//	Parallelism	14a, 14b
x	Obvious mistake	
∧	Obvious omission	
#	Space needed	
℘	Delete	
?	Unclear	
∼	Transpose	

THE MACMILLAN COLLEGE HANDBOOK

THE
MACMILLAN
COLLEGE
HANDBOOK

Second Edition

Gerald Levin

Professor Emeritus, University of Akron

Macmillan Publishing Company
New York

Collier Macmillan Canada
Toronto

Editor: Eben W. Ludlow
Development Editor: Sharon Balbos
Production Supervisor: Linda Greenberg
Production Manager: Valerie A. Sawyer
Text and Cover Designer: Eileen Burke

This book was set in 10/11 New Aster by Waldman Graphics, Inc., and printed and bound by Arcata Graphics/Fairfield. The cover was printed by The Lehigh Press, Inc.

Acknowledgments appear on pages A-1 and A-2, which serve as an extension of the copyright page.

Macmillan Publishing Company
866 Third Avenue, New York, New York 10022

Collier Macmillan Canada, Inc.
1200 Eglinton Avenue East, Suite 200
Don Mills, Ontario, M3C 3N1

Library of Congress Cataloging-in-Publication Data

Levin, Gerald Henry, 1929–
    The Macmillan college handbook / Gerald Levin.—2nd ed.
        p.   cm.
    Includes index.
    ISBN 0-02-370231-1
    1. English language—Rhetoric—Handbooks, manuals, etc.
    2. English language—Grammar—1950— —Handbooks, manuals, etc.
    I. Title.
    PE 1408.L4133   1991
    808'.042—dc20   90-36315
                              CIP

Printing: 1 2 3 4 5 6 7   Year: 1 2 3 4 5 6 7

PREFACE

□

□

The Macmillan College Handbook, Second Edition, has been designed to serve as an accessible and comprehensive reference guide and as an effective teaching text. The handbook includes a thorough and practical discussion of rhetoric, grammar, and the logic of the essay. The handbook offers full explanation of *how* to write, and provides unusually detailed discussion of choices open to the writer. Thus students can use this handbook to increase their understanding of various aspects of writing rather than merely to acquire a set of rules and principles. In this second edition, we retained the features that have successfully set this handbook apart—the comprehensive coverage of rhetoric and grammar and the extensive treatment of sound reasoning. But we have also made some substantial revisions to enhance the overall content and accessibility of the handbook for you and your students.

The changes in the second edition include:

- **Expanded discussion of the writing process** with more extensive coverage of planning, drafting, revising, and editing.
- **Two new chapters on writing in several fields,** including writing in the humanities, social sciences, natural sciences, and applied sciences—with sample student papers.

- Discussion of ways to **avoid sexist language.**
- **Five full chapters on writing the research paper,** including coverage of **MLA and APA documentation styles,** new coverage of **CBE documentation style,** and a **newly annotated MLA sample research paper.**
- New and useful in-chapter screened **checklists** that provide a quick review of crucial information.
- A **new chapter on writing with a word processor** that stresses the value of the word processor in drafting and revising.
- A new chapter on vocabulary enrichment.

The second edition also retains unique end-of-chapter **summaries** that act as a **"handbook-within-a-handbook"** by providing students with the opportunity to review the main points of each chapter.

Approach

The Macmillan College Handbook **treats writing as a continuous act of planning, drafting, revising, and editing.** The steps of the writing process are explored in Chapters 1–4; however, the handbook does not treat the topic in a reductive or prescriptive manner. Instead, this handbook encourages student writers to make *choices* based on appropriateness to the writing situation; thus the writing process is shown to be a recursive series of writing acts that vary with the type of writing the student does. Few if any practiced writers proceed in the same way in every writing situation. Some writers use the traditional topic or sentence outline in preparing to write the essay or later in revising it; others benefit from freewriting and the other techniques of invention described in Chapter 2, sometimes drawing on these in successive drafts of the paper. Some writers revise extensively and edit in the course of writing the first and later drafts; others revise and edit only after producing a full draft. *The Macmillan College Handbook* thus does not insist on a single approach or suggest that all successful writers follow identical procedures.

The Macmillan College Handbook also seeks to increase the student's skill in writing paragraphs and widen the student's repertory of styles and inventive skills. To achieve this aim, the book teaches by example, illustrating the styles of standard written English through numerous sentences and paragraphs from contemporary writers in various fields and several student essays typical of those written in college courses. This book assumes that we do not learn to write effective sentences, paragraphs, and essays only by experimentation and constant writing, though these activities are essential. We learn to write as we learn to speak—by hearing and reading sentences—and we discover ways of improving our writing in the same way. Both the unpracticed and the practiced writer need models of effective sentences, paragraphs, and essays. Writing models, indeed, are indispensable. **This handbook includes numerous professional models from a wide range of contemporary writers,** many of whom have influenced contemporary prose style. It also includes **seven samples of successful student essays.** Admittedly, a handbook alone cannot turn the student into an active reader or a better one. But it should encourage the student to make reading and writing integral activities, as in fact they must be in most academic work.

As a basic grammar and correction guide, this handbook emphasizes effective writing. It includes a review of parts of speech and their function in the sentence; the parts of the sentence; full instruction on difficult matters of sentence construction; and rules and current conventions of punctuation in standard written English. But unlike handbooks that merely state rules and principles, *The Macmillan College Handbook* does more: grammar problems that prove most troubling to students (fused sentences, fragments, comma splices, etc.) receive full attention, but the book does not restrict itself to these problems. It discusses *why* sentences are effective or ineffective and gives a full explanation of *how* to build sentences and correct them.

The elements of reasoning have an important role in student writing. **This text devotes an entire part—four full chapters—to sound reasoning.** The handbook contains a full discussion of inductive and deductive reasoning, persuasive argument, and logical fallacies. The discussion of persuasive writing draws on traditional methods of analysis as well as on Toulmin's distinctions between warrants, claims, and backing. Toulminian argumentation is presented, not as a substitute for traditional deductive procedures, but as a highly useful way of stating and defending premises. A student's persuasive essay is included to illustrate the concepts covered here.

The Plan of the Handbook

The Macmillan College Handbook is organized into eleven parts and two glossaries. Although chapters may be assigned in any order that suits your needs, they can be assigned and discussed sequentially.

Part One discusses the writing of the whole paper, including ways of finding and analyzing a subject—illustrated through the development of one student's expressive essay from the initial choice of subject through successive revisions and final editing. Part Two shows how to organize and develop paragraphs. Part Three contains a description of the sentence and its parts, followed by a systematic description of the traditional parts of speech and a thorough discussion of agreement and pronoun case and reference. In this way, matters of grammar are presented as knowledge necessary in writing effective sentences—the subject of Part Four.

By demonstrating ways to vary sentences, make them clear and concise, and give ideas proper emphasis, Part Four prepares for the discussion of sentence correction in Part Five. Topics covered in Part Five include sentence fragments, comma splices, fused sentences, mixed constructions, misplaced modifiers, and shifts and omissions. Part Six opens with chapters on punctuation—the uses of the comma, the semicolon, the colon, the apostrophe, and other punctuation marks. The concluding chapters discuss capitalization, abbreviations, numbers, and the rules of spelling. Like the earlier chapters on sentence effectiveness, these chapters stress choices in punctuation open to the writer.

Turning in Part Seven to matters of diction, the handbook discusses standard English as a dialect; abstract and concrete, general and specific words, slang, and jargon; uses of the dictionary; and uses of figurative language. Part Seven also includes a new chapter on building a vocabulary. Part Eight returns to the whole essay: four chapters are devoted to the forms of argument, the persuasive essay, and the reasoning it employs and should avoid. The four chapters of Part Nine describe in detail research techniques and the writing of the documented paper—finding and interpreting evidence, organizing and documenting the research paper according to the new MLA citation method, the use of footnotes and endnotes, and APA and CBE documentation styles. Part Ten discusses writing in special fields, including the humanities, social sciences, and natural sciences. Later chapters in this part provide specific instruction on writing course notes, examination answers, business letters, resumes, and memorandums. The chapters in Part Eleven summarize the formatting of student papers and discuss the uses of the word processor in writing papers. The text concludes with glossaries of usage and grammatical terms that provide additional help with diction and grammar. Charts on the inside front and back covers of the book provide a plan of the book, revision symbols, and a guide to topics of major concern in revising and editing papers.

Accompanying Materials

A newly expanded, complete package of supplements for instructors and students accompanies *The Macmillan College Handbook.*

- A new and uniquely comprehensive **Instructor's Annotated Edition** contains suggestions for teaching with the handbook, references to articles and books on particular topics, alternate writing assignments, and suggested answers to most of the exercises.
- **The Macmillan Guide for Teachers of Writing** by Maggy Smith, director of English Education, University of Texas at El Paso, contains useful material for teaching assistants, including detailed discussions of composition theory and teaching methods.
- **The Macmillan College Workbook**, Second Edition, by Alice MacDonald, University of Akron, offers students an opportunity to increase mastery of basic skills through varied and interesting exercises and self-tests. Although the workbook parallels the organization of the handbook and uses its definitions, it is a self-contained text appropriate for use independent of the handbook. An *Answer Key* accompanies *The Macmillan College Workbook*.
- By special arrangement with Conduit Educational Software, **Writer's Helper: Prewriting and Revising Software** by William Wresch, University of Wisconsin, Stevens Point, is available with *The Macmillan College Handbook* in student and instructor versions for the IBM and Macintosh. Further information on this award-winning software and other supplements may be obtained from your Macmillan representative.
- The **Test Bank** contains two parallel sets of diagnostic tests keyed to specific sections of the handbook, and is available in a printed form and as *Microtest® Test Preparation System* software for IBM and Macintosh computers.
- **Transparency Masters** consisting of writing samples and revisions, charts, and other valuable information draw from and supplement the handbook for classroom use.
- An **Instructor's Correction Chart** replicates the front and back inside covers of the handbook—with revision symbols—for convenient reference.

- *Study Guides* have been prepared for the **CLAST** exam in Florida and the **TASP** exam in Texas.

Acknowledgments

I wish to acknowledge advice on the first edition and suggested examples given by colleagues at the University of Akron. I owe a particular debt to William Francis, Bruce Holland, Robert Holland, Martin McKoski, Kenneth Pakenham, Sally Slocum, and Linda Weiner. Alice MacDonald gave invaluable criticism of the whole manuscript and again advised me on the chapter on business writing. I am grateful to Steven Carroll and other University of Akron students for their interest and cooperation. I owe special thanks to Glenn Grube, a student at Trinity College, Hartford, Connecticut, for the essay in Chapter 4 and the paper on Emily Dickinson in Chapter 43. I owe thanks also to Patricia Skovran, whose comments on Glenn Grube's essay about the Division of Motor Vehicles are the basis of questions and comments in Chapter 4. I express thanks also to Barbara Bailey, Welles-Turner Memorial Library, Glastonbury, Connecticut, for help in securing reference materials, and to Lynne M. Olver of the Online Research Services, West Hartford, Connecticut Public Library, for help in updating the documented paper on cholera in Chapter 42.

I wish to thank the following reviewers who added to the book immeasurably through their criticism of one or more drafts: Joe Benson, North Carolina Agricultural and Technical State University; Barbara Carr, Stephen F. Austin State University; Mark Coleman, SUNY College at Potsdam; Carol David, Iowa State University; Joyce R. Durham, University of Dayton; Thomas E. Gaston, Purdue University; Opal W. Hawkins, North Carolina Agricultural and Technical State University; Alice MacDonald, The University of Akron; Ellen McManus, University of Illinois at Chicago; Robert G. Noreen, California State University, Northridge; William Peirce, Prince George's Community College; Delma M. Porter, Texas A&M University; Kenneth Risdon, University of Minnesota, Duluth; Barbara R. Sloan, Santa Fe Community College; Maggy Smith, University of Texas at El Paso; John W. Taylor, South Dakota State University; and Sally T. Taylor, Brigham Young University.

I wish also to acknowledge the following writers and texts from whom I have learned much about English grammar, logic, and rhetorical theory over many years:

Cohen, Morris R., and Ernest Nagel. *An Introduction to Logic and Scientific Method.* New York: Harcourt, 1934.

Copi, I. M., and C. Cohen. *Introduction to Logic.* 8th ed. New York: Macmillan, 1990.

Corbett, Edward P. J. *Classical Rhetoric for the Modern Student.* 2nd ed. New York: Oxford UP, 1971.

Kinneavy, James L. *A Theory of Discourse.* Englewood Cliffs, NJ: Prentice-Hall, 1971.

Kolln, Martha. *Understanding English Grammar.* 3rd ed. New York: Macmillan, 1990.

Quirk, Randolph; Sidney Greenbaum; Geoffrey Leech; and Jan Svartik. *A Grammar of Contemporary English.* New York: Seminar Press, 1972.

Sledd, James. *A Short Introduction to English Grammar.* Chicago: Scott, Foresman, 1959.

Toulmin, Stephen. *The Uses of Argument.* Cambridge, Eng.: Cambridge UP, 1958.

I also wish to thank the following people at Macmillan: the development editor, Sharon Balbos, for her detailed comments on all aspects of the handbook; the production editor, Linda Greenberg, for her consideration and care in guiding the manuscript to book form; the production manager, Valerie Sawyer, for her contributions to the manufacturing process; the copyeditor, Wendy Polhemus-Annibell, for her painstaking editing and unerring sense of style; the designer, Eileen Burke, for the imaginative design and improved readability of the text; and the executive editor, Eben W. Ludlow, for suggesting this book, and for his reliable judgment and advice. I also could not have written this book without the strong support and help of my wife, Lillian Levin. Finally, Christopher and Daniel Rubin and Matthew Ziegler were always in mind.

G.L.

TO
THE
STUDENT

Using This Handbook

Once you are familiar with the plan of this book, you will develop your own ways of using it. Note that many of the topics discussed in separate chapters are closely related. Thus, knowing how to use the comma depends on knowing how to use the semicolon and colon; knowing how to place clauses to prevent misreading depends on knowing how to place words and phrases in the most effective order in the sentence. You will find it useful to consult both discussions. Extensive cross-references direct you to related topics. You also may want to keep a log of sections you consult often, and a list of ideas and examples you turn to frequently. These are but a few ways you can utilize this handbook to serve your needs as a writer. Also, be aware of the following features, which will enable you to locate information quickly:

- Top of page **tabs** contain section numbers and symbols that correspond to the material under discussion on specific pages.
- The **brief contents** on the inside back cover, the detailed table of contents at the start of the handbook, and the detailed index are excellent means of locating topics.

- **End-of-chapter summaries** act as chapters in miniature and offer you the opportunity to review an entire chapter's contents at a glance.
- In-chapter **checklists** on important topics offer you quick summaries. These checklists are screened in blue and are easy to spot. They are also listed in the table of contents.
- The inside front cover contains a listing of **"Sections Consulted Often"** for your reference and **"Revision Symbols"** that your instructor may use in correcting your papers.

CONTENTS

Contents

Contents

Contents

Contents

Contents

Contents

Contents

Contents

PART ONE

WRITING ESSAYS

Purpose and Audience 1

Purpose and audience are essential considerations in writing a paper. Writing a set of instructions for a beginner on the use of a power saw and writing a research paper on various methods of timber cutting require different decisions. So does a persuasive essay on the issue of deforestation. Purpose and audience in each instance determine the kind and amount of detail you should give in the paper.

In this first chapter, we explore the roles that purpose and audience play in writing papers. The remaining chapters in Part One discuss the stages of the writing process—from the initial planning and drafting of the paper, to its revision in additional drafts, and the final editing and proofreading. Chapter 4 traces these stages through a student paper similar to the type you may be asked to write for a college composition course.

1a Purposes in writing

Decisions on how to organize and what to include in an essay depend on your **purpose** or aim as well as on your audience—the readers you have chosen to address. A piece of writing may satisfy a variety of purposes. These fall into four main groups:

- **Expressive writing** aims to state or express one's feelings and beliefs.
- **Informative** or **expository writing** is used to give information.
- **Persuasive writing** aims to convince.
- **Literary writing** seeks to delight or create pleasure.

Following are examples of each purpose:

General Purposes	Specific Examples
- *Expressing feelings and beliefs*	Stating a personal, religious, or political credo
- *Giving information*	
Revealing one's history, interests, and character	Stating one's personal history in a job application
Exploring the natural world	Exploring the Rockies on a backpacking trip
Exploring the human world	Describing the difficulties of being a working mother
	Recalling a friendship
Giving directions	Explaining how to write with a word processor
Giving advice	Suggesting how to behave at a job interview
Analyzing a problem	Defining drug addiction, comparing and contrasting various kinds of addiction, analyzing causes, predicting effects
Considering solutions	Presenting solutions to drug addiction
Reporting research	Interpreting studies of drug addiction
Evaluating	Evaluating solutions and research

3

- *Persuading*

Generalizing from observations and experiments	Describing the general effect of nitric acid on a series of metals
Drawing inferences from established truths	Arguing that the First Amendment guarantees the news media certain rights
Urging someone to accept a truth or belief	Defending or attacking the right to own an assault rifle
Urging readers to take action	Urging support for or opposition to a bill banning assault rifles
Making a request	Asking an insurance company to renew a policy

- *Giving pleasure*

	Narrating an exciting sports event
	Describing a California beach

A piece of writing usually has more than one aim. In the course of expressing your feelings or beliefs, for example, you may also need to give your readers information about the experience that prompted you to write. In protesting a policy, you are expressing your feelings about it, giving information about the policy, and trying to convince your readers to support your position. Often you can identify one of these purposes as your primary or main one, in which case you refer to the piece of writing as expressive, informative or expository, persuasive, or literary. This handbook is concerned with the first three types of writing. These are types that you will encounter most in your college courses. Let us consider each aim or purpose in detail, showing how all three join in particular writing situations.

1 Expressing feelings and beliefs

Many of your statements merely express a personal feeling or attitude—like the exclamation "Wow!" that expresses joy or amazement over an unexpected happening. **Expressive writing** conveys emotions generated by friendships, sports, books and films, travel, experiences in the world of nature, observations, personal achievements. The novelist and essayist Virginia Woolf expresses her feelings about a London street observed in springtime:

London is enchanting. I step out upon a tawny colored magic carpet, it seems, and get carried into beauty without raising a finger. The nights are amazing, with all the white porticos and broad silent avenues. And people pop in and out, lightly, divertingly, like rabbits; and I look down Southampton Row, wet as a seal's back or red and yellow with sunshine, and watch the omnibuses going and coming and hear the old crazy organs.

—*The Diary of Virginia Woolf*, May 26, 1924

Personal essays also express the writer's own religious credo or beliefs. The purpose of the following writer is to testify to the values he lives by—not to encourage others to change their opinions or character, though he would admire them for doing so:

The people I admire most are those who are sensitive and want to create something or discover something, and do not see life in terms of power, and such people get more of a chance under a democracy than elsewhere.

—E. M. Forster, "What I Believe"

In contrast, political manifestos and protests like the *Declaration of Independence* usually express anger or some other feeling, at the same time seeking to correct a wrong.

If the purpose of your writing is unclear, your reader will be unsure how to respond. If your aim is to express your feelings about a situation or to protest a wrong, convey your feelings clearly and directly, as E. M. Forster does. If your aim is expository, be specific about why you are giving the information. If your aim is to convince your readers to change their attitude or to take some action, state what is wrong and what should be done to correct the wrong. However, you need not state your purpose directly ("My purpose in writing is to . . ."). Readers will discover your purpose in how you present and develop the subject of your paper.

2 Giving information

Informative or **expository writing** takes many forms. Your purpose may be to share an experience or perhaps a discovery about a person, place, or the world of nature. In giving information, you are satisfying the curiosity of your readers and inviting them to share the pleasure of your discovery. Lists, explanations, reports, encyclopedia articles, and the like also give information. In addition, informative writing some-

5

times evaluates or makes judgments and argues a thesis or proposition.

The amount of detail you should provide depends on the purpose of your explanation. The report of a scientific experiment or a technical process gives as complete an account as possible so that others can test your findings. A set of directions or a description of a process must also be complete if the reader is to perform it. If, as in the following paragraph on opening a beehive, the writer is describing the process to make a point, the explanation may be a general one:

> The first thing to do in a beeyard after zipping oneself into a bee suit is to take the bee smoker from its metal carrying can and light it. A bee smoker is a cylindrical firebox, compact enough to hold easily in one hand, with a small bellows attached to its edge and a hinged, cone-shaped top with a hole in it. Fuel is put in through the top opening, and the air is forced across it after it is lighted and smoldering by squeezing the bellows. This directs the smoke out of the hole in the top in puffs that will quiet the bees. The smoke makes them act as if their hives were on fire: they forget about tending their home and prepare to abandon it by filling themselves with honey; when their bodies are filled, it is difficult for the bees to bend themselves into a stinging posture.
>
> —Sue Hubbell, *A Book of Bees*

Hubbell is informing her reader about her experiences as a beekeeper; she also is writing to encourage the reader to keep bees. She provides sufficient detail to realize her purpose. As in all writing, one's purpose guides the choice of words and sentence structure as well as the amount of the detail and organization. Hubbell uses nontechnical language in her exposition; she defines each word and relates it to the process described. She also presents the steps **chronologically**—the usual order in giving directions and tracing a process. An explanation departs from chronological order for special reasons. A memo to automobile mechanics describes, chronologically, the installation of a newly designed part; but since the mechanics are familiar with the general process, the memo focuses on new steps or procedures that require special attention.

Not all informative or expository essays are concerned with giving directions; not all are chronologically arranged. Census reports and encyclopedia articles have no special reason to be chronological. Much informative writing examines problems and solutions from various perspectives. You may write informative essays that give a precise definition of an idea on the basis of new observations and experiments. You may on occasion show that an idea is the outcome of other ideas, or that an idea is supported by particulars of experience, as in a lab report that generalizes from an experiment you performed. These informational kinds of argument may be used persuasively. You may also synthesize various theories and findings before evaluating them and perhaps draw further conclusions.

Informative writing is the basis of many college writing assignments. You will write useful and interesting informative essays if you keep the following points in mind.

A mere outlining of the subject will not achieve your purpose in giving information. The reader at best will have a vague idea of what you saw but not what you experienced and felt. The following writer gives us the details we need to share his experience in the Arizona desert:

> Walking back to the highway, I saw a coil of sand loosen and bend itself into a grainy S and warp across the slope. I stood dead still. A sidewinder so matched to the grit only its undulating shadow gave it away. And that's something else about the desert: deception. It can make heat look like water, living plants seem dead, mountains miles away appear close, and turn scaly tubes of venom into ropes of warm sand. So open, so concealed.
> —William Least Heat Moon, *Blue Highways*

Too much detail will blur the explanation and confuse your readers. Include background information and details on related points only if they are relevant to the experience or the process you are describing. In deciding what to include, put yourself in the place of your readers and consider their response.

In the course of reporting what you saw and experienced, show your readers how you reached insight and understanding. In showing them, you need not talk about yourself, but you do need to give the details that captured your attention. You need also to present details in an organized way, keeping distinct each of the devices or techniques you use to convey the experience and your ideas about it. If you use narrative, description, and analysis of some kind (e.g., definition, classification, comparison and contrast) you need to keep each aspect of the discussion separate and distinct. Your reader should be aware of your purpose at each stage of the essay or discourse.

3 Persuading

The purpose of **persuasive writing** is to *convince*. When writing a persuasive essay, you are encouraging your readers to change their thinking or beliefs or to take action. You are doing more, then, than stating arguments or giving reasons. Consider the following statements asking for payment of a bill:

> I will appreciate your paying this bill as soon as possible.
> Please remit payment on receipt of this bill.
> Pay up or else!

These persuasive statements seek to convince in different ways. The first two statements are disguised commands, and the third statement is threatening. The person asking for payment has the choice of persuading by making a polite request or by commanding or threatening. This person also has the choice of providing reasons why the bill should be paid (e.g., responsible people pay their bills on time, irresponsible people lose their credit) or giving none.

Since the purpose of persuasive writing is to convince, you want to gauge the character of your audience in shaping the argument or answering opponents. In an essay on animal rights, the columnist Meg Greenfield tells us that, though she is not in favor of ending the use of animals in laboratory experiments, she is in favor of ending "wanton, pointless cruelty" in research, training, and food production. Greenfield recognizes that a segment of her audience considers supporters of animal rights to be zealots. Addressing this concern, she discusses "vivid, cringe-inducing" photographs that have been criticized as fanatical. Greenfield agrees the photographs are powerful but admits they have influenced her thinking on the issue. "Eventually they get your attention," she writes. "And eventually you at least feel obliged to weigh their arguments and think about whether there may not be something there."

Persuasive arguments often answer objections and present counterarguments. Greenfield does this in defending the photographs that led her to consider old prejudices:

> The objection to our being confronted with these dramatic, disturbing pictures is first that they tend to provoke a misplaced, uncritical and highly emotional concern for animal life at the

direct expense of a more suitable concern for human suffering. What goes into the animals' account, the reasoning goes, necessarily comes out of ours. But I think it is possible to remain stalwart in your view that the human claim comes first and in your acceptance of the use of animals for human betterment and *still* to believe that there are some human interests that should not take precedence. For we have become far too self-indulgent, hardened, careless and cruel in the pain we routinely inflict upon these creatures for the most frivolous, unworthy purposes. And I also think that the more justifiable purposes, such as medical research, are shamelessly used as cover for other activities that are wanton.

—"In Defense of the Animals," *Newsweek,* April 17, 1989

Greenfield's paragraph is persuasive in another way. Persuasive writing often seeks a common ground or understanding between opponents in a debate. Greenfield is seeking to reconcile the conflicting views of an audience that holds different opinions on the use of animals in laboratory experiments. Greenfield's image of her audience guides her decisions—in organization, strategy, sentence structure, diction, and other features that determine how her essay is understood and received.

EXERCISES

1. Rewrite the following messages as requests, commands, and threats, and be ready to discuss the differences in wording.
   a. Everyone should have handed in the paper by Monday.
   b. We need volunteers for the cookie sale.
   c. Your club dues are two months overdue.
   d. Papers free of spelling errors will receive special consideration.
2. What is the chief purpose of each of the following statements or paragraphs? Be ready to discuss any subordinate aims or purposes as well.

   a. All rights reserved including the right of reproduction in whole or in part in any form.
      —Statement on the copyright page of a book

   b. I have faith that for every piece of information there is someone somewhere who wishes to receive it. In that spirit I am putting down a few notes on the topic, "How to raise a woodchuck." Admittedly this is not a problem on everyone's mind; but if you live in woodchuck country, which in the East is almost anywhere, it is possible you will find yourself holding a baby woodchuck and wondering what to do with it.

—Faith McNulty, "How to Raise a Woodchuck"

c. During two decades of work among blacks and Spanish-speaking Americans of the Southwest (in the Rio Grande Valley they often prefer to be called Chicanos, but up in the hills of New Mexico some shun that word in favor of Hispanic-Americans), and among Pueblo and Hopi Indians, as well as some Athabaskan Indians in Alaska, I have tried to gain some sense of how words such as "race," "ethnic heritage," and "class," not to mention "history" itself, become for particular children moments—and longer—of self-observation, reflection, hopeful anticipation, or sheer dread.

—Robert Coles, "Minority Dreams, American Dreams," *Daedalus*, Spring 1981 ∎

Checklist: Purposes in Writing

1. What is my purpose in writing? Do I wish to express my feelings and beliefs? Am I writing to declare my position on an issue or to protest a practice, policy, attitude, or idea?
2. Is my purpose to explore an aspect of the world, perhaps through an experience or observation of my own? Do I want to explore a problem by analyzing it and considering solutions to it? Do I want to propose my own solution to the problem?
3. Do I want to give information about a person, place, or object? How do I want my readers to use this information?
4. Is my purpose also persuasive? Do I wish to change my readers' opinions and attitudes? Do I want my readers to take some action?
5. Do I want to achieve more than one purpose in writing? Do I want to give information about a situation, express my feelings and beliefs about it, *and* persuade my readers to accept and act on them?
6. How much detail do I need to give to realize my purpose in writing?

7. What is the best way to organize these details and my discussion of them?
8. In planning and drafting my paper, have I changed my purpose? Has it broadened or narrowed? Do my revisions take account of these changes?

1b Defining your audience

When you write, you do so with a specific **audience** in mind. Audiences vary in size, nature, interests, and knowledge of the subject. Your audience may be a single person or a multitude. In making a list of chores or keeping a diary or journal, you are writing for an audience of one—yourself. In writing a letter or taking down a telephone message, you are writing to someone else. Much of your writing is for larger audiences. Your audience may be, as in Meg Greenfield's article on laboratory animals, a group of people with a variety of interests and varying knowledge of the subject. Or your audience may be limited to a small group of people with the same interests and concerns, such as physiologists who use animals in their research.

Purpose and audience are twin considerations. Assume that you are writing an instruction manual for users of a new computer model. How you write the instructions depends on the nature of your audience and the jobs they will be performing. If your audience consists solely of people who have worked with computers, you may decide not to give instructions on basic operations. But if your audience includes those unfamiliar with computers, you want to give full instructions. A physicist reporting on an experiment in a scientific journal similarly gauges the knowledge and background of the audience. These factors determine the description of the project, technical explanation and detail, and other features of the report. Writing the same report for a popular magazine, however, the physicist presents the same facts and conclusions in a nontechnical style suited to a different audience.

The writer of a persuasive essay similarly gauges the knowledge of the audience. Attitudes, beliefs, and interests are especially important, for the writer must know what arguments will carry the most weight and what strategies will be the most effective in shaping attitudes and beliefs that the writer wants the audience to possess. The writer will probably do research on the topic. The audience needs to know the background of the particular controversy, and the facts presented must be accurate and pertinent to the argument.

Attention to audience is crucial in writing because your readers are not present to tell you what they understand and what they don't understand. Defining your audience is, therefore, essential in any writing situation if you hope to communicate and be understood. To be understood, you need to do the following:

- Define your audience and keep it in mind as you write.
- Consider the knowledge and interests of your audience in organizing the essay and introducing the subject.
- Define unfamiliar terms and illustrate unfamiliar ideas.

1 Writing to general and special audiences

A **general audience** varies in background and knowledge of the subject; the audience varies most when the subject of the essay is scientific or technical, and less when the writing concerns everyday experiences. A **special audience,** by contrast, shares the same knowledge and background.

We see this difference in the readership of popular magazines. Some magazines choose to address a wide audience of varying interests, background, and knowledge. Even magazines that focus on a particular subject or interest such as sports or astronomy may view their audience as a general one. Other magazines address a special audience of rather similar background and knowledge. For example, an article on a long-distance truck driver in a magazine of general circulation defines the term *semi-trailer* for readers who don't know how long-distance trucks are rigged:

> The majority of long-distance commercial vehicles in America are semis—short for tractor (cab, engine, steering axle, power train, single or tandem drive axles with four tires per axle, and, perhaps, a sleeper) and semi-trailer. A semi-trailer, whether it is a flatbed, such as Lonnie pulls, or a van, a tank, or a hopper, has permanent axles only toward its rear. It cannot move down the

road unless it is supported in front. In Lonnie's rig, the support comes from the tractor itself.

—Bryan Di Salvatore, "Truck Driver," *The New Yorker,*
September 12, 1988

The author defines a key term *(trailer)* fully and gives a partial definition of another *(semi-trailer).* He pauses throughout his article to define terms and explain matters that would not require explanation in a specialized magazine directed to truck drivers.

The more specialized the magazine, the more technical may be the vocabulary and discussion. The following instructions on how to buy a portable tape player are from a magazine column directed to readers who own or know something about stereo equipment:

> First, narrow your range of choice. If you're like most readers of *Stereo Review,* you would be unlikely to buy a home or auto tape deck without a noise-reduction system (Dolby, dbx, or DNR), and by requiring noise reduction in any portable tape player you are considering, you can eliminate perhaps 80 per cent of the players on the market. As in shopping for any hi-fi equipment, avoid brand names that are totally unfamiliar or that sound suspiciously similar to famous brand names. For example, if you come across a "Xony Walkaway," simply walk away.
>
> —Myron Berger, "Choosing a Personal Portable,"
> *Stereo Review,* September 1983

The author of this article knows his audience well enough to gauge its knowledge about portable tape players and its buying habits. Knowing what kind of information to provide, he names the noise-reduction systems as a reminder of the kind used in home and auto tape decks but he does not describe or define these systems. He does describe the kind of equipment the buyer should not consider. The author is certain that his readers know enough about stereo equipment but may not know much about fake or unreliable products.

The information may be even more specialized if the audience consists of a single person or a small number of readers. In this case, the writer may present the information in language suited to the reader, using specialized but familiar terms. However, it is usually a good idea to recognize the reader with less knowledge and experience. Writers of articles in professional journals like *Nature, Journal of Sociology,* and *Yale Law Review* usually assume that their readers are familiar

13

with technical terms and ideas. Much of their writing is therefore technical and theoretical, often highly abstract in vocabulary and statement of ideas. If these writers were instead addressing a general audience, they would probably write less technically. They would look for ways to explain technical matters in everyday language, with the help of examples and comparisons with familiar objects.

2 Gauging your audience

Differences in audience need to be addressed when you are planning your writing and deciding how to begin and develop it. Following are some considerations to keep in mind.

Level of interest and knowledge.   Gauging the interests and knowledge of your audience is essential. Unless you have a specific audience in mind, you cannot decide what terms or ideas need to be defined. As noted earlier, in writing for a general audience, you need to define terms essential to understanding the discussion and to explain and interpret ideas and processes that may be unfamiliar. It is wise to do the same for a special audience by defining important terms and showing the way they are used. Even readers familiar with the subject need a reminder of these meanings. Take these same considerations into account when organizing your essay. Unless the subject requires a chronological presentation of details, a good procedure is to build from familiar to unfamiliar details or ideas, or from fundamental to more complex ones.

Beliefs and background.   The beliefs and background of your audience are important considerations in writing persuasive essays. In organizing your essay, you might begin by identifying points on which you and your readers probably agree and build to controversial points. On highly controversial issues like abortion and gun control, you probably will persuade few if any readers to change their stand. But you may lead readers to question their beliefs.

Kinds of evidence.   Expressive, informative, and persuasive writing use one or more of the following kinds of evidence:

Personal experience
Facts
Observations

Experimental and statistical data
Inferences
Evaluations and judgments
Secondary sources (newspapers, magazines, journals, books)

These kinds of evidence may occur in essays addressed to general readers, but you will do best to present facts and experimental and statistical data with a minimum of technical explanation. If your audience is a limited one and is familiar with technical language and details, you can write in a technical style.

3 Generating interest

A successful essay holds the reader's interest throughout. One way to hold the reader's interest is to capture it in the very first paragraph, by stating or showing why the subject interests you and why it should interest your reader.

The following opening paragraph of a book on recent discoveries in astronomy generates interest by explaining why the theoretical object called a black hole is so fascinating:

> A black hole is one of the most fantastic things ever predicted by modern science. It is a place where gravity is so strong that nothing—not even light—can escape. It is a place where gravity is so strong that a hole has been rent in the very fabric of space and time. Surrounding this yawning chasm is a "horizon" in the geometry of space where time itself stands still. And inside this hole, beyond this horizon, the directions of space and time are interchanged.
> —William J. Kaufmann, III, *Black Holes and Warped Spacetime*

Kaufmann gives the general reader a brief, clear definition of the complex phenomenon to be discussed; his definition arouses our interest as we try to picture the object. Kaufmann also tries to capture our attention through riddles or paradoxes about black holes. He is sensitive to his audience, aware that technical details early in the book would probably distract the reader from the topic of the paragraph. He knows that the attention of the reader will wane if details are excessive or unnecessary.

It is possible to generate interest in your audience by combining details with more general comments. The author of the following paragraphs holds the attention of her readers by skillfully moving between details of a notorious chemistry

15

course and general comments on its reputation and effect on students:

> When I was in college, there was an infamous course known as Chem 20. Organic chemistry was the sieve into which was poured every pre-medical student in the university. But only those who came through it with an A or B could reasonably expect to get into a medical school.
>
> Chem 20, therefore, became a psychological laboratory of pre-med anxiety. Every class was a combat mission. Each grade was a life-or-death matter. It reeked of Olympian anguish and Olympic competitiveness. It taught people whose goal in life was the relief of pain and suffering that only the fittest, the most single-minded, would survive.
>
> —Ellen Goodman, "The Chem 20 Factor"

Your readers may lose interest if you give unnecessary explanatory detail—for example, an account in the first paragraph of topics covered in organic chemistry. Whatever the interests and background of the audience, writing that gives details without interpretation or commentary may prove as boring as a general statement presented without detail or illustration. Yet it is better to err in giving too much detail than in giving too little; even the specialist may need a reminder of basic terms and illustrations of them.

Your writing will be most successful when you have a clear and accurate picture of your audience and an idea of the attitudes and beliefs you want your audience to possess.

Checklist: Defining Your Audience

1. What audience am I addressing? Is my audience an individual or a group of people? If a group, is my audience a general one whose knowledge of the subject varies? Or is it a special audience that shares the same knowledge?
2. How can I capture the attention and interest of my audience? What kind of introduction will best achieve my purpose in writing?
3. What examples will best illustrate my points and realize my purpose?

4. What interests and attitudes should I take into account in organizing my essay? What attitudes and beliefs do I want my audience to hold? Should I acknowledge or call attention to them?
5. What organization will best achieve the effect I have in mind? If my essay is informative, is a chronological organization best? Or should I begin with familiar steps or ideas and proceed to unfamiliar ones? If my essay is persuasive, should I begin with ideas that are least controversial and proceed to ones that are most controversial?
6. What vocabulary is appropriate for my audience? What terms need to be defined? What ideas or processes need explanation?
7. What tone is appropriate? Should I address my audience as if I were conversing with them? Or should I address my audience in an objective tone?

1c Choosing a writing style

Once you have defined your audience, you are ready to choose an appropriate style for your paper. The word **style** generally refers to the manner in which you address your audience and specifically refers to the various means by which you do so. Speaking and writing styles differ according to the formality of the occasion and your familiarity with your listeners or readers. Usually custom or established ways of speaking and writing tell you what style is appropriate.

If you are writing to friends and acquaintances, you may decide to write informally, as if you were conversing about the subject. **Informal English,** both in speech and writing, assumes a familiarity between speaker and listener, writer and reader, that permits you to be less precise and more conversational or colloquial. In informal English, you use everyday words and expressions, and on occasion you may use slang. Although it maintains many of the patterns of spoken English, informal writing is neither repetitive nor loosely organized. As

17

in conversation with friends, it may make personal references or allusions to familiar people and events, but these references are usually kept to a minimum.

Formal English tends to be what the word *formal* suggests—speech and writing that are "at attention," each idea stated precisely, in tightly constructed sentences. A formal writing style or use of words is usually appropriate in papers on abstract or technical subjects. A formal style is also appropriate in writing term papers, reports, and letters of applications. Although you may converse with your college instructors, it would be inappropriate to write a lab report or a research paper as if you were chatting about the subject. A formal occasion, such as an application for a scholarship, also requires a formal tone and formal style.

Formal and *informal* are best defined as the extreme limits of a wide spectrum of words, phrases, and sentence constructions. Sharing qualities of both formal and informal is **general English**—the speech that you hear on radio and television and read in magazines, journals, and newspapers. General English is the prevailing standard of communication in the school and in business and governmental affairs. Flexible and highly adaptable, general English often combines the exact sentence structure and sometimes the abstract and technical words of formal English with the looser conversational sentence structure and vocabulary of informal English. Most of the examples in this handbook are of this kind.

Despite the labels given to various words and phrases, the borders between formal and informal language are not exact. Their defining features, indeed, are inseparable from their use. This handbook distinguishes formal or informal usage when writing departs in a striking way from general usage. (See 30b and 30c for additional discussion of general and special audiences and formal and informal styles of writing.)

In the course of writing a paper, you will probably choose words and sentence structures that you sense are inappropriate to your audience and occasion. For example, you may inadvertently use a slang expression that would be appropriate in speaking to friends but would be inappropriate in addressing a teacher or employer. Writing frequently requires continual adjustments in style and tone. However, when you have a clear image of your audience in mind as you write, you are likely to write in a consistent and appropriate style.

EXERCISES

1. Be ready to discuss the decisions you would need to make as a writer in explaining how to parallel park to (a) a student driver and (b) a person who has never driven.

2. For each of the following writing situations, write down your decisions about the amount of information and the degree of formality you would use to write about them.

   a. a note taped to the refrigerator asking someone not to eat the breakfast plums

   b. a note to a mechanic explaining why the refrigerator is not working

   c. a note to a friend giving unasked-for advice

   d. a letter of complaint to a department store about a defective toaster

   e. a letter to the same store applying for a job

   f. a letter to a bank explaining why a check bounced

3. Write a note or letter for one of the preceding items illustrating some of your decisions about the amount of information and degree of formality.

4. Write a paragraph for a general audience explaining an idea or institution that you have come to understand through reading or study (e.g., the theory of the big bang or the electoral college as an institution). Assume that your audience possesses some knowledge of the general subject but no detailed knowledge of the idea or institution. Then rewrite your paragraph for an audience that possesses no knowledge of the subject.

5. The following are opening paragraphs of essays and newspaper and magazine articles. What does each author assume that his or her readers know about the subject? What type of audience is each author addressing—a general or a limited audience? How does the author seek to generate interest in the subject? Does the author succeed in capturing your interest?

   a. "Size," Julian Huxley once remarked, "has a fascination of its own." We stock our zoos with elephants, hippopotamuses, giraffes, and gorillas; who among you was not rooting for King Kong in his various battles atop tall buildings? This focus on the few creatures larger than ourselves has distorted our conception of our own size. Most people think that *Homo sapiens* is a creature of only modest dimensions. In fact, humans are among the largest animals on earth; more than 99 percent of animal species are smaller than we are. Of 190 species in our

own order of primate mammals, only the gorilla regularly exceeds us in size.
—Stephen Jay Gould, "Sizing Up Human Intelligence"

b. What is thinking? Introspection supplies preliminary answers. Some thought is verbal: a kind of silent talking to oneself. Other mental processes seem to be visual: images are called to mind and wordlessly manipulated. Evident though they are, the mechanisms of thought long eluded experimental analysis and quantification. How can these seemingly inaccessible, subjective processes be measured and investigated scientifically?
—Lynn A. Cooper and Roger N. Shepard, "Turning Something Over in the Mind," *Scientific American*, December 1984

c. In the early evening, I take my seat in a natural amphitheatre of limestone boulders, in the Texas hill country; at the bottom of the slope is a wide, dark cave mouth. Nothing stirs yet in its depths. But I have been promised one of the wonders of our age. Deep inside the cavern, twenty million Mexican free-tailed bats are hanging up by their toes. They are the largest known concentration of warm-blooded animals in the world. Soon, at dusk, all twenty million of them will fly out to feed, in a living volcano that scientists call an "emergence." They will flood the September sky with their leathery wings and ultrasonic cries, and people in cities as far as fifty miles away, without realizing it, will rarely be more than seventy feet from a feeding bat.
—Diane Ackerman, "Bats," *The New Yorker*, February 29, 1988 ■

Summary

1a Have a clear purpose in mind in writing a paper. You can have one or more of the following purposes in writing an essay or other piece of writing:

Express your feelings and beliefs for their own sake (**1a 1**).

Describe a personal experience or observation you have made about the world (**1a 2**).

Convey information (**1a 2**).

Persuade your readers to change their thinking or to take some action (1a 3).

1b Define the audience for your paper. Determine whether your audience is a general one with little or no knowledge of your subject, or a special one that shares knowledge of your subject.

Choose details and examples that are appropriate for a general audience or for a special or limited one (1b 1–2).

Gauge the knowledge and background of your audience in deciding how to begin the essay (1b 3).

Capture the attention and interest of your readers through details of the subject (1b 3).

1c Write in a style and tone appropriate to your purpose and audience.

Preparing to Write

2

It sometimes seems that experienced writers put words on paper without preparation or planning, that their ideas and details fall into place effortlessly. Most writers, however, not only prepare to write but also do considerable thinking and imagining in the course of drafting and revising. For most, writing is an act of continuous rethinking and revision.

Writers prepare to write in a number of ways. They read extensively, browse in newspapers and magazines, keep diaries and journals, make lists and outlines, ask questions of themselves and others. Sometimes writers quickly discover a topic or central idea and methods of developing it during the initial planning. At other times, they must give their ideas considerable thought, working them out in trial paragraphs and longer drafts.

As you may know from experience, few writers produce finished sentences or paragraphs without having to revise and edit them. Many writers let their ideas and supporting details take shape slowly. In an hour or a day, a week or even a month, they return to these ideas and details and begin shaping them into an essay. They do so in their heads as well as on paper, organizing ideas and details, making lists, outlining, and drafting sentences and introductory and concluding paragraphs. In the course of drafting the paper and later in revising it, a writer may decide to change the tone, point of view, or even the subject of the essay.

This chapter discusses ways of finding a subject and analyzing it to discover relationships among ideas—and possibly new ideas, impressions, and details. The techniques of invention discussed here will help you in the planning and revising of your papers.

2a | Understanding the writing process

Sitting down to write a letter or an essay, you may have your audience and purpose clearly in mind. Sometimes your purpose becomes clear only in the act of writing a first or second draft. The **writing process** refers to the series of activities you usually perform in writing a paper.

First among these activities is the **planning** of the paper, sometimes called **prewriting.** In planning, you search for and narrow a subject or topic, think of ways to develop the topic, use one or more techniques of invention to discover details, organize through lists and outlines, formulate a thesis, and write trial sentences or paragraphs.

After planning, you usually write a draft of the paper. In **drafting,** you sometimes write down your ideas without pausing; at other times you pause to recast or rephrase an idea, to define terms, or to find new examples. When you have completed a satisfactory draft, you are ready to revise it. In **revising,** you reconsider the point of view and thesis of the draft, its organization and development, and perhaps even your subject. This revision is sometimes called "global" because you are looking at the whole essay, not at individual paragraphs or sentences only. Having examined what you have written, you may write a second and even a third draft. In the course of drafting and revising the paper, you may pause to make corrections in spelling, punctuation, and grammar. However, these corrections are your chief concern in **editing** the paper and **proofreading** it a final time.

Planning, drafting, revising, and editing are rarely performed step by step. The process each of us follows is usually the sum of individual writing habits that we develop with practice. Moreover, few of us proceed in the same way in every writing situation. Some writers produce essays that satisfy all readers in a single draft; some write several drafts, particularly when the paper is long and its ideas and details are complex. Some depend on the traditional topic or sentence outline in planning the essay; others find freewriting and other techniques of invention useful, sometimes drawing on them in successive drafts of the paper. Some writers revise extensively and edit in the course of writing the first and later drafts; others revise and edit only after producing a full draft.

Each writing assignment or situation requires different decisions. A memorandum does not call for the same decisions or process that a term paper or literary essay does. But the kinds of questions you ask and the decisions you make are much the same. As you plan your paper, for example, you may find that your purpose needs to be sharpened. In selecting a topic, you may find it necessary to ask questions about purpose and audience that you didn't think of asking at the start. You may discover that your original topic is too broad, and that you must reformulate your topic or narrow your focus. Your image of the audience, your sense of what it knows and believes about the subject, probably will come into sharper focus as you plan the paper.

In general, the act of writing is usually one in which you return to earlier stages to rethink your subject, organization, and presentation of ideas and then rewrite some or all of the draft. As we will see in Chapter 4, the kind of questioning and thinking that occurs in planning the paper occurs also in drafting and revising it.

Checklist: The Writing Process

1. **Planning**—finding a subject, thinking of ways to develop it, inventing ideas and details, organizing the paper, outlining, and formulating a tentative thesis.

2. **Drafting**—writing trial sentences and paragraphs, and writing one or more drafts or versions of the essay.
3. **Revising**—reconsidering the point of view, organization, development of the subject, and perhaps even the subject itself.
4. **Editing**—making corrections in spelling, punctuation, and grammar.
5. **Proofreading**—making a final check before presenting the essay to readers.

2b Finding a subject

Writing begins when you are given a writing assignment or are prompted to write by some experience or event. Much college writing is assigned writing—essays of various types, quizzes and examinations, field and lab reports, research papers. Much of the writing you will do in your career will be assigned writing: you may be asked to write memorandums, reports, case histories, briefs, and other kinds of writing important to business and the professions. Much of your daily writing is also a response to reading of some kind. Reading is indeed the counterpart of writing and an activity indispensable to the accomplished writer.

In your composition course, you may be asked to write a particular type of paper—perhaps an expressive or personal essay, an informative or persuasive paper, or a literary piece such as a short story or an imaginative dialogue. Your instructor may specify an audience and purpose for the paper or ask you to define them. If a general topic is assigned, you will have an opportunity to narrow it to one that you make your own. The topic becomes your own if it

- reveals your personal interests and concerns;
- uses your knowledge, experience, and insight;
- says something interesting and important about you and your world;
- is limited enough to be explored in depth.

25

These concerns should guide you in searching for a subject and limiting it to a specific topic.

1 Reading and discussion

A writer "must read widely and thoughtfully" and "must learn to read not as an amateur spectator but as an engaged professional," the poet and essayist John Ciardi recommends. In reading thoughtfully, you become aware of possible subjects for papers and of choices in developing and organizing ideas. Your command of sentence structure depends not just on your hearing sentences but also on seeing how writers shape them. You build your vocabulary and learn to use words in the same way.

Mark Twain described his own dependence on reading in this way: "Let us guess that whenever we read a sentence and like it, we unconsciously store it away in our model-chamber; and it goes with the myriad of its fellows to the building, brick by brick, of the eventful edifice which we call our style." Much of your writing depends in the same way on your reading, though you may not be aware of this fact. The ideas and experiences of other people and the ways they express them inspire you to write about your own. Books, magazines, and newspapers provide a constant source of ideas and impressions that may later suggest the subject for an essay of your own or a way of developing it. A newspaper editorial or letter to the editor may prompt you to write about your own view of an issue.

Many valuable ideas and details for papers may come out of discussions with friends and, on occasion, interviews you participate in or conduct. In some of your college courses, you will engage in extensive discussion; you certainly will do so informally with your classmates. These are valuable sources of topics and ideas. Jotting them down in a notebook or recording them in a journal can be of immense help later, as you prepare to write.

2 Keeping a journal

Many writers find that keeping a record of thoughts and impressions in a journal helps to generate ideas and to serve as an aid to memory. Journals have different uses—some writers use them to jot down reflections and musings recorded at various times; others record daily accounts of their experiences and impressions. The columnist William Safire suggests that the journal or diary is a valuable means of recovering forgotten ideas and details:

> Diaries remind us of details that would otherwise fade from memory and make less vivid our recollection. Navy Secretary Gideon Welles, whose private journal is an invaluable source for Civil War historians, watched Abraham Lincoln die in a room across the street from Ford's Theater and later jotted down a detail that puts the reader in the room: "The giant sufferer lay extended diagonally across the bed, which was not long enough for him. . . ."
>
> —"On Keeping a Diary"

The novelist Virginia Woolf kept a diary throughout most of her career, recording thoughts and impressions that she constantly put to use in her writing. In one entry, she discusses the value of writing rapidly and freely:

> I note however that this diary writing does not count as writing, since I have just re-read my year's diary and am much struck by the rapid haphazard gallop at which it swings along, sometimes indeed jerking almost intolerably over the cobbles. Still if it were not written rather faster than the fastest typewriting, if I stopped and took thought, it would never be written at all; and the advantage of the method is that it sweeps up accidentally several stray matters which I should exclude if I hesitated, but which are the diamonds of the dustheap.
>
> —*The Diary of Virginia Woolf*, January 20, 1919

Woolf suggests an excellent reason for keeping a journal—to sweep up "the diamonds of the dustheap," the stray thoughts and perceptions that may serve the writer later.

In your composition course, you may find it useful to keep a journal of ideas and impressions suggested by your reading, class discussions, and other experiences. Such a journal can help in preparing to write both brief class papers and longer essays. A journal entry may even provide the impulse to write an essay, perhaps one in which you use an idea or perception to explore your feelings or discover a truth about the world or about yourself. These ideas and perceptions can be the starting point of your exploration, and you may turn to them in the course of writing to discover other ideas. You may, indeed, want to jot down ideas for use at another time.

Scientists use journals to keep careful records of their findings, for they cannot risk trusting the details and results of their research to memory. These records must be precise—more so than the recording of daily impressions and ideas. The notebook in your science course serves the same purpose. In it you may keep a record of your experiments, giving an orderly account of each one and making notes on your findings. You may also make notes on other possible lines of investigation.

3 Observing and reflecting

Ideas and impressions come from reading, reflection, even day-dreaming. Many come from day-to-day observations recorded at random. The randomness of these observations is a means of discovery; the imagination has an opportunity to explore the world without guidance. Your journal can do for you what the sketchbook does for the artist: permit you to record the colors, sounds, smells, and shapes of the world. You need not see a point or an idea in the impressions you record. Those you do record are like photographs of a fascinating or beautiful scene or object.

You may decide to record these impressions in words and phrases that you can later form into sentences and paragraphs. However, words and phrases need a context—a noting of their connection, perhaps a note on their significance—when you prepare to write. Imagination provides this context. So does reflection. At a later time, you may think about the observations recorded in your journal. Or you may do so at the time of your observation or experience. Thinking is often thought of as a conscious, systematic activity. But you probably have had the experience of waking after a night's sleep and discovering a way to organize ideas or solve a problem that puzzled you the day before. Many writers habitually wait a few hours or longer before they put their ideas on paper, organize, and begin writing. Having found a topic that you wish to write about, you may benefit from letting the ideas, impressions, and details in your journal "incubate" in your mind.

The teacher and writer William Least Heat Moon suggests that we often see things when we don't look directly at an object:

> Reading my notes of the trip—images, bits of conversations, ideas—I hunted a structure in the events, but randomness was the rule. Outside, sheltered by a live oak, a spider spun a web. Can an orb weaver perceive the design in its work, the pattern of concentric circles lying atop radiating lines? When the mys-

tical young Black Elk went to the summit of Harney Peak to see
the shape of things, he looked down on the great unifying hoop
of peoples. I looked down and saw fragments. But later that afternoon, a tactic returned to me from night maneuver training in
the Navy: to see in deep darkness you don't look directly at an
object—you look to the left; you look at something else to see
what you really want to see. Skewed vision.

—*Blue Highways*

"Skewed vision" is a way of letting your imagination play on a
subject, of bringing imagination and reflection into play.

EXERCISE

Topics are often generated from what you have read. Reading
may suggest ideas or comparable situations in your life that are
worth exploring. After reading the two paragraphs that follow,
write down some ideas or situations for writing suggested by one
of them.

a. Communication, whatever it is, is more than a matter
of words, and in some familiar situations it is a great
deal more than words. When in ordinary social and
business life we identify ourselves before others (or
indeed before ourselves), when we convey attitudes
and information, when we take in the intentions of
our fellow creatures, we use several of our senses at
once, and we use them in complicated ways. We are
present, clothed and combed, three-dimensional, taking up space and filling the air with our peculiar personal accents. We present ourselves by being present.
The fact that we do this, as often as not, with non-
chalant ease should not obscure the variety and richness of our communicating.

—Walker Gibson, *Tough, Sweet and Stuffy*

b. Let's examine a typical American conversation. Joan
and Sandra meet on the sidewalk. Preliminary greet-
ings over with, Joan begins to talk. She starts by looking right away from Sandra. As she hits her conversational stride, she glances back at her friend from
time to time at the end of a phrase or a sentence. She
does not look at her during hesitations or pauses but
only at natural breaks in the flow of her talk. At the
end of what she wants to say, she gives Sandra a
rather longer glance. Experiments indicate that if she
fails to do this, Sandra, not recognizing that it is her
turn to talk, will hesitate or will say nothing at all.

—Flora Davis, "The Language of the Eyes" ■

29

2c	Limiting the topic

A broad topic like the first week of college or the first day on a job leaves little room for development in a short essay. In the space of a few pages, you will have little room to develop any single experience or impression if you describe everything that happened. Your paper might consist of a series of miscellaneous details from which you draw no conclusions. A broad topic like air pollution or political changes in China, on the other hand, invites a highly abstract or technical discussion that contains few specific details or personal observations. The topic is so broad that you cannot explore it in depth.

If you don't limit your topic properly, your essay may turn out to be overly abstract or overly detailed, lacking any interpretation or conclusions. Although some essays consist solely of ideas and others solely of facts or details, the most interesting essays contain a weaving of ideas, details, and examples. Readers are fascinated by observations, details, and ideas when they enrich each other. The more specific and well focused an essay, the more readers are able to relate their experiences to those of the author.

The degree to which a topic should be limited depends on the length of the paper as well as your audience and purpose in writing. In college writing, length is often specified in an assignment; newspapers and magazines often prescribe a length for letters and articles. Sometimes you will make the decision about length, a decision sometimes guided by the nature of your audience. An explanatory paper addressed to a special audience, perhaps scientists interested in the greenhouse effect, probably will be longer than a nontechnical description for readers of newspapers.

However, your purpose in writing is your chief consideration in limiting the topic. Assume that you are thinking of writing a letter to a newspaper complaining about various city services—street repair, emergency health assistance, garbage collection. These are all matters of concern to you. You even consider discussing other city services like welfare and recreation. Obviously, a letter discussing so many topics would have to be many pages in length. (The figure on page 54 in Chapter 3 shows how many topics might be discussed if your purpose in writing is to encourage improvement in city services.)

Usually you have a limited purpose in mind when writing—in this case, to give your local official information about a specific city service and to gain the support of the newspaper and its readers for improving that service. You are generally concerned about inefficiency, but you are particularly concerned about a certain nuisance. Your purpose is perhaps to get a pothole on your street repaired. Assume that you want to call attention to inefficiency and indifference. Can you do both in the same letter? You can if you make the pothole—your specific concern—your *main* topic and your general concern with city services your *subordinate* topic. The narrower the topic, the more specific your details will be. The broader your topic, the more general your examples will be (e.g., dangerous streets and roads rather than a specific street and a particular pothole). Both can be discussed in a short letter, but not at the same length or in the same amount of detail.

Limiting the topic thus requires careful attention to the main topic of the paper and to subordinate topics. If your topic still covers too much, you might consider further limitations, some of which can also be introduced as subordinate topics. Here are some examples of how broad topics can be limited:

Subject	Broad Topic	Limited Topic	Further Limitations
Impressions of college	First week of college	First day of college	First-day impressions of college instructors or classes
			Comparison of a high school and a college English class
Air pollution	Los Angeles smog	Causes of smog	A major cause of smog
		Proposed solutions	Controlling car emissions
		Health effects	Lung diseases
		Economic effects	One serious economic effect
Political conflict in China	Student protests in June 1989	Crushing of protest at Tiananmen Square	Causes of protest
			Effects on students and universities
			Political effects
			World response

31

Checklist: Limiting the Topic

1. How can I limit a broad topic to a specific one?
2. What limitation of topic will best serve my purpose in writing?
3. What limitation of my topic will help me to discuss and illustrate my central idea fully?
4. Does my paper have a prescribed length? If not, what length would be appropriate, given my purpose and audience?
5. Should I limit my topic further to fit the length prescribed?

EXERCISES

1. Assume that you narrowly miss an accident on a crowded expressway on the way home from school. A driver cut across two lanes of traffic in order to reach an exit. Arriving home, you decide to write a letter to your newspaper about the risks of driving on expressways. Think about the kind of letter you would write, and then answer the following questions:
    a. What purpose would your letter serve? Would the letter be expressive, informative, or persuasive—or all of these? To what audience would you write?
    b. What general limitation of the subject (dangers of driving) would help you best satisfy your purpose in writing and communicate most effectively with your audience?
    c. What more specific limitation or focus would help you be more detailed and persuasive?
2. Write a letter on a topic of your choice. Limit your topic in a way best suited to realize a particular purpose and reach a particular audience.
3. How might one of the following statements be limited to meet the criteria discussed in 2b?

    a. You might as well fall flat on your face as lean over too far backward.
                    —James Thurber, *The Bear Who Let It Alone*

    b. I've got to relearn what I was supposed to have learned.
                    —Sylvia Ashton-Warner, *Myself*

c. If you have to keep reminding yourself of a thing, perhaps it isn't so.
> —Christopher Morley, *Thunder on the Left*

d. We want the facts to fit the preconceptions. When they don't it is easier to ignore the facts than to change the preconceptions.
> —Jessamyn West, Introduction to *The Quaker Reader* ■

2d | Inventing ideas and details

Reading and discussion, keeping journals and notebooks—these are important ways of finding a subject and limiting the topic. These and other techniques—such as freewriting, brainstorming, and clustering—also help the writer to invent ideas and details that develop the topic. They may be useful at later stages of writing as well, perhaps after you have formulated a thesis and outlined a draft of your paper.

1 Freewriting

Freewriting is continuous, uninterrupted writing, in which you put ideas and impressions on paper without pausing to make changes in content or to correct grammar, spelling, or punctuation. Some writers use the journal as a means of freewriting; others engage in freewriting before beginning the first draft of a paper; and yet others do freewriting in the course of writing the first and second drafts. Freewriting is helpful in generating ideas and details; it can jog the memory as well as bring the imagination into play. It gives you an opportunity to capture images and ideas not always easy to summon when your attention is focused on an idea or a sequence of ideas worked out in a preliminary outline. Sometimes freewriting loosens a block that arises when you have trouble defining the topic or finding ways to develop it.

The success of freewriting depends on putting words on paper as rapidly as possible. This procedure is similar to the improvisations of the musician whose fingers wander over the piano keyboard or trumpet keys at random. As new combinations of sound emerge in improvisation, so do surprising images and ideas in freewriting. The imagination is brought to play upon a theme that takes shape in this exploration.

The following is an example of freewriting. The author was prompted to write it by a car ride into Cleveland from the city of Akron to the south:

> Coming in from the south on I-71, first a view of Cleveland on a bluff above a wide valley. Another interstate crosses the valley from east to west. Then a sign for Broadview Heights, but already the view is lost. No sense of height. Just ragged-looking frame houses and just after you pass into Cleveland the steelworks, belching smoke, one tall stack that looks on fire. The car turns toward Terminal Tower past a huge lot with what seems like hundreds of post office delivery cars. Enormous lots on the other side of the interstate. The turn of the road suddenly to downtown and north. If you miss the turn into downtown or up the Inner Belt to the lake, you pass over the river that cuts the city in half. It doesn't look like much of a river but it once caught fire, maybe the only river in the U.S. that's happened to. What you notice as you drive is what you expect to see.

Although the writer has chosen a subject for her paper—Cleveland viewed on entering the city from the south—she does not yet have an idea or thesis that will organize the details of her trial paragraph. Reading the paragraph, she realizes that her details develop her concluding statement:

> What you notice as you drive is what you expect to see.

Rewriting the paragraph, she uses her concluding statement as a topic sentence that states the central idea (see 5b):

> In driving into an unfamiliar city, you see what you expect to see. Driving into Cleveland from the

```
south on I-71, the city comes into view across a wide
valley--on what seems a bluff. Perhaps you notice the
site, knowing you would pass through Broadview Heights
first....
```

The writer then develops the paragraph by describing the sights referred to in her freewriting and by drawing a conclusion:

```
But all of these are mistaken impressions. The Cleve-
land you see from the interstate is not the city as it
really is.
```

Here may be the thesis of a complete essay. The writer is ready to write a draft of an essay describing Cleveland as it appears to an interstate driver and as it really is. In looking over the draft, she jots down ideas and details as well as ways of developing the essay. For it is always helpful to jot down phrases that state purposes and ideas and keep them close at hand in planning the paper and writing a draft. Comparison and contrast will be important to her development, so the writer makes a note of possible topics—the industrial center of Cleveland, the Cuyahoga River that divides the city, the rich ethnic diversity that marks Cleveland and its suburbs. On any one of these topics, she might freewrite another paragraph.

Neither freewriting nor any other technique of invention works for everyone in the same way or works successfully at all times. By experimenting with several techniques, you can determine which of them can best help you in writing papers.

EXERCISE

Do the following activities as you prepare to write an essay on a topic of your choice. (Your instructor may modify these procedures or suggest additional ones.)

1. For at least one week, keep a journal. Record your observations and impressions of friends or fellow students without regard to their possible meanings. Any trait or act that you find interesting or unusual is worth recording.
2. Choose one of the observations recorded in your journal and freewrite about it, writing quickly every idea

35

or image that it calls to mind. Don't be concerned with the meaning of your ideas or images.

3. Choose one of the ideas you arrive at, and write freely on it or any other topic suggested by it. You need not have a point or central idea in mind as you do so. If a point or idea does occur to you, record and mark it for later use. Probably a number of such ideas will occur to you in the course of your writing.

4. Rewrite your paper with a specific purpose and audience in mind. New ideas and details will probably come to mind in the course of rewriting. You may even drop some of the ideas and details of your original draft. ■

2   Listing and brainstorming

As you plan your paper, you will want to keep lists of possible topics, ideas, and details. You may also make lists later in drafting and revising the paper. At any of these stages, you can also brainstorm the subject.

Brainstorming is a special kind of listing that works through a process of rapid association. Often a group activity, brainstorming is used by teams of scientists, government officials, businesspeople, and other groups to discover promising ideas and approaches to a problem. Writers use brainstorming for the same purpose. In the planning stage, brainstorming is useful in finding a topic and inventing or discovering ideas and details.

Brainstorming is similar to freewriting in that you quickly write down words and phrases that you associate with a general subject or specific topic. For instance, assume that you are asked to write an essay on some personal experience for a purpose of your choice. Your audience in this case is your instructor and classmates. You begin by jotting down several possible subjects for the paper and discover that a recent audition for the college orchestra seems most promising. You begin brainstorming by quickly writing down a few words and phrases suggested by the audition:

```
getting ready
auditions in high school
psyched for tests in college
skills
reasons for joining the orchestra
```

You continue brainstorming by listing everything else that comes to mind:

practicing	sight-reading
talking to orchestra	intonation
members	timing
high school orchestra	ensemble playing
audition	not letting the mind
playing in high school	wander
orchestra	listening to other
college-entrance exams	players
math tests	knowledge of music
performing for friends and	talking to orchestra
family	head
playing for pleasure	self-confidence
performing with a group	overcoming jitters

One of these words or phrases may suggest a limited topic and perspective. For example, *sight-reading* suggests a paper on the skills required for a successful audition. In a paper on this topic, you might have one or more purposes—to express your feelings about auditions, to reveal your interests and special talents, or to explain how to prepare for an audition. Although the immediate purpose of brainstorming is to generate ideas and details, it also can help you define a topic and purpose.

3 Clustering

Another method for arriving at ideas is called **clustering.** This technique, recommended by the writing teacher Gabrielle Lusser Rico, involves writing down the key ideas suggested by a word. The clustering of the word *audition*—your main topic— might begin like this:

You continue clustering by writing down other words and phrases suggested by the key ideas. These words and phrases, in turn, suggest others. The items are circled and connected with lines, as shown in the accompanying diagram.

Clustering

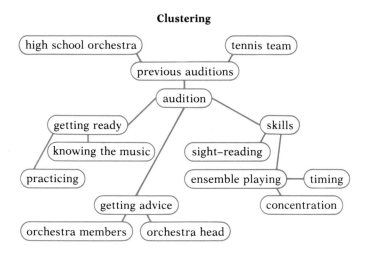

As in brainstorming, success in clustering depends on your ability to write down words and phrases quickly and to allow your imagination to play on them. Clustering helps you to visualize the possible relationships between ideas and details. Of course, you will make many chance associations that you will decide not to use in your paper.

Brainstorming and clustering need not be as involved as the examples just illustrated. You may find a quick jotting down of ideas and details sufficient to arrive at an idea for a paper. Planning longer essays may require more work, and you will have occasion to use these and other techniques of invention during the drafting and revision of the essay.

EXERCISE

The following words and phrases suggest various connections. Connect them into single clusters, in the manner shown above. Then write down several topics suggested by these clusters and list ideas and details.

looking for defects
       tire tread   oil consumption
          condition of engine
                warranty
engine wear
       upholstery
              reputation of dealer
     buying a used car
  buying from a friend
       buying from a dealer
                financing
  biking
             newspaper ads
       cheap transportation
    paying for college
  student loan
      commuting
renting an apartment   sharing an apartment
      college dorms
taking the bus   living at home

4 Sorting

Another invention technique involves classifying or sorting the items you discovered through brainstorming. In **sorting,** you discover thematic relationships or groupings like the following:

Skills to be tested	Previous experience
sight-reading	high school orchestra
ensemble playing	tryout
knowledge of music	playing in the high
breath control	school orchestra
intonation	college-entrance exams
timing	writing under pressure
	trying out for the
	chess team

<pre>
                                  Qualities needed
          Preparing for audition   for success
            talking to orchestra   self-confidence
              members   overcoming jitters
            talking to orchestra   concentration
              head
            practicing
</pre>

Large groupings may suggest further breakdowns. For example, the grouping "Previous experience" might be divided as follows:

<pre>
          Previous experience
            Other auditions
            Playing in the high school orchestra
</pre>

These subgroupings may suggest a limited topic that you can write about from experience and observation.

EXERCISES

1. Sort the following topics into two or more groupings that show their relationships. Then suggest several subjects that the topics might develop.

aerating the soil	destroying insects
clearing brush	harvesting
seeding	furrowing
weeding	propping young plants
fertilizing	pruning young plants
raking	watering

2. Write down as quickly as you can as many ideas and facts or experiences suggested by one of the following:
   a. pop music
   b. reading the newspaper
   c. comic strips
   d. greeting cards
   e. household chores

Now look for patterns in your ideas and facts, grouping them in various ways. Select one of these patterns and use it to organize an essay that says something important about you and your world.

5 Asking questions

Newspaper and magazine writers cannot afford to miss important information about a story. They therefore **ask questions** about the nature of the event, the people involved, time and place, means and circumstances, results and consequences:

What?	What happened?
Who?	Who is responsible?
Where?	Where did the event occur?
When?	When did it occur?
How?	How did it occur?
Why?	Why did it occur?

The following opening paragraphs of an eyewitness account of the army assault on protesters in Tiananmen Square, in Beijing, China, on June 4, 1989, answer the preceding questions. The Hong Kong newspaper that first published this report identified the writer as a twenty-year-old university student.

Where?	Beijing—In the predawn hours of June 3, I was sitting on the steps of the Monument to the People's
Who?	Heroes. I saw with my own eyes what happened
What?	when the army opened fire on the students and citi-
How?	zens quietly sitting in the square.
	By the afternoon of that Saturday, we had already heard that the army would carry out the order to crack down. An anonymous phone call—to a pub-
Why?	lic phone in a nearby alley—had come around 4 P.M.
When?	to tell us that the army was about to clear Tianan-
	men by force. Alerted by the news, we had an emergency meeting, at which we decided what measures we would take to defuse the confrontation and avoid a blood bath.

—*New York Times,* June 12, 1989

The remainder of this account gives additional information on what happened at Tiananmen Square and why.

If you were investigating the assault at Tiananmen Square for a report of your own, you would have to ask these same questions to gather the important facts, including those necessary to understanding what happened. Remember that what is obvious to you may not be obvious to your readers. Some readers, for instance, may not be aware of the events leading up to the student demonstrations, or of the leaders of China, or of other events in that country during the 1980s. You will not miss important facts if you look at the event as your readers would.

EXERCISE

Analyze a newspaper or magazine report of an important event to find out if it answers all of the questions listed on page 41. Be ready to discuss how informative you find the report. ∎

6 Particle, wave, field

In a special form of analysis (called *tagmemic analysis*), a particular thing is looked at in three different ways or perspectives:

- as **particle** or **object**—something existing at one particular moment, without concern for how it behaves or interacts with other objects;
- as **wave** or **process**—something in the state of moving or changing;
- as **field**—something acting or functioning as part of a field or system, as part of an organization of interrelated parts.

Here is an example of these three perspectives from a report on laser lifts, devices that control spacecraft from the ground:

Object
Process
Field

> A brilliant beam of laser light lances up from the ground, reflects off a mirror orbiting hundreds of miles away, and reaches toward a small rocket nozzle attached to one of the satellites. The rocket flares to life, propelling the satellite toward its desired final destination—an orbit higher than the shuttle can reach. Within a few minutes, each of the satellites has been sent on its way, propelled by the energy of the laser's beam.
> —Ben Bova, "A Laser Lift," *Science 84,*
> September 1984

We know what a laser lift is because we are told *what kind of object it is* ("a brilliant beam of light"), *how it behaves* (it "reflects off a mirror" and "reaches toward a small rocket nozzle"), and *how it fits into a system or field* (it is responsible for the ignition of the rocket and propulsion of the satellite).

Tagmemic analysis may give additional information about the object through the following:

Contrast—how laser lifts differ from similar objects, perhaps other kinds of devices that control spacecraft.

Variation—how much variation exists in the class or type, perhaps in the design of laser lifts.

Distribution—where laser lifts fit as a source of energy in the general class of rocket fuels or propellents.

The author contrasts laser lifts with the chemical rocket:

Unlike a chemical rocket, whose fiery power comes from the release of the fuel's inherent chemical energy, a laser rocket acts more like a huge teakettle. The laser itself never leaves Earth but fires an intense beam of light up into the spacecraft where it heats the propellant to such high temperatures and pressures that it comes spewing out the nozzle with tremendous energy.

—Ben Bova, "A Laser Lift"

Analysis of particle, wave, and field is often useful in deciding on a topic or focus for an essay and discovering ideas and details. Assume that you are asked to analyze your composition course as part of an overall evaluation of your school. You can view the composition course:

- as an *object*—the subject matter and aims of the course;
- as a *process*—the day-by-day activities, the process of learning to read and write; and
- as a *field*—the place of the course in the curriculum or degree program of the college.

You might further develop the analysis by asking how the course differs from another in content and teaching methods:

- How does the course differ from similar courses at other schools?
- How does the course relate to other courses in the same field at the college?

The techniques of invention discussed in this section can be used individually or in combination, at various stages in writing the paper. Once you have selected a topic and formulated a thesis, you may need to search for additional ideas and details that will help you develop the paper. If your paper concerns a topic that may be analyzed as object, process, and field, you may wish to conduct a full analysis at this point, perhaps in company with further brainstorming or clustering.

43

Checklist: Techniques of Invention

1. Make notes on my reading.
2. Keep a journal of my observations and thoughts.
3. Write freely on my topic.
4. Brainstorm my topic.
5. Connect or link my ideas and details.
6. Arrange my ideas and details in clusters or sort them.
7. Ask questions.
8. Analyze my topic as object, process, and field.

EXERCISE

Show how one of the following can be viewed as (a) object, (b) process, and (c) field:

1. planting a vegetable garden
2. a city street
3. quarterback, center fielder, or center (basketball)
4. a tire jack
5. a chemistry experiment

What topics for an essay does your analysis suggest?

2e   A note on writing with a word processor

Word processors are especially useful in preparing to write papers. Chapter 48 focuses on the uses of a word processor, but we should note a few of its advantages here.

A word processor is a small computer designed to perform some of the mechanical acts of writing. Although it cannot perform the mental processes necessary in writing, it can perform many of the mechanical jobs involved in planning, drafting, revising, and editing the paper. For example, you might use the word processor to list the topics you came up with while brainstorming. You can also use it to brainstorm a topic or experiment with a topic or sentence outline. Some word-processing programs allow you to keep your original lists of topics, ideas, and details in on-screen "windows" for reference.

At the drafting stage, the word processor allows you to delete words, phrases, sentences, and paragraphs, or transfer them to other parts of the draft with the help of various commands and functions keys. Successive drafts can be stored in the computer, in case you need to consult them later on. These same functions are useful during the revision stage as well. The word processor is especially valuable as an editing tool, and many programs contain special features that help you with punctuation, spelling, and grammar. The word processor does not displace paper and pencil; indeed, you may prefer to plan and write with pencil or typewriter.

Summary

2a The writing process consists of planning, drafting, revising, editing, and proofreading the paper.

2b There are numerous ways of finding a subject.

You can use your reading and discussion of ideas to find subjects and generate ideas and details **(2b 1)**.

You can keep a journal to store your observations, ideas, and details **(2b 2)**.

Your personal experiences and observations are dependable sources of subjects **(2b 3)**.

2c Take account of your purpose, audience, and paper's length in limiting your subject to a specific topic.

2d There are numerous ways of inventing ideas and details.

Freewriting is a useful way of discovering ideas and details and relieving writing blocks **(2d 1)**.

Brainstorming helps to recall ideas and images stored in memory **(2d 2)**.

Clustering and sorting ideas and images helps in discovering patterns and common themes **(2d 3–4)**.

By asking the journalist's six questions—What? Who? Where? When? How? Why?—you can avoid missing important details of a story **(2d 5)**.

Analyzing a person, place, thing, or activity as an object, process, or field can help you to discover its qualities **(2d 6)**.

2e   A word processor can assist in planning the paper.

Organizing the Paper

3

In planning an essay, you must define your purpose and audience, limit your topic, decide on ways to develop it, and search for ideas and supporting details. You must also formulate a working thesis or central idea and decide on a general organization, perhaps with the help of an outline. Before writing a complete first draft, you also want to choose a specific focus or point of view, a physical angle from which you can describe a scene. These activities need not occur in this order. You may have a firm thesis in mind when you select your topic and define your purpose and audience. Your working thesis may, indeed, turn out to be your final thesis. Often, in writing a paper, you discover what you want to say in the process of trying to say it.

3a Choosing a thesis

1 Thesis as controlling idea

The word *thesis* refers to the central idea of a piece of writing. In expressive writing, the thesis may be a reflection or personal truth. In informative writing, the thesis is usually an assertion or statement of fact. In a persuasive essay, it is a proposition, sometimes presented as a proposal that the writer intends to prove:

> Children, of any age, should have the right to work for money and to own and use, spend or save, the money they earn. This right, like the right to vote or to manage one's own learning, can stand alone. It could be granted to young people even if no other adults rights were granted.
>
> —John Holt, "The Right to Work"

A thesis is not the same as a statement of intention or a statement of subject. A letter to the editor of a newspaper might begin as follows:

```
Potholes are a danger to drivers. A large pothole is

causing accidents on my street.
```

These sentences indicate the purpose and subject of the letter. Neither sentence is a substitute for the thesis—the direct statement that you want the pothole repaired:

```
To prevent more accidents, the city must repair the

pothole now.
```

The thesis in persuasive, philosophical, and scientific writing is usually *explicit*; in personal and informative essays it is often *implicit*, the reader inferring the thesis from the details of the essay.

Not all essays contain a thesis. Essays that express personal feelings or develop impressions of people or places may have no central idea or point; the essay instead is organized through a central feeling or impression. A set of directions usually makes no point about the process to be performed, but an essay comparing two ways of performing the process may argue that one is better than the other.

Regardless of where it appears, the thesis serves as the central, organizing idea of the essay. It always states or implies the purpose of the essay. A detailed thesis statement sometimes reflects the organization of the essay.

2 An effective thesis

An effective thesis makes a limited assertion that is supported fully in the essay. An ineffective thesis makes a broad generalization that is not supported.

In planning your paper, your first concern is to think of an idea that can serve as a working thesis—the tentative idea that you want to develop. In sorting and classifying the details and ideas you gathered, you may find a common theme or idea that is worth developing. As you work with the idea, you will probably rephrase it, limiting the assertion in light of the details and ideas that develop it. Surprised with new implications and truths, you may decide to work with another idea. This is the way you turn your working thesis into your final one. The process is continuous as you plan, draft, and revise the paper.

In formulating a working thesis, you will produce a number of statements, not all of them satisfactory. An unsatisfactory working thesis can be a broad generalization that you find difficult or impossible to support in drafting the paper. You may, however, be able to convert the generalization into a limited observation or thesis that can be supported by the evidence you gathered. Here are several examples:

Broad Generalization	**Limited Observation or Thesis**
Accidents increase in heavy traffic.	I take greater risks when traffic is heaviest, and I see others doing the same.
Popular music is an effective vehicle of social protest.	The lyrics of country music idealize American rural life in protesting the values of urban society.
Urban crowding has changed the way Americans live.	Many Los Angeles residents spend more time in their cars than in their houses or outdoors.

An effective thesis engages the interest of readers. A good way of engaging readers' interest is to lead into the thesis statement with a limited generalization that in some way relates to their own experience:

> Most of us are not in control. My own life is an unending battle against clutter.
>
> —Ada Louise Huxtable, "Modern Life Battles: Conquering Clutter"

In generalizing your experience in this limited way, you gain the attention of readers who see your ideas as having a bearing on their lives. Restating the thesis at various points in the essay helps to maintain interest in the same way.

3 Placing the thesis

Where should you place the thesis or central idea? At the beginning of the essay, in the middle, or at the end?

The answer depends on how much help your readers need in understanding your point. You have the choice of introducing the thesis close to the beginning of the essay, or building up to it through explanatory detail. Most contemporary essayists present the thesis or central impression early to guide the reader through the discussion and details. In scientific reports, the thesis usually appears in the opening paragraph or as part of the introductory summary or abstract. In argumentative essays, the thesis is usually stated toward the beginning and restated at the end. In general, it is best to state the thesis early, unless you think it will not be understood without explanatory details or it is so controversial that you want to present the evidence in its favor first. On occasion, you may want the details you are presenting to make their effect before you interpret them.

The thesis of an essay, then, can express the central idea, control the amount of detail, and establish a focus and dominant tone. In these ways, the thesis creates in the reader expectations of what the essay will try to accomplish.

Checklist: Testing the Thesis Statement

1. Does my thesis statement make a complete assertion?

2. Does it express a single idea?
3. Is my thesis statement limited enough to be supported in the essay?
4. Does it refer to a specific area of experience?
5. Does it convey the purpose of my essay or paper?

EXERCISES

1. Identify the thesis in a letter to the editor of a newspaper. Be ready to discuss whether the letter would be more effective if the thesis was presented in a different place and in a different way.
2. Rewrite the letter, presenting the thesis in a different place. Make any other changes that you think will improve the letter, and be ready to justify your changes. ■

3b Developing the thesis

Having limited your thesis in a satisfactory way, you must look for ways to develop it. Ways of developing the thesis include the following:

- **Narration**—an account of related events, in the order they occur.
- **Description**—a picture in words of a person, place, or object.
- **Definition**—an explanation of what something is (by placing it in a familiar class of objects and stating how it differs from other members of the class, or by shedding light on the current meaning of a word by looking at its origin).
- **Classification**—placing various objects in a single group or class (e.g., classifying as *vertebrates* mammals, reptiles, birds, and other animal groups that have a backbone or spinal cord).
- **Division**—naming the subgroups or divisions of a broad class.
- **Illustration**—giving one or more examples of an idea or principle.
- **Comparison** and **contrast**—starting the similarities or differences between two or more things.
- **Analogy**—point-by-point comparison of unlike things that share a few important characteristics.
- **Process analysis**—tracing a chain of interconnected, repeatable events.
- **Causal analysis**—tracing the causes and/or effects of an event.

51

You will find these methods or modes of exposition at work in many of your college texts. For example, definition, classification, and division are basic to explanations of species, categories, and relationships. Biology and chemistry texts use these methods to classify species and compounds. You will use them in your own explanations and demonstrations in examinations and papers. Your literature text may use comparison and contrast to show how two poets develop the same theme. Historians, sociologists, economists, and scientists are all concerned with process and causal analysis.

You will have many opportunities to use the methods of development in your college writing. Often you will need to consider which kinds of development are appropriate to your purpose and topic. In a biology paper, for instance, you may be asked to define the term *vertebrate* before dividing the class of vertebrates (mammals, reptiles, fish, and others). In a chemistry exam, you may be asked to trace a chemical reaction and explain why it occurs. In a paper for a political science course, you might trace the events that produced an important act of Congress or its effects on a particular industry or group of Americans. In most writing assignments, you will use these methods in combination. Thus, you might also make brief comparisons with other legislation, citing similar causes or different effects. Definition is often a necessary step in classifying words and analyzing their divisions or subclasses; process analysis is usually an integral part of tracing a chain of causes and effects. Your writing in every discipline will require description, narration, illustration; your examples may take the form of analogy. Comparison and contrast are essential in making judgments or evaluations.

Expressive and persuasive writing use the same methods of development. In an autobiographical essay, you might classify the reading you do or the sports you play; you might describe an unusual place or narrate an important event in your life. In a persuasive essay, you might define key terms in debating a current issue, illustrate the use of these terms, and compare opposing arguments in the course of refuting them. Few essays depend on a single method of development or analysis. In organizing your paper, then, you need to consider the best way to present these methods. (Chapter 6 shows how these methods of development are used in building paragraphs.)

☑

Checklist: Developing the Thesis

1. What methods of development does my thesis call for? Does it call for definition, classification, comparison, process analysis, or some other method?
2. Does the writing assignment call for special methods of development? In writing a paper or answering an exam question, should I define terms, compare ideas and attitudes, trace a process, or analyze causes or effects?
3. What use can I make of description and narration in my writing?
4. If I use examples to develop my thesis, which ones will best fit my purpose and audience?

EXERCISE

Suggest different ways the following topics might be developed in an informative essay addressed to beginning drivers who have received driving instruction but have had little driving experience. Then choose one topic and suggest what methods of development might serve in organizing an expository essay for a particular audience.

1. parking on a hill
2. backing into a narrow space
3. entering a heavily traveled expressway
4. parallel parking

■

3c Choosing a focus

Once you limit your topic, you are ready to choose a **specific focus** or point of view. In the letter to the newspaper, we began with a **broad focus** that covered a wide range of problems. In writing from a broad focus, we would discuss various problems from the viewpoint of someone standing at a distant place and observing the streets of the city, its places of recreation, and other sites. Obviously, at such a distance, it would be impossible to describe very much.

Limiting the focus decreases that physical distance. Assume that you want to describe a dangerous pothole in the middle of your street. You are able to write about a specific problem in depth, but you must first select a specific focus from which to view the pothole. A useful focus might be to describe it as an approaching driver or pedestrian sees it. Each of these viewpoints has its advantages. The pedestrian would give a broader picture of the dangers of the pothole to the driver, but the driver could better describe the experience of driving over the pothole. In photographing a scene, you try to focus the camera from the best angle and distance and in the best light. You do the same in writing—in this case in describing the hazards of the pothole. The solution might be to describe the pothole from more than one physical angle or perspective. The difference between a broad and restricted focus is illustrated in the following figure:

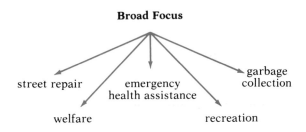

Broad Focus

street repair   emergency
health assistance

welfare   recreation

garbage
collection

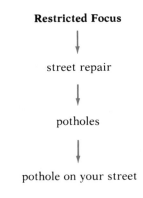

Restricted Focus

street repair

potholes

pothole on your street

3d | Organization and unity

The **order of ideas** in your essay depends on the methods you choose to develop them. If your essay contains a description of a city street, that part of the essay is spatial in organization: you are showing how the details look to an observer at a particular place. If your essay also contains a narrative of events, such as an account of a car accident, that part of the essay is temporal or chronological in organization. Process analysis is usually chronological; so is an analysis of a chain of causes and effects.

The order of ideas depends also on your audience and purpose in writing. Repairing a flat tire, for example, can be explained in various ways. The most obvious way is to present the steps chronologically. Other ways of organizing the explanation are possible if the audience is familiar with the general process. Auto mechanics probably don't require a full description of how a new tire jack works. And, though a chronological account is customary in expositions of this kind, you need not present steps chronologically. You might begin instead with less familiar or more difficult steps, giving brief attention to familiar and easy ones in the course of your explanation. In writing a persuasive letter, you might begin by reminding your readers that you and they agree on some points and then build to ideas on which you disagree. Persuasive arguments often proceed from less controversial ideas to more controversial ones. Here are the most common ways of ordering ideas:

- From specific details to general ideas and conclusions (as in causal analysis)
- From general ideas to specific details
- From the simple to the complex
- From the less to the more emphatic or important (order of climax)
- From the more (or less) familiar to the less (or more) familiar
- From the least to the most controversial (in persuasive arguments)

Since most writing uses a combination of methods, you can order ideas in various ways. In the letter to the newspaper, the facts of the case would be stated before recommending that the pothole be repaired. Since the purpose of this letter is to convince the city to take action and also gather support for your position, you make decisions about how much detail and explanation to include. You also make decisions about the order of your reasons or arguments and the arrangement of the main divisions of the letter—the description of the pothole, the explanation of its hazards, and the argument weighing the cost and benefit of repair. The arrangement of these parts depends on your purpose in writing; in this case, it is to get the pothole repaired. You may decide that your description of the pothole and account of the accident will be more effective if you present them before explaining why safe streets are a wise investment. You will be most persuasive if you conclude with your most important points. What comes toward the end of the letter stays with the reader, particularly if you state your points emphatically.

The greater the number of parts or divisions, the more attention the **unity** of the essay requires. Unity means that the essay develops one idea at a time, and develops it fully. It also means that when you develop the essay in various ways, such as by joining description and narration to develop an explanation, you do not switch from one method to another abruptly. (See 4b on unifying the paper.)

Checklist: Organizing the Paper

1. From what point of view should I write? And how broad should my focus be? Does my focus or limitation of topic fit the length prescribed? Have I limited the topic enough to explore it in depth?
2. What should be my working thesis? How should I introduce it? Where should I restate it?
3. What does my audience know about the subject? How much explanation must I give of important terms, ideas, and processes? How much detail should I give on any of these?
4. What organization will best serve my purpose? How should I order my ideas and details?
5. Have I unified my paper by ordering my ideas and details?

3e | Outlining the paper

In organizing your paper, you may find it helpful to use an outline to relate your ideas. A **topic outline** consists of short phrases, arranged to show the relationship of ideas. It is particularly useful in limiting the topic and choosing a focus. A **sentence outline,** consisting of complete sentences, provides an opportunity to state ideas exactly and to determine if they are adequately developed.

Following are a topic and sentence outline for a letter to a newspaper asking for the repair of a city street:

```
                    TOPIC OUTLINE

TOPIC: Repairing a pothole
   I.  Neglect of city streets
       A.  Causes
           1.  Rising costs
           2.  Official apathy
           3.  Public resistance to tax hikes
       B.  Effects
           1.  Increasing number of accidents
           2.  Serious injuries and deaths
  II.  History of a large pothole
       A.  Characteristics
           1.  Size
           2.  Location
       B.  Effects
           1.  Accidents
           2.  Deaths
 III.  Action needed
       A.  Repair of pothole
       B.  Maintenance of city streets
       C.  Support of tax hikes
```

SENTENCE OUTLINE

WORKING THESIS: City streets must be kept in good condition to reduce serious accidents and prevent needless
deaths.

   I. Our city streets are crumbling.

      A. They are crumbling for several reasons.

         1. Costs of repair are rising.

         2. City officials are apathetic.

         3. Voters have resisted proposed tax hikes.

      B. The effects have been serious.

         1. The number of serious accidents is in-
creasing.

         2. Drivers and pedestrians are suffering in-
jury and death.

  II. A large pothole is causing numerous accidents.

      A. The pothole is one of the worst in the city.

         1. It looks like a small pond.

         2. It is located in the middle of a busy
street.

      B. The pothole has caused property damage and
physical injury.

         1. It has caused several car collisions.

         2. People have been crippled or killed in
accidents.

 III. The city and the public must act now.

      A. The city works department must repair the
pothole without delay.

      B. The department must keep all streets in bet-
ter repair.

      C. The public must support higher taxes.

    You will write useful outlines if you observe the following
guidelines.

Consistency. In topic and sentence outlines, ideas are broken down into component ideas. The word *breakdown* means division: a breakdown must have two or more subdivisions. This is why every *A* has a *B*, and every *1* a *2*. If a single topic or sentence appears in the breakdown, it should be combined with the heading.

Indentation. The breakdown is indented to show the *relationship* between ideas and details. But notice that the headings (A, B, C) don't necessarily express the more important ideas. You may decide to give the details (shown in the breakdown) greater emphasis in the paper.

Parallelism. The wording and structure of parallel topics and sentences is roughly parallel ("The department must keep," "The public must support"). Parallelism is desirable because it shows whether ideas and details serve the same purpose in the paragraph.

Thesis statement. The outline may include a thesis statement at the beginning or at the end. Note that the outline states the ideas and details of the essay only; it does not show which ideas serve as the introduction and conclusion.

Outlines are valuable not only in planning but also in drafting and revising papers. In outlining a first draft, you may find an idea that stands without supporting ideas or details. Here is another opportunity to discover additional ways of developing the essay. The sentence outline may suggest that the development of the topic is too broad for the purpose you have in mind. When you begin revising the paper, you may decide to reduce the number of your examples. At the revision stage, the outline is also valuable in testing the organization of ideas.

The outline is a preliminary plan only—a plan that you are likely to change several times in the course of drafting and revising the paper. As you write the paper, you may think of more desirable ways to limit the topic or develop it. The longer the essay, the more backtracking and rewriting of the draft you are likely to do—a time when outlines can be especially helpful.

Summary

3a Your thesis should be the central idea, personal truth, directive, or proposition of your essay.

Use a working thesis as the controlling or organizing idea (**3a 1**).

Make your working thesis an idea that your evidence supports fully (**3a 2**).

Place your thesis toward the beginning of the essay unless you have reason to build the discussion toward it (**3a 3**).

3b Use one or more methods—definition, classification and division, illustration, comparison and contrast, analogy, process and causal analysis—to develop your thesis.

3c The more narrow the focus of your discussion or the scene you are describing, the greater the clarity of your details must be.

3d Consider your purpose in writing and your audience in organizing your ideas and details.

3e A topic or sentence outline is useful in organizing the essay and testing its structure.

Writing the Paper

4

In writing your paper, you put your plan to work. You begin by writing a single draft, and sometimes you write more than one. In this instance, your first draft is a trial effort, an attempt to understand the subject that sometimes ends without your reaching a definite conclusion or thesis. For this reason, the first draft is sometimes called a "discovery" draft. In your second draft, you incorporate ideas and details from your trial draft into your original plan and outline. Revision begins with your second draft and perhaps later ones.

This chapter describes the process of writing one or more drafts of the paper and revising and editing it. The chapter then illustrates the whole process—from the initial planning to the final editing—through the composition of a student essay.

4a | Drafting the paper

1 Writing a first draft

As you draft, you will probably make several false starts before ideas and details begin to flow. One false start may occur if you write in a tone or voice that is unsuited to your subject or audience (see 29c). Other false starts include narrating an event without clarifying the time and place or giving sufficient information about the participants, or describing a scene from the wrong angle or point of view. Drafting is similar to taking a photograph from several angles and then choosing the best angle from which to take more pictures. "I make use of two or three cameras almost all the time," the film director Akira Kurosawa has said. "I cut the film freely and splice together the pieces which have caught the action most forcefully, as if flying from one piece to another."

As you write the first draft, you want to keep your notes and outline close at hand, for you may want to consult them in writing your opening paragraphs. Your first draft is a test of your plan; it is also a means of discovering what you want to say. For this reason, write without pausing to consult your notes and outline even if you depart from them. Your writing may take an unexpected direction through which you may discover valuable ideas and details or a new and better approach to the topic. Note these new possibilities in the margin of the page. If you depart from your notes or outline, don't feel obliged to return to them to get your paper on track. Don't pause to rethink the paper or write a new outline. When you revise your latest draft you will have an opportunity to evaluate these possibilities in light of your purpose and the needs of your audience.

You may find it helpful to get the response of your instructor or classmates to your first draft or a few paragraphs from it. Your instructor may be able to point out problems in focus, organization, and other features (see page 76) that will save you time later on. Your instructor may also call attention to sentence style and to errors in spelling, punctuation, and grammar. You may wish to ask another reader questions that will help in revising your paper (see page 80).

2 Writing a second draft

In writing your second draft, you will again have your outline and notes in hand, but you should not use them mechanically. For, as in your first or trial draft, you will want to incorporate new ideas and details and perhaps reorganize parts of the paper. Here are additional suggestions for writing your second draft:

Open each of your paragraphs with a topic sentence.   A topic sentence states the central idea of the paragraph and develops the central idea or thesis of the essay. Don't spend time on the wording of these sentences at this point. If a topic sentence suggests a different idea, develop that idea. You will have an opportunity later on to revise the sequence of ideas and perhaps restate your topic sentences. (See 5b on using topic sentences to focus paragraphs.)

Develop your paragraphs in ways suggested by your working thesis and topic sentences.   If, for example, your topic sentence mentions an important term, define and discuss that term in the paragraph; if the topic sentence suggests a resemblance between people, compare and contrast those people. If other ways of developing your paragraphs occur to you in the course of drafting them, make a note of these possibilities for later use. See Chapters 5 and 6 on ways of developing and organizing paragraphs. See 5b especially on using topic sentences.

Write the paper in blocks.   In your preliminary plan or outline, you arranged your ideas and details in segments or blocks. Write your draft block by block to maintain continuity. You will probably need to rewrite your introductory and concluding paragraphs after your main discussion takes shape, but don't be concerned with this now. See 5e for help with opening and closing paragraphs.

As in your first draft, if you are uncertain about names, dates, and other details, make a note in the margin to check them later on. Don't interrupt your writing of the paper to do so.

4b | Revising the paper

1 The process of revision

Although you reconsider your plan for the paper at all stages of the writing process, it is your main concern in revising. The process of revision includes:

- **adding** and **deleting** ideas and details;
- **substituting** words, phrases, and sentences;
- **moving** ideas and details to other parts of the essay.

As you revise, you should look at what you have written through the eyes of your readers. You should read not only for accuracy of details and consistency of thought but also for overall unity and effectiveness.

Unity.   Your essay has **unity** if your ideas and details develop the topic sentences of your paragraphs, and the paragraphs together develop your thesis. If you notice inconsistencies in reading the draft, you should look carefully at your working thesis to see whether it covers all ideas and details. If it does not, you need to revise it and perhaps map a revision of the whole essay, working out a new organization and perhaps adopting a new point of view or tone. In revising, you also rephrase or recast sentences and check words for exactness of meaning.

Coherence.   In organizing the essay, you need to give the essay **coherence.** You want to show your reader how the sentences in your paragraphs form a whole. Your paragraphs are the larger units of your essay, so they too must form a whole. To make your paragraphs and essay coherent, you may need to add linking words or formal transitions (words like *thus, however,* and *therefore*). Pronouns are an important means of coherence, and so are sentence coordination and subordination and other means of showing the relationship between ideas. (See 5c on ways of making paragraphs and essays coherent.)

Relevance. Your ideas and details are relevant if they serve the purpose of the essay. A colorful description of a car may make an idea concrete in an expressive essay but distract the reader of an informative essay on repairing a car engine. Your ideas and details must fit the knowledge and interests of the general or special audience.

Consistent style. The style of your paper—word usage, tone, sentence structure, and other features—should be consistent as well. The paper should not swing from formal sentences and an abstract vocabulary to informal sentences and slang. You need to watch out for inappropriate shifts in tone—for example, from an impersonal, objective tone to a chatty one. (See 1c and 30a–b for discussion of diction and formal and informal writing styles.)

2 Improving your introduction

In drafting the paper, your main concern is getting your ideas on paper. You therefore write your introductory paragraphs without considering their effectiveness. In revising the draft, you should evaluate the effectiveness of your introduction and consider how your readers will respond to it.

An effective introduction announces the topic of the paper. Your opening paragraph should not leave your readers in doubt about the subject or topic of the paper. One way to introduce the topic is to begin with a general statement of the subject (*generalization*) and then limit the subject to a specific topic (*restriction*). Another way is to proceed from an opening statement of the topic to specific details, or to begin the paragraph with these details so to build to the thesis statement. (See 5c for examples of these kinds of opening paragraphs.)

You will gain the attention of your readers by stating your thesis early, perhaps in your first or second paragraph. Your readers want to know not only the subject or topic of the paper but also what you have to say about it. You should give your readers this information early in the paper unless you have reason to delay your thesis. The following opening paragraph introduces the thesis through a question:

I was writing not long ago about a team of Purdue engineers who foresaw that by 2001 practically everything would be done by remote control. The question I asked—because such a "projection" *forces* one to ask it—was, *Where does satisfaction come from?* I concluded that there probably wouldn't be much satisfaction in such a world. There would be a lot of what passes for "efficiency," and lot of "production" and "consumption," but little satisfaction.

—Wendell Berry, "Home of the Free"

If you decide instead to build to your thesis statement, you may want to hint at it early on, as the student writer Glenn Grube does in his essay later in this chapter. (See 5d for additional ways of introducing the thesis.)

You will engage the readers' interest immediately by appealing to their curiosity and imagination. In doing so, you are showing your readers why the subject is important and interesting to you. You can use details, images, and metaphors to appeal to their imagination:

The men have left a gigantic 6600 combine a few yards from our grove, at the edge of the stubble. For days it was working around the farm; we heard it on the east, later on the west, and finally we could see it grinding back and forth over the windrows on the south. But now it has been simply squatting at the field's edge, huge, tremendously still, very professional, slightly dangerous.

—Carol Bly, "Getting Tired"

To hold the interest of your readers, add details that develop your introductory generalizations. You might also add a quotation that suggests the importance of the topic or presents an unusual way of viewing or discussing it, or ask a question of the reader, as Wendell Berry does.

A formal opening statement like the following probably won't capture the interest of many readers:

```
In this essay, I will describe my experiences
working on a farm.
```

And opening an informative or persuasive essay with the thesis can seem abrupt:

```
Life in the future may be more efficient, but it
won't give much satisfaction.
```

Notice, however, that scientific papers often open with the thesis or the central finding of the researchers or scientists:

> The United States is likely to be headed for another major energy crisis for a number of reasons. These include (i) recent developments in the world oil markets, (ii) the resultant crippling of the U.S. petroleum industry, (iii) the continued existence of the Organization of Petroleum Exporting Countries (OPEC) cartel, (iv) instability in the Middle East, (v) the inherently long times necessary to change the U.S. and world energy systems, and (vi) the short-term orientation of the U.S. public, government, and industry. The background for this unfortunate situation is described below.
> —Robert L. Hirsch, "Impending United States Energy Crisis,"
> *Science,* March 20, 1987

3 Improving your conclusion

Writing an effective conclusion requires the same care as writing an effective introduction. In revising your draft, you should check for the following:

An effective conclusion reminds readers of the importance of the subject to you.   The reader has been occupied with following your discussion and may have lost sight of the main topic and its importance. Your concluding paragraph should remind the reader of this importance through reference to the ideas introduced in your opening paragraphs. Many effective conclusions build to a general statement or a series of generalizations that give this reminder.

An effective conclusion sometimes restates the thesis.   If you state your thesis toward the beginning of the essay, you will help the reader by restating it at the end. In a long essay, it is a good idea to remind the reader of the thesis in the middle paragraphs. One way of restating the thesis is to present it as a call for action or as a forecast or prediction:

> It is clear that there are a number of options that could stop the current slide into extreme national dependence on foreign

oil. However, because none are simple, because people are generally happy with lower energy prices, and because the country tends to be short-term oriented, there appears to be a low probability of action before the problem becomes severe. It is for these reasons that a future national energy crisis seems likely, probably sometime in the early to mid-1990s, when U.S. oil dependence is above 50% and OPEC has regained control of world oil markets.

　　—Robert L. Hirsch, "Impending United States Energy Crisis"

An effective conclusion completes the discussion. An ineffective conclusion ends the paper inconclusively or ambiguously, leaving the reader uncertain about whether the discussion has come to an end. To make your conclusion effective, you might end with a call to action, a forecast, or a final question that engages a response to the essay. But don't tell the reader directly that you are concluding the essay or inviting their response:

```
Having presented my reasons for believing we are facing
a new energy crisis, I ask the reader to consider ways
to avoid one.
```

Hirsch makes no direct appeal in his concluding paragraph, yet his forecast suggests why we should consider taking action.

4 Improving your sentences and diction

In the course of revising your draft, you want to improve your sentences and diction. Revising sentences involves much more than making them grammatical—you also want them to express your ideas most effectively. The effectiveness of a sentence may be improved in several ways, such as by reducing wordiness (see 15a) or by subordinating ideas and details to give greater prominence to the main idea (see 12c). You can also use parallelism to highlight similar and contrasting ideas (see 14a). You will make the greatest improvements in your sentences if you concentrate on how they function in your paragraphs and in the whole essay. As you read your draft, listen to how the sentences connect. Your reader should hear your voice in your sentences, though your written sentence style should be tighter in structure than your spoken one. When you hear a sentence that jars the ear, recast it.

Choices in language or diction depend on whether you are writing in an informal, general, or formal style (see 1c, 29b). You need to consider the tone you want to convey in the paper. Your choice of tone should be based on the nature of the subject and the relationship you wish to establish with your readers. In general, the more you focus on personal experience, the more informal your choice of words is likely to be. The more you focus on facts, processes, and ideas, the more formal your tone will be in vocabulary and sentence structure. Just as you continually make adjustments in the amount of discussion and detail, so do you make adjustments in diction and tone.

Revision takes many forms. There are no fixed rules that fit every written situation and purpose. You will reconsider earlier decisions and make new choices, perhaps redefining your purpose and focus and even your audience. In some papers, your main concerns in revision will be sentence style and diction. Revision is complete when you consider the paper satisfactory. But even then you may decide to return to the paper a month or so later to make further revisions.

5 Titling the paper

You may have given your first or second draft a working title. As you write your paper, jot down other titles that occur to you. In revising the paper, choose the title that best fits your topic and approach to it and engages the interest of the reader. The title should point to the topic of the paper; it may also suggest the nature of the essay and your approach. If your title is too general, it probably won't interest many readers:

```
Changing Jobs
```

If the title is too specific, it may give the impression that your essay is highly technical:

```
Learning to Drive a Twenty-ton Semitrailer
```

The following title states the general topic of the essay:

```
On First Driving a Semitrailer
```

4c | Editing the paper

In the course of drafting and revising the paper, you may pause to edit it for grammar, punctuation, and spelling. However, these are your main concerns during the final editing and proofreading stages. In editing the final draft, you correct errors in grammar, punctuation, and spelling that you did not correct earlier. Revision and editing, of course, are not wholly separate processes. But while you edit the draft by spotting mistakes and correcting them, you now concentrate on making these types of corrections. A final proofreading of your typed or printed final copy is also essential. You need to do this job well. On occasion, you may want to return to a finished paper to make additional changes and corrections.

Editing calls for a practiced eye. Although you may find it easy to recognize misspelled words, inaccurate punctuation, or lack of agreement in the writing of others, it is far more difficult to recognize your own errors, particularly those resulting not from carelessness but from habit. For example, you may have difficulty with sentence fragments and comma splices, or with pronoun agreement and reference. One solution is to keep a list of the grammatical and punctuation errors you tend to make and have had to correct on earlier papers; this list should also include the sections in this handbook that discuss how to correct such errors. In addition, the summaries at the end of each chapter will help you in correcting these errors.

As noted earlier, it is important to put yourself in place of the reader as you revise. You can do the same as you edit the final draft. It is also helpful to read the paper aloud; your ears may discover errors that your eyes missed.

Finally, keep a dictionary close at hand for checking the spellings and meanings of words. It may also be helpful to keep a list of the words you tend to misspell in your writing. (See 28g for a list of commonly misspelled words.)

Whatever advice you receive on a draft from your instructor or classmates, the decisions on what to change and what to retain are entirely your own. It is up to you to determine if your essay is satisfactory in form and content and ready to be submitted to readers. For this reason, you must learn to look at your writing with a critical eye, recognizing its good qualities but also its faults and inadequacies. Good writers, John Ciardi says, have "a second attention lurking in the mind at the very moment they have felt the need to be most indivisibly absorbed in what they are doing." This "second attention," though important in drafting, is indispensable to revision and editing.

Checklist: Revising and Editing the Paper

1. What changes will improve the paper as a whole? Have I fully explained my ideas? Do I need to add supporting ideas and details? Do I need to illustrate any of them?

2. Have I chosen ideas and details that fit the interests and knowledge of my audience? Have I appealed to their curiosity and imagination?

3. Is my paper unified? Do all of my ideas and details connect to my thesis? Have I discussed one idea at a time?

4. Is my discussion coherent? Do I need to add transitional words or sentences to clarify the relationship of my ideas and details or to indicate a change in topic?

5. Does my introduction suggest the purpose and nature of my essay? Does it introduce or state my thesis? Is it concise?

6. Does my conclusion restate my thesis and adequately summarize the essay? Does it pull together the main points of the discussion? Is it concise?

7. Are any of my sentences awkward or unclear? If so, how should I recast them? Have I used standard punctuation and grammar? Have I misspelled any words?

8. Is the level of usage right for my subject, audience, and occasion? Are any of my words inexact or inappropriate?

9. Does my title describe the essay accurately and concisely?

4d | Paper in progress: Glenn Grube, "Mild Protest at the DMV"

1 Planning the paper

Glenn Grube was prompted to write about his experiences at a local office of the Connecticut Department of Motor Vehicles (DMV), where he had recently gone to register a new car and secure license plates. His visit to the DMV office was not his first; he had come as a teenager to take a driving test and had returned several times to renew his driving license and car registration. On his most recent visit, Glenn realized that his feelings and impressions of the office were different from those of his first.

Glenn decided to write about these changed perceptions and feelings. His essay would be expressive, though he would be giving information about the DMV in creating a setting for his experiences. Glenn also had another motive for writing. He had participated in a brief episode—probably a common occurrence in a large public office and certainly insignificant to the others involved, yet significant enough to Glenn at the time to prompt him to explore its meaning in his essay.

Glenn wanted to express his feelings about the DMV office; but he did not want his essay to be a complaint about the long lines and confusion he had experienced there. He needed to give information about the office, but his essay would not be a warning to readers about what to expect. His audience would be a mixed one, including those who had visited the office and those who had not. Glenn's general purpose, then, was to share an experience and perhaps make a point about it. In planning the essay, he would need to define his purpose exactly, choose a specific focus, and decide on a central impression or idea.

A list of topics. Glenn's planning began by quickly writing down a list of images and ideas recalled from his visit:

```
License & Registration Room signs hung on wire
snaking lines
plastic waiting chairs
Public Room--locked at 4:15--closed at 4:30
people locked out
```

```
forms and number
pictures
  squat, brick
  columns in front
  tiled floors, gray paint like school or hospital
  gift shop--magazines, cigarettes, candy, soda
constant hum of fans
blinking electric sign giving numbers
lines to left and right of the sign
seat belt and DWI posters on wall
"Public Welcome"
```

Glenn organized these details into several groups, noting that they fell under several general topics:

```
The building outside
The building inside--halls, gift shop, etc.
License and Registration Room--posters, signs,
regulations, furniture, lines of people
```

A preliminary outline. Drawing on his lists, Glenn produced a topic outline for a draft of his paper. The center of the paper would be his experience waiting to register his car.

```
  I.  Entering the building
      A.  The building seen from the outside
      B.  The building seen from the inside
          1.  Rooms and corridors
          2.  Signs to the License and Registration
              Room
 II.  Entering the License and Registration Room
      A.  Signs and posters
      B.  Lines of people
III.  Waiting to register my car
      A.  A walk through the corridor outside
      B.  Talking with people
      C.  An episode at closing time
```

1. A woman locked out of the room
2. Attitude of officials in the room
3. Attitude of the people waiting

This topic outline suggested to Glenn how to relate his ideas and details. The outline did not, however, show what weight he would give these ideas and details in the paper (see 3e). As it turned out, Glenn decided to make the episode he originally placed in a subordinate position the center of his discussion. He did not realize he would do so when he began to plan the paper. It was only through drafting and revision that Glenn was able to discover the focus of his discussion and the weight of the ideas and details suggested in the outline.

Glenn's outline also suggested a possible working thesis. He considered making his center of discussion the behavior of the people waiting in the office in response to the episode that occurred at closing time. Glenn did not yet have a clear idea of what the episode said about these people or about the DMV. But he knew that he wanted also to convey the atmosphere of a public place and its effect on people. Drafting the paper would perhaps bring his subject and purpose in writing into focus and show him a way to unite the several themes he had in mind.

2   Drafting the paper

Glenn proceeded to write a first draft of his paper. The opening and middle paragraphs of his first draft, with the marginal and interlinear changes that Glenn made, follow. These paragraphs contain a few additional changes in phrasing and punctuation.

First Draft—Opening Paragraphs

From the outside, the Connecticut State
Department of Motor Vehicles (DMV) looks much like
most institutional buildings. It is large, squat and
brick. The pillars around the main entrance facing
the street give it a slightly imperial feel, but other
than that, it could easily pass for any public school. *with its drab red brick and simple structure.*
It is nestled in a residential corner of ~~suburban~~ *a suburb of Hartford.*
Wethersfield. The first time I went there was to take

my driving test to get my ~~lisence~~ *license*, three years ago.

The area surrounding the DMV ~~is a veritable~~ *does not look threatening,* *with its large, single-family houses and tree-lined streets, but on closer inspection it is a veritable obstacle* ~~obsticale~~ course for drivers. There are numerous yeild signs, one-way streets, *and* divided roads, ~~and for~~ *to trip up sixteen year olds taking their driving test. And for the truly difficult test,* ~~the truly vicious driving tester~~, the busy Silas Deane Highway is not far away. *Also,* It has ~~even~~ been rumoured that the DMV pays nearby residents to grow bushes high enough to partially block street signs, further complicating the driving tests. But despite all these ~~obsticals~~ *obstacles*, I passed that test, ~~and now~~ three years *ago,* *and now* two traffic tickets, and one totaled car later, I am back at the DMV registering a used car I just bought.

First Draft—Middle Paragraphs

I hear a young woman giving directions to an elderly man, and follow him to my line. The room is rectangular with a high ceiling. I stand in a line leading to a desk in the center of the room, and

~~After~~ *R*egaining my bearings, I ~~managed to get~~ *glance around to find the* ~~in the~~ correct line ~~through a combination of signs and overheard conversations.~~ There ~~were~~ *are* at least ~~five~~ *four* ~~separate~~ *other* lines snaking through this room, all of them curving down roped-off aisles. Despite the numerous lines, the majority of the people seemed to be sitting in rows of plastic chairs in the back of the room, and I soon learned why.

After ten minutes in this line, I got to the front and was given two forms to fill out and a number and then curtly dismissed. Confused, I wandered away.

I write down my name, address, insurance company and the rest of the things people always want to know about you on the yellow sheets.

Then I ~~happened~~ *happen* to look up, and I ~~saw~~ *see* a large number "63" displayed on a screen near the ceiling. The number in my hand was 112. Discouraged, I ~~settled~~ *settle* down with the rest of the unlucky numbers in an uncomfortable plastic chair. They were up to number 69 when I finished filling in my forms.

Following is Glenn's complete second draft and marginal comments and suggestions such as you might receive from an instructor on a first or second draft:

Second Draft

From the outside, the Connecticut State
Department of Motor Vehicles (DMV) looks much like
most institutional buildings. Seen from a distance it
is a large building; seen close, it is squat and brick.
The pillars around the main entrance facing the street
give it a slightly imperial feel, but other than that, it
could easily pass for any public school with its drab,
red brick and simple structure. It is nestled in a
residential corner of Wethersfield, a suburb of

ref

Hartford. The first time I went(there) was to take my
driving test to get my license, three years ago.

The area surrounding the DMV does not look
threatening with its large, single-family houses and

*Weak adjective-
let the noun
do the work.*

tree-lined streets, but on closer inspection, it is a
(veritable) obstacle course for new drivers. (There are

*Your sentence will
be emphatic if you
open with this
compound subject.*

numerous yield signs, one way streets, and divided
roads to trip up sixteen-year-olds nervously taking
their driving test.) And for the truly difficult driving

*You manage
this double
view well.
Will all this
detail relate
to your
central
impression
or thesis?
The less you
say about
yourself,
the more
the building
comes into
focus.*

test, the busy Silas Deane Highway is not far away.
Also, it has been rumoured that the DMV pays nearby
residents to grow bushes high enough to partially
block street signs, further complicating the driving
tests. But despite all these obstacles,(I) passed that
test three years ago, and now two traffic tickets, and
one totaled car later,(I) am back at the DMV
registering a used car I just bought.

As(I) walk through the automated doors

*Notice the
distracting
rhyme.*

prepared for an afternoon of boring bureaucracy,(I)
am once again struck by how much all of
Connecticut's public buildings look the same. (The
vibrant green of the bucolic scene)outside fades into a

dull green-tiled floor and cement brick walls, coated
in grey paint. It(reminds me)of a prison, or even a

*Tense problem
- see 9a-2.*

hospital,(if the atmosphere were more sterile.) I need
to find the "General Information, License and
Registration Room." Following the directions on the
large plastic signs hanging by chains from the ceiling,
I walk down the hall and up a large stairwell and
then turn right. Entering through one of the many

*What does
the room
look like
from the
doorway?*

sets of double doors, I(stop). All the noise and action
in this room confuse me. Up until now, I had
encountered only a few employees sipping coffee and
one or two other people strolling the halls looking at

*Your narrative
shifts tense.
See 18a-4
on literary
present
tense.*

signs. But in this large room there(were)at least one
hundred people milling around.

After a few moments I am able to regain my
bearings, and I begin to glance around at the signs
trying to find the correct line. I overhear a young
woman giving directions to an elderly man, and follow
him to my line. The room is rectangular with a high
ceiling. I stand in a line leading to a desk in the
center of the room, and(there are)at least four other
lines snaking through this room, all of them curving
down roped-off aisles. Despite the numerous lines,
the majority of the people seem to be sitting in rows
of plastic chairs in the back of the room, and I soon
learned why.

*Your central
impression seems
to begin here —
confusion, leading
to discouragement,
finally tedium.
Can you highlight
these
impressions?*

After ten minutes in this line, I get to the front
and am given two car registration forms to fill out
and a number and then curtly dismissed. Confused, I
wander away. Then I happen to look up, and I see a
large number "63" displayed on a screen near the
ceiling. The number in my hand(was)112.
Discouraged, I settle down with the rest of the

77

unlucky numbers in an uncomfortable plastic chair.
I write down my name, address, insurance company,
and the rest of the things people always want to know
about you on the yellow sheets. (They) were up to
number 69 when I finished filling in the forms.

Watch for vague pronouns. See 11e.

As the number changed every three to four
minutes, a green arrow would flash, showing (you)
which line to get into. One line was for receiving (your)
number, one was for automobile dealerships only, and
one was to have your photograph taken for your
license. I would go to one of the other two lines. I (sat)
waiting and reading all the pro–seatbelt and
anti–drunk/driving posters ~~which~~ *that* were tacked up
around the room. I (soon bored) of this, and decided to
take a stroll around the building.

You can omit these words without changing your meaning See 11e.

On my walk, I discovered a cafeteria, an
emissions–testing appeal office, a small shop that sold
cigarettes, candy and magazines ("Public Welcome"
read the sign outside it) and innumerable soda
machines and rest rooms. When I returned to my
vigil in the registration room the number *on the* screen said
89.

Can you relate these details to your central impression?

For a while I (entertained myself) by
eavesdropping on conversations around me. One
man, looking rather uncomfortable and nervous, was
discussing strategy with another man, who I assumed
to be his lawyer, as they prepared to go to a hearing
on the suspension of his driver's license. After those
two left, I began *to* chat with those nearby. The
atmosphere seemed very friendly, since we all knew
no one had anything better to do. When you are
bored, even the most mundane conversation seems
interesting. We all joked about the slow advance of

the numbers, and cheered on those with lower numbers soon to be called. The flash of the camera and the low hum of large industrial fans faded into the background, and we began to enjoy one another's company. Some say that tragedy brings people closer together. Tedium seemed to have the same effect here.

Nice build to this point. A thesis perhaps?

Good trans.

Most of us had been waiting for more than an hour, and as the time got closer and closer to 4:30 (closing time for the DMV), some of us with higher numbers began to worry that we might not be served. But at 4:15, our fears were allayed. A brown uniformed(employee)announced that the outside doors would be locked, and only those who already had numbers would be served. I was relieved(and only four numbers from being called,)so I relaxed. Suddenly there was a loud pounding on the door. A middle-aged woman with greying hair was peering through the small, square window in the door, and I saw her lips moving excitedly. I recognized her as one of the people who had been sitting with me earlier. The DMV employee who had just locked the doors saw her, pointed to his watch, and shook his head. As he turned to walk away, the woman(futilely) held up a paper with the number 110 printed on it. She had been waiting for hours and had just gone outside for a moment perhaps to smoke a cigarette. Almost simultaneously, all of us waiting in the chairs began to yell at the employee. We all knew how frantic that lady must feel; we had all been waiting just as long. (There was a feeling of ~~comradary~~ *comradery* among us.) Despite the fact that she would probably delay our service for five minutes or so, we all shouted at

A guard?

See 14b

She hasn't yet been refused.

Did the tedium mentioned earlier lead to this reaction?

Is this your thesis?

Parallelism
for emphasis.
Your crucial
paragraph —
give more
specific
details.

the employee to let her in.(Perhaps) fearing a riot,(or
~~perhaps~~
maybe) just to be nice, the man went back and opened
the door for her. She came over to us and thanked us
(graciously) and then her number flashed on the
screen.

I was called soon after, and got my license
plates and registration papers. As I walked out of the
DMV I felt strangely happy despite the tedium of the
afternoon. I had spent hours waiting and I had to
pay over $100 in fees, and yet I still felt good.

*A good draft — interesting subject and approach. I see the building
and the room. Your feelings come across. But take your time with
key moments and key details. For example, if one's number is called,
why get into another line? You may want to cut down on details
that draw the reader away from your central impression and
emerging thesis. Which is? I see a number of ideas but no
central or dominant one. I look forward to your revision.*

3 Revising the second draft

In revising the second draft of his paper, Glenn used the marginal comments of his instructor as well as some advice from
a friend to reconsider his purpose and focus of interest.

Comments on his draft.   Here are the questions that Glenn
asked a friend about his second draft and the answers he
received:

- Is the purpose of my essay clear?
  As far as I can tell, your purpose is to describe a place and
  narrate how people, all strangers, form a group. The group is
  analogous to army recruits in basic training. All types of people
  are thrown together, to wait in what resembles a foxhole. The
  strangers at the end form a vanguard and protect one of their
  own. Your essay is more about these people than about the
  Motor Vehicle Department.
- Is the thesis or central impression clear?
  I see a central impression—boredom, tediousness, the atmosphere of a public waiting room. Toward the middle of the paper
  you say that tedium has the same effect as tragedy—it brings
  people together. But the episode that follows doesn't show that
  tedium led to the protest. So you must have another idea in

mind—that people form a vanguard when they are pressed together. You make this point well.

■ Do you see what happened? Is the focus clear?

A very good opening description, but the focus shifts too quickly in some of your paragraphs. It would be better if you said more about the setting—the hallway, lines, posters. And what were the people like? The later scenes need the most detail.

■ Is the tone consistent?

The tone is consistent. The feeling of tedium is felt up to the end of the essay. That feeling gives way to other feelings at the end, but you prepare the reader for them.

■ How effective are my sentences?

Some of your sentences need to be revised. Some are awkward. Perhaps shorter, more concise sentences would be more effective.

Sharpening the focus. Glenn's first concern in beginning his revision of the second draft was to sharpen the focus of his opening paragraphs. Both of his readers noted the sense of tedium and aimless activity—a place where nothing seems to be happening. Glenn wanted to show that those working in the building sensed this feeling and were affected by it, but he decided not to stress this point. To describe the workers would shift the focus from the tedium of waiting. Glenn wanted his details to develop this idea. He realized that he had been working with a half-formed idea in writing his first and second drafts.

Choosing a thesis. Glenn realized that he had made a point worth developing—tedium, like tragedy, brings people closer together. Was this the point he had in mind in showing how the people waiting to register their cars acted when they saw the woman locked out of the room? Both of Glenn's readers raised this question in their comments.

In his first draft, Glenn referred to the growing sense of comradery among the people waiting at the DMV. But he wondered whether the same unity of feeling and action occurs in similar situations, such as in a crowded bus, where people are also pressed together and immobile. Glenn decided not to generalize about how people behave. Although he wanted to explain the behavior of the people involved in the episode at the DMV, he knew that to generalize about human nature was beyond the scope of his essay. He therefore rephrased his working thesis to refer indirectly to the episode:

```
Frustration and tedium have created a bond.
```

Having revised his thesis, Glenn was ready to undertake an overall revision that combines description, narration, and commentary. His chief concern was to build the essay up to the climactic episode. He needed to eliminate some details in order to highlight the ideas and details that support his thesis. In his first and second drafts, he had focused on the Motor Vehicles Department, assuming it was his subject. But in thinking about the draft and the comments of his readers, he realized that his subject was the brief protest he had witnessed. So he reworked his second draft, sharpening its focus and refining his thesis. He also needed to make each detail contribute to the central impression and thesis, and to give more attention to his sentences.

Sentence style.   Glenn wrote his first draft in the past tense. As the revised paragraph from his final draft shows (see page 87), Glenn turned to the literary present tense (see 18a 4) to report his experiences as if they are occurring at the

Second Draft—Middle Paragraph

The room is rectangular with a high ceiling. It is easy to lose one's bearings in such a place.
~~After a few moments I am able to regain my bearings, and I begin to~~ glance around ~~at the signs~~
trying to find the ~~correct line.~~ *registration counter* I overhear a young woman giving directions to an elderly man, and follow him to ~~my~~ *a* line. ~~The room is rectangular with a high ceiling. I stand in a line leading to a desk in~~ the center of the room and there are at least four other ~~lines snaking through this room,~~ all of them curving down roped-off aisles. ~~Despite the numerous lines,~~ the majority of ~~the~~ people ~~seem to be~~ sitting in ~~rows of~~ plastic chairs ~~in~~ *at* the back of the room and I soon ~~learned why.~~

that begins near
This line leads to a desk, where one is given a number. From the desk radiate at least three other lines,
They have also come to register new cars.

One line is for automobile dealers, another for those having a photograph taken for a driving license, and still another for those renewing their licenses. As I wait to get my number, I notice

moment of narration. Glenn gave his essay greater immediacy and liveliness in making this change.

One of Glenn's readers commented that awkward sentences could be improved by shortening them. In revising his paragraphs to give full details on a single action, Glenn decided to separate some of his longer sentences. Following is a revised sentence from his first draft:

First Draft

```
There was a choice of only two for those with numbers,
since one line was for receiving your number, one was
for automobile dealerships only, and one was to have
your photograph taken for your license.
```

Second Draft

```
One line was for receiving your number, one was for au-
tomobile dealerships only, and one was to have your
photograph taken for your license.
```

Could this sentence be improved further? Glenn tried omitting unnecessary words and reducing the number of second-person pronouns (*you, your*). He also revised the tense:

Final Draft

```
One line is for automobile dealerships, another for
those having a photograph taken for a driving license,
and still another for those renewing their licenses.
```

Glenn also omitted the second-person pronoun from other sentences where it proved unnecessary:

Second Draft

```
As the number changed every three to four minutes, a
green arrow would flash, showing you which line to get
into.
```

Final Draft

```
As the numbers change, every three or four minutes,
flashing green arrows point to different lines, where
people whose numbers have been called are standing.
```

83

Glenn made some of his sentences emphatic by dropping the opening expletives *there* and *it* and beginning with the subject:

Second Draft

```
There are numerous yield signs, one-way streets, and
divided roads to trip up sixteen year olds nervously
taking their driving test.
```

Final Draft

```
Numerous yield signs, one-way streets, and divided
roads, and crowded Silas Deane Highway not far away,
trip up the sixteen-year-old....
```

Diction. Decisions in diction involve choosing words appropriate to the subject and audience. Glenn's essay is written in a general style that at times borders on the informal and colloquial:

```
When you are bored, the most aimless conversation seems
interesting. We joke about the slow advance of the num-
bers and cheer those with numbers soon to be called.
```

The tone of the sentence is ironic and perhaps even amused. Glenn did not want the tone of the paragraph to be grave.

In revising his paper, Glenn gave considerable attention to his choice of adjectives. Often the choice was whether to use a stronger adjective or to omit an unnecessary adjective. He took the advice of his teacher in the following revised sentence:

```
But on closer inspection, it proves to be an [a verita-
ble] obstacle course for the driver.
```

4 Editing the final draft

Glenn edited his third and final draft for spelling, punctuation, and grammar. He had already made corrections and changes in writing his second draft. He needed now to look at these features of his essay in a more systematic way.

Glenn admits that he is not a confident speller. He therefore uses his dictionary when in doubt about the spelling of a word. Some of the words he misspelled are among those in the list of commonly misspelled words in Chapter 28.

Glenn had fewer decisions to make about punctuation. For example, he caught a missing hyphen in his first draft and another in editing his final draft. With the addition of details in his second and final drafts, he made increasing use of semi-colons to connect related ideas. He described the DMV building in these words in his first draft:

```
It is large, squat and brick.
```

In his second draft, he sought to show how a building could look both large and squat:

```
Seen from a distance, it is a large building; seen
close, it is squat and brick.
```

Here is Glenn's final revision:

```
Seen from a distant point, it is a large building; seen
from a closer point, it is squat and brick.
```

Two sentences in Glenn's first draft used the third-person *they* without specific reference:

```
They were up to number 69 when I finished filling
in my forms.
They announced that the outside doors would be
closed....
```

Glenn gave these pronouns specific reference in his final revision. In drafting and later editing the paper, he corrected obvious grammatical errors. His overuse of indefinite pronouns required much of his attention.

Satisfied with the revision and editing of his final draft, Glenn chose a title for the paper. Before presenting the paper to readers, though, he proofread it and then typed his final copy.

5 Third and final draft

The third and final draft of Glenn's paper appears on the following pages. The marginal annotations point out aspects of the paper's organization, focus, and thesis.

Final Draft

Mild Protest at the DMV

by Glenn Grube

From the outside, the Connecticut State
Department of Motor Vehicles looks much like most

Double view
of the DMV

institutional buildings. Seen from a distant point, it
is a large building; seen from a closer point, it is
squat and brick. The pillars that surround the main
entrance facing the street give the building an
imperial look, but other than that, it could easily pass
for a public school, with its drab, red brick and
simple structure. The department is nestled in a quiet
residential corner of Wethersfield, a suburb of
Hartford. I visited the building for the first time
three years ago, when I came to take my driving test.

Double
mental
view

Preview of
the
registration
office

To the new driver, the area surrounding the
DMV, with its large, single-family houses and
tree-lined streets, does not look threatening. But on
closer inspection, it proves to be an obstacle course
for the driver. Numerous yield signs, one-way
streets, and divided roads, and crowded Silas Deane
Highway not far away, trip up the sixteen-year-old
nervously taking a driving test. I faced these
obstacles three years ago, in taking my own. I am
back at the DMV to face another test. I have come to
register a used car I just bought and get license plates
for it.

As I walk through the automated doors, the
green outside fades into a dull green-tiled floor and
cement walls coated in gray paint. The corridors
remind me of a prison or perhaps a hospital. Yet I

Central
impression
introduced

Restless-
ness,
immobility

Anxiety and
confusion

Focus
narrows

Reason for
confusion

Earlier
impression
reinforced:
restless-
ness,
immobility

have the sense that nothing is happening. A sign directs me to the "General Information, License and Registration Room." Following the directions on the large plastic signs hanging by chains from the ceiling, I walk down the hall and up a large stairwell; I turn right to a large room. Entering through one of several sets of double doors, I find myself surrounded by lines of restless people and busy but motionless workers, who seem locked in their places behind the counters. In the hall I had encountered a few workers sipping coffee and one or two visitors anxiously looking at signs. In this large room, at least two hundred people are milling around.

The room is rectangular, with a high ceiling. It is easy to lose one's bearings in such a place. I glance around, trying to find the registration counter. I overhear a young woman giving directions to an elderly man and follow him to a line that begins near the center of the room. This line leads to a desk, where one is given a number. From the desk radiate at least three other lines. all of them curving down roped-off aisles. One line is for automobile dealers, another for those having a photograph taken for a driving license, and still another for those renewing their licenses. As I wait to get my number, I notice people sitting in plastic chairs at the back of the room. They have also come to register new cars.

Reaching the front of the line ten minutes later, I am given duplicate registration forms to fill out and a number and am curtly dismissed. Confused and annoyed, I wander toward the rows of chairs. Happening to look up, I see a large "63" displayed on a screen near the ceiling. The number in my hand is 112. Discouraged, I join the restless people in the chairs. Sitting down, I fill out the forms, giving my name, address, insurance company, and the miscellaneous information that interests people who register cars. The people at the registration and licensing windows are up to number 69 by the time I finish.

Details reinforce central impression: aimless activity

As the numbers change, every three or four minutes, flashing green arrows point to different lines, where people whose numbers have been called are standing. As I sit waiting, I read the pro–seat belt and anti–drunk driving posters tacked up around the room. Soon bored, I decide to take a walk in the

Boredom, tedium

corridor. On my walk, I discover an empty cafeteria and a half–empty emissions–testing appeals office. People are wandering aimlessly in a small shop that sells cigarettes, candy, and magazines. The sign

Ironic comment on scene

outside the shop says "Public Welcome." Others are standing around soda machines. When I return to my vigil in the registration room the number on the screen is 89.

A different kind of anxiety

For a while I entertain myself by eavesdropping on conversations around me. One man, looking uncomfortable and nervous, discusses strategy with another who I assume to be his lawyer; they are waiting for a hearing on suspension of his driver's

New perception and discovery: friendliness born of tedium

license. When these men leave, I turn to chat with people sitting nearby. The atmosphere is friendly. When you are bored, the most aimless conversation seems interesting. We joke about the slow advance of the numbers and cheer those with numbers soon to be called. The flash of the camera and low hum of large industrial fans fade as the talk increasingly engages

Thesis introduced

us. Some say that tragedy brings people closer together. Tedium seems to have the same effect here.

Most of us have been waiting for more than an hour, and as the time gets closer to 4:30--closing time at DMV--some of us with lower numbers begin to worry that we may not be called. At 4:15 our fears

Lead into climactic episode

are allayed. A brown uniformed guard announces that the outside doors are to be locked; only those with numbers will be called to the windows. Only four numbers from being called, I relax.

Suddenly we hear a loud pounding on the door. A middle-aged woman with graying hair is peering through the small, square window; she seems frantic; her lips are moving excitedly. I recognize her as one of the people sitting near me earlier. The guard who has just locked the doors sees her, points to his watch, and shakes his head. As he turns to walk away, the woman holds up a card with the number 110 printed on it. She has been waiting for more than an hour and, like others, has gone outside for a

Unity of feeling and action

moment, perhaps to smoke a cigarette. Simultaneously, all of us waiting to register our cars begin shouting at the guard. We know what the woman in the hall is feeling. We have been waiting

Thesis restated

just as long. Frustration and tedium have created a bond. Despite the fact she will delay our being served, we continue shouting at the guard to let her into the room. Perhaps fearing a small riot, perhaps wanting to please us, the guard grins with embarrassment and opens the door. The relieved

Grube 5

Ironic
comment
on system

woman comes over to thank us, then walks quickly to the counter. Her number has flashed on the screen.

I am called soon after to present my forms and receive my license plates and registration papers. As I walk out of the DMV, I feel strangely happy. I have spent hours waiting and I have paid over $100 in fees, but I am not surprised at my strange mood.

4e The writing process summarized

This chapter and those preceding it trace a general process followed by many writers. This process begins with considerations sometimes referred to as prewriting—choosing a topic, finding supporting ideas and details, limiting the topic, considering a possible organization and working thesis, perhaps outlining and writing trial paragraphs.

These considerations continue in drafting the essay. But your major concern in drafting is to work your plan and perhaps discover new ideas or even a new approach to the subject. You may also limit your focus and reorganize parts of the paper. Revision is often an integral part of drafting. Following a first or trial draft and sometimes a second draft, you begin the process of full-scale, systematic revision in which you look at the draft as a whole. You test your organization and unity, perhaps narrow the focus of discussion or choose a new focus, reorganize parts of the essay or perhaps the whole essay, and revise your working thesis into your final one. You also give increasing attention to your sentence style and choice of words.

In the course of revision, you may ask friends for advice on one or more of your drafts. Your instructor may also comment on the drafts and perhaps discuss them with you, and you may receive additional advice from classmates. In drafting and revising the paper, you may edit for grammar, punctuation, and spelling, but your editing probably won't be systematic at this point. When you edit your final draft, though, you should take a more systematic approach to the task. You should also proofread the final draft for typing and other errors you missed while editing.

As noted earlier, not all writers follow the steps of the writing process in a particular order. Drafting, revising, and editing are for many writers overlapping processes. Many find outlines distracting and prefer to think out the paper as they write. Others find outlines and other techniques indispensable to planning and writing the paper, particularly for writing long essays. The more writing you do, the more you will develop habits of prewriting, writing, revision, and editing that fit you best.

EXERCISE

The following drafts of an essay were written by a student in response to a *Newsweek* article by Martin Krovetz entitled "Going My Way." Read both drafts, noting especially the changes made by the writer in the second draft. Then decide whether the revisions add to the effectiveness of the essay. Explain your responses.

```
                DRAFT 1: GOING MY WAY

        From time to time, each of us takes a moment
   to stand and evaluate where we have been and on
   which path we are headed in life. In doing so, it
   seems necessary to relate or compare one's accom-
   plishments, failures, adventures, and values to
   those of other persons and groups. Has life been
   rewarding and satisfying to me? Does the future
   hold promise? Or could I have possibly chosen an-
   other avenue of approach in my search for happi-
   ness and fulfillment?

        Most of my acquaintances in high school were
   just that--acquaintances and nothing more. How-
   ever, there is one individual I consider my best
   friend who lives close by and keeps in touch on
   a regular basis. We continually make judgments
   about each other to justify how we live our
```

lives. Observing this friend and his life-style, which is different from mine, gives me a sense of security about my own way of handling life.

My friend is single and I am married. He has his own business; I am employed by another. Traveling is a frequent event in his life; I am lucky to break away for the weekend. He is a social extrovert, and I like to spend most of my free time with my wife. Free time seems to be more abundant in his schedule than in mine. He has diabetes; I am in excellent health. So you see, we are quite different in many respects, with a strong friendship the one thing we hold in common.

So how is it that I derive security from observing and evaluating the way my best friend lives? To begin, I must say that owning and operating your own business sounds very prestigious, but at times it presents an inescapable dilemma. My friend is a photographer and is in constant demand. If he is not running out at nine at night to drive 75 miles to photograph for insurance purposes a lady with a broken leg, then he is tied up all day Sunday with a wedding. When not on the scene shooting pictures, then it is downstairs to his dark room to develop film. How much free time does he have? This grinding schedule may endure for days, weeks, or months and then suddenly business stops. I rather enjoy the predictability of my forty-hour week. Though time off is seldom at best, I have the advantage of planning ahead.

Being single certainly rids an individual of many responsibilities that married people enjoy. No one to report to, a smaller grocery bill--the single life sure keeps things fresh with the dating scene. I have been married a few years and love my wife dearly, but on occasion I envy that novelty that accompanies a date with a different woman every week. On the other hand, my friend seems to envy the security and stability of my relationship with my wife.

Sharing responsibility is a wonderful feeling. Although problems seem to arise more frequently in a marriage, having someone to help work them out is an experience impossible when one is single. I gather this from conversations with my friend. He seems troubled often and appears to need someone to overcome his dismay at life and his apathy. For these reasons and many more, I find marriage a rewarding institution.

DRAFT 2: GOING MY WAY

From time to time we take a moment to stand back and look at where we have been in life and where we are going. Comparing oneself with a friend helps in taking this measure. Has life been rewarding and satisfying for me? Does the future hold promise? Or could I have possibly chosen another avenue in my search for happiness and fulfillment?

Most of my acquaintances in high school were just that--acquaintances. However, one person I consider my best friend lives nearby and keeps in touch. We continuously make judgments about each other to justify what we do and how we live. Observing this friend and his life-style, so opposite to mine, gives me a sense of security about my own handling of life.

My friend is single while I am married. He has his own business; I am employed. Traveling is a frequent event in his life; I am lucky to break away for the weekend. He is a social extrovert; most of my free time is spent with my wife. So you see we are quite different in many respects, with a strong friendship, at times, the only thing we share.

You may wonder why I derive security from observing and judging the way my friend lives. To begin, I must say that owning and operating your own business sounds prestigious but at times it makes life hectic. If my friend is not running out at nine at night to drive seventy-five miles to photograph for insurance purposes a lady with a broken leg, he is tied up Sunday afternoon with a wedding. When not on the scene shooting pictures, he ventures downstairs to the darkroom to develop film. How, you may ask, does he have a free moment? This grinding schedule may endure for days, weeks, or months, and then suddenly a void. I rather enjoy the predictability of my forty-hour week. Though I seldom have time off, at least there is the advantage of being able to plan ahead.

Being single certainly rids an individual of many responsibilities of married life. No one to report to, a smaller grocery bill, and the single status--these keep things fresh with regard to dating. I have been a husband nearly four years and love my wife dearly, but on occasion I miss the novelty that accompanies a date with a different woman each week. By contrast, my friend seems to envy the security and stability of our marriage. I have come to value my marriage with

its strength seeming to increase as the days
progress. Considering the unity marriage has
given me, I believe life continues to have a good
deal of the "positive" in store for me.

     Having two incomes is a benefit, certainly.
A few years ago, misfortune struck when I was
laid off. My wife went back to work in order to
pull us through. Having the support of your wife
spiritually and emotionally through troubled
times is a strength unfelt by those who are single. For a marriage to be strong there must be
love. Love in marriage is unlike that developed
in a friendship or between parents and children.
It is the most powerful of all feelings and it is
that power which gives me gratitude for the past
and optimism for the future. Through my friend I
realize life has bestowed on me a gift to which
there can be attached no price. ■

Summary

4a In drafting your paper, be ready to revise your plan if better ideas and a better approach to the subject occur to you.

4b In revising the latest draft of your paper, look at the organization, focus, sentence structure, and diction of the whole paper, not of individual paragraphs only.

Make your subject and focus clear in your introductory paragraphs, and introduce your thesis early unless you have reason to build up to it later in the paper (4b 2).

In your conclusion, restate your thesis or refer to it, and perhaps remind your readers of why your subject is important (4b 3).

4c Edit your final draft for spelling, grammar, and punctuation, and proofread the paper carefully before giving it to readers.

95

PART TWO

EFFECTIVE PARAGRAPHS

Organizing Paragraphs

5

Effective essays contain well-organized and well-developed paragraphs. An essay that presents ideas and details in a single undivided mass would be difficult, perhaps impossible, to read. Paragraphs are therefore an important help to the reader. They are also essential to the writer, because they help in thinking about the subject and in keeping the discussion on track.

Part Two focuses on ways of organizing and developing paragraphs. Chapter 5 shows how to write opening and closing paragraphs, connect paragraphs, and give them focus, unity, and coherence. In Chapter 6, the discussion turns to the development of paragraphs through various patterns or methods of analysis, including definition, classification, example, and comparison and contrast. As we will see, these methods are important not only in developing paragraphs but in developing the whole essay as well.

5a Defining the paragraph

A **paragraph** is a group of sentences, the first line of which is indented to distinguish it as a whole. The basic unit of the essay, the paragraph can center on a single idea or on several ideas.

Not all paragraphs develop a single idea. Some paragraphs simply mark changes in tone, point of view, or speaker, particularly if the essay consists largely of dialogue. Newspapers routinely break paragraphs that develop several ideas into a series of short paragraphs, each consisting of a single idea or fact. The following introductory paragraphs on Yemen, a country in the Middle East, illustrate this use of short paragraphs for emphasis and dramatic effect:

> The old is very old here, and the new is very new. Sometimes, the collision is painful.
>
> The Queen of Sheba, it is said, once ruled these lands, sending frankincense and myrrh by caravan across Arabia to far-flung Gaza, bound for Jerusalem, Athens and Rome. These days the trade across the desert is in bootlegged Toyota Land Cruisers and compact disc players.
>
> In this land at the tip of the Arabian peninsula, young men tote automatic rifles on their backs, and some tribes have tanks and armored cars left over from the country's civil war, say people who have travelled extensively, encountering tribal roadblocks that set the boundary between new Government and old fiefdom.
>
> —Alan Cowell, "Wadi Dahr Journal," *New York Times*, October 24, 1989

Summary paragraphs draw conclusions and often consist of one or two sentences. Cowell uses a dramatic single-sentence summary paragraph to comment on changes brought about by the Yemenite civil war:

> The changes, thus, were even more abrupt than those that modernized oil-producing Arab countries like Saudi Arabia and Kuwait.

Transitional paragraphs briefly introduce the topic of succeeding paragraphs, sometimes by asking a question:

99

During the "working" day, she labored beside—not behind—my father in the fields. Her day began before sunup, and did not end until late at night. There was never a moment for her to sit down, undisturbed, to unravel her own private thoughts; never a time free from interruption—by work or the noisy inquiries of her many children. And yet, it is to my mother—and all our mothers who were not famous—that I went in search of the secret of what has fed that muzzled and often mutilated, but vibrant, creative spirit that the black woman has inherited, and that pops out in wild and unlikely places to this day.

But when, you will ask, did my overworked mother have time to know or care about feeding the creative spirit?

The answer is so simple that many of us have spent years discovering it. We have constantly looked high, when we should have looked high—and low.

—Alice Walker, "In Search of Our Mothers' Gardens"

Most paragraphs, of course, are longer than one or two sentences because they answer questions and develop ideas. The paragraphs you will write in essays, term papers, and reports will usually develop an idea fully. Thus, the remainder of this chapter illustrates ways of organizing and developing a single idea or a series of related ideas in a paragraph. Such a paragraph often resembles a miniature essay, with a beginning, middle, and conclusion. The beginning sentence sometimes states the subject or central idea, the middle sentences develop the idea through explanatory details and related ideas, and the concluding sentences describe the central idea fully or restate it. This type of paragraph is the heart of the essay or paper.

5b   Focusing through topic sentences

Paragraphs often begin with a statement of the writer's central idea, called the **topic sentence.** With the central idea in focus, you guide your reader through the paragraph, showing how various details and ideas connect. The following paragraph opens with the central idea that the creatures of sea forests rise upward in gradations; it then shows us how they do so:

Topic sentence: central idea

Life in a sea forest rises toward the top in sharp gradations of movement. Brittle stars, purple sea fans, lavender sponges, ostrich-plume hydroids, flowery sea anemones, and lobsterlike crayfish ring the rockbound holdfast. Above this almost immobile layer of life cruise small sand sharks and rays flapping their robelike wings like finny Draculas. Above them schools of shimmering sardines pass like rain showers, and bass, sheepshead, spiny sculpin, and dainty senoritas dart about. On the outskirts of the forest bonita, barracuda, and albacore sprint like animated steel arrows, and above the surface the seabird swirls, occasionally lighting on the brown canopy.

Details: various kinds of movement

—Wesley Marx, *The Frail Ocean* (emphasis added)

By referring to "sharp gradations of movement" in the opening topic sentence, Marx suggests how the supporting ideas and details of the paragraph are organized: according to the various kinds of *movement* above the immobile ocean floor.

You can use similar techniques to open and develop your own paragraphs. However, you do not have to open your paragraph with your central idea. You may instead choose to begin with an introductory statement of your subject or topic and then build to a statement of your central idea in the middle of the paragraph or at the end, as Sue Hubbell does in the following paragraph:

Statement of topic

I am good friends with a woman who lives across the hollow. She and her husband sell cordwood to the charcoal factory in town. Her husband cuts the logs because a chain saw, in the Ozarks, is regarded as a man's tool, and she helps him load and unload the logs. Even though the wood is going to be turned into charcoal, it is traditional to cut it to four-foot lengths. A four-foot oak log is heavy; a strong man can lift it, but a woman has to use all her strength to do her part. My friend returns from her mornings sick with exhaustion, her head throbbing. She and I talk sometimes about how it would be if women were the woodcutters: the length would be less than four feet. *Having to do work beyond her strength makes my friend feel weak, ineffectual, dependent and cross.*

Details on woodcutting

leading into

topic sentence

—Sue Hubbell, "Felling Trees" (emphasis added)

Occasionally, you may decide to delay your topic sentence in order to introduce a complex or controversial idea. In this instance, you might open with a question and lead through a series of details to the central idea or answer. You may also open the paragraph with a series of details that leads to the topic sentence (see 5d 2).

In deciding how to open and organize your paragraphs, you should also consider your audience and whether your essay is expressive, informational, or persuasive. Ask yourself what your readers know about the subject and how they will respond to your ideas.

EXERCISE

Write a paragraph that opens with one of the following ideas or one of your own choosing. Experiment with the placement of the topic sentence in the paragraph.

1. The identity of a school depends on more than its academic program and its teachers.
2. Waiting in line tells you much about people.
3. Repairing household appliances requires different skills.
4. Music makes different demands on listeners.
5. We read books in different ways, depending on our purpose in reading.

5c Unifying the paragraph

A **unified paragraph** connects details and subordinate ideas to a central idea. Although your ideas and details may seem connected when you write a paragraph, in revising the paper you may discover that a paragraph contains ideas or details that belong in separate paragraphs or that need to be subordinated to a main idea or made to support it.

Here is a disunified paragraph:

```
College athletics puts a strain on students and

faculty when it is the chief activity of the school.

Classroom cheating creates a strain, too. The wide-

spread belief of the public that a school's worth is to
```

```
be measured by its teams encourages players to win at
any cost, and teachers sometimes find themselves under
pressure to give passing grades to players doing poor
work. Students and teachers thus are victims of a sys-
tem not of their making. And cheating in the classroom
increases the pressure on everyone--students, teachers,
administrators.
```

This paragraph is not unified because it fails to discuss one idea at a time. The opening sentence talks about college athletics. The second sentence introduces a new and unrelated idea—classroom cheating; the word *too* suggests that the rest of the paragraph will focus on college athletics and cheating, but it does not. The remainder of the paragraph discusses teams. The final sentence returns to the matter of cheating, without reference to college athletics.

This paragraph can be unified by mentioning college cheating briefly and then discussing it in a separate paragraph where the idea can be fully developed:

```
    College athletics puts a strain on students and
faculty when it is the chief activity of the school.
The widespread belief of the public that a school's
worth is to be measured by its teams encourages players
to win at any cost, often putting teachers under pres-
sure to give passing grades to players who cheat or do
poor work. Students and teachers thus are victims of a
system not of their making.

    One sign of strain is the common view that cheat-
ing in the classroom is a normal part of college
life....
```

The central topic of the paragraph (college athletics) is now in focus. The paragraph is unified.

You can unify your own paragraphs by presenting one idea and developing it fully before turning to another idea. The more ideas and details you present in the paragraph, the more help your reader will need in following your train of thought. You need to distinguish between your main ideas and your subordinate ideas. And you will sometimes need formal transitions or connectors (words and phrases like *however* and *by contrast*) to show how ideas and details relate. Pronouns, key words, and sentence parallelism are also essential in making paragraphs cohere or hold together.

1 Coordinating and subordinating ideas

Coordinate ideas have the same importance in the paragraph in developing the main or central idea; **subordinate ideas** support or develop ideas of greater importance or weight. To make the paragraph easy to read, you need to make the relative importance of your ideas clear to your reader.

In the following example, the topic sentence makes a general statement about cooking meat outdoors. The series of subordinate ideas and examples that develop this idea are themselves coordinate ideas of equal weight and construction, as the indentations show.

A   A large piece of meat suspended over the fire must be turned frequently, because only the side toward the fire gets the effect of the rising hot air and the radiation [*topic sentence*].

B   The rig known as a dingle fan, probably from the logging-camp shed called a dingle, is helpful in this task.

C   To make the apparatus attach a short chain to the upper end of a stick that is angled upward over the perimeter of the campfire.

C   Suspend the meat from the chain by a string attached to a hook in one end of the meat.

C   Tie a short stick to the string.

D   One end of the stick holds a fan made of wire or branches wrapped in aluminum foil or leaves.

D   To the other end attach a small rock to serve as a counterweight to the fan.

C   Orient the plane of the fan somewhat off the vertical and arrange the entire assembly so that the fan is in the hot air rising from the campfire.

B   The meat is not in that convection current but is exposed to the radiation from the fire.

—Jearl Walker, "The Amateur Scientist,"
Scientific American, August 1985

The coordinate ideas B,B develop the topic sentence in showing how to cook a piece of meat over an open fire. The coordinate ideas C,C,C illustrate how to construct a dingle fan. The coordinate ideas D,D explain how to tie a short stick to a string.

The ideas of the paragraph in this way form a hierarchy. We know that the series of coordinate ideas are subordinate because they explain and illustrate the preceding idea. Note that the topic sentence (A) may be coordinate with the topic sentences of the preceding and the following paragraphs.

2   Using transitions

In revising a complex paragraph of your own, determine whether the relation of ideas is clear. If the connections are not immediately clear, try adding formal transitions or recast the paragraph to clarify it.

Assume you have written a paragraph with some care and are satisfied that your ideas connect clearly. But will your reader see that they do?

Consider how much misunderstanding can arise in speaking to people: you routinely repeat statements, backtrack to earlier parts of the conversation, point out connections, underscore important words, ask whether you are being understood. In your writing, you are usually more careful in connecting your statements because you cannot see or respond to the effect of your words on the reader. **Transitional words and phrases** are helpful in marking shifts in idea and explanation that may not be immediately apparent to the reader.

The following paragraph uses formal transitions to clarify the relations between ideas and details and change in focus:

Topic sentence	*I think it is a human trait to exaggerate difference—to imagine an odd thing as odder than it really is.* I expected, when I first met elephants, to have
Contrast	exaggerated their size in my imagination. *But* elephants are so big, so much bigger than any other creature we meet on land, that I found the opposite to be true: I had actually reduced them in my mind,
Change in focus	diminished their size and their difference. *Up close,* within reach, an elephant is a transcendent thing, entirely alien. Elephants resemble us in funny ways—they catch colds, get sunburns, babysit each
Addition	other's children. Rosy and I *even* have the same body temperature. *But* I am really nothing like Rosy, and
Qualification	she is nothing like me; *still,* as I watch her and her kin pass by, my strongest feeling is one of society and relation.

—Sallie Tisdale, "The Only Harmless Great Thing,"
The New Yorker, January 23, 1989
(emphasis added)

In revising your essays, add a formal transition where you must pause to guess a connection. Try reading Tisdale's paragraph quickly, omitting the transitions. You probably will grasp the thread of ideas, but you will have to pause several times to guess at connections. Writers today often omit formal transitions where the connection of ideas and details is clear.

Notice a significant feature in the organization of Tisdale's paragraph: the author weaves ideas and examples together, moving from idea to example or supporting details, from the abstract to the concrete. This weaving of ideas and examples into a whole would not be possible without transitions.

Here are some common transitional words and phrases used to highlight the connections among ideas or to signal shifts in the discussion that need to be made clear to the reader.

Common Transitions

To add: and, also, too, furthermore, moreover, in addition, then, indeed, even

To signal time: before, earlier, since, afterward, later, now, meanwhile, in the meantime, until, soon

To indicate place: here, there, elsewhere, above, below, behind, on this side, on the other side, to the right, to the left, to the north, to the south, nearby, far from here

To qualify, limit, modify, and state exceptions: but, however, nevertheless, notwithstanding, nonetheless, while, though

To repeat for emphasis and clarity: to repeat, once again, in other words, in particular, in short, in summary

To illustrate: for example, for instance, that is, specifically

To show cause and effect: as a result, consequently, accordingly, therefore, then, for this reason

To compare and contrast: similarly, by comparison, likewise, in the same way, as, but, despite, by contrast, on the contrary, on the one hand, on the other hand

To summarize: in summary, in brief, in short, in conclusion, finally

3 Using pronouns and key words

Pronouns help to make paragraphs concise and coherent by keeping the subject of the paragraph in focus. In the following example, the authors mention Napoleon Bonaparte in the first sentence and use pronouns to refer to him in the remainder of the paragraph. Pronoun reference is clear because the authors discuss no other person. The paragraph is coherent and concise.

> Until 1810 Napoleon could forgivably feel that *he* had been true to the Revolution's second goal—equality. *He* had upheld and spread the equality of all before the law. *He* had established not an impossible equality of abilities and merits, but an equality of opportunity for all talents, wherever born, to develop themselves in a society offering education, economic opportunity, and political eligibility to all; perhaps this *carrière ouverte aux talents* [career open to talents] was *his* most lasting gift to France. *He* almost ended corruption in public life; *this* alone should immortalize *him*. *He* gave to all the example of a man using *himself* up in administration when not called to the battlefield. *He* remade France.
> —Will and Ariel Durant, *The Age of Napoleon* (emphasis added)

Key words, like pronouns, may be repeated to keep the central idea in focus. The words *constant* and *change* keep the central idea in focus in the following paragraph:

> The soil exists in a state of *constant change,* taking part in cycles that have no beginning and no end. New materials are *constantly* being contributed as rocks disintegrate, as organic matter decays, and as nitrogen and other gases are brought down in rain from the skies. At the same time other materials are being taken away, borrowed for temporary use by living creatures. Subtle and vastly important chemical changes are *constantly* in progress, converting elements derived from air and water into forms suitable for use by plants. In all these *changes* living organisms are active agents.
> —Rachel Carson, *Silent Spring* (emphasis added)

4   Using parallelism

Parallelism is the use of phrases and clauses having the same grammatical structure for the same purpose in the sentence (see 14a). Parallelism is an important way of giving ideas equal weight in the paragraph. For example, in the earlier paragraph on Napoleon Bonaparte, key words in each sentence are parallel (*he had been true, He had upheld and spread, He had established, He almost ended, He gave, He remade*). In arranging ideas of similar weight and meaning, the authors build the paragraph to the climactic final sentence. Notice also that parallelism is used for contrast in the third sentence:

He had established
not an impossible equality of abilities and merits,
but *an equality of opportunity for all talents.* . . .

EXERCISES

1. Write a paragraph on a topic of your own choosing. Use key words and parallel phrases to connect your ideas and details and to focus on your central idea.
2. The following paragraph needs to be unified. Rewrite the paragraph by connecting phrases and sentences and by restating or rearranging ideas and details as needed to achieve unity.

> Moving into a new apartment can be an exciting experience, but it also can strain the nerves. When you arrive at the apartment with a loaded car, finding a parking space nearby may seem the least of one's problems but it can be the worst. New neighbors sometimes want to be of help, but it's hard to find a telephoᵤe when the lights won't go on. You may have hired a mover to bring some of your furniture, and you can't find the janitor who has the key. Sometimes you find the water turned off. Your neighbor across the hall invites you in for some coffee just as the mover arrives with your furniture. It's hard to keep a sense of humor when things go wrong. A stray dog or cat may wander into the apartment because you left the door open. ■

5d | Organizing the paragraph

Most of the paragraphs discussed in the preceding sections open with a statement of the topic sentence or central idea. However, there are other ways to open paragraphs. Following are the four main ways of opening and organizing paragraphs:

- Open with the central idea, followed by supporting details and ideas.
- Open with details that build to the central idea.
- Open with a statement of the topic, followed by its restriction and illustration.
- Open with a question or statement of a problem, followed by an answer or solution.

1   Generalization–details

Most of the paragraphs you write will probably open with the central idea and provide supporting details. The italicized words and phrases in the following paragraph refer to the core idea of the opening sentence:

Topic sentence: core idea	What I have most wanted to do throughout the past ten years is *to make political writing into an art.* My starting point is always a feeling of *partisanship,* a sense of injustice. *When I sit down to write a book,* I do not say to myself, "I am going to produce *a*
Restate-ment	*work of art."* *I write* it because there is some lie that I want to expose, some fact to which I want to draw attention, and my initial concern is to get a hearing.
Restate-ment	But I could not do the work of *writing a book,* or even a long magazine article, if it were not also *an aesthetic experience.* Anyone who cares to examine my work will see that even when it is downright propaganda it contains much that a full-time politician would consider irrelevant. I am not able, and I do not want, completely to abandon the world view that I acquired in childhood. So long as I remain
Detailed restate-ment	alive and well I shall continue to *feel strongly* about prose style, *to love* the surface of the earth, and to *take a pleasure* in solid objects and scraps of useless information. It is no use trying to suppress that side of myself. The job is to reconcile my ingrained likes and dislikes with the essentially public, nonindividual activities that this age forces on all of us.

—George Orwell, "Why I Write" (emphasis added)

In long paragraphs of this kind, you will help your reader by restating the central or core idea as Orwell does. Opening the paragraph with the central idea emphasizes its importance. Restating it at the end of the paragraph gives it even greater importance, for readers tend to remember new information given at the end of sentences and paragraphs.

2   Details–generalization

You can give unusual emphasis to your central idea by building the paragraph through a series of details, creating a sense of climax. The following paragraph is the dramatic opening to a book on the bubonic plague that struck Europe in the fourteenth century:

Details of plague and its effects

Example leads into the topic sentence: general statement on the Black Plague

In October 1347 a Genoese fleet made its way into the Messina harbor in northeast Sicily. Its crew had "sickness clinging to their very bones." All were dead or dying, afflicted with a disease from the Orient. The Messinese harbor masters tried to quarantine the fleet, but it was too late. It was not men but rats and fleas that brought the sickness, and they scurried ashore as the first ropes were tied to the docks. Within days, the pestilence spread throughout Messina and its rural environs and, within six months, half the region's population died or fled. *This scene, repeated thousands of times in ports and fishing villages across Eurasia and North Africa, heralded the coming of the great natural disaster in European history—the Black Death.*

—Robert S. Gottfried, *The Black Death* (emphasis added)

Such a dramatic build to the topic sentence is found in the opening paragraphs of many articles and books. When this type of paragraph appears in the middle or at the end of an essay, its effect is even more dramatic.

3 Topic–restriction–illustration

Another useful method of organization is to open your paragraph with a broad generalization or statement of the topic, restrict that topic to one area of experience or thought, and then illustrate it. The writer Paul Horgan begins the following paragraph with a broad statement about American humor, immediately restricts the topic to humorous sounds, and illustrates these sounds in the remainder of the paragraph:

Topic Restriction

Illustration

American humor rested less on inherent wit or sharp observation of human failings than on rough *drolleries* full of exaggeration and strange usage for its own sake. The speech became noisy and profuse. It imitated sounds of sucking and smacking and cracking and slicing and chopping and sawing and thumping and poking and digging and clapping and exclaiming and hushing. It stuck in extra syllables for elegance and comic surprise. It liked to repeat in the same word the sound of dental consonants that gave a jerky, droll effect. It made comedy out of mouth-widening vowel sounds and speech-yodels whose effect depended upon a swallowed *1*—the gobble of the North American turkey. It was at times almost an abstract sound. Its character stripped of known words and their meaning, and left only with sound, might still suggest the meaning intended, along with the hard, simple, and at times lyrically beautiful life from which it came.

—*Sons of Democracy* (emphasis added)

It is useful to think of this kind of paragraph as a funnel that opens broadly and increasingly narrows. This kind of paragraph is particularly useful when you want to focus on details.

4 Question–answer

You may sometimes want to begin a paragraph with a question or problem and then answer that question or suggest a solution. This method of organization is most useful in writing informational papers and technical reports. The following paragraph asks a question and then answers it in the remainder of the paragraph:

Opening question	*What is "shooting a film," then?* If I were to ask this question of everybody, I would no doubt obtain quite different responses, but perhaps you would all
Topic sentence: central idea hinted at	agree on one point: shooting a film is doing what is necessary in order to transport the contents of the manuscript onto a piece of film. *In doing so, you would be saying quite a lot and yet not nearly enough.*
Details	For me, shooting a film represents days of inhumanly relentless work, stiffness of the joints, eyes full of dust, the odors of make-up, sweat and lamps, an indefinite series of tensions and relaxations, an uninterrupted battle between volition and duty, between vision and reality, conscience and laziness. I think of early risings, of nights without sleep, of a feeling keener than life, of a sort of fanaticism cen-
Central idea	tered about a single task, *by which I myself become, finally, an integral part of the film,* a ridiculously tiny piece of apparatus whose only fault is requiring food and drink.

—Ingmar Bergman, "What Is 'Film Making'?"
(emphasis added)

And here is a paragraph that states a problem and then proposes a solution:

Problem

Solution

    Why are the more massive stars hotter stars? The weight of the outer layers of a massive star causes great pressure at the center. If the star is not to collapse, it must attain a high temperature, since only then can the gas pressure balance this weight. The higher temperature increases the energy production, which maintains the star against its own gravity—which would otherwise cause it to fall in upon itself. If such a star overheats, it expands. The expansion cools the center, and the energy-production rate decreases, again stabilizing the star. Thus a star is a stable, giant, thermonuclear furnace—a ball of gas held together by gravity and saved from collapse by the internal pressure of gas heated by the nuclear fuel.

                —Jesse L. Greenstein,
                "Natural History of a Star"

    The methods of organization described in this section can be combined in a paragraph. For example, the question or problem that opens a paragraph may be stated generally and then restricted and worked out in detail.

Checklist: Paragraph Organization

1. Is each of my paragraphs a unit of thought? Do my details and subordinate ideas connect to the central idea?
2. Does my central idea or topic sentence appear in a prominent place in the paragraph? Have I shown my reader that this idea is clearly my central one?
3. If my central idea appears at the end of the paragraph, does my opening sentence state the subject or topic?
4. Is my paragraph unified? Have I discussed one idea at a time?
5. If my paragraph contains several ideas, is their weight and purpose clear?
6. Do I need to restate my central idea in the course of the paragraph for special emphasis?

7. If my central idea is a broad one, can I restrict and illustrate it?
8. If my paragraph begins by asking a question or posing a problem, have I answered that question or suggested a solution to that problem?
9. Do I need transitions to connect the ideas and details in my paragraph? Have I used key words and parallelism, as well as transitions, to make the paragraph coherent?

EXERCISES

1. Write a paragraph that opens with an idea suggested by a recent experience at home, school, or work. Illustrate this idea with details of this and other experiences.
2. Rewrite your paragraph by building to your central idea, using the same details. You may want to open the paragraph with a brief statement of the topic.
3. Use one of the following sentences in a paragraph of your own. Restrict your central idea to a particular area of experience and conclude the paragraph with illustrations of that experience.
   a. The borrower is servant to the lender.
      —Proverbs 22:7
   b. There is no new thing under the sun.
      —Ecclesiastes 1:9
   c. It is good to have an end to journey towards; but it is the journey that matters, in the end.
      —Ursula K. Le Guin, *The Left Hand of Darkness*
   d. The worst cynicism: a belief in luck.
      —Joyce Carol Oates, *Do with Me What You Will* ∎

5e	Opening and closing paragraphs

1 Opening paragraphs

In the **opening paragraph,** you want to introduce the subject of the essay and try to generate interest in it. The narrower your focus, the more interesting your essay will be. But you need to assess the knowledge and concerns of your audience in narrowing the focus. Addressing the general readership of a magazine on science, the author of the following paragraph begins an article on robot space exploration with a personal address to the reader:

> There is something about the topic of outer space that induces hyperbolic expectations. With no difficulty at all I can think of a billion-dollar space mission before breakfast any day of the week and a multibillion-dollar mission on Sunday. Ordinarily I do not inflict such visions on my fellow citizens, but I note that proposals of comparable or lesser merit and of much greater cost receive public attention, and some are influential in high circles of government. I submit that the proposed permanently manned space station is in this category.
>
> —James A. Van Allen, "Space Science, Space Technology and the Space Station," *Scientific American*, January 1986

Van Allen appeals to the interest and concern of his general audience in the following ways:

- by stating his subject (the cost and merit of manned space stations);
- by noting the expectations that space exploration generates;
- by addressing the concern of the American public with the cost of space programs;
- by informing his readers of his thesis—that manned space stations discourage other kinds of important space exploration.

An effective opening paragraph captures your reader's attention. If your purpose is expressive or expository, you want to appeal to the reader's curiosity or personal interest in the subject. If your purpose is persuasive, you want to make the reader receptive to your thesis. We saw earlier that you can open a paragraph effectively by stating a problem or asking a question. However, there are many other effective ways of opening paragraphs.

Consider these examples:

Personal Reference

We weren't all Okies during the Great Depression, even though the photographs of abandoned farms and ramshackle cars loaded with household goods are the best-known symbols of those hard times. Many of us had roofs over our heads—but not always our own roofs. One way or another, we helped each other; we managed, we rose to the occasion. What we needed—

5e

¶

or gave—might be as substantial as a place to live or as intangible as maintaining self-respect.

—Sally A. Adams, "We Had a Roof and Happiness,"
Christian Science Monitor, June 5, 1988

Anecdote

A young woman I know started her first year of college feeling hopeful. The horrors of high school were over. Like others before her, she had an airbrushed picture of college life in general and dormitory life in particular. She had a roommate she liked a lot. She found a boyfriend.

—Susan Walton, "Hers," *New York Times*, July 2, 1987

Description

From the center of downtown Tucson the ground slopes gently away to Main Street, drops a few feet, and then rolls to the banks of the Santa Cruz River. Here lies the sprawling center of the city known as El Hoyo. . . .

—Mario Suarez, "El Hoyo"

Dramatic Statement

I do not believe in Belief. But this is an age of faith, and there are so many militant creeds that, in self-defense, one has to formulate a creed of one's own. . . .

—E. M. Forster, "What I Believe"

Humor

They are called Malapropisms, Spoonerisms, "Archie Bunkerisms," or, simply, "tips of the slongue."

—John Sherwood, "Malapropisms,
Oft Apt Even If Inappropriate"

Reference to a Current Event

As disasters go, this one was terrible, but not unique, certainly not among the worst on the roster of U.S. air crashes. There was the unusual element of the bridge, of course, and the fact that the plane clipped it at a moment of high traffic, one routine thus intersecting another and disrupting both. . . .

—Roger Rosenblatt, "The Man in the Water"

Quotation

"I could be bounded in a nutshell and count myself a king of infinite space," boasts Hamlet and immediately cancels the claim with the qualification, "were it not that I have bad dreams."

115

He expresses the predicament of the individualist ever since
the Renaissance. . . .
—Stephen Spender, "The Connecting Imagination"

Facts and Statistics
The health-care system of this country is a staggering enterprise, in any sense of the adjective. Whatever the failures of distribution and lack of coordination, it is the gigantic scale and
cope of the total collective effort that first catches the breath, and
its cost. The dollar figures are almost beyond grasping. They vary
from year to year, always upward, ranging from something like
$10 billion in 1950 to an estimated $140 billion in 1978, with
much more to come in the years just ahead, whenever a national
health-insurance program is installed. The official guess is that
we are now investing a round 8 percent of the GNP in Health; it
could soon rise to 10 or 12 percent.
—Lewis Thomas, "The Health Care System"

Warning
For the first time in the history of the world, every human
being is now subjected to contact with dangerous chemicals,
from the moment of conception until death. . . .
—Rachel Carson, *Silent Spring*

As these examples show, there are many ways for writers to
open paragraphs. You can refer to your own interests or concerns, or make only a brief reference to personal interests and
focus instead on details about the subject. Although some
writers prefer to open paragraphs by stating the thesis fully,
others prefer to introduce it gradually. How early you present
the thesis depends again on your audience—a difficult or
highly controversial thesis often requires an extended introduction.

2 Closing paragraphs

A **closing paragraph** signals the end of the discussion and
reminds the reader of the thesis and importance of the subject.
Just as the beginning and end of a sentence are special points
of emphasis, so are the opening and closing paragraphs of an
essay. Because the beginning and ending of paragraphs are so
prominent, they are good places to state and restate the thesis.
Van Allen restates his thesis as he argues the competitive need
for other than manned space flight:

In the meantime the European Space Agency, Japan, and the U.S.S.R. are forging ahead with important scientific missions. The progressive loss of U.S. leadership in space science can be attributed, I believe, largely to our excessive emphasis on manned space flight and on vaguely perceived, poorly founded goals of a highly speculative nature. Given the current budgetary climate and a roughly constant level of public support for civil space ventures, the development of a space station, if pursued as now projected, will seriously reduce the opportunities for advances in space science and in important applications of space technology in the coming decade.

— "Space Science, Space Technology and the Space Station"

In scientific writing, the concluding paragraph usually makes suggestions for further research. An expository essay may conclude with a summary of the analysis or the process described. A persuasive essay may conclude with a dramatic appeal for action. A successful closing paragraph reaffirms the importance of the subject and restates or reminds the reader of the thesis of the essay. Like the opening paragraph, it may employ humor or use any of the other strategies discussed earlier for introductions. In short, a successful conclusion leaves no loose ends.

5f Linking paragraphs

Paragraphs do not work alone; together they must link to form the whole essay. For example, an opening paragraph may state a generalization, illustrated in the succeeding paragraph, and then developed further:

Generalization

The Old Testament described the multiplicity of languages as affliction visited on mankind, and history is replete with confusions resulting from language barriers. Modern examples are at hand:

Series of examples

A Venezuelan shipper sends an order for automobile spare parts to Italy—and is shipped tractor parts instead. The British Foreign Office uses the word *requérir* ("to demand") incorrectly—and an incensed French general demands an apology. American tourists in a Far Eastern metropolis attempt to communicate in sign language—and are severely mauled because their signs are interpreted as insults. People drown unnecessarily in a sea disaster (the *Andrea Doria*) because they cannot understand rescue directions given in a tongue other than their own.

Comment on examples
Transitional question

Surely we were better off during the Middle Ages, when everything of international importance was expressed in Latin. Can't we appreciate the advantages of a universal language and devise one? . . .

—Jacob Ornstein and William W. Gage, "The Dream of a World Language"

You can link your paragraphs in several ways:

- Add *transitional words or phrases* (e.g., *nevertheless, for this reason, further, moreover*—see the list on page 106.)
- Give a *preview of the topic* of the following paragraph ("Modern examples are at hand").
- Pose a *transitional question* ("Can't we appreciate the advantages of a universal language and devise one?").
- Present an *interpretation of the preceding paragraph* or *a conclusion based on the evidence* presented ("Surely we were better off during the Middle Ages").
- Make a *reference to an idea, detail, or example* discussed in the preceding paragraph.

EXERCISE

Read Bland Blanshard's paragraph carefully, then write answers to the following questions:

1. Where does the central idea (or topic sentence) of the paragraph appear? What does the author gain in placing the central idea where he does?
2. How many main divisions does the paragraph have, and how does each division develop the central idea?
3. What kind of transitions mark these divisions?
4. What use does the author make of transitional pronouns and parallel sentence structure?
5. What key words help to unify the paragraph?
6. Do you find the organization of the paragraph effective? In what other ways might the author have organized the paragraph?

First, then, let us ask the critics a question. You are insisting that the college prove its usefulness: just what do you mean by usefulness? You imply that a thing is useful when it contributes to success, but how do you measure success? Is it success, for example, to make a great deal of money? That is certainly not the whole story, for money is not an end in itself; it too is prized because it is useful, that is, because it is a means to something beyond. Money in itself has no value. If you were on an island, cut finally off from civilization, and your pockets were bulging with bills of large denominations, what would the money be worth? A little, perhaps; it would save one the trouble of gathering leaves if one wanted to build a fire; but that would be about all. Money is literally not worth keeping; its only value is that we can get rid of it in exchange for other things. Well, what are these other things? A better house, we say, a better car, the chance to travel. But then we prize these too for their usefulness, for the something further that they bring us. The ampler house brings us comfort and rest and quiet and a sense of freedom and dignity; the car brings to our family the pleasures of the open road, and their pleasure is reflected in ours; travel enriches us with new impressions and ideas. These are the ulterior things, the self-validating things, that make money and possessions useful. Comfort and quiet and richness of mind are not good because they are good *for* something; they are simply good, good in their own right. And you will notice that all these values are goods of the spirit, goods that lie not in things but in the minds that enjoy them. In the end all useful things are useful because they produce these useless goods that are valued for nothing further; or if you wish, it is precisely the useless things of the world that in the end alone are useful, since only they will give us what we want.

—Bland Blanshard, "The Uses of a Liberal Education" ■

Summary

5a Organize your paragraphs as units of thought. Break the paragraph if necessary to mark changes in tone, point of view, speaker, or emphasis.

5b Focus on your central idea by stating it in a topic sentence—at the beginning, middle, or end of the paragraph.

5c Unify the paragraph by connecting the ideas and details to the central idea.

Show your reader which ideas are coordinate and which are subordinate (5c 1).

Use transitional words and phrases to connect ideas and details and show their relationship (5c 2).

Highlight ideas through parallelism, and keep the subject in focus by using pronouns and key words (5c 3–4).

5d Organize each paragraph in a systematic way.

If appropriate, develop your opening statement through a series of details or build these details to the thesis statement (5d 1–2).

State the topic of the paragraph, restrict it, and then illustrate it (5d 3).

State a problem or pose a question and then discuss its solution or answer (5d 4).

5e Take advantage of the beginning and end focus of your opening and closing paragraphs.

Use your opening paragraphs to state the subject of the essay, generate interest in it, and possibly state the thesis (5e 1).

Use your closing paragraphs to reaffirm the importance of the subject, restate your thesis, or recommend further investigation (5e 2).

5f Link your paragraphs through transitional words and phrases and other means.

6

Building
Paragraphs

A paragraph may be well organized but still unsuccessful if it is not fully developed with details and a pattern of development. Patterns of development include description, narration, definition, classification and division, example, comparison and contrast, analogy, process analysis, and causal analysis. They may be used singly or in combination in a paragraph or essay. For example, an introductory paragraph for an essay on the federal budget might define the word *deficit* and classify kinds of deficits. Succeeding paragraphs may illustrate present and past deficits, compare personal and family budgets, trace the process by which government deficits occur, and analyze the causes and effects of the current federal deficit.

The patterns of development employed depend on the nature of the idea being discussed and the purpose of the analysis. In this chapter, we survey the various patterns of development and show how they are used. Two of these patterns are basic to most writing—description and narration.

6a   Description

In **descriptive writing** you give a picture in words of a person, an object, or a scene. The organization of details in descriptive writing is **spatial;** that is, you observe the subject from a particular physical point of view or angle, which you may or may not specify. Sometimes the description encompasses a broad area, perhaps a park or a river seen from the air. At other times the description may be narrow in focus, as in the following description of Yosemite Falls in California:

> Physical point of view: Fern Ledge
>
> Ascent to Fern Ledge
>
> Description

During the time of the spring floods the best near view of the fall is obtained from Fern Ledge on the east side above the blinding spray at a height of about 400 feet above the base of the fall. A climb of about 1400 feet from the Valley has to be made, and there is no trail, but to anyone fond of climbing this will make the ascent all the more delightful. A narrow part of the ledge extends to the side of the fall and back of it, enabling us to approach it as closely as we wish. When the afternoon sunshine is streaming through the throng of comets, ever wasting, ever renewed, the marvelous fineness, firmness and variety of their forms are beautifully revealed.

—John Muir, *The Yosemite*

Muir is specific about height and distance; he is specific, too, about changes in physical point of view. He tells us where he is walking and where he is standing in viewing the falls. Often his description focuses on an aspect of the scene to which the details build. Muir focuses our attention on a narrow ledge from which we view the falls.

In an effective description, the details create a central impression. The following description of a Mexican revolutionary focuses on a single physical detail that is repeated in the course of the paragraph. This detail makes us aware of the "ominous ripeness" of a vain and deluded man:

> Key physical detail

Braggioni catches her glance solidly as if he had been waiting for it, leans forward, *balancing his paunch between his spread knees,* and sings with tremendous emphasis, weighing his words. He has, the song relates, no father and no mother, nor even a friend to console him; lonely as a wave of the sea he comes and goes, lonely as a wave. His mouth opens round and yearns sideways, his balloon cheeks grow oily with the labor of song. *He bulges marvelously* in his expensive garments. Over his lavender collar, crushed upon a purple necktie, held by a diamond hoop: over his ammunition belt of tooled leather worked in silver, buckled cruelly *around his gasping middle:* over the tops of his glossy yellow shoes Braggioni *swells with ominous ripeness,* his mauve silk hose stretched taut, his ankles bound with the stout leather thongs of his shoes.

Physical detail repeated

Repeated again
Climactic repetition

—Katherine Anne Porter, "Flowering Judas"
(emphasis added)

Description helps to capture and hold the attention of your readers. In expressive writing, it allows them to share your experience. In expository writing, it gives them essential information about an object. In persuasive writing, it helps them to visualize the situation you are discussing. Description appeals to the senses of the reader through concrete words, imagery, and figurative language (see 30a and 31a). Porter appeals to our senses as she names the colors and gives exact details of Braggioni's clothes and jewelry; she also chooses specific verbs and adjectives (*bulges, crushed, buckled*) and uses metaphor (*balloon cheeks*).

6b | Narration

Basic to many kinds of writing, **narration** presents a series of events, usually in chronological order. Newspaper stories often narrate the facts without much explanation or description. In historical accounts, the writer may narrate bare facts, pausing perhaps to interpret them. You will have an opportunity to use narration in fictional stories, historical accounts, reports of experiments, and personal histories.

A clear focus and consistent point of view are as important in narration as they are in description. In the following narration of a parachute jump from an airplane over Massachusetts, the author keeps the central experience—the fall from the plane—in focus:

Moment before jump	When my turn came, I suddenly felt a stab of pain for all the forgotten soldiers who balked and were kicked out, perhaps shot, for their panic and for delaying the troops. I was hooked to a static line, an automatic opening device, which made it impossible to lie down or tie myself to something. The drillmaster could not hear all that I shouted at him. But he knew the signs of mutiny and removed my arms from his neck. He took me to the doorway, sat me down, and yelled "Go!" or "Now!" or "Out!" There was nothing to do but be punched by the wind, which knocked the spit from my mouth, reach for the wing strut, hold on hard, kick back the feet so weighted and helpless in those boots, and let go. The parachute opened with a plop, as Istel had sworn to me that it would. When my eyelids opened as well, I saw the white gloves on my hands were old ones from Saks Fifth Avenue, gloves I wore with summer dresses. There was dribble on my chin; my eyes and nose were leaking. I wiped everything with the gloves.
Identification with earlier jumpers	
Preparation for jump	
Thoughts of mutiny	
The jump	
Details of ascent	

—Gloria Emerson, "Take the Plunge . . ."

Emerson reports the events chronologically. And she is careful to specify the changes in point of view ("He took me to the doorway, sat me down"). But Emerson does not attempt to tell her readers everything that happens. She selects key details that reveal both what happened and what she felt when making the jump. Narrative used in this way joins with description: the author pauses to describe her gloves and her physical appearance. Narration and description usually work together in creating a central impression or effect.

EXERCISES

1. Suggest how description can be used to develop one of the following topics in an expressive, an informative, and a persuasive essay:
   a. buying a used car
   b. driving in heavy traffic
2. How might narration be used to develop each of the preceding topics?
3. Write a short account of a recent event you witnessed or an unusual experience. Include the following in your account:
   a. a narrative of the event or experience.
   b. a description of the scene and people involved. ▪

6c | Definition

Definition gives the current meaning of a word, the meaning of the word as used in the past, or special meanings given to it by certain occupations or groups of people. Definition is essential in the many kinds of writing you do in college. Quizzes and exams usually ask for definitions. In expository and persuasive essays, you explain words unfamiliar to your readers.

1 Denotative definition

A **denotative definition** states the characteristics fully in a sentence like the following:

> The phrase *on background* is a term used by reporters and government employees to describe a statement of fact or opinion that may not be quoted or attributed to the speaker.

Your own definition of such a term probably would be *informal* unless you were asked to define the term fully, perhaps on a political science exam. In an informal discussion, you probably would define a word partially by citing one or two but not all of its defining characteristics. How much information you provide depends on what your readers know about the subject and the word.

On occasion you may want to weave a definition into the discussion, as in the following explanation of speaking "off the record":

> In fact, off the record is used more as a device for giving out information than for hiding it, since there is little reason for a public figure to tell a reporter something that will never turn up in print or influence what does turn up. Reporters sometimes go back to their sources to put off-the-record remarks on the record, or else to use them under other traditional rubrics.
>
> —" 'I Don't Want to Be Quoted'," *Newsweek*, August 27, 1984

Many denotative definitions place the thing being defined in a class or genus and then state the specific differences—characteristics that set the thing apart from all other members of the class. Not all definitions state these differences. The following definition places an object (*bearings*) in a class of objects (*flat strips of metal*), describes the object, and tells us what it does:

> Bearings are flat strips of metal, formed into half-circles about as thick as a matchbook match and about an inch wide. The bearing surface itself—the surface that *bears* the crankshaft and that *bears* the load imposed by the fire-induced pressure above the piston—is half as thick.
>
> —Don Sharp, "Under the Hood," *Harper's*, June 1980

How broad the class you choose depends on the purpose of your definition and on your audience. How complete your definition should be depends on how much information you believe your readers need. Like Sharp's, most definitions begin at the point at which readers need explanation of special terms. Sharp might have assigned car bearings to another class, perhaps *engine parts*:

> A car bearing is an engine part that . . .

Sharp assumes that his audience knows that bearings are engine parts and he therefore defines bearings more narrowly. His definition of bearings occurs in a discussion of how cars work, directed to a nontechnical audience. A technical dictionary directed to a special audience of mechanics and engineers would give the more detailed definitions needed in manufacturing, study, and experimentation.

2 Connotative definition

You will have occasion to use other kinds of definition in your writing. **Connotative definition** gives the general and special associations made with a word or the positive or negative feelings that the word arouses. You would use connotative definition in explaining the associations made with country music or another kind of popular music. You might give a connotative definition after telling your readers what country music is, or you might discuss only the connotations. The following definition defines the lyrics of country music and suggests the feelings they arouse in the listener:

> The South, as it is presented in country music, is the best possible place to live, the standard for comparing all other places, especially the Northern city. The North, in general, is a cold, gray, hazy area at the periphery of country music's map, as far from

home as one can get. Listen to one song or a hundred, the pattern is the same. If a song is about someone being unfaithful, drunken, jobless, or lonely, it will be in a city, probably in the North. If a song is about family, security, childhood, love, or other pleasant things, it will be in the South, probably on a farm. Texas usually appears as a land of heroic men and romantic women. Canada and Alaska show up as our new frontiers, important places for individualists. And California is an ambiguous place with both Southern and Northern characteristics, perhaps a reflection of the conflict between the agricultural and urban parts of that state.

—Ben Marsh, *A Rose-Colored Map*

3 Etymological definition

Etymological definition gives the derivation or origin of a word. This kind of definition is useful in shedding light on current meanings by tracing the history of a word. The following writer gives the origin of the word *mustang* in giving a history of wild horses in the American West:

Nor could the horse itself be contained any longer. So many were scattered in the confusion of the perpetual rustling that stray horses sighted by the Spaniards were dubbed "mestenos" (belonging to the *mesta*, a Spanish word referring to stock growers). In time, this word became mustang, the name by which we still call our wild horses.

—Hope Ryden, *America's Last Wild Horses*

Other kinds of definition are common in persuasive writing and in philosophical and scientific writing.

4 Other kinds of definition

Theoretical definition gives an explanation of sometimes controversial words like *comedy, tragedy, democracy, obscenity.* Writers who use controversial words often argue or give reasons, and in the course of doing so propose a theory of something in opposition to another theory or belief. Abraham Lincoln was giving a theoretical definition in defining conservatism:

What is conservatism? Is it not adherence to the old and tried, against the new and untried?

A special kind of theoretical definition, called a **precising definition,** seeks to make an existing definition as exact as

127

possible. Judicial opinions and political statements are often precising definitions, and the writer of the definition may note this fact:

> In order to discuss democracy intelligently it will be necessary, therefore, to define it, to attach to the word a sufficiently precise meaning to avoid the confusion which is not infrequently the chief result of such discussions.
>
> —Carl Becker, *Modern Democracy*

You may on occasion wish to create a word and define it for your readers because you cannot find a word to describe a new situation or thing. **Stipulative definition** proposes a new word instead of redefining an existing one. A recent example is the word *prosumer*—coined by Alvin Toffler to describe "do-it-yourselfers" who help produce what they consume. Stipulative definitions sometimes come into general use. The word *quark*, borrowed from a twentieth-century novel by the physicist Murray Gell-Mann, is now the accepted term for a particle of the atom.

In writing paragraphs of definition, you may wish to combine two or more of these types. You might first state what a thing is and then give its connotations, referring also to its etymology. In addition, you want to be sure that your reader knows what kind of definition you are presenting. You don't have to use the technical names of definitions to do so. For example, after stating what an object is, you might note that people make different associations with the word used to describe the object. You might introduce a theoretical definition by stating that people hold different ideas about democracy or obscenity.

(See 32b–e for additional discussion of definition.)

EXERCISES

1. Assume that you are writing a set of directions for a mechanical process you often perform:
   a. What questions do you need to ask about your audience before you begin?
   b. What terms do you need to define? What terms don't require definition? How does knowledge of your audience help you decide?
   c. What kind of definitions would be appropriate in explaining a stage of the process?
2. Compare definitions of the word *democracy* in two college dictionaries. How do the definitions differ in conception or theory?

6d | Classification and division

Closely related to definition, classification and division are integral to explanations of relationships among objects or ideas. **Classification** groups similar objects or ideas into a single category or class: for example, classifying robins, orioles, crows, and eagles as birds. **Division** breaks down a single class into its component parts or classes.

You will have occasion to use classification in reports that require a grouping of objects like those in the following paragraph. The author places a number of systems into a single class and then defines it:

Name of class	Computer systems that monitor or control processes in the real world are rapidly growing in number. They deal with such things as air traffic
Members of class	control, the equivalent routing and signaling system for the railroads, the operation of nuclear power plants, the distribution of electric power, the telephone network, the autopilot and other control systems of an aircraft, the operation of elevators, the control of robots and machine tools, the indoor environment of buildings, production lines in manufacturing plants, the flight of spacecraft and so on.
Definition of class	One distinctive characteristic of a process-control computer is that its primary function is to communicate with the physical world rather than with a human operator (although it may display information about the state of the process to the operator). Another feature is that a process-control computer cannot set its own pace; it must respond on cue to events in the world at large.

—Alfred Z. Spector, "Computer Software for
Process Control," *Scientific American*,
September 1984

Whereas classification creates a class, division breaks down a class, usually according to a single principle or method of analysis. For example, you might divide the class *horses* according to their *use*.

draft horses used for work
light horses used for riding and herding

You could in turn divide subclassifications according to another principle or the same one; for example, by also dividing light horses according to use:

> saddle horses (American saddle horses)
> harness racing horses (trotters)
> racing horses (thoroughbreds)
> herding horses (the Appaloosa and Pinto)

In the following paragraph, Appaloosa horses are divided according to *color type:*

Class	These *Appaloosa horses,* named after the Palouse River along which they once grazed, have been facetiously called the two-toned, polka-dotted ponies, and the description can hardly be more accurate.
Principle of division	rate. There are six *color types,* but the two most common patterns are as follows: The front half of the animal is either white or roanish, meaning that it is a solid color, interspersed with white hairs, giving that part of the horse an almost iridescent cast—
Types	much like "shot silk"—when the light hits it in a particular way. If the basic color of the roan is black, this half of the animal sometimes appears blue; if the basic color is brown, it reflects shades of red. The rear half of the Nez Percé horse is either white, spattered with small roan polka dots, or roan with a scattering of small white polka dots. A third type of Appaloosa is called the leopard phase, and an animal so marked is covered with round polka dots over its entire white or gray body.

> —Hope Ryden, *America's Last Wild Horses*
> (emphasis added)

The division must be consistent but it need not be complete. In dividing, you may not know all of the parts that form the class. In this instance, you should tell your reader that the division is not complete.

Division and classification are complementary forms of analysis. In college courses, you will have occasion to classify and divide evidence. For example, you might sort out various chemical substances into classes such as acids and bases. Having made this general classification, you might then divide or subclassify—for example, acids—into organic and inorganic acids. In a literature course, you might classify writers on the basis of the age in which they lived (*Romantic writers*), then divide this general class on the basis of genre (*Romantic novelists, Romantic poets, Romantic dramatists*).

In writing a paragraph that classifies or divides, be sure to identify the class (e.g., "The general class of acids includes . . ."). You need not state that you are classifying or dividing, but the process of analysis should be clear. Telling your reader what you are doing can make the paragraph wordy. Avoid comments like "I will now state the classes into which acids fall."

EXERCISES

1. Assume that you are writing an account of sports for an audience and you decide to divide the class *sports* on the basis of place (e.g., sports played on water). How many divisions will you have?
2. Assume that later in your account of sports you divide the class *ballgames*. How many ways might this class be divided?
3. Assume that one of your subdivisions or subclassifications is baseball. How many ways might this subclass be divided?
4. Are the following divisions of each class consistent? Why, or why not?
   a. *Fruit of the vine:* grapes, raspberries, blackberries, blueberries, strawberries
   b. *Organic acids:* citric acid, phosphoric acid, carbonic acid, lactic acid, sulfuric acid
   c. *Armies:* divisions, regiments, battalions, infantries ■

6e | Example

Examples are essential in most writing. In an exam answer, you do best always to illustrate your ideas, making an abstract idea concrete wherever possible. An apt illustration shows that you understand the idea. It also provides your reader with a context, a sense of the area of experience to which the idea relates.

The range of experience to which your ideas apply may be so wide that your reader will find them vague without examples. The idea of "runaway industrial dynamism" in the following paragraph can refer to so many phenomena that the reader needs the extended example of fluorocarbons to clarify it:

131

Idea illustrated

Example: fluorocarbon spray can

Details of production and distribution

Focus on "runaway dynamism"

Consider only one recent, well-publicized example of our runaway industrial dynamism. A number of American, European, and Japanese companies develop the fluorocarbon spray-can dispenser—a commercial novelty of relatively minor economic significance to the corporate interests of these societies. For nearly two decades, the product is blithely mass-produced, advertised, and marketed on a world-wide scale. It is in daily use everywhere before anybody can collect evidence of its environmental effects—or perhaps even thinks of making such an investigation. Then, a few inquisitive scientists, acting on the basis of their own private research, suggest the possibility that the fluorocarbons may be capable of doing cataclysmic damage to the ozone layer. Their research is disputed and a public debate ensues. Meanwhile, the fluorocarbons already released continue to rise skyward beyond retrieval, perhaps to rend the biosphere permanently and globally.

—Theodore Roszak, *Person/Planet*

You may want to illustrate the central idea of your paragraph through a single extended example like Roszak's or through a series of short examples like the following:

Time

Space

Queuing gets more things through a space-time bottleneck by lining them up in space or time. Schedules and appointment calendars line things and people up in time: queues, lists, or priority systems line them up in space. Like things can be lined up or queued to get more of them into a limited space. Canners do it when they line the anchovies up head by tail to get more into the can at a time (the anchovies *share* the time-space of the can when they are curled around something else, like a caper). You queue in space when you put all the tall books on one tall shelf so that you can get more shelves and hence more books on the wall at the same time.

—Caroline Bird, *The Crowding Syndrome*

Notice that Bird presents a parallel series of examples: she develops her idea first by briefly discussing things that we line up in time, then by discussing things we line up in space. Presenting contrasting examples or details in a single paragraph has the advantage of keeping the central idea and the subordinate ideas and details in focus. If your paragraph contains a number of contrasting ideas, restate each of them as Bird does ("You queue in space") to keep the sequence of ideas and details clear.

EXERCISES

1. In a paragraph, use illustration to explain one of the following statements or one of your own choosing. Develop your paragraph through an extended example or a series of brief examples.
   a. I read novels and textbooks in different ways.
   b. People in my family have different eating habits.
   c. My friends (or members of my family) respond to personal criticism in different ways.
2. Develop the following paragraph by adding examples to make the idea concrete.

```
        Television can generate conflicting emotions
   in the viewer in the space of an evening or an
   hour--in newscasts particularly. The sequence of
   facts, ideas, images is often so rapid that the
   viewer experiences a welter of emotions. The re-
   sult is an emotional short-circuit, a diminishing
   of thought--if thinking occurs at all. Marshall
   McLuhan must have had this effect in mind in his
   famous statement "The medium is the message."
```

 Comparison and contrast

Comparison illustrates a point or argues a thesis by pointing to similarities between objects or ideas; **contrast** does this by pointing to differences. In explaining why aspirin and codeine kill pain, you would discuss their similarities; you would also discuss differences in explaining that one drug is not addictive and the other is addictive. A paragraph can contain both comparison and contrast.

The things or ideas being compared and contrasted usually are of equal importance in the analysis. For example, in explaining the painkilling effects of aspirin and codeine, you would give equal attention to both—citing similarities as well as differences. Comparisons of this kind present a *relative estimate*: the qualities of one object are weighed or measured by comparison with another. In this case, the qualities of aspirin are measured against those of codeine.

In comparing or contrasting, you can present the similarities or differences in two ways—*point by point* or *subject by subject* (sometimes called **block comparison** or **contrast**). The following paragraph contrasting European and American circuses develops point by point, the differences between clowns, acts, and performing styles discussed one at a time:

Topic: European vs. American circuses
1. Clowns
2. Acts

3. Performing styles

European circuses are more familial in atmosphere than our American brand, and their stars—like the great dapper Russian clown Popov—tend to work from a presumption of good health and good will. Popov depicts a playful, intelligent well-dressed man at the top of his form, whereas American clowning stresses lunacy, poverty, misery, weirdness. American thrill acts are just that: lean toward the possibility that the man may plunge down before our eyes and die. But in Europe the same performers will use nets or "mechanics" (wires to the roof) because the premium is on dexterity and grace, not simply nerve. Often there is something of a gulf between the European stars brought to this side of the ocean who keep to the friendly, upbeat motif, and the ones who go whole hog instead for our circuses' preference for suffering and the bizarre.
—Edward Hoagland, "Pathos and Perfection"

You can organize the paragraph in blocks—for example, by first stating the features of the European circus (clowns, acts, style) then stating the similar or contrasting features of the American circus (clowns, acts, style). But a paragraph that presents both similarities and differences is best developed point by point—first dealing with similarities between European and American circuses, then with differences. Block comparison and contrast risks becoming blurred because of the extended presentation required. A point-by-point comparison and contrast might follow this pattern:

Point-by-Point Comparison/Contrast
Clowns
   Similarities
   Differences
Acts
   Similarities
   Differences
Performing styles
   Similarities
   Differences

Like definition and other patterns of development, comparison (and contrast) are indispensable in much of the writing you do in college and later. At some point in college writing, you will need to make brief comparisons and sometimes extended ones. You may be asked to compare personal experiences, writers in different periods of American or English literature, presidents, or government policies. In your business courses, you will discover that comparison is an essential method of analysis in judging the merits of particular products or marketing campaigns and policies.

EXERCISES

1. Choose two objects—such as two cars you have driven or two houses you have lived in—and make a list of their similarities and differences. Write a paragraph discussing these similarities and differences point by point.
2. Rewrite your first paragraph, using block comparison and contrast as patterns for development. ■

6g Analogy

Analogy is a special form of comparison used for illustration. It uses *point-by-point comparison* to explain or illustrate one thing through another thing that resembles it in some ways but not in all ways. The things compared in analogy are usually strikingly unlike but share a few important characteristics. For example, you might give a point-by-point comparison to form an analogy between writing an essay and drawing a picture in order to show how similar the two mental acts are. The following example makes an analogy between amplifier power in stereo systems and horsepower in cars:

Thing analogized: amplifier power	Amplifier power, usually measured in watts per channel, is rather like horsepower in cars: it's handy in the tight spots. You don't always drive with the gas pedal jammed to the floor, pulling every bit of available power from the engine. Similarly, an amplifier or receiver rarely operates at full output. But there are moments in music—just as there are moments on the road—when ample power helps you over the hurdles. On the road, you may need the extra power to pass a truck. In music, the equivalent of such a critical moment may be an orchestral fortissimo, a pianist's exuberance in striking a sforzando, or the stentorian proclamations of a great pipe organ. If not enough power is available at such moments, the sound grows harsh and the thrill of the climactic moment turns into sonic hash. The point is that—contrary to popular belief—power doesn't equate with loudness but rather with the purity of sound in loud passages.
Analogy	
Similarities developed	

—Hans Fantel, "Sound," *New York Times,*
March 13, 1983

Notice that amplifier power is not like horsepower in all respects. Since analogies are always limited in the number of similarities they can make, it may sometimes be necessary to warn the reader not to draw other unwarranted conclusions. The analogy is useful if the differences do not cloud the explanation. Indeed, the purpose of the analogy is to make the similarities stand out. As Fantel's paragraph shows, analogy is an important device of exposition. Science writers depend on analogy to make difficult ideas clear to readers who have little knowledge in the field. In science and other fields, analogy must be used with caution, for it depends on similarities between things, not on identities, and the differences between these things are fundamental though not always apparent.

Your own paragraphs may consist entirely of analogy, or you may wish to combine analogy with other patterns of development, perhaps pausing to define your terms. Whereas comparison can be developed point by point or subject by subject, an analogy is usually developed point by point. Block comparison would blur the analogy.

(See 34c on the use of analogy in argument.)

EXERCISES

First write down the similarities between driving a car and riding a bicycle (or between two other similar activities). Use these similarities to write a paragraph of analogy directed to a person learning to drive, to ride a bicycle, or to perform another activity. At the end of your paragraph, state the limits of the analogy—that is, the points of dissimilarity between the two things you have compared.

6h | Process analysis

Process analysis informs readers about a series of connected acts, each act leading to the next. An instruction book enables you to assemble or operate a stereo or other piece of machinery. In maintaining lab notes, you are keeping records of various processes. Similarly, lab manuals describe a series of processes. So in many ways does the handbook you are reading. Some paragraphs trace processes—perhaps a natural process like the circulation of the blood or a mechanical process like assembling a bicycle. As in Jearl Walker's instructions on cooking meat over an open fire (see page 104), a process analysis is usually chronological, the steps presented in the order of occurrence.

In giving instructions, you must make a decision on where to begin. Again, your decision depends on an estimate of your audience. Giving a recipe to an inexperienced cook, you would begin with the first steps and describe each in full detail; giving the same recipe to an experienced cook, you might skip over some of the steps if they are obvious. If you present any of the steps out of order, perhaps to give some of them special attention, you may wish to indicate the natural order. In giving instructions, you want to define special terms and give a detailed explanation of difficult steps.

Not all process analysis is instructional. You may wish to give information about a process, perhaps to tell your readers something about the people who perform it. In the following paragraph, Elizabeth Marshall Thomas demonstrates the amazing ingenuity of the Kung Bushmen of the Kalahari Desert in southern Africa, who discovered a species of beetle that is poisonous only in the pupa stage. One of thousands, the species is difficult to find.

General process: making poisoned arrows	Kung Bushmen, who use metal arrows obtained by trading animal skins for wire with the Bantus, have a complicated system of poisoning in which they use several ingredients for the poison paste. One of these is a binding fluid, used because the pure poison squeezed from the grub will not adhere well to metal but must be made binding and sticky. The binding material comes from the bark of a tree. They chew the bark thoroughly and spit the mash into a little mortar made from the knee bone of an antelope, a nice little cup, into which the Bushmen have squeezed the milky juice of sansevieria plants, got by wringing the heavy, thick leaves. This juice has an irritating effect when it is dissolved in a wound and causes the antelope to rub and scratch its wounded spot against a tree, which stimulates circulation in the area, which carries the poison more quickly through the body, which hastens death.
Process of making binding fluid	
Source	
Deriving juice from bark	
Effect	

—*The Harmless People*

Thomas is not giving instructions on performing the process; rather, she is illustrating the complex technology of a native people mistakenly thought to be unskilled because of their simple living conditions. In writing to give information, define and explain only those terms and steps that your readers need to understand the point you are making.

EXERCISE

In a humorous essay, Russell Baker describes the seemingly impossible job of opening the safety cap of a plastic bottle:

> Approaching the bottled acid, I grip the cap, press down— there's the trick to conquering the "safety cap": pressing down before turning—and unscrew.
>
> —"Openings"

Baker eventually finds that the cap refuses to come off the bottle.

Write a set of instructions on how to perform another difficult job. Assume that you are giving instructions to a frustrated person who has asked for your help. ◼

6i | Causal analysis

Causal analysis demonstrates a chain or interconnection of acts and events. Tracing causes and effects is probably the most complex way to develop paragraphs. The economist traces **causes** to show that inflation usually occurs when demand exceeds supply. The biologist or medical researcher asks about causes when examining a series of physiological events that seem related. In answering an exam question in an economics or biology class, you may trace a series of events and discuss their **effects.** In an essay written in your composition course, you might discuss the immediate and not-so-immediate events that led to your decision to attend college, or the effects of a book that influenced your choice of a career.

Sometimes the chain of causes and effects is a simple one, as in this explanation of why car bearings wear out:

> If the oil level falls too low, the oil pump sucks in air. The oil gets as frothy as whipped cream and doesn't flow. In time, oil pressure will fall so low that the "idiot" light on the dashboard will flash, but long before then the bearing may have run "dry" and suffered considerable amounts of its metal to be peened away by those 3,500-pound hammer blows.
> —Don Sharp, "Under the Hood"

Or the process may be a complex one, as in a series of related chemical experiments. In writing a lab report, you would report each experiment separately and comment on the relationship among the experiments in your opening and concluding paragraphs.

Note that the word *cause* has various meanings. One meaning distinguishes **mediate** or **remote causes**—those distant in time—from **proximate** or **immediate causes**—those close in time. Thus a defect in the manufacturing of a tire may cause a flat at a later time: this cause is a remote one. The immediate cause, closer in time, is a hard bump that flattens the weakened tire. A mediate cause of low oil in the crankshaft might be the ignorance or neglect of the car owner. In a paragraph that distinguishes mediate from immediate causes, you need to specify each kind and keep your analysis of each from overlapping.

Other meanings of the word *cause* distinguish

the *material* out of which an object is made (wood, graphite, metal and rubber—materials of a pencil);

the *form or shape* given to the object (the mold, form, or shape used in its manufacture—the encasing of a thin rod of graphite in wood, with the eraser attached);

the *maker* of the object (the manufacturer of the pencil);

the *purpose* or use of the object (the application of pencil to paper).

The following causal analysis focuses on material and shape in explaining why the longbow is inefficient by comparison with other bows:

Material and formal cause

Although the longbow, a simple curved stick with a string connecting the ends, figured prominently in Britain's Hundred Years' War and sustained generations of American Indians, it is short on efficiency. The Indians' hunting success, in fact, was due more to their stalking expertise than to technology. The bow is huge, typically 72 inches long, so much of the energy expended in drawing the bowstring goes into returning the massive limbs to their original position rather than shooting the arrow.

Formal cause

—Laura B. Ackerman, "The Bow Machine," *Science 85*, July/August

In your own informative paragraphs or essays, you may focus on a single cause or on several. How many you discuss depends on the purpose of your analysis. For example, an analysis of an unknown substance dumped into a lake to find out whether it is toxic might require you to focus on these causes:

Cause	Focus of Investigation
Material	Identity of substance
Formal	Chemical structure
Effective (Maker)	Manufacturer
Final (Purpose)	Purpose of substance

(See 34d on the use of causal analysis in argument.)

✓ Checklist: Patterns of Development

1. What patterns of development or analysis will help me develop the central idea of my paragraph or essay?
2. Which of these patterns will best help my audience understand the central idea of my paragraph or the thesis of my essay?
3. How much do my readers know about the subject of my paragraph or essay? How much detail should I provide to help them understand my comparison or analogy, the process I am explaining, or the causes and effects I am tracing?
4. What is the best way to organize my paragraph or essay, given the patterns of development I have chosen?

EXERCISES

1. Write a paragraph distinguishing immediate from mediate causes of some important event in your life, perhaps an achievement that involved long preparation and the help of many people. In the course of your paragraph, discuss which of these causes contributed most to your success.
2. Write a paragraph distinguishing the materials, form, maker, and purpose of one of the following:
   a. the book you are reading
   b. an essay you wrote recently
   c. the vehicle that brought you to school
   d. a piece of sports equipment
   e. a mechanical device

6j Combining patterns of development

You will have frequent occasion to combine the patterns of development discussed in this chapter. In describing a process, for instance, you may need to define basic terms and classify tools or ingredients. In paragraphs that trace cause and effect, you may need to use process analysis. Few paragraphs develop ideas without illustrating them. Here is a paragraph that illustrates the western influence on Asia through the failure of some Asian countries to industrialize rapidly:

General topic	At this point we reach one of the consequences of the western impact which, though unintended, may have given a decisive setback to Asian devel-
Example	opment. Until the nineteenth century China and India were exporters to Europe of manufactures— hand-loom textiles, silks, pottery. In addition, peasant income all through the vast countryside was
Comparison	supplemented by local handicrafts. In Britain such centers of artisan enterprise were often the starting
Contrast	points of mechanized industry. In Japan after 1870, they were to prove so again as thousands of small workshops were moving to production with power
Causes of failure	and machines. But in India and China as the nineteenth century developed, this widespread preindustrial system of manufacture was wiped out by the flooding in of machine-made textiles and gadg-
Effects of failure and British economic policy	ets from the West. Local centers were extinguished. Peasant income fell. Indigenous growth ceased. Later in the century, modern factory industry began; but often, as in China, it was overwhelmingly foreign. In India, given Britain's doctrines of free trade and *laissez faire,* Indian enterprise did not secure full tariff protection until after the First World
Central idea	War. Industrialization was thus slow in spreading and would have been even slower if two world wars had not hastened it a little.

　　　　　　　　　—Barbara Ward, "The Economic Revolution"

Notice the importance of transitions in a paragraph that combines several patterns of development. The words *in addition, but,* and *thus* help Ward to organize a diverse series of ideas and details. Transitions show where the discussion has come from and where it is going. They are essential to following the writer's train of thought.

The devices of paragraph unity and coherence discussed in Chapter 5 are also important in building paragraphs. The more patterns of development that you combine, the more attention you must pay to how ideas and details in the paragraph form a whole. A disunified paragraph lacks a central focus—a central idea to which the ideas and details connect. These connections depend, finally, on how your paragraphs fit into the essay. In revising the essay, you have an opportunity to test not only the unity and coherence of your paragraphs but also the unity and coherence of the whole essay.

EXERCISES

1. Write a letter to a newspaper arguing in favor of some change in the law. Use at least three of the methods of analysis discussed in this chapter to develop your argument.
2. Revise your letter, directing it instead to a relative or a friend. To fit this new audience, change the methods of analysis used to develop your argument as needed. Be ready to justify these changes.

Summary

6a Use description to give details about persons, places, and objects.

6b Use narration to explain events.

6c Use the appropriate kind of definition in explaining terms or ideas.

Use a *denotative definition* to give the properties or characteristics of an object or idea (6c 1).

Use a *connotative definition* to convey the ideas and feelings associated with a word (6c 2).

Use an *etymological definition* to explain the current and past meanings of a word (6c 3).

Provide *your own defintion* of a word to make its usage more precise. (6c 4).

Stipulate a new word and definition or give your own theoretical definition if you find the current ones unsatisfactory (6c 4).

6d Classify objects or ideas to show their common properties. Divide a class of objects or ideas to distinguish among them.

6e Make your ideas clear through examples.

6f Compare and contrast to show similarities and differences among objects or ideas.

6g Present an analogy for the purpose of illustration.

6h Analyze a natural or mechanical process for the same purpose.

6i Distinguish distant or remote causes from immediate ones. Discuss the materials of a thing, or its form or shape, or its maker, or its purpose or use, or all of these, to analyze a cause.

6j Combine methods of development and analysis where appropriate.

PART THREE

SENTENCE GRAMMAR

The Sentence
and Its Parts

7

Grammar is the system by which we form sentences. The grammatical system of a language describes its sentence patterns, names the forms or classes of the words that fill these patterns, and explains how these classes work. English sentences convey meaning in systematic ways. As a speaker and writer of English, you have the ability to form a wide variety of sentences, using a relatively small number of sentence and word patterns as models.

To form sentences, you need not be conscious of these sentence patterns or classes of words. You speak and write sentences, often of great complexity, without summoning grammatical patterns or structures to mind, and without being able to describe them. You were a skilled speaker long before you learned to write, and you became a skilled speaker without attaining knowledge of grammar. Why, then, should you study grammar? Although grammatical knowledge alone cannot make you a better writer of sentences, it can help you analyze the sentences you write and provide a common vocabulary for discussion of sentences and essays. Your knowledge of grammar will be particularly useful in revising and editing your papers.

Thus, before we can turn to a discussion of how to revise and edit sentences (the topics of Parts Four and Five of the *Handbook*), we first need an understanding of the grammatical definitions and patterns used to form sentences—our focus in Part Three. In this chapter, we begin our survey with the patterns of the English sentence. Chapter 8 describes the words and phrases that form these patterns, and Chapters 9–11 deal with agreement and pronoun case and reference—aspects of English grammar important in achieving clarity and coherence.

7a Sentence sense

In a recent conversation, you may have asked someone to repeat an unclear statement or complete an unfinished one. In most conversations, speakers must often clarify their statements by rephrasing or explaining them. The same is true of written communication. In receiving a puzzling note or letter, you may write asking the writer to clarify a statement.

In fact, confusion over words and sentences is exceptional in spoken and written communication. When confusion does occur, it is usually momentary. When in conversations you misunderstand a word or phrase, you mentally make the correction by substituting the right word or by putting the misplaced words into their correct order. When you read a confusing statement, you usually guess at what the writer meant, and you probably guess correctly.

Why are you able to clear up confusion over words so easily? A **sentence** consists of a subject and something said about it. As a speaker and listener you have a **grammatical** or **sentence sense** that tells you that certain information has been given. This sentence sense does not depend on your ability to analyze the parts or constituents of the sentences you hear or read or on a knowledge of the system by which they are formed. Thus, you sense that the following groups of words are not sentences:

all the apples
red are

147

You probably sense also the meaning of the following string of words:

apples not are red all

And you easily turn this string of words into a sentence:

Not all apples are red.

Yet recognition of sentences does not depend on seeing or hearing words alone. It depends also on intonation and pitch of voice and the setting of the statement. Sentence sense depends on knowing how words are pronounced and in what **context** or situation. **Intonation** or **vocal stress** further identifies the nature of your statement and your tone or attitude. For example, without the context of spoken conversation, you would not know how to interpret the following:

going home

These words have four possible interpretations, depending how they are spoken and in what context they are used:

Going home!
Going home?
Going home.
. . . going home,

Pitch of voice by itself is not an infallible test of a complete sentence, but it is often useful in determining whether a group of words forms a sentence.

EXERCISES

1. How far do the following groups of words depart from familiar English sentences? Do the words suggest more than one meaningful sentence?
   a. laughed the children at the clown
   b. to solve the problem hard was
   c. I took the hardest subject was calculus
   d. over spilt milk is there to cry no time
   e. can I in this adventure without your help not succeed or your encouragement
   f. equally to all students interesting can be few subjects with no background especially those
2. The following sentences have different meanings depending on how they are pronounced. Pronounce each sentence in two different ways and describe the difference in meaning:

a. is he crazy
b. what a robin
c. going to the beach in this weather
d. we are going to the beach
e. nothing doing

 7b Sentence constituents

Your grammatical sense tells you what **parts** or **constituents** come together to form units in the sentence. Consider the following words, phrases, and clauses:

The tall man	Those
on stage	who drank
is	the polluted water
the dramatist	became ill
who wrote the play	afterward

We know that the word groups in each column are constituents of larger groups:

The tall man on stage is the dramatist who wrote the play.	Those who drank the polluted water became ill afterwards.

Knowing how to speak and write sentences also depends on knowing the meaning of words—a knowledge independent of your sentence sense. Notice that you would introduce a vocal pause or break to clarify the following sentence:

We hope that good will prevail.

The words *good* and *will* belong to different sentence constituents: *will prevail* is the verb of the sentence.

The following sentence is spoken and marked in a different way:

She is a woman of goodwill.

A sentence consists of a **subject** and a **predicate.** The subject of the sentence may be a person, a place, an object, an idea, or an activity:

149

> She
> That woman
> Alaska
> Inflation
> Soccer

The predicate of the sentence makes a statement about the subject:

> She / *is my sister.*
> That woman / *owns a blue car.*
> Alaska / *has vast natural resources.*
> Inflation / *has undermined many democratic governments.*
> Soccer / *is becoming a popular sport.*

If the subject is performing an action, the predicate names or describes the action:

> The men / *argued.*

The predicate may contain **complements**—words that complete the naming or description. The **direct object** receives the action:

> The artist drew *a picture* on the pad.
> The golfer hit *the ball* into the water.

The **indirect object** is the receiver of the direct object, usually in sentences containing the verb *give.* The indirect object usually precedes the direct object:

> The coach gave *the team* instructions.
> The artist gave *me* the picture.

The **subjective complement** is the person or object equivalent to the subject (*predicate noun*) or a word descriptive of it (*predicate adjective*). The subjective complement follows the verb *to be* or other linking verb (*is, are, was, were, will be, seems, becomes*), or a verb of sense:

> The tall woman in the white jacket is *a chemist.*
> She seems *a woman of ability.*
> She becomes *head of the department* tomorrow.
> The head of the company is *intelligent* and *ambitious.*
> Lemons taste *sour.*

The **objective complement** describes or gives information about the direct object:

The voters elected the former congresswoman *governor.*
Jim called me *his friend.*
I consider her *somebody indispensable.*

An **appositive** is a word or phrase that describes or gives an alternate name to another word or phrase adjacent or close to it:

Mary Smith, *my former roommate,* lives in Atlanta.

Modifiers may be attached to any of these constituents. Modifiers include *single words (former, loud, silvery, quietly)* as well as *phrases* (see 7c). An important kind of modifier is the **prepositional phrase**—a combination of words like *to* and *of* and a complement:

to the expressway   on the table
of the company   by the river

The **absolute phrase** attaches to the beginning or end of a sentence, modifying the whole sentence:

The performance having ended, the curtain came down.
He bolted the door, *his arms shaking.*

EXERCISES

1. Name the function served by the noun *Jupiter* in the following sentences:
   a. The astronomer explained that the planet Jupiter has several moons.
   b. The largest planet in our solar system, Jupiter is possibly a small star.
   c. She gave me a large book with pictures of Jupiter.
   d. The largest planet of the solar system is Jupiter.
   e. NASA voted the next planet for exploration Jupiter.
2. Write sentences that use the noun *athlete* (and any necessary modifiers) in the following positions:
   a. subject
   b. direct object
   c. indirect object
   d. subjective complement
   e. appositive
   f. objective complement
   g. prepositional phrase

151

7c | Forming sentences

1 Sentence patterns

Words can be arranged in endless ways, yet the number of possible arrangements or patterns used to form complete sentences is limited. Think of the sentence as consisting of two parts: (1) a **noun phrase** (e.g., a single word like *fish* or a combination of words like *The two men*), and (2) a **verb phrase** (e.g., a single word like *swim* or a combination of words like *were arguing*).

Sentence

Noun phrase (NP) ←—————————→ Verb phrase (VP)

Patterns in English sentences arise not from variations in the subject noun phrase but from variations in the predicate verb phrase, as the following list of patterns shows.

    NP   VP
1. *Subject + intransitive verb*:

> Fish swim.
> The two men were arguing.

    NP   VP
2. *Subject + linking verb + subjective complement*:

> That animal is a wolf.
> Lemons taste sour.

    NP   VP
3. *Subject + transitive verb + direct object*:

> The artist drew a picture on the wall.
> The voters rejected the amendment.

    NP   VP
4. *Subject + transitive verb + direct object + objective complement*:

> The newspapers called the statement a lie.
> His opponent called the candidate unqualified.

    NP   VP
5. *Subject + transitive verb + indirect object + direct object*:

> The artist gave me the picture.
> Her aunt sent Barbara a pass to the dog show.

These sentence constituents—subject, predicate, complements—consist of, and may also be modified by, single words, phrases, and clauses. For example, the subject of the sentence may be followed by appositive words and phrases:

The capital of Connecticut, *Hartford,* is north of New Haven.
George Washington, *first president of the United States,* died in 1799.

Sentences are classified according to their purpose.

Declarative sentences make direct statements:

The eggs are four weeks old.

Interrogative sentences ask questions:

How old are the eggs?

Imperative sentences issue commands or requests:

Make me an omelet.

Exclamations express wonder, surprise, anger, horror, and other attitudes and emotions:

The eggs taste rotten!

EXERCISE

Identify the sentence pattern of each of the following sentences.

1. The books on the shelf are dusty.
2. We walk every morning.
3. The controversy deadlocked the convention.
4. She called the compromise a fraud.
5. The compromise is indeed a fraud.
6. The sauce in the pan smelled garlicky.
7. Interstate 70 connects Columbus, Indianapolis, and St. Louis.
8. The judge gave the defendant a large fine and time in jail.
9. Few of the people on my block have traveled out of the state.
10. The judge called the act criminal.

2 Phrases and clauses

A **phrase** is a group of words that functions as a part or constituent of the sentence. Phrases are usually classified according to the part of speech that governs them—thus **noun phrases** (*The woman*), **verb phrases** (*is going*), **prepositional phrases** (*to the airport*), **participial phrases** (*driving in a pickup*), **infinitive phrases** (*to drive a pickup*), and so on. As noted earlier, noun phrases and verb phrases sometimes consist of a single word (*Fish swim*). (Chapters 8 and 9 define the four parts of speech that provide meaning—nouns, verbs, adjectives, and adverbs—as well as other classes of words.)

A **clause** is a group of words that contains a subject and predicate. Clauses sometimes serve as complete sentences, sometimes as sentence constituents, sometimes as modifiers that add information about the subject, the predicate, or the whole sentence.

Independent clauses (or **main clauses**) stand alone as whole statements or assertions:

I am going home.
We drank.
The men in the hall drank water from the tap.

Dependent clauses (or **subordinate clauses**) serve as constituents or modifiers. Dependent clauses are classified as *noun clauses, adjective clauses,* or *adverb clauses,* according to their function as nominals, adjectivals, or adverbials.

3 Nominals

A **nominal** is a word, phrase, or clause that serves as a subject, object, complement, or optional modifier in any of the positions taken by nouns or noun phrases:

Word
Juneau is the capital of *Alaska.*
Walking is more beneficial than *jogging,* some doctors say.

Phrase
The capital of Alaska is south of Anchorage.
The person at the tollbooth gave the driver directions to the fair-
   grounds.
To win the presidency will require money and energy.

Clause
Whoever gets sick should call the Health Department.
The winner is *whoever reaches the finish line first.*
They ate *whatever grew in the fields.*

4 Adjectivals

An **adjectival** is a word, phrase, or clause that functions as an adjective or as a word that modifies a noun:

Word
The *blue* hotel stood at the end of the street.
I can find my way *home.*

Phrase
The people *next door* are friends of my parents.
The boy *running across the street* is my brother.

Clause
The only person *who can help you* is not in the office today.
The book *that fell on the floor* has a broken spine.
The essay contest, *which Mary won last year,* will offer a cash prize for the first time in its history.

5 Adverbials

An **adverbial** is a word, phrase, or clause that functions as an adverb or as a word that modifies a verb:

Word
He ran *quickly* down the stairs.

Phrase
He came *flying down the stairs.*
She reached out *to catch the falling chair.*

Clause
We applauded *when the curtain came down.*
Review the chapter carefully *before you do the problems.*

(Chapters 8 and 9 discuss other grammatical structures that serve as nominals, adjectivals, and adverbials.)

7d Sentence types

Sentences are sometimes classified by the number of independent and dependent clauses they contain. A **simple sen-**

tence consists of a single independent clause—a subject and predicate that can stand alone as a self-contained statement. Simple sentences can vary in length and degree of modification, as the following examples show:

> The first case was that of a man called Milliken, an enormous, hulking fellow in his late thirties, swarthy, hairy-chested and with arms and legs on him fit for the strong man in the circus. He ran a milk route at one end of the town.
> —William Carlos Williams, "Old Doc Rivers"

In a **compound sentence** two or more independent clauses are joined through a coordinating conjunction (*and, but, yet, for, or, nor, so*), correlative conjunctions (for example, *both/and, not only/but also*), or a semicolon:

> Rivers was fidgeting / *and* I wasn't in a particularly pleasant mood myself.
> I could feel my face flush / *but* I didn't say anything.—"Old Doc Rivers" (emphasis added)

A **complex sentence** consists of a single independent clause and one or more dependent clauses, introduced by subordinating conjunctions (for example, *because, since, after, although, when, whenever,* and *than*) or the pronouns *who, which,* and *that*.

> *When he'd been there a month or so,* he'd begin to ask the Superintendent, *who was a friend of his,* whether he didn't think [*that*] *he could go out to work again.*
> Rivers made a hobby one time of catching rattlesnakes, *which abound in the mountains of North Jersey*—"Old Doc Rivers" (emphasis added)

A **compound-complex sentence** consists of two or more independent clauses and one or more dependent clauses:

> He had been in bed in the front of the house *and* I shall never forget my surprise and the shock to my sense of propriety *when I saw Frankel, whom I knew,* coming down the narrow, dark corridor of the apartment in his bare feet and an old-fashioned nightgown *that reached just to his knees.*—"Old Doc Rivers" (emphasis added)

Notice that this classification of sentences tells us nothing about the length of the sentence or the number of phrasal or clausal modifiers. As the first example above shows, a simple sentence may be longer than a sentence containing additional clauses. However, the classification is sometimes convenient in discussing ways to expand a sentence or join sentences closely related in idea.

EXERCISES

1. Expand the following phrases into independent clauses:
   a. the black Labrador retriever
   b. her long-awaited twenty-first birthday celebration
   c. is waiting impatiently
   d. courageously volunteered to test the water
   e. running down the path toward the lake
   f. to explain why the plan succeeded
   g. the long white trailing scarf
   h. someone waiting outside
   i. the eagerly awaited qualifying match
   j. watching from the sidelines
2. Add modifying words, phrases, or clauses to five of the preceding independent clauses. ∎

Summary

7a Your "sentence sense" helps you recognize a complete sentence.

7b A sentence contains a subject and a predicate.

> The subject describes a person, a place, an object, an idea, or an activity.
> The predicate makes a statement about the subject.

7c Sentences consist of a noun phrase and a verb phrase.

The noun phrase consists of a noun or a pronoun with or without modifiers (**7c 1**):

The verb phrase consists of an intransitive verb or a transitive verb taking one or more of the following complements (**7c 1**):

NP   VP
Subject + intransitive verb:

> The two men were arguing.

NP   VP
Subject + linking verb + subjective complement:

> That animal is a wolf.
> Lemons taste sour.

157

NP   VP
Subject + transitive verb + direct object:

    The voters rejected the amendment.

NP   VP
Subject + transitive verb + direct object + objective complement:

    The newspapers called the statement a lie.
    His opponent called the candidate unqualified.

NP   VP
Subject + transitive verb + indirect object + direct object:

    Her aunt gave Barbara a pass to the dog show.

Declarative sentences make direct statements. *Interrogative sentences* ask questions. *Imperative sentences* issue commands or requests. *Exclamations* express wonder, surprise, anger, horror, and other attitudes and emotions (7c 1).

Single words, phrases, and clauses form sentences (7c 2):

A *phrase* is a group of words that functions as a subject, predicate, or modifier in the sentence.

A *clause* is a group of words containing a subject and predicate and serving as complete sentences or sentence constituents and modifiers.

Nominals are words, phrases, or clauses of various types that serve as subjects, objects, complements, or optional modifiers in any of the positions taken by nouns or noun phrases (7c 3).

Adjectivals are words, phrases, or clauses that function as adjectives or words that modify nouns (7c 4).

Adverbials are words, phrases, or clauses that function as adverbs or as words that modify verbs (7c 5).

7d A *simple sentence* consists of a single independent clause. A *compound sentence* consists of two or more independent clauses joined by a coordinating or correlative conjunction or by a semicolon. A *complex sentence* consists of an independent clause and one or more dependent clauses. A *compound-complex sentence* consists of one or more independent clauses and one or more dependent clauses.

Nouns, Pronouns, Adjectives

8

Words serve two functions in the sentence. Nouns, pronouns, verbs, adjectives, and adverbs refer to the people, objects, actions, and qualities that sentences discuss. Prepositions, conjunctions, determiners (words like *a, an,* and *the*), auxiliaries (words like *have* and *must*), interrogatives (words like *who* and *where*), expletives (such as *there* and *it*), and qualifiers (words like *very* and *even*) give structure to sentences by introducing and connecting phrases and clauses. Qualifiers also convey information about nouns, verbs, adjectives, and adverbs in sentences. Pronouns act as stand-ins for nouns, contributing to both the content of the sentence and its structure.

Note that some words belong to more than one class or part of speech. The word *college,* for example, is classified as a noun (*the college I attend*) or an adjective (*my college roommate*), depending on its use in the sentence. Content words thus have different functions in the sentence—as nominals, adjectivals, and adverbials (see 7c). We take note of these multiple functions in this chapter on nouns, pronouns, and adjectives as well as in the following chapter on verbs and adverbs. Chapter 9 also discusses prepositions, conjunctions, expletives,

159

and interjections. In reading later chapters, you may want to return to Chapters 8 and 9 to refresh your understanding of parts of speech. Although familiarity with parts of speech will not make you a better writer, it will help you in analyzing sentences and revising them.

8a | Nouns

English has a wide variety of **nouns** that make it possible to name people, places, and things exactly. Nouns thus give sentences specific content. This section describes these types and their forms. Later sections discuss how to use nouns effectively in sentences.

1 Defining nouns

A **noun** (e.g., *city*) or **noun phrase** (e.g., *New York*) names or identifies a person, place, object, idea, or the like. A noun may appear in the subject, object, or other positions in the clause (see 7b). Nouns have three **cases**—*nominative, possessive, objective* (page 166). Nouns are identical in form in the nominative and objective case but not in the possessive.

Types of Nouns

Classification	Function	Examples
Common nouns	Nouns that point to people, objects, or places	man, woman, wall, street, car
Proper nouns	Nouns that name particular persons, objects, or places	Abraham Lincoln, Lake Erie, Yale University
Concrete nouns	Nouns that identify things known through sight, taste, smell, touch, hearing	star, salt, perfume, jazz, sandpaper, running
Abstract nouns	Nouns that name ideas or qualities	courage, democracy, tyranny, ambition
Collective nouns	Singular nouns that name groups of people or objects	class, crowd, band, chorus, family

| **Count nouns** | Nouns that refer to things that can be counted, that have singular and plural forms | man, men; hall, halls; car, cars |
| **Mass (noncount) nouns** | Nouns that refer to things that cannot be counted; that have no plural forms | health, grease, news, tennis |

These traditional noun classes often overlap. For example, some abstract nouns may also be count nouns (such as *democracy*). Some words can even serve as count and noncount nouns:

Noncount Noun	**Count Noun**
a drink of *water*	*waters* of the Niagara
a basket of *food*	*foods* of various nations

The following nouns take plurals and therefore are count nouns:

classes	bands
crowds	choruses
regiments	teams

The distinction between count and noncount nouns is important in determining agreement with subjects and verbs (see 10a). Noun phrases combine nouns with determiners (*a, an, the, this, your,* etc.) and sometimes with one or more modifiers:

a boy, a girl
the red-haired boy
the girl with the white scarf

2 Noun forms

Noun forms include the singular, plural, and possessive. The base form of nouns is singular:

boy, girl, radio, tomato, fox, baby, foot, mouse, child

Most nouns become plural by adding *-s, -es,* or *-ies*:

boy*s*, girl*s*, radio*s*, tomato*es*, fox*es*, bab*ies*

Singular nouns express possession by adding the inflection *-'s*.

161

Most plural nouns ending with *s* express possession by adding an apostrophe only:

girl*'s* hat, girls*'* hats

The -*'s* indicates ownership or possession in these words. Singular proper nouns ending in *s* add *'s* instead of just an apostrophe:

Venus*'s* orbit, Keats*'s* odes

Note that some nouns do not change in form in the plural:

deer, sheep

Seven nouns form the plural by changing the base word:

foot, feet   woman, women
goose, geese   mouse, mice
louse, lice   tooth, teeth
man, men

Some nouns form the plural with the -*en* ending:

brothers, breth*ren* (members of a religious organization)
child, child*ren*
ox, ox*en*

The singular and plural possessives of these nouns form the same way as that of other nouns—through addition of the inflection -*'s*:

child*'s* hat, children*'s* hats

The word *of* can substitute for -*'s*:

hat *of* the child, hats *of* the children
hat *of* the girl, hats *of* the girls

In some phrases, *of* has the same meaning as *about*:

the story *of* the Brontës (*or* the story *about* the Brontës)

Sometimes the ending -*'s* or -*s'* and the word *of* are both used in phrases like the following to clarify the possessive meaning:

the novels *of* the Brontë sisters*'* (i.e., the novels *by* the Brontës, not novels about the Brontës)

3 Determiners

Nouns and noun phrases often are introduced by **determiners,** which give information about quantity (*three* books) or relationship (*my* sister, *your* sister).

The **article** is an important class of determiner. The **in-definite articles** *a* and *an* identify nouns for the first time:

I found *a* book in the hall.

The **definite article** *the* is used with nouns previously identi-fied in a sentence or paragraph:

The book is an automobile repair manual.

Note that the indefinite article *a* is used before words sounded as consonants:

a book
a horse (the *h* sounded)
a youth
a union (the *u* sounded as a consonant *y*)

The indefinite article *an* is used before words beginning with or sounded as vowels:

an apple
an upper floor
an SOS (*S* is pronounced as a vowel)

Some nouns and pronouns serve as determiners of nouns. Numbers also serve as determiners. Following is a partial list of determiners:

	Determiners
Demonstrative pronouns	*this* book, *that* book, *these* books, *those* books
Possessive nouns	*my* book, *your* book, *his* book, *her* book, *its* book, *our* books, *their* books, *whose* book
Indefinitive pronouns	*several* books, *more* books, *many* books, *few* books, *most* books, *each* book, *every* book, *some* books, *any* book, *all* books, *no* book, *either* book, *neither* book
Numbers	*one* book, *two* books, *three* books

4 Noun functions

Nouns and noun phrases have various functions in sentences, depending on their position in a sentence:

Subject	*Water* is scarce in August.
	Polluted water ran from the tap.

Direct object	The officials asked *a question*.
Indirect object	They asked *the landlord* a question.
Subjective complement	Those men are *officials* from the Health Department.
	The water tastes *bitter*.
	She became *president*.
Objective complement	The landlord branded the statement *nonsense*.
Appositive	The men who tested the water, *officials* from the Health Department, issued a report.

Nouns and noun phrases also serve various functions in phrases:

Object of preposition	The women are officers of *the company*.
Absolute phrase	*The river being polluted,* the city had to find another source of water.

An **absolute phrase** (or **noun absolute**) consists often of a noun and a participle that modifies the whole sentence.

Nouns and noun phrases belong to the broad class of *nominals* (7c)—words, phrases, and clauses that serve in the same positions that a noun can. Nouns and noun phrases can also serve as *adjectivals* and *adverbials* (7c)—words, phrases, and clauses that serve in the same positions as adjectives and adverbs. As adjectivals and adverbials, nouns and noun phrases serve as modifiers:

the way home
the meeting this afternoon

EXERCISE

Create sentences of your own using the following types of nouns in the positions indicated:

1. a common noun as subject
2. a common noun as subjective complement
3. a count noun as subject
4. a mass (or noncount) noun as direct object
5. a proper noun as objective complement
6. a proper noun as appositive
7. a common noun as indirect object
8. a count noun as direct object
9. a count noun as objective complement
10. a mass (or noncount) noun as subject

Pronouns are important tools in achieving concision in sentences, paragraphs, and essays. Consider how overloaded with words a sentence or paragraph would be if you were forced to repeat a noun instead of using a pronoun to refer to it. The absence of pronouns also would force conversations to slow down considerably. Pronouns single out and give essential information about the quantity and other qualities of nouns. They also connect ideas and specify the topic. The effective writer knows how to use pronouns for these purposes.

1 Defining pronouns

Pronouns are words that substitute for nouns and noun phrases in the same positions in the clause. In these positions, they refer to an *antecedent* or earlier noun, noun phrase, or pronoun in the sentence or paragraph.

Some pronouns have separate forms to distinguish *gender* (masculine, feminine, neuter) or *number* (single, plural). Some pronouns also have separate forms as subjects (*I, we*), objects (*me, us*), and possessives (*my, our*). The exception is the pronoun *you*, which serves as subject and object.

Different types of pronouns serve different functions. Pronouns fall into the following classes:

Types of Pronouns

Classification	Function	Examples
Personal pronouns	Refer to people or things	I, you, he, she, it, we, you, they, me, my, his, hers
Demonstrative pronouns	Point to specific things	this, these, that, those
Indefinite pronouns	Point to general things; do not specify a particular person or object	another, everybody, anybody, nobody, nothing, many, several, few, both
Relative pronouns	Introduce clauses that modify nouns	who, whom, whose, whoever, whomever, which, whichever, that

165

Interrogative pronouns	Begin questions	who, what, which, whoever, whomever, whatever, whichever
Reflexive pronouns	Refer to nouns or pronouns—the subject of a clause	(I hurt) myself, yourself, himself, herself, itself, ourselves, yourselves, themselves
Intensive pronouns	Stress the noun or pronoun referred to earlier in the sentence	I *myself* am going (in place of someone else) She is going herself
Reciprocal pronouns	Express mutual relationship	each other, one another

2 Pronoun forms

The **case** of the pronoun indicates its role in a phrase or clause. Pronouns in the **subjective case** serve as subjects and subjective complements. Pronouns in the **objective case** serve as direct and indirect objects, objective complements, and objects in prepositional phrases (*to me, from him*). Pronouns in the **possessive case** modify nouns to show possession (*her* book). Separate forms in the possessive case serve when the noun is absent (*That book is hers*).

Personal pronouns refer to individuals and groups of people and things. Here are their singular and plural forms in the subjective, objective, and possessive case:

Subjective Case

First person	I	we
Second person	you	you
Third person	he, she, it	they

Objective Case

First person	me	us
Second person	you	you
Third person	him, her, it	them

Possessive Case

First person	my (mine)	our (ours)
Second person	your (yours)	your (yours)
Third person	his, her, its (his, hers, its)	their (theirs)

Other classes of pronouns also have different forms in the singular and plural (e.g., *this, these; that, those*). The relative pronoun *who* has case forms:

Subject	*Who* is that man?
Object	*Whom* are you calling?
Possessive	*Whose* dog is that?

The relative pronoun *whoever* has the object form *whomever*:

Give this package to *whoever* comes.
Give this package to *whomever* the office sends for it.

3 Pronoun functions

Pronouns substitute for nouns in the same positions that nouns take in sentences:

Subject	*He* answered the question sarcastically.
Subjective complement	The tenant is *he*, not the woman on the stairs.
Direct object	She answered *him*
Indirect object	They handed *her* the lab report.
Objective complement	He considers her *somebody* important.
Object of preposition	She is going to the play with *him*.

Since you give so much attention to pronouns in revising sentences, you may assume that they are difficult to use. The fact is, in speaking, you seldom if ever pause to find the "right" pronoun, though you do pause at times to find the right noun or adjective. Most of the time, your sentence sense tells you what pronoun to use; you habitually use pronouns in highly versatile ways without confusing them.

However, a few pronouns like *none* and *whom* may pose special concerns in writing in general or formal styles (see 10a and 11c), but even when ungrammatical they are almost always understood. Those errors that make sentences ambiguous or unclear receive attention in later chapters. The following sections discuss matters of pronoun usage in greater detail:

10b—Pronouns and their antecedents
11a—Object pronouns
11c—*Who* and *whom*, and Vague pronouns
11e—Ambiguous pronoun reference
30e—Sexist use of pronouns

EXERCISE

Write sentences using the personal pronoun *she* in its various forms in the following positions:

1. as subject
2. as direct object
3. as indirect object
4. as subject complement
5. as appositive
6. as object complement
7. as object of preposition

8c Adjectives

In their descriptive function, **adjectives** help the reader to see the qualities of people, places, and objects. To use adjectives effectively, you need to know where to place them in the sentence and how to make them emphatic. This section deals with the placement of adjectives. Later sections deal with placing them in emphatic positions in the sentence.

1 Defining the adjective

Adjectives modify or attribute qualities to nouns and pronouns (*the polluted stream; he is tired*).

An adjective can stand in various positions in a sentence, but it most commonly appears immediately before the noun:

> She is an *intelligent, hardworking* woman.
> It is a *red* and *gold* cover.

When an adjective follows the noun, it gains emphasis:

> She is an intelligent woman, *hardworking* and *gifted* in physics.

In the predicate position, adjectives serve as subjective complements:

> Daisies are *yellow* and *gold*.
> The milk smells *sour*.
> She felt *tired* after the long ride home.

Adjectives also serve as objective complements, as in these sentences:

We considered the explanation *convincing.*
She found the water *clean* enough to drink.

Adjectives belong to the larger class of *adjectivals* (7c), words that modify nouns. Adjectivals include nouns (*horse* show, *word* processor, *desert* island), noun phrases (*this morning's* paper), prepositional phrases (house *on the corner*), and dependent clauses (the quiz *that I passed*). Adjectivals also include verb forms called *participles* (see 9a).

2 Adjective forms

Some adjectives have special forms and words to show comparison. The comparative suffix *-er* or the substitute words *more* and *less* indicate a degree or quality higher than that expressed by the basic adjective:

friend*ly*, friendl*ier*
more friendly, *less* friendly

The superlative suffix *-est* or the words *most* and *least* combine with the simple adjective to compare three or more persons or objects:

more friendly (of the two)
most friendly (of the three)

Adjectives consisting of more than two syllables generally use the words *more* and *most* rather than suffixes to show degree:

furious, *more* furious, *most* furious
noticeable, *more* noticeable, *most* noticeable

Here are some of the suffixes used to form adjectives:

-able: objectionable, remarkable
-ant: deviant, radiant
-ary: revolutionary, mercenary
-en: heathen, woolen
-ful: artful, beautiful
-ible: terrible, possible

-ic: arctic, classic
-ical: classical, comical
-ive: active, imaginative
-ory: illusory, compensatory
-ous: generous, devious
-y: chilly, sleepy

Like pronouns, the form and position of adjectives seldom pose problems for writers. One common error in adjective usage is the double comparative, which occurs when the words *more* or *most* are attached to an adjective that already shows comparison:

Incorrect	Correct
more friendlier	friendlier, *or* more friendly
most happiest	happiest, *or* most happy

Errors of this sort can be easily corrected during the revision stage. Just look for adjectives ending in *-er* or *-est*, checking that they are not preceded by *more* or *most*.

EXERCISES

1. Give the simple, comparative, and superlative forms of the following adjectives. Consult your dictionary if you are unsure about whether the comparative or superlative is expressed with *-er* or *-est*.
   - **a.** spare
   - **b.** thin
   - **c.** revolutionary
   - **d.** careless
   - **e.** pungent
   - **f.** illegible
   - **g.** grumpy
   - **h.** delicate
   - **i.** repulsive
   - **j.** beautiful

2. Each of the suffixes or word endings listed on page 169 has a particular meaning. For example, *-ory* means "having the nature of"; thus, the word *illusory* means having the nature or the qualities of an illusion. Use your dictionary to determine the meanings of the other suffixes in that list, and then give one or two adjectives for each suffix.

3. Use the same list of suffixes to form adjectives from the following words, or add other suffixes:
   - **a.** mountain
   - **b.** dirt
   - **c.** joy
   - **d.** evolution
   - **e.** laugh
   - **f.** fuss
   - **g.** photograph
   - **h.** Germany
   - **i.** England
   - **j.** Japan

4. Use the following words as nouns and adjectives in sentences of your own.

   Examples:
   David Copperfield is a classic of English literature.
   Pasta is a classic food of Italy.

   - **a.** team
   - **b.** military
   - **c.** satellite
   - **d.** lawn
   - **e.** picnic

5. Use your dictionary to find the adjective forms of the following words:
   - **a.** automobile
   - **b.** president

c. government
d. grammar
e. family

Summary

8a Nouns.

Nouns name persons, places, objects, events, and ideas in the subject, object, and other positions in the clause.

> *Noun phrases* are word groups that function as nouns **(8a 1)**:
>
> > the girl with the white scarf
>
> *Common nouns* identify people or objects by class **(8a 2)**:
>
> > man, hall, water, tap, wall
>
> *Proper nouns* name particular persons, places, and things:
>
> > Thomas Jefferson, Eleanor Roosevelt, White House
>
> *Concrete nouns* identify things known through sight and the other senses:
>
> > star, salt, perfume, jazz, sandpaper
>
> *Abstract nouns* name ideas or qualities:
>
> > courage, democracy, tyranny, ambition
>
> *Collective nouns* are singular nouns that refer to groups:
>
> > class, crowd, regiment, band, chorus, team
>
> *Count nouns* refer to things that can be counted; they have singular and plural forms:
>
> > man, men; woman, women; tap, taps; wall, walls
>
> *Mass (noncount) nouns* refer to things that cannot be counted; they have no plural forms:
>
> > health, grease, tennis, wisdom, news

Determiners identify or give information about nouns **(8a 3)**:

> The *indefinite articles a* and *an* identify nouns.
> The *definite article the* refers to nouns identified previously in the sentence or paragraph.

171

Demonstrative pronouns (*this* book), *possessive nouns* and *pronouns* (*Mary's* coat, *her* coat), *indefinite pronouns* (*each* book), and *numbers* (*one* book) function as qualifiers and determiners.

8b   Pronouns.

Pronouns substitute for nouns and other nominals in the same positions in the clause **(8b 1)**:

Personal pronouns identify people or things **(8b 2)**:

Subjective: I, you, he, she, it, we, you, they
Objective: me, you, him, her, it, us, you, them
Possessive: my, mine, your, yours, his, her, hers, its, our, ours, their, theirs

Demonstrative pronouns (*this, these*) refer to specific things close to the speaker or writer.

Indefinite pronouns (*another, some, everybody, nothing*) do not specify a particular person or object; they point to general things.

Relative pronouns (*who, which, that*) introduce certain dependent clauses.

Interrogative pronouns (*who, which, that*) begin questions.

Reflexive pronouns (You hurt *yourself*) refer to the subject of a clause.

Intensive pronouns (I *myself* am going) refer to and stress an earlier noun or pronoun in the sentence.

Reciprocal pronouns (We like *one another*) express mutual relationship.

8c   Adjectives.

Adjectives attribute qualities to nouns and pronouns or make statements about them in the predicate:

She is an *intelligent* woman.
Mary is *intelligent*.

Verbs and Adverbs

9

The forms and functions of verbs and adverbs give structure to the sentence. So do prepositions, conjunctions, expletives and interjections, other important classes of words.

9a | Defining the main verb

The **verb** is the heart of the predicate of the sentence. As part of the predicate, it makes a statement or assertion about the subject. These statements may convey action, a state of being, and present, past, and future circumstances:

> The travelers *boarded* the plane.
> They *are* Puerto Rican.
> They *lived* for many years in San Juan.

The main verb is always a **finite verb** (walk, walks, walked)—it conveys tense, voice, and other features. Some finite verbs also have singular and plural forms (*is, are*). The subject of the clause determines whether a verb is used in the first, second, or third person.

All verbs have a **base form** or **infinitive** (*walk*) that names the verb. The base form is also used as the present-tense form, except in the third-person singular (*she walks*). All verbs except *to be* add the ending -*s* in the third-person singular.

All verbs also have two participial forms. The **present participle** ends in -*ing*:

> walk*ing*, runn*ing*, eat*ing*, sleep*ing*

The **past participle** ends in -*ed, -d, -t, -en,* or -*n,* or changes the vowel of the base verb:

> walk*ed*, she*d*, buil*t*, shav*en*, r*u*ng (ring), c*a*ught (catch)

The past participle of most verbs has the same form as the past tense (*walked*). These forms are different for a small number of irregular verbs (see page 178).

Participles combine with auxiliary verbs (forms of *be* and *have,* modal verbs like *will* and *must*) to form verb phrases:

> am walking
> have walked
> must have walked

Participles also serve as modifiers (see 7c on adjectivals).

Verb phrases, a combination of auxiliaries with the base form or a participle, also serve as predicates. (Section 9b later in the chapter explains how to form verb phrases.)

1 Transitive, intransitive, and linking verbs

Main verbs are classified as transitive, intransitive, or linking.

Transitive verbs take a complement—a direct object and sometimes an indirect object and objective complement (see 7b):

> The convention elected *Bill secretary.*

Intransitive verbs express action not directed to an object and therefore do not take a complement:

> We *complained* to the manager.
> She *walks* often in the woods.

Some verbs may be transitive or intransitive depending on whether the direct object is named:

The children *ate* their *food* noisily.
The children *ate* noisily.

Linking verbs connect the subject to a subjective complement. Some linking verbs use a form of *be*:

She *is* an excellent student.
The apples *are* ripe.

Other linking verbs include *become, look, remain,* and *seem*:

I *become* grouchy around four o'clock.
She *looks* happy in the photograph.
She *remains* happy in her job.
She *seems* happy in the class.

Notice that forms of the verb *be* (I *am* grouchy, she *is* happy) can be substituted for the linking verbs in the preceding sentences.

Yet other linking verbs include verbs of sense:

The blanket *feels* soft.   The music *sounds* loud.
The cherries *taste* sour.   The stew *smells* garlicky.

Classes of Verbs
Main verbs
  Transitive verbs
  Intransitive verbs
  Linking verbs
    Forms of the verb *be*
    Verbs like *become* and *seem*
    Verbs of sense
Auxiliary verbs
  Forms of the verb *be*
  Modal verbs
  Do

---

2 Tense

The **tense** of the main verb tells us whether the action or state of existence expressed is in the present (*walks, is*) or the past (*walked, was*):

	The Verb *walk*		
Present tense		*Past tense*	
I walk	We walk	I walked	We walked
You walk	You walk	You walk	You walked
He, she, it walks	They walk	He, she, it walked	They walked

Verbs in the **past tense** tell us that the action being described is completed. Verbs in the **present tense** tell us that the action is happening at the moment of speaking or writing. Other uses of the present tense include the following:

Uses of the Present Tense

- To state what is happening at the moment of speaking or writing:

    The sun shines into the kitchen.

- To state what happens at intervals:

    I often walk to school.

- To report ideas and opinions in books, articles, and the like:

    Lincoln states in the Cooper Union Address that "right makes might."

- To describe actions in stories, plays, novels, and so on:

    Huck Finn travels past the island on a raft.

- To generalize, state a truth, or express an opinion:

    Verbs express action.
    Sour apples make delicious pies.

- To state a future action:

    The performance begins at eight o'clock.

To express tense, the main verb changes in form (*is, was, are, were*) or adds a suffix (*walks, walked*). In the present tense, the verb *walk* adds the suffix -*s* in the third-person singular only. We express ideas about the future through verb phrases formed with auxiliaries (see 9b).

The Verb *be*			
Present tense		*Past tense*	
I am	We are	I was	We were
You are	You are	You were	You were
He, she, it is	They are	He, she, it was	They were

Tense combines with a quality of verbs called **aspect** to indicate whether the action is ongoing or when it began or ended (see 9b).

3 Voice

Voice tells us whether the subject of the sentence is the performer or the receiver of the action. In a sentence in the **active voice,** the subject is the actor:

The pilot (*flies, is flying, flew*) the plane through the storm.

In a sentence in the **passive voice,** the subject is acted upon:

The plane *was flown* by the pilot through the storm.

Sentences containing transitive verbs usually can be transformed into the passive voice. To switch a sentence from the active to the passive voice, you make the direct object of the sentence (*plane*) the subject. The passive verb is formed through a form of the auxiliary verb *be* (*was*) and the past participle of the transitive verb (*flown*).

Notice that the pilot is the actor in both sentences. The difference is in the shift in emphasis. (For further discussion of the active and passive voice, see 12e.)

4 Mood

Mood describes the use of the verb to indicate whether the speaker or writer is making a declaration of fact, issuing a command, making a request, or expressing a doubt, possibility, or wish. A sentence in the **indicative mood** states a fact:

I walked to the park.

A statement in the **imperative mood** issues a command:

> Walk!
> Please begin.

A statement in the **interrogative mood** asks a question:

> Did I walk far enough?

A verb in the **subjunctive mood** shows the speaker is *wishing*:

> Wish I were ten years younger!

supposing something contrary to fact:

> If I were able to bike to work, I would never drive.

recommending, demanding, or suggesting:

> She demanded that the meeting adjourn.
> They requested that everyone walk to work.
> Let freedom ring!

or *doubting*:

> I doubt the statement is true.

Notice that the subjunctive form of the verb is the base form of the word in clauses beginning with *that*:

> that the meeting *adjourn*
> that everyone *walk*

Were these statements declarative sentences, the verb would take the inflection *-s*:

> She told us that the meeting *adjourns* at noon regularly.
> They know that everyone in the office *walks* to work.

In formal English, *if* clauses that suppose something contrary to fact use the verb *were*:

> If I *were* able to bike to work . . .

In general and informal English, the verb *was* is common, except in the expression *As it were.*

5 Regular and irregular verbs

A **regular verb** forms the past tense and the past participle usually by adding *-ed* or *-d* to the base form (*walked*). An **ir-**

regular verb has different forms for past tense and past participle.

To show the past tense and past participle, irregular verbs substitute *-t* or *-en* for *-ed* (past tense and past participle *built*, past participle *broken*), or change the vowel (past tense *broke* and *brought*). Some irregular verbs use the base form for the present tense, past tense, and past participle (*cut*, *hit*, *let*, *put*, and *shut*).

Although few in number, irregular verbs include many of the most commonly used English verbs. Following is a list of the base or infinitive, past tense, and past participle forms of irregular verbs:

Irregular Verbs

Base Form	Past Tense	Part Participle
arise	arose	arisen
be	was (were)	been
bear	bore	borne
begin	began	begun
bid	bid	bidden
bite	bit	bitten, bit
blow	blew	blown
break	broke	broken
bring	brought	brought
buy	bought	bought
catch	caught	caught
choose	chose	chosen
come	came	come
dig	dug	dug
dive	dove, dived	dived
do	did	done
draw	drew	drawn
drink	drank	drunk
eat	ate	eaten
fall	fell	fallen
fight	fought	fought
find	found	found
flee	fled	fled
fly	flew	flown
forget	forgot	forgotten
freeze	froze	frozen
get	got	gotten
give	gave	given
go	went	gone
grow	grew	grown
hang	hung	hung (referring to objects)

179

Irregular Verbs (continued)

Base Form	Past Tense	Past Participle
have	had	had
keep	kept	kept
know	knew	known
lay	laid	laid
lead	led	led
lie	lay	lain
lose	lost	lost
pay	paid	paid
prove	proved	proved, proven
ride	rode	ridden
ring	rang	rung
rise	rose	risen
run	ran	run
say	said	said
see	saw	seen
shrink	shrank	shrunk
sing	sang	sung
sink	sank, sunk	sunk
sit	sat	sat
speak	spoke	spoken
spring	sprang	sprung
stand	stood	stood
steal	stole	stolen
swim	swam	swum
take	took	taken
tear	tore	torn
tell	told	told
throw	threw	thrown
wake	woke	woken, waked
wear	wore	worn
wring	wrung	wrung
write	wrote	written

9b Building the verb phrase

The verb of the predicate takes the form of a main verb (*walks*) or a phrase formed with the base or participial form and one or more auxiliaries (*will have walked*). Grammarians refer to the verb of the predicate as the **verb phrase.**

1 Auxiliary verbs *have, be,* and *do*

Auxiliary verbs are helping verbs that combine with the base form of the verb or with the present or past participle to form verb phrases.

We saw earlier that forms of *be* serve as main verbs (*I am sick*). The same is true of forms of *have* and *do* (meaning *to perform*):

> I *have* the flu.
> He *did* wrong.

Forms of *have, be,* and *do* also serve as primary auxiliaries by combining with the base verb or with a participle for various purposes, including the following:

- To refer to an action completed at some time in the past:

  > We *had left* the house by the time you called.

- To refer to an action in progress:

  > We *are washing* the dog.

- To refer to a coming action:

  > We *are moving* to Seattle.
  > We *will call* you tonight.

- To make a statement negative:

  > John *does*n't *want* to go.

- To ask a question:

  > *Do* you *want* to go to Boston?

- To make a statement emphatic:

  > I *do want* to go.

Note that forms of *do* are obligatory in questions when the *have* or *be* auxiliary forms are omitted.

> *Do* (*don't*) you walk to school?
> *Did* (*didn't*) you walk to school?

2 Modal auxiliaries

Modal auxiliaries express the attitude of the speaker or writer toward the action or circumstances being described. Like the

181

auxiliaries *have, be,* and *do,* modal auxiliaries also can combine with the base form of the verb to form verb phrases:

Attitude Conveyed	Modals	Examples
Intent, will	*shall, should*	I should walk.
	will, would	You will walk.
Capability	*can, could*	I can walk.
Possibility	*may, might*	I may come.
		We might call.
Permission, denial		You may (not) go.
Obligation, need	*must*	You must leave.
	ought to	You ought to come.
Absence of, obligation	*need*	You need not come. (Used with the negative.)
Courage	*dare*	I dare come.
Lack of courage, fear		I dare not come. (Used with the negative.)

Modal auxiliaries also combine with other auxiliaries and participles:

> They *will be walking* home.
> They *would have walked* if they missed the bus.
> You *should have walked.*

Modals always precede the *be* auxiliary and the *have* auxiliary in verb phrases.

The idea of possible or conditional action is expressed through the modal *would* in combination with the base form or an auxiliary and participle:

> I *would walk.*
> I *would be walking.*
> I *would have walked.*

We predict future action through the modal *will* or the more formal and less common modal *shall* in combination with other auxiliaries and verb forms:

> I *will walk.*
> I *will be walking.*
> I *will have walked.*

These combinations are traditionally referred to as the *future tense* even though the English main verb does not change in form or add a suffix to express future time. We saw earlier that verbs change in form or add special endings to show tense and number (in the third-person singular of the present tense).

English has no future tense parallel to present and past tense in form.

3 Aspect

Tense tells us whether an event occurred in the present or the past. **Aspect** is the feature of a verb that tells us whether the action is in progress or is finished.

Progressive aspect tells us whether the action is, was, or will be ongoing or continuing:

I *am (have been, will be) writing* to several companies.

Progressive aspect also stresses the habitual nature of the action or gives special emphasis to it:

Habitual action: He *is* always *shouting*—never *talking.*
Emphasis: I *am walking* as fast as I can.

Perfect aspect tells us about the inception of the action and its duration—when the action began and whether it was completed or is continuing into the present:

I *have written* to several companies.

The verb phrase gives us information about progressive and perfect aspects in the following ways:

Aspect	Information Conveyed	Examples
Present progressive	An ongoing event or in progress in the present.	I am still running twelve miles a day.
Past progressive	An ongoing event or in progress in the past.	I was running ten miles a day last year.
Future progressive	An event that will be in progress in the future.	I will be running in the marathon.
Present perfect	An event begun in the past that continues into the present.	I have run everyday since June.
Past perfect	An event begun in the past and completed before a stated time or event of the past.	I had run in marathons before the Boston marathon last year.

183

Aspect	Information Conveyed	Examples
Future perfect	An event in the future completed at a predicted time.	By the time you reach Boston, I will have run in the marathon.
Present perfect progressive	An ongoing event begun in the past that probably will continue.	I have been running in the park everyday.
Past perfect progressive	An ongoing event occurring before a stated time or event in the past.	Before I entered last year's marathon, I had been running in local contests.
Future perfect progressive	An ongoing event in the future that will be completed at a predicted time.	By the time you read this letter, I will have been running in several marathons.

EXERCISES

1. Use the base or infinitive verb *eat* to form finite verbs in the first- and third-person singular as follows:

   Example
   Present indicative: I eat. He, she, it eats.

   a. past indicative
   b. future indicative
   c. imperative
   d. present progressive
   e. past progressive
   f. future progressive

2. Do the same with the following:
   a. present perfect
   b. past perfect
   c. future perfect
   d. present perfect progressive
   e. past perfect progressive
   f. future perfect progressive

3. Change the following sentences from the active to the passive voice:
   a. The third contestant answered the question correctly.
   b. The coach praised the basketball team for their win at the tournament.
   c. Lightning struck the tree.
   d. The storm, which blew in from the west, caused no damage to the town.
   e. The woman on the bus gave me this map of the city.

4. Write sentences that express the following:
   a. an action that took place in the past
   b. an action that was ongoing in the past
   c. an action in progress in the past continuing into the present
   d. an action in progress in the previous summer that continued into the fall
   e. an action that will occur in the future
5. Write sentences that combine modals with verbs (and auxiliaries) to express the following:
   a. an action that will take place
   b. an action that might take place
   c. an action that must take place
   d. an ongoing action that might have taken place
   e. an ongoing action that must have taken place

9c | Verbals

Participles and infinitives are called **verbals** because they derive from verbs. They have other functions in addition to forming verbs and verb phrases.

The **participle** functions as an adjectival in modifying nouns (see 7c):

the *walking* doll
the *walked* dog
Walking slowly, she saw an old friend coming toward her.
Walked everyday by his owner, the dog was well exercised.

The participle also functions as an adverbial:

I wrote my chemistry report *sitting* on the front steps.

The infinitive (*to walk*) functions as a nominal:

To walk would be sensible.
I like *to walk.*
The best exercise is *to walk.*
They let us *pick* our own apples. [*to* omitted]

The infinitive also functions as an adjectival:

I have no reason *to walk.*

and as an adverbial:

I went to the library *to study* for the exam.

Another verbal, the **gerund,** always functions as a nominal. Like the present participle, the gerund adds *-ing* to the base verb. *Walking* is a gerund in the following sentences:

Walking is good exercise. [*subject*]
I stumbled on a rock while *walking* to school. [*subject of dependent clause*]
I enjoy *walking.* [*direct object*]

But notice that *walking* is a present participle in the following sentence:

Walking to the store, I met John.

Verbals are occasionally the chief component of sentence fragments. The participial phrase *Walking down the street* is not a complete sentence, nor is the infinitive phrase *To walk down the street,* nor the gerund phrase *Walking home at midnight.* (See 16b for a discussion of fragments that contain verbals.)

9d   Adverbs

1   Defining the adverb

The **adverb** modifies the verb, giving us information about place, time, duration, frequency, manner, condition, and other qualities:

Place	Put the chair *there,* not *downstairs.*
Time	She left for college *yesterday.*
Duration	She is *still* on the road.
Frequency	She calls home *often* but *never* on weekends.
Manner	He spoke *angrily* to the manager.

Like adjectives, adverbs often stand next to the words they modify. But they also have great freedom of movement in the sentence:

Fortunately, the storm caused little damage.
The storm, *fortunately,* caused little damage.
The storm caused little damage, *fortunately.*

This freedom of movement of the adverb is of great advantage to the writer, making it possible to give exact emphasis to particular words and phrases.

Adverbs are the most prominent class of *adverbials* — words that modify verbs (see 7c). Prepositional phrases, noun phrases, dependent clauses, and other grammatical structures have an adverbial function in the sentence. Following are lists of common adverbial phrases and clauses as well as some common adverbs.

Prepositional Phrase
He walks *with difficulty*.

Noun Phrase
She is arriving *this month*.
The newspaper costs *thirty cents*.

Infinitive Phrase
I volunteered *to write the letter*.

Dependent Clause
We began car pooling *when the buses stopped running*.
The bank cashed the check *even though it was not endorsed*.

Common Adverbs

Place	above, below, up, down, indoors, outdoors, upstairs, downstairs, here, there
Time	then, now, tonight, tomorrow, yesterday, afterwards, soon, later, shortly
Degree	almost, hardly, quite
Duration	never, always, forever, momentarily, widely
Frequency	much, often, seldom, frequently, occasionally, once, twice, weekly, monthly, daily
Manner	also, fast, slowly, quickly, heavily, lightly, softly, kindly, weakly, strongly, deeply, brightly, noisily, quietly, definitely, reluctantly, sadly, happily, confidently, carefully, probably, really, certainly

2 Adverb forms

A few adjectives end in *-ly*:

a likely story
a homely fact

Many adjectives add *-ly* to form adverbs:

softly, loudly, nicely, rapidly

To express the **comparative** and **superlative,** adverbs ending in -*ly* take the function words *more* and *most*:

> more softly, most softly
> more loudly, most loudly
> more rapidly, most rapidly

Some adverbs have the same form as adjectives and can add the inflections -*er* and -*est*:

Adjective Forms
> the *early* showing, the *earlier* showing, the *earliest* showing

Adverb Forms
> showed it *early,* showed it *earlier,* showed it *earliest*

The adverb *soon* is one of a few that use the inflections -*er* and -*est* for the comparative and superlative:

> arrived *soon,* arrived *sooner,* arrived *soonest*

A small group of adverbs form the comparative and superlative with different base words. These adverbs include the following:

> laughed *much,* laughed *more,* laughed *most*
> cried *little,* cried *less,* cried *least*
> spoke *well,* spoke *better,* spoke *best*

Some adverbs end with the suffixes -*where* or -*wise*:

> going *nowhere*
> said *otherwise*

Some adverbs are dual in form, occurring with and without the -*ly* ending.

> close, closely   rough, roughly
> deep, deeply   second, secondly
> even, evenly   slow, slowly
> fair, fairly   tight, tightly
> loud, loudly   wrong, wrongly

The short form occurs most with single-syllable or short words:

> He always drives *slow* on icy roads.
> She parked *even* with the other car.
> They gave the directions *wrong.*

Some shortened forms are used mainly in informal speech and writing:

Informal	**Formal**
close-knit family	*closely* knit family
quick-acting remedy	*quickly* acting remedy

Note that the -*ly* form is always required before the verb:

She *quickly* ran to the window.
They *wrongly* gave directions.

3 Qualifiers

Closely related to adverbs are words that qualify or intensify adjectives and adverbs. This class of words, called **qualifiers,** were traditionally called adverbs. The following are the most common:

quite fast
rather angry
really frightening
too violent
very amusing

A large number of adverbs ending in -*ly* are used to qualify adjectives. These include the following:

absolutely dangerous
especially troubling
particularly complex
politically savvy
technically feasible

Some qualifiers are used with comparative adjectives and adverbs:

even better
much sooner
no farther
still later
right away

Other qualifiers are used informally in conversation:

real good eating
right pretty

You may find the alternate forms of adverbs and qualifiers confusing at times. The confusion arises most often in formal writing, which favors the *-ly* form of the adverb. The adverb *badly*, for example, is used informally without the *-ly* ending:

> The quarterback played *bad*.

Compare this formal usage:

> The violinist played the concerto *badly*.

Notice that the word *bad* is used most often as an adjective:

> The quarterback made a *bad* play.

The role of adverbials and qualifiers in the sentence is discussed further in these sections of the *Handbook*:
12c—Placement of modifiers
18b—Omitted adverbs
20d—Placement of adverbial clauses

9e Prepositions, conjunctions, expletives

1 Prepositions

Prepositions relate nouns, noun phrases, and pronouns to other words in the sentence. The relationships that prepositions show may be of possession (*hat of the woman*), place (*house by the river*), or destination (*trip to Houston*), among others. Unlike some other parts of speech, prepositions do not change in form.

You form phrases with prepositions by adding a noun or noun phrase, as in the following:

about the city	*in* Chicago
at school	*of* the school
at the center	*on* the shelf, *on* it
by the river	*to* the river, *to him*
before the window	*toward* the library
beside the chair	*on* the chair
between the walls	*with* the hammer, *with* it
from the sidelines, *from* her	

Phrasal prepositions are compounds of words. They include the following:

according to the latest census
along with her mother
as a result of the election
at the expense of failing
by means of arithmetic
except for Mary
in case of war
in connection with the case
in back of the building
in place of the lecture
in spite of the cold
instead of the book
in view of the threat
on behalf of my father and mother
with regard to your letter of May 14

2 Conjunctions

Conjunctions are words or phrases that connect other words, phrases, and clauses. Conjunctions fall into several classes. **Co-ordinating conjunctions**—*and, but, for, yet, or, nor*—connect independent clauses:

I grow tomatoes, *but* I don't like eating them.
It may be October, *yet* the leaves have not started falling.

They also connect words and phrases of the same weight or importance:

bread *and* butter
quiet *yet* firm *and* sometimes insistent
to bake bread *and* churn butter
to debate *but* not to slander *or* libel an opponent

The word *so* is used informally as a coordinating conjunction:

The plums are for breakfast, *so* don't eat them.

Conjunctive adverbs resemble conjunctions in stressing the close relationship between independent clauses when they follow a connecting semicolon:

It is already October; *however,* the leaves have not started to fall.
It's been raining since Monday; *consequently,* we're postponing our trip.

Conjunctive adverbs include the following:

also	indeed	moreover	so
besides	instead	nevertheless	therefore
furthermore	likewise	otherwise	thus
however	meanwhile	similarly	yet

Subordinating conjunctions join dependent or subordinate clauses to independent clauses:

Although it is October, the leaves have not started to fall.
We are postponing our trip *because* it has been raining since Monday.

Here are some common subordinating words and phrases:

after	as soon as	provided that	though	whenever
although	before	since	unless	wherever
as	even though	so that	until	
as if	if	than	when	
as long as	in order that	that	where	

The relative pronouns *who, which,* and *that* also function as subordinators, linking dependent to independent clauses:

The woman *who asked the question* is running for mayor.
The car *that we rented at the airport* broke down as we entered the expressway.
We boarded the bus, *which had just arrived from Portland.*

Correlative conjunctions show mutual or complementary relationships in phrases and clauses. Here are some common correlatives:

both/and:	She ran for *both* class secretary *and* class president.
either/or:	She wants to be *either* secretary *or* president.
neither/nor:	She is *neither* secretary *nor* president of the class.
not only/but also:	She is *not only* the secretary *but also* the president of the class.
on the one hand/on the other hand:	*On the one hand,* she wants to hold both offices; *on the other* (*hand*), she knows she doesn't have time for both jobs.
just as/so:	*Just as* runners warm up before a race, *so* do musicians before a concert.

The following sections of the *Handbook* discuss problems that sometimes arise with adverbs and conjunctions:

10a—Using *or* and other conjunctions with compound subjects
11a—Comparisons with *as* and *than*
18b—Omitted adverbs
20a—Single-word modifiers
20b—Squinting modifiers

3 Expletives

Expletives are "dummy" or empty words that open sentences when the subject is moved to a later position for emphasis. The expletive adds nothing to the meaning of the sentence.

There is a dog on the porch.   A dog is on the porch.
It's good to be home.   To be home is good.

Delaying the subject in the first sentence above gives emphasis to the fact that the dog is on the porch. The expletive makes the second sentence idiomatic or characteristic of English as spoken and written. The formal equivalent to the right is a stilted sentence.

Expletives also introduce nominal clauses:

We trust *that* the city will rebuild the bridge.

The expletive *that* can be omitted in midsentence without disturbing the meaning of the sentence:

We trust the city will rebuild the bridge.

However, *that* cannot be omitted when the sentence opens with the nominal clause:

That it will snow I can promise you!

(See 10a and 12e for further discussion of the role of expletives in sentence agreement and clarity.)

Interjections

Interjections, important in expressive speech and writing, are words and phrases that express strong emotion—joy, anger, approval, disapproval, surprise. Sometimes interjections stand alone, punctuated with an exclamation point:

Oh!
Wow!
How absurd!

At other times interjections are used as sentence modifiers:

Oh, is that what you're talking about?
All right, do what you think best.

(See 21b for examples of interjections and their punctuation in works of fiction.)

EXERCISES

1. Form simple adverbs from the following adjectives. Then give their comparative and superlative forms.
   a. sure
   b. tame
   c. right
   d. near
   e. loose
   f. careful
   g. poor
   h. generous
   i. reasonable
   j. natural
2. Use the correlatives listed on page 192 in sentences of your own.
3. Write sentences containing three of the coordinating conjunctions and three of the subordinating conjunctions listed on pages 191–92.
4. Write sentences using three of the conjunctive adverbs listed on page 192.

Summary

9a–9b Verbs and verb phrases.

Verbs and *verb phrases* make statements about subjects in the predicate, describing actions, states of existence, and present, past, and future circumstances.

Transitive verbs take direct objects and sometimes indirect objects and object complements (9a 1):

The convention *elected* Bill secretary.

Intransitive verbs do not take direct objects:

The storm *petered* out.

Linking verbs (*be, seem, become,* verbs of sense) connect subjects with subjective complements:

> She *is* an excellent student.
> She *seems* happy.
> The milk *tastes* sour.

Verbs give information about the following (**9a 2–4**):
  Tense—present (*lives*) or past (*lived*)
  Voice—active (*ate*) or passive (*was eaten*)
  Mood—indicative (*I go*), interrogative (*Are you going?*), subjunctive (*If I were to go*), imperative (*Go!*)
  Aspect—progressive (*am living*) or perfect (*have lived, had lived, will have lived*)

Regular verbs have the same forms for the past tense and past participle (*walked, walked*). *Irregular verbs* have different forms for each (**9a 5**).

All verbs have a *present participle* (*writing, walking*) and a *past participle* (*walked, written*) that help to form verb phrases:

> am walking, has walked, is writing, has written

The auxiliary verbs *have, be,* and *do* combine with the base form of the verb or with participles to form verb phrases (**9b 1**):

> are leaving, had left, do believe

Modal verbs can combine with the base verb alone (**9b 2**):

> I must walk.
> I can walk.

Modal verbs can also join with auxiliaries and participles:

> I must have walked.
> I must be walking.

Progressive aspect and *perfect aspect* indicate whether the action is in progress or is finished (**9b 3**)

9c Verbals.

Verbals function as nominals, adjectivals, and adverbials.

The *participle* also functions as an adjectival:

> *Walking* slowly, she saw an old friend coming toward her.

The infinitive phrase functions as a nominal:

> *To walk* should be sensible.

195

as an adjectival:

> I have no reason *to walk.*

and as an adverbial:

> She is going *to walk.*

Gerunds function as nominals:

> *Walking* is good exercise.

9d   Adverbs.

Adverbs and adverbial phrases and clauses modify the verb, giving information about place, time, duration, frequency, manner, condition, and other qualities:

> He *seldom* walked *quickly.*
> She walks *everyday.*
> He walks to work *when traffic is heavy.*

9e   Prepositions, conjunctions, expletives.

Prepositions relate nouns, noun phrases, and pronouns to other words in the sentence and never change in form **(9e 1)**:

> to, from, of, upon, toward, on, with

> Prepositions form phrases by adding a noun phrase (*by the river*).
> Phrasal prepositions are compounds of words (*according to, by means of, as a result of*).

Conjunctions are words or phrases that connect other words, phrases, and clauses. Conjunctions fall into the following classes **(9e 2)**:

> *Coordinating conjunctions* (*and, but, for, yet, or, nor*) connect independent clauses.
> *Conjunctive adverbs* (*however, therefore, thus*) stress the relationship between independent clauses following the connecting semicolon.
> *Subordinating conjunctions* (*since, because, when*) join dependent or subordinate clauses to independent clauses.
> *Correlative conjunctions* (*not only/but also, both/and, either/or, neither/nor*) show mutual or complementary relationships in phrases and clauses.

Expletives are words that add nothing to the meaning of the sentence but give additional emphasis to the subject by pushing it to a later part of the sentence **(9e 3)**:

There is a dog on the porch.
It is good to be home.
We trust *that* the city will rebuild the bridge.

9f Interjections.

Interjections are words and phrases that express strong emotion—joy, anger, approval, disapproval, surprise.

Agreement 10

Nouns, pronouns, and verbs agree or match in number, person, and gender—subject and verb agree in the predicate of the clause; sentence pronouns and the antecedents or words they refer to agree. Few of these matching forms give us trouble. Those that do cause confusion fall into certain patterns. This chapter discusses these patterns of agreement and ways of recognizing them in revising your sentences.

10a Subject and verb agreement

A subject in the third-person singular agrees with the *-s* form of the verb in the present tense (*Mary walks*). All other subjects agree with the base form of the verb (*I walk, you walk, they walk*). The form of the verb in the past tense is the same in all three persons, singular and plural (*Mary walked, they walked*). Your ear sometimes tells you that forms are mismatched (*I walks, Mary walk*), but it is not a dependable guide in every instance.

1 Agreement with mass and count nouns

Mass (noncount) nouns (8a) refer to things that we cannot count, such as food, drink, health, and news. When the subject of the sentence is a mass noun, the verb is always singular:

The food *is* spoiled.
Wet grass *is* hard to mow.

Mass nouns always take the singular and therefore are never preceded by *a* or *an*. However, when nouns like *food* and *grass* are referred to in the plural to distinguish among types—*various foods, various grasses*—they become count nouns.

Unlike mass nouns, **count nouns** (8a) refer to things or groups of things that can be singled out and counted; they have both singular or plural forms:

Chemicals *are defined* by their molecular structure.
Politicians *have* different speaking styles.

Plural count nouns always take plural verb forms.

2 Agreement with collective nouns

Collective nouns (8a) have a singular form even though they refer to groups of people or things. The collective nouns *committee, family, jury, group,* and *team* have a singular meaning when they refer to a group acting as a unit. In this instance, the verb is singular:

The family *is gathering* for the wedding.
The jury *has reached* its verdict.
The committee *is filing* a unanimous report.

Collective nouns have a plural meaning when they refer to independent actions of the group. In this instance, the verb is plural:

The committee *continue* to disagree about amending the constitution.
The jury *disagree* over the verdict.
The committee *are* filing conflicting reports.

If the sentence sounds awkward in the plural, specify the members of the group instead:

The family members are coming . . .
Members of the committee are filing . . .

Phrases that state a unit of measurement take the singular:

Two-thirds of a pint *is* the amount of milk required by the recipe.

However, the plural is used when the subject refers to independent units:

Two pints of milk *are* in the refrigerator.

Note that words derived from Latin and Greek may form their plurals with different affixes. For example, the singular word *memorandum* forms its plural as *memoranda*. Occasionally, the plural word *data* appears with singular verbs even though the form and sense of the word are plural:

The data presented *is* probably flawed.

Data is used with the plural verb in scientific writing. The word *media* is always used with the plural verb:

The media *have* enormous influence over political opinion.

3   Agreement with indefinite pronouns

Indefinite pronouns (8a) do not refer to specific people or things; rather, they point to people or things in general. Some indefinite pronouns are singular, some are plural, and some can be both depending on how they are used. Those singular in form include the following:

anybody	everybody	nothing
anyone	everything	one
anything	neither	somebody
each	nobody	someone
either	no one	something

Those plural in form include these:

both	many
few	several

Singular indefinite pronouns take singular verbs; plural indefinite pronouns take plural verbs.

A small number of indefinite pronouns—including *all, any, more, most, none,* and *some*—take singular or plural verbs depending on their referent in the sentence:

None of these apples *are* for sale.
None of this fruit *is* ripe.

Note that the referent in the first sentence is a plural count noun (*apples*); in the second sentence, it is a singular mass noun (*fruit*).

4 Agreement with titles

Titles always take a singular verb, even when the title is plural:

Bananas is one of Woody Allen's early movies.
The American is one of Henry James's early novels.
"The Sisters" *is* the opening story of James Joyce's *Dubliners*.

5 Agreement with delayed subjects

In sentences beginning with the expletives *there* and *it* (9e), the verb agrees with the delayed subject, not with *there* or *it*. The subject shifts to the position following the verb.

Because *there* and *it* appear in the subject position, it is easy to forget to make the verb agree with the delayed subject:

Lack of Agreement	**Revised**
There *isn't* and never have been barges this far up the river.	There *are not* and never have been barges this far up the river.

The word *it* is both a pronoun and an expletive. Used as a pronoun, *it* takes a singular verb:

It *is* the call I've been waiting for.

Used as an expletive, *it* functions like *there*, as the transformed sentences in the right-hand column show:

Cooking is fun.	It is fun to cook.
Ohio is colder than Georgia in the winter.	It is colder in Ohio than in Georgia in the winter.

Following the expletive *it* the verb is always singular, regardless of what follows in the sentence:

It *is* Margaret who's coming, not Barbara.
It *is* her sisters who are coming, not her college roommates.

6 Agreement with inverted subjects

When the sentence inverts or reverses the subject and verb, the verb agrees with the subject, *not* with the noun or pronoun of the opening modifier:

Lack of Agreement	**Revised**
Outside the restaurant *was* parked twelve red *cars*.	Outside the restaurant *were* parked twelve red *cars*.

This sentence is a transformation of the following, in which the subject begins the sentence:

Twelve red *cars were* parked outside the restaurant.

If you are in doubt about the agreement, test it by beginning the sentence with the subject.

7 Agreement between subject and complement

A verb agrees with its subject, *not* with its complement:

Lack of Agreement
The *cause* of the epidemic *were* the brown *rats*.

Revised
The *cause* of the epidemic *was* the brown *rats*.

The writer of the first sentence anticipates that the subject complement *rats* names the cause.

8 Intervening words

Don't mistake words that come between the subject and verb for the subject of the sentence:

Lack of Agreement	**Revised**
The *book*, like others on the subject, *are* failing to win a large audience.	The *book*, like others on the subject, *is* failing to win a large audience.
The nineteenth-century woman *novelist*, like George Eliot and the Brontës, *were* anxious to be taken seriously.	The nineteenth-century woman *novelist*, like George Eliot and the Brontës, *was* anxious to be taken seriously.

If in doubt about the agreement, recast the sentence:

Nineteenth-century women *novelists* like George Eliot and the Brontës *were* anxious to be taken seriously.

The longer the intervening phrase or clause, the greater the risk of missing agreement with the subject.

9   Agreement with compound subjects

Compound subjects (those joined by *and* and other coordinating conjunctions) usually take plural verbs:

> Minneapolis *and* St. Paul *are* cities in Minnesota.

However, a compound subject that begins with *each* or *every* takes a singular verb because the compound subject is referring to the same thing:

> *Each* city and county in the state *levies* taxes.
> *Every* man and woman in this town *opposes* the tax levy.

The conjunction *or* takes the singular subject when the sense of the sentence tells you that the verb cannot be plural:

> I don't know whether Minneapolis *or* St. Paul *is* the capital of Minnesota.

This sentence states two alternatives, only one of which can be true. The decision is more difficult when the subjects are different in number. The sense of the sentence is no longer a reliable guide. In this situation, the verb should agree with the nearest subject:

> I don't know whether organic chemistry only or *calculus and physics are* required for the major.

When phrases like *along with, as well as, besides, in addition to,* and *together with* follow a singular subject, the verb is singular:

> Organic chemistry, *in addition to* calculus and physics, is a requirement for the degree.

The italicized modifier (called *nonrestrictive*) presents important but not essential information. The sentence says that organic chemistry is a requirement for the degree; it adds the information that calculus and physics are also requirements. This information is important but nonessential because organic chemistry would be required even if physics and calculus were not. Notice also that the modifying phrase is set off by commas.

Single phrases or ideas consisting of compound subjects take the singular verb:

> *Ham and eggs is* a popular dish in England and America.

When referred to individually, compound subjects that form a single phrase take plural verbs:

Ham and eggs are popular American foods.

The same is true of performers, composers and dramatists, and others who form a team:

> Katherine Hepburn and Spencer Tracy *are* remembered through their many films.

10 Agreement with subjects joined by correlatives

Correlative conjunctions (*either/or, neither/nor, not only/but also*) take singular verbs when the correlative subjects are singular:

> *Either* Minneapolis *or* St. Paul *is* the capital of Minnesota.
> *Neither* St. Cloud *nor* Rochester *is* on the Mississippi River.
> *Not only* calculus *but also* physics *is* a requirement for the degree.

Correlatives take the plural verb when both subjects are plural:

> Neither *Latin and Greek* nor *logic and advanced composition are* requirements for the major.

When some of the subjects are singular and some plural, the verb agrees with the nearest subject:

> Neither *Latin and Greek* nor *logic is* a requirement.
> Neither *logic* nor *Latin and Greek are* requirements.

The same rule governs subjects different in person:

> Neither *she* nor *I am* invited.

Sentences of this sort usually sound awkward. The following revision is preferable:

> I'm not invited, nor is she.

Checklist: Subject–Verb Agreement

1. Do the subjects and verbs in my sentence agree?
2. If my subject is a mass noun, have I used a singular verb? If my subject is a plural count noun, have I used a plural verb?

3. Have I used a singular verb with a collective noun that refers to the group as a whole? Have I used a plural verb in referring to members of the group individually?

4. Have I used the appropriate verb with singular and plural indefinite pronouns?

5. Have I used a singular verb with titles and people acting as a team?

6. Have I made the verb agree with an inverted or a delayed subject that follows it?

7. Have I made the subject agree with the verb and not with intervening words or with the complement?

8. If a compound subject is joined by *or* or a correlative conjunction, have I made the verb agree with the nearest subject?

EXERCISES

1. Write sentences that use the following nouns as subjects. Make the subject agree with the verb in each sentence.
   a. *class* in the singular
   b. *class* in the plural
   c. *medium*
   d. *media*
   e. *committee* in the singular
   f. *committee* in the plural

2. Write sentences that use the indefinite pronouns *anybody, each, either, none,* and *some* as subjects.

3. Choose the correct verb in each of these sentences:
   a. Each of us (*is, are*) going to the beach.
   b. Some of us (*is, are*) not going.
   c. The committee (*is, are*) arriving at different times.
   d. The board of governors (*is, are*) making a decision about the scholarships this afternoon.
   e. *Wings* (*was, were*) one of the first sound films.
   f. Gravel (*was, were*) shoveled on the driveway.
   g. It (*was, were*) the apples that spoiled, not the peaches.
   h. Throughout the novels of Thomas Hardy (*occurs, occur*) amazing coincidences.
   i. Not a single person in the room, not even the people who paid beforehand for their tickets, (*was, were*) told that the flight had been rescheduled.
   j. There (*was, were*) not one in the room who (*was, were*) willing to volunteer for the committee.

10b Pronoun and antecedent agreement

The considerations that govern agreement between subjects and verbs also apply to pronouns and their antecedents. An **antecedent** is a noun or pronoun mentioned earlier in the sentence or paragraph, to which the pronoun refers:

Walking up the stairs is my *wife*, not *her* twin sister.
He knows *himself* better than *his* parents do.
We presented *our* case to the board of governors.
They presented *their* case to the board of governors.

Agreement is essential to the clarity of the sentence or paragraph. Without agreement your reader would be delayed by having to identify the referent of the pronoun.

1 Agreement with nearest compound subject

Compound subjects usually take plural pronouns:

Chicago and Evanston have *their* own police departments.

A compound phrase that expresses a single idea or entity takes a singular pronoun:

Mutt and Jeff, the popular cartoon strip, had *its* own special humor.

When the conjunction *or* joins a singular and a plural noun or pronoun in a compound subject, the pronoun agrees with the antecedent closest to it:

I can't remember whether Cleveland alone or *all cities in Ohio are holding* an election Tuesday.

2 Agreement with indefinite pronouns

The indefinite pronouns *each, every, everyone, everybody, no one, nobody, someone, something, nothing,* and *everything* usually take singular pronouns:

With respect to the proposals, *each* has *its* benefits and risks.

Some indefinite pronouns (*all, any, more, none, some*) take a singular verb if the antecedent is a mass noun:

The *fruit* looks fresh. *Is some* for sale?

A plural antecedent makes the verb plural:

The *apples* look fresh. *Are some* for sale?

Earlier in the chapter (10a) we saw that the pronoun *none* is singular or plural depending on its referent in the sentence. The convention is the same between *none* and its antecedent:

All of the apples have been picked, but none *are* for sale.
Though all the fruit is ripe, none *is* for sale.

Agreement with other indefinite pronouns depends on the sense of the sentence:

The woman from Ohio was *the only one* of the visitors [who *was*] *stricken with food poisoning.*
The woman from Ohio was *only one* of the visitors who *were* stricken with food poisoning.

The singular *was* is required in the first sentence because only one person—the woman from Ohio—was stricken with food poisoning. The plural *were* is required in the second because several of the visitors were stricken, not just the woman from Ohio.

3 Avoiding the generic *he*

A special problem arises when a singular subject refers to human beings. The generic *he* and *his* were traditionally used to refer to both men and women:

Each of us is donating *his* salary for the benefit.

An increasing number of careful writers are rejecting the generic *he* because it excludes women from the statement.

A useful way to show that a statement refers to men and women is to pluralize the subject:

Wordy
Each of us is donating his or her salary for the week.

Revised
All of us are donating our salary for the week.

(See 30e for a discussion of other ways to avoid sexist use of pronouns.)

4 Agreement with collective nouns and pronouns

The rules of agreement between collective nouns and verbs are the same for pronouns and their collective antecedents. A pronoun agrees with a singular antecedent and verb if the pronoun refers to the group as a whole; it agrees with a plural antecedent and verb if the pronoun refers to the members of the group individually:

> Although the committee *has its* special rules or procedures, *it* governs *itself* through the House rules.
>
> The committee *have their* own separate codes of ethics governing *their* individual staffs, but the committee as a whole acts according to the House code. The members govern *themselves*.

In less formal English, the singular is used, even when the sense of the sentence is plural:

> The committee has its own separate codes of conduct. . . .

The words *anybody, everybody,* and any other indefinite pronoun formed with *-body* and *-one* may be followed by a plural or collective pronoun when the meaning is plural and collective and the sentence refers to animate or human beings:

> Anybody can enter if *they* have a pass.
> Everyone has a right to *their* opinion.

EXERCISES

1. Choose the correct verb and pronoun forms in each of the following sentences:
   a. Each of the suburbs (*has, have*) (*its, their*) mayor and council.
   b. New York, Washington, Boston, and Chicago (*has, have*) (*its, their*) airports close to heavily populated areas.
   c. Every city and suburb (*need, needs*) to protect (*its, their*) water supply from chemical pollution.
   d. The team (*is, are*) practicing for (*its, their*) last game.
   e. Either you or your lab partners (*is, are*) to clean (*your, their*) equipment before leaving.

    f. The principal, along with the teachers and counselors, (*is, are*) meeting with (*her, their*) lawyer at three o'clock.

    g. Neither the pilot nor the flight attendants (*is, are*) able to explain (*his, her, their*) disappearance from the airport.

    h. Either John or his brothers (*was, were*) in Vietnam during (*his, their*) years in the army.

    i. Not one of the students and not one of the teachers (*is, are*) attending the meeting.

    j. Few of the students and even fewer of the teachers (*is, are*) attending the meeting.

2. For the following sentences, correct those that lack agreement. Note that some of the sentences may be correct as written.

    a. Hydraulics is concerned with the laws of movement in liquids and its application in engines.

    b. Hydraulics and aeronautics are closely related sciences, though each are taught in different departments of the college.

    c. Among the novels of Willa Cather is *My Antonia*.

    d. Among the novelists who have written about Chicago is Saul Bellow and Nelson Algren.

    e. One of Toni Morrison's novels is *Beloved*.

    f. Each of Saul Bellow's novels and each of Toni Morrison's have been published in Great Britain.

    g. The committee on scholarships will announce their decisions in April.

    h. Elizabeth, in addition to taking organic chemistry and physics, is taking genetics.

    i. Belgium, along with Holland, Denmark, and Norway, were occupied by Germany during World War II.

    j. No one who has owned a dog want to support so harsh a law.

3. Complete the sentence using the appropriate present tense form of the verb shown:

    a. Either Marge or Barbara (verb *work*)

    b. Neither Barbara nor her sisters (verb *work*)

    c. The three R's—reading, writing, arithmetic—(verb *be*)

    d. The two sisters, together with their brother (verb *attend*)

    e. Together with the ingredients called for in the recipe, the three tablespoons of sugar (verb *make*)

    f. The ingredients, in addition to the honey called for in the recipe (verb *be*)

    g. The whole family, including the cousins from Stamford (verb *be*)

    h. The manager, as well as the office workers (verb *work*)

    i. The phrase *bread and butter* (verb *be*)

    j. Few of the candidates (verb *buy*)

Summary

10a Subjects and verbs agree in number.

When the subject is a mass noun, the verb is singular. When the subject is a plural count noun, the verb is plural **(10a 1)**:

> The *food is* spoiled.
> Various *foods* in the warehouse *are* rotting.

When the sentence refers to members of a group individually, the verb is plural. When the sentence refers to the group as a unit, the verb is singular **(10a 2)**:

> The *committee continue* to disagree on amending the constitution.
> The *jury has* reached its verdict.

If the indefinite pronoun is singular in form (*anybody, everything*), the verb is singular; if plural in form (*few, many*), the verb is plural **(10a 3)**.

Indefinite pronouns like *none* and *some* are singular or plural depending on their referent in the sentence:

> *None* of the tomatoes *is* spoiled, but *some* of the apples *are*.

Titles take singular verbs **(10a 4)**:

> "The Sisters" *is* the opening story of James Joyce's *Dubliners*.

In sentences beginning with the expletive *there*, the verb agrees with the delayed subject **(10a 5)**:

> There *is* no *explanation* for what happened.

The verb is always singular following the expletive *it*:

> *It is* her sisters who are coming, not John's.

The verb agrees with the inverted subject, not with an opening modifier **(10a 6)**:

> Outside the restaurant *were* parked ten red *cars*.

The verb agrees with its subject, not with its complement **(10a 7)**:

> The *cause* of the epidemic *was* the brown rats.

Verbs agree with their subjects, not with intervening modifiers (**10a 8**):

> The *book*, like others on the same subject, *is* failing to win a large audience.

Subjects joined by *and* usually take plural verbs (**10a 9**):

> Minneapolis *and* St. Paul *are* cities in Minnesota.

Compound subjects beginning with *each* and *every* take singular verbs:

> *Each* city and county in the state *levies* taxes.
> *Every* man and woman in this town *opposes* the tax levy.

When *or* joins singular nouns or pronouns of a compound subject, the verb is singular. When some of the nouns or pronouns are singular and others plural, the verb agrees with the nearest subject (**10a 9**):

> Minneapolis *or* St. Paul *is* the capital of Minnesota.
> Neither Milwaukee *nor* Minneapolis and St. Paul *are* on the Missouri River.

When phrases like *in addition to* and *as well as* follow a singular subject, the verb is singular:

> Organic chemistry, *in addition to* calculus and physics, *is* a requirement for the degree.

Compound subjects that form a single phrase take singular verbs:

> *Ham and eggs is* a popular dish.

Correlatives take singular verbs when the subjects are singular and plural verbs when the subjects are plural (**10a 10**):

> *Either* Minneapolis *or* St. Paul *is* the capital of Minnesota.
> *Either* Minneapolis and St. Paul *or* Milwaukee and Madison *are* on the Mississippi.

When some of the correlative subjects are singular and some plural, the verb agrees with the nearest subject:

> Neither *Latin and Greek* nor *logic is* a requirement.

10b Pronouns agree with their antecedents.
Compound subjects usually take plural pronouns (**10b 1**):

Chicago and Evanston have *their* own police departments.

A compound phrase that expresses a single idea takes a singular pronoun:

The comic strip *Mutt and Jeff* had *its* own special humor.

The indefinite pronouns *all, any, more, none, some* take a singular verb if the antecedent is a mass noun. A plural antecedent makes the verb plural **(10b 2)**:

The *fruit looks* fresh. *Is some* for sale?
The *apples look* fresh. *Are some* for sale?

The pronouns *each* and *every* make the subject singular:

Each of the proposals has *its* benefits.

Pluralizing the subject is a way to avoid excluding women from a statement **(10b 3)**:

All of us are donating our salary.

The pronoun is singular if its antecedent is a collective noun; the pronoun is plural if the antecedent refers to the members of the group individually **(10b 4)**:

Although the committee *has its* special rules or procedures, *it* governs *itself* through the House rules.
The committee *have their* own separate codes of ethics governing *their* individual staffs, but the committee as a whole acts according to the House code.

A plural pronoun may follow *anyone, everybody,* and similar indefinite pronouns if the meaning is plural and the sentence refers to animate or human beings:

Everyone has a right to *their* opinion.

Pronoun Reference

11

Putting the right pronoun in the subject position is something we do out of habit. We rarely say "Me is going home." Occasionally, though, we do confuse subject and object positions, putting the subject pronoun in the object position (*between you and I*) and the object pronoun in the subject position. In the subject position, *we guys* sounds strange to many even though the phrase is grammatically correct:

> We guys are taking the plane to Seattle.

Some uses of pronoun case and reference are matters of exactness and clarity, such as exact reference of *who* and *which*. Other uses of pronoun case and reference are matters of convention that vary across the spectrum of people who speak and write English. These uses and conventions are the subject of this chapter.

11a   Personal Pronouns

Some **personal pronouns** change in form to show singular and plural and to show case. The subject pronoun has separate forms in the three persons and three cases:

	Subjective Case	**Objective Case**	**Possessive Case**
First person:	I, we	me, us	my, mine, our
Second person:	you, you	you	your, yours
Third person:	he, she, it, they	him, her, it, them	his, hers, its, theirs

To use the correct form, you must know how the pronoun is used in the sentence.

1   Subjective case

Pronouns in the **subjective case** occur in the same subject positions filled by nominals:

> The coach and *I* watched the play from the sidelines.

The subject form also fills the subject complement position as the equivalent of the subject (see 7b):

> The tennis pro is *she,* not her sister.

This sentence would be pronounced with full stress on *she.* In a less emphatic sentence, the new information would follow the verb:

> *She* is the tennis pro, not her sister.

The objective case is common in informal speech:

> The tennis pro is Mary, not her.
> It's me.

The subjective case is preferred in writing, though it is awkward to say or write "It is I."

In the subject and other positions, a pronoun is **ambiguous** when its referent or antecedent is uncertain:

Ambiguous
Neither Wilson nor Hughes doubted *he* would be elected.

If *he* refers to Wilson and Hughes both, you can try to clear up the ambiguity by rewording the sentence:

> Wilson did not doubt he would be elected, nor did Hughes.

But the ambiguity remains, for the second clause can mean:

> . . . nor did Hughes doubt that Wilson would.
> . . . nor did Hughes doubt that he himself would.

The solution is to specify the antecedent even at the cost of repetition:

Revised
Neither Wilson nor Hughes doubted *Wilson* would be elected.

The following revision is appropriate in referring to both men:

> Neither Wilson nor Hughes doubted that *he himself* would be elected.

In an appositive phrase, pronouns take the case of the nouns they stand next to:

> Those in the front row, my classmates and *I*, cheered loudly.
> The speaker recognized us—my classmates and *me*.

2 Objective case

Pronouns in the **objective case** serve as objects in the following positions:

Direct object	We sent the tickets to Mary, but she returned *them*.
Indirect object	We sent *her* the tickets.
Object of preposition	We received the tickets from *her*.

The errors in the following sentences probably occur because the writer loses sight of the object in each sentence. Note the revisions:

Nonstandard	**Revised**
The lawyer wrote to my husband and *I* that the claim had been settled.	The lawyer wrote to my husband and *me* that the claim had been settled.
She asked her the question, not *he*.	She asked her the question, not *him*. [indirect object of *asked*]

The ear is an unreliable guide in making decisions about pronoun case. The tendency to use the subjective case in object positions again arises from the sense that the pronouns in the subjective case sound correct in prepositional phrases like the following:

> They gave the tickets to you and *I*.
> Between you and *I* he's greedier than he knows.

3 Possessive case

Although pronouns in the **possessive case** seldom give us problems in speaking or writing, they can create ambiguous and awkward sentences when they are not used carefully. To avoid ambiguous sentences, always make sure that a possessive pronoun has a clear referent in the sentence.

The following sentence is ambiguous because it has two possible meanings:

Ambiguous
Smith is famous for his indictment.

The sentence does not clarify whether Smith made a general condemnation or indictment or was formally charged or indicted by a grand jury for an offense. Here are possible clarifications of the sentence:

Revised
Smith is famous for his indictment of judicial corruption in the county.
Smith is famous for his indictment by a grand jury on the charge of judicial corruption.

A sentence will also sound awkward if it contains a reference to a possessive noun used as a modifier:

Awkward
In Emily Dickinson's poetry, *she* often uses complex metaphors.

Although the subject pronoun *she* has an antecedent in *Emily Dickinson*, the reference is to a noun functioning as an adjective (see 8c), a momentary source of confusion for the reader. The revision here is a simple matter:

Revised
In her poetry, Emily Dickinson often uses complex metaphors.

4 Pronoun case after *as* and *than*

The case of the pronoun in an elliptical clause introduced by
as or *than* depends on its function in the whole clause. An
elliptical clause deletes words and phrases unnecessary to the
meaning of the sentence:

> She is as smart *as I* [*am smart*].
> He gave James more *than she* [*gave him*].

In these sentences, the subjective case of the pronoun is used
because it serves as the subject in an elliptical cause beginning
with *as* and *than*. But the meaning is the same when the object
form is used informally:

Informal	**Formal**
She is as smart *as me.*	She is as smart *as I.*
She is smarter *than me.*	She is smarter *than I.*

Deletions can create confusion. The meaning is not the
same in the following sentences:

> He gave James more *than she* [*gave him*].
> He gave James more *than* [*he gave*] her.

The correct pronoun case is obligatory in each of these sentences.

If in doubt about the correct pronoun case after *as* or *than,*
complete the construction as shown above.

5 Reference to an implied word

Always be sure that pronoun references have a clear antecedent or earlier referent in the sentence or paragraph. The following sentence is ambiguous because it has no specific
antecedent for the italicized word:

> **Ambiguous**
> In debating gun control, she stated the number of *them* in private
> hands.

The word *them* refers to the modifying word *gun,* not to a
specific antecedent. To make the sentence clear, specify the
antecedent:

Revised
In discussing gun control, she stated the number of *guns* in private hands.

(See 10b on pronoun and antecedent agreement.)

Checklist: Pronoun Reference

1. Are my subject, object, and possessive pronouns in the right case?
2. Do my pronouns have clear referents or antecedents?
3. Have I used the appropriate pronoun case following *as* and *than*?
4. Have I used *that* and *which* consistently in introducing dependent clauses?
5. Have I used *whom* following a preposition? Have I used demonstrative pronouns with clear reference?
6. Have I used *you* and *it* consistently and clearly?

EXERCISES

1. Choose the pronoun in the correct case in each of the following sentences:
   a. An agreement exists between Bill and (*they, them*).
   b. She is taller than (*he, him*).
   c. The manager gave the tickets to (*she, her*).
   d. Give them to (*he, him*), not (*she, her*).
   e. Few people make mistakes as foolish as (*they, them*).
   f. I know the Smith brothers and (*their, they're*) sister.
   g. There are few in the class smarter than (*she, her*).
   h. Give the book to no one but (*he, him*).
   i. The best photo is of (*they, them*), not (*we, us*).
   j. The argument is between (*they, them*) and (*we, us*).
2. Some of the following sentences contain pronouns in the wrong case. Change the pronoun form where necessary.
   a. They forgot to tell Frank and I that the road was closed.
   b. They told Bill, the students who had been waiting in the hall, and them that the performance had been canceled.
   c. I would rather hear the bad news from you than from her.

d. We could not explain to the bank official or to the police officer or she where we lost the blank checks or when.
e. They gave us campers directions to the lake.
f. We were certainly as experienced as they.
g. Me and my friends would like to reserve a campsite.
h. To me and my friends it seemed the longest way to go.
i. She herself is to blame, not us.
j. She and myself are to blame, not you and him. ∎

Reflexive pronouns

The **reflexive and intensive pronouns** have the following forms:

Singular	**Plural**
myself	*ourselves*
yourself	*yourselves*
himself	*themselves*
herself	
itself	

Reflexive pronouns show that the actor and the person acted upon are the same:

Direct object	She injured *herself* in the accident.
Indirect object	We did not give *ourselves* enough time.
Object of preposition	Tom bought tickets for Jane and *him-self.*

Note that reflexive pronouns are used in informal speech as complements, with more than the usual stress:

They asked Frank and *myself* to go.

The following usage is nonstandard:

She sold the car for *himself.*

The following is standard:

She sold the car for *him*.

Reflexive pronouns require a stated antecedent.
Intensive pronouns are used as emphatic appositives:

I *myself* am going.

219

The intensive pronoun gains additional emphasis at the end of the sentence:

They must do the job *themselves.*

The third-person pronoun *itself* is also used as an emphatic appositive:

The building *itself* needs repair.

These are also nonstandard forms:

Nonstandard	**Revised**
He *hisself*	He *himself*
We *ourself*	We *ourselves*
You *yourself*	You *yourselves* (if plural)
They *theirselves*	They *themselves*

11c Relative pronouns

The **relative pronouns** *who, which,* and *that* refer to persons and things.

Who refers to people:

They are the couple *who* bought our house.

That refers to objects and occasionally to people when introducing a relative clause that restricts or limits the meaning of the noun it modifies:

The people *that bought our house* are friends of my sister.
The toolbox *that I put in the garage* [not the toolbox which I put in the yard] is gone.

However, *which* usually introduces a nonrestrictive clause—one that does not limit the meaning—and is set off by commas:

The toolbox, *which I put in the garage,* is gone. [The speaker owns one toolbox, not two.]

1 Vague use of *which*

The relative pronoun **which** has a clear reference in the following sentence:

On my next trip to Washington, I intend to visit the Smithsonian Air Museum, *which* has World War II airplanes on display.

When the reference is to an idea rather than a thing, the pronoun reference is often unclear:

Ambiguous
The historians give various explanations for Napoleon's blunder, *which* is why the question continues to be debated.

Here the word *which* has two possible antecedents: the fact that historians give various explanations for the blunder—an idea expressed in the whole first clause—and the word *blunder* itself. The following sentence clarifies the reference:

Revised
The historians give various explanations for Napoleon's blunder, *and these explanations* show why the question continues to be debated.

The sentence can be tightened:

The various explanations of historians for Napoleon's blunder continue to be debated.

This revision is still more concise:

Historians continue to debate Napoleon's blunder.

Despite the reduction in words, the sense of the original sentence is retained because the word *debate* implies that historians give different explanations for Napoleon's blunder.

Note that some writers use the pronoun *whose* to avoid an awkward use of *which*:

Awkward
The toolbox the latch *of which* is broken is in the garage.

Revised
The toolbox *whose* latch is broken is in the garage.

2 Who and whom

Who and **whom** give trouble because in speaking we don't require the *-m* ending (*whom*) to identify a word in the object position. The position of many words, not their special ending, gives us this information. So important is position in distinguishing subject and object forms that we commonly say:

Who did he give the tickets *to*?

We use *who* and not the formally correct *whom* (the object of the preposition *to*) because it appears in the subject position.

Occasionally, we hear or say the following—with full stress on *who*:

He gave the tickets *to who*?

The objective form always follows the preposition, with ordinary stress:

To whom did you give the tickets?

In everyday speech and informal writing, *who* is common as the object except before the preposition *to*. *Whom* is required in this position at all levels. In other positions, *whom* is found most in formal writing.

A special problem arises when forms of *who* and *whom* introduce dependent clauses. Compare the following:

Nonstandard
Give the tickets to *whomever* asks for them.

Standard
Give the tickets to *whoever* asks for them.

The correct form is *whoever* as subject of the noun clause *whoever asks for them*. The confusion arises because *whomever* at first glance seems to be the object of *to*. The object is in fact the noun clause *whoever asks for them*.

If in doubt about which form to use, isolate the dependent clause and then try to substitute *he, she,* or *they* as follows:

Give the tickets to (*whoever, whomever*) asks for them.
Dependent clause: she asks for the tickets
Give the tickets to *whoever* asks for them.

He wondered (*who, whom*) had sent the tickets.
Dependent clause: she sent the tickets
He wondered *who* had sent the tickets.

EXERCISE

Correct the misuse of *who* and *whom* in the following sentences as necessary. (Some of the sentences may be correct as written.) Distinguish between informal and formal usage.

1. Many people on whom we depend in turn depend on us.

2. Give this message to whoever calls.
3. Give the message to the person who calls at six.
4. The actress who I talked with after the play lives in Boston.
5. The people who we saw driving to the lake waved as they drove by.
6. She was willing to explain the problem to whomever asked.
7. Whoever you tell, don't tell everything that happened.
8. I know where I'm going and whom I'm going with.
9. Tell whomever you want to the full details of the accident.
10. Those whom you tell will repeat the story to whoever asks them.

11d Demonstrative pronouns

In speaking, you habitually use the **demonstrative pronouns** *this, that, these,* and *those* without specifying their antecedents because the object is in sight:

This is easy for anyone to fix.

If your listeners look confused, you may pause to clarify the pronoun reference:

I mean the flat tire over there.

In writing, you should take care to specify the antecedent if the context does not make your pronoun reference clear. The pronoun is most likely to be vague when it refers to an idea. In the following example, the word *that* refers to a series of ideas expressed in the first two sentences:

Vague
Napoleon let ambition guide him in planning military strategy. He was also vain and overconfident. *That* is why he did not take the advice of his generals in planning the invasion of Russia.

Revised
These qualities explain why *Napoleon* did not take the advice of his generals in planning the invasion of Russia.

11e Indefinite pronouns *you* and *it*

The pronoun **you** is often used with indefinite meaning in conversation:

> *You*'ve no idea the trouble we've had with the new stove.

In the following sentence, *you* has the meaning of *me*:

> It gives *you* no end of trouble.

The indefinite *you* makes the following sentence awkward and repetitious:

> **Repetitious**
> *You*'ve no idea the fun *you* can have with sailboats.

Substituting the formal indefinite pronoun *one* makes the sentence stilted, shifting it awkwardly from third-person *one* to first-person *you*:

> **Awkward**
> *One* has no idea the fun *you* can have with sailboats.

The following revision is awkward whether spoken or written:

> *One* has no idea of the fun with sailboats.

One is correct but formal, however, in a short sentence like the following:

> *One* can have fun with sailboats.

The following revision loses nothing in meaning:

> **Revised**
> Sailboats are fun.

The pronoun **it** is ambiguous when it has no clear referent in the sentence. In the following sentence, *it* has two possible referents—*character* or *political behavior*:

> **Ambiguous**
> Historians disagree on the character and political behavior of Franklin Roosevelt. *It* seems to be not just a concern of historians but also of novelists and filmmakers.

Here are possible revisions of the second sentence that remove these ambiguities:

Revised

His character [or behavior] seems a major concern not just to historians but also to novelists and filmmakers.

Novelists and filmmakers, not just historians, seem to be concerned with his character [or behavior].

Notice that *it* also may be an expletive when used without an intended reference (see 9a, 10a).

EXERCISE

Correct any faulty pronoun reference in the following sentences:

1. Each of us knows their limitations.
2. Einstein and Bohr debated his rejection of the quantum theory that he had helped to create.
3. Neither changed their position on quantum theory in the course of debate.
4. Inflation increased as wages fell, which was difficult to explain.
5. Gun control remains a controversial issue, particularly in areas where crime is increasing. That is not surprising.
6. The invasion of Normandy surprised the Germans, which the Allied command hoped would happen.
7. The speaker on dog obedience explained that they respond to consistent commands.
8. The popularity of rock music is shown by the huge crowds that attend their concerts.
9. In the senator's campaign for the presidency, reporters discovered his persistence and idealism.
10. Animal ecology is the study of their distribution and breeding habits.
11. The circus performers—tumblers, clowns, highwire acrobats—they are as exciting as ever to see.
12. Nobody knows how much math they will need later in life.
13. Either Jim or Bill will get the job, and he knows it.
14. Fire, flood, famine, plague—that has been a continual source of suffering of people, rich and poor.
15. One needs all the help you can get.
16. Jefferson had foresight and an understanding of the importance the West would have. It explains his decision to make the Louisiana Purchase.

17. The storm buried the city in snow and closed the highways, which is why we canceled our trip.
18. In Fawn Brodie's biography, she presents new facts about Thomas Jefferson.
19. John worked overtime during the week, and he spent the weekend in the office which is why he is taking this week off.
20. Neither of the sisters guessed she would win the scholarship.

Summary

11a Position determines the case of a personal pronoun.

The pronoun appears in the *subjective case* when it serves as subject or subjective complement (**11a 1**):

> *She* is the tennis pro, not her sister.
> The tennis pro is *she*, not her sister.

Pronoun appositives take the case of the nouns they stand next to:

> The two of us, my sister and *I*, cheered loudly.

Give pronouns clear antecedents (**11a 1**):

Ambiguous	**Revised**
Neither Wilson nor Hughes doubted *he* would be elected.	Neither Wilson nor Hughes doubted *Wilson* would be elected.

Put a pronoun in the *objective case* when it serves as direct object, indirect object, or object of the preposition (**11a 2**).

Make *possessive* pronouns clear in their reference (**11a 3**):

Ambiguous	**Revised**
Smith is famous for his indictment.	Smith is famous for his indictment *of* judicial corruption.
In Emily Dickinson's poetry, she often uses complex metaphors.	In her poetry, Emily Dickinson often uses complex metaphors.

The subject form of the pronoun is used after *as* and *than* when verb and object are deleted in the elliptical clause (**11a 4**):

> She is as smart *as I*.

A pronoun should not refer to an implied word (**11a 5**):

Unclear
In debating gun control,
she stated the number of
them in private hands.

Revised
In debating gun control,
she stated the number of
guns in private hands.

11b Reflexive pronouns require a stated antecedent.

Nonstandard
She sold the car for
himself.

Revised
She sold the car for *him.*

11c Give the relative pronouns *who, which,* and *that* specific and consistent references.

Vague
The historians give various
explanations for
Napoleon's blunder,
which is why the
question continues to be
debated.

Revised
The various explanations of
historians for Napoleon's
blunder continue to be
debated.
Or: Historians continue to
debate Napoleon's
blunder.

Nonstandard
Give the tickets to
whomever asks for them.

Revised
Give the tickets to *whoever*
asks for them.

11d Demonstrative pronouns most often create problems when the referent is a previous series of ideas:

Ambiguous
Napoleon let ambition
guide him in planning
military strategy. He
was also vain and
overconfident. *That* is
why he did not often
take advice.

Revised
These qualities explain why
Napoleon did not often
take advice.

11e The pronouns *you* and *it* sometimes make sentences awkward and repetitious.

Repetitious
You've no idea the fun *you*
can have with sailboats.

Revised
You can have fun with
sailboats.
Or: Sailboats are fun.

It doesn't make sense to
leave *it* on the street.

It doesn't make sense to
leave the car on the
street.

PART FOUR

EFFECTIVE SENTENCES

Sentence Unity and Emphasis 12

In writing your papers, you continually make decisions about sentence unity, emphasis, variety, and other matters of sentence construction and effectiveness. Your sentences will be effective if you make these decisions with your readers in mind.

An effective sentence states your point without confusion. In conversing, you form sentences naturally, without deliberately shaping them for emphasis or clarity. You also address a visible audience that reacts immediately to your words. When you are misunderstood, you can pause to rephrase what you said or to give particular words a different emphasis. The situation in writing is different: here you address an audience you cannot see; your readers are not present to convey their misunderstanding and you cannot pause to clarify your statements. Thus, in writing you need to anticipate their response to your words. This is why you need to examine your sentences from the point of view of your readers. Doing so will ensure that your sentences are pleasing and effective.

The chapters in Part Four of the *Handbook* focus on how to write effective sentences. In this chapter, we consider ways of giving sentences unity and proper emphasis. Chapters 13–15 turn to other features of effective sentences—variety, parallelism, clarity, concision.

12a   Sentence unity

An effective sentence is **unified:** it deals with one idea at a time. The details that convey the idea must form a whole. A disunified sentence lacks a central idea or focus. The sentence jumps from one idea or detail to another, attaching unrelated details to the sentence as trailing modifiers:

Disunified
The tall, red-haired man in the white jacket is the swimming coach—hot-tempered but understanding, competitive but not ruthless, a tournament swimmer himself for many years, having trained in high school for state meets, and later in college, from which he graduated with honors in American history and political science.

The details about the coach's high school and college swimming and academic career shift abruptly from the new information—that the man is the new swimming coach—to qualities unrelated to his new job. The sentence lacks a central idea and focus; the topic shifts as the sentence progresses. Here are two possible revisions of the sentence that unify the details and omit those irrelevant to the new information:

First Revision
The tall, red-haired man in the white jacket is the swimming coach—hot-tempered but understanding, competitive but not ruthless. A tournament swimmer himself for many years, he trained in high school for state meets, and later in college.

Second Revision
The tall, red-haired man in the white jacket is the swimming coach. A hot-tempered but understanding man, he is competitive but not ruthless, having been a tournament swimmer himself for many years. . . .

In constructing your sentences, keep closely related ideas together. The following sentence effectively combines a large number of related ideas without losing focus:

> But I remember the smell of the big schoolroom, a smell of ink and dust and boots, and the stone in the yard that had been a mounting block and was used for sharpening knives on, and the little baker's shop opposite where they sold a kind of Chelsea bun, twice the size of the Chelsea buns you get nowadays, which were called Lardy Busters and cost a half-penny.
> —George Orwell, *Coming Up for Air*

Orwell's sentence describes different but not unrelated things—things of the past that connect in the act of remembering them. He unifies his sentence by presenting one thing at a time, and fully.

12b Beginning and end focus

Your sentence is unified, but have you given emphasis to the ideas and details you consider most important?

You can do so by taking advantage of the positions of most stress in the sentence—the beginning and the end. The end of the sentence usually is the more emphatic. In reading a sentence, you look to the beginning to see who or what performed the action and to the end to see what happened. What appears at the end of the sentence is most often the focus of your attention, particularly if the words themselves are emphatic:

> The third wave moved forward, *huge, furious, implacable.*
> —Stephen Crane, "The Open Boat" (emphasis added)

Notice how the emphasis of the sentence shifts in the following rewriting of Crane's sentence:

> Huge, furious, implacable, *the third wave moved forward.*

Important as the opening adjectives are, the emphasis now falls to the forward movement of the wave.

The natural emphasis found at the end of the sentence is called the **end focus.** The opening of the sentence usually presents information given to the reader previously, and the end of the sentence gives information that is new:

Given information   *New information*
The booklet, the one on the table, / is an instruction manual for
  computer programmers.

Notice that when you use the passive voice (12e), you take
advantage of end focus by stressing the agent of the action
described by the verb. Compare the following:

Active Voice   **Passive Voice**
The manager of the store   The instruction book was
  wrote the instruction book.   written *by the manager of
                                              the store.*

If you want to stress who wrote the book, you switch the subject to the end of the sentence, using the passive voice.

New information occasionally appears at the beginning of
the sentence, the position of second most emphasis. With a
beginning focus, the new information receives unusual stress
in speaking the sentence:

Who wrote the booklet? *The store manager* did!

End focus is indispensable in constructing effective sentences. Because the sentence pushes forward to new information, the predicate generally is able to take greater modification than the subject. When the information given at the end
of a sentence seems less important than the information at the
beginning, the result is anticlimactic:

Speeding like a shadow through the water, hurling the crystalline
spray and leaving the long glowing tail, an enormous fin was seen
by the correspondent.

The passive voice (*was seen by the correspondent*) awkwardly
shifts the emphasis to the less important idea in the sentence.
Crane's actual sentence wonderfully emphasizes the effect of
the fin upon the water:

The correspondent saw an enormous fin speed like a shadow
through the water, hurling the crystalline spray and leaving the
long glowing trail.

— "The Open Boat"

Usually your ear will tell you when you have stressed a less
important idea at the end of a sentence. In revising your sentences, listen carefully to how they begin and end.

12c Emphasis through subordination

In an effective sentence, the central or core idea stands out. However, your reader needs to see not only the core idea but also the relationship of ideas and details in the sentence. Grammatical subordination and coordination are ways of showing the relative importance of ideas and, at the same time, of emphasizing the core idea of each main clause.

Subordination makes ideas and details grammatically dependent in the clause. Words, phrases, and clauses all serve as modifiers. Details that explain, illustrate, and qualify the core idea most often appear in subordinate clauses, participial and prepositional phrases, and appositives:

Walking toward Third Avenue, she bumped into a neighbor, *a dancer at City Center, who lived in her building.*

Following is a list of common words and phrases used to subordinate elements in the sentence.

Common Subordinators

Purpose	Subordinating words and phrases	Examples
▪ To state where an event occurred	that, where, which	The park *where* we hiked is in Simsbury.
	along, besides, by	We visited the museum *by* the mall.
▪ To state the time of an event	after, before, since, when, while	The day *after* we drove to Tulsa it snowed.
▪ To identify a person or thing	that, which, who	The woman *who* wrote the letter is sitting there.
▪ To state causes, purposes, reasons	because, in order to, since, so that, that,	She wrote *because* she could not reach you on the telephone.

Common Subordinators (continued)

Purpose	Subordinating words and phrases	Examples
▪ To concede, qualify, or state an exception	although, even though, unless	We will drive to Tulsa *unless* it rains.
▪ To state a condition or requirement	as if, however, if, provided that, whatever	We will hold the meeting only *if* all voting members attend.

1 The process of subordination

When you subordinate an idea, you turn an independent clause into a dependent clause or phrase or a single-word modifier (see 20a). These modifiers are attached to the core subject, verb, or complement. Subordination is the chief way of giving emphasis to the core idea of the sentence. The following sentence contains various ideas and details, yet the core sentence stands out clearly:

> At the top of a ridge *I caught sight of Devil's Tower* upthrust against the gray sky as if in the birth of time the core of the earth had broken through its crust and the motion of the world was begun.
>
> —N. Scott Momaday, "The Way to Rainy Mountain"
> (emphasis added)

Notice in the following breakdown of Momaday's sentence that the independent clauses in the left column appear as subordinate elements in the actual sentences in the right column:

Modifying Phrase

I stood at the top of a ridge.	At the top of a ridge I caught sight of Devil's Tower
Devil's Tower thrust up against the sky.	upthrust against the sky

Modifying Clause

In the birth of time the core of the earth broke through its crust and the motion of the world began.	as if in the birth of time the core of the earth had broken through its crust and the motion of the world was begun

Momaday uses other kinds of subordination in the following sentence:

> Yellowstone, it seemed to me, was the top of the world, a region of deep lakes and dark timber, canyons and waterfalls.
> —"The Way to Rainy Mountain"

Parenthesis

It seemed to me that Yellowstone was the top of the world.	Yellowstone, it seemed to me, was the top of the world,

Appositive

Yellowstone is a region of deep lakes and dark timber, canyons and waterfalls.	a region of deep lakes and dark timber, canyons and waterfalls

If your sentence contains a single main clause, as Momaday's sentence does, you will make it most effective by opening with the core of the sentence and attaching modifying phrases and clauses to it. The sentence cumulates information, as in the following example:

Core idea   *The impulse to write things down is a peculiarly compulsive one,* inexplicable to those who do not share

Modifiers   it, useful only accidentally, only secondarily, in the way that any compulsion tries to justify itself.
> —Joan Didion, "On Keeping a Notebook"
> (emphasis added)

2 Modifying the verb

The verb (or verb phrase) of your sentence will accept as many modifiers as you wish to add. But you want to add them without making the sentence difficult to read. Notice in the following sentence how modifying words and clauses expand the verb:

> Denser and denser *grows* this dome of vapors, descending lower and lower upon the sea, narrowing the horizon around the ship.
> —*The Mirror of the Sea* (emphasis added)

Conrad might have added more details to his description of the sea, but at the risk of blurring the action stressed.

If the core idea still does not stand out after revising your sentence, reduce the number of modifiers, build to the core idea, or change the voice of the sentence. And watch for un-related modifiers that distract attention from the core idea:

Faulty
Ferguson won the cross-country race, *which he entered at the last moment, persuaded by his wife that he might win, having almost succeeded on three previous tries, the last in 1980—the year he retired as a cargo pilot.*

As in the faulty sentence analyzed on page 231, the information provided in the italicized modifiers in this sentence is not directly related to its topic or core idea—the fact that Ferguson won the race. Here is an acceptable revision of the sentence:

Revised
Persuaded by his wife that he might win, Ferguson entered the cross-country race at the last minute and won. He almost succeeded on three previous tries, the last in 1980—the year he retired as a cargo pilot.

3 Modifying the subject

Expanding the subject with a series of modifiers gives the sentence greater emphasis, indeed a dramatic quality:

The brown mats of seaweed that appeared from time to time were like islands, bits of earth.
The captain, rearing cautiously in the bow after the dinghy soared on a great swell, said that he had seen the lighthouse at Mosquito Inlet.
—Stephen Crane, "The Open Boat" (emphasis added)

Crane expands the modifying phrase (*marked by dingy clouds and clouds brick-red*) in the following sentence with another modifying phrase:

A squall, marked by dingy clouds and *clouds brick-red, like smoke from a burning building,* appeared from the southeast.
—"The Open Boat" (emphasis added)

Note that your sentence will be ineffective if the details do not develop the main idea. The miscellaneous details that open the following sentence are distracting because they again have nothing to do with the core idea:

Piloting his own plane, which he had learned to fly in the Air Force, which he joined in 1951 at the start of the Korean War, Ferguson won the cross-country race [*core idea*].

If the information about when and where Ferguson learned to fly is important, the sentence should state it in a separate sentence:

> Piloting his own plane, Ferguson won the cross-country race. He had learned to fly in the Air Force, which he joined at the start of the Korean War.

Your paragraphs and essays will gain emphasis if you group related ideas and details into a series of well-constructed sentences. But doing so requires close attention. Don't be tempted to break a heavily modified sentence into component sentences until you have tested its unity and connected it clearly to the rest of the paragraph. In revising a paper, read each paragraph carefully to make sure your sentences form a whole and give proper emphasis to key ideas.

See 13a for discussion of cumulative sentences that open with the core sentence and for periodic sentences that build to the core.

4 Misplaced emphasis

You may have to recast a sentence several times before you find the best way to make the core idea prominent. If your supporting ideas and details blur the core idea, they probably belong in a separate sentence. When a phrase or clause describes a highly dramatic or exciting action, it is best to take advantage of end focus by placing it late in the sentence—preferably in the main clause:

Unemphatic	**Emphatic**
While the car caught fire we were *talking about the weather*.	While we were talking about the weather, *the car caught fire*.

The sentence to the left puts the end focus on *talking about the weather*, but weather is probably not the idea the writer wants to emphasize. In the sentence to the right, the emphasis is properly on the important idea—that the car caught fire.

Achieving proper emphasis is not always so simple. We saw that end focus gives weight to concluding dependent or subordinate clauses, particularly when they express action:

> [Woodrow] Wilson was a Southerner by birth and breeding, *although he made his career in the North*.
> —Gerald W. Johnson, "The Cream of the Jest"
> (emphasis added)

The italicized subordinate clause receives approximately the same emphasis as the main clause; it could receive more. If placed at the end, the main clause would receive full emphasis:

> Although he made his career in the North, *Wilson was a Southerner by birth and breeding.*

A subordinate element may, in fact, contain the most important idea of the sentence:

> Traffic was heavy but spry, until it bogged down on the far side of O'Hare. Hemmed in by dozens of trucks of every size, we rolled on degraded roads through thick, blasphemous air lit by a hydrocarbon-red sun, passing under screaming jets and over huge railroad switching yards full of piggyback flatbed railcars, slowing time after time to pay money to sullen tolltakers, *in a vehicle held in bouncing thrall by an indifferent world of gray, gritty commerce, of haphazardness and uncommunity.*
> —Bryan DiSalvatore, "Truck Driver,"
> *The New Yorker*, September 12, 1988

End focus is crucial in this sentence. But so is the idea expressed—an idea given dramatic emphasis in the phrasing.

Word order is also essential in controlling emphasis. The following sentences have the same meaning, but in neither do we have a sense of misplaced emphasis:

> Looking at pictures requires active participation, and a certain amount of discipline *in the early stages*.
> Looking at pictures requires active participation, and, *in the early stages*, a certain amount of discipline.
> —Kenneth Clark, *Looking at Pictures* (emphasis added)

The difference between the two sentences is in the idea given emphasis at the end of each sentence.

Notice that a sentence sounds awkward when the main clause is squeezed between two subordinate clauses of similar construction. The awkwardness increases when the subordinate clauses begin with the same word:

Awkward
> *Although people generalize about good and bad art,* they are really talking about pictures and books that have given them pleasure, *although they never say so.*
> *Since crime makes people feel unsafe,* gun sales increase *since people believe guns are their only protection.*

The dependent clauses in the first example are not parallel in meaning. The revision requires the change of a single word:

239

Revised

When people generalize about good and bad art, they are really talking about pictures and books that have given them pleasure, although they never say so.

The dependent clauses in the second sentence are parallel in meaning and therefore should stand together (see 14a).

Revised

Since crime makes people feel unsafe and they believe guns are their only protection, gun sales increase.

Reducing a clause to a phrase may also correct the problem:

Gun sales increase because people, *feeling unsafe*, believe guns are their only protection.

(See 20d for ways to revise misplaced clauses.)

Exercise

Revise the following sentences to correct faulty subordination or misplaced emphasis:

1. Driving to Seattle to ride the monorail, which had been constructed during the World's Fair, held when she was a child, she stopped to visit an old friend.
2. She could not find the house, which she thought was on the main street which was a mile from the interstate, which cut north in Seattle.
3. After driving from one end of the street to the other, she stopped to call her friend, after making sure she was in the right town.
4. The person who answered was not her friend, who had driven to Portland that morning.
5. Because he is a poor speaker, Hanson was not elected because he failed to persuade the audience.
6. At the end of the street, where the fire was out of control, the warehouse had burned to the ground, the neighboring drugstore now in flames.
7. The man with the injured foot finished second in the race, in the face of competition from some of the fastest runners in the state, including San Francisco and Los Angeles, which produced the winners of the last marathon.
8. Knowing that the qualifying exam would test knowledge of genetics, I reviewed my notes, believing they would be more helpful than the text.
9. As soon as I read the exam questions, I began to write as soon as I decided which ones to answer first.

10. Writing with increasing confidence, I remembered facts and ideas I thought I had forgotten, writing an answer to the first question. ■

 ## Emphasis through coordination

Your sentence may contain two or more ideas that you want to emphasize. **Coordination** refers to ways of joining ideas of equal weight into a single sentence. Coordination is also possible between single words, phrases, and clauses in the sentence:

Oak, maple, and beech grow in the Berkshires. [*single words*]
We *complained about the bad food* but *continued to eat it.* [*phrases*]
Rain fell all night, yet *the stream did not flood.* [*clauses*]

Here is a list of the kinds of words and punctuation used to coordinate ideas:

Means of Coordination

- **Coordinating conjunctions:** *and, but, for, yet, or, nor*
- **Correlative conjunctions:** *either/or, neither/nor, not only/but also, both/and*
- **Semicolon (sometimes followed by a conjunctive adverb):** *furthermore, however, moreover, nevertheless, therefore, thus*
- **Colon**

Coordinating conjunctions are the most common means of coordinating independent clauses. At times, you may choose to substitute a colon or a semicolon, sometimes following the semicolon with a conjunctive adverb. Here are some examples:

Coordinating Conjunctions
It is silly to talk to bees—for one thing, they can't hear—*but* I often do anyway. I tell them encouraging things, ask them for help *and* always thank them for doing good work.
—Sue Hubbell, *A Book of Bees* (emphasis added)

241

Colon
There is always something to talk about with the other hands, because farming is genuinely absorbing. It has the best quality of work: nothing else seems real.

—Carol Bly, "Getting Tired"

Semicolon
Still, cornpicking and plowing is a marvelous time of the year on farms; one of the best autumns I've had recently had a few days of fieldwork in it.

—Carol Bly

Semicolon Followed by a Conjunctive Adverb
The net increment to human health and cheerfulness is hard to exaggerate; *indeed*, it now requires an act of imagination to understand what infectious disease formerly meant to humankind, or even to our own grandfathers.

—William H. McNeill, *Plagues and People* (emphasis added)

These sentences reflect the emphatic forward movement of spoken English, and, as in Hubbell's first sentence, the break for a parenthetical comment. Pauses give emphasis to the words that follow; so do semicolons and colons.

The following sentences also reflect the emphasis of speech, with trailing coordinate clauses marked by the words *and* and *even* and a dash to stress the importance of the ideas:

Newton is said to have recalled, near the end of his life, that this inspiration came to him when he saw an apple fall from the tree in front of his mother's house. The story may be true—Newton's desk in his bedroom looked out on an apple orchard, *and even* a Newton must occasionally have interrupted his work to gaze out the window—*and* it serves, in any event, to trace how he arrived at a quantitative description of gravitation that drew together the physics of the heavens and the earth.

—Timothy Ferris, *Coming of Age in the Milky Way*
(emphasis added)

As Ferris's paragraph shows, coordination and subordination combine to emphasize ideas and details in the sentence and the paragraph. Often a lack of emphasis arises from excessive coordination. If you give every idea and detail the same emphasis, no single idea or detail will stand out. In revising a sentence that lacks emphasis, look to see how it connects with other sentences. You may wish to reduce, or perhaps increase, the amount of coordination in the whole paragraph.

☑

Checklist: Achieving Emphasis

1. Is my sentence unified? Does it discuss one idea at a time and keep related ideas and details close together?
2. If I added a series of modifiers to the core of the sentence, are the modifiers connected directly to it? If the core idea seems distant or blurred, have I added too many modifiers?
3. If I expanded my subject with a series of modifiers, have I made the sentence top-heavy or drawn attention away from the core idea?
4. In revising an unclear or awkward sentence, have I experimented with different emphasis and arrangement of modifiers?
5. Have I used the active and passive voice for proper emphasis (12e)?
6. Are the sentences of the paragraph clearly connected? In the whole paragraph, do they give proper emphasis to the key ideas?

EXERCISE

Combine each of the following groups of sentences into one or two sentences, deleting unnecessary words. Use subordination and coordination to give emphasis to the main idea.

1. We ordered dishes in the restaurant and ordered them by name.
    We did not know what the names of the dishes meant.
    We found we had ordered dishes that were highly peppered or seasoned.
2. The trees were budding by the middle of May.
    The shrubs that flowered in April were now in full blossom.
    So were the early spring flowers.
3. A good pair of shoes should have these qualities.
    They should have stitches that are even and not visible.
    They should have soles that will last long.

They should fit well but not to be so tight that they pinch.
The soles should be flexible.

4. A number of bands performed at the concert.
Some had two members, and some had three or more.
Some played rock, and some played country and bluegrass music.

5. Not many buildings on campus were built before 1970.
Those built before 1970 have thicker walls and higher ceilings.
Classes in these buildings are quieter than those in newer buildings.

6. We discussed *Hamlet*.
We discussed Hamlet as a character and read various interpretations of his behavior.
Then we saw a videotape of the play.
We discussed how closely the performance realized the character of Hamlet.

7. Not many of us had read *Hamlet* before.
Only a few had seen a performance of it.
None had seen a performance of *Hamlet* in a theater.
Those who had seen performances of it watched it on television or at the movies.

8. Talking about a character is easier than writing about a character.
Writing about Hamlet is an example.

9. Hamlet is so complex a character that I find it impossible to identify a central quality.
Hamlet makes too many statements about himself to do so.

10. The car looked as if it had been driven long and hard.
The wheels were caked with mud.
The windshield was spattered with mud.
The bumper on the front of the car was badly dented. ■

12e The active and passive voice

You use the active and passive voice in your everyday speech. Your speech would be artificial if you spoke in one voice only. You need to use both voices in your writing for the same reason.

1 Uses of the active and passive voice

English sentences in the **active voice** focus on the *action*. The **passive voice** increases the focus on the *actor* by shifting the subject of the sentence to the position following the verb—taking advantage of end focus:

Active Voice
Shakespeare wrote many plays.
The war impoverished the middle class.

Passive Voice
Many plays were *written by Shakespeare.*
The middle class was *impoverished by the war.*

These sentences say the same thing but with a different emphasis. In the sentences to the right, the passive voice emphasizes the agent of the action. The sentences would be spoken with full stress on the final words *Shakespeare* and *war*.

By shifting the actor to the position following the verb, you can add various modifiers without making the sentence awkward or unclear:

The house was destroyed by the fire, which raged through the neighborhood until fire fighters arrived.

Opening the sentence with lengthy information about the fire makes it awkward:

The fire, which raged through the neighborhood until fire fighters arrived, destroyed the house.

The passive voice also will help you avoid a long, awkward opening subject:

Awkward
That the storm struck without a public warning by the Weather Bureau upset many people.

Improved
Many people were upset that the storm struck without a public warning by the Weather Bureau.

2 Misuses of the passive voice

Overuse of the passive voice makes writing sluggish in playing down or ignoring the actor. The following sentence is awkward because the actor has played an important role in the action and deserves mention:

The car was wrecked by me in the accident.

The passive voice is used here to soften the impact of the statement. Notice that the passive voice does not produce an awkward sentence when the actor is not mentioned:

> The car was wrecked in the accident.

In the active voice, the sentence is blunt and courageous:

> *I* wrecked the car in the accident.

The subject *I* would probably be pronounced with more than ordinary stress in this sentence.

3 Seeking objectivity

Overuse of the passive voice also can make writing impersonal and objective in playing down the actor. It can create the impression that personal feelings play no role in the activity or in the reporting of it. Technical writing frequently uses the passive voice to achieve an objective tone, as in statements like the following:

> It will be demonstrated in this paper that . . .
> The molecular structure of heavy water will be discussed in this paper . . .
> The conclusion to be drawn from this study is that . . .
> It is to be hoped that these findings will . . .
> Objections may be raised to examining Shakespeare's sonnets from the point of view of . . .

To achieve an objective tone, you need not depend on the passive voice exclusively. The following paragraph, which opens an article addressed to a general audience, shows that an objective tone may also be achieved through the active voice:

> Many machines imitate nature; a familiar example is the imitation of a soaring bird by the airplane. One form of animal locomotion that has resisted imitation is walking. Can it be that modern computers and feedback control systems make it possible to build machines that walk? We have been exploring the question with computer models and actual hardware.
> —Marc H. Raibert and Ivan E. Sutherland,
> "Machines That Walk," *Scientific American*, January 1983

Personal references are rare in reports on research in scientific journals, though not in reports delivered to scientific conferences or in scientific articles directed to a general audience.

EXERCISE

Revise the following passages to make the verbs active and to reduce wordiness:

1. That is the car that was hit by me.
2. The car that was struck on the right by the truck had just been stolen.
3. The dance that was attended by my sister and her boyfriend was sponsored by the senior class.
4. A fine will be levied by this magistrate upon drivers convicted by this court.
5. The paper was not written by me in time to meet the deadline.

12f Climactic order

Clauses and phrases can be arranged in **climactic order** to give ideas increasing emphasis:

Clauses
I came, I saw, I conquered.

Phrases
It was not, in short, particular environments that determined the American character or created the American type but the whole of the American environment—the sense of spaciousness, the invitation to mobility, the atmosphere of independence, the encouragement to enterprise and to optimism.
—Henry Steele Commager, *The American Mind*

Commager creates a sense of climax by setting off the four concluding appositive phrases and by ending the sentence with important qualities (independence, enterprise, optimism) that took advantage of particular environments.

Descriptive details can also build in importance. The following passage builds to the most significant physical feature of the woman described:

Her arms were folded and as she mounted the prominence, she might have been the giant wife of the countryside, come out at some sign of danger to see what the trouble was. She stood on two tremendous legs, with the grand self-confidence of a moun-

tain, and rose, up narrowing bulges of granite, to two icy blue
points of light that pierced forward, surveying everything.
                    —Flannery O'Connor, "The Displaced Person,"

O'Connor's sentence shows that climactic order is particularly
useful in building to a key detail or point.

However, like other unusual sentence structures, climactic
order should be used sparingly. The fewer climactic sentences
or peaks of emphasis in the paragraph, the more striking will
be the ideas and details that you do emphasize. You need also
to watch for anticlimax in your sentences and paragraphs. If
the content does not warrant a dramatic buildup, the sentence
or paragraph may sound flat or even comical.

For a discussion of climactic order in periodic sentences
that build to the core idea, see 13a.

Summary

12a Unify your sentence to make it emphatic.

Disunified	**Unified**
The tall, red-haired man in the white jacket is the swimming coach—hot-tempered but understanding, competitive but not ruthless, a tournament swimmer himself for many years, having trained in high school for state meets, and later in college, from which he graduated with honors in American history and political science.	The tall, red-haired man in the white jacket is the swimming coach—hot-tempered but understanding, competitive but not ruthless. A tournament swimmer himself for many years, he trained in high school for state meets, and later in college.

12b Use the beginning and ending of your sentences to
emphasize the actor and action.

Emphasis on action	**Emphasis on actor**
The manager of the store wrote the instruction book.	The instruction book was written by the manager of the store.

12c In adding modifiers to the subject and predicate, don't hide your core sentence.

Faulty	**Revised**
Ferguson won the cross-country race, which he entered at the last moment, persuaded by his wife that he might win, having almost succeeded on three previous tries, the last in 1980—the year he retired as a cargo pilot.	Persuaded by his wife that he might win, Ferguson entered the cross-country race at the last minute and won. He almost succeeded on three previous tries, the last in 1980—the year he retired as a cargo pilot.

Take advantage of end focus to emphasize the important idea:

Unemphatic	**Emphatic**
While the car caught fire we were talking about the weather.	While we were talking about the weather, the car caught fire.

12d Give emphasis to ideas of equal weight by coordinating them.

Rain fell all night, yet the stream did not flood.

12e Use the active and passive voice appropriate to avoid writing awkward sentences.

Awkward	**Revised**
That the storm struck without a public warning by the Weather Bureau upset many people.	Many people were upset that the storm struck without a public warning by the Weather Bureau.

12f Use climactic order to give ideas and details in the sentence unusual emphasis.

Sentence Variety

13

Effective sentences are, in part, grammatically correct. But grammatical sentences are not necessarily effective with all readers. A formal sentence style is more suited to a professional audience than to one made up of nonprofessionals. Therefore, in drafting and revising an essay you adjust the form or structure of your sentences and the meaning you want to express with your audience and subject in mind.

You cannot hope to hold the attention of your readers if you don't write sentences that have **variety.** Although English has certain rules governing words, order, deletions, and other features of grammar, the language also allows you to vary your sentences in numerous ways. Just as you can choose different arrangements of words, phrases, and clauses to achieve emphasis, so too may you choose to combine several short sentences into a single long sentence, or to break up a long sentence into separate ones. You also have choices in opening and closing your sentences. These and other matters of sentence style and variety are our focus in this chapter.

13a Varying sentence structure

In varying the structure of your sentences, you make your paragraphs more interesting. Your sentences carry different points of emphasis, reflecting the varied emphasis of your spoken sentences.

We noted earlier (12b) that the most prominent points of emphasis in the sentence occur at the beginning and the end:

> Mary objected to details of the proposal.

The opening of the main clause of the sentence receives stress in stating the subject; the end position usually receives greater stress in expressing the action and providing information about it. We call this way of emphasizing new information *end focus* (12b).

Beginning and end focus are important in deciding where to place modifiers. The following sentence stresses Mary's *objection:*

> *When she heard the details of the proposal,* Mary objected.

This revision stresses the *reason* for Mary's objection:

> Mary objected *when she heard the details of the proposal.*

Each sentence takes advantage of end focus but for a different purpose.

The principle of end focus explains why we begin most of our sentences with the core idea in the main clause and add a sequence of modifiers to it. In conversing, we state the core idea and then push ahead to explanatory details and other new information. What comes at the end of the sentence is stressed even though it appears in a subordinate phrase or clause. The same principle is at work when you coordinate two or more main clauses. A sentence of this type has several peaks of maximum stress or emphasis, not just one.

You need not always begin a sentence with a core clause. You may instead want to give the core idea special emphasis by building to it through the sequence of modifiers that ordinarily follows it. This principle is at work in the preceding sentence beginning with the adverbial clause *When she heard the details of the proposal.* We call this kind of sentence *periodic*, in contrast to the "loose" or *cumulative* sentence that opens with the core clause and then amplifies it. The *mid-branching* sentence achieves a different kind of emphasis by interrupting the core clause with explanatory details. Yet another kind of emphasis is possible with the *inverted* sentence, which reverses the subject and verb. As we will see in the discussion that follows, these different kinds of sentences—cumulative, periodic, mid-branching, and inverted—can give variety to your paragraphs by distributing the points of emphasis.

1 Cumulative sentences

The **cumulative sentence**, sometimes called the "loose" or "right-branching" sentence (because the modifiers follow or branch from the core), opens with the core of the main clause and adds to it a series of explanatory details or afterthoughts:

> *They listened,* all ears and eager minds, picking here and there among the floating ends of narrative, patching together as well as they could fragments of tales that were like bits of poetry or music, indeed were associated with the poetry they had heard or read, with music, with the theater.
> —Katherine Anne Porter, "Old Mortality" (emphasis added)
> *Jockeys bounced lightly,* their knees almost level with the horse's back, rising and falling like a rubber ball.
> —Katherine Anne Porter (emphasis added)

Both of these sentences state the core idea immediately and then amplify the idea with a series of exact details. Both push forward to new information about the subject.

When a sentence consists of two or more coordinated clauses, the details of the first idea lead into the second and the two coordinate ideas form a single unified idea:

> *A cloud in the sky suddenly lighted* as if turned on by a switch; *its reflection just as suddenly materialized on the water upstream,* flat and floating, so that I couldn't see the stream bottom, or life in the water under the cloud.
> —Annie Dillard, *Pilgrim at Tinker Creek* (emphasis added)

The trailing modifiers in this sentence may be grammatically subordinate, but they contain important information. End focus keeps our attention on these explanatory or amplifying details.

2 Periodic sentences

In the **periodic sentence** (sometimes called a "left-branching" sentence because the modifiers come before the core clause), you take advantage of end focus to give unusual emphasis to an idea or to generate surprise. This effect is possible because the full sense or meaning is incomplete until the period of the sentence is reached:

Unusual Emphasis
Water is a universal symbol. Tamed and trickling out of the tap, softened and fluoridated, warmed in the boiler by fires burning million-year-old oil, it is still not quite a commodity.
—Elizabeth Janeway, "Water"

Surprise
Head erect, a prompt payer of taxes, yearly subscriber to the preacher's salary, land owner and father of a family, employer, a hearty good fellow among men, *Mr. Thompson knew*, without putting it into words, *that he had been going steadily down hill.*
—Katherine Anne Porter, "Noon Wine" (emphasis added)

These sentences build to the core idea through a series of modifiers.

The dramatic effect natural to the periodic sentence lessens when the delayed core idea is lengthy:

Starting from the greatest city in the world, almost invisible on a fair-sized map of the continent, one must push the wheels for three quarters of a day before reaching the midland seas that are the country's crown.
—Jacques Barzun, "Innocents at Home"

The periodic sentence is sometimes shorter than Janeway's and sometimes longer than Barzun's. Most writers today use the periodic sentence for special emphasis only. And most, like Barzun, keep the opening modifiers short to avoid making the sentence top-heavy—a risk to the writer in opening with a long string of modifying phrases and clauses. The periodic sentence is also less common today than the cumulative sentence because in delaying the core subject it tends to make the sentence more formal (unlike the cumulative sentence) and dramatic or suspenseful.

3 Mid-branching sentences

In interrupting the core clause with modifiers, the **mid-branching sentence** resembles the cumulative sentence in suggesting the forward movement of conversation. Like the periodic sentence, the mid-branching sentence generates suspense in delaying the predicate:

> *Science fiction once prophesied*, in its apparently wild flights of fancy, *many of the aerial feats that have come to pass.*
> —Nancy Hale, "The Two-Way Imagination" (emphasis added)
> *The hanging judge*, that evil old man in scarlet robe and horsehair wig, whom nothing short of dynamite will ever teach what century he is living in, but who will at any rate interpret the law according to the books and will in no circumstances take a money bribe, *is one of the many symbolic figures of English.*
> —George Orwell, "England Your England" (emphasis added)

As Orwell's sentence shows, the mid-branching sentence also allows you to group modifiers as a unit, framed by the opening subject and the concluding predicate.

4 Inverted sentences

An **inverted sentence** reverses the subject and predicate. Sentence inversion is a valuable way of highlighting new information by placing it at the end of the sentence:

> Near to her in the boat, and clearly visible to her although she was not looking at them, *were Willy and Theo.* Perhaps she could perceive them so sharply because their image had occurred so often during the terrible confusions and indecisions of the afternoon and evening.
> —Iris Murdoch, *The Nice and the Good* (emphasis added)

An inverted sentence can be awkward and unfocused if it opens with a chain of modifiers that gives diverse information about the subject:

Awkward	Revised
Ordered by the judge to stand at the bar, their hands in cuffs, their heads bowed, were the young man and woman arrested the night before.	Their hands in cuffs, their heads bowed, the young man and woman arrested the night before were ordered by the judge to stand at the bar.

Revised
The judge ordered the young man and woman arrested the night before, their hands in cuffs, their heads bowed, to stand before the bar.

The sentence to the left rightly stresses the identity of the people at the bar by putting that information at the end. But the sentence is awkward because the information is diverse and the focus is blurred: we are given details about the order of the judge, immediately followed by details of the appearance of the man and woman. The first of the revised sentences in the right column focuses on the order of the judge. The second revised sentence focuses on the condition of the man and woman. In revising sentences like this one, you need to experiment with various arrangements to gain the focus you want.

EXERCISE

Identify the following sentences as cumulative, periodic, mid-branching, or inverted. Then rewrite two of them, altering their structure and, if necessary, rephrasing sentence elements. Briefly explain how the rewritten sentences differ in emphasis from the originals.

Example:

Periodic sentence:
Living in the modern world, clothed and muffled, forced to convey our sense of our bodies in terms of remote symbols like walking sticks and umbrellas and handbags, it is easy to lose sight of the immediacy of the human body plan.

—Margaret Mead, *Male and Female*

Cumulative sentence:
It is easy to lose sight of the immediacy of the human body plan, living in the modern world, clothed and muffled, forced to convey our sense of our bodies in terms of remote symbols like walking sticks and umbrellas and handbags.

1. All matter, and even the seemingly smooth flow of light itself, is grainy, all made of tiny units of one sort or another whose myriad combinations and interrelations weave the fabric of events.
   —Philip Morrison, "Cause, Chance and Creation"

2. Around us on every side, in the clear, cool September light, rose the roofs and spires of London. Above them were already slowly rising thirty or forty cylindrical balloons.
   —Winston S. Churchill, *The Gathering Storm*

3. Each human being is a superbly constructed, astonishingly compact, self-ambulatory computer—capable on occasion of independent decision making and real control of his or her environment.
   —Carl Sagan, *Broca's Brain*

4. The tragic, the trivial, the violent, the easily grasped and understood—these were and continue to be the staples of broadcasting, as they are in all of the mass media.
   —Robert Lewis Shayon, *The Crowd-Catchers*

5. Miranda and Maria, disheartened by the odds, by their first sight of their romantic Uncle Gabriel, whose language was so coarse, sat listlessly without watching, their chances missed, their dollars gone, their hearts sore.
   —Katherine Anne Porter, "Old Mortality" ■

13b Varying sentence length

Sentences vary in length from a few words to more than fifty. How long should a sentence be? Is there a limit to sentence length that you should observe?

Some features of sentence style are determined by convention or social agreement as well as by individual preference. Many contemporary writers favor long sentences to express their ideas. Some twentieth-century writers of fiction have produced sentences a page or more in length; others have written a page or more of very short sentences. An increasing number of today's writers favor short, lightly modified sentences.

Short sentences have their uses, but so do long sentences. The belief that a sequence of short sentences (like a sequence of short paragraphs) is easier to read than a sequence of long sentences is mistaken. A string of disconnected short sentences can be difficult to read, and so can a long sentence. Whether long or short, a sentence is easy to read when it presents a sequence of ideas and details with clarity and conciseness. A highly effective long sentence may express a single continuous idea, with pauses for qualifications and explanatory detail.

1 Effective long sentences

You can do many things with a long sentence that you can't do with short sentences. A **long sentence** can convey a single, unbroken impression through a series of connected details:

> If you happen to be in Hoboken at six in the morning, you can stand on a broad wharf made of cobblestone and concrete, part of which is collapsing into the Hudson River, and look across three-quarters of a mile of open water at Manhattan, a blue silhouette against a sickly-pink sky, and see to your right the World Trade Center, then Brooklyn and, dimly, the Verrazano Bridge; to your left you can see all the way to the George Washington Bridge.
>
> —"Hoboken Terminal," Talk of the Town,
> *The New Yorker*, August 22, 1983

This cumulation of detail compresses a single moment's viewing: we look across the Hudson from the Hoboken wharf—first at the Manhattan skyline, across the river, then south to the Verrazano Bridge, and finally north. Breaking up this sentence would destroy this single focus.

You can also show simultaneous action in a long sentence, as in this description of caged chimpanzees in a research lab:

> As we approached the nearest cage, its two inmates bared their teeth and with incredible accuracy let fly great sweeping arcs of spittle, fairly drenching the lightweight suit of the facility's director. They then uttered a staccato of short shrieks, which echoed down the corridor to be repeated and amplified by other caged chimps, who had certainly not seen us, until the corridor fairly shook with the screeching and banging and rattling of bars.
>
> —Carl Sagan, *The Dragons of Eden*

This description would lose its effectiveness if it were broken down into separate sentences.

Grouping ideas and details into a long sentence can provide a single focus. A paragraph that groups ideas and details into a series of well-constructed sentences is easier to read than a choppy paragraph.

2   Effective short sentences

Short sentences also have an important place in the paragraph. They are useful in highlighting key ideas or, as in the following paragraph, the topic idea:

> A story is not merely an image of life, but of life in motion—specifically, the presentation of individual characters moving through their particular experiences to some end that we may accept as meaningful. And the experience that is characteristically presented in a story is that of facing a problem, a conflict. To put it bluntly: *No conflict, no story.*
> —Robert Penn Warren, "Why Do We Read Fiction?"
> (emphasis added)

Short sentences can create a dramatic effect and therefore are most effective when they are used sparingly:

> When I was a boy growing up in the city, I was afraid to walk the streets after dark. Then came years in which I was fearless. I was part of the night. It could hide me, change me, free parts of me that didn't come to life while the sun shone. Now, as close to a man as thirty years have teased me, I feel the old fears returning. I listen. I read. I am convinced the night streets are unsafe. Full circle the darkness is inhabited by a bestiary of threatening shapes that daylight only partially dispels. I sleep with a bayonet under my bed.
> —John Wideman, "Fear in the Streets"

With a string of short sentences, transitions are essential. A paragraph becomes monotonous and confusing when one short idea follows another in a disconnected, choppy manner—a sentence style sometimes referred to as "primer style." Notice how little impact the short sentences to the left have in comparison to the carefully constructed sentences to the right. The author is describing the hunting of wildebeests in the Kalahari Desert, in Southwest Africa:

Choppy

They threw up their heads. They snorted like horses. They galloped away, leaving behind them a great cloud of dust. Gai ran after. His heels were pounding. He was gone in a few great perfect strides. It

Revised

They threw up their heads, snorting like horses, and galloped away, leaving behind them a great cloud of dust. Gai ran after, his heels pounding, and was gone in a few great perfect strides, as if a

was as if a hawk had left us with a few stiff beats of its wings.

hawk had left us with a few stiff beats of its wings.
—Elizabeth Marshall Thomas, *The Harmless People*

By combining a series of related actions into a single sentence, the author sharpens the focus of the paragraph.

A useful guideline is not to break up a long sentence unless you have reason to do so. If you have to read a long sentence twice to understand it, try reducing it to its component ideas and then recasting it. You may wish to keep the ideas in a single sentence or to present them in separate sentences. A good way to keep attention focused on key ideas is to avoid using long or short sentences exclusively in a paragraph.

3 Sentence fragments

Writers occasionally use a **sentence fragment**—usually a detached phrase or clause—for special emphasis:

> Technology has its own inner dynamic. When it was possible that technology could bring off a moon landing, then it was certain that sooner or later, the landing would be brought off. *However much it cost in human lives, dollars, rubles, social effort.*
> —C. P. Snow, "The Moon Landing" (emphasis added)

More common is the detachment of an appositive from the core sentence:

> With each step she feels the painful press of the coins against her foot. *A sweet, endurable, even cherished irritation, full of promise and delicate security.*
> —Toni Morrison, "The Bluest Eye" (emphasis added)

Morrison might have attached this long appositive to the preceding sentence with a colon or dash, but in so doing, she would lose the emphasis:

> With each step she feels the painful press of the coins against her foot—a sweet, endurable, even cherished irritation, full of promise and delicate security.

Morrison detaches the appositive to give it special emphasis.

As with strings of short sentences, the dramatic emphasis achieved through detached phrases and clauses ends quickly. For this reason, fragments are best used sparingly. (See 16b on the weak sentence fragment.)

Revision gives you an opportunity to vary your sentences and tighten their structure. It may take several tries before you discover which ideas to highlight in short sentences. Your decisions will depend both on the content of your sentences and the effect you want to achieve. You probably will want to return to these sentences for additional revision after you have worked through the whole paper and tested the unity and coherence of each of your paragraphs.

Checklist: Sentence Variety

1. Have I taken advantage of beginning focus and end focus in building my sentences?
2. Have I varied my sentences to avoid monotony?
3. Should I recast any of my sentences as cumulative or periodic sentences?
4. If I used sentence inversion, did I do so without making the sentence awkward or blurring the focus?
5. Have I used short sentences effectively in my paragraphs? Can I combine any of my short sentences into longer sentences that group related ideas and details?
6. Do my sentences open with the same words or with similar ones? Should I vary these sentence openers?

EXERCISE

Find examples of very short sentences and possibly sentence fragments in a current magazine article. Find examples also of unusually long sentences. Be ready to discuss their use and effectiveness. ■

  Varying sentence openers

You probably have written a series of sentences that open with the same word—often the personal pronoun *I*. Repeating the same word at the beginning of successive sentences is a valuable way of achieving emphasis and coherence in a paragraph, but excessive repetition can be distracting and monotonous:

Monotonous

```
      Few people know how to listen to music. They
like to hear music playing in the background as
they work. They do not have the patience to listen
to music without doing something else. They do not
take the time to learn about music. They know only
that music is loud or soft, fast or slow.
```

Your sentences won't be monotonous if you vary your opening words, perhaps with modifying or transitional phrases, as in the following revision:

Revised

```
      In America today, few people know how to lis-
ten to music. At work they like to hear music play-
ing in the background. They do not have the pati-
ence to listen to music without doing something
else. Indeed, most do not take the time to learn
about music. They know only that music is loud or
soft, fast or slow.
```

Combining the last two sentences of this revised paragraph will add variety:

```
Knowing only that music is loud or soft, fast or
slow, most do not take the time to learn about
music.
```

Here are other ways to vary your sentence openers:

- Begin with the subject and verb of the main clause:

  Few people know how to listen to music.

- Begin with a prepositional phrase:

  At work they like to hear music playing in the background.

261

- Begin with a transitional adverb:

  Indeed, most do not take the time to learn about music.

- Begin with a participial phrase:

  Knowing only that music is loud or soft, fast or slow . . .

- Begin with a dependent clause:

  Because they know only that music is loud or soft, fast or slow . . .

- Begin with an infinitive phrase:

  To listen to music well, people must know something about its characteristics.

- Begin with an absolute phrase:

  To be sure, listening to music requires concentration.

EXERCISE

Revise the following paragraphs so to vary the openings and the sentences. Add words, phrases, and clauses as needed. Combine sentences to improve concision and focus.

1. I know little about the physical world around me. I know little about the things that grow near my house and how they form what scientists call an "ecosystem." I know little about how people can upset this ecosystem. People used to call this ecosystem the "balance of nature." People talk about flooding and other "natural" disasters. They do not realize that flooding and other "natural" disasters often occur when the ecosystem is upset. I discovered what an ecosystem is when I experienced a natural disaster. Land was cleared near my house to build a shopping mall. All the trees were cut down. Our basement started flooding everytime it rained. Storm sewers in the neighborhood overflowed. I learned a lesson about nature from this experience.

2. Writing is a skill that requires practice. Playing a musical instrument comes no more naturally than writing. Practice is essential. Practice is essential, too, in dancing. Writing calls for a much different kind of practice. The words put on paper must have meaning. The words must form a meaningful whole. The sounds produced in practicing a musical instrument need not form a meaningful whole. Dance steps need not either.

Summary

13a Vary the types of sentences you use in a paragraph to distribute the points of emphasis.

Cumulative sentences stress the core idea at the beginning **(13a 1)**:

> *Jockeys bounced lightly,* their knees almost level with the horse's back, rising and falling like a rubber ball.
> —Katherine Anne Porter

Periodic sentences build to the core idea **(13a 2)**:

> Water is a universal symbol. Tamed and trickling out of the tap, softened and fluoridated, warmed in the boiler by fires burning million-year-old oil, *it is still not a commodity.*
> —Elizabeth Janeway

Mid-branching sentences interrupt the core idea with explanatory details **(13a 3)**:

> *Science fiction once prophesied,* in its apparently wild flights of fancy, *many of the aerial feats that have come to pass.*
> —Nancy Hale

Inverted sentences reverse normal word order to stress new information **(13a 4)**:

> Near to her in the boat, and clearly visible to her although she was not looking at them, *were Willy and Theo.*
> —Iris Murdoch

13b Vary the length of your sentences to increase interest and to maintain focus in your paragraph.

Combine short sentences to revise a choppy paragraph **(13b 1)**.

Use a moderate number of short sentences for special emphasis or dramatic effect **(13b 2)**.

Use sentence fragments sparingly for special emphasis **(13b 3)**.

13c Vary your sentence openers to avoid monotony.

Parallelism, Balance, Antithesis 14

In this chapter, we turn to another important feature of effective sentences—parallelism. Balance and antithesis are special uses of parallelism that highlight similar and contrasting ideas.

14a Parallelism

Parallelism is a natural part of the way you construct sentences. When you coordinate subjects and other sentence elements, you use the same (or parallel) grammatical structure. Usually you do so without being aware of the process. Sometimes, though, parallelism requires special attention, such as when you omit necessary words or use parallelism in a misleading way. By showing that certain words, phrases, and clauses have the same function in the sentence, parallelism helps to give ideas proper emphasis, to clarify their relationships, and to make the sentence concise and pleasing to read.

1 Parallel words, phrases, and clauses

Words, phrases, and clauses that serve the same grammatical function in the sentence take the same grammatical form:

skate	to skate	skating	while skating
ski	to ski	skiing	while skiing
sled	to sled	sledding	while sledding

Coordinating conjunctions (9e) join these parallel forms into parallel subjects, verbs, complements, and modifiers:

Parallel Subjects
Skating, skiing, and sledding are popular winter sports.

Parallel Verbs and Complements
I usually *ride my bike to school* but *drive my car to work.*

Parallel Modifiers
I enjoy hiking *when the weather is sunny* but not *when it's raining.*

When you begin a series like the preceding ones, you usually continue the series by using the same grammatical forms but you do not repeat words or phrases that are understood. For example, in the following sentence it is not necessary to repeat the phrase *you have to*:

To make a good fire outdoors, you have to *use dry wood, use plenty of kindling,* and *stack the wood properly.*

In most cases, your ear tells you when a sentence lacks parallelism. The following sentences to the left are awkward and unemphatic and clearly nonparallel. The parallel sentences to the right are emphatic, clear, and concise:

Nonparallel

Dry wood, plenty of kindling, and *stack the wood properly* to make a good fire.

I usually use dry wood, *plenty of kindling,* and stack the wood properly.

I make a fire by using dry wood, *use plenty of kindling,* and *stack the wood properly.*

Parallel

Dry wood, plenty of kindling, and proper stacking make a good fire. [*parallel subjects*]

I usually use dry wood, use plenty of kindling, and stack the wood properly. [*parallel verbs*]

I make a fire by using dry wood, using plenty of kindling, and stacking the wood properly. [*parallel complements*]

When parallel words, phrases, and clauses follow **correlative conjunctions** (*either/or, neither/nor, not only/but also*) they have the same grammatical form:

> We're either *going hiking* this weekend or *going swimming*—we haven't decided.
> Either *we're going hiking* or *we're going swimming.*
> We haven't decided whether *to go hiking* or *to go swimming.*
> We're not only *going on a hike* but also *going swimming.*

Sentences that lack parallelism are awkward or unclear:

Awkward	**Revised**
We're going either *to hike* or *swimming.*	We're going either *to hike* or *to swim.*

The correlative conjunctions *either/or* and *neither/nor* occur most frequently in formal writing. In informal speech and writing, they are often omitted:

> We're going hiking or swimming.

2 Uses of parallelism

Parallelism is used to give equal emphasis to ideas and details and to make sentences concise:

> It was when I found out I had to talk *that school became a misery, that the silence became a misery.*
> —Maxine Hong Kingston, *The Woman Warrior*
> (emphasis added)

> There we chanted together, voices rising and falling, loud and soft, *some boys shouting, everybody reading together, reciting together* and not alone with one voice.
> —Maxine Hong Kingston (emphasis added)

> Most commonly we come to books with blurred and divided minds, asking *of fiction that it shall be true, of poetry that it shall be false, of biography that it shall be flattering, of history that it shall enforce our own prejudices.*
> —Virginia Woolf, "How Should One Read a Book?"
> (emphasis added)

Parallelism is also used to join a large number of related ideas into a concise, emphatic sentence like the following:

> Apart from ethnic differences, the very nature of migrancy makes it possible to isolate certain values and social characteristics commonly found among

Parallel
phrases

migrants: a spirit of resignation; a sense of being trapped; an astonishing lack of bitterness; a fierce family loyalty; a buoyant, often subtle wit; a tendency to spend money, when they have it, to meet not only immediate needs but immediate desires; a longing to be somebody, manifested sometimes as a blatant groping for status, more often as a craving for recognition as a human being; a longing for a better life for their children; a quick and generous sympathy for neighbors in trouble; a high incidence of stamina and courage.

—Louisa R. Shotwell, *The Harvesters*

In constructing paragraphs, parallelism is useful in highlighting ideas and details of equal importance in adjacent sentences:

Today Rodney's Landing wears the cloak of vegetation which has caught up this whole land *for the third time, or the fourth, or the hundredth. There is something Gothic* about the vines, in their structure in the trees—*there are arches,* flying buttresses, towers of vines, with trumpet flowers swinging in them for bells and staining their walls. *And there is something of a warmer grandeur* in their very abundance—*stairways and terraces and whole hanging gardens* of green and flowering vines, with a Babylonian babel of hundreds of creature voices that make up the silence of Rodney's Landing.

—Eudora Welty, *The Eye of the Story* (emphasis added)

Parallelism helps in yet other ways to construct effective sentences and paragraphs. It can add coherence and balance to sentences and paragraphs, highlight similar or contrasting ideas, and make the relationships among items in a list or set of directions easier to understand.

Coherence. You can add coherence to your writing by using similar or parallel phrases to describe a sequence of ideas. When you state your ideas in parallel phrases, you help the reader in following your train of thought. You may also find formal transitions (*similarly, likewise*) unnecessary. Notice how the parallel phrases *there is* and *there are* connect the series of impressions in Welty's paragraph, making formal transitions unnecessary.

Comparison and contrast. Parallelism is essential in comparison and contrast. Parallel words and phrases highlight the similarities and differences between the people, things, or ideas being compared. (See 6f for examples of effective uses of parallelism in paragraphs of comparison and contrast.)

Lists and outlines. The items in lists, recipes, and sets of directions will stand out if you arrange them in parallel order:

> Making a perfect omelet
>> Using fresh eggs, milk, and butter
>> Heating the pan
>> Mixing the eggs and milk
>> Adding the butter and mixture to the hot pan
>> Turning the eggs quickly . . .

Topic and sentence outlines also use parallel phrases and clauses to show the relationships among ideas and details (see 3e).

Stylistic and rhythmic effect. Parallelism is a means of achieving sentence balance and antithesis—of giving ideas special emphasis and of giving sentences rhythm and a pleasing balance. Sentence balance and antithesis, special uses of parallelism, are discussed in detail later in the chapter (14c).

EXERCISE

Complete each of the following sentences by creating a pattern with the italicized words. Make sure that the completed sentences are parallel.

> Example
> The dog *raced out of the house*, leaped into the parked car, and jumped into the back seat where the children sat.

1. He was tired of *mowing the lawn*
2. We need to *trim our spending*
3. *Either* we go to the movies
4. We *either* go the movies
5. We are going *either* to the movies
6. We are *not only* going to the movies
7. *Not only* are we going to the movies
8. *Whether* we go to the movies
9. She is *both* president of the club
10. We *neither* elected him vice president

14b Faulty parallelism

When revising your sentences for parallel structure, make sure that words, phrases, and clauses serving the same function in the sentence have the same grammatical structure. A sentence that sounds awkward or unclear may lack necessary parallelism or the parallelism of the sentence may be misleading.

1 Missing parallelism

In correcting sentences that lack necessary parallelism, look for structures that have the same grammatical function in each sentence. Note the faulty parallelism in the following sentence:

Faulty Parallelism
She believed her plan would succeed and which would earn her a promotion.

The first dependent clause [*that*] *her plan would succeed* is the direct object of *believed*. The second dependent clause *which would earn her a promotion* is also a direct object of *believed*. Elements in a series or pair of elements need to be parallel:

Revised
She believed [that] her plan would succeed and [that it] would earn her a promotion.

Lack of parallelism following correlative conjunctions is usually easier to revise:

Faulty Parallelism
Jim and his wife are learning not only *Italian* but also are *learning French.*

Revised
Jim and his wife are learning not only *Italian* but also French. [*stress on the languages*]
Jim and his wife are not only *learning* Italian but are also *learning French.* [*stress on the act of learning*]

269

Often the addition of a missing relative pronoun, preposition, or article corrects a sentence that lacks parallelism:

Missing Relative Pronoun
We stopped to repair the rental car we were driving to Detroit and had broken down twice on the way.

Revised
We stopped to repair the rental car *that* we were driving and *that* had broken down twice on the way.

Missing Preposition
We decided not to stay at the motel on the lake or the road we had passed.

Revised
We decided not to stay at the motel on the lake or *on* the road we had passed.

Missing Article
We cooked a large slice of bacon and egg.

Revised
We cooked a large slice of bacon and *an* egg.

2 Misleading parallelism

Sentences may sound awkward or be misleading if parallel phrases and clauses do not express parallel ideas:

Awkward
He wants *to learn chess* and *to find enough time* to do so.

Revised
He *wants to learn chess* and *hopes to find enough time* to do so.

The awkward sentence to the left shifts from what the person wants (*to learn chess*) to what the person requires (*to have enough time to do so*). The revised sentence clarifies the meaning by adding the necessary verb to the second part of the sentence.

The shift in meaning is not as obvious in the following sentence to the left. The subject complements seem parallel in idea but are not:

Awkward
She is anxious about the interview and determined not to call us unless it goes well.

Revised
She is anxious about the interview and *is* determined not to call us unless it goes well.

The sentence to the left shifts from what the person feels (*is anxious about the interview*) to what she plans to do (*is deter-*

mined not to call us). The simple addition of *is* makes the meaning exact.

Checklist: Achieving Parallelism

1. Can I highlight any words, phrases, or clauses by using a coordinated or parallel series?
2. Are the series I have used parallel in structure?
3. Can I use parallelism to highlight similar or contrasting ideas?
4. Can I use parallelism to give equal emphasis to ideas and details of the same importance?
5. Have I checked my sentences for missing parallelism and misleading parallelism?
6. Should I use balance and antithesis for additional highlighting of similar or contrasting ideas?

EXERCISE

Identify and correct the faulty parallelism in the following sentences.

Example
We left the expressway at the third exit, drove two miles down the highway, *turning* at the gas station to the lake.

Revised
We left the expressway at the third exit, drove two miles down the highway, *and turned* at the gas station to the lake.

1. They know that a nice house costs money and which is hard to find unless you have enough for a down payment.
2. Either we look for a new car or spend money fixing our old one.
3. The house needs a coat of paint, new window sashes, and expensive new roof.
4. She is not only good in math but is in political science and French.
5. You need patience to train a dog, make it sit on command, and not jumping on people.

6. To train a dog, you need both patience and the dog needs to see your firmness.
7. The dog doesn't know whether to sit or do you want it to lie down.
8. She wants not so much to train the dog as it should not jump on people.
9. The committee made the decision to support her candidacy and to notify her of its decision.
10. I am ready whenever you are and when John is. ∎

14c Balance and antithesis

Parallelism emphasizes the similarities or differences among ideas in a series. These similarities or differences can be highlighted further by using parallelism to give the sentence balance. One kind of sentence balances or gives equal weight to similar or complementary ideas. A second kind of sentence gives equal weight to antithetical or contrasting ideas. **Balance** and **antithesis** are most often used in a single sentence or adjacent sentences, but they can also be extended throughout a paragraph.

Since balance and antithesis create highly emphatic sentences, they are less commonly used in contemporary writing than other sentence structures. They nevertheless have important uses. Expository writing that employs comparison and contrast uses moderately balanced sentences. Occasionally, heavy balance and antithesis are used in political addresses and other persuasive writing. In your own writing, you want to use balance and antithesis when your ideas warrant special emphasis and a highlighting of their similarities and differences.

1 Uses of sentence balance

In a balanced sentence, phrases and clauses of *similar* structure and length emphasize similar ideas. In some sentences, all elements of the sentence are exactly parallel in structure and length:

> When young people are as free to walk out of a classroom where they are bored by a dull teacher as grown-up people are to walk

out of a theater where they are bored by a dull playwright, the schools will be far more crowded than the theaters, and the teachers far more popular than the actors.

—George Bernard Shaw, *Sham Education*

Here are the parallel phrases and clauses:

When young people are as free to walk out of a classroom where they are bored by a dull teacher	as grown-up people are [free] to walk out of a theater where they are bored by a dull playwright
the schools will be far more crowded than the theaters	the teachers [will be] far more popular than the actors

Few writers today follow Shaw in balancing sentences so exactly. The following passage is more typical of the sentence balance found in contemporary prose:

The Greeks were *keenly aware, terribly aware,* of *life's uncertainty* and the *imminence of death.* Over and over again they emphasize *the brevity and the failure of all human endeavor, the swift passing of all that is beautiful and joyful.*

—Edith Hamilton, *The Greek Way* (emphasis added)

In contrast to Shaw's, not all of Hamilton's parallel phrases are the same length. The two sentences point up ideas in an intense way, but the varying length of Hamilton's phrases reduces the intensity somewhat. In both of Hamilton's sentences, ideas and sentence balance and reinforce each other. Similarity in ideas makes us sensitive to the balance, at the same time that the rhythm created by this balance highlights the similarity. Sentence balance requires attention to the arrangement of sentence elements.

Most contemporary writers follow Hamilton in using sentence balance moderately for dramatic emphasis. A heavily balanced sentence like Shaw's is more common in legal documents, treatises, technical discussions addressed to professional audience, and public addresses, where the occasion warrants a strong, sometimes highly emotional emphasis:

Let the word go forth from this time and place, to friend and foe alike, that the torch has been passed to a new generation of Americans—*born in this century, tempered by war, disciplined by a hard and bitter peace, proud of our ancient heritage*—and unwilling to witness or permit the slow undoing of those human rights *to which this Nation has always been committed,* and *to which we are committed today at home and around the world.*

—President John F. Kennedy, Inaugural Address, 1961 (emphasis added)

If you have occasion to use sentence balance, use a moderate balance unless you wish to achieve an emphasis as strong or as emotional as President Kennedy's. If you do use a heavily balanced sentence, try to lighten the stress of surrounding sentences. Your sentences will be effective if they don't depart too often from the looser patterns of everyday speech and writing.

2 Uses of antithesis

Antithesis is the balancing of *contrasting* phrases and clauses:

> We observe today *not a victory of party but a celebration of freedom*—symbolizing *an end as well as a beginning*—signifying *renewal as well as change*.
> —President John F. Kennedy (emphasis added)

Like the balancing of similar phrases and clauses, antithesis can be carried through a series of sentences:

> An unjust law is a code that is out of harmony with the moral law. To put it in the terms of St. Thomas Aquinas: An unjust law is a human law that is not rooted in eternal law and natural law. *Any law that uplifts human personality is just. Any law that degrades human personality is unjust.* All segregation statutes are unjust because segregation distorts the soul and damages the personality. It *gives the segregator a false sense of superiority* and *the segregated a false sense of inferiority*.
> —Martin Luther King, Jr., "Letter from Birmingham Jail," 1963 (emphasis added)

A less pointed antithesis is common in expository prose that contrasts ideas:

> If a future directed by America was not wholly clear, neither was it a blank, and those who knew that nation best were satisfied that it meant intensely and meant good. For the America that would shape the unknown future was an America whose character had been formed in the known past, and if the lineaments of that character had not yet hardened into fixed patterns, they were at least recognizable and familiar.
> —Henry Steele Commager, *The American Mind*

As the King passage shows, antithesis can have a highly dramatic effect. Like sentence balance, antithesis makes sentences emphatic as well as highly concise. These qualities make it particularly useful in summary statements and conclusions:

> Civilization does not die, it migrates; it changes its habitat and its dress, but it lives on. The decay of one civilization, as of one

individual, makes room for the growth of another; life sheds the old skin, and surprises death with fresh youth.

—Will Durant, *The Life of Greece*

EXERCISE

Rewrite the following sentences to loosen the balance and antithesis, and be ready to discuss what is gained or lost as a result:

1. The young are developing superior powers for sharing their attention. Many youngsters watch one game on television while listening to another over the radio through transistor headphones. Brokers can watch the ticker while talking over the telephone, most adults can confer while eating lunch, and mothers learn to mend while keeping watch on a playground bully.

   —Caroline Bird, *The Crowding Syndrome*

2. Where necessity ends curiosity begins, and no sooner are we supplied with everything that nature can demand, than we sit down to contrive artificial appetites.

   —Samuel Johnson, "On Idle Curiosity" ■

Summary

14a Use parallelism to make your sentences clear and concise.

Make words, phrases, and clauses that perform the same function in the sentence parallel in form **(14a 1)**:

Skating, skiing, and sledding are popular winter sports.

Make words, phrases, and clauses follow parallel correlative terms **(14a 1)**:

We are either *going hiking* this weekend or *going swimming*.

Use parallelism to give equal emphasis to ideas of the same importance **(14a 2)**:

It was when I found out I had to talk *that school became a misery, that the silence became a misery.*

—Maxine Hong Kingston

14b   Revise sentences that contain faulty parallelism.

Supply missing relative pronouns, articles, and prepositions to complete parallel structures (**14b 1**):

Awkward	**Revised**
He wants *to learn chess* and *have enough time* to do so.	He wants *to learn chess* and *hopes to have enough time* to do so.

Avoid misleading parallelism (**14b 2**):

Misleading	**Revised**
She is anxious about the interview and eager to call us if it goes well.	She is anxious about the interview and *is* eager to call us if it goes well.

14c   Use sentence balance and antithesis to highlight ideas.

Sentence balance highlights similar ideas in the sentence (**14c 1**):

> Over and over again they emphasize the brevity and the failure of all human endeavor, the swift passing of all that is beautiful and joyful.
>
> —Edith Hamilton

Antithesis gives equal emphasis to contrasting ideas of the same weight in the sentence (**14c 2**):

> We observe today *not a victory of party but a celebration of freedom*—symbolizing *an end as well as a beginning*—signifying *renewal as well as change*.
>
> —President John F. Kennedy

Concise Sentences

15

An effective sentence is a clear sentence, exact and unambiguous in meaning. It is also a **concise sentence,** stating an idea without elaboration that adds nothing to the meaning. In the give and take of conversation, you may pause to clarify a statement or repeat a point. But you don't always choose words as you speak to make your statements clear and concise. In drafting a paper, you may write in the same way you speak. At later stages of writing, however, you take the opportunity to consider the clarity and concision of your sentences. Unlike a conversation, a piece of writing offers no opportunity for restatement, once you give the final edited paper to your reader. It is therefore essential to put yourself in the place of your reader in the course of revising your sentences.

15a Deletion and reduction

Deleting unnecessary words and **reducing** unnecessarily long phrases and clauses will help to unify your sentences and make them clear and concise. Deletion also makes it easier to expand the sentence with modifiers. The more unnecessary words a sentence contains, the fewer details and ideas you can add.

1 Deleting words

We normally delete identical subjects, verbs, predicates, and complements to avoid needless repetition in sentences:

Identical Subjects
The coach is talking excitedly, and *the coach* is waving his arms. He is talking to the rival coach.

Revised
The coach is waving his arms and talking excitedly to the rival coach.

Identical Predicates
The coach *is talking* excitedly, and the rival coach *is talking* excitedly, too. They *are talking* about the winning field goal.

Revised
The two coaches *are talking* excitedly about the winning field goal.

Identical Complements
The coach *is a native Chicagoan* and the team captain *is a native Chicagoan.* They roomed together at college. They are friendly rivals as a result of their long friendship.

Revised
Native Chicagoans and college roommates, the two coaches have long been friendly rivals.

Deletion also helps you avoid ambiguous pronoun reference:

Wordy
Explaining to a child why wars happen is difficult for *someone. They* lack experience and knowledge.

Revised
Children lack the experience and knowledge to understand why wars happen.

You can also add modifiers to this revised sentence without loss of unity or concision:

Children lack the experience and knowledge, of people and life, to understand why wars happen.

2 Deleting clauses

Reducing clauses to phrases is another useful way of making sentences clear and concise. Compare the following sentences:

Wordy	**Revised**
The woman is tall and *she is also red-headed,* and *she is instructing* the team of runners consisting of boys and girls.	The tall, red-haired woman is instructing the boy-and-girl running team.

The sentence to the right gains focus and clarity by reducing independent clauses to modifying phrases.

The same reduction is possible with dependent clauses:

Wordy	**Revised**
As she demonstrated how to gain speed on the track, she lowered her head.	Demonstrating how to gain speed on the track, she lowered her head.

Notice the different emphasis given the modifying phrase when it precedes the main clause:

Lowering her head, she demonstrated how to gain speed on the track.

You can also achieve clarity and conciseness in your sentences by reducing clauses to phrases:

Wordy	**Revised**
Beethoven, who was becoming increasingly deaf, wrote a famous letter to his brothers that concerned his affliction.	Becoming increasingly deaf, Beethoven wrote a famous letter to his brothers concerning his affliction.
The box that is on the chair contains books. They are on World War II.	The box on the chair contains books on World War II.

Independent clauses can be reduced to a single clause if they contain closely related ideas:

Doctors are increasing rapidly in *number,* but *doctors are not increasing* in rural areas of the United States, and they are needed in these areas.	The number of doctors is increasing rapidly in the United States but not in rural areas where they are needed.

Once again, the more concise your sentence, the more you can expand it without loss of focus or clarity:

> The number of doctors is increasing rapidly in the United States but not in rural areas—particularly in the Southeast and the West—where they are needed.

3 Deleting phrases

Reducing and subordinating phrases is another way to make sentences clear and concise:

Wordy	Revised
The foreman sat in the front row of the box reserved for the jury. He listened intently to the witness.	The foreman, sitting in the front row of the jury box, listened intently to the witness.

The following sentences have the same meaning, but phrase reduction changes the emphasis or focus of the sentence:

In his loneliness Beethoven found solace in nature.	The lonely Beethoven found solace in nature.

The sentence to the left emphasizes Beethoven's loneliness; the sentence to the right focuses instead on the solace found by the deaf composer. In the following example, the sentence to the right gives greater emphasis to Beethoven's deafness—the cause of his resolute character:

Beethoven as a deaf man was more resolute in character than Beethoven as a man in possession of his hearing.	Deaf, Beethoven was more resolute in character than Beethoven possessed of hearing.

EXERCISE

Delete words and reduce clauses and phrases where necessary to make the following sentences concise:

1. It rained last year on the Fourth of July, and it rained the previous Fourth, but I don't think it will rain this coming Fourth of July.
2. The sky filled with clouds put a halt to our picnic in the backyard. We had been planning a long time to have the picnic in the backyard. We moved the picnic into the house.

3. Good summers come in cycles, and bad summers come in cycles. Good winters and bad winters come in cycles, too. These cycles occur especially in the Midwest.
4. Stating the matter as clearly as I know how, I believe the play cannot succeed even if it is revised.
5. The explanation that the defendant gave failed to convince the jury.

15b Repetitive sentences

Emphatic repetition of words and phrases is common in advertisements that continually remind the viewer of the name of a company or product. We find the same emphatic repetition in political statements like the following, by British Prime Minister Winston S. Churchill, at the start of World War II:

> Victory at all costs, victory in spite of all terror, victory however long and hard the road may be; for without victory there is no survival. (May 13, 1940)

Repetition is effective when it is used sparingly for special emphasis; however, continuous repetition blurs the focus of a paragraph or essay, reduces its conciseness, and quickly tires the reader.

1 Necessary repetition

A sentence is wordy if it needlessly repeats a name:

> *Johnson* explained the budget proposal; then *Johnson* turned the meeting over to his assistant.

Johnson's name is repeated needlessly. We usually delete the name in a successive clause, substituting a pronoun or omitting the name because it is understood:

> *Johnson* explained the budget proposal, then [*he*] turned the meeting over to his assistant.

However, a sentence will be ambiguous or confusing if it fails to specify one of several antecedents or omits essential words. In this case, repetition is often necessary to avoid ambiguity:

281

Ambiguous
Johnson explained the budget
proposal, then turned the
meeting over to his as-
sistant, who said *he* would
comment on other features
of the budget later.

Clear
Johnson explained the budget
proposal, then turned the
meeting over to his as-
sistant, who said that *Johnson* would comment on
other features of the
budget later.

Give the job to Johnson not
to Wilson, unless *he* protests.

Give the job to Johnson, not
to Wilson, unless *Johnson*
protests.

Implied words may be deleted to make a sentence concise.
The relative pronoun *that* is commonly deleted in sentences
like the following:

We know [*that*] John isn't coming.

But the pronoun should be stated to avoid confusion in reading
the sentence:

We just found the book assigned is out of print.
We just found *that* the book assigned is out of print.

If the pronoun is omitted, the reader may stumble over the
words that open the sentence:

We just found the book assigned . . .
We just found *that* the book assigned . . .

(See 11c on vague and ambiguous pronoun reference and
18b on omitted words.)

2   Redundancy

A **redundant statement** uses different words to repeat an idea
needlessly:

Redundant
This morning we will *now* search for the missing cash.
The *result* of the investigation was the *consequent* dismissal of
the cashier and his *resulting* arrest.

Your ear probably alerted you to the redundancy of the first
statement but perhaps not to that of the second. In the first
sentence, the words *this morning* and *now* say the same thing.
In the second, the words *result*, *consequent*, and *resulting* have
the same meaning. Here are satisfactory revisions of the
sentences:

Revised
This morning we will search for the missing cash.
The result of the investigation was the cashier's dismissal and
arrest.

Redundancy is hard to spot in a sentence like the following:

Redundant
His failure as secretary of state is partly to blame for his ineffective conduct of foreign policy.

This sentence repeats in the predicate what it says in the subject: failure and ineffectiveness are the same thing. Here is a
satisfactory revision of this sentence:

Revised
As secretary of state he failed to conduct foreign policy effectively.

3 Same words, different meanings

Using the same word with different meanings in a sentence
can create momentary confusion and awkwardness:

Awkward	**Revised**
He will *present* the report of the committee *presently*.	He will present the commit-tee report *soon*.
Surely, she is *sure* to come.	She is *sure* to come.
The investigation *reportedly* will lead to a bad *report* on the agency.	The investigation *supposedly* will lead to a bad report on the agency.
I am still *doubtful* about the verdict, but my opinion will *undoubtedly* change.	I am still *skeptical* about the verdict, but my opinion will undoubtedly change.

A sentence may sound awkward even if the repeated words
or phrases have different meanings:

Awkward	**Revised**
In point of fact, we have *the facts* to prove the case.	*Indeed*, we have the facts to prove the case.

EXERCISE

Revise the following paragraph to eliminate unnecessary or awkward repetition:

Prime Minister Winston S. Churchill spoke of "victory at all costs," in his speech to the House of Commons, on May 13, 1940. Prime Minister Churchill spoke also of "victory in spite of all terror." In that same speech, Churchill added in the same sentence that "without victory there is no survival." In the same speech, Prime Minister Churchill made the famous statement, "I have nothing to offer but blood, toil, tears, and sweat," a renowned statement that definitively, more than any other of the wartime prime minister's public pronouncements on Britain's war effort, defined Churchill as Great Britain's leader in war. ∎

15c Nominalized sentences

Nominalization is the process of transforming a verb or adjective into a noun phrase. Note the following examples:

Verb or Adjective	Noun Phrase
he says	his statement that
they fight	their fighting
I paint	my paintings of
she corrects	her correction of
to correct	the correcting of
the painful cut	the pain of the cut
the foolish remark	the foolishness of the remark
named the boat	the naming of the boat
explained the mistake	the explanation of the mistake

Nominalization is useful when you want to focus on the action being described in a sentence. Consider the following statements:

I *painted* the house in a month.
It took me a whole month *to paint* the house.
The painting of the house took me a month.

The word *painting* nominalizes the verb *painted* and the infinitive *to paint*. The nominalized subject of the third sentence allows the writer to focus on the house painting as an activity. Nominalization gives the act of painting weight and emphasis.

Nominalization is often used to describe technical processes:

A further refinement of servo control is possible through the addition of a *phase-locked loop* (PLL), perhaps in conjunction with a quartz-crystal oscillator.
—Alan Lofft, "Choosing a Turntable," *Stereo Review*, May 1983

Lofft might have written:

> Manufacturers can refine servo control by adding a phase-locked loop. . . .

But the desired emphasis is lost in this rephrasing. The focus of Lofft's discussion in his original statement is on the refinement of servo control, not on the manufacturers.

Nominalization is an important means of emphasis, as the following sentences show:

> The *Fifth Symphony* expresses Beethoven's faith in life.
> The *Fifth Symphony* is an expression of Beethoven's faith in life.

The first sentence focuses on the act of expression, the second sentence on the *Fifth Symphony* itself.

Notice that nominalization may even change the meaning of a sentence. In the second of the following sentences, the writer nominalizes the adjective *expensive* with a change in meaning:

> He bought *an expensive car.*
> He bought a car *at great expense.*

Meaning must be your first concern in deciding whether to nominalize an adjective or verb. Unless your sentence gains in meaning by nominalizing, use an adjective or verb in place of the nominal.

When overused, nominalization can exact a price in conciseness and tone. Nominalized sentences are often wordy, and they create a formal effect often unsuited to a plain statement of fact. They also can sound lofty and authoritative. Of course, an authoritative, impersonal tone may be what the writer wants. Consider the following request for payment of a bill:

> Nonpayment of this bill will necessitate our taking legal action.

This statement is a threat, and threats gain force by sounding impersonal. The full weight of the law presumably stands behind the writer. In general, the more nominalized the sentence, the more objective and the less personal it will sound.

Here are three ways to make overnominalized sentences clear and concise:

1. *Change nouns to verbs:*

Wordy	**Concise**
Their fighting is a frequent occurrence.	They fight a lot.

285

Wordy	**Concise**
The idealization of America by immigrants from Eastern Europe occurred in different ways.	Immigrants from Eastern Europe idealized America in different ways.
Nonpayment of this bill will necessitate legal action.	We will sue if you don't pay this bill.

2. *Change nouns to adjectives or adverbs:*

Wordy	**Concise**
Their donation of money to the Cancer Society is an annual occurrence.	They donate money to the Cancer Society annually.
The loudness of the bark awakened the sentry.	The loud bark awakened the sentry.

3. *Reduce prepositional phrases to adjectives or verbals:*

Wordy	**Concise**
It was a day of sunshine.	It was a sunny day. The day was sunny.
We began a period of study for the exam.	We began studying for the exam.

Checklist: Making Your Sentences Concise

1. Can I improve the clarity and concision of my sentences by deleting unnecessary words or reducing unnecessarily long phrases or clauses?
2. Is it necessary to repeat any words to make my sentence clear?
3. Have I repeated any words needlessly or awkwardly?
4. Have I checked my sentences for redundant statements?
5. Do any of my statements create momentary confusion as a result of using the same word with different meanings in the same sentence?
6. Have I nominalized a verb or an adjective needlessly? Can I make any statements less formal or less impersonal by using a verb or adjective instead of a nominal?
7. Do my sentences contain details that have nothing to do with the main point?

8. Have I made a needless or meaningless qualification in any of my sentences?
9. Can I delete any circumlocutions or other wordy phrases?

EXERCISE

In the following sentences, change the nominalized noun phrases to verbs or adjectives. Be ready to discuss how your revisions change the meanings of the sentences.

1. Correction of this paper requires a number of steps.
2. She has experience with music and dance.
3. The falsification of the evidence was a disturbance to the judge.
4. The fact of significance is that no person has received a citation under the new law.
5. The chair is responsible for the submission of the report.
6. Affording an opportunity for discussion is the purpose of the meeting.
7. The appointment of a committee for revision of the bylaws shall be the responsibility of the chair.
8. The supply of the required electric power source and fittings to operate the equipment is the responsibility of the customer.
9. The favor of a response is requested.—a wedding invitation.
10. "The disciplinary power of the university is inherent in its responsibility to protect its educational purposes and processes through the setting of standards of conduct and scholarship for its students and through the regulation of the use of its facilities."—From a statement of university regulations ■

15d Unnecessary details

In revising your sentences, look for **unnecessary details** that have nothing to do with your central idea and may distract your reader:

287

Overly Detailed
President Franklin Delano Roosevelt, former governor of New York, thirty-second president of the United States, and architect of the New Deal, sponsored ambitious social legislation in the 1930s to relieve poverty and unemployment. President Lyndon Baines Johnson, former Senate majority leader, the thirty-sixth president, and architect of the Great Society, sponsored an equally ambitious social legislation in the 1960s.

Journalists occasionally make a statement dramatic by giving the full name and title of an important person. In most instances, however, including name and title is distracting and pretentious. Notice that the first names of President Roosevelt and President Johnson, at first mention of them, must be supplied if the context of discussion (perhaps social welfare in the 1930s and the 1960s) is not sufficient to distinguish them from presidents Theodore Roosevelt and Andrew Johnson. But to understand the points made about them, we don't require their middle names, the number of their presidencies, or the information that Roosevelt was governor of New York and Johnson Senate majority leader.

The following revision gives the information necessary:

Revised
President Roosevelt, architect of the New Deal, and President Johnson, architect of the Great Society, sponsored ambitious social legislation in the 1930s and 1960s, respectively.

In descriptive writing, additional details are not distracting if they make a scene or experience vivid. But these details must be selected and organized carefully. Needless details blur the description instead of enhancing it.

15e Overqualification

Qualification is often necessary to make statements accurate and to avoid overgeneralizing. The italicized qualifications in the following sentences are normal in speech and writing:

With change, *it seemed,* prosperity was coming. Many of the new buildings of Dublin might be unlovely, but *at least* they were earnests of success.

— Jan Morris, *Travels* (emphasis added)

For like it or not, whatever your opinions, the drums of tragedy sound still in Dublin, muffled but unavoidable, as they sound nowhere else on earth.

—Jan Morris

These qualifiers don't clutter the sentences; the author's main idea in each sentence emerges clearly.

Needless qualifiers, however, can draw attention from the main idea of the sentence. The italicized phrases in the following sentence obscure the core idea by delaying it:

Overqualified

It takes no great intelligence, *I should add,* and no great amount of knowledge, *it seems to me,* to realize how impossible *a thing* a flying saucer is.

Qualifiers can also weaken the words modified:

Weak

He is *quite* furious that the bill was passed and *very* determined to work for its appeal.

The following revisions of these sentences gain clarity and concision by omitting the qualifying phrases:

Revised

It takes no great intelligence and no great amount of knowledge to realize how impossible a flying saucer is.

He is furious that the bill was passed and determined to work for its appeal.

EXERCISE

Reduce each sentence to the fewest words possible without changing its original meaning:

1. Though we seldom know the exact reasons why wars occur, we usually know the general reasons why.
2. The book that is second from the left on the first shelf contains the essay that is assigned for Monday.
3. The astronaut whose name is Scott is not the same man as the explorer of the Antarctic whose name is Scott, too.
4. The play that concerns the life of Winston S. Churchill gives a picture of his life that is tragic.
5. The house that is the third from the corner on the north side of the street is where I live.
6. Snow that falls rapidly and is wet is hard to shovel.

289

7. Sores that are red and swollen and painful and hot are in-fected sores.
8. The last person who is in the room should shut the doors and the windows that are open.
9. The part of Italy that is on the border with Switzerland is one of the parts of the country that is the most beautiful.
10. The north of Italy that is in the wide region that includes Milan and Turin is the region of Italy that is industrial.

15f | Circumlocution

Circumlocution means taking the long way around in making a point:

Pretentious
There is a not unlikable actor in the cast who has attracted the interest of all those delighting in the thespian arts. His per-formance is not all one might have been hoping for. It was, in-deed, much less than one might have expected.

The statement attempts to say that a likable actor gave a poor performance. But the writer takes the long way around with the circumlocutions *a not unlikable actor in the cast* and *the interest of all those delighting in* to generate suspense and avoid harsh criticism. Our attention begins to lag as we wait for a specific reference or plain statement of opinion. The phrase *thespian arts* is also circumlocution—a flowery, indirect way of saying *theater* or *the movies*. In trying to avoid the com-monplace statement through an "elegant variation," the writer instead says something pretentious.

A string of inflated phrases can also take the long way around, making a statement difficult to understand:

The quasi-peaceable gentleman of leisure, then, not only con-sumes of the staff of life beyond the minimum required for subsistence and physical efficiency, but his consumption also undergoes a specialization as regards the quality of the goods consumed.
—Thorstein Veblen, *The Theory of the Leisure Class*

Note the needless substitution of *staff of life* for the simple *bread*, the needless repetition of *consume, consumption,* and *consumed,* and substitution of *as regards the* for the simple *of*.

The phrase *gentleman of leisure,* joined with other noun phrases, weighs down the sentence. Veblen is saying that rich people eat more than necessary and are fussy eaters. Probably few readers will understand the sentence even after a second or third reading.

We sometimes use circumlocutions to make a statement sound authoritative, or sometimes to avoid sounding blunt. If you discover circumlocutions in your writing, try restating the idea in plain words, without sounding rude or blunt:

Inflated	**Improved**
The decision cannot be made at this point in time.	Sorry, but I can't decide now.
He is leaving for Atlanta due to the fact that he was offered a job there.	He is leaving for Atlanta where he was offered a job.
She broke the engagement on account of family differences.	She broke the engagement because she didn't like his family.
His childish temper was another factor in the cause of her decision.	She also didn't like his childish temper.
What is your question in regards to?	What are you asking about?
She talked in terms of her impressions of the family.	She gave her impressions of the family.

A great number of popular phrases also engage in circumlocution, inflating sentences without adding to their meaning. The popular circumlocutions in the following list should be avoided in your writing.

Common Circumlocutions to Avoid

a factor in the cause of	in the modern world of today
a reason for why	in the nature of
all things considered	in the process of
as far as can be determined	in this day and age
as to the outcome of	in the nature of
at this point in time	in the process of
by means of	more or less
due to the fact that	no matter what may be said
for the purpose of	not the less because
for the reason that	notwithstanding
in connection with	on account of
in spite of the fact that	with (*or* in) regards to
in terms of	with respect to
in the event of	without regard for

In revising your sentences, you can reduce wordiness in several ways.

- Watch for sentences that have the wordiness or rambling quality of ordinary conversation. Think of your paper as a conversation with your reader—a conversation tighter in its lack of repetition and qualification.
- Don't use qualifiers like *perhaps, maybe,* or *it seems* unless your generalization needs to be limited.
- If you use the words *very* and *quite* to intensify an adjective (*very pretty, quite wet*), try to find a stronger adjective (*beautiful, soaked*).
- Look for repetition in your paragraphs. One sentence may repeat another in different words.
- If your sentences contain strings of phrases (*the donation of a book of great value to the library*), try reducing prepositional phrases to adjectives and transforming noun phrases to verb phrases or adjectives (*donated a valuable book*).
- Look for words with an uncertain meaning in the sentence. They may be redundant or take the long way around in making a statement.

Your writing can be concise without seeming spare or impersonal. Make personal references when these are appropriate, but try not to open too many sentences with *I*. An effective writing style avoids extremes.

EXERCISE

1. Eliminate the circumlocutions in the following sentences. Make the sentences as direct as you can.
   a. In the not unlikely event that the storm blankets the area, we will not venture out.
   b. I want to discuss your policy with regards to work that is presented to you late.
   c. We are in the process of deciding whether to close the office in the event of the impending national celebration.
   d. He explained the change in personnel in terms of the rapid fall in productivity.
   e. There is a not inconsiderable amount of money that exists for the purpose of guaranteeing the election of the candidate.

2. Identify circumlocutions in letters to a newspaper or magazine. Be ready to discuss their effect.

Summary

15a Delete unnecessary words and reduce clauses and phrases to make your sentences concise.

15b Needless repetition can make a sentence wordy.

Revise a sentence that contains needless repetition (**15b 1**):

Repetitious	**Revised**
Johnson explained the proposal; then *Johnson* turned the meeting over to his assistant.	*Johnson* explained the proposal, then turned the meeting over to his assistant.

Repeat a name when a pronoun has two possible antecedents (**15b 1**):

Johnson explained the budget proposal, then turned the meeting over to his assistant, who said that *Johnson* would comment on other features of the budget later.

A redundant statement repeats an idea needlessly in different words (**15b 2**):

Redundant	**Revised**
The *result* of the investigation was the *consequent* dismissal of the cashier and his *resulting* arrest.	The investigation led to the cashier's dismissal and subsequent arrest.

Avoid repeating a word with different meanings (**15b 3**)

Repetitious	**Revised**
He will *present* the report of the committee *presently*.	He will *present* the committee report *shortly*.

15c When nominalized nouns do the work of other parts of speech, sentences become excessively formal and hard to read.

Wordy	**Revised**
He made the statement that he is coming.	He said he is coming.

15d Omit details unrelated to the central idea.

Wordy
President Franklin Delano Roosevelt, former governor of New York, sponsored ambitious social legislation in the 1930s.

Revised
President Franklin Delano Roosevelt sponsored ambitious social legislation in the 1930s.

15e Don't qualify a sentence needlessly.

Overqualified
It takes no great intelligence, *I should add,* and no great amount of knowledge of the subject, *it seems to me,* to realize how impossible *a thing* a flying saucer is.

Revised
It takes no great intelligence and no great amount of knowledge of the subject to realize how impossible a flying saucer is.

15f Circumlocution makes sentences inflated and unclear.

Inflated
She talked in terms of her impressions of the family.

Revised
She gave her impressions of the family.

PART FIVE

CORRECTING
SENTENCES

Sentence Fragments

16

In Part V of the *Handbook* we turn to the faults and problems of most concern during the drafting and revising of papers: sentence fragments, comma splices, fused sentences, dangling and misplaced modifiers, mixed constructions, omissions, and shifts in person and tense. As with faulty pronoun reference, these faults sometimes arise from carrying habits of speech into writing. Because written English lacks some of the resources of speech, it has special rules for writing complete sentences and making their connections exact. You will have more control over your writing if you know what resources are available to you in speaking and writing. We begin, therefore, by considering some of these resources.

16a | Writing and speech

Fragments are faults in writing because they impede communication. But they are not always faults in speech, where we clip or fragment sentences to single out or stress an idea. The following statement by Sam Crawford, a major-league baseball player, is typical of informal speech:

> "Yeah, I'm sort of hard to find. Still bounce around a lot, you know. Always on the move. Probably a hangover from all those years in baseball—Boston today, Detroit tomorrow, never long in one place. I do have a house down in Hollywood, but I can't take that town. Too much smog. Too many cars, all fouling up the air. Can hardly breathe down there. Too many people, too. Have to stand in line everywhere you go. Can't even get a loaf of bread without standing in line."
>
> —Quoted in Lawrence S. Ritter, *The Glory of Their Times*

Sam Crawford's sentences are spontaneous and highly expressive. Your own speech contains the same pauses and halts that punctuate spoken English. To be vital and expressive, written sentences must not depart too widely from the rhythms of speech. Indeed, writers occasionally use clipped sentences—as Crawford does—for special emphasis (see 13b). At the same time, though, these rhythms and speech habits can make written sentences confusing when they momentarily interrupt the flow of ideas. When these habits occur in written English, we call them *fragments* to call attention to the problems. *Comma splices* and *fused* and *stringy sentences* sometimes are also transfers from speech (see Chapter 17). Because it is difficult to reproduce the pauses and intonation of speech, our written sentences must be tighter in structure than the sentences we speak. To communicate effectively in writing, then, we must take care with structure and punctuation.

EXERCISE

Rewrite the statements of Sam Crawford, turning the shortened or clipped sentences and the phrases into complete sentences. Be ready to discuss what is gained or lost in your rewriting.

16b Fragments

If you can't find a core idea or main clause in your sentence, check to see whether you have detached a phrase, clause, or appositive from the previous sentence or the sentence that follows. Join the fragments to the core of the sentence.

1 A test for fragments

The **sentence fragment** is a detached phrase or clause whose meaning depends on the whole sentence. The fragment is usually a dependent clause or a participial phrase like the following:

> when the cruiser turned the corner
> turning the corner

Detached clauses and phrases impede communication in written English because they usually lack clear and immediate reference.

If you have trouble spotting sentence fragments, you can test your sentences to see whether they contain a core or main idea that makes a complete assertion. The following sentence contains a core or main idea, a modifier, and an appositive:

> Walking down the street, the man waved frantically at the car—
> a blue and white police cruiser parked at the curb.

Here is the *core sentence:*

> the man waved frantically at the car

Here is the *modifier:*

> walking down the street

And here is the *appositive*—the phrase that names or identifies the car:

> a police cruiser

The appositive is itself *modified*:

> a blue and white police cruiser parked at the curb

The main sentence makes the assertion that the man waved at a car. By contrast, the appositive—*a blue and white police cruiser parked at the curb*—makes no assertion; it merely identifies the car.

If in doubt whether a group of words constitutes a whole sentence, try turning the words into a yes/no question:

> The man walking down the street waved frantically at the blue
> and white police cruiser parked at the curb, didn't he?

By contrast, the appositive cannot be turned into a yes/no question:

A blue and white police cruiser parked at the curb, didn't he?

Listening to the way you speak a sentence sometimes tells you that you have written a fragment. In speaking the following phrases, you usually do not drop your voice on reaching the end:

walking down the street ⟶
a police cruiser ⟶
a police cruiser parked at the curb ⟶

Notice that the pitch of your voice normally drops when you reach the period of a complete sentence:

The man waved frantically at the car parked at the curb. ⟍

At the end of a question and at the end of an exclamation, your voice also drops in pitch, even though the final word is given greater than ordinary emphasis:

Am I hungry? ⟍
Am I hungry! ⟍

But when you intend to continue the sentence, your voice usually neither rises nor falls. This unchanging pitch is sometimes the signal that your sentence is incomplete.

With the core sentence, you raise the pitch sometimes lightly, sometimes heavily, to signal the subject, verb, or modifier, depending on which word you want to stress:

Who was waving?	The *man* was waving frantically at the car parked at the curb.
What was the man doing?	The man *was waving* frantically at the car parked at the curb.
How was the man waving?	The man was waving *frantically* at the car parked at the curb.

Stress on the first or second word of the sentence occurs when you are answering a question or wish to give the subject special emphasis. Ordinarily, stress falls on the verb or, as in the preceding example, an adverb (*frantically*) or other word you want to emphasize. With fragments you may stress the first word (as well as later words), as in these statements of the baseball player quoted earlier:

still bounce around a *lot,* you know
always on the *move*
probably a *hangover* from all those years in *baseball*
too much *smog*

Here, then, is a possible test of sentence fragments: they sometimes begin with a word pronounced at a higher than ordinary pitch, no matter what other words in the sentence are stressed.

Checklist: Types of Sentence Fragments

1. A subject that lacks a verb
2. A verb that lacks a subject
3. A detached dependent clause (beginning with *because, when, that, which, who,* etc.)
4. A detached modifying phrase (for example, *parked at the curb*)
5. A detached appositive (for example, *a blue and white police cruiser*)
6. A detached absolute phrase (for example, *the street flooding rapidly*)

2 Detached subjects and predicates

Fragments occasionally take the form of **detached subjects, verbs,** or **complements.** Here are completions of the sentences spoken by the baseball player:

Detached Subject
Too many cars, all fouling up the air [*are on the street*].
[*There are*] too many people, too.

Detached Verb
[*I*] can hardly breathe down there.

Detached Complement
[*Hollywood has*] too much smog.

These detached subjects, verbs, and objects are usually clear when spoken. In a piece of writing, though, they may confuse the reader.

3 Detached modifiers

Fragments occasionally take the form of **detached modifiers.**
You probably have the least trouble with phrases like the
following:

> a dark red, two-door sedan
> parked at the curb
> looking out of the window

These phrases are easily attached to a main sentence:

> *Looking out of the window,* we saw *a dark red, two-door sedan
> parked at the curb.*

A long introductory modifier, combined with a dependent
clause, is easy to mistake for a complete sentence:

> At the intersection of Main and Elm, where the dark red sedan
> had stalled and was slowing the late afternoon traffic . . .

Dependent clauses are easier to mistake for complete sentences because they contain subjects and verbs:

> that had turned the corner
> because the car was speeding
> although the police cruiser signaled the car to stop
> whenever you want
> since you went away

Dependent clauses are easily attached to a word or phrase in
the main sentence:

> The dark red sedan *that had turned the corner* began to speed.
> The police cruiser turned on its siren *because the car was
> speeding.*
> *Although the cruiser signaled the car to stop,* it continued down
> the street.
> Leave *whenever you want.*
> The neighborhood has changed *since you went away.*

The opening words of these clauses can help in deciding
whether the sentence is a fragment. Each of these attaching
words gives a signal, telling you to connect the clause to a word
in the main sentence:

> The dark red sedan *that* . . .
> The cruiser turned on its siren *because* . . .
> Leave *whenever* . . .

4 Detached appositives

The fragment may take the form of a **detached appositive.**
An appositive names or identifies the noun usually adjacent to
it:

> The car, *a dark red sedan,* picked up speed when it approached
> the intersection.

Commas usually punctuate the appositive. If the appositive
contains internal punctuation, it is set off with dashes from
the rest of the sentence:

> The car—*a dark red, two-door sedan, with a broken rear window*—
> picked up speed when it approached the intersection.

An appositive that modifies the whole sentence is usually set
off with a dash:

> An accident occurred at the corner of Main and Elm—*a mishap*
> *that could have been averted.*

(See 25b on punctuation of appositives.)

5 Detached absolute phrases

An **absolute phrase** (see 8a), normally attaches to a main sentence without a connecting word or a conjunction. Absolute
phrases are noun phrases followed by a modifier, often a participial phrase or an adjective or prepositional phrase:

> The governor declared a state of emergency, *the hurricane having*
> *flooded the coastal towns.*
> *The street flooding rapidly,* she considered crossing on foot.
> *A small brown dog at her feet,* she picked it up and started to cross
> the street.

Set apart from the main sentence, a **detached absolute
phrase** becomes a fragment:

> The hurricane having picked up force over the gulf
> The stream flooding rapidly
> A small brown dog at her feet

Absolute phrases are usually found in written rather than
spoken English, a reason perhaps for the trouble they sometimes give writers.

EXERCISE

Some of the following groups of words are fragments. Turn them into a complete sentence by attaching them to the core sentence of a main clause.

1. the mower standing near the curb needs repair
2. running down the street without looking ahead of him
3. except for the answer you forgot to finish
4. giving as much help as the class needs to solve the equation
5. which tells you something about calculus
6. no matter who comes to the door
7. give no money to whoever comes to the door even if it is my neighbor
8. after the game ended and the fans started running toward the players
9. nine times out of ten
10. whenever you are ready lock the door and come out to the car
11. that we found in the backyard near the fence
12. explain your reason for not rejoining the club
13. whoever drives the Ford should have the tires checked
14. the mural completed and ready to be shown
15. his having argued that the policy would bankrupt the school district
16. the first person who entered the classroom
17. wondering when the results of the bar exam would be announced
18. they disagreed that dues should be raised
19. the dues having been raised without the consent of the members
20. however the results of the exam appear to you

Summary

16a   Sentence fragments often originate in loose patterns of speech.

16b   Turn a sentence fragment into a complete sentence.

A test of a spoken fragment is that it often begins at a higher pitch than a complete sentence (**16b 1**):

still bounce around a lot, you know

Attach subjects or complements to verbs (16b 2):

Too many cars on the street	*There are* too many cars on the street.

Attach phrases and dependent clauses to an independent clause (16b 3):

Speeding down the street	Speeding down the street, the car jumped the curb.
That turned the corner	The car that turned the corner began to speed.

Attach appositives to the words they modify (16b 4):

The blue and white car parked at the corner	The police cruiser—the blue and white car parked at the corner—turned on its siren.

Attach absolute phrases to an independent clause (16b 5):

The stream flooding rapidly	The stream flooding rapidly, she considered crossing on foot.

Comma **17** Splices and Fused Sentences ☐

☐

Like the sentence fragment, the comma splice, the fused sentence, and the stringy sentence can momentarily confuse your reader and make the sequence of ideas difficult to follow. Correcting these problems calls for attention to both the structure and sound of the sentence.

17a Comma splices

Commas usually divide independent clauses connected by a coordinating conjunction (*and, but, for, yet, or, nor*). A semicolon or colon (see 23a, 23b) often substitutes for the comma when the coordinating conjunction is omitted. **A comma splice** results when a comma joins independent clauses without a coordinating conjunction:

Comma Splice
The biologist from England is reading a paper at the meeting on Thursday, she

Revised
The biologist from England is reading a paper at the meeting on Thursday, *and*

will speak to a small group of researchers on Friday.	she will speak to a small group of researchers on Friday.
She drove to Boston despite the snowstorm, she was worried the turnpike would close.	She drove to Boston despite the snowstorm, *for* she was worried the turnpike would close.

If the two parts of the sentence are closely related in meaning or form a single idea, the second part perhaps containing an explanation of the first part or an example, restore the coordinating conjunction, as in the preceding revised sentences, or do the following:

- *Substitute a semicolon for the comma:*

   The biologist from England is reading a paper at the meeting on Thursday; in addition, she will speak to a small group of researchers on Friday.

- *Substitute a colon:*

   She drove from Boston despite the snowstorm: she was worried the turnpike would close.

- *Subordinate one of the independent clauses:*

   She drove from Boston despite the snowstorm *because* she was worried the turnpike would close.

- *Reduce one of the independent clauses to a modifying phrase:*

   She drove from Boston despite the snowstorm, *worrying* that the turnpike would close.

Comma splices usually occur in short sentences like these, where the second sentence begins with a pronoun.

The comma splice also can occur within a series of short sentences or independent clauses:

Comma Splice	**Revised**
Jane circled the lot looking for a parking space, she spotted one at the end of a lane, another car pulled into the space before she could reach it.	Jane circled the lot looking for a parking place *until* she spotted one at the end of a lane. *But* another car pulled into the space before she could reach it.

The comma splice is easier to spot when the subject of the second clause is different from the subject of the first:

Everyone admires courage, *the climbers* continued to ascend the mountain, knowing that a storm was rising.

If the two parts of the sentence have different subjects and are not closely related in meaning, each may be made a separate sentence. If the ideas are closely related, a colon or semicolon will better show their relationship:

Everyone admires courage: the climbers continued to ascend the mountain, knowing that a storm was rising.

Note that the comma occasionally divides "contact clauses"—explanatory or complementary clauses that form a single idea:

Artists always seek a new technique, and will continue to do so as long as their work excites them. But form of some kind is imperative. *It is the surface crust of the internal harmony, it is the outward evidence of order.*
—E. M. Forster, "Art for Art's Sake" (emphasis added)

If you have trouble with comma splices, take time to look at sentences in which you use a single comma to divide clauses. The sentence contains a comma splice if both clauses are independent and are not connected by a coordinating conjunction. Take time also to refer frequently to the chapters of the *Handbook* on the comma (22), the semicolon and colon (23), and other punctuation marks in revising your sentences. The more familiar you are with their uses, the more control you will have over your sentences.

Checklist: Comma Splices

1. Have I spliced two sentences that begin with the same subject (*John, he*)?
2. Have I spliced two sentences, the second of which begins with a conjunctive adverb or adverbial phrase (for example, *as a result, however, moreover, nevertheless, thus*)?
3. Have I spliced a statement and a subsequent example?
4. Have I spliced statements containing unrelated ideas?

EXERCISE

Correct the comma splices where necessary in the following sentences:

1. Most scientists today work in teams, some work alone in laboratories and observatories, but even these scientists depend on other scientists in testing their discoveries.
2. Football, baseball, and tennis, but not ice hockey or soccer, are sports with a wide television audience.
3. You have no basis for a claim if you have no witnesses, you can send in a report of the accident, but I doubt it will do any good.
4. Give this envelope to the man at the front door, don't give it to the woman at the desk.
5. We came to the fork in the road and paused, we decided to turn back and ask directions.
6. No one stopped to help, each car slowed down to observe the accident and then drove away.
7. Waste not, want not.
8. Michael, who told you about Los Angeles traffic, has never been there. ■

17b Fused sentences

The **fused sentence** (also called the **run-on sentence**) joins independent clauses into a single sentence without intervening punctuation:

Don't forget to fill the tank you're out of gas.
Management and labor reached agreement yesterday on the contract however they are waiting to announce the details.
The negotiations were long and bitter in fact they were almost broken off several times.

As with comma splices, the second clause may contain an explanation of the first clause or an example.

You can revise the fused sentence in these ways:

■ *By writing separate sentences:*

Don't forget to fill the tank. You're out of gas.

■ *By using a comma or other appropriate punctuation:*

> Management and labor reached agreement yesterday on the contract; however, they are waiting to announce the details.
> Management and labor reached agreement yesterday on the contract, but they are waiting to announce it.
> The negotiations were long and bitter; in fact, they were almost broken off several times.

If you have trouble with fused sentences, try reading your sentences aloud. In doing so, listen for the normal break and drop in voice that marks the end of a clause or sentence. If your voice drops midway, the sentence is probably fused.

EXERCISE

Correct the following fused sentences by breaking them into shorter sentences, by subordinating a clause or a phrase, or by adding the necessary punctuation:

1. I am taking a course in computer science as a matter of fact I am taking it for the second time.
2. Listening to music requires complete attention you will hear sound but you won't hear the music if you are reading a book or working a puzzle.
3. The report of a fifth physical force called "hypercharge" challenged current theory of gravity several years ago however few scientists have accepted the evidence as indisputable, little has been written about "hypercharge" recently.
4. Few people know him as well as I do I met him in high school later however we lost touch moving as we did from job to job.
5. I have several reasons for not making a decision now I will notify you when I have made it I won't make it now.
6. People have mistaken ideas about dogs they do have feelings they do understand words and they do think.
7. Dr. Watson met Sherlock Holmes shortly after Watson returned from India he had been wounded there in the Second Afghan War.
8. Watson first saw Holmes in a chemical lab studying blood stains "Why, man, it is the most practical medico-legal discovery for years," Holmes said to him, referring to haemoglobin.
9. Watson and Holmes thus discovered their common interest in medicine indeed they shared other interests in the days following.

10. Watson discovered strange habits in Holmes his friend would sit for hours silently he walked for miles he had immense energy.

17c Stringy sentences

Stringy sentences are long, rambling sentences that string together clauses and phrases and quickly lose the reader's attention:

> Old soldiers never die, the old song says, they just fade away as everyone knows who tries to remember the name of a famous politician whom everyone talked about once but whom nobody now remembers though his face was in the papers daily, and everyone has had the same experience with long-retired actors and actresses.

Length is not the cause of stringy sentences. A long sentence will ramble only if it fails to subordinate ideas and details properly or fails to focus on the core idea. In a tightly knit sentence, we see the relation of part to part as we read it. (See 13b on long sentences.)

Like other confusing sentences, the stringy sentence often originates in the continuous and unvaried clauses common in speech:

> You know he's lonesome and he wants to talk to somebody, and there you are and you can't talk to him. There's one person who feels badly and you can't do anything.
>
> —Studs Terkel, *Working*

The change of topic ("and there you are," "There's one person") makes this sentence ramble on. We may get the same impression when the topic of successive clauses is the same:

> He's lonesome and he wants to talk to somebody. . . .

In persuasive and literary writing, we occasionally find two independent clauses—seldom more than two—coordinated in this way to suggest intense emotion, resolve, or even boredom:

> She listened in a quiet, slow way and thought the notes out like a problem in geometry so she would remember. *She* could see the shape of the sounds very clear and *she* would not forget them.
>
> —Carson McCullers, *The Heart Is a Lonely Hunter*
> (emphasis added)

This kind of repetition is rare in expository writing, which seldom requires such heavy emphasis.

Stringy sentences can be tightened by subordinating one or more of the clauses or by writing separate sentences:

Stringy
It rained heavily in September and the first snow fell the first week of October and it was the earliest snowfall anyone could remember.

Revision 1: Subordination
Following the heavy rain in September, the first snow fell the first week of October—the earliest snowfall anyone could remember.

Revision 2: Separate Sentences
It rained heavily in September. The first snow fell in the first week of October, the earliest snowfall anyone could remember.

The revision you choose depends on the emphasis you wish to give to the various ideas in the sentence.

EXERCISE

Correct the following stringy sentences by eliminating unnecessary words, breaking them into shorter sentences, or revising the punctuation as necessary:

1. Mow the lawn without touching the flowers, and pick up the grass instead of leaving it on the ground, and trim the hedges, but don't cut them too short, and weed where you can, too.
2. The last person I met on my trip to Los Angeles was an agent for a famous television actress, a man who introduced himself, and it was obvious he had no other talk except about her—he talked about nothing else.
3. Few people know as much about the fourteenth century as Barbara Tuchman does, as we see in her book about the fourteenth century, *A Distant Mirror*, which is mainly about the black plague which killed thousands of people and the social and political consequences of the plague.
4. I would like to answer that question frankly and honestly, but we all realize that discretion is a virtue in talking about matters still in the courts, and I am sorry to disappoint you in not being able to say more than I have said already.

311

5. The train stopped at the viaduct—for what reason none of us in the coach could discover, though we could see people on the track, including several who had been riding in our coach and someone whom we had seen at the station in Denver where we had boarded. ∎

Summary

17a Comma splices.

To correct a comma splice, add a coordinating conjunction before the comma or substitute a semicolon or a colon for the comma:

Faulty	Revised
The biologist is speaking tonight, she will speak on Friday to a smaller group.	The biologist is speaking tonight, *and* she will speak on Friday to a smaller group.
	The biologist is speaking tonight; she will speak on Friday to a smaller group.
She drove to Boston despite the snowstorm, she was worried that the turnpike would close.	She drove to Boston despite the snowstorm, *for* she was worried that the turnpike would close.
	She drove to Boston despite the storm: she was worried that the turnpike would close.

17b Fused sentences.

Divide the independent clauses of a fused sentence with the appropriate punctuation:

Faulty	Revised
The negotiations were long and bitter in fact they were broken off several times.	The negotiations were long and bitter; in fact, they were broken off several times.

17c Stringy sentences.

Tighten a long, rambling sentence by subordinating one or

more of the clauses or by putting the ideas in separate sentences:

Faulty

It rained heavily in September and the first snow fell the first week of October and it was the earliest snowfall anyone could remember.

Revised

Following the heavy rain in September, the first snow fell the first week of October—the earliest snowfall anyone could remember.

Shifts and Omissions

18

In everyday conversations, shifts and omissions are common and create little confusion because a frame of reference guides speaker and listener. This frame permits rapid shifts in grammatical form and subject as well as omissions of certain words. If the listener looks confused, the speaker can immediately clarify the shift or omission. This kind of correction occurs frequently throughout a conversation.

In written English, you have the opportunity to consider how well your sentences communicate. This is the job of revision and editing in writing papers. Any unwarranted shift or unwarranted omission of words makes a written sentence ambiguous and confusing. Your readers may have to read the sentence several times before they understand it. In this chapter, we turn to ways of revising sentences that make unwarranted shifts and omissions.

314

18a Shifts

Shifts in person and number of pronouns (from *I* to *you* or from *I* to *we*) and in tense, mood, and voice (see 9a) are common in spoken communication—in brief exchanges, conversations, interviews. The following sentences contain common shifts in spoken English where context clarifies the statement. However, these shifts are unacceptable in standard written communication:

Shift in Person
Politicians who want to bury chemical wastes close to where people get their drinking water forget *you* will need their votes in November.

Shift in Tense
When we *talked* to the people downtown, they *say* chemical wastes will be kept out of the water, but we don't believe they will.

Shift in Mood
If we *had* a say in the matter, these wastes *won't* be dumped near where people get their drinking water.

1 Person

The writer of the first sentence above makes a **shift in person**—from the third-person *politician* to the second-person *you*. The shift is confusing because these words refer to the same people. The following revision removes the awkwardness:

Politicians who want to bury chemical wastes close to where people get their drinking water forget *they* will need the votes of these people in November.

The following sentence also contains a shift in person:

One hardly knows what to do, particularly when *you* can't get help from people paid to give it.

The shift from the third-person *one* to the second-person *you* makes the sentence awkward and confusing. Revising this sen-

315

tence calls for a change to *you* at the beginning or a change to *one* in the remainder of the sentence. A change to one makes the sentence excessively formal:

> *One* hardly knows what to do, particularly when *one* can't get help from people paid to give it.

Repeated in a string of clauses and phrases, *one* produces a stilted and unclear sentence:

> *One* should realize that *one* will lose the confidence of *one's* voting constituents.

A similar problem occurs with the repetition of the informal *you*. In a string of clauses, *you* produces a monotonous sentence, particularly if the word is used often in the paragraph:

> *You* should realize that *you* will lose the confidence of *your* voting constituents.

The following revisions are not stilted or monotonous:

> One should realize that voters will lose confidence. [*formal*]
> You will lose the confidence of voters. [*informal*]

Shifts in person also can be troublesome in paragraphs and essays. Compare the following paragraphs:

Awkward	**Revised**
We seldom think of the problems a candidate faces in talking to an audience on television rather than face to face. You have to take into consideration the pressure when you can't see how they are taking your words. Candidates who are effective speakers before live audiences become tongue-tied when facing a camera.	We seldom think of the problems a candidate faces in talking to an audience on television rather than face to face. We have to consider the pressure on candidates who cannot witness the response to their words. Effective speakers become tongue-tied when facing a camera and a live audience.

The paragraph to the left makes a series of awkward and illogical shifts in person. The revision to the right uses the pronoun *we* consistently and reduces the wordiness of the paragraph.

2 Number

Shifts in number occur when a plural pronoun is part of the antecedent:

> *Each* of us should write *their* representative.

Their mistakenly agrees with *us* rather than with *each*—the subject of the sentence. This mistake probably occurs because the closest pronoun to *their* is the plural *us* and therefore confuses the writer. The writer may also be avoiding the sexist use of the pronoun *his.*

The opening pronoun *each* focuses on the individual, not on the group. The following sentences are correct:

> *Each* of us should write to *his or her* representative.
> *All* of us should write *our* representatives.

(See 10a on number agreement in pronouns.)

EXERCISE

Correct the faulty shifts in person and number in the following sentences:

1. You can get help in emergencies if one dials 911.
2. If a person parks in a yellow zone without their permit, they may find their car towed away.
3. Nobody should have to pay more than their share.
4. If you can get a mechanic to repair the car on Sunday, expect to pay them overtime.
5. One can't help giving their opinion on the matter when asked.
6. People should realize that you can't clean up the environment without spending money.
7. You can clean up toxic-waste dumps near populated areas if they do care about a clean environment.
8. The property owners in the neighborhood has his drinking water threatened by toxic waste.
9. The city of Dayton is threatened by toxic wastes leaking into their underground water.
10. Each of us property owners has a view of their own on the issue. ∎

3 Tense

Needless **shifts in tense** may give the reader the mistaken impression that different people are speaking or that different events are occurring:

Ambiguous
When we *talked* to the people downtown, they *say* chemical
wastes will be kept out of the water, but we don't believe they
will.

The writer here shifts from the past *talked* to the present *say.*
The sentence will be ambiguous to some readers because the
writer is using *say* in the sense of "They'll say anything." The
tenses are consistent in the following sentence:

When we *talked* to the people downtown, they *said* chemical
wastes will be kept out of the water, but we don't believe they
will.

However, the sentence is still ambiguous: the second *they* can
refer to both *people* and *wastes* earlier in the sentence.
Here are satisfactory revisions of the original sentence:

Revised
When we talked to the people downtown, they said chemical
wastes will be kept out of the water, but *we don't believe they
will be.*
When we talked to the people downtown, they said chemical
wastes will be kept out of the water, but *we don't believe them.*

4 Literary present tense

Summaries of novels, stories, movies, plays, and essays use the
literary present tense, not the past tense. The summary tells
us what is happening in the time frame created by the author
rather than in actual time:

It is delightful when the characters are real, when Shakespeare
does bother about them. Brutus is real, so is Cassius, so is Antony, so perhaps is Caesar himself. Brutus is an intellectual who
can do things, who is not (like Hamlet) hampered by doubts. He
can do things—but he always does them wrong: his advice is
invariably fatal, from the moment of the murder to the battle of
Philippi.
                                    —E. M. Forster, "Julius Caesar"

In the final scene of *Abe Lincoln in Illinois,* Lincoln says farewell
to the townspeople of Springfield at the train station, his wife
standing at his side.

In writing a summary of a literary work, be careful not to shift to the past tense:

Lincoln *finishes* his address, and then the train *departed.*

The same rule applies to statements made in the past tense. Note that an unchanging truth stated by someone in the past is reported in the present tense:

Faulty Tense	**Revised**
Lincoln said at Gettysburg that the United States *was* "one nation indivisible."	Lincoln said at Gettysburg that the United States *is* "one nation indivisible."

The verb *was* suggests that the truth or application of the statement ended in the past. But the Gettysburg Address continues to proclaim "one nation indivisible" to anyone who reads it.

EXERCISE

Correct the faulty shifts in tense in the following sentences:

1. *Star Wars* was a western movie disguised as science fiction.
2. When we saw *Star Wars,* we understood now why it was so popular a movie.
3. Before we could ask them to our house for Thanksgiving, they ask us to theirs.
4. The floor had to be swept, then it should have been washed with a detergent.
5. Einstein stated in his special theory of relativity that mass was a form of energy.
6. In *Sunrise at Campobello,* Franklin Roosevelt was stricken with polio but makes the decision to continue his career in politics.
7. The press seldom photographed President Roosevelt as he sits in his wheelchair.
8. Not everyone agrees that the press disclose the full details of presidential illnesses.
9. Certainly everyone agrees that the fact that the president is ill must be reported and what the outcome was.
10. In John Steinbeck's *The Grapes of Wrath,* victims of the Oklahoma drought in the 1930s sought work in California fields and orchards.

■

5 Sequence of tenses

When you join two clauses describing related actions, the **sequence of tenses** shows the exact relation of the actions in time and aspect (see 9b). For example, in describing an event in the **past tense,** you are showing that the event was completed in the past:

> Scott *returned* to the Antarctic to lead an expedition to the South Pole.

If you wish to refer to an event prior to that named in the sentence, you use a verb in the **past perfect tense**:

> Scott *had visited* the Antarctic before he *returned* to lead the expedition.

In another sequence of tenses, you use a verb in the **present perfect tense** to follow a verb in the present or past tense:

> We *know* (*knew*) that scientific expeditions to the Antarctic *have produced* useful knowledge.

The verb of the dependent clause tells the reader that useful knowledge was produced in the past and continues to be produced in the present.

A parallel sequence of tenses occurs with the use of **past progressive** and **present progressive** verbs:

> Scott *had been thinking* of an expedition before he *returned* to England.
> The newspaper *reports* that the ozone layer *has been thinning* over the Antarctic and the Arctic.

In describing future events, you also use verb phrases in sequence:

> Some scientists *believe* that the situation *will worsen.*
> The newspaper *reports* that the vaccine *will have been tested* by the end of the year.

Remember that a verb in the **present tense** expresses a general truth in a dependent clause, whether the preceding verb is in the present or the past tense:

> The newspaper *states* that ozone *protects* the atmosphere.
> The newspaper *stated* that ozone *protects* the atmosphere.

Participles and infinitives also distinguish actions in the present and the past. You use the **present participle** (*protect-*

ing) to show that the action expressed is happening at the time expressed by the verb of the clause:

Vaccines are miraculous inventions, *protecting* us from disease.

The **past participle** shows that the action occurred prior to or at the time expressed by the verb:

Protected from disease, humans often thrive in harsh climates.

By contrast, you combine the **present infinitive** (*to protect*) with the verb to express a present or a future action:

I *wear* sunglasses *to protect* my eyes.
I *intend to protect* my health in other ways.

The **perfect infinitive** (*to have protected*) points to action in the past:

Natural immunity seems *to have protected* many populations from disease.

Participles and infinitives seldom cause problems with simple present and past verbs. But they can create inexact and awkward sentences when used with verbs in perfect aspect.

Many awkward sentences arise because the verb in the dependent clause does not show an exact time relationship to the verb in the independent clause. Consider the following examples.

■ *Present tense verb in the independent clause:*

Inexact
The meeting *is succeeding* because it *had been planned* well.

Exact
The meeting is succeeding because the committee *planned* it well.

Since the plan was made before the ongoing meeting, the revised sentence changes the verb in the dependent clause to the past tense.

Inexact
The book *explains* that cosmic rays *bombarded* the earth since its formation.

Exact
The book explains that cosmic rays *have bombarded* the earth since its formation.

Cosmic rays bombarded the earth in the past and continue to bombard it today. The verb in the dependent clause is therefore changed to the present perfect.

- *Past and present perfect tense verbs in the independent clause:*

Inexact
The conference succeeded because it *has* been well chaired.

Exact
The conference succeeded because it *was* well chaired.

Since the conference is not ongoing, it is no longer being chaired. The past tense makes this point clear.

Inexact
The conference *has issued* weekly reports when it met.

Exact
The conference *issued* weekly when it met.

Since the conference met in the past, it could no longer be issuing weekly reports. The simple past verb *issued* makes the time relationship clear.

- *Past perfect tense in the independent clause:*

Inexact
Elizabeth *left* for Akron by the time I arrived.

Exact
Elizabeth *had left* for Akron by the time I arrived.

The ambiguity in the sentence to the left is cleared up by changing the verb to the past perfect.

- *Verb phrases expressing future action:*

Inexact
Elizabeth *will stay* in Akron if I *decided* to come.

Exact
Elizabeth will stay in Akron if I *decide* to come.

- *Participles and infinitives:*

Inexact
Calling from home, Mary arrived at the hotel expecting to find a reservation in her name.

Exact
Having called from home, Mary arrived at the hotel expecting to find a reservation. . . .

The revision clarifies that Mary called before leaving from home.

Inexact
The president was thought *to make* the decision before the meeting began.

Exact
The president was thought *to have made* the decision before the meeting began.

The revision clarifies the fact that the president was not in the process of making the decision.

(See 9a and 9b for a complete discussion of the tense and aspect of verbs.)

EXERCISE

Complete the following dependent or independent clauses using verbs in the appropriate tense:

1. The law of gravity predicts that
2. The plan failed because
3. The bureau had warned of an earthquake before
4. The indictment charges that
5. Having sighted the lifeboat, the pilot
6. She trimmed the bushes while
7. She was trimming the bushes when
8. He had written to the company just before
9. We have written to the company even though
10. Inflation occurs when

6 Mood

Shifts in mood also make sentences awkward and confusing. Recall (9a) that verbs in the **indicative mood** state a fact or ask a question (*I walked home. Did you walk home?*); verbs in the **imperative mood** give commands or make polite requests (*Stop! Watch your step!*); verbs in the **subjunctive mood** state a wish, a demand, or a condition contrary to fact (*I wish the meeting were over. I ask that the meeting be adjourned.*).

Compare these statements in the indicative mood:

If I go, I will look for you.
Walk out if the meeting is adjourned.

These sentences state alternative actions, one of which must occur: the speaker will either go or not go, walk out or not walk out. The sentence does not state what the speaker will do.

The following sentence opens in the subjunctive and shifts awkwardly to the indicative:

Were I to go, I will look for you.

This sentence illustrates the same kind of awkward shift in mood:

If we *had* a say in the matter, chemical wastes *won't* be dumped near where people get their drinking water.

The sentence begins in the subjunctive ("if we had a say in the matter") and shifts to the indicative ("chemical wastes won't be dumped because we do have a say").

Here are possible revisions in both the subjunctive mood and the indicative mood:

Subjunctive
If we *had* a say in the matter, these wastes *wouldn't* be dumped near where people get their drinking water.

Indicative
If we *have* a say in the matter, chemical wastes *won't* be dumped near where people get their drinking water.

The subjunctive mood is used in formal demands, statements contrary to fact, statements of desire beginning with *I ask* or *I wish,* and statements of possibility:

We demand that the meeting *be adjourned.*
I wish that Elizabeth *were* here to argue the case.
If it please the court, I shall present the case in favor of my client.

Here is how to revise a sentence that shifts from the subjunctive to the indicative:

Inexact	**Revised**
If they *had veto power,* the bill *will be sent* to the committee for redrafting.	If they had veto power, the bill *would be sent* to the committee for redrafting.

A sentence that shifts from the imperative to the indicative mood is particularly awkward:

Awkward	**Revised**
Don't write a business letter on both sides of the sheet, and the letter will make a good impression if the page looks uncrowded.	Your business letter will make a good impression if you write on one side of the sheet and don't crowd the page.

7 Voice

Shifts in voice—from the active to the passive voice or vice versa—are also awkward. Use the active voice unless you have reason to make the verb passive (see 12e):

Awkward	**Revised**
We *finished* the discussion but agreement *was not reached* by us.	We *finished* the discussion but *did not reach* agreement.

324

Awkward
The race *was won* and the ski team immediately *left* for the Olympic trials in Vermont.

Revised
The ski team from California *won* the race and immediately *left* for the Olympic trials in Vermont.

EXERCISE

Correct the faulty shifts in mood or voice in the following sentences:

1. If I were king, you will be queen.
2. He smashed the fender and the door was dented.
3. He said he had a suit my size and would I try it on.
4. The beginning writer can learn something from reading for style, but don't imitate apishly.
5. The exam was finished at twelve and then we had lunch.
6. If you were not sick, come to the meeting with us!
7. Though she went to the play against her will, it was much enjoyed.
8. After we had built the fence, we decided to sell the lot.
9. I hammered the door shut and the windows were sealed.
10. Watch for the railroad crossing, and then the road will turn sharply to the right.

18b | Omitted words

We routinely omit words clearly implied in the sentence:

We know (*that*) he walks four miles every morning.

But **omitted words** sometimes make a sentence ambiguous and awkward.

1 Omitted determiners

When necessary determiners are omitted from a sentence, the meaning is blurred:

Ambiguous
She saw an enormous dog and bicyclist on the road.

Revised
She saw an enormous dog and *a* bicyclist on the road.

325

We cannot tell whether *enormous* describes just the dog or the dog and the biker both. The word *bicyclist* takes the modifier *a*.

The omission of the determiner *the* can also make a sentence ambiguous:

> We need advice of the doctor.

This sentence means either that we need advice *about* the doctor or that we need advice *from* the doctor. Here are revisions that clarify the meaning:

> **Revised**
> We need the advice of the doctor.
> We need advice about the doctor.
> We need the doctor's advice.

2   Omitted expletive *that*

Omission of the expletive *that* can make a sentence momentarily ambiguous:

Ambiguous
I remember none of the students enrolled in the course.

Revised
I remember *that* none of the students enrolled in the course.

3   Omission in verb phrase

Omission of part of the verb phrase can make a sentence awkward or ambiguous:

Awkward
I am not and will never smoke.

We are driving to Tulsa on Tuesday and may on Friday to Stillwater.

Revised
I am not and *will never be* a smoker.

We are driving to Tulsa on Tuesday and may *drive* on Friday to Stillwater.

If necessary, repeat the whole verb phrase to clarify a statement:

Ambiguous
I no more think about how you spend your money than you think about mine.

Revised
I no more think about how you spend your money than you think about *how I spend mine.*

4 Omitted adverb

You must sometimes repeat an adverb to clarify your meaning. Consider the following sentence:

> Jim never loses his temper and blames others if they do the same.

If the sentence means that Jim never loses his temper and never blames others, repeat the adverb:

> Jim never loses his temper and *never* blames others if they do.

You need not repeat the adverb if the sentence is worded as follows:

> Jim never loses his temper or blames others if they do.

5 Omitted preposition

Omission of a preposition can create awkwardness or confusion. Compare the following:

Confusing	**Revised**
She is curious and looking forward to visiting French Canada.	She is curious *about* and looking forward to visiting French Canada.

The sentence to the left says that the woman is a curious person. The writer probably meant to stress the object of her curiosity—French Canada.

In the following example, the sentence to the left is probably clear at first reading, but the omission of the preposition *by* makes the sentence awkward:

Awkward	**Revised**
He is as fascinated and deeply involved in city politics as his wife is.	He is as fascinated *by* and deeply involved in city politics as his wife is.

In revising your sentences for shifts and omissions, read your paper quickly for consistency in person, number, tense, and other grammatical forms. Look for shifts in your sentences, paragraphs, and the whole paper. Circle any doubtful shifts or omissions you are uncertain about and check them in the *Handbook*.

EXERCISE

Correct the faulty shifts and omissions in the following sentences. Rephrase the sentence if necessary.

1. I see few of the people signed up to work came.
2. We always have and always will like country music.
3. He is tired and angry with the constant bickering at committee meetings.
4. They want help of their parents.
5. He has no knowledge or interest in scuba diving.
6. She has knowledge and will continue on the life of early settlers in Minnesota.
7. They watched the fire with concern and not knowing what to do.
8. I am worried as you and will more until this crisis is over.
9. She seldom asked for favors and offered to do favors for others.
10. In the waiting room of the office sat an old man and young woman.
11. It never rains on Memorial Day and also rains on Labor Day.
12. If you were in my position, you will make the same decisions.
13. In his book *Plagues and People*, William McNeill described how bubonic plague and other diseases influenced European history.
14. Since they wanted to see the outcome of the trial, the week's adjournment was resented.
15. She never called and never will her former employer.

18c Incomplete comparisons

When someone introduces a comparison, you usually expect the person to complete it. For example, if someone says to you "There's nothing more tiring," you would probably ask "More tiring than what?" The person would then complete the comparison:

There's nothing more tiring than standing in line for an hour.

Incomplete comparisons omit essential words and make sentences ambiguous:

I like Mary more than Jane.

Either of the following revisions clarifies the meaning:

I like Mary more than I like Jane.
I like Mary more than Jane does.

The following sentences to the left are also ambiguous:

Ambiguous	Revised
Pizza is as popular with grown-ups as teenagers.	Pizza is as popular with grown-ups as (it is) *with* teenagers.

The addition of *with* avoids momentary confusion in reading the sentence.

Pizza in this restaurant is as good if not better than home.	Pizza in this restaurant is as good as, if not better than, *the kind my father makes* at home.

The revision here also removes the momentary ambiguity and awkwardness.

EXERCISE

Correct the incomplete comparisons in the following sentences:

1. He likes eating more than Jane.
2. My sister dislikes ice cream more than him.
3. I enjoy tennis more.
4. Growing tomatoes is hard as lettuce.
5. Hamburgers are just as popular with Europeans.

Summary

18a   Shifts.

Avoid awkward shifts in person, number, tense, mood, and voice:

Shift in Person	Revised
Politicians forget *you* will need support from people like us.	Politicians forget *they* will need support from people like us.

Shift in Number	**Revised**
Each of us should write to *their* representative.	All of us should write to *our* representatives.

Shift in Tense	**Revised**
When we *talked* to the people downtown, they *say* chemical wastes will be kept out of the water.	When we talked to the people downtown, they *said* chemical wastes will be kept out of the water.

Shift in Sequence of Tenses	**Revised**
The meeting *was* a success because it *has* been planned carefully.	The meeting was a success because it *had* been planned carefully.

Shift in Mood	**Revised**
Were I to go, I *will* look for you.	Were I to go, I *would* look for you.

Shift in Voice	**Revised**
We *finished* the discussion but agreement *was not reached* by us.	We *finished* the discussion but *did not reach* an agreement.

18b Omissions.

Add omitted determiners, expletives, parts of verb phrases, adverbs, and prepositions to eliminate ambiguity:

Ambiguous	**Revised**
She saw an enormous dog and bicyclist on the road.	She saw an enormous dog and *a* bicyclist on the road.
She expected the owner of the growling dog was nearby.	She expected *that* the owner of the growling dog was nearby.
I am not and will never smoke.	I am not and *will never be* a smoker.
Jim never loses his temper and blames others if they do.	Jim never loses his temper and *never* blames others if they do.
She is curious and looking forward to visiting French Canada.	She is curious *about* and looking forward to visiting French Canada.

18c Incomplete comparisons.

Complete comparisons to avoid ambiguity and awkwardness:

Ambiguous

There's nothing more
   tiring.

Pizza is as popular with
   grown-ups as teenagers.

Revised

There's nothing more
   tiring than standing in
   line.

Pizza is as popular with
   grown-ups as *with*
   teenagers.

Mixed Constructions and Other Faults

19

The sentence faults described in this chapter—mixed constructions, false equations, and faulty predication—are sometimes hard to analyze and correct. Think of them as mistrials—a necessary and unavoidable part of casting sentences and revising them.

19a | Mixed constructions

In the course of writing, you may open a sentence with one kind of structure and switch to another, forgetting the pattern you have in mind. This is called a **mixed construction.** The following classification of mixed constructions will help you detect them in your sentences and correct them.

1 From phrase to predicate

Opening a sentence with one kind of structure and switching midway to another results in a mixed construction. The sentence is usually awkward and confusing:

Awkward
On meeting his uncle was a surprise.

The confusion arises because the sentence mixes the following:

on meeting his uncle—a prepositional phrase where the reader
  expects a subject
was a surprise—a predicate

The sentence may be read in two ways:

Revised
On meeting his uncle he showed his surprise.
Meeting his uncle was a surprise.

If in doubt about how to revise this kind of sentence, ask "What
is the surprise?"—that is, "What is the subject of the verb?"—
and revise the sentence to give the answer.

2 From dependent clause to predicate

Confusion also arises when a dependent clause awkwardly appears where the reader expects a subject:

Awkward
If Alice comes should be the time to discuss the matter.

To revise the sentence, ask this question:

If Alice comes, what will happen or who will do what?

Then complete the sentence by giving the answer:

Revised
If Alice comes, we can discuss the matter.

Here is an alternate revision that stresses when the discussion
is to take place:

We can discuss the matter if Alice comes.

Compare the following awkward sentences with their revisions:

Awkward	**Revised**
Because Alice was late made us angry.	We were angry because Alice was late.
Even though you didn't get a part in the play shouldn't	The fact that you didn't get a part in the play shouldn't

333

<table>
<tr>
<td>discourage you from trying out again.</td>
<td>discourage you from trying out again.
Don't be discouraged from trying out again because you didn't get a part in the play.</td>
</tr>
</table>

3 From independent clause to predicate

Another type of mixed construction occurs when an independent clause is mistakenly used to form the subject of the sentence:

Awkward
He protested was the reason for his being fired.

To revise the sentence, change the independent clause to a dependent one:

That he protested was the reason for his being fired.

Then recast the sentence so the important information comes at the end:

Revised
The reason for his being fired is *that he protested*.

Here are other satisfactory revisions:

He was fired because he protested.
His protest led to his firing.

EXERCISE

Correct the mixed constructions in the following sentences:

1. After talking to the teacher was when he made the decision.
2. Everyone missed the final question and that there had been no time to cover the final chapter in class.
3. By explaining your absences may persuade him to give you a makeup.
4. The exam was easy surprised her.
5. In looking at the car was the mechanic who had looked at it the week before.
6. In all the years we lived in Pittsburgh were the happiest of our lives.
7. She is going to Pittsburgh by plane is what worries me.

8. On entering the room led to their meeting.
9. Since the book contained no index made it difficult to use.
10. The whistle blows at five is the time to quit working.

 19b False equations

A **false equation** misleads the reader about what the predicate will say about the subject:

Misleading
The one movie I saw was in August.

The word *one* and the verb *was* suggest that the movie title will follow. Here is a satisfactory revision:

Revised
The one movie I saw in August was *Rain Man*.

The confusion arises because *to be* verbs (*is, are, was, were*) equate similar ideas or similar things (see 9a) and express time relationships:

Equivalent Things
The movie I saw was *Rain Man*.

Time
The showing was in August.

In the preceding false equation, the word *one* suggests that the title will follow, not the time the speaker saw it.

In a grammatical sentence, subject and subjective complement are equivalent in meaning, whatever form the complement takes:

Doubling a recipe is how you feed a large group.

However, the sentence can sound awkward when subject and subject complement are not equivalent things or ideas:

The only help I need is how to wire the speakers.

The following revision changes the subject complement to an equivalent term:

The only *help* I need is *being shown* how to wire the speakers.

But this revision is wordy and needlessly formal. The following is not wordy:

I need help in wiring the speakers.

Another kind of false equation mixes things with activities:

Hunter's stew is where you cook meat with vegetables.

The false equation in this sentence mixes a thing (*stew*) and an activity (*where you cook*). The following revision correctly equates stew with meat and vegetables:

Hunter's stew is meat cooked with vegetables.

Note that the word *where* is often used informally to refer to a place:

A veterinary college is *where* you learn to care for animals.

General and formal English state the equivalent term:

A veterinary college is a school that teaches care of animals.

EXERCISE

Rewrite each of the following sentences to correct the false equation:

1. College is when you find out how important friends are.
2. The only baseball game I ever played was in junior high.
3. The one composer we truly liked was at the end of the course.
4. The symphony we heard of Beethoven was in New York.
5. Lacrosse is when you play with webbed rackets rather than sticks.
6. The official explanation for the accident was because a control valve failed to open.
7. Air pollutants are a reason to know chemistry.
8. Organic chemistry and biochemistry are where you study complex molecules and enzymes.
9. The overture is when the conductor starts the performance.
10. Chili is where you mix ground beef, tomatoes, and ground red pepper and other spices.

19c Faulty predication

Faulty predication occurs when you fail to state in the subject position who or what is performing the action. The following sentence makes an assertion or predication about the subject:

> Word processors may soon replace typewriters.

You can ask the following question about the subject:

> What will word processors soon replace?

The predicate provides the answer—typewriters. The predicate makes a statement about the subject.

But notice what happens in the following sentence:

Faulty
The convenience of word processors may soon replace typewriters.

At first glance the sentence seems to be talking about word processors, but a second glance shows that the predicate is referring to an aspect of word processors—their convenience. Putting the word *convenience* in the subject position exposes the faulty predication:

> *The convenience* may soon replace typewriters.

The following revision clarifies the sentence:

Revised
Because of their convenience, word processors may soon replace typewriters.

Faulty predication is less obvious in the following example:

Faulty
Agreement between subject and verb causes many writers problems.

It is not agreement that causes problems but uncertainty over how some subjects and verbs agree in sentences:

> Uncertainty over agreement between subject and verb causes many writers problems.

337

The fault here is that *uncertainty* and *problems* overlap in meaning. Here is a satisfactory revision:

Revised
Many writers are uncertain about the agreement between subject and verb.

In the course of revision, listen for sentences that sound awkward or don't make sense. If you suspect your sentence may contain a mixed construction, false equation, or faulty predication, check to see whether the predicate refers directly to the subject. You may spot what is wrong at first glance, or you may have to analyze the sentence. Your instructor may point out a particular fault. If you don't see what is wrong, recast the sentence. You will discover much in rephrasing your ideas.

EXERCISE

Correct the mixed constructions, false equations, or faulty predication as appropriate in the following sentences:

1. The one book I read was during spring vacation.
2. The fact he must give a talk is the reason he's nervous.
3. Her reputation was her chocolate cake.
4. The rise in the cost of money requires many people to put off buying new houses.
5. A hurricane is when the winds rise above seventy-three miles per hour.
6. The popularity of country music will soon catch up with rock in other countries.
7. The risk of stereotypes fuel racial prejudice.
8. People watching a crime and not even calling the police is because they think someone else will report it, an article in *Psychology Today* suggests.
9. When the stew overcooks makes it hard to clean the pot.
10. The lack of exercise makes many people take up jogging.
11. The last time we drove to Detroit and stopped in Toledo on the way.
12. We wondered if we should stop in Bowling Green on the way home?
13. The only person I knew well was in the army.

14. Calculus is where you find out if you're suited for engineering.
15. Because the bus broke down is why I'm late this morning.
16. The United States has a long way to catch up with China's population.
17. Mountain climbing probably exceeds the hazards of other outdoor sports.
18. The safety of airbags may soon become standard equipment in cars.
19. An eclipse is where astronomers measure the curving of starlight passing near the sun.
20. The two books by George Orwell we read was at the beginning of the course.
21. The unexpected result of the examination is the reason she is switching from chemistry to physics.
22. Getting into college is when you start making decisions for yourself.
23. Americans eat more fat than they should explains the increase in coronary disease.
24. On arrival at the airport was a long delay at customs.
25. Cooperation among the nuclear powers causes worry around the world.

Summary

19a Mixed constructions.

Mixed constructions begin with one kind of structure and continue or end the sentence with another.

Don't use a phrasal modifier in place of the subject (**19a 1**):

Faulty	**Revised**
On meeting his uncle was a surprise.	On meeting his uncle he showed surprise.
	Meeting his uncle was a surprise.

A dependent clause in the subject position can make a sentence awkward (**19a 2**):

Faulty	**Revised**
If Alice comes is the time to discuss the matter.	We can discuss the matter if Alice comes.

An independent clause cannot serve as the subject (19a 3):

Faulty	**Revised**
He protested was the reason for his being fired.	The reason for his being fired was that he protested. He was fired because he protested.

19b False equations.

Make the subject and the subjective complement equivalent things or ideas:

Faulty	**Revised**
The one movie I saw was in August.	The one movie I saw in August was *Rain Man*.

19c Faulty predication.

Make the predication about the actual subject and not about an aspect of it:

Faulty	**Revised**
The convenience of word processors may soon replace typewriters.	Because of their convenience, word processors may soon replace typewriters.

Misplaced Modifiers

20

This chapter discusses ways of placing modifiers effectively in the sentence. **Misplaced modifiers**—words, phrases, and clauses—can make sentences awkward and unclear. Like other kinds of sentence revision, faults in word order sometimes arise from the way we talk: sentences that are clear when spoken may be unclear when written. In these instances, revision requires a tightening of spoken patterns—but not an extreme departure from them.

20a Single-word modifiers

If a sentence seems awkward or confusing, the trouble may be a misplaced word. A **single-word modifier** can change the meaning of a sentence when it appears in different positions. In the following examples, the modifier *only* expresses different ideas in different positions of the sentence:

Modification of the Subject—*Jane*
Only Jane raised her hand.   No one but Jane raised her hand.

Modification of the Verb—*raised*

Jane *only* raised her hand.   Jane raised her hand but said nothing.

Modification of the Object—*finger*

Jane raised *only* a finger.   Jane raised a finger, not her whole hand.

Modification of an Adverb—*once*

Jane raised her hand *only* once.   Jane did not raise her hand more than once.

Often single-word modifiers can occur in different parts of informal sentences without a change in meaning, as in the following:

I *just* have one thing to say.
I've *just* one thing to say.

In revising an awkward sentence, check to see if you placed an adjective or adverb close to the word or phrase it modifies. Listen particularly to the emphasis you give words like *only* and *just*. Notice that, in the first three preceding examples, you pronounce *only* with more than usual stress, as shown in the marking of the word. Written sentences usually convey the meaning and added stress of a word without special marking. Occasionally, you may want to use italics to show emphasis (see 26d), but you should do so sparingly. If you find it necessary to italicize more than a single word, the sentence probably needs recasting.

EXERCISE

The following sentences use the single-word modifier *only* or *even* in different positions to convey different meanings. State the exact meaning of each sentence.

1. She is going to class only today.
2. She is only going to class today.
3. Only she is going to class today.
4. She is even going to class.
5. Even she is going to class.

20b Squinting modifiers

A sentence may be confusing because a modifier placed between two words seems to modify both words, blurring the meaning. This is called a **squinting modifier** because it looks in opposite directions—at the word or phrase that precedes and the word or phrase that follows:

Ambiguous
People who watch television *rarely* read a great deal.

The sentence has two possible meanings:

Revised
People who *rarely* watch television read a great deal.
People who *rarely* read a great deal watch television.

Each of these sentences is a satisfactory revision of the original sentence depending on the writer's intended meaning.

EXERCISE

Revise the following sentences that contain squinting modifiers. Some of the sentences may be correct as written.

1. The team that practices often wins.
2. The teacher said after class she would discuss the exam.
3. The surgeon said presently the scar would fade.
4. People who eat green apples once in a while will get bad stomachaches.
5. Not everyone who eats green apples immediately gets sick.
6. She explained during the recess she wanted to talk further about my decision.
7. She urged us strongly to defend our ideas.
8. Runners who fail to warm up slowly lose agility.
9. The tree that grew in the shade quickly lost its leaves.
10. Those who saw her fall suddenly called for help.

20c Misplaced phrases

Phrasal modifiers often can be placed in various parts of the sentence. Where they appear depends on the emphasis desired:

> She described her mistake *with a grin*.
> She described her mistake, *grinning*.
> *With a grin* she described her mistake.
> *Grinning*, she described her mistake.

When another modifier intervenes between a noun and its modifier the sentence will be understood if you punctuate it properly. The following sentence is ambiguous because it lacks the necessary punctuation:

Ambiguous
He described his mistake to the man with a grin.

A comma clarifies the sentence:

Revised
He described his mistake to the man, with a grin.

Placing a phrasal modifier in other positions may produce an unidiomatic sentence that departs widely from spoken patterns:

> He described, *with a grin*, his mistake *to the man*.
> He described his mistake, *with a grin*, *to the man*.

If the sentence sounds awkward, place the phrase next to the word it modifies:

> *With a grin*, he described his mistake *to the man*.
> *Grinning*, he described his mistake *to the man*.

Dividing the modifier from its subject sometimes makes a sentence momentarily ambiguous. If this happens, move the modifier next to its subject or add a comma:

Ambiguous	**Revised**
We saw the bear driving down the highway.	Driving down the highway, we saw the bear.
	We saw the bear, driving down the highway.

Ambiguous

Hunting for food, you must drive into the backcountry where grizzlies roam.

Revised

You must drive into the backcountry where grizzlies roam, hunting for food.

In revising your sentences, read them from the perspective of your reader. If you pause to guess at the meaning, recast the sentence. You may have to recast a sentence several times before you find a way to make it clear.

EXERCISE

Correct any of the following sentences that you find unclear or awkward because of misplaced phrases.

1. She, paper and pencil in hand, made a list of the people in the room.
2. She made a list of the people, with pencil and paper in hand, in the room.
3. He explained with some reluctance how the accident had occurred to the police officer.
4. He explained how the accident occurred with some reluctance.
5. An accident at the corner was seen, leaning out of the window.
6. Barking on the rocks, we watched the seals.
7. To keep alive during the winter, you should water the shrubs heavily in the fall.
8. The children on the swings ignored their mothers, pushing one another gleefully.
9. Not wanting to drive back for the water jar we had left on the porch meant looking for a place to get water on the road.
10. We caught sight of the steamer, coming around the bend near the inlet.

20d Misplaced clauses

1 Adjective clauses

Adjective clauses are dependent clauses that perform the same functions as single-word adjectives. Adjective clauses follow the words they modify, except when separated by other modifiers of the noun.

The following sentence sounds awkward because the adjective clause is separated from the word it modifies:

Awkward
His letter arrived on Tuesday, *which he had mailed from Akron*.

Revised
His letter, *which he had mailed from Akron*, arrived on Friday.
His letter, *mailed from Akron*, arrived on Friday.

Momentary ambiguity can arise when the adjective clause has two possible antecedents:

Ambiguous
The letter was forwarded with other mail *that she had left at the office*.

The following revision removes the ambiguity but makes the sentence awkward and unidiomatic:

With the forwarded mail came the letter that she had left at the office.

The following revision is idiomatic:

Revised
The letter *that she had left at the office* was forwarded to her with other mail.

Notice that the adjective clause in the revised sentence identifies the letter, in contrast to the following sentence where the adjective clause comments on a letter already identified:

The letter from her son, *which she had left at the office*, was forwarded to her with other mail.

In spoken English, we often use the word *which* with broad reference at the end of the sentence:

My basement is filled with litter, *which* is why I'm cleaning it Saturday.

In written English, the word *which* is given exact reference. (See 11c on the vague use of *which*.)

2 Adverb clauses

Adverb clauses are dependent clauses that function like single-word adverbs (see 9d). Unlike noun and adjective clauses, adverb clauses have greater freedom of position in the sentence:

> I like Dickens *because he combines humor with pathos.*
> *Because he combines humor with pathos,* I prefer Dickens to other novelists.

A sentence may sound awkward if the adverb clause follows an adjective clause:

Awkward

> I like Dickens, who wrote *David Copperfield*, because he combines humor with pathos.

The following revision makes the sentence even more awkward:

> Because he combines humor with pathos, I like Dickens, who wrote *David Copperfield*.

This sentence is awkward and confusing because it emphasizes the less important information placed at the end. The focus of the sentence is not that Dickens wrote *David Copperfield* (this information merely identifies Dickens as the author) but that Dickens combines humor and pathos. The solution is to reduce the adjective clause to a phrase so to emphasize the more important information:

Revised

> I like Dickens, the author of *David Copperfield*, because he combines humor with pathos.

EXERCISE

Rewrite any of the following sentences that contain misplaced clauses:

1. The snow caused the flooding, which melted quickly.
2. Because the streams overflowed, the people near them had to be taken to high ground.
3. The people had to be taken to high ground when the streams overflowed, because they were in danger.
4. Not many people knew that she was the writer's first wife, who did not know him well.
5. Whatever the cost, we better have the car repaired, which our insurance should cover.
6. No matter what you are told, read all the chapters assigned, which the exam will cover.

7. Read all the chapters assigned, except the final chapter, which the exam will cover.
8. The final chapter of the chemistry text discusses the molecule, the whole of which was assigned for the exam.
9. Not one of the experiments we performed was on the exam, which I assumed would be.
10. She is one of several women in the course whose aim is to enter medical school.

20e | Dangling modifiers

Consider again this sentence from earlier in the chapter:

Hunting for food, you must drive into the backcountry where grizzlies roam.

The verbal phrase *hunting for food* is misplaced in the sentence, connecting to the word *you* instead of to the word it modifies—*grizzlies*. It is called a dangling modifier when it hangs or "dangles" in the sentence without a subject:

Hunting for food, you must go into grizzly country.

1 Participial phrases

Participial phrases are verb forms that function as adjectives (see 9c). A sentence may be unclear if a participial phrase dangles or hangs awkwardly in the sentence, without a subject:

Unclear
Driving down the highway, a grizzly was seen.

To correct the sentence, begin the main clause with the subject of the verbal:

Revised
Driving down the highway, *we* saw the bear.

As this example shows, dangling modifiers often arise in using the passive voice (*a grizzly was seen*). Shifting the sentence to the active voice easily corrects the problem. Whenever a verbal phrase opens the sentence, the subject of the verbal should be the subject of the main clause.

Note that **absolute phrases** (see 8a) are not dangling modifiers since they modify the whole sentence and not particular words:

No objection being heard, the meeting adjourned.
The plan having failed, the committee is proposing another.

2 Gerund phrases

Gerunds are verb forms (or verbals) that end in *-ing* and function as nouns (see 9c). Like nouns, gerunds can take objects. As verbals they also take adverbial modifiers:

Chopping wood requires a sharp axe.
Running slowly is just as tiring as *running fast*.

Like participial phrases, gerund phrases dangle in the sentence when the doer is not mentioned or named:

Unclear
In chopping wood, the axe must have a sturdy handle and a strong blade.

To correct the sentence, name the doer in the main clause:

Revised
In chopping wood, *a person* needs an axe with a sturdy handle and a strong blade.

3 Infinitive phrases

Like the participle and the gerund, the **infinitive phrase** is a verbal—a verb form that adds the preposition *to* and functions as a nominal, adjectival, or adverbial (see 7c). Infinitive phrases also require a specific reference in the sentence. In the following sentence, the lack of specific reference creates momentary ambiguity:

Ambiguous
To hit a golfball off the tee, a good driver is needed.

Revised
To hit a golfball off the tee, the golfer needs a good driver.

Changing the verb to active voice usually corrects the reference.

The following sentence is common in spoken English:

More work is required to pass the course.

In written English, the subject is specified:

To pass the course, you need to do more work.

The opening infinitive modifier *To pass* creates the expectation that the subject will refer to the person taking the course.

4   Reduced clauses

Reduced or **elliptical clauses** can also dangle in the sentence:

Ambiguous
When told the fire was out, the order to evacuate the building was cancelled.

To correct the sentence, make the subject of the main clause the person who was confronted by the facts:

Revised
When told the fire was out, *the manager* cancelled the order to evacuate the building.

EXERCISE

Correct any of the following sentences that contain dangling modifiers:

1. After hammering the nails, the wood should be treated with shellac.
2. The registrar was notified on hearing that the transcript had not been sent.
3. An application will be sent, once the transcript is received.
4. To write well, a good dictionary is essential.
5. Dragging under the car, it was impossible to remove the limb while climbing the steep hill.
6. Forced to climb the stairs, the top floor was hard to reach.
7. Considering how far Los Angeles is from Denver, it's remarkable how short the flight was.
8. On hearing the motion, there was a call for the question.
9. Given the different opinions expressed, it's no wonder the motion lost.
10. Far up the mountain was seen a herd of elk, taking photos.

20f Split constructions

Split constructions can make sentences awkward. But not all split constructions have this effect. The "rule" that infinitives are *never* split is, in fact, not a rule at all. Effective sentences often contain split infinitives. The following are guidelines on effective and ineffective ways to split constructions in a sentence.

1 Splitting subject and verb

Splitting a pronoun subject from its verb usually makes a sentence awkward:

Awkward
We, wondering what had caused the explosion and fire, *whispered* about the accident anxiously.

Revised
Wondering what had caused the explosion and fire, *we whispered* about the accident anxiously.

When a split of this kind does occur, the opening pronoun is given more than double stress:

He countersigned the check. *She*, knowing the check was forged, *refused*.

Notice that the split is not awkward when the subject is a noun or noun phrase:

The crowd of people, wondering what had caused the explosion and fire, *whispered* about the accident anxiously.

2 Splitting a verb phrase

Verb phrases are occasionally split by single words and absolute phrases—usually with full stress when spoken:

I have *fully* considered the matter.
I have, *to be honest about it*, not yet considered the matter.

But splitting a verb phrase with a long adjective modifier usually makes the sentence sound awkward:

351

Awkward

I have, *wanting to make a decision at this time*, considered the matter.

Revised

Wanting to make a decision at this time, I have considered the matter.

3 Splitting an infinitive

Writers occasionally split the infinitive to achieve emphasis or to avoid ambiguity:

The ability of water *to readily evaporate and condense* in the atmosphere has a profound effect on monsoon circulation.
— Peter J. Webster, "Monsoons" (emphasis added)

Placing the adverb *readily* before the words *evaporate* and *condense* shows that it modifies both words, not just one or the other as in the following ambiguous revisions:

Ambiguous

The ability of water *readily* to evaporate and condense in the atmosphere has a profound effect on monsoon circulation.
The ability of water to evaporate and condense *readily* in the atmosphere has a profound effect on monsoon circulation.

If you do split an infinitive, it is best to restrict the splitting to a single word or short phrase.

EXERCISE

Correct those sentences that contain awkward or confusing split constructions:

1. We decided, having discussed whether we were doing the right thing, the future so uncertain, not to buy the car.
2. We, uncertain what size car we would need, thought it best to wait until spring.
3. The mayor asked the council to, given the extent of the flooding, vote to make money available for relief.
4. They voted to quickly as possible deal with the emergency.
5. Only those people who have had, recently, first-aid training should assist.
6. He is willing to as soon as possible transfer the deed.

(continued on page 354)

*The crew can no longer tolerate Captain Bligh's
ruthless splitting of infinitives.*

Drawing by Handelsman; © 1989 The New Yorker Magazine, Inc.

7. The remaining campers, certain that the weather forecast was mistaken, decided to remain in the park.
8. One, if on the highway for a long trip, should carry sufficient supplies and food for an emergency.
9. We don't intend to foolishly sacrifice our advantage by discussing our moves with reporters.
10. Spring is the best season to, after preparing the soil, transplant flowers and shrubs.

Summary

20a To avoid awkwardness and ambiguity, place single-word modifiers as close as possible to the word or phrase they modify.

20b Avoid squinting modifiers that point to the words or phrases that precede and follow them.

Ambiguous	**Revised**
People who watch television *rarely* read a great deal.	People who *rarely* watch television read a great deal.

20c To avoid ambiguity, place phrasal modifiers immediately before or after the words they modify, or add a comma.

Ambiguous	**Revised**
She described her mistake to the man with a grin.	With a grin, she described her mistake to the man. She described her mistake to the man, with a grin.
We saw the grizzly driving down the highway.	Driving down the highway, we saw the grizzly.

20d Place clausal modifiers next or close to the words they modify.

Put adjective clauses next to the words they modify (**20d 1**):

Ambiguous	**Revised**
The box arrived with the mail, which he had left on the bus.	The box *that he had left on the bus* arrived with the mail. The box, *which he had left on the bus,* arrived with the mail.

Put adverb clauses close to the verb (**20d 2**)

20e Revise sentences that contain dangling modifiers.

To correct a dangling modifier, begin the main clause with the word that the modifier is meant to describe (**20e 1–3**):

Ambiguous	**Revised**
Driving down the highway, a grizzly was seen.	Driving down the highway, *we* saw a grizzly.

Begin the main clause with the word that a reduced or elliptical clause is meant to describe (**20e 4**):

When told the fire was out, the order to evacuate the building was cancelled.	When told the fire was out, *the manager* cancelled the order to evacuate the building.

20f Split constructions can make sentences awkward and confusing.

Don't split the subject and predicate or a verb phrase with a long modifier (**20f 1**):

Awkward	**Revised**
We, wondering what had caused the explosion and fire, *whispered* anxiously about the accident.	Wondering what had caused the explosion and fire, *we whispered* anxiously about the accident.

Split infinitives with single words or short phrases if necessary (**20f 2**).

PART SIX

PUNCTUATION AND MECHANICS

21

End Punctuation

□

In the eight chapters of Part Six, we turn to the rules and conventions that govern sentence **punctuation** and **mechanics.** Some rules are fixed: question marks punctuate direct questions, never indirect questions. Other uses of punctuation are conventional; these can vary and sometimes even change over time. The semicolon and colon, for instance, are used less in writing today than in earlier writing. Journalism has influenced this change. Most newspapers and magazines favor short sentences and paragraphs, assuming that short paragraphs are easy to read and hold the audience's attention. A short paragraph usually has minimal punctuation, containing two or three related ideas that are stated in separate sentences without semicolons or colons. These and other punctuation marks are necessary in longer paragraphs that group main and subordinate ideas and details instead of dividing them.

A series of short paragraphs is not necessarily easier to read than a long paragraph that organizes a series of related ideas and details. An essay consisting of one- or two-sentence paragraphs is, in fact, as difficult to read as an unparagraphed essay. Your readers will not grasp the thought of your essay if you shift focus every two or three sentences. Thus, in a well-developed paragraph, commas, semicolons, colons, dashes, and other punctuation marks keep ideas in focus by indicating how ideas and details are related. Knowing how to use the various marks of punctuation is essential in organizing effective paragraphs.

Chapters 21–26 cover the rules of punctuation as well as the conventional uses and choices available to the writer. In many instances, you can choose the punctuation that best expresses the relationship of ideas and nuances of meaning. Chapter 27 turns to the mechanics of writing—how to use capitals, abbreviations, and numbers. Rules of spelling are then discussed in Chapter 28. Since errors in punctuation and spelling are connected to how we pronounce words and speak sentences, we begin with the connection between vocal intonation and writing.

21a Punctuation and meaning

1 Voice and meaning

When you speak a sentence, you punctuate it with your voice to convey meaning and emotion. Your listener hears the stops and pauses and changes in pitch. Your reader depends also on punctuation to understand the same sentence.

Consider the following unpunctuated words:

The law requires dogs to be leashed

End punctuation—periods, question marks, exclamation points—indicates your intention in a general way:

Statement of fact	The law requires dogs to be leashed.
Exclamation of surprise, shock, or outrage	The law requires dogs to be leashed!
Question	The law requires dogs to be leashed?

Punctuation indicates that the sentence is a statement, an exclamation, or a question, though it cannot always express the exact intent or meaning of a statement. For its interpretation, you sometimes depend on its context or surrounding statements. If neither punctuation nor context can do so, you may state your intention directly:

> I am surprised (or shocked or outraged) that the ordinance requires dogs to be leashed.

2 What punctuation does

Punctuation allows you to control meaning in sentences in the absence of vocal inflection or pitch. The inflections and tones of the many dialects of English vary so much that written punctuation can express only a few of them. But most speakers of these dialects share a written standard: written punctuation marks conform to established conventions of usage, their main purpose being to set off complete sentences and clarify the relationship between phrases and clauses.

Thus, in written English we know that a dependent clause defines or expresses essential information, when commas do not set it off:

> Most of Morocco is so desolate *that no wild animal bigger than a hare can live on it.*
> —George Orwell, "Marrakech" (emphasis added)

> One day a poor old creature *who could not have been more than four feet tall* crept past me under a vast load of wood.
> —George Orwell (emphasis added)

By contrast, we know that a dependent clause is nonessential, commenting on the main clause, when it is set off by commas:

> She answered with a shrill wail, almost a scream, *which was partly gratitude but mainly surprise.*
> —George Orwell (emphasis added)

Speakers distinguish among similar parenthetical or explanatory details through pauses, marked by intonation or pitch. However, these markers vary among the many dialects of English, and in some dialects they are barely distinct. Therefore, punctuation is not always a reliable way to indicate these pauses in speech.

In fiction, punctuation is often used expressively. Novelists and short story writers occasionally italicize and capitalize words to convey the feelings, tone, or attitude of characters:

> "What's going to happen to him now?" I asked again.
> "They'll send him away some place and they'll try to cure him." He shook his head. "Maybe he'll even think he's kicked the

habit. Then they'll let him loose"—he gestured, throwing his cigarette into the gutter. "That's all."

"What do you mean, that's *all?*"

But I knew what he meant.

"I *mean*, that's *all.*" He turned his head and looked at me, pulling down the corners of his mouth. "Don't you know what I mean?" he asked softly.

—James Baldwin, "Sonny's Blues"

As soon as the children saw they could move their arms and legs, they scrambled out of the car, shouting, "We've had an ACCIDENT!"

—Flannery O'Connor, "A Good Man Is Hard to Find"

Even when used expressively in fiction, punctuation is still limited in what it can convey. In the first passage, Baldwin uses italics to convey nuances of meaning, yet he tells us that the final speaker asked the question softly. In the second passage, O'Connor tells us directly that the children shouted.

In nonfictional prose, punctuation is typically used less expressively and italics are used rarely for emphasis. Still, punctuation offers wide opportunities to convey attitude and emotion. If, for example, you want to stress a particular idea, you can place it between dashes. To show that an idea is an aside or a momentary interruption, you can place it in parentheses. To show that two ideas are parts of a single idea or thought, you can join them with a semicolon. To show that one statement explains or amplifies another, you can join them with a colon.

EXERCISES

1. Write down the various ways the following sentences can be punctuated, and give the corresponding meanings:
    a. The dog bit the letter carrier
    b. More people watch television than read newspapers
    c. Stop smoking
    d. Please stop smoking
    e. Is that why you turned off the radio
    f. The election ended in a landslide
2. Describe how the punctuation of the following passage helps to convey the meaning of the statements and the tone or attitude of the speaker.

    We had a lady come in about six months ago. She wanted her car in the same spot. I said, "Sorry lady, can't put it in a certain spot." She said, "I want it in *that* spot." She came back and I had it in *that* spot. She said, "Thank you."

I said, "Okay, lady." She came back again and we was filled up. She wanted *that* spot again, and I said, "No, I'm filled, lady. I can't get you *that* spot. I can't get you *any* spot."

—Studs Terkel, *Working* ◼

21b | Uses of end punctuation

1 The period

Use a **period** (.) to mark the following:

Plain Statement of Fact
The meeting was canceled.

Indirect Question
She asked why the meeting had been canceled.

Compare this statement with the following direct question:

She asked, "Why was the meeting canceled?"

Unemphatic Request or Command
Ask for a seat on the aisle.
Give the dog the bone.

Compare these statements with the following emphatic requests:

Insist on a seat on the aisle!
Don't tease the dog!

2 The question mark

Use a **question mark** (?) to punctuate a direct question:

Why was the meeting canceled?

We just saw that the indirect question omits the question mark:

The woman asked why the meeting had been canceled.

Notice that the question mark always follows the question, never the speaker tag:

Nonstandard	Revised
"When does the class meet," the student asked?	"When does the class meet?" the student asked.

Notice also that the question mark is always used without other punctuation when a speaker tag follows.

In giving dates, use a question mark to show that a date is uncertain:

> The English dramatist and poet Ben Jonson (1573?–1637) wrote comedies and tragedies.

You can also use a question mark in parentheses to show that a fact or figure is uncertain:

> The destruction of Troy about 1200 B.C. (?) was the subject of the many heroic poems woven into the *Iliad*.

Occasionally, the question mark appears in a series of questions that forms a single sentence:

> Will the forest be squeezed dry in a few years or can the farming, mining, or whatever go on forever? Who will benefit from the new use—the people of the forest? the poor of the country? a domestic elite? foreign consumers?
> —Catherine Caufield, *In the Rainforest*

3 The exclamation point

Use the **exclamation point** (!) to punctuate *commands:*

> Sit!

But omit the exclamation point in making requests:

> Turn in your exams by three o'clock.

The exclamation point is always used without other punctuation. Omit the comma that normally separates a quotation from the speaker tag when an exclamation point is used:

> "Sit!" he commanded the dog.
> "Don't tease the dog!" the old woman shouted from the porch.

Compare these statements with the following unemphatic request that uses a comma:

> "Please sit down," the woman said to her visitor.

As in indirect questions, omit the exclamation mark in reporting a command:

Nonstandard	Revised
I told the dog to sit!	I told the dog to sit.

Use the exclamation point with **interjections** (9f) when you want them to express amazement, pleasure, or a similar emotion:

Wow!
Nothing doing!
I don't believe it!

His son was too strong—of course!—to need medicine.
          —Doris Lessing, "The Temptation of Jack Orkney"

Use the exclamation point sparingly to express surprise or shock. A paragraph or an essay containing a string of exclamation points loses its force:

We saw a falling star just before ten o'clock! It set the sky ablaze! It may not have been a falling star! It may have been an unknown object!

EXERCISE

Punctuate the following items as statements, questions, or exclamations as appropriate. Refer to the examples on page 359 of the meanings possible through punctuation.

1. Hands over your head
2. Please turn off the lights when you leave the room
3. Down in front
4. The street flooded minutes after the rain began
5. Who says all politicians are crooks
6. I wonder why the traffic took so long to clear
7. I asked why did the traffic take so long to clear
8. What a movie
9. Explain yourself
10. You're joking

Summary

21a In speaking, you stop, pause, and change the pitch of your voice to convey meaning and emotion. In writing, punctuation conveys the meaning of sentences.

21b End punctuation indicates the intention of a statement.

Use the *period* to mark a plain statement of fact, an unemphatic request or command, and an indirect question (**21b 1**).

> The cat is sitting on the piano.
> Ask for a seat on the aisle.
> She asked why the class had been canceled.
> The police officer asked who had found the dog.

The *question mark* appears after a direct question (**21b 2**):

> "Why was the meeting canceled?" the woman asked.

Omit the question mark after an indirect question:

> The woman asked why the meeting had been canceled.

Use the *exclamation point* with commands, certain emphatic statements, and interjections (**21b 3**):

> Sit!
> I don't believe it!
> Wow!

The Comma **22**

□

In writing a sentence, we cannot depend on the vocal markers we depend on in speaking; pauses and pitch changes vary widely from speaker to speaker. If writers attempted to punctuate their sentences exactly as they speak them, punctuation would vary so widely that much writing would be difficult to read. For this reason, commas and other punctuation marks are necessary in setting off phrases and clauses in the written sentence. This chapter describes the conventional uses of the **comma,** beginning with the separation of independent and dependent clauses.

22a Clauses

1 Independent clauses

Use a comma before a *coordinating conjunction* that joins **independent clauses**—clauses that can stand alone as self-contained sentences:

It is raining today, *and* it will probably rain tomorrow.
It will not rain today, *but* it surely will rain tomorrow.
Take the course next semester, *for* it won't be offered again.
Take the course, *or* go to the dean and ask for an exemption.
He made good sense about why I should take the course, *yet* I
   was unconvinced.
The bear did not move or make any noise, *nor* did I.
His argument made good sense, *so* I took his advice.

You can omit the comma when the clauses are short and
have the same grammatical form:

The bear looked at me and I looked at it.
It did not move nor did I.

Remember that a *comma splice* (17a) results when a
comma appears between independent clauses without a coordinating conjunction. Complementary clauses that form a
single idea are the exception:

Tartuffe is not a hypocrite, he is the hypocrite.
                       —Edith Hamilton, *The Greek Way*

2   Dependent clauses

Commas set off **dependent clauses** and other modifiers that
comment on or add nonessential information to the main
clause. These clauses and modifiers are called **nonrestrictive.**
Dependent clauses and other modifiers are **restrictive** when
they define or identify the referent of the noun, add essential
information, or complete the main clause. Omission of a restrictive modifier changes the meaning of the sentence; omission of a nonrestrictive modifier does not.

Nonrestrictive
Herman Melville, *who spent eighteen months on a whaling ship*,
used his experiences in writing *Moby Dick.*

Restrictive
Moby Dick is one of many novels *that Melville wrote about his sea
experiences.*

Dependent clauses serve as nominal, adjectival, and adverbial clauses—clauses that perform the same functions as
nouns, adjectives, and adverbs (see 7c). *Noun clauses* function

367

as subjects and complements and therefore are not set off with commas:

> *Whoever scores the highest points* wins the game.
> Give the trophy to *whoever wins the game*.

Use commas to set off nonrestrictive **adjective clauses** from the nouns and noun phrases they modify:

> The speaker was Seymour Karnow, *who wrote Vietnam: A History*.
> I read Seymour Karnow's *Vietnam: A History*, *which describes the Vietnam War*.
> The family moved in June from San Diego, *where they lived for almost fifteen years*.

Don't use commas (or any other punctuation) to set off restrictive adjective clauses. Compare the following sentences:

Restrictive	**Nonrestrictive**
The Elizabeth Taylor *who wrote numerous stories and novels* is not Elizabeth Taylor the actress.	The British writer Elizabeth Taylor, *who wrote numerous stories and novels*, is not the actress Elizabeth Taylor.

In the sentence to the left, the adjective clause (*who wrote numerous stories and novels*) identifies Elizabeth Taylor as the British writer, not the actress. In the sentence to the right, the same clause comments on the British writer, already identified by the opening noun phrase (*The British writer*).

The relative pronoun *that* always introduces a restrictive clause (see 8b). The relative pronoun *which* usually introduces a nonrestrictive clause:

Restrictive
The Dickens novel *that* I saw dramatized is *Nicholas Nickleby*.

Nonrestrictive
The Mystery of Edwin Drood, *which* Dickens left unfinished, has also been dramatized.

In deciding whether to separate an adjective clause from the word it modifies, consider the sense of the sentence first.

Adverbial clauses modify the verb of the main clause, adjectivals, other adverbials, or the whole sentence (7c). The *sub-*

ordinating conjunctions that introduce adverbial clauses include the following:

after	before	once	whenever
although (though)	except that	since	where
as	if	unless	whereas
as soon as	in order that	until	wherever
because	in that	when	while

Don't set off restrictive adverbial clauses that follow the
main clause:

> The weekend is the time *when you probe to see how much people
> really like you.* During the week they are forced to be with you
> and be nice to you *because their work requires it.*
> —Max Gunther, "The Weekend World" (emphasis added)

But set off adverbial clauses that open a sentence, whether the
clause is restrictive or nonrestrictive. The following sentence
opens with a restrictive clause, set off with a comma. The sentence concludes with a restrictive clause that is not set off:

> *Although we had been driving for several hours in heavy rain,* we
> decided not to stop *until we arrived home.*

Writers occasionally omit the comma when the subject of
a short opening adverbial clause and the subject of the main
clause are the same:

> When *he* came to the highway *Neil* turned right, toward Olinger,
> instead of left toward the Turnpike.
> —John Updike, "The Happiest I've Been" (emphasis added)

If you decide to omit the comma from a short opening
clause or phrase, make sure that the omission does not make
the sentence confusing:

Confusing	**Revised**
A few weeks before she be- came ill with a high fever.	A few weeks before, she be- came ill with a high fever.
Of the team of twenty one or two will qualify for the Olympics.	Of the team of twenty, one or two will qualify for the Olympics.
On our visit to Boston that night we stayed at a hotel downtown.	On our visit to Boston, that night we stayed at a hotel downtown.

EXERCISE

Add commas where needed in the following sentences:

1. I won't go unless you do.
2. The book that earned Annie Dillard the Pulitzer Prize is *Pilgrim at Tinker Creek.*
3. The third game of the World Series which is now in the seventeenth inning has already broken the record.
4. The election will take place as scheduled even though one of the candidates has withdrawn.
5. The issue of *Newsweek* that arrived yesterday contains a report on the greenhouse effect.
6. The one red-covered book you find on the shelf is the book I need for the course.
7. Few of the people who heard her speak knew that she was the woman who ran for Congress.
8. When she received word of her election, she resigned from her law firm.
9. None of us who had ever seen the couple were surprised that they won the contest.
10. The one previous tornado that struck the town at noon on April 4 did more damage than any storm in the history of the town. ■

Series

1 Clauses, phrases, and words

Use commas to divide words, phrases, and clauses that form a series or list:

Clauses

If you knew about the fundamental substance, you could do much more than make simple money: you could boil up a cure-all for every disease affecting humankind, you could rid the world of evil, and, while doing this, you could make a universal solvent capable of dissolving anything you might want to dissolve.
                              —Lewis Thomas, "Alchemy"

Phrases

The cell membrane is no longer a simple skin for the cell; it is a fluid mosaic, a sea of essential mobile signals, an organ in itself

[*noun phrases*]. Cells communicate with one another, exchange messages like bees in a hive, regulate one another [*verb phrases*].
—Lewis Thomas, "Making Science Work"

Words
The East River area had such gangs as the Buckaroos, Hookers, Daybreak Boys, and Swamp Angels, while the Chrystie, Forsyth, and Elizabeth street region had the notorious Slaughter House gang.
—Robert E. Riegel, *Young America, 1830–1840*

Use a comma to separate three or more items in a series, like those in Riegel's sentence. Although some writers omit the final comma of the series—the comma preceding *and*—its omission can create ambiguity. For instance, omitting the comma after the phrase "Daybreak Boys" would suggest to some readers that the name of the gang is "Daybreak Boys and Swamp Angels."

2 Coordinate adjectives

Use commas to separate a series of **coordinate** or **parallel adjectives** that modify the same word:

He was a man of about fifty, tall, portly, and imposing, with a massive, strongly marked face and a commanding figure.
—Sir Arthur Conan Doyle, *Adventures of Sherlock Holmes*

Coordinate adjectives are interchangeable, a fact you can test by reversing their order or putting *and* between them:

He was a man of about fifty—portly, tall, *and* imposing. . . .
Tall, imposing, portly—he was a man of about fifty. . . .

Each adjective modifies the phrase *man of about fifty*.

Don't use a comma to separate superimposed adjectives or determiners from noun phrases consisting of an adjective and a noun:

A double carriage–sweep, with a snow-clad lawn, stretched down in front to two large iron gates which closed the entrance.
—Sir Arthur Conan Doyle (emphasis added)

Here the determiner *two* modifies the phrase *large iron gates,* and the adjective *large* modifies *iron gates.* The adjectives *large* and *iron* cannot be interchanged; neither can the determiner *two* and the adjectives.

EXERCISE

Add commas where needed in the following sentences:

1. The gray cloudy sky promised rain.
2. She described herself as friendly curious interested in music somewhat ambitious but not excessively so.
3. In the driveway is a battered 1973 coal gray Plymouth.
4. Hand this book to the tall blonde man talking to the woman on the stairs.
5. The dogs barked the cats snarled and the children hooted.
6. The tattered discolored dark green pages made the book impossible to read.
7. The discolored dark green tattered pages made the book impossible to read.
8. The very long dark green worn carpet showed the true age of the house.
9. To find the source of the noise, she looked first to the north then to the west and finally to the south.
10. She asked that we collect the specimens sort and tag them according to type and finally write a brief description of each.

22c Words and phrases

1 Single words

Use commas to set off words that qualify or change the emphasis of the sentence:

> *However,* we need facts to make the decision.
> There is, *consequently,* something you can do.

Omit the comma when the adverb is essential to the meaning of the sentence and is not a qualifying or parenthetical comment:

> He noted that prices had remained stable throughout the year.
> But he *also* explained that prices would probably increase.

A comma is used to set off a concluding modifier even though the modifier restricts the meaning:

The price of food had already risen. He speculated that the price of oil would rise, *too.*

2 Modifying phrases

Don't set off short introductory phrases that restrict the meaning of the sentence:

> John usually acts cautiously. *In this matter* he showed bad judgment.

Use a comma to set off a long introductory phrase, whether or not the phrase restricts the meaning, except when the verb immediately follows:

> *In deciding to quit school,* John showed bad judgment.
> *In front of the former city courthouse* stands a statue of George Washington.

In the second example, a comma is unnecessary because the verb *stands* immediately follows the introductory phrase.

Always set off introductory participial and infinitive phrases with a comma (see 9c):

Opening Participle
Shouting, the old man waved a white cloth at the passing cars.

Opening Infinitive Phrase
To explain how the heart pumps blood, the teacher used a diagram.

Always use a comma to set off nonrestrictive modifiers that follow the main clause:

> She ate rapidly, *worrying that she would miss her train.*

Use commas to set off transitional or parenthetical phrases, no matter where they appear in the sentence:

> We need, *as a result,* more facts to make the decision.
> *In fact,* the winter was longer than we had expected.

But don't set off restrictive modifiers or objective complements that identify or define the noun:

> The woman *holding the violin* is the soloist.
> The engineering report left Sylvia *feeling a success.*

3 Contrasting phrases

Set off **contrasting phrases** with commas, no matter where they appear in the sentence:

Scott, *not Amundsen*, died in the Antarctic.

Make an exception for phrases introduced by *but* meaning "except":

No one *but Mozart* could have written that concerto.

Here the phrase *but Mozart* restricts the meaning.

4 Absolute phrases

Always set off an **absolute phrase** with a single comma. Unlike the participle, which modifies a specific word or phrase, the absolute phrase modifies the whole clause or sentence, connecting to no single element grammatically:

Participle
Falling in torrents, the rain soaked the ground.

Absolute phrase
The rain having soaked the ground, we had the picnic indoors.

As the following examples show, the absolute phrase may follow the main clause and may occur in a series:

Six boys came over the hill half an hour early that afternoon, running hard, *their heads down*, *their forearms working*, *their breath whistling*.
     —John Steinbeck, "The Red Pony" (emphasis added)

He could see the two other boys down below, *the ball going back and forth between them as if they were bowling on the grass*, and *Glennie's crew-cut head looking like a sea urchin*.
     —Richard Wilbur, "A Game of Catch" (emphasis added)

5 Appositives

An **appositive** is a noun or noun phrase that explains or further identifies the word or words it precedes or follows as in the following sentences:

Robert Falcon Scott, *the English explorer*, died in the Antarctic in 1912.

A naval commander who had visited the Antarctic in previous expeditions, Scott knew the hazards that he probably would face in trying to reach the South Pole.

Use commas to set off nonrestrictive appositives, wherever they appear in the sentence. The appositives in the preceding sentences are nonrestrictive—in the first sentence the appositive gives additional information about Scott; in the second it comments on his qualifications. In the following example, the long appositive phrase both identifies and comments on the subject of the sentence:

The baby's first gropings and touchings, *those various mouthings and tastings and smellings that become increasingly purposeful during the first year of life*, may be seen as the beginnings of play.
—Marie Winn, *The Plug-in Drug* (emphasis added)

Most appositives are nonrestrictive. But some are restrictive, forming a single phrase with a noun or noun phrase they immediately follow:

Scott *the explorer* died in the Antarctic whereas Scott *the astronaut* is still living.

Restrictive appositives are not set off with commas.

When an appositive comes at the end of the sentence, it is set off with a comma:

We spent three days in Juneau, *the capital of Alaska.*

(See 25b on uses of the dash with long appositives and emphatic short ones.)

EXERCISE

Add commas where needed in the following sentences and explain why they are necessary:

1. Contrary to what you heard the court will be in session.
2. Herman Melville's first novel *Typee* describes his experiences in the Marquesas Islands in the South Pacific.
3. George Plimpton's *Paper Lion* an account of his training with a pro-football team was first published in 1966.
4. She found the book interesting her curiosity about the life of the professional player growing from page to page.

5. He insisted finally that no action be taken.
6. We cannot take action no matter what happens.
7. The empty boat began to sink its keel gashed by the submerged rock at the entrance to the harbor.
8. Nothing happened except for the scuffle in the street.
9. Joe Louis the heavyweight boxer wrote an autobiography.
10. The heavyweight boxer Joe Louis wrote an autobiography.

22d   Quotations

Use commas to set off a **speaker tag** that interrupts a quotation:

> "But if thought corrupts language," *George Orwell wrote*, "language can also corrupt thought."

Notice that the comma that sets off the speaker tag precedes the quotation mark.

Omit the comma if the quotation contains a question mark or exclamation point and the speaker tag follows:

> "Was the meeting canceled?" the woman asked.
> "Give me liberty or give me death!" Patrick Henry said.

Also omit the comma when the speaker tag includes the word *that:*

> Thomas Jefferson wrote to James Madison *that* "a little rebellion now and then is a good thing."

(See 21b on the punctuation of indirect quotations.)

22e   Other uses of commas

1 Dates and numbers

Use a comma to divide the day of the month from the year:

> May 17, 1930

Omit the comma when you give only the month and year or when you invert the day and month:

May 1930
12 May 1930

A comma follows the year when the date appears before the end of the sentence:

She was born February 14, 1934, in Boston, Massachusetts.

Commas are used to divide units in numbers of four or more digits:

1,180
10,180
100,180
1,000,000
100,000,000

The comma is optional in four-digit numbers:

1,000 *or* 1000
1,180 *or* 1180

Omit the comma in street addresses:

13527 Fourth Avenue

And omit it in page numbers and four-digit years:

page 1250
1990 *but* 20,000 B.C.

Use a comma in giving measurements that contain two or more parts:

twelve feet, two inches

2   Addresses

Use a comma to separate a city from the state:

Cuyahoga Falls, Ohio

A comma follows the state when it appears before the end of a sentence:

She lives in Cuyahoga Falls, Ohio, a city north of Akron.

Commas separate the units of an address but not the street

number from the name of the street or the state from the ZIP code:

250 Elm Street, Cuyahoga Falls, Summit County, Ohio   44221

3 Names, titles, degrees, and identifying phrases

Use a comma when inverting a proper name:

Dole, Elizabeth
O'Connell, Mary D.

Commas separate full and abbreviated titles that follow the proper name:

Elizabeth Dole, Secretary of Labor
Mary D. O'Connell, M.D.

Don't use a comma when the name precedes the title:

Secretary of Labor Elizabeth Dole
Dr. Mary D. O'Connell

Use a comma in addressing a person in an informal letter:

Dear Jim,

But use a colon in formal address:

Dear Secretary Dole:
Dear Dr. O'Connell:

A comma is also used in the closing phrase of a letter:

Sincerely,
Yours truly,

The following procedures will help you use commas more effectively in drafting and revising your papers:

- If you set off a clause with a pair of commas, look to see whether the clause defines the subject or provides essential information. Read the sentence aloud, omitting the clause to see if the sentence changes in meaning. If the clause is restrictive, omit the commas.
- Watch for single commas. These correctly follow participial and absolute phrases; single commas also separate a nonrestrictive adjective clause from the noun or noun phrase it modifies. Single commas don't separate the main constituents of the sentence

---

✔

Checklist: Using Commas

1. Have I set off introductory qualifiers and transitional words and phrases (*however, moreover, to be sure*) with commas?
2. Have I used commas to set off opening participial phrases (*Failing to reach the English coast*) and opening absolute phrases (*The Armada having failed to reach the coast*)?
3. Have I set off opening adverbial clauses (those beginning with words like *since, because,* and *although*) with commas?
4. Have I used commas to set off nonrestrictive clauses and other modifiers that comment on the main clause? Have I misused commas with restrictive clauses and other modifiers essential to the meaning of the sentence?
5. Have I set off contrasting phrases with commas?
6. Have I used a comma to separate a speaker tag from a direct quotation?
7. Have I separated dates, addresses, and numbers with appropriate commas?

(subject, verb, complement) unless modifiers intervene, and they don't separate independent clauses without a coordinating conjunction. (See 17a on the comma splice.)

■ If you use a comma in a position where it does not belong—for example, between the subject and predicate—try recasting the sentence. The problem in punctuation may arise from an awkward construction or arrangement of words.

EXERCISE

Add commas where appropriate in the following sentences:

1. The year 1939 marks the beginning of World War II.
2. Germany invaded Poland on September 1 1939 on the pretext that it was protecting German nationals living in the country.
3. He lives at 3255 Westlawn Avenue Akron Ohio a city in the northeastern part of the state.

4. The official census of the ward showed 32550 residents of voting age.
5. The woman on the platform is Elizabeth McClintock Nobel Prize Laureate.
6. The woman on the platform is Nobel Prize Laureate Elizabeth McClintock.
7. "Ask not what your country can do for you" President Kennedy said in his inaugural address of January 20 1961 "ask what you can do for your country."
8. President Kennedy was shot on November 22 1963 in an open automobile in Dealy Plaza in Dallas Texas.
9. Marcus Welby M.D. was a popular television show in the 1960s.
10. Send your letter to William R. Rehnquist The Chief Justice The Supreme Court Washington D.C. 20540. ■

22f | Misuses of the comma

Unnecessary commas make sentences difficult to read. The comma is misused when it sets off restrictive words, phrases, and clauses (see 22a and 22c). It is also misused when it separates independent clauses without a coordinating conjunction (see 17a on the *comma splice*). Following are other common misuses of the comma.

1 Unnecessary comma between subject and verb

Nonstandard
The course scheduled for
eight o'clock three days a
week**,** will be scheduled at
another hour.

Revised
The course scheduled for
eight o'clock three days a
week will be scheduled at
another hour.

In the sentence to the left, the single comma unnecessarily separates the subject from the predicate. The longer the subject noun phrase, the greater the risk of reading it as a modifying phrase.

Note that this rule does not apply if a qualifying or explanatory word or phrase appears after the subject. In this situation, commas are used in pairs:

The course, *in fact*, is required for graduation.

2 Unnecessary comma between verb and direct object

Nonstandard
The judge said, that she was levying a heavier fine than usual.

Revised
The judge said that she was levying a heavier fine than usual.

The needless comma in the sentence to the left possibly arises because the writer mistakes it for the comma that follows a speaker tag introducing a direct quotation:

Necessary Comma
The judge said, "I'm suspending the fine for this first offense."

3 Unnecessary comma between verb and subject complement

Nonstandard
The reason for the hike in food prices is, that the drought reduced the corn harvest.

Revised
The reason for the hike in food prices is that the drought reduced the corn harvest.

Although the long noun phrase seems to invite a comma, it is nonstandard. To decide whether you need a comma, reduce the subject to its core.

The reason is that the drought reduced the corn harvest.

4 Unnecessary comma between coordinate nouns

Nonstandard
I see no difference between my sentence, and your sentence.

Revised
I see no difference between my sentence and your sentence.

The compound objects form a single phrase with the preposition, making a comma unnecessary.

5 Unnecessary comma between coordinate verbs

Nonstandard
He explained his absence, and promised to be punctual in the future.

Revised
He explained his absence and promised to be punctual in the future.

The coordinate verbs in the sentence form a single phrase, broken by the comma in the sentence to the left. We sometimes need a comma to prevent misreading. Inserting a comma after the opening phrases clarifies the following sentences:

Necessary Comma
A few weeks before, he arrived home with a bad cold.

On the team of twenty, one or two will qualify.

EXERCISE

Add or delete commas where necessary in the following sentences. Note that some sentences may be punctuated correctly.

1. More errors result from carelessness, than neglect.
2. Many years after he wrote that he was returning to Idaho, where he had been raised.
3. The tall pine tree, which we planted a few years ago is dying.
4. Among the ninety six students held scholarships.
5. At twenty degrees below the car is hard to start.
6. I have more faith in their honesty, than you have.
7. She addressed the class that was graduating mid-year.
8. She reasoned, that the water would be warmer on the south shore than on the north.
9. She told the class about the strange animal, swimming close to shore.
10. On the ledge above the fire continued to burn out of control.

Summary

22a Commas with clauses.

Separate coordinate clauses with a comma and a coordinating conjunction (**22a 1**):

It is raining today, *and* it will probably rain tomorrow.

Set off nonrestrictive adjective clauses with commas
(**22a 2**):

> John, *who still has tickets to sell*, will be home later.

Set off opening adverbial clauses with a comma:

> *When you reach the highway*, you turn right.

Omit the comma when a restrictive adverbial clause follows the main clause:

> She is walking to school even though it is raining.

22b   Commas with series.

Use commas to divide words, phrases, and clauses that form a series (**22b 1**):

> Her sisters are a teacher, a lawyer, and a doctor.

Use commas to divide a series of coordinate adjectives if they are interchangeable (**22b 2**):

> He was short, thin, and bald.

22c   Commas with words and phrases.

Use commas to set off introductory words and phrases that qualify or change the focus of the sentence (**22c 1–2**):

> *To explain the process clearly*, you need a diagram.
> *However*, we need facts to make the decision.

Use commas to set off nonrestrictive words and phrases (**22c 1–2**):

> She ate rapidly, *worrying that she would miss her train.*

Don't use commas to set off restrictive words and phrases essential to the meaning of the sentence (**22c 1–2**):

> He also explained that prices would probably increase.

Always set off contrasting words and phrases with commas, no matter where they appear in the sentence (**22c 3**):

> Scott, *not Amundsen*, died in the Antarctic.

Always set off absolute phrases with a comma (**22c 4**):

> *The motion to adjourn having been made*, the meeting ended.

Set off a nonrestrictive appositive with commas but not a restrictive one (22c 5):

> Robert Falcon Scott, *the explorer*, died in the Antarctic in 1912.
> Scott *the explorer* died in Antarctic whereas Scott *the astronaut* is still alive.

22d Commas with quotations.

Use a comma to separate the speaker tag from a direct quotation (22d):

> *Patrick Henry said*, "Give me liberty or give me death!"

22e Other uses of the comma.

Use a comma to divide the month and day from the year (22e 1):

> May 17, 1930

Divide units in numbers of four or more digits with commas (22e 1):

> 10,543
> 10,543,230

Separate the units of an address with commas but not the street number from the street name or the state from the ZIP code (22e 2):

> 250 Elm St., Cuyahoga Falls, Summit County, Ohio   44221

Use a comma to separate a title or degree that follows a proper name (22e 3):

> Elizabeth Dole, Secretary of Transportation

22f Misuses of the comma.

Don't divide the main constituents of the sentence—the subject and verb and their complements—unless modifiers intervene:

Nonstandard
The course scheduled for eight o'clock three days a week, will be rescheduled.

Revised
The course scheduled for eight o'clock three days a week will be rescheduled.

Nonstandard	Revised
The judge said, that she was levying a heavier fine than usual.	The judge said that she was levying a heavier fine than usual.
The reason for the hike in food prices is, that the drought reduced the corn harvest.	The reason for the hike in food prices is that the drought reduced the corn harvest.

Don't use a comma with coordinate nouns or verbs or co-ordinate noun phrases or verb phrases:

Nonstandard	Revised
He is my friend, and your friend.	He is my friend and your friend.
He is my friend, and wants to be yours.	He is my friend and wants to be yours.

The Semicolon 23
and Colon

□

Semicolons and colons are important in achieving sentence and paragraph unity. Your readers are unlikely to see the relationships among your ideas and details if you do not connect words and phrases with proper punctuation. In connecting phrases and clauses, semicolons and colons serve as transitions, signaling the reader that ideas are closely related or that an idea is to be developed or amplified by what follows in the sentence or paragraph. This chapter shows how to use semicolons and colons and clarifies their roles in sentence and paragraph unity.

23a │ The semicolon

1 Semicolon with independent clauses

Use the **semicolon** (;) to join *independent clauses* in the absence of a period or a coordinating conjunction (*and, but, for,* *yet, so, or, nor).* The semicolon shows that ideas are closely related:

> Night fell quickly; at about four o'clock the fog poured down the San Francisco hillsides, covered the bay, and clouded the windows.
>
> —Maxine Hong Kingston, *China Men*

And the semicolon sets closely related ideas apart from other ideas:

> When I was a child I thought we lived at the end of the world. It was the eternity of the subway ride into the city that first gave me this idea. It took a long time getting to "New York"; it seemed longer getting back.
>
> —Alfred Kazin, "The Open Street"

Occasionally, the semicolon replaces the comma before a coordinating conjunction to give extra emphasis to what follows. In the following examples, the emphasis falls on an amplifying clause and an afterthought:

Amplifying Clauses

Ours is an age of fiendish competition; *and the constant effort,* not so much to get ahead as to keep afloat, is hardly calculated to make us less frantic. Ours is an age of incessant anxiety; *and our vivid awareness* of the fact is scarcely calculated to make us less anxious. Ours, all too graphically, is an age of violence; *and being reminded* of the fact at every turn is hardly calculated to make us less scared.
—Louis Kronenberger, "Unbrave New World" (emphasis added)

Afterthought

Sale of land could never be more than temporary; so when Indians, from Plymouth Rock to Oregon, sold land, they thought of the sale as a temporary arrangement. The moment that the payment ceased to come the land returned to the tribe; *or so they thought* as long as they could.
—Mari Sandoz, "Some Oddities of the American Indian" (emphasis added)

2   Semicolon with conjunctive adverbs

Adverbs often introduce independent clauses. In this position, they are followed by the comma:

> Inflation rose over 300 percent as a result of the war. *Therefore,* the government devalued the currency.

Economics is hard for me to understand. *In fact*, the English writer Thomas Carlyle called it "the dismal science."

If a semicolon connects these independent clauses, the adverb (*therefore*) or adverbial phrase (*in fact*) strengthens the conjunction of the clauses—thus the term *conjunctive adverb* (see 9e for a list):

Inflation rose over 300 percent as a result of the war; *therefore,* the government devalued the currency.

Economics is hard for me to understand; *in fact,* the English writer Thomas Carlyle called it "the dismal science."

Notice that you can put the adverb or adverbial phrase in various positions in the second clause, depending on the stress you wish to give it:

Inflation rose over 300 percent as a result of the war; the government *therefore* devalued the currency.

Economics is hard for me to understand; Carlyle, *in fact,* called it "the dismal science."

Always set off an adverb or adverbial phrase with a single comma when it opens the clause.

3 Semicolons and commas in a series

When one or more members of the series contain commas, use semicolons to separate the main parts of each member:

We visited Columbus, the capital of Ohio; Lansing, the capital of Michigan; and Springfield, the capital of Illinois.

Semicolons are optional if the members of the series are distinct without them. In the following passage, the author uses commas to punctuate the six-part series in his first sentence; he uses semicolons to punctuate the three-part series in the second sentence:

These years witnessed the passing of the old West, the disappearance of the frontier line and of good, cheap farm land, the decline of the cattle kingdom, the completion of the transcontinentals, the admission of the Omnibus States, and the final territorial organization of the trans-Mississippi area. They revealed a dangerous acceleration of the exploitation of natural resources; the seizure of the best forest, mineral, range, and farm land by corporations; and the beginnings of the conservation and reclamation movement.

—Henry Steele Commager, *The American Mind*
(describing America in the late 1800s)

Notice that the second member of the series in Commager's second sentence contains several parts (*the seizure of the best forest, mineral, range, and farm land by corporations*). This second sentence would be difficult to read if its three members were punctuated with commas instead of semicolons.

Writers sometimes use semicolons to combine a series of independent clauses into a single impression or idea:

> A large raw wound constantly oozes out protein; the body burns up calories trying to heal the wound; bacteria settle on open wounds.
>
> —Elizabeth Morgan, *The Making of a Woman Surgeon*

> He wore a flimsy shirt of material that must have been imitation silk; it opened on the chest on the dirty hem of an undershirt; his light cotton suit was soiled.
>
> —Saul Bellow, *The Victim*

Semicolons are particularly useful in grouping a large number of related ideas and details into a single paragraph:

> The whole world is in flood, the land as well as the water. Water streams down the trunks of trees, drips from hat-brims, courses across roads. The whole earth seems to slide like sand down a chute; water pouring over the least slope leaves the grass flattened, silver side up, pointing downstream. Everywhere windfall and flotsam twigs and leafy boughs, wood from woodpiles, bottles, and saturated straw spatter the ground or streak it in curving windrows. Tomatoes in flat gardens are literally floating in mud; they look as though they have been dropped whole into a boiling, brown-gravy stew. The level of the water table is at the top of the toe of my shoes. Pale muddy water lies on the flat so that it all but drowns the grass; it looks like a hideous parody of a light snow on the field, with only the dark tips of the grass blades visible.
>
> —Annie Dillard, *Pilgrim at Tinker Creek*

4 Semicolons with phrases

Occasionally, semicolons divide a series of phrases to stress similarity or parallelism in ideas. In the following passage, the author uses semicolons to separate noun phrases for this purpose:

> Education is about civilization. Lose sight of that and you lose sight of humanity. Then education is divorced from the great virtues: truth, justice, compassion, humility. Special interests dictate their own ends: *the individual's concern for looking out for*

No. 1; economic interests' concern with expanding their earnings at any cost; governments' concern with controlling and directing their citizenry and with extending their hegemony.
—Hilary Thimmesh, "Education Is about Civilization," *Chronicle of Higher Education,* June 20, 1984 (emphasis added)

Although none of the parallel noun phrases in this passage contains commas, semicolons make the series of long phrases easier to read.

In using semicolons, you will find the following guidelines helpful:

- Use a semicolon to join closely related ideas that form a complex idea. But limit the number of ideas you join to two or three. Too many attached clauses may blur your central idea.
- Check your paragraphs for sentences that open with an adverb (*thus, however, therefore*) or adverbial phrase (*in fact*). If the sentence is closely related to the one that precedes it, consider using a semicolon to connect the two sentences. If you want to give unusual emphasis to the second one, separate the sentences with a period.
- The longer the paragraph, the more useful the semicolon. A long paragraph usually contains several important ideas; supporting ideas and details may develop these ideas. Semicolons help to keep your main ideas distinct and in focus.
- Use the semicolon sparingly to add an explanatory statement or an afterthought to an independent clause. An explanation or afterthought may deserve a separate sentence.
- The semicolon is useful in correcting comma splices. If in doubt, apply the tests for comma splices described in 17a.

5 Misuses of the semicolon

Use a comma, not a semicolon, to separate the main clause from a *phrasal modifier:*

Nonstandard	**Revised**
They opened a pizza shop near the factory; *hoping to attract workers coming off shift.*	They opened a pizza shop near the factory, hoping to attract workers coming off shift.
They also serve calzones; *a turnover containing ham and cheese.*	They also serve calzones, a turnover containing ham and cheese.

Use a comma, not a semicolon, to separate the main clause from a *dependent clause:*

Nonstandard	Revised
The shop is in a yellow building; *which was once a grocery store.*	The shop is in a yellow building, which was once a grocery store.

Use a colon or a dash, not a semicolon, to separate the main clause from a *series:*

Nonstandard	Revised
The shop serves other popular food; *hamburgers, spaghetti, chili, frankfurters.*	The shop serves other popular food—hamburgers, spaghetti, chili, frankfurters.

See 23b and 25b on uses of the colon and the dash.

EXERCISE

Add commas and semicolons as necessary to the following sentences:

1. However difficult you find talking with him about your problems be as forthright as you can.
2. You will find him difficult to talk to about your problems however you will gain from being direct and honest.
3. The meeting began with a welcome from the mayor the head of the Revenue Office outlined the budget for the coming year using charts of city services one of her assistants discussed a tax increase reduction of administrative costs and better coordination with the state Budget Office.
4. At the county fair we ate hot dogs pizza and corn on the cob rode the ferris wheel drove Dodge-'Em cars and parachuted and watched the dog trials the baking competition and the cattle auction.
5. He was so sick that he had to be taken to the hospital and he was not the only person who became sick from overeating.
6. The Algonquin family of Indians included the Chippewas living between Lake Erie and what is today North Dakota the Cheyennes living in what is today Nebraska and the Blackfeet living northeast of the Rocky Mountains.
7. She is unwilling to run for president nevertheless I recommend our nominating her.
8. The blackfish includes the sea bass and tautog the herring includes the pilchard and the sprat the carp includes the minnow the dace and the goldfish.

9. The concerts this summer include an all-Handel program an all-Beethoven program an overture the Fifth Symphony the Third Piano Concerto a Mozart and Mahler program a Mozart concerto and the Mahler Fourth Symphony.

10. The exhibition now on display includes Manet Cézanne and Picasso the exhibition opening in May will present Spanish painters of different periods. ▪

23b The colon

1 Colon with explanation and summary

Use the **colon** (:) to introduce ideas or details that explain or amplify the idea of the preceding clause:

Explanatory Details
We visited Columbus, Lansing, and Springfield: these are the capitals of Ohio, Michigan, and Illinois.
The range of cures or terminations of boredom is a wide one: migration, desertion, war, revolution, murder, calculated cruelty to others, suicide, pornography, alcohol, narcotics.
—Robert Nisbet, "Boredom"

Explanatory Statement
So it is with the ascendancy of political parties: the more powerful a party-in-office becomes, the greater the boredom it produces in the public mind.
—Robert Nisbet
Terror continues to be used by totalitarian regimes even when its psychological aims are achieved: its real horror is that it reigns over a completely subdued population.
—Hannah Arendt, *The Origins of Totalitarianism*

Use the colon to introduce or, as in the following example, to restate a question you posed earlier in the paragraph or essay:

Question
What about Force, though? While we are trying to be sensitive and advanced and affectionate and tolerant, an unpleasant question pops up: does not all society rest upon force?
—E. M. Forster, "What I Believe"

You may also use the colon for a dramatic summary or restatement of a preceding idea:

Summary and Restatement
Historians divide the past into epochs, years, and events, as thought divides the world into groups, individuals, and things; but history, like nature, knows only continuity and change: *historia non facit saltum*—history makes no leaps.
—Will Durant, *The Life of Greece*

2 Colon with quotations

Use a comma or the more formal colon to introduce a direct quotation:

She said, "I can't decide who is the better candidate."
The speaker replied: "I'm the better candidate!"

Quotations introduced by long introductory phrases and clauses usually take the colon:

She said after listening to the speeches and thinking about them: "I can't decide who is the better candidate."

A colon, not a comma, always follows a speaker tag or introductory statement ending with the word *following:*

Emily Dickinson wrote the *following*: "How dreary to be somebody!"

3 Colon with final appositive

Use the colon to introduce a final appositive:

Several of the New England states have extensive coastlines: Connecticut, Maine, Massachusetts, Rhode Island.
Most heroes, whatever magazine they came from, looked like members of one of two families: Pat Ryan's or Flash Gordon's.
—Jules Feiffer, *The Great American Comic Book Heroes*

The dash, common in general and informal statements, is more emphatic in this position (see 25b):

Two diseases attacked the colonists—malaria and yellow fever.

4 Additional uses of the colon

Use the colon in the following writing situations:

- To show time:

    4:30 a.m.

- To give biblical citations:

    Exodus 4:16

- To separate title and subtitle:

    Michael Crichton, *Five Patients*: *The Hospital Explained*

- In bibliographical references (see 41a):

    New York: Macmillan, 1990.
    PMLA 104 (1988): 177–89.

- To close salutations in business letters:

    Dear Mr. Smith:

5 Misuses of the colon

Use the colon following a complete sentence; don't use the colon after a fragment:

Nonstandard	**Revised**
One cause of inflation: is low interest rates.	One cause of inflation is low interest rates.

Don't use the colon to introduce an indirect quotation:

Nonstandard	**Revised**
Hannah Arendt states: that totalitarian regimes never give up the use of terror.	Hannah Arendt states that totalitarian regimes never give up the use of terror.

Don't use the colon to divide a participial, infinitive, or any other modifier from the main clause:

Nonstandard	**Revised**
Robert Ardrey gives numerous examples of the territorial imperative: drawing on Konrad Lorenz and other zoologists.	Robert Ardrey gives numerous examples of the territorial imperative, drawing on Konrad Lorenz and other zoologists.
To give examples of the territorial imperative: Ardrey draws on numerous studies of animal behavior.	To give examples of the territorial imperative, Ardrey draws on numerous studies of animal behavior.

EXERCISE

Punctuate the following sentences with commas, semicolons, and colons as necessary:

1. A major source of medical compounds is the vast rain forest of northern and central Brazil that rain forest like those of Africa and Central America is disappearing.

2. The vast South American rain forest is disappearing it is falling to developers hungry for grazing and farming land.

3. Catherine Caufield in her book on rain forests states "Tropical rain forests are being destroyed faster than any other natural community."

4. The movie *The Emerald Forest* shows the effects of the disappearance of rain forests on Indian tribes tribal warfare loss of Indian culture the denuding of the land itself.

5. The son of an American dam builder disappears into the rain forest years later the father enters the forest to search for the boy.

6. The course includes the following writers the novelists Mark Twain Henry James and Kate Chopin the nineteenth-century poets Walt Whitman and Emily Dickinson the twentieth-century poets Robert Frost Hart Crane and Wallace Stevens.

7. Mozart was a late eighteenth-century composer Ravel was a composer of the early twentieth century.

8. She called at 12 15 in the afternoon and later at 5 20 she apologized for missing the session.

9. She gave these reasons for not coming her car was not running smoothly and the distance was too great to drive having had a mechanic look at the engine she didn't want to arrive late.

10. The street was crowded with carts trucks large vans filled with furniture from the building marked for demolition construction workers spectators from the neighborhood children on the way home from school. ∎

Summary

23a The semicolon.

Use the semicolon to connect independent clauses in the absence of a period or coordinating conjunction (**23a 1**):

> Inflation rose over 300 percent as a result of the war; the government therefore devalued the currency.

Use the semicolon to connect independent clauses joined by a conjunctive adverb (23a 2):

> Inflation rose over 300 percent as a result of the war; therefore, the government devalued the currency.

Use semicolons to divide a series when one or more of the members contain commas (23a 3):

> We visited Columbus, the capital of Ohio; Lansing, the capital of Michigan; and Springfield, the capital of Illinois.

Don't use a semicolon to introduce a phrasal modifier, dependent clause, or series (23a 5):

Nonstandard	**Revised**
They opened a pizza shop near the factory; *hoping to attract workers coming off shift.*	They opened a pizza shop near the factory, hoping to attract workers coming off shift.
The shop is in a yellow building; *which was once a grocery store.*	The shop is in a yellow building, which was once a grocery store.
The shop served other popular food; *hamburgers, spaghetti, chili, frankfurters.*	The shop served other popular food— hamburgers, spaghetti, chili, frankfurters.

23b The colon.

Use a colon to introduce ideas or details that explain or amplify the preceding clause (23b 1):

> We visited Columbus, Lansing, and Springfield: these are the capitals of Ohio, Michigan, and Illinois.

Use a colon to introduce a direct quotation, particularly after a long speaker tag (23b 2):

> The candidate, who had risen to his feet, replied angrily: "I'm the better candidate!"

Use a colon to introduce final appositives (23b 3):

> Several of the New England states have extensive coastlines: Connecticut, Maine, Massachusetts, Rhode Island.

Use colons to show time, cite biblical passages, separate titles from subtitles, and close salutations (23b 4):

4:30 a.m.
Exodus 4:16
Michael Crichton, *Five Patients*: *The Hospital Explained*
Dear Mr. Smith:

Use a colon only after a complete statement, not after a fragment (**23b 5**):

Nonstandard
One cause of inflation is:
low interest rates.

Revised
One cause of inflation is
low interest rates.

Don't use a colon to introduce an indirect quotation or to separate a modifier from the main clause (**23b 5**):

Nonstandard
He said that: he was
coming.
He gave numerous
examples: drawing on
studies of animal
behavior.

Revised
He said that he was
coming.
He gave numerous
examples, drawing on
studies of animal
behavior.

The 24
Apostrophe

The **apostrophe** is used mainly to show possession (*Mary's books*) and to form contractions (*I'm, you're*). Sometimes it is used to form plurals. Although the apostrophe has fewer uses than the comma or semicolon, it gives many writers trouble. A brief history of the apostrophe may help to explain why.

Early English was a highly inflected language; like Latin and modern German, it depended on **inflections** or word endings to indicate the grammatical functions of words. Modern English depends more on word order, though it retains some word endings from its early form. For example, today we distinguish the subject and direct object by their position in the sentence, not by word ending; but we still inflect some verb forms, such as when we add *-ed* to indicate the past tense. We also still use a word ending to show possession. Early English showed possession through various word endings, including *-es* (and related spellings), which eventually displaced others. Chaucer, for instance, refers in a poem to "fortunes sharp adversitee." Notice that Chaucer did not use an apostrophe to show possession. Writers who mistakenly omit the apostrophe in the equivalent modern phrase *fortune's sharp adversity* are unknowingly in accord with the practice of Chaucer's time. Later in the development of English, the apostrophe was introduced to show contraction or omission of a letter in a written word, usually *e* as in *call'd*. This practice was common in Shakespeare's time in writing noun plurals and singular nouns that showed possession. The use of the apostrophe with plural nouns gradually ended, but its use in showing contraction and possession continues to this day.

For many writers today, using the apostrophe to show possession is complicated by the function word *of*, which provides an alternative way of showing possession. In other words, writers can choose between the possessive noun with the apostrophe (*girl's*) and the alternate phrase that uses the function word *of* (*of the girl*). These and other modern uses of the apostrophe are the subject of this chapter.

24a Possession

The apostrophe is used to show **possession.** To form the possessive of a singular noun, add an apostrophe and an *s*:

the girl**'s** hat
the boy**'s** hat

To form the possessive of a plural noun ending in *s*, add only the apostrophe:

Singular	**Plural**
the student**'s** opinion	the students**'** opinions
the baby**'s** bottle	the babies**'** bottles

For plural nouns that do not end in *s*, add both the apostrophe and the *s*:

the media**'s** role
children**'s** books
women**'s** studies
men**'s** coats

Note also that the full -'*s* is used to form the possessive of singular proper nouns that end in *s* and *z*:

Liz**'s** sister Sylvia
Keats**'s** poems
Jones**'s** dog [*but* the Joneses**'** dog]

If the singular noun contains two or more syllables and ends in *s* or *z*, you may omit the possessive *s* and use an apostrophe only:

> Dickens' novels
> Kansas' weather

To show possession in compound phrases, add *-'s* to the last word only:

> his brother-in-law**'s** hats
> his sister-in-law**'s** coat
> the Secretary of State**'s** address

Phrases using the function word *of* are an alternative way of showing possession:

> the student**'s** opinion   the opinion *of* the student
> anyone**'s** opinion   the opinion *of* anyone
> my friend**'s** car   the car *of* my friend
> my friends**'** cars   the cars *of* my friends

Inanimate objects possess things, not in the sense of owning them but in the sense of having a property or attribute. To describe a property or attribute of an inanimate object, we say *rind of the orange* or *orange rind,* not *orange's rind,* and *door of the car* or *car door,* not *car's door.*

Phrases with *of* are useful in focusing on the component:

> The cook saved the rind *of* the orange to make candy.
> The tractor smashed a door *of* the car parked in the road.

The phrases *orange rind* and *car door* are less emphatic:

> *Orange rind* makes delicious candy.
> Please don't slam the *car door.*

Note that some sentences require both the apostrophe and the function word *of* for clarity. Compare the following:

> She owns a picture *of* Picasso [a likeness of the Spanish painter].
> She bought a picture *of* Picasso**'s** [a picture painted by Picasso].

24b Contraction

Use the apostrophe to show omission in **contractions,** such as contracted words:

I'm	he'll	can't	don't
you're	she'll	couldn't	doesn't
we're	who's	wouldn't	wasn't
they're	I'll	won't	weren't

Use the apostrophe to show the omission of numerals and letters:

Spirit of '76
Crash of '29
five o'clock

Use the apostrophe also to show omission of opening, closing, or unstressed vowels in reproducing dialect and speech:

"good ol' boy"
"S' long, ev'rybody!"

The following passage from a contemporary novel uses apostrophes to show contraction and omission in the dialect of a southern woman:

had	"I wish *I'd* known you was going begging!" Aunt
would have	Nanny cried to her through the others' laughter. "*I'd*
	opened both arms so fast! I always prayed for me a
would	girl—though *I'd* have taken a boy either, if answer
Miss	had ever been sent." She puffed on. "*Mis'* Hanks
	carried you straight to the orphan asylum and
Here is	handed you in. 'Here's a treat for you,' she says to
them/It is	'em. '*It's* a girl. I even brought her named.' She
	named you after her trip to Ludlow. It was a glo-
	rious day and she was sorry she had to cut her visit
	so short. Gloria Short."

—Eudora Welty, *Losing Battles* (emphasis added)

24c Plurals

The apostrophe is sometimes used to show the **plural** forms of letters of the alphabet, abbreviations, numbers, and words discussed as words:

P's, *Q*'s, and *U*'s
7's and 8's
Four-H's [Four-H Clubs]
BA's
the number of *I*'s in the essay

The apostrophe may be omitted if the plural meaning is clear:

*P*s and *Q*s [but not *U*s]
7s and 8s
the 1960s
SATs, VCRs

24d The apostrophe misused with possessive pronouns

The words *hers, his, its, yours, theirs,* and *whose* show possession and therefore do not use an apostrophe:

I have a coat of *hers*.

Here are the nonstandard and standard uses of possessive pronouns to show possession:

Nonstandard	Standard
hers'	hers
his'	his
it's, its'	its
yours'	yours
theirs'	theirs
whose'	whose

The most confusion arises in the distinction between the possessive pronoun *its* and the contraction *it's* (*it is*). The word *its* does not require an apostrophe when used as the possessive form of the pronoun *it*. Compare the following:

Possessive *its*
The dog chased *its* tail.
Walking past the building, we could not see *its* upper floors.

Contracted *it is—it's*
It's the chance I've been waiting for.
It's time to eat dinner.

The following suggestions will help in checking for missing or misused apostrophes:

- In proofreading, watch for nouns that end in *-s*. Look to see whether these words are simple plurals (*girls*) or possessive nouns (*girl's*). Add any missing apostrophes to the possessive nouns.

- Look for possessive pronouns like *his* and *theirs*. These words are possessive in form and don't require the apostrophe.
- Look for contracted pronouns like *you're* and *they're*, and add any missing apostrophes. Watch especially for misuses of the possessive pronoun *its* and the contraction *it's*.
- Look for plurals of numbers, letters, and abbreviations that may require apostrophes.

EXERCISES

1. Add apostrophes where necessary in the following sentences:
  a. The womans coat is on the couch.
  b. We cant come on Saturday because we are going to my sister-in-laws wedding.
  c. The child pulled the three cats tails.
  d. All of the cats scratched after having their tails pulled.
  e. No ones coming to the party.
  f. You have used too many buts in this paper.
  g. The number of PhDs in chemistry is decreasing.
  h. Those whose degree is in biology are decreasing, too.
  i. Shes fortunate to have a job in so crowded a field.
  j. She knows the as, bs, and cs of computer programming.
2. The following phrases use the function word *of* to show possession. Rewrite them using the apostrophe to form the possessive.
  a. the sister of the Rosses
  b. the grandchildren of the mothers-in-law
  c. a play of Plautus
  d. the son of Venus
  e. the skin of the banana
  f. a novel of Dumas
  g. reunion of her son and daughter-in-law
  h. the library of each of the three presidents
  i. a sonnet of William Butler Yeats
  j. the uniform of the marine

Summary

24a Use the apostrophe to show possession.

To form the possessive of a singular noun, add -'s to the word:

the girl's hat
the boy's coat

For plural nouns ending in *s,* add only the apostrophe:

> my friend**s'** cars

For plural nouns that do not end in *s,* add both the apostrophe and the *s:*

> the children**'s** toys
> the men**'s** coats

To form the possessive of singular proper nouns ending in *s* and *z,* add -*'s:*

> Keat**s's** poems
> Li**z's** sister Sylvia
> Jone**s's** dog [*but* the Joneses' dog]

The function word *of* is an alternative way of showing possession:

> the student**'s** opinion   the opinion *of* the student

Use the function word *of* to describe the properties or attributes of inanimate objects:

> door of the car [*or* car door]

24b   Use the apostrophe to form contractions.

The apostrophe shows omission in contracted words:

> I'm   you're   isn't   won't   wasn't
> we're   they're   aren't   you're   it's

24c   Use the apostrophe to form some plurals.

The apostrophe is sometimes used to show the plural forms of letters of the alphabet, abbreviations, numbers, and words discussed as words:

> *P*'s and *Q*'s
> Four-H's
> BA's
> 7's and 8's
> the number of I's in the essay

24d   Misuses of the apostrophe.

The words *hers, his, its, yours, theirs,* and *whose* show possession and therefore do not use an apostrophe.

Hyphen, Dash, Parentheses, Brackets, Slash

25

This chapter discusses other important punctuation marks—hyphens, dashes, parentheses, brackets, and slash. These are important in clarifying the relationship of words, showing the relative importance of ideas, making additions to parenthetical material, and contrasting terms. These punctuation marks also have other important uses.

25a The hyphen

1 Compound words and phrases

Use the **hyphen** (-) to connect compound words that form a single idea:

Italian-American
life-style
Boston-New York-Washington corridor
composer-conductor

These and other multisyllabic words and phrases are hyphenated to distinguish the component words.

But hyphenation is not consistent in multisyllabic words. Some words formed from two-word phrases do not require hyphenation to distinguish them:

flimflam
doubleheader
checkbook
cordwood

When in doubt about the hyphenation of multisyllabic words, consult your dictionary.

Familiar phrases like the following are not hyphenated:

He waited until the *last minute* to call.
Her speech was *long awaited.*
The tennis match was *hard played.*

But these and similar phrases are hyphenated when you use them as modifiers:

He made a *last-minute* call home.
She delivered her *long-awaited* speech to a packed hall.
The *hard-played* tennis match earned an ovation.

Some modifying phrases require hyphenation to distinguish them from the word modified:

a short-armed robber [i.e., a robber with short arms]
a short armed robber [i.e., an armed robber short in height]

The hyphen is omitted in adverb-participle phrases when the adverb ends in *-ly:*

badly needed rain
happily married couple

Hyphenation is not needed when the modifying phrase follows the word modified. Compare the following:

last-minute purchase
purchase made at the *last minute*

A hyphen is used to join a prefix to a capitalized word:

non-English
post-World War II [*but* postwar]

2 Compound numbers, fractions, letters

Use the hyphen to make the following compounds easy to read:

555-0111 [phone number]
pages 1-20
four hundred sixty-eight thousand dollars
X-cars
one-third
1990-99
forty-four and nine-tenths

Hyphenate two-word numbers from twenty-one to ninety-nine when you spell them out.

EXERCISE

Add the appropriate hyphens to the following items. Consult your dictionary as needed.

1. life time guarantee
2. ten light years from Earth
3. object lesson
4. over flight
5. present participle
6. ill fated life
7. namby pamby
8. post Impressionism
9. Rocky Mountain spotted fever
10. scorched earth policy

25b | The dash

It is easy to confuse the hyphen with the dash. The hyphen merely connects phrases; the **dash** marks a break in the sentence. Note that, in typing, two hyphens (--) equal a dash(—). See Chapter 47 on mechanics of the paper.

1 Appositives

Use a dash to set off a short *appositive* that appears at the end of a sentence:

There is one cure for boredom—*work*.
The neighborhood I grew up in was actually one street—*Brown Street*.
—Charlayne Hunter-Gault, "I Remember" (emphasis added)

A dash is less formal than a colon in setting off a longer appositive (see 23b):

My sister has always been interested in that sort of thing—*spaghetti in a bucket, chicken in a basket, pig in a blanket.*
—Calvin Trillin, *American Fried* (emphasis added)

Always use a dash to set off appositives that open the sentence, as in this statement on the upper Amazon region:

Rays, piranhas, anacondas, electric eels—I make it sound a dangerous place, even without mentioning crocodiles.
—Marston Bates, *The Forest and the Sea* (emphasis added)

Note that an independent clause (*I make it sound a dangerous place*) always follows an opening appositive.

Dashes often set off an appositive that occurs in the middle of a sentence:

The virtues of the American Puritan—*the ones portrayed in colonial American literature*—sustained the Massachusetts colonists in a harsh world.

In the following sentence, dashes are necessary to prevent misreading:

One of the remarkable things is that very few of the major plant or animal types—phyla or classes—have become extinct.
—Marston Bates

Always use dashes to set off a series of appositives appearing in the middle of the sentence:

The virtues of the early Massachusetts colonists—*piety, honesty, fortitude*—helped them survive a harsh world.

2 Explanation and illustration

A dash or pair of dashes often sets off an example or explanatory detail:

Perhaps it is only the cold-blooded animals—*anacondas and boas and pythons, for example*—that find a special opportunity for bigness in the rain-forest environment.
—Marston Bates, *The Forest and the Sea* (emphasis added)

He was coming to meet us—*that is, making his way down through the field.*

—Eudora Welty, "Kin" (emphasis added)

In the following sentences, the dashes set off explanatory phrases and clauses:

He was a ferocious enemy of Germany in both world wars, yet after each he begged the British government—*in vain*—to dispatch emergency shipments of food to its starving people.

—William Manchester, *The Last Lion: Winston Spencer Churchill* (emphasis added)

He despised the thump of staplers—*the only sound he hated more was whistling*—so in fastening pages he used a paper punch and threaded tape through the holes.

—William Manchester (emphasis added)

His niche in history—*it is a big one*—is secure. And so is his place in our affections.

—William Manchester (emphasis added)

A dash that sets off an appositive close to the beginning of a sentence creates an unusually dramatic effect:

Dinosaurs—the word itself is rich in associations: one remembers the huge creatures glimpsed on grammar school field trips to the natural history museum; the teetering brontosaurus skeleton that obsessed poor Cary Grant in the movie "Bringing Up Baby," and the sad gray and orange monsters lumbering off to their deaths in "Fantasia."

—Michiko Kakutani, "Dinosaur Mysteries," *New York Times,* November 8, 1986

3 Qualification

Use a dash or a pair of dashes to emphasize a qualification or an exception to a statement:

Qualification
When I say that we have ended nature, I mean not that natural processes have ceased but that we have ended the thing that has—*at least, in modern times*—defined nature for us: its separation from human society.

—Bill McKibben, *The End of Nature* (emphasis added)

Exception

The Magellanic Clouds are well-known features of the night sky—*only to be seen from the Southern Hemisphere of the Earth, however.*

—Fred Hoyle, *The Nature of the Universe* (emphasis added)

4 Interruption

Use dashes to show an interruption or break in thought or speech, to mark a deliberate pause, and to convey shock, surprise, hesitation, or some other attitude:

Interrupting Question

John Alden—*or do I mean Miles Standish?*—proposed marriage to Priscilla Mullens in Longfellow's poem.

Emphatic Pause

I hoped—for nothing.

Hesitation

He rolled over in the big bed, his heart still beating in quick, dull throbs, and with every throb he felt his energy escaping him, his—his inspiration for the day stifling under those thudding blows.

—Katherine Mansfield, "Mr. Reginald Peacock's Day"

Abrupt Break in Statement

She scrambled up again. "Watch me do a handspring. Watch me do a—"

—Carson McCullers, *The Heart Is a Lonely Hunter*

If the break is not abrupt, the ellipsis (three spaced periods; see 26c) is used instead of a dash to show that the voice is trailing off:

"Your face is certainly familiar," she murmured, scrutinizing him. "Now let's see . . ."

—Flannery O'Connor, *A Circle in the Fire*

Breaking words and phrases with dashes has the same dramatic effect in fictional dialogue:

How—very—extraordinary!" said she.

Katherine Mansfield, "The Man without a Temperament"

Dashes are most effective when they are used sparingly. A paragraph crowded with dashes loses emphasis and is difficult to read.

25c Parentheses

Use **parentheses** to set off unemphatic explanatory ideas and details:

The virtues of the American Puritan (*the ones portrayed in colonial American literature*) sustained the Massachusetts colonists in a harsh world.

A comma or other punctuation mark that belongs to the sentence goes outside the closing parenthesis:

Penguin eggs have red yolks, because of the orangy krill they feed on (just as flamingos have pinkish feathers because of their diet), and translucent whites.

—Diane Ackerman, "Penguins," *The New Yorker,* July 10, 1989

When the parenthetical statement is itself a sentence that stands apart from other sentences, open it with a capital letter and put the end punctuation (period, question mark, or exclamation point) inside the closing parenthesis:

One newly calved iceberg lies like a chunk of glass honeycomb, spongy from being underwater. (*At some point, it was other side up.*) Another has beautiful blue ridges like muscles running along one flank.

—Diane Ackerman (emphasis added)

If the parenthetical statement is a question or exclamation, put the question mark or exclamation point inside the closing parenthesis:

He was also fond of streetcar rides (*could the system have been municipally owned?*), soldiers' monuments, cemeteries, big, coarse flowers like cannas and cockscombs set in beds by city gardeners.

—Mary McCarthy, *Memories of a Catholic Girlhood*
(emphasis added)

EXERCISE

Add dashes and parentheses to the following sentences, depending on the amount of emphasis you think the appositive or interrupting phrase should receive. Also add any other punctuation required.

1. Three cars in the lot the blue sedan, the red hatch-back, the yellow convertible were sold yesterday.
2. The blue sedan the sedan with the yellow stripe not the one without has a dent on the hood.
3. The rumble seat the folding seat in open cars years ago probably will never come back into style.
4. The rumble seat but I'd better define the term for you before explaining what it was for.
5. Lincoln the large city west of Omaha not the small town in north central California is the site of a large university.
6. The blue sweater the one I wore last night is missing.
7. I am missing my blue sweater not the one you gave me but the one I wore last night.
8. *Tosca* the opera by Puccini not Verdi is a melodrama.
9. Several of Bach's sons Johann Sebastian Bach the great eighteenth-century organist and composer were famous composers in their own day.
10. Not all of J. S. Bach's twenty children born from his two marriages survived infancy.

25d Brackets

Brackets enclose parenthetical material that appears within a statement in parentheses. Use brackets, not parentheses, to add your own explanation or comment to a quotation. The brackets are necessary to distinguish your parenthetical comment from those of the author you are quoting:

> Of mass in its slow-moving, relatively unenergetic terrestrial state, Einstein remarked, "It is as though a man who is fabulously rich [i.e., mass] should never spend or give away a cent [i.e., of its energy]; no one could tell how rich he was," and on that ground Einstein excused his nineteenth-century predecessors for failing to notice what he called the "tremendous energy" in mass.
> —Jonathan Schell, *The Fate of the Earth*

The parenthetical explanation may interpret and comment on the source material being quoted:

> "Morton has been at work," Arnold writes in a private diary, "for his sake gave 1 P.T. [that is, allowed him one pupil-teacher as an assistant] but this is the last whole [writing illegible] . . . with the bad. . . ."
> —Park Honan, *Matthew Arnold: A Life*

Brackets also enclose letters omitted from words that you are quoting from a document. The following passage adds omitted letters and an explanatory comment in brackets to an early seventeenth-century reference to Shakespeare:

> On December 23rd he wrote "to my Cousin Shakespeare the copies of all our oaths m[a]de then [in the council]; also a note of the inconveniences would gr[ow] by the inclosure.
> —S. Schoenbaum, *Shakespeare's Lives*

When quoting a statement, add the Latin word *sic* in brackets—[sic]—meaning "thus" or "as I found it," following a possible error or unusual form of a word:

> Thomas Jefferson wrote in the first draft of the Declaration about "rights inherent and inalienable [sic]," and in the final draft about "certain unalienable rights."

Use brackets to substitute the name of a person who is referred to by a pronoun in the passage you are quoting:

> Schoenbaum states, "About the origins of [Shakespeare's] professional career that made possible his rise to eminence in his home town, the records are frustratingly mute."

The inserted word *Shakespeare's* substitutes for the pronoun *his* in the original passage.

EXERCISE

Assume that you are quoting the following statement and wish to define the italicized terms. Consult your dictionary, and then use brackets to add your definitions of the terms to the quotation:

> Dinosaurs lived during the *Mezozoic Era.* Dinotheres lived during the *Miocene Epoch,* and like the dinosaurs are now extinct.

25e | The slash

Use the **slash** (/) to mark alternate or contrasting terms:

either/or
credit/noncredit courses
pass/fail option

The slash also marks off lines of poetry quoted without indentation. However, always indent a quotation that consists of four or more lines of poetry. The quotation is introduced by a line of text and is indented ten spaces from the left margin:

```
Milton's poem "L'Allegro" contains these famous lines:
             Sport that wrinkled Care derides,
             And Laughter holding both his sides.
             Come, and trip it as ye go
             On the light fantastic toe.
```

When you quote fewer than four lines of poetry, you need not separate and indent them. Instead, use a slash to mark each line break:

```
Milton's poem "L'Allegro" contains these famous lines:
"Come, and trip it as ye go / On the light fantastic
toe."
```

Note that a space appears before and after the slash in quoting poetry.

Summary

25a The hyphen.

Use the hyphen with compound words and phrases and to add a prefix to a capitalized word (**25a 1**):

Italian-Americans   life-style
non-English   post-World War II

Some modifying phrases require hyphenation to distinguish them from the word modified (**25a 2**):

a *short-armed* robber

Hyphens ease the reading of compound numbers and fractions:

> 555-1003
> one-third
> four hundred and forty-four dollars

25b   The dash.

Use dashes to set off appositives at the beginning or in the middle of the sentence (25b 1):

> *Ohio, Illinois, Michigan*—these are large manufacturing states.
> The three large manufacturing states of the Midwest—*Ohio, Illinois, Michigan*—have had high unemployment.

Explanatory or illustrative words and phrases may be set off with dashes (25b 2):

> His niche in history—*it is a big one*—is secure.
> —William Manchester

Use dashes to give special emphasis to parenthetical statements (25b 3):

> The virtues of the early Massachusetts colonists—*those portrayed in early colonial literature*—sustained them in a harsh climate.

Use dashes to set off interrupting questions and comments (25b 4):

> John Alden—*or do I mean Miles Standish?*—is a character in a Longfellow poem.

25c   Parentheses.

Use parentheses to set off unemphatic explanatory comments:

> The virtues of the early Massachusetts colonists (*those portrayed in early colonial literature*) sustained them in a harsh climate.

25d   Brackets.

Use brackets to enclose your own explanatory comments in quotations:

> The budget director told the congressional committee, "This fiscal year [1990] will bring a higher deficit."

25e The slash.

Use the slash to mark a contrast in terms and to set off lines of quoted poetry:

> either/or
> credit/noncredit courses
> "Come, and trip it as ye go / On the light fantastic toe."

When quoting more than three lines of poetry, indent each line and omit the slashes.

Quotation 26 Marks, Ellipsis, Italics

In papers written for your college courses, you will have frequent occasion to quote from articles, books, and other source material. Chapters 40 and 41 discuss the use of quotations in documented papers, which are usually based on secondary sources. This chapter briefly reviews the use of quotations and gives the rules for using quotation marks, ellipsis points, and italics.

26a | Using quotations

In a paper for a course in English, history, or another subject, you may present research you have conducted, summarize the findings of other researchers, or use published and unpublished research to support a thesis. In such papers, **direct quotations** serve one or more of the following functions:

- Define the thesis of the paper or the problem to be discussed.
- State important background.

417

- Illustrate an idea.
- Give primary evidence for the thesis.
- Provide additional evidence.
- State ideas and opinions that you wish to dispute.
- Provide contrary evidence.

Quotations serve the same purpose in personal, expository, and persuasive essays. You may wish to quote a phrase or one or more sentences from one or more sources, perhaps to state a thesis and establish its importance. In presenting evidence or illustrating an idea, however, you should quote only what cannot be adequately summarized or paraphrased exactly. Often the tone or nuance of a statement is impossible to convey; it you wish to call attention to tone or nuance, quote the statement. But keep the quotation short, and be careful not to change its meaning or intent in omitting its context. To do so is to "quote out of context."

(For additional discussion of quotations and their punctuation, see 40c.)

26b | Quotation marks

In quoting a statement or passage, you reproduce it word for word, exactly as it appears in the original source. You also enclose it in **quotation marks** to indicate that the statement or passage is reproduced exactly as in the original.

1 Quoting sentences and passages

Put a quoted sentence in quotation marks following the speaker tag and perhaps identification of the source:

```
Virginia Woolf states in her essay "How Should One Read
a Book?": "After all, what laws can be laid down about
books? The battle of Waterloo was certainly fought on a
certain day; but is Hamlet a better play than Lear?"
```

When the quotation consists of no more than four typed lines, enclose it in quotation marks and incorporate it into your

418

paragraph. However, when the quotation consists of more than four typed lines, indent the quotation ten spaces from the left margin and omit the quotation marks:

```
Virginia Woolf states in her essay on how to read a
book:

        After all, what laws can be laid down about
        books? The battle of Waterloo was certainly
        fought on a certain day; but is Hamlet a bet-
        ter play than Lear? Nobody can say. Each must
        decide that question for himself. To admit
        authorities, however heavily furred and
        gowned, into our libraries and let them tell
        us how to read, what to read, what value to
        place upon what we read, is to destroy the
        spirit of freedom which is the breath of
        those sanctuaries. Everywhere else we may be
        bound by laws and conventions--there we have
        none.
```

2 Punctuating quotations

Note the following conventions in punctuating quotations:

- The period is always positioned inside the final quotation mark:

    Thomas Jefferson wrote to James Madison, "A little rebellion now and then is a good thing."

- The final period of the quotation changes to a comma when the speaker tag follows:

    "A little rebellion now and then is a good thing," Thomas Jefferson wrote to James Madison in 1787.

- The semicolon appears outside a closing quotation mark:

    Jefferson wrote to Madison about the worth of "a little rebellion"; the seventeenth-century John Bradshaw wrote that "rebellion to tyrants is obedience to God."

- The question mark and the exclamation point appear outside the final quotation mark when they are not part of the original quotation:

> Why did the crowd chant the word "traitor"?
> They chanted the word "traitor"!

Note that the exclamation point and the question mark punctuate the whole sentence, not only the single word *traitor*. The first sentence asks a question; the second expresses amazement.

- When the question mark or exclamation point is part of the original quotation, it appears inside the final quotation mark:

> Jefferson asked William Stevens Smith in a letter in 1787, "What country before ever existed a century and a half without a rebellion?"

3   Quoting words and phrases

Put quoted words and phrases in quotation marks and incorporate them into your paragraph:

> What used to be known as artificial respiration ("Out goes the bad air, in comes the good") has given way to "rescue breathing."
> —Paul Fussell, "The Boy Scout Handbook"
> And throughout there is a striking new lyricism. "Feel the wind blowing through your hair," the scout is adjured, just as he is exhorted to perceive that Being Prepared for life means learning to "live happy" and—equally important—"to die happy."
> —Paul Fussell

> To its young audience vulnerable to invitations to "trips" and trances and anxious self-absorption, the book calmly says: "Forget yourself."
> —Paul Fussell

Don't put a slang or inappropriate phrase (*fink, nerd, sweet guy*) in quotation marks. Use the expression without quotation marks or substitute a more appropriate expression. But use quotation marks in discussing a particular word or phrase in a source:

> Fussell refers to the "anxious self–absorption" of the young reader.

In quoting poetry, incorporate a phrase or short line into your sentence, enclosing it in quotation marks:

> The words "O wild West Wind" open one of Shelley's odes.

(See 25e on punctuating lines of poetry quoted in an essay.)

4 Quotations within quotations

A quotation may itself contain a quotation. Enclose a quotation within a quotation in **single quotation marks:**

> One historian says the following about Jefferson: "His political temper is best revealed in his statement to Madison, 'A little rebellion now and then is a good thing.' "

> "Sometimes a friend will come over while I'm watching TV. I'll say, 'Wait a second. Just let me finish watching this,' and then I'll feel bad about that, letting the machine take precedence over people. And I'll do that for the stupidest programs, just because I *have* to watch, somehow."
>
> —Marie Winn, *The Plug-in Drug*
> (quoting a woman addicted to television)

5 Divided quotations

If you interrupt a compound sentence with a speaker tag or a personal comment, don't capitalize the beginning word of the continuing quotation:

Original Quotation
You may object that Defoe is humdrum, but never that he is engrossed with petty things.

—Virginia Woolf, "Defoe"

Nonstandard
"You may object that Defoe is humdrum," Virginia Woolf
states, "<u>But</u> never that he is engrossed with petty
things."

Revised
"You may object that Defoe is humdrum," Virginia Woolf
states, "<u>but</u> never that he is engrossed with petty
things."

Note that a divided quotation requires a semicolon (*following* the interrupting phrase) if the original sentence is divided by one:

Original Quotation
The mind, the throat, are clogged; forgiveness, forgetfulness, that have arrived so often, fail.

—John Updike, "The Dogwood Tree"

421

Nonstandard

```
"The mind, the throat, are clogged," John Updike
writes, "forgiveness, forgetfulness, that have arrived
so often, fail."
```

Revised

```
"The mind, the throat, are clogged," Updike writes;
"forgiveness, forgetfulness, that have arrived so
often, fail."
```

26c Ellipsis

In quoting a passage, you may wish to omit words that are not essential to the meaning. Omitting the words reduces the length of the quotation and highlights the important ideas. Ellipsis points show this omission.

1 Ellipsis in quotations

An **ellipsis** (. . .), consisting of three evenly spaced periods or ellipsis points, indicates that words have been omitted from the original quotation:

Original Passage

Linguistics is the scientific study of language. At first sight this definition—*which is one that will be found in most textbooks and general treatments of the subject*—is straightforward enough. But what exactly is meant by "language" and "scientific"? And can linguistics, as it is currently practised, be rightly described as a science?

—John Lyons, *Language and Linguistics* (emphasis added)

Omission of Words within a Sentence

```
Lyons states: "Linguistics is the scientific study of
language. At first sight this definition... is
straightforward enough. But what exactly is meant by
'language' and 'scientific'?"
```

In the following passage, the ellipsis occurs at the end of the first sentence. The omitted passage gives important information about the American elm, but the passage is not essential to the point being made:

Original Passage

The survival of the robin, and indeed of many other species as well, seems fatefully linked with the American elm, *a tree that is part of the history of thousands of towns from the Atlantic to the Rockies, gracing their streets and their village squares and college campuses with majestic archways of green.* Now the elms are stricken with a disease that afflicts them throughout their range, a disease so serious that many experts believe all efforts to save the elms will in the end be futile.

—Rachel Carson, *Silent Spring* (emphasis added)

Omission of Words at the End of a Sentence

Rachel Carson states: "The survival of the robin, and indeed of many other species as well, seems fatefully linked with the American elm.... Now the elms are stricken with a disease that afflicts them throughout their range, a disease so serious that many experts believe all efforts to save the elms will in the end be futile."

The period following *American elm* is the normal period of the sentence; the three spaced periods of the ellipsis follow. The ellipsis tells the reader that the end of the first sentence and perhaps one or more additional sentences have been omitted. (See 40c for additional examples and discussion.)

2 Other uses of ellipsis

The ellipsis marks a pause as the author seeks the right phrase or wants to surprise the reader:

In a surgical operation, a risk may flash into reality: the patient dies . . . of *complication.*

—Richard Selzer, *Mortal Lessons*

The ellipsis also shows the narrator pausing or trailing off:

It glared at them a moment and then . . . went out.

—Katherine Mansfield, "The Daughters of the Late Colonel"

> She scrambled out, over the pile of loose earth that had fallen back into one end of the grave, calling to Paul that she had found something, he must guess what . . .
> —Katherine Anne Porter, "The Grave"

The ellipsis can also be used to imply that there is more to say on a topic:

> It is possible for literary students to spend more time reading criticism and criticism of criticism than they spend reading poetry, novels, biography, stories. A great many people find this state of affairs as quite normal, and not sad and ridiculous. . . .
> —Doris Lessing, Preface to *The Golden Notebook*

Some uses of the ellipsis are more common in fiction than in nonfictional prose. In the following passage from Joseph Conrad's *Typhoon*, a tenacious ship captain, trying to navigate through a storm, shouts in broken phrases to his first mate:

> "Keep on hammering . . . builders . . . good men. . . . And chance it . . . engines. . . . Rout . . . good man."

But in another passage from the same story, the rapid shouts of the first mate are punctuated with dashes instead:

> "Watch—put—in—wheelhouse—shutters—glass—afraid—blow in."

26d   Italics

1   Emphasis

Use *italics* (or <u>underlining</u> in typing) to give special emphasis to an important word or phrase, or to suggest the inflection or stress given a word in speaking the sentence:

> Before the teacher came my father took me aside to ask *why* she was coming, what *interest* she could possibly have in our house, in a boy like me.
> —James Baldwin, *Notes of a Native Son*

Use italics sparingly for this purpose. The emphasis diminishes if too many words are italicized.

2 Titles

Italicize the titles of books, magazines, newspapers, movies, plays, long poems, art objects, musical compositions, and similar titles:

Novel
E. M. Forster, *A Passage to India*
Toni Morrison, *Beloved*

Biography, History, Memoir
Elizabeth Longford, *Queen Victoria: Born to Succeed*
Barbara W. Tuchman, *The Guns of August*
James Watson, *The Double Helix: A Personal Account of the Discovery of the Structure of DNA*

Textbook, Critical Study, Treatise
I. Copi, *Introduction to Logic,* 6th Edition
E. D. Hirsch, Jr., *Validity in Interpretation*
Suzanne K. Langer, *An Introduction to Symbolic Logic*

Journal, Magazine, Newspaper
Journal of Sociology
Newsweek
New York Times [Omit *The* in giving titles of newspapers.]

Edited Collection of Articles and Essays
Roger Fowler, ed., *Style and Structure in Literature: Essays in the New Stylistics*
David Landy, ed., *Culture, Disease, and Healing: Studies in Medical Anthropology*

Theatrical Work
All in the Family [television series]
Empire of the Sun [film]
Wendy Wasserstein, *The Heidi Chronicles* [play]

Long Poem
Edna St. Vincent Millay, *The Murder of Lidice*
Alfred Lord Tennyson, *In Memoriam*

Artwork
Leonardo da Vinci, *Mona Lisa*
Michelangelo, *David*

Musical Work
Johann Sebastian Bach, *The Goldberg Variations*
Giuseppe Verdi, *Falstaff*

Do not italicize works identified by musical form, number, key, or opus unless the form is part of the title:

Ludwig van Beethoven, Symphony no. 3 in E flat Major ("Eroica")
Hector Berlioz, *Symphony Fantastique*, Opus 14

Do not italicize the titles of essays, chapters, short poems, articles, and editorials; these appear in quotation marks:

Article
Holliday, Robin. "A Different Kind of Inheritance." *Scientific American* June 1989: 60–73.

Chapter
Chapter 2, "Things Are Not Always What They Seem," in Paul Davies, *Other Worlds: Space, Superspace, and the Quantum Universe*

Essay
Henry David Thoreau, "Life without Principle"

Poem
Marianne Moore, "The Fish"

(On styles of bibliographical entries and note forms in documented papers, see 41a–b.)

3 Words discussed as words

Italicize a word that you are discussing as a word or defining:

The word *rodeo* derives from a Spanish word meaning to surround.

Compare *chef* with *cook, tailor* and *seamstress,* and *poet* with *poetess.* In each case, the masculine form carries with it an added degree of excellence. In comparing the masculine *governor* with the feminine *governess* and the masculine *major* with the feminine *majorette,* the added feature is power.
—Alleen Pace Nilsen, "Sexism in English: A Feminist View"

Do the same with letters and numbers that you are discussing:

The sounds *s* and *z* mark the possessive form of nouns in spoken English.

The term *1984*, derived from George Orwell's novel of this name, is a popular description of totalitarian regimes.

Note that some writers use quotation marks in place of italics, particularly in quoting from a source (see 26b). Use italics or quotation marks in a consistent way.

4 Foreign words

Most foreign words and phrases should appear in italics. The following sentence refers to the Russian novelist Aleksandr Solzhenitsyn's imprisonment in a *sharashka*, a Soviet scientific institute that employed convicted scientists and engineers:

> Despite all these preoccupations, Solzhenitsyn did not omit his daily "linguistic exercises" with Dahl's dictionary, which he had religiously kept up since the *sharashka*.
> —Michael Scammell, *Solzhenitsyn*

However, foreign words and phrases that have been assimilated into English through frequent use are not italicized:

laissez-faire	genre
cliché	versus
détente	etc.
et al.	raison d'être

When in doubt about foreign words in this category, consult your dictionary. If the word isn't listed there, it should be italicized.

EXERCISES

1. Assume you are quoting the following statement in the course of a paragraph:

> I claim not to have controlled events, but confess plainly that events have controlled me.
> —Letter to A. G. Hodges, April 4, 1864

In an introductory phrase, identify Abraham Lincoln as the author and identify the source of the statement and its date. Then quote the statement, incorporating it into your sentence or paragraph.

2. Assume that you wish to quote the following passage in a paper on the effects of a library on one's interests or career.

First decide what words and phrases can be omitted from the passage without changing what the author is saying about the experience of doing research in Widener Library, at Harvard University. Then write out the passage, omitting these nonessential words and phrases and showing your reader that you have made omissions:

> In the process of doing my own thesis—not for a Ph.D., because I never took a graduate degree, but just my undergraduate honors thesis—the single most formative experience in my career took place. It was not a tutor or a teacher or a fellow student or a great book or the shining example of some famous visiting lecturer—like Sir Charles Webster, for instance, brilliant as he was. It was the stacks at Widener. They were *my* Archimedes' bathtub, my burning bush, my dish of mold where I found my personal penicillin. I was allowed to have as my own one of those little cubicles with a table under a window, queerly called, as I have since learned, carrels, a word I never knew when I sat in one. Mine was deep in among the 942s (British History, that is) and I could roam at liberty through the rich stacks, taking whatever I wanted.
> —Barbara W. Tuchman, "In Search of History"

Be ready to discuss these omissions.

Summary

26a Using quotations.

Quotations are useful in most types of college papers. They can define a thesis, provide important background or evidence, illustrate ideas, and state opinions that you wish to dispute.

26b Quotation marks.

Put direct quotations of no more than four typed lines in quotation marks **(26b 1)**:

> Thomas Jefferson wrote to James Madison, "A little rebellion now and then is a good thing."

If the quotation consists of more than four typed lines, indent it and omit the quotation marks **(26b 1)**.

The period that ends a quoted sentence appears before the final quotation mark. The final period of the quotation changes to a comma if the speaker tag follows (**26b 2**):

> "A little rebellion now and then is a good thing," Thomas Jefferson wrote to James Madison.

Semicolons appear after the closing quotation mark:

> Jefferson wrote to Madison about the worth of "a little rebellion"; the seventeenth-century John Bradshaw wrote that "rebellion to tyrants is obedience to God."

Put quoted words and phrases in quotation marks (**26b 3**):

> What used to be known as artificial respiration ("Out goes the bad air, in comes the good") has given way to "rescue breathing."
>
> —Paul Fussell

A quotation within a quotation appears in single quotation marks (**26b 4**):

> One historian says the following about Jefferson: "His political temper is best revealed in his statement to Madison, 'A little rebellion now and then is a good thing.' "

If you interrupt a quotation with a speaker tag or personal comment, do not capitalize the beginning word of the continuing quotation (**26b 5**):

> "You may object that Defoe is humdrum," Virginia Woolf states, "*but* never that he is engrossed with petty things."

A divided quotation requires a semicolon if the original sentence is divided by one:

> "The mind, the throat, are clogged," Updike writes; "forgiveness, forgetfulness, that have arrived so often, fail."

26c Ellipsis.

The ellipsis marks the omission of words in quotations:

> The survival of the robin, and indeed of many other species as well, seems fatefully linked with the American elm. . . . Now the elms are stricken with a disease that afflicts them throughout their range, a disease so serious that many experts believe all efforts to save the elms will in the end be futile.
>
> —Rachel Carson

429

26d   Italics.

Use italics to emphasize an important word or phrase, or to suggest the inflection or stress given a word in speaking the sentence (26d 1):

> Before the teacher came my father took me aside to ask *why* she was coming, what *interest* she could possibly have in our house, in a boy like me.
>
> —James Baldwin

Italicize the titles of books, magazines, newspapers, movies, plays, long poems, art objects, musical compositions, and similar titles (26d 2).

Italicize words discussed as words (26d 3):

> The word *rodeo* derives from a Spanish word meaning to surround.

Put foreign words and phrases in italics unless they are now common English words (26d 4).

Capitalization, **27** Abbreviations, Numbers

□

This chapter describes the conventional use of capitals and common abbreviations. It also describes conventional ways of reporting numbers.

27a Capitalization

1 Sentence openers

Capitalize the first word of a declarative sentence, a question, or an exclamation:

> **T**he temperature is below zero.
> **I**s the temperature below zero?
> **I**'m cold!

Capitalize the first word of a question following an introductory statement:

> There are many legitimate scientific issues relating to origins and ends: **W**hat is the origin of the human species? **W**here did plants and animals come from?
> —Carl Sagan, "A Sunday Sermon"

Lowercase is standard following a colon. But writers sometimes capitalize the first word of a complete sentence following a colon, particularly if the second sentence itself contains a colon:

> This leads to the second characteristic of the symbol: **I**t participates in that to which it points: the flag participates in the power and dignity of the nation for which it stands.
> —Paul Tillich, "Symbols of Faith"

2 Quotations

Capitalize the first word of a quoted sentence or line of poetry:

> A character in Shakespeare's *Julius Caesar* gives the famous warning, "**B**eware the Ides of March."
> Wordsworth opens his sonnet with the lines, "**T**he world is too much with us; late and soon, / **G**etting and spending, we lay waste our powers."

But don't capitalize the first word of a full or partial quotation that you have made part of your sentence:

> Wordsworth tells us that "**t**he world is too much with us."

Capitalize the first word of a quotation when it is introduced by a speaker tag or a phrase that identifies the source:

> Erich Kahler states in his essay "The Nature of the Symbol," "**O**nly consciously formed images are real symbols."

Don't capitalize the first word of the second half of a divided quotation:

> "If money, success or the nation is someone's ultimate concern," Paul Tillich asks, "**c**an this not be said in a direct way without symbolic language?"

(For other conventional uses of capitalization in quotations, see 26b.)

3 Names and titles

Capitalize first words, last words, and all principal words including nouns, pronouns, verbs, adjectives, adverbs, and sub-

ordinating conjunctions. Do not capitalize the articles preceding them, prepositions, coordinating conjunctions, and the *to*
in infinitives.

Names and Titles
Abraham Lincoln
Associate Justice Sandra Day O'Connor
Father John Murray [priest]
Rabbi Susan Gottlieb

Places and Geographical Regions
the Rocky Mountains
the Pacific Ocean
La Paz, Bolivia
Mojave Desert
East Coast, West Coast
the North, the South
South Glastonbury, Connecticut
Jefferson City, Missouri

Months of the Year
February 14, 1934
14 February 1934

Historical Periods, Events, Holidays
Italian Renaissance
the Roaring Twenties
World War II, Vietnam War
Thanksgiving, Christmas, Hanukkah

Religions
Buddhism, Buddhist
Islam, Islamic, Muslim, Black Muslim
Greek Orthodox Church, Greek Orthodox
Judaism, Jewish, Judaic
Protestant Episcopal Church, Episcopalian
Roman Catholicism, Roman Catholic Church, Roman Catholic

Organizations and Members
AFL—CIO
Boston Symphony Orchestra
Cancer Society
Los Angeles Dodgers
Republican party, Republicans

Racial and Ethnic Groups
Caucasian
African-American
Hispanic-American

Titles of Works
Beloved; Huckleberry Finn [novels]
In Memoriam [long poem]
Sonnets from the Portuguese [sequence of poems]
Hamlet; The Heidi Chronicles [plays]
Annie Hall; Indiana Jones and the Temple of Doom [movies]
48 Hours; Murphy Brown; McNeil-Lehrer Report [television programs]
Harvard Business Review; Newsweek; Washington Post [periodicals]

Scientific Theories
Big Bang
Special Theory of Relativity

Languages
American English
Gaelic
Scots Gaelic
Swahili

Brand Names and Trade Names
Anacin, Coke, Quaker Oats
GM, IBM, Sony, Xerox

Note: Generic names are not capitalized: aspirin, cola.

4 Unnecessary capitalization

Don't capitalize the seasons:

last winter, next summer, this fall, this spring

And don't capitalize nouns that designate general classes:

the early symphonies and quartets of Beethoven
the letters of Emily Dickinson
moonlight, sunlight, starlight
the moons of Jupiter, the rings of Saturn
elms, maples, chestnuts
the interstate highways

Compare:

> **S**ymphony no. 3 ("**E**roica") of Beethoven
> **I**o, **G**anymede, **E**uropa, and **C**allisto are moons of Jupiter.

Don't capitalize the names of diseases or medicines unless the disease includes the name of its discoverer or a region associated with it:

> malaria, polio myelitis, yellow fever, cortisone, insulin
> **B**roca's aphasia, **H**odgkin's disease, **R**ocky **M**ountain spotted fever

Don't capitalize the word *earth* except when mentioning it with other planets:

> The planet earth has one moon.
> The space ship is now earthbound.
> **M**ercury, **V**enus, **E**arth, and **M**ars are the inner planets of the solar system.

Don't capitalize nouns that state familial relationships or refer to a position or job:

> Wilson is president of the company.
> She was the governor of Kentucky in 1982.
> My mother and father are coming for a visit.

The titles of high officials of government are occasionally capitalized:

> She is now **G**overnor of Kentucky.
> George Bush was elected **P**resident of the United States in 1988.

Note the alternative usage in expressions like the following:

> fall semester, **F**all semester
> sophomore French, **S**ophomore French
> senior prom, **S**enior **P**rom

EXERCISE

Add the necessary punctuation to the following sentences:

1. the full title and subtitle of steven weinbergs book is the first three minutes a modern view of the origin of the universe.
2. the phrase rumble seat has almost disappeared.
3. steven spielberg who directed jaws also directed close encounters of the third kind and e. t.

4. the course is being offered on a credit noncredit basis.

5. the following cities on the southern atlantic coast perrine miami coral gables hollywood fort lauderdale are connected by an interstate highway.

6. william faulkners novel the town is about the snopes family so is his novel the mansion.

7. in his autobiographical novel the cancer ward aleksandr solzhenitsyn describes events in the year of stalins death 1953.

8. the italian phrase buon giorno is used to greet people in the morning buona sera to greet people in the evening buona notte to say goodnight.

9. the concluding chapter of noam chomskys book language and mind is titled language and philosophy.

10. the word boost comes from a nautical word meaning to haul.

27b | Abbreviations

Abbreviations help to make writing concise and emphatic by giving the minimum information needed to identify a person, place, or thing in as brief a form as possible. For example, we usually abbreviate the names of television networks (ABC, CBS, NBC) and academic degrees (B.A., M.A., Ph.D.). Writing out the words for these items would load a sentence with unnecessary words. This section discusses conventions of abbreviation and provides convenient lists of many standard abbreviations.

1 Titles and names

First and middle names are often abbreviated:

John F. Kennedy   C. P. Snow

Note in the second example that a space separates the first and middle initials.

Abbreviate titles and terms like *junior, senior,* and *doctor* only when they appear with proper names:

Dr. Mary Jones   Mary Jones, *M.D.*
William Jones, *Jr.*   William Jones, *Sr.*

Nonstandard	**Revised**
He is the *jr.* member of the firm.	He is the *junior* member of the firm.

Use abbreviations for *company, incorporated,* and the like only when they appear with proper names:

She is an employee of Smith and Jones, *Inc.*

Nonstandard	**Revised**
She has been a member of the dance *co.* since 1985.	She has been a member of the dance *company* since 1985.

Periods may be omitted from abbreviations when no confusion in meaning results:

MA   NY   Phd   USA

Acronyms, or abbreviations formed from the initial letters of a compound name and pronounced as a single word, dispense with periods when the reference is clear:

AIDS (acquired immunodeficiency syndrome)
UNICEF (United Nations International Children's Emergency Fund)

Other abbreviations, formed from the initial letters of compound names and pronounced letter by letter, also dispense with periods:

AFL-CIO (American Federation of Labor-Congress of Industrial Organizations)
IBM (International Business Machines)

Names of important people are sometimes abbreviated without periods when they consist of more than two letters:

FDR (Franklin Delano Roosevelt)
LBJ (Lyndon Baines Johnson)

If you use abbreviations like these, always spell out the full name at the first reference.

2   Units of measurement, time of day, addresses

The following conventions govern the use of abbreviations to describe units of measurement, time of day, and street addresses.

Units of measurement.   Scientific and technical writing abbreviate units of measurements:

14 in.   42 ft.   200 yds.   54 qts.

Note that abbreviations appear only with figures or numerals. Always spell out the unit of measurement when referring to it without a numeral or when the number is spelled out:

Nonstandard	**Revised**
The runner was *sixteen* *in.* from the finish line.	The runner was *sixteen* *inches* from the finish line.

Time of day.   Use the abbreviations *a.m.* and *p.m.* to express time of day only when you use numerals:

5 a.m.   five o'clock in the morning
4:30 p.m.   four-thirty in the evening

Addresses.   Give an address in numerals:

1226 N. Ridge Rd.

You may abbreviate words like *street, avenue, drive, North,* and *South* in giving addresses:

345 14th St.
154 Park Ave., So.

(See 27c on the conventional uses of numerals.)

3   Place names

Even though newspapers and magazines frequently abbreviate the names of states and countries to save space, don't abbreviate the name of a state or country in the text of your paper:

Nonstandard	**Revised**
Plains, *Ga.,* is south of Atlanta.	Plains, *Georgia,* is south of Atlanta.

Initial abbreviations like USA and USSR are the exceptions:

He has lived in the *USA* since 1934.

4 Some common abbreviations

Following are some common abbreviations for words used in lists, with proper names and numerals, and in bibliographical entries (see 41 a–b).

Common Abbreviations

A.D.	Precedes the date: A.D. 12 [Latin: *anno Domini,* "year of the Lord"]
a.m., A.M.	before noon [Latin: *ante meridiem*]
anon.	anonymous
assn.	association
assoc.	associate
ave.	avenue
b.	born
B.A.	Bachelor of Arts
B.C.	Before Christ [20 B.C.]
B.S.	Bachelor of Science
C.	Centigrade
c., ca.	about [used with inexact dates: c. 1536]
©	copyright [© 1983]
cf.	compare [used in notes to refer readers to another passage]
ch., chs.	chapter, chapters
col., cols.	column, columns
colloq.	colloquial
comp.	compiled by, compiler
d.	died
dept.	department
diss.	dissertation
div.	division
ed.	editor, edited by, edition
eds.	editors, editions
e.g.	for example
esp.	especially
et al.	and others
etc.	and so forth
ex.	example
F.	Fahrenheit
fig.	figure
g.	gram, grams [14 g. *or* fourteen grams]
govt.	government
GPO	Government Printing Office
i.e.	that is

Common Abbreviations (*continued*)

illus.	illustrator, illustrated by, illustration
inc.	including, incorporated
introd.	writer of introduction, introduced by, introduction
Jr.	junior
l., ll.	line, lines
m.	meter, meters [100 m. *or* one hundred meters]
M.A.	Master of Arts
M.D.	Doctor of Medicine
M.S.	Master of Science
ms., mss.	manuscript, manuscripts
NB	note carefully [Latin: *nota bene*]
n.d.	no date [used in notes when date of publication is unknown]
no.	number
n.p.	no place (of publication) or no publisher [used in notes when the place of publication or the publisher is unknown]
obj.	object, objective
op.	opus or work [Beethoven Symphony No. 5. op. 67]
Ph.D.	Doctor of Philosophy
pl.	plate; plural
p.m., P.M.	after noon [Latin: *post meridiem*]
poss.	possessive
pref.	preface, writer of preface
pt.	part
qtd.	quoted
rept.	report, reported by
rev.	revised, revision, review, writer of revision or review
rev. ed.	revised edition
sc.	scene
sec., secs.	section, sections
ser.	series
[sic]	thus so
sing.	singular
soc.	society
subj.	subject, subjective, subjunctive
trans.	translator, translated by, translation
vol., vols.	volume, volumes
vs.	versus

27c | Numbers

The treatment of **numbers** varies in the disciplines. In business writing, the numbers one through nine are spelled out and the numbers 10 and above are written in numerals. In scientific and technical writing, all numbers are usually expressed as figures. In most other types of nontechnical writing, where numbers are discussed infrequently, whole numbers that can be written in one or two words are spelled out and those that cannot are expressed in numerals.

1 Words versus figures

In general and formal writing use words instead of numerals to state quantities or to indicate position in a series.

> first, second, third, fourth, etc.
> hundredth, thousandth, millionth, billionth

Use numerals, not words, in expressing a series of numbers:

Wordy
The backyard measures *twenty-five* by *forty-five* feet, *twenty* by *thirty-three* feet, and the house itself *one hundred twenty* by *one hundred fifty-seven* feet.

Improved
The backyard measures *25* by *45* feet, the front yard *20* by *33* feet, and the house itself *120* by *157* feet.

Use no more than two words in writing out round numbers:

> *three* apples, *thirty-three* apples, *432* apples
> *3,325* applications [*not* three thousand three hundred twenty-five applications]

Use the word *thousand* in expressing an even number of thousands:

> *six thousand* people

For an odd number in the thousands, express the figure in hundreds:

sixty-five hundred people

Use a combination of figures and words for round numbers in the millions and higher:

The U.S. population is more than *200 million*.
The star is thought to be *4 billion* years old.

When you start a sentence with a number, write it out using no more than two words:

Two hundred people live in the building.

If more than two words are necessary, use numerals and put them later in the sentence:

Nonstandard   **Revised**
Three thousand three hundred   Taxpayers filed *3,320* returns
  and twenty tax returns   in 1990.
were filed in 1990.

2   Other conventional uses

The following conventions govern the use of numbers to indicate fractions, percentages, inclusive numbers, temperature, time of day, dates and centuries, and addresses:

Fractions and decimals.   Use figures in writing fractions and numbers containing decimals:

a poster measuring 14¾ by 22½ inches
grade point average of 3.2

Percentages.   Use figures in writing percentages:

25% (in scientific and technical papers)
25 percent (in papers in the humanities)

Inclusive numbers.   In papers in the humanities, if the years cited are in one century, give the last two digits only:

1900–45

Give the full year if the dates fall in different centuries:

1899–1905

Inclusive pages are not abbreviated when the numbers are less than 100:

75–76

From 100 up, include the changed digits only:

554–72 (554–572)
1554–652 (1554–1652)

In papers in the social sciences and the biological sciences, pages numbers are usually given without abbreviation. See the style manuals cited on p. 709.

Temperature.   Use numerals and symbols if you make frequent reference to a temperature in a paper:

90°F.
10°C.

If you refer to a temperature only occasionally, state the temperature in words:

ninety degrees Fahrenheit
ten degrees Centigrade

With monetary units, use a numeral following the dollar symbol:

$100

You can combine numerals with words to express large amounts of money:

$100 million
$2.5 billion

Time of day.   Use numerals with *a.m.* and *p.m.* to give the time of day:

5 p.m.
10 a.m.

In general and formal writing, give the time of day in words, not in numerals:

five o'clock [*not* five p.m.]
five in the evening
twenty to seven
a quarter past eight
half past eight

Always spell out the number before the word *o'clock.*

Dates and centuries.   Use numerals to give dates:

May 30, 1929
30 May 1929

Writers occasionally give a date in words:

the thirtieth of May 1929

But not:

the 30th of May 1929

Don't write out the year except when it occurs at the beginning of a sentence:

The market crash of *1929* [*not* nineteen hundred twenty-nine]
marked the beginning of a worldwide economic depression.
Nineteen twenty-nine was the year of the market crash.

If possible, recast the sentence:

The market crash occurred in 1929.

Always spell out centuries; decades can be written as words or figures:

twentieth century
the 1990s *or* the nineties

Addresses.   Give an address in numerals:

1226 N. Ridge Rd.

Writers occasionally spell out a numbered street to avoid confusion:

1226 Twenty-sixth Ave.

Give highway numbers in numerals:

I-77 [Interstate 77]
Ohio 176

3   Roman numerals

Roman numerals have been largely replaced by arabic numerals, but they still have special uses.

Roman numerals are used to identify the acts and scenes of plays:

King Lear, I, iii [act 1, scene 3]

Capitalized roman numerals mark individual volumes of multivolume works; lowercase roman numerals mark the pagination of the front matter or introductory pages to a book:

G. Jean-Aubry, *Joseph Conrad: Life and Letters*, I, xi. [volume 1, page 11 of the introduction]

The following seven letters form roman numerals:

I, i, 1	X, x, 10	C, c, 100	M, m, 1,000
V, v, 5	L, l, 50	D, d, 500	

Here are the roman numerals from one to twenty:

I, 1	VI, 6	XI, 11	XVI, 16
II, 2	VII, 7	XII, 12	XVII, 17
III, 3	VIII, 8	XIII, 13	XVIII, 18
IV, 4	IX, 9	XIV, 14	XIX, 19
V, 5	X, 10	XV, 15	XX, 20

EXERCISE

Abbreviate and use numerals where possible in the following:

1. The Jones Company, Incorporated
2. Linguistic Society of America
3. Association of American University Professors
4. I. M. Copi, *Introduction to Logic*, Sixth Edition
5. Erwin H. Ackerknecht, *A Short History of Medicine*, revised edition
6. forty-seven degrees Fahrenheit
7. 777 Seventy-seventh Avenue, North Canton, Ohio
8. Figure seven, page twenty-one, volume forty
9. Pages 1127–1642
10. Plate number eight

Summary

27a Use capitals in consistent ways.

Capitalize the first word of a declarative sentence, a question, or an exclamation (27a 1).

I'm cold!

Capitalize the first word of a quoted sentence or line of poetry (27a 2):

> A character in Shakespeare's *Julius Caesar* gives the famous warning, "**B**eware the Ides of March."

Don't capitalize the first word of a full or partial quotation that you have made part of your sentence:

> Wordsworth tells us that "**t**he world is too much with us."

Capitalize the first word of the quotation when it is introduced by a speaker tag or a phrase that identifies the writer and work:

> Erich Kahler states in his essay "The Nature of the Symbol," "**O**nly consciously formed images are real symbols."

But don't capitalize the first word of the second half of a divided quotation:

> "If money, success or the nation is someone's ultimate concern," Paul Tillich asks, "**c**an this not be said in a direct way without symbolic language?"

Capitalize proper nouns (*America*) and proper adjectives (*American*), but not the articles that precede them (**27a 3**):

> **A**braham **L**incoln
> the **P**acific **O**cean

Don't capitalize the seasons (**27a 4**):

> last winter, next summer, this fall, this spring

Don't capitalize common nouns that designate general classes:

> the early symphonies and quartets of Beethoven

Don't capitalize nouns that state familial relationships or refer to a position or job:

> Wilson is president of the company.
> My mother and father are coming for a visit.

27b Use abbreviations consistently.

First and middle names are often abbreviated (**27b 1**):

> John F. Kennedy
> C. P. Snow

Abbreviate titles only when they appear with proper names:

> Dr. Mary Jones   Mary Jones, M.D.

Acronyms and other abbreviations formed from the initial letters of names dispense with periods when the reference is clear:

AIDS (acquired immunodeficiency syndrome)
IBM (International Business Machines)

Use conventional abbreviations for units of measurement, time of day, and addresses (27b 2):

14 in. *or* fourteen inches
5 p.m. *or* five o'clock in the evening

Spell out the name of a state or country in the text of a paper (27b 3):

Plains, *Georgia,* is south of Atlanta.

27c   Use words and figures in reporting numbers.

Use numerals in expressing large numbers that cannot be written in one or two words (27c 1):

3,325 applications [*not* three thousand three hundred twenty-five applications]
thirty-three applications

Use the word *thousand* in expressing an even number of thousands:

six thousand people

For an odd number in the thousands, express the figure in hundreds. Use a combination of figures and words for numbers in the millions and higher:

sixty-five hundred people
200 million
4.5 billion

Always use numerals to express numbers using fractions, decimals, and percentages:

Employment increased by 14 percent in the service industries.
His grade point average is 3.4 [*not* three point four].

Abbreviate numbers from 110 up by including the changed digits of the changed number:

110–12

Use conventional words and figures in reporting temperature, dates, time of day, and addresses (27c 2):

15°C.	74°F.
5:15 a.m.	11:30 p.m.
777 Elm St.	777 Seventy-seventh St.

Don't write out the year except at the beginning of the sentence:

The market crash of 1929 [*not* nineteen hundred twenty-nine].

Spell out centuries; use words or numerals for decades:

nineteenth century
the 1990s *or* the nineties

Use roman numerals to identify the acts and scenes of plays, the individual volumes of multivolume works, and the front matter or introductory pages of a book (27c 3).

Spelling   *28*

□

□

This chapter gives help with common spelling problems. Many of these problems arise from inconsistencies between the **spelling** and the **pronunciation** of words, others from a confusion between words that resemble one another in sight and sound. Although the dictionary remains your best resource in spelling, knowledge of certain groupings or patterns can help you with troublesome words.

28a Spelling and pronunciation

In trying to spell a word, we often follow the spelling of another word that looks or sounds alike. Because the words *outrage* and *courage* look alike, we assume that the adjectives derived from them are spelled the same way. Using the spelling of *courageous* as our guide, we attach the *-ous* suffix to *outrage* to form the adjective *outrageous*. Because the words *receive* and *conceive* sound alike, we assume the adjectives derived from them (*receivable, conceivable*) are also spelled alike. These assumptions are often correct.

But the eye and ear are not always reliable guides in spelling. For example, the eye may deceive us into misspelling the word *ridiculous*. Remembering the *-eous* in *courageous*, we might misspell the word as *ridiculeous*. The ear will not correct the misspelling because we do not hear the suffix *-e* even if we break *courageous* into syllables in pronouncing it. The ear again deceives us: we may misspell the word *apparatus* as *apparatous* because the ending sounds like that of *courageous*.

Many words that look alike are not pronounced alike: *enough, dough, through, rough.* Vowels in unstressed syllables, as in the final syllable of *dictionary,* are not distinct, and we don't pronounce all consonants or syllables in words like *condemn* and *foreign.* In addition, the pronunciation of many words varies widely in the United States and in other English-speaking countries: we accent and slur over sounds in different ways:

> In American [English] the secondary accent in *necessary,* falling upon *ar,* is clearly marked; in English only the primary accent on *nec* is heard, and so the word becomes *nécess'ry.* . . . The same difference in pronunciation is to be observed in certain words of the *-ative* and *-mony* classes, and in some of those of other classes. In American the secondary accent on *a* in *operative* is always heard, but seldom in English.
> —H. L. Mencken, *The American Language*

There is no certain guide to spelling in all situations. But we can learn much from common features of English spelling and from common spelling errors.

28b Words that look and sound alike

We often misspell words that are pronounced alike or are similar enough in sound to lead us to confuse them. We misspell other words that look somewhat alike but are different in form. Knowing that words can differ in these ways can help you identify the words you are most likely to misspell in your writing.

1 Homonyms

Homonyms are words that are pronounced alike but have different meanings and usually different spellings. Since homonyms are responsible for so many misspellings, you will find it helpful to become familiar with them. In this partial listing of homonyms and the other listings in this section, one or more meanings of a word are given in brackets to distinguish it from a similar word:

Common Homonyms

assent [agreement]	ascent [act of climbing]
bare [empty]	bear [*noun:* furry mammal; *verb:* hold, endure]
boar [male hog]	bore [*noun:* drill; *verb:* weary, someone or something uninteresting]
board [plank]	bored [made weary, uninterested]
born [given birth]	borne [carried]
brake [restrain]	break [shatter]
buy [purchase]	by [beside]
cite [refer to]	sight [power of seeing]
	site [place]
coarse [crude]	course [path]
discreet [careful]	discrete [separate, independent]
fair [impartial]	fare [price of transportation]
forth [forward]	fourth [preceded by three others]
hear [listen]	here [at this place]
heard [listened]	herd [group of animals]
hole [cavity]	whole [unit]
its [possessive of *it*]	it's [contraction of *it is*]
know [be acquainted with]	no [not]
lead [*noun:* heavy metal; *verb:* give direction]	led [gave direction; past participle of *lead*]
meat [flesh]	meet [come face to face]
new [original]	knew [was acquainted with]
passed [met a requirement; past participle of *pass*]	past [history, previous events]
patience [endurance]	patients [sick people]
peace [tranquillity]	piece [segment]
plain [unadorned, open, level surface]	plane [flat surface; aircraft]
presence [appearance]	presents [gifts]

Common Homonyms (*continued*)

principal [foremost]	principle [rule, guideline]
rain [precipitation]	reign [govern]
	rein [restrain, hold back]
right [correct]	rite [ceremony]
	write [put words on paper]
road [highway]	rode [past participle of *ride*]
scene [place]	seen [observed]
straight [direct]	strait [narrow channel of water]
their [possessive of *they*]	there [in that direction]
	they're [contraction of *they are*]
to [in the direction of]	too [also]
	two [preceded by one]
waist [part of body between hips and ribs]	waste [unused material]
weak [lacking strength]	week [seven days]
weather [atmospheric conditions]	whether [either]
which [what one]	witch [sorcerer]
who's [contraction of *who is*]	whose [possessive of *who*]

Some words are similar in pronunciation and in some dialects or varieties of English are pronounced the same. Yet like homonyms, these words are different in spelling and meaning. They are especially easy to confuse because they differ only by a letter or two. Here is a partial list:

Words That Sound Alike

accept [receive with approval]	except [leaving out]
aisle [narrow walkway]	isle [small island]
allude [refer to indirectly]	elude [evade]
allusion [indirect reference]	illusion [false perception or belief]
capital [chief importance; assets; uppercase letter]	capitol [seat of government]
complement [something that completes]	compliment [statement of praise]
descent [act of climbing down]	dissent [disagreement]
desert [barren place]	dessert [a sweet food eaten at the end of a meal]
elicit [draw out]	illicit [unlawful]
formally [following custom or rules]	formerly [at an earlier time]

Words That Sound Alike

gorilla [large ape]	guerrilla [irregular soldier]
lessen [decrease]	lesson [something learned]
loose [free, unbound]	lose [mislay]
moral [upright]	morale [spirit, sense of dedication]
quiet [not noisy]	quite [almost]
raise [lift up]	raze [level to the ground]
stationary [unmoving]	stationery [writing paper]
than [except]	then [at that time]
your [possessive of *you*]	you're [contraction of *you are*]

Certain compound phrases are easy to confuse with single words that resemble them in spelling and sometimes meaning. The following definitions will help you identify their misspellings:

already [by now]	all ready [prepared]
altogether [completely]	all together [acting as a unit]
anybody [anyone]	any body [any single person]
anymore [any longer]	any more [another]
anytime [whenever]	(at) any time [whatever time]
everybody [all]	every body [each person]
maybe [perhaps]	may be [auxiliary *may* and verb *be*]
(a) somebody [important person]	some body [unidentified person]
sometime [having once been]	some time [at a time to come]

2 Words with similar roots and affixes

Many words are easy to confuse because they share the same root or affix yet have different meanings. A **root** is a unit of sound that conveys meaning (e.g., *act*). An **affix** is a sound that we attach to the beginning or end of a root to form other words. We call these attached sounds **prefixes** and **suffixes**. For example, we attach the prefix *re-* to *act* to form the word *react;* we attach the suffixes *-ion* and *-s* to *act* to form the words *action* and *actions*. Following is a partial list of words that have the same roots or affixes:

Words with Similar Roots and Affixes

assure [confirm]	ensure, insure [guarantee]
beside [by]	besides [in addition]

453

Words with Similar Roots and Affixes (*continued*)

censor [person who forbids publication]	censure [criticize, condemn]
climatic [adjective form of *climate*]	climactic [coming at the peak]
conscientious [diligent]	conscious [aware of]
continual [occurring at regular intervals]	continuous [occurring without interruption]
credible [believable]	credulous [easily convinced]
deduce [infer]	deduct [subtract from]
detract [defame]	distract [divert attention]
eminent [highly respected]	imminent [about to happen]
incredible [unbelievable]	incredulous [doubtful]
irritate [bother]	aggravate [intensely annoy]
off [away from]	of [derived from, belonging to]
practicable [workable]	practical [useful]
precede [ahead or in front of]	proceed [to continue, move forward]
respectful [courteous]	respective [relating to each of several things]
sensual [excessive gratification of the senses]	sensuous [appealing to the senses]

3 Similar noun and verb forms

The spelling of many noun and verb forms are easily confused, often because they differ by only a single letter. Here is a partial list:

Noun	**Verb**
advice [counsel]	advise [to counsel or give advice]
affect [stimulus]	effect [to produce a change]
belief [conviction]	believe [to accept as true]
breath [single inhalation of air]	breathe [to inhale and exhale air]
choice [the alternative selected]	choose [to select from a number of alternatives]
descent [a climbing or coming down]	descend [to climb or come down]
device [mechanical object]	devise [to construct, plan]
entrance [passageway]	enter [to go into]
envelope [paper container]	envelop [to surround, enclose]
expense [cost]	expend [to spend]
prophecy [forecast]	prophesy [to predict or forecast]

Noun	**Verb**
receipt [written statement that money or goods were received]	receive [to get, take possession of]
speech [a talk]	speak [to talk to]

Some of the words in this and earlier listings are discussed further in the Glossary of Common Usage (page G-1).

EXERCISES

1. Choose the appropriate word in each of the following sentences. Consult your dictionary as needed.
   a. It's the book he (*cited, sighted*) in his speech.
   b. Their house is built on the (*cite, site*) of the old city hall, on (*Forth, Fourth*) Street.
   c. The doctor examined two (*patience, patients*) that morning.
   d. We waited through several (*scene, seen*) changes for (*their, there*) appearance on the stage.
   e. He's the senator (*who's, whose*) speech they (*heard, herd*) in Washington.
   f. I (*accept, except*) your apology with thanks.
   g. She (*alluded, eluded*) to the apology in her letter.
   h. The senator addressed the audience (*formally, formerly*) on the issue of jobs in the 1990s.
   i. He spoke of our (*loosing, losing*) jobs if inflation remains higher (*than, then*) last year.
   j. He said, "If inflation remains (*stationary, stationery*) or goes down, (*your, you're*) going to benefit."

2. Use the following words in sentences that show their meaning:
   a. affect
   b. continual
   c. continuous
   d. credible
   e. climactic
   f. descent
   g. devise
   h. imminent
   i. practicable
   j. respective

28c Forming plurals

1 Regular plurals

Knowing how to form the plurals of words is helpful in avoiding spelling errors. Although most plural forms fall into regular

455

patterns, a small number of English words have irregular plurals. Here are the patterns for regular plurals:

Nouns Ending in -s	**Examples**
■ Most nouns form plurals by adding -s to the singular form.	books, hats, shoes
■ If the plural ending adds a syllable to the word, the word takes -es.	churches, boxes, bushes
■ Some words have no separate plural forms.	spacecraft, pliers, sheep, Japanese, Iriquois

Nouns Ending in -y	**Examples**
■ Nouns with a vowel before the -y usually form plurals by adding -s.	boys, monkeys
■ Nouns with a consonant before the -y change -y to -i and add -es.	cherry, cherries
■ Names ending in y usually add -s.	Murphys, Cassidys
■ Some place names (*Rocky Mountains*) change -y to -ies.	Rockies

Nouns Ending in -o	**Examples**
■ Most nouns ending in -o form plurals by adding -s.	radio, radios
■ Nouns ending in a consonant and -o add -es.	potato, potatoes
■ Some words ending in -o have alternative plurals.	mosquitos, mosquitoes

Nouns Ending in -f and -fe	**Examples**
■ Most nouns ending in -f and -fe take the plural -s.	roof, roofs safe, safes
■ Other nouns change -f to -v and add -es.	elf, elves
■ However, some plural nouns can take either -s or -ves.	hoofs, hooves

Compound Words	**Examples**
■ Add the plural -s to the end of compound words, except when the first word is more important.	police cars sisters-in-law

Consult your dictionary about these and other spellings when in doubt.

2 Irregular plurals

The small number of English words that have irregular plural forms often confuse the speller.

child, children	louse, lice	ox, oxen
foot, feet	man, men	tooth, teeth
goose, geese	mouse, mice	woman, women

Note that the plural word *brothers* has the alternative form *brethren,* used in references to members of a civic, religious, or professional organization.

3 Plurals of foreign words

English words derived from other languages, particularly Latin and Greek, sometimes form their plurals by using the suffix of the original language. These words can also confuse the speller. Here is a partial list:

alumnus, alumni	medium, media
alumna, alumnae	memorandum, memoranda
antenna, antennae	phenomenon, phenomena
appendix, appendices	psychosis, psychoses
crisis, crises	radius, radii
criterion, criteria	syllabus, syllabi
datum, data	thesis, theses
genus, genera	

Some of these words have an alternate English plural:

antennas	radiuses
appendixes	syllabuses
memorandums	

EXERCISE

Form the plural of each of the following words and phrases:

1. heroine
2. lady-in-waiting
3. criterion
4. quiz
5. ratio
6. father-in-law
7. truck rig
8. scarf
9. Kennedy
10. rap session

**Using spelling rules
to avoid errors**

The following general rules of spelling will help you avoid spelling errors.

1 Words with *-ie* and *-ei*

Words that sound like *be* and *see* usually take *-ie:*

bel*ie*ve, n*ie*ce, rel*ie*ve, s*ie*ge, w*ie*ld

Words in which the *c* is sounded like *sh* take *-ie* also:

consc*ie*nce, defic*ie*nt, suffic*ie*nt

But words in which the *c* is sounded like *see* take *-ei:*

conc*ei*ve, dec*ei*t, dec*ei*ve, rec*ei*pt, rec*ei*ve

Words with long *a* or *i* vowels that sound like *hay, might,* or *air* also take *-ei:*

n*ei*ghbor, r*ei*gn, S*ei*ne, v*ei*n
h*ei*ght, sl*ei*ght
h*ei*r, th*ei*r

Exceptions to these rules include the words *friend, mischief, sieve,* and *view.*

2 Words with final *-e*

Before the suffixes *-able, -ary, -ing,* and *-ous,* the final *-e* is usually dropped:

us*e*, us*able*	reliev*e*, reliev*ing*
imagin*e*, imagin*ary*	fam*e*, fam*ous*

Some words maintain the final *-e* to prevent confusing them with other words. Compare the following:

dying, dy*e*ing

Before the suffixes *-less, -ly, -ment, -ness, -some* and others beginning with a consonant, the final *-e* is kept:

nam*e*, nam*eless*, nam*ely*	sam*e*, sam*eness*
stat*e*, stat*ement*	whol*e*, whol*esome*

Exceptions to this rule include the word *wholly.*

458

Words ending in *-ce* or *-ge* (pronounced with a soft-sounded *c* or *g*) retain the *-e* before suffixes beginning with *a* and *o:*

advanta*geous*, coura*geous*, notic*eable*

3 Words that double final consonants

Some words double the final consonant before a suffix that begins with a vowel:

- One-syllable words ending in a single vowel and a consonant:

slip	sli*pped*	sli*pping*
trot	tro*tted*	tro*tting*
nap	na*pped*	na*pping*

- Two-syllable words in which the second syllable ends in an accented single vowel and a consonant:

occur	occu*rred*	occu*rring*
submit	submi*tted*	submi*tting*

Note that words ending in *l* may or may not double the consonant even though the accent falls on the first syllable:

travel	traveller, traveler
label	labelled, labeled

Don't double the consonants in the following instances:

- Single-syllable words containing two vowels or two consonants:

loo*k*	looked	looking
loc*k*	locked	locking

- Two-syllable words containing two vowels or two consonants in the second (accented) syllable and words ending in *x:*

remark	remarked	remarking	remarkable
detain	detained	detaining	detainable
box	boxed	boxing	boxable

- Words with suffixes beginning with a consonant:

star	starless
deter	determent

- Two-syllable words in which the accent falls on the first syllable or shifts to it:

defer	deference
refer	reference

4 Words ending in -*ic*

For words ending in -*ic*, add *k* before a suffix that starts with *i, e,* or *y:*

panic	panic*k*ed, panic*k*ing, panic*k*y
picni*c*	picnic*k*ing
traff*ic*	traffic*k*ing

5 The suffixes -*able* and -*ible*

The suffix -*able* forms adjectives from verbs:

affordable, readable, notable

The suffix -*able* is also used with stems ending in a hard-sounded *c* or *g:*

amicable, navigable

The suffix -*ible* is used with stems of adjectives derived from Latin verbs and with stems of nouns ending in -*ion:*

divisible, negligible, permissible

Consult your dictionary when in doubt about these spellings.

6 The suffix -*ly*

When adding the suffix -*ly* to a word ending in -*l*, retain the *l:*

final, finally	real, really
formal, formally	regional, regionally

If the word ends in a double *l*, merely add *y:*

hill, hilly

If the word ends in a consonant and *le*, drop the *e* and add only *y:*

remarkable, remarkably

7 The suffix -*cede*

The normal suffix is -*cede:*

intercede, precede, recede, secede

Three words end in -*ceed:*

exceed, proceed, succeed

Only one word ends in -*sede:*

supersede

28e Techniques for improving your spelling

The following techniques will help you to improve your spelling:

- Always keep your handbook and dictionary handy to check the spelling of words you are unsure about. If the word is an unfamiliar one, check the dictionary definition to be sure that you do not confuse the word with another that resembles it (see 28b).
- Use the dictionary to check your pronunciation of misspelled words. Although pronunciation is not always a reliable guide to spelling, the dictionary guide may be of help with words you consistently misspell.
- Become familiar with the prefixes and suffixes in section 33a. As your familiarity increases, you will become adept at spelling words in special fields like biology and medicine. You will also add words to your vocabulary.
- Your word-processing programming disk may include a spelling check. This is a valuable resource, but it cannot tell you if you have used the wrong word (such as *there* instead of *their*) and it cannot catch homonyms (28b) or the inappropriate use of words spelled correctly. Always supplement a computer spelling check with one of your own.
- Keep a log of the words you tend to misspell, noting their correct spellings. Your instructor may call your attention to these words in a draft paper. Check the correct spelling in your dictionary, and from time to time analyze your list of misspelled words for the patterns analyzed in this chapter. Keep a record of these patterns, and check to see whether other words that you tend to misspell fit them.

Following is a list of words that are commonly misspelled. You will find it helpful to keep this list handy for reference during spelling checks. It includes homonyms and other commonly misspelled words discussed earlier in the chapter. (For further discussion, see pages G-1–G-20 of the Glossary of Common Usage.)

Commonly Misspelled Words

absence
absorbable
academy
acceptable
accessible
accidentally
accommodate
accuracy
accustom
achievement
acknowledgment
acquainted
acquitted
acreage
across
address
adolescent
advice
advise
adviser (*or* advisor)
affect
aggravate
aggressive
aisle
all right
allude
analysis
annihilate
annoying
anonymous
apiece
apparent
appreciate
aquatic
assassin
associate
athletics
attendance

bargain
basically
believe
beneficial
biased

breadth
bureaucracy
business

calculator
calendar
camouflage
capital
capitol
carrying
category
ceiling
cemetery
changeable
characteristic
chief
cite
coarse
colossal
column
commercial
committee
complementary
complimentary
conceited
conceive
condemn
conscience
conscientious
consensus
convenient
criticism
criticize
curiosity

deceit
deceive
descendant
desperate
develop
diabetes
dialogue (*or* dialog)
dilapidated
disappear

disappoint
discernible
discipline
disease
dissipate
distinct

ecstasy
effect
efficient
eighth
elicit
elude
embarrass
environment
equipped
especially
exaggerate
exceed
exercise
exhaust
exhilarate
existence
exorbitant
experience
explanation
extraordinary

fascinate
fiend
finally
forego
foreign
foresee
foretell
foreword
forfeit
forty
fragmentary
frivolous
futilely

gauge
genealogy
government

Commonly Misspelled Words (*continued*)

grammar
grievance
guarantee
guard
guerrilla (*or* guerilla)
guidance

hangar
hanger
happened
happily
harass
harmonious
heard
height
heroes
heroines
hindrance
holiday
hoping
humane
humorous
hundreds
hurriedly
hypocrisy

idiosyncrasy
illicit
illusion
immediate
immensely
incalculable
incredible
independent
indestructible
inflammable
initiative
innocuous
innuendo
integrate
interference
interrupt
intramural
irrefutable
irrelevant
irreparable

its
it's

jeopardy
jewelry
judgment (*or* judgement)

laboratory
legitimate
leisure
length
lessen
lesson
liaison
lightning
likelihood
loneliness
loose
lose
luxurious
lying

magazine
maneuver
material
meanness
mediocre
memento
military
millennium
miniature
mischief
missile
mortgage
muscle
mysterious

necessary
nevertheless
niece
noncommital
noticeable
nowadays

occasion
occurrence
ongoing
opportunity

parallel
paralysis
particular
pastime
peaceable
perceive
permissible
phase
physical
physiology
picnicking
playwright
portentous
possess
precede
prejudice
prevalent
prey
principal
principle
privilege
procedure
proceed
professor
pronunciation
prophecy
prophesy
psychiatry
psychology
psychosomatic
publicly
pursue

quandary
questionnaire
quiet
quite
quizzes

ransom
receipt
re-create
referring
recommend
rehearsal
relief
relieve

Commonly Misspelled Words (*continued*)

religious	strategy	unanimous
reminisce	strength	unconscious
repentance	stubbornness	undoubtedly
resemblance	subtlety	unifying
resources	suburban	unimaginable
restaurant	successful	unnecessary
rhetoric	succession	unshakable
rhythm	succumb	urgent
ridiculous	sufficient	usable (*or* useable)
rigmarole	suffrage	usage
roommate	summary	using
	superintendent	
sacrifice	supersede	vacillate
sandwich	suppress	vacuum
satellite	surprise	vegetable
scarcity	susceptible	vengeance
schedule	symmetry	victorious
secede	synonym	visible
secretary		
seize	technical	waive
separate	technique	warring
sergeant	temperature	weather
sheriff	tendency	Wednesday
shriek	testament	weird
significant	thorough	whether
similar	threshold	wholly
skiing	through	withhold
sophomore	tobacco	worshiped (*or* worshipped)
sovereign	toward	worthwhile
specimen	tragedy	writing
speeches	traveler (*or* traveller)	
statistics	truly	yeoman
stayed	twelfth	yield
stony	tyranny	
straight		zoological

Summary

28a Pronunciation is not always a reliable guide for spelling words correctly.

28b Words that look and sound alike can confuse the speller.

Homonyms are pronounced alike but have different meanings and spellings (**28b 1**):

their, there, they're
cite,sight, site

Other words are similar in pronunciation but different in spelling and meaning (28b 1):

than, then
elicit, illicit

Words with the same roots or affixes are easily confused. So are the noun and verb forms of many words (28b 2–3):

assure, ensure, insure
advice, advise

28c   Knowing how to form plurals helps in spelling words.

Regular nouns add -s or -es to form the plural (28c 1):

books, hats, shoes
churches, boxes, bushes

Nouns ending in -y form the plural by adding -s or by omitting the y and adding -ies (28c 1):

day, days
cherry, cherries

Nouns ending in -o form the plural with -s or -es (28c 1):

radio, radios
potato, potatoes

Most nouns ending in -f form the plural with -s; many change -f to -v and add -es (28c 1):

roof, roofs
hoof, hooves

Compound nouns add -s to the final word, except when the first word is more important (28c 1):

police cars, sisters-in-law

Irregular plurals and the plurals of foreign words can confuse the speller (28c 2–3):

child, children
foot, feet
mouse, mice
alumnus, alumni
syllabus, syllabi

28d Knowing other rules of spelling helps in avoiding errors.

Words that sound like *be* take *-ie*, except after *c* when it's sounded like *see* (**28d 1**):

> believe, deceit, conscience

Words with long *a*, long *i*, and some other vowels take *-ei* (**28d 1**):

> neighbor, height, heir

The final *-e* is usually dropped before the suffixes *-able*, *-ary*, *-ing*, and *-ous* (**28d 2**):

> usable, imaginary, relieving, famous

The final *-e* is kept before the suffixes *-less*, *-ly*, *-ment*, *-ness*, and *-some:*

> nameless, namely, statement, sameness, wholesome

Words like *notice* and *courage* that end in *-ce* or *-ge* retain the *-e* before suffixes beginning with *a* or *o:*

> noticeable, courageous

The final consonant usually doubles before a suffix starting with a vowel (**28d 3**):

> slipped, occurred

Words ending in *-ic* add *k* before suffixes starting with *-i*, *-e* or *-y* (**28d 4**):

> panicked, panicking, panicky

The suffixes *-able* and *-ible* form adjectives (**28d 5**):

> affordable, readable, divisible, permissible

When the suffix *-ly* is added to a word ending in *-l*, the *l* is retained (**28d 6**):

> formally, regionally

The usual suffix is *-cede* (**28d 7**):

> intercede, precede, secede

One word ends in *-sede* and three words end in *-ceed:*

> supersede, exceed, proceed, succeed

PART SEVEN

DICTION

Using Appropriate Words

29

Each of us has a formal and informal language that we use in talking at home, at work, and at school. Some of us may also speak several languages or dialects that we share with people in our region of the country and with special groups. Yet what is considered appropriate language or dialect with one group or occasion may not be appropriate with another. For example, formal usage is appropriate in writing a college term paper or a letter applying for a job; general or informal usage is appropriate in a letter to family or friends. Since we write for different audiences, we need to know the conventions that govern various dialects and their formal and informal usage.

Part Seven deals with **diction**, or matters of usage. This chapter begins with a description of the three levels of standard English—formal, informal, and general—and discusses ways of finding your own voice. Chapter 30 turns to abstract and concrete words, general and specific words, slang and jargon, technical words, and sexist language. Chapter 31 discusses the uses of figurative language, including metaphor, simile, and personification. Chapters 32 and 33 focus on how to use the dictionary and other ways to build your vocabulary.

29a Dialects and standard English

1 What is a dialect?

We commonly talk about speaking and writing "English," as if English were a uniform language. Yet English varies considerably in pronunciation, vocabulary, and grammar in different areas of the United States and in other English-speaking countries. These variations may be regional, ethnic, or occupational. They also may be specific to an ethnic or age group.

A **dialect** is a special variety of language spoken by people in one or more regions of a country or by a group of people in all regions. The dialect may be distinctive in its pronunciation, vocabulary, and grammar, or in some of these. American English has numerous regional and local dialects. For example, people in the South accent and pattern their words in ways quite different from those in the North. Differences exist even within a state; many Chicagoans and people in southern Illinois speak different dialects.

Ethnic dialects are not limited to a region or state. Speakers of Black English throughout the United States use distinctive pronunciation, vocabulary, and grammatical structures and usage, including the use of *look* for *looked* and the auxiliary *been* for *has, have,* and *had.* The linguist Geneva Smitherman explains that the Black English speaker relies on the context of the sentence or the conversation to signal time, with the result that the past tense and past participle omit *-ed.* Smitherman gives these examples: *I look for him last night. This guy I know name Junior. . . .* Smitherman notes that "some Black Dialect speakers may be more bi-dialectal than others, preferring to use White English around whites, Black English around blacks."[1]

Several dialects usually prevail in a community. Some of these may be *social dialects,* such as those spoken by particular age groups. Even in families where English is the single language, differences usually exist. Although grandparents, parents, and younger members of the family speak and write the same language, each age group often has its own unique

---

[1] *Talkin and Testifyin* (Boston: Houghton Mifflin), pp. 26, 31.

words, idioms, even sentence phrasing. And each family member usually shares a dialect with friends and groups outside the family. Los Angeles teenagers—Chicanos, blacks, "Valley girls"—have special languages, some shared with teenagers in other parts of the country. Richard Bernstein describes a general teenager's language as consisting of "invented words; some . . . absorbed from street language, rap music, ethnic jargon; others are twists on the special vocabulary of a generation." He points out that the expression *cool it* has given way to *chill*:

> *Chill* also seems to have replaced *to stand somebody up,* or *to fail to turn up for a date.* "She chilled on me," the young man said, after waiting disconsolately for several hours. (On the other hand, the word *chillin',* with origins in rap music, means *first rate, terrific,* as in "The concert was chillin'.").
> —"Youthspeak," *New York Times Magazine,* December 11, 1988

Technical and *occupational dialects* are distinguished by a technical jargon or vocabulary shared by members of a special group, such as sports fans, music fans, hobbyists, computer engineers, or car mechanics. A technical discussion of stereo equipment in a specialized magazine with a national circulation refers to "crossover frequency" and "directivity patterns," terms familiar to those who know this special jargon. Like the social dialect described by Bernstein, technical dialects are not limited to a region or class.

2 Standard English as a dialect

Despite the many differences among English dialects, they share a common structure or arrangement of sentence parts, even in sentences condemned by many as incomprehensible and "bad English." A southern white speaker is quoted as follows:

> "I *ain't* gonna sit in *no* chair and let *no* crazy lawyer tell me *no* lies about *no* law that *no* judge has in *no* law books that *no* smart politician wrote or *nothin'* like that, *nohow.*"
> —Cited in Elizabeth Closs Traugott,
> *The History of English Syntax*

Despite the nonstandard *ain't* and string of double negatives, probably few of us have trouble understanding this speaker. We understand the sentence because it is English in its basic structure. Features of a particular dialect are often features of English no longer current in the standard dialect: the intensive use of negatives is typical of sentences in Chaucer's and Shakespeare's day. Noting that "triple and quadruple negatives are the sole province of Africanized English," Geneva Smitherman quotes a Black English speaker: "Don't nobody never help me do my work."[2]

If English varies in so many ways, what do we mean when we refer to "English" as a language? And how is the "standard English" we are taught in school, hear on radio and television, and read in newspapers and magazines related to regional and social dialects?

Like other special languages spoken and written in the United States, the standard English we learn in school is a dialect. It is a social dialect used by those who govern the country, operate the judicial system, make laws, run schools, and conduct commercial business. Because of its wide public use and social prestige, this dialect is widely referred to as **standard English**. In some communities, standard English is the dialect of the majority; in other communities, it may be the dialect of the minority, even though schools and businesses in these communities teach and use the prevailing standard.

The term **nonstandard English** refers to usage that departs from the standard dialect in one or more ways. To many who speak the standard dialect, nonstandard English is considered unacceptable or inferior. They sometimes argue that nonstandard English is unclear or inexpressive. Yet even defenders of a "pure standard" often recognize that the dialects of the southern white, the black speaker, and others are just as clear and expressive as the standard dialect. Thus, standard English is not "better" or more "correct" or more expressive or more beautiful than other dialects. Why, then, should you study or seek to improve your use of it?

Standard English is a cultivated or learned dialect, and a highly flexible one, capable of dealing with concrete experience and abstract ideas because of its large and varied vocabulary. It is the accepted language of general and scholarly discourse in newspapers, magazines, and professional journals. Its syntax and vocabulary have wide use throughout the United States; a person must speak and write the prevailing standard to make a career in politics, to teach school, or to find a white-collar job. These are important reasons for improving one's skills in standard English.

[2]*Talkin and Testifyin*, p. 30.

Standard English has never been a fixed dialect; it changes over time, often enriched by nonstandard dialects. In an ethnically and culturally diverse country like the United States, few who master a dialect that is not their own willingly give up their own. Mastering standard English, then, does not require the sacrifice of a personal dialect. Indeed, few people give up their special dialects in the process of improving their command of English.

29b Levels of usage

At times you want to write formally, as in letters of job application; a personal tone will not do. At other times you want to write informally and personally, as in letters or notes to family and friends. Some words and sentences are appropriate to particular personal, social, and business situations; others are not. Standard English offers you a range of choices in diction and sentence structure at levels commonly referred to as *formal, informal,* and *general.* Usage is usually defined according to these levels or varieties. Although the distinction among formal, general, and informal usage is not exact, knowing their defining features is helpful in choosing the appropriate usage.

1 Formal English

Formal English is appropriate in writing about subjects that require unusual precision. Technical papers, insurance policies, contracts, and letters from corporations are usually written in formal English. So are the official correspondence of government officials, statements of goals and requirements in college catalogs, scholarly articles, textbooks, and occasional magazine and newspaper articles, editorials, and columns.

Often technical in nature, formal writing usually requires exact statement and choice of words, in contrast to the looser wording of everyday conversation. Here are some of the most distinctive qualities of formal English:

Characteristics of Formal English
- Filled-out constructions and few contractions (e.g., *is not* in preference to *isn't*)

- Occasional sentences opening with the third-person *one* (*"One finds. . . ."*) and infrequent use of the second-person pronoun *you*
- Frequent mid-branching and periodic sentences (see 13a)
- Prominent sentence parallelism, balance, and antithesis (14a–c).
- A large number of technical and abstract words, many of Latin and Greek origin (30a)

The following passage is typical of the highly formal usage of technical essays directed to a special audience:

> What is often unrecognized or ignored is the fact that the "races" about which many scientists speak and write are those perceived and delineated by particular groups of people who interact in given sociopolitical contexts. Comparative studies of these popular racial typologies show them to vary from place to place; studies of popular racial classifications also show them to vary from one historical period to another.
>
> —Gloria Marshall,
> "Racial Classifications: Popular and Scientific"

Marshall's sentences are tight and carefully planned—each idea is stated precisely and moderately balanced (*vary from place to place, vary from one historical period to another*). The passage contains none of the pauses or qualifications common in everyday speech. Many of the words and phrases are abstract (*sociopolitical contexts, racial typologies*), a large number of them are Latin and Greek in origin (*perceived* and *political*).

Formal essays directed to a general audience are sometimes closer to spoken English in their personal references. Abstract words and phrases (e.g., *social group* and *burdens and crises*) and careful parallelism make the following passage formal:

> When I think of what makes me a dedicated member of a social group I realize that burdens and crises are more effective than benefits. Perceived threats to the common good stir us to work and sacrifice to a degree that appeals to self-interest never can. This behavior in turn reinforces our sense that the "tribe" we sacrifice for is *our* tribe.
>
> —Andrew Oldenquist, "On Belonging to Tribes,"
> *Newsweek*, April 5, 1982

But formal writing need not and does not avoid personal reference. The writer refers to himself in this sentence, at the same time depending on sentence balance for special emphasis. Formal speech and writing need not be stiff or impersonal.

473

2 Informal English

Informal English is appropriate in writing about everyday concerns and personal experiences. Here are the most distinctive qualities of informal English:

> **Characteristics of Informal English**
> - Sentence patterns that are typical of conversational English
> - Frequent use of contractions (*didn't, shouldn't*)
> - Cumulative and mid-branching sentence construction (see 13a)
> - Frequent use of the second-person *you*
> - Everyday expressions or colloquialisms (*all kinds of stuff*)
> - Many concrete words like *job* and *think about* and fewer abstract or general words like *employment* and *contemplate* (30a)
> - Occasional use of slang (30c)

In sentence structure and vocabulary, informal English seldom departs from the sentence patterns and vocabulary of conversational or **colloquial English**. Informal English assumes a familiarity between you and your listener or reader that permits you to be less exact in references to people and things and more colloquial (see 1c). Colloquial sentences are usually looser in structure than formal sentences. When they are periodic and build to the subject, they often include the pauses that mark our common talk.

The writer of the following passage converses with the reader about growing up in the 1930s. His use of colloquial sentence patterns (*So I'd climb on roofs*), frequent contractions, cumulation of clauses, and concrete words and colloquialisms (*I shouldn't have bitten that one off*) makes the writing informal:

> The main reason people hired me was the Depression. They didn't have any money to fix their radios, and they'd hear about this kid who would do it for less. So I'd climb on roofs to fix antennas, and all kinds of stuff. I got a series of lessons of ever-increasing difficulty. Ultimately I got some job like converting a DC set into an AC set, and it was very hard to keep the hum from going through the system, and I didn't build it quite right. I shouldn't have bitten that one off, but I didn't know.
>
> —Richard P. Feynman, *Surely You're Joking, Mr. Feynman!*

3 General English

General English may be concrete or abstract; it may deal with everyday experiences and ideas and blend formal and informal features. Here are the common features of general English:

Characteristics of General English

- Frequent use of cumulative sentences and occasional use of periodic and moderately balanced sentences (see 13a)
- A mix of concrete, abstract, and technical words (30a, 30d)
- Occasional use of contractions
- Colloquial expressions (30b–c)

The English you hear on radio and television and read in magazines, journals, and newspapers is most often at this general level. General English is spoken and written by people in their business and other public and everyday communications. Much of your college writing will be at this general level.

The following definition of the term *entropy* is typical of general English: it mixes abstract and concrete words (*entropy, torn-down buildings*), colloquialisms (*one-way street, messy*), cumulative and moderately periodic and balanced sentences, and occasional contractions (*Once it's created*):

> Disorder, alas, is the natural order of things in the universe. There is even a precise measure of the amount of disorder, called entropy. Unlike almost every other physical property (motion, gravity, energy), entropy does not work both ways. It can only increase. Once it's created, it can never be destroyed. The road to disorder is a one-way street.
>
> Because of its unnerving irreversibility, entropy has been called the arrow of time. We all understand this instinctively. Children's rooms, left on their own, tend to get messy, not neat. Wood rots, metal rusts, people wrinkle and flowers wither. Even mountains wear down; even the nuclei of atoms decay. In the city we see entropy in the rundown subways and worn-out sidewalks and torn-down buildings, in the increasing disorder of our lives. We know, without asking, what is old. If we were suddenly to see the paint jump back on an old building, we would know that something was wrong. If we saw an egg unscramble itself and jump back into its shell, we would laugh in the same way we laugh at a movie run backward.
>
> —K. C. Cole, *New York Times*, March 18, 1982

Although philosophical and other academic writing is usually formal in style, philosophers sometimes prefer a general style:

> The molecular theory of gases emerged as an ingenious metaphor: likening a gas to a vast swarm of absurdly small bodies. So pat was the metaphor that it was declared literally true, thus becoming straightway a dead metaphor; the fancied miniatures of bodies were declared real, and the term "body" was extended

475

to cover them. In later years the molecules have even been observed through electron microscopy; but I speak of origins.
—W. V. Quine, *Theories and Things*

Quine uses common words to state an abstract idea. Familiar
phrases give us the sense of a philosopher conversing about
the role of metaphor in science. The general style in no way
diminishes the seriousness or depth of what Quine has to say.

In drafting a paper, you may write much of it in an informal style to get your ideas down on paper. You probably will
not think about usage or sentence structure in composing each
sentence, though you may pause to rephrase an idea or choose
a different word. But consistent usage will be one of your main
concerns in revising and editing the paper. Frequent use of
contractions, slang, and other informal features of your draft
would be inappropriate in a paper that calls for a general or
formal style. Your sentence structure will also need closer attention than you gave it in the draft. In editing the paper, you
have an opportunity to make a final check of usage. You should
make all necessary changes at this stage, even though you may
have to retype one or more pages.

EXERCISE

Using subject matter, vocabulary, and sentence construction as
your guides, identify the level of usage—formal, informal, or general—used in the following passages:

1. Nothing is truer than Pasteur's famous statement that
   only "the prepared mind" makes discoveries. But little
   thought has been given up to now to the process by
   which the mind is prepared. A mere knowledge of
   certain facts is not enough, nor the presence of certain concepts and ideas, if they are hidden away in a
   different brain compartment. An astonishingly high
   proportion of major new concepts and theories is
   based on components that had long before been available but which no one had been able to tie together
   properly. This must be remembered in any search for
   external influences in the development of scientific
   ideas.
   —Ernst Mayr, *The Growth of Biological Thought*

2. Having heard less about the awful consequences of
   study, the Middle Atlantic Colonies seem to have been
   more willing to gamble, and the Dutch who settled
   New York tolerated girls in their primary schools

from the very beginning. These were church sponsored, and strict and total segregation was the rule. Smaller towns with one building at their disposal specified that "Boys and Girls should be separated as much as possible from each other." Girls again got the drafty back rows and the chilly corners. The good burghers of New Amsterdam took particular pains to guarantee that their thrifty mixing of the sexes did not encourage social evils.

—Elaine Kendall, "Beyond Mother's Knee," *American Heritage*, June 1973

3. We were talking of the first discoveries of uniqueness—of being oneself and no one else. Not your father, not your mother, not your sister, not your brother. I. Me.

It is then—when you begin not only to know it, but act it—that society moves in. Society says it wants people to be different but it doesn't really mean it. Parents like to believe their children are different from other children—smarter, of course, better-looking and so forth—but most parents are secretly disturbed when their children are *really* different— not like others at all. In fact, very early they start to pigeonhole you in certain ways.

—Marya Mannes, "Who Am I?"

4. I get great satisfaction every time I regulate and stoke the furnace. It is like a winter-long chess problem, with the impetus of necessity thrown in to make it all real. For example, the six p.m. filling must provide heat for an evening at play downstairs, but must also end up consuming all the wood in the furnace, leaving a bed of hot coals, and plenty of room for loading in the upright night fire. Other times have other requirements, and the moderate intricacy of it all gets to be second nature after a while. Last winter I felt I'd turned into a human thermostat, and then realized that's what I'd been all along.

—Mark Kramer, "Wood Heat" ■

29c Finding your own voice

Your writing always has a **voice** that reflects the tone of your statements and the way you stress words and phrases. On occasion, you become aware of voice when a sentence or paragraph doesn't "sound right." In a letter of application, you sense that your opening sentences are too chatty or, conversely, are stiff and even unfriendly. The letter is probably not in the voice you want to convey.

Usually you are not aware of voice as you speak or write. Writing to a familiar audience is often like a conversation with friends. You may not finish a sentence, certain that your listeners know what you mean; you may choose a less exact word for the same reason. Most conversations are characterized by an interplay between old and new knowledge, perhaps a return to something said earlier in the conversation or repetition of a statement or explanation. Writing that resembles conversation is probably closest to your everyday voice.

The less familiar you are with your audience, the less shared knowledge you can depend on. In giving directions to a friend, you probably nod or talk less precisely, referring to "the house over there" rather than to the "white house with the picket fence, on the southwest corner of Main and Sixth Streets." Giving directions to a stranger, you gesture carefully and choose your words and sentences with care. Giving the same directions in writing, you are also more precise. Your voice is therefore more formal, less personal.

Even in highly formal writing, the reader hears the voice of the writer. At this level, you need not depart entirely from colloquial patterns or vocabulary. Just as informal writing can sound chatty and overfamiliar, formal writing can sound stuffy and impersonal. Indeed, writing that departs too far from colloquial patterns risks sounding stiff and distant.

You are likely to make several new starts to find a proper voice before continuing with your writing. You also may make additional adjustments in voice and tone in the course of writing. You want to consider your audience in making decisions about sentence structure and choice of words. Your subject may be more suited to a formal treatment than an informal one, and so may be the writing situation—for example, a midterm report on laboratory work in a science course. These factors influence the voice in which you write. A chatty, informal presentation would be inappropriate in term papers and reports. But so would a stiff, impersonal presentation. In drafting and revising your papers, listen for a voice that isn't your own. Even in a formal essay, the reader should hear your voice, not someone else's.

EXERCISE

Write instructions for each of the following groups of people on how to find a particular street or neighborhood. Be ready to discuss the decisions you made about language or diction in writing the instructions.

1. Friends who live in a neighboring town or city
2. Children
3. Teenagers
4. English-speaking visitors from another country ■

Summary

29a Standard English is one dialect among many spoken and written dialects.

29b Choose a level of usage appropriate to the subject and occasion.

Formal English is appropriate in writing about subjects that require unusual precision and that are of wide public concern **(29b 1)**.

Informal English is appropriate in writing about personal matters and everyday concerns and experiences **(29b 2)**.

General English, a blend of formal and informal usage, is appropriate in writing about business, political, and other everyday concerns **(29b 3)**.

29c Consider your audience in establishing a voice in a piece of writing.

Choosing **30**
Effective Words

Your choice of words in an essay depends on your subject as well as on your audience. If your audience is a general one, technical or unfamiliar terms will need thorough explanation; some of your readers are likely to know the meanings of these words, but some will not. In writing to a special audience, one fully acquainted with your subject and terminology, a thorough explanation of terms is usually unnecessary. A physicist addressing other physicists probably would not define terms, whereas a physicist addressing the general public would have to define those same terms thoroughly. Thus, words that are effective in addressing one kind of audience may be ineffective in addressing another kind. In this chapter, we turn to the effective and ineffective uses of various classes of words—abstract and concrete words, general and specific ones, slang, technical jargon, and sexist language.

30a Abstract and concrete words

Abstract words refer to abstract things like ideas, not to specific things. Although ideas are abstract, they can be illustrated through **concrete words** that refer to the objects, events, and persons that embody these ideas. Compare the following examples:

Abstract	**Concrete**
Historical novels often contain symbolic characters.	Ivan Denisovich, in Solzhenitsyn's novel about Soviet prisons, represents millions victimized by Stalin and his police state.
The media influence aggressive public behavior.	Televised fights between baseball and other sports players encourage spectators to fight in the stands and on the field.
Scientific achievement often has a price.	Many pesticides that increase crop production at the same time pollute water and air.

One or more paragraphs, indeed an entire essay, may discuss an idea using only abstract words and phrases. Definitions are often abstract, as in the following passage that defines the abstract word *industry* through other abstract words and phrases:

Abstract

The first important word is *industry,* and the period in which its use changes is the period which we now call the Industrial Revolution. *Industry,* before this period, was a name for a particular human attribute, which could be paraphrased as "skill, assiduity, perseverance, diligence." This use of *industry* of course survives. But in the last decades of the eighteenth century, *industry* came also to mean something else; it became a collective word for our manufacturing and productive institutions, and for their general activities.

—Raymond Williams, *Culture and Society*

By contrast, the following passage uses concrete words to describe a specific industrial process:

Concrete
    Toward the middle of the nineteenth century William E. Ward of Port Chester, New York, developed machinery for the hot-forging of nuts and bolts. In this procedure bar stock is heated to about 870 degrees Celsius (1,600 degrees Fahrenheit) and fed into the forming dies. Later Ward developed machinery to do the work by cold-forming. The procedure is much the same except that the bar stock is not heated. The dies must be strong, and the machine that holds them must be capable of exerting powerful forces. A cold-formed product can be made to closer dimensional tolerances than a hot-formed one and is stronger. Cold-forming is now the basic method of manufacture for mass-produced nuts, bolts and screws.
                                    —Frederick E. Graves, "Nuts and Bolts,"
                                      Scientific American, June 1984

    Abstract words are essential in writing about ideas. When you state an abstract idea, though, make it concrete by using an example. This allows your reader to visualize the idea through particular people and events that embody it. In writing to a general audience, many of whom are likely to be unfamiliar with the idea, you need to define and illustrate the idea with concrete words. Your writing will be most effective when you combine the abstract and the concrete, weaving ideas and concrete details and examples into a whole.

 30b | General and specific words

    General words name a class; **specific words** name the members of a class. Thus, general words are appropriate in discussing a class of objects, events, or persons (*weapons, wars, soldiers*). To describe a specific object, event, or person, concrete words are appropriate (*armored tanks, Invasion of Sicily, General Patton*).
    Words and phrases have different degrees of generality. Although the following words all refer to the same thing, they differ greatly in degrees of generality:

implement
tool
hammer
claw hammer
small-headed claw hammer
small iron-headed claw hammer

Compare the following statements:

General
I used a special tool to insert the nail.

Specific
I used a small iron-headed claw hammer to pound the nail into the wall.

If your point is simply to identify the type of tool you are using, you don't require adjectives (*small iron-headed claw*):

I pounded the nail with a hammer.

You do need adjectives if the features of the hammer are important to your discussion:

The small claw hammer made the job easier.

Don't use more adjectives than you need; superfluous details can mislead the reader. The adjective *iron-headed* would be superfluous in the preceding example unless you wanted to stress the metal.

How specific you should be in a paragraph or essay depends on your purpose in writing. If your purpose is to give general information, details that are too exact may distract the reader from the point you are making. The writer of the following paragraph chooses words suited to general statements and specific details:

In early childhood girls' and boys' clothes are often identical in cut and fabric, as if in recognition of the fact that their bodies are much alike. But the T-shirts, pull-on slacks and zip jackets intended for boys are usually made in darker colors (especially forest green, navy, red and brown) and printed with designs involving sports, transportation and cute wild animals. Girls' clothes are made in paler colors (especially pink, yellow and green) and decorated with flowers and cute domestic animals. The suggestion is that the boy will play vigorously and travel over long distances; the girl will stay home and nurture plants and small mammals. Alternatively, these designs may symbolize their wearers: the boy is a cuddly bear or a smiling tiger, the girl a flower or a kitten. There is also a tendency for boys' clothes to be fullest at the shoulders and girls' at the hips, anticipating their adult figures.

—Alison Lurie, "The Language of Clothes"

Lurie provides enough details for us to visualize the different clothing. Her detail is specific and never excessive. The girls' clothing is "decorated with flowers and cute domestic animals." These details are sufficient; Lurie would have blurred her point by naming the flowers and the animals.

EXERCISE

Make the following sentences specific without adding superfluous words:

1. Several phenomena of nature are killing the forest.
2. He rode several vehicles to get to school.
3. She put several objects for painting the house on the porch.
4. The shelf was full of different reading materials.
5. He passed the driving test even though he made several mistakes.
6. The variety of courses she took shows her many interests.
7. She used an implement to collect things scattered in the yard.
8. He prepared the chicken in a special way to make it less fattening.
9. The weather turned nasty.
10. We had engine trouble on the trip to Cincinnati.

 Slang

Slang is showy, often metaphorical, and usually short-lived language, originating in a subculture. Invented words or coinages like *glitzy* and *sleaze* are examples of slang. These words sometimes pass into general usage, at which point they become *colloquialisms*—everyday words and phrases used mainly in informal conversation (see 29b).

Slang is common in informal speech and writing and is occasionally used in general discourse, usually for a humorous effect. It is seldom used in formal writing. Slang is meant to be colorful and ostentatious. "We all knew each other," a politician is quoted in a newsmagazine:

> There was a lot of talk about who might be available—a lot of massaging. . . . There were a few elbows bent and a few stories told. But in St. Louis, everybody was hot to trot.
>
> —*Newsweek*, August 1, 1983

The speaker is showing his cleverness and political agility through the slang he uses.

The origin of the word *slang*, possibly from the Norwegian word *slengjenamn* for nickname, suggests one reason for its popularity. Slang offers a shortcut in speaking, often through images. As in the colorful talk of the politician, slang depends on clipped phrases (*a lot of massaging*) and flashy metaphors (*hot to trot*)—a way of speaking and writing that depends on a confidential relationship with the listener or reader. Slang may be short-lived because it loses its confidentiality as it spreads to people outside the group. One linguistic theory suggests that slang is a game of words that loses interest when the words become overfamiliar. This theory helps to explain why colorful metaphors fade in interest, making the slangy talk of a television talk-show host stale quickly.

Slang is usually ineffective in general and formal writing because it is current for so short a time. At any level of writing, though, frequent slang can tire even the reader familiar with it. However, don't hesitate to use everyday expressions, colloquialisms, and common words if these express your meaning adequately. The word *think* may be adequate for the idea you want to express; the colloquial *mull over* (meaning to linger over or ponder an idea) may be appropriate, too. But the slang expression *roll it over* is inappropriate in general and formal writing. Everyday expressions or colloquialisms keep writing from sounding overly formal and stuffy. Effective sentences never depart too widely from colloquial patterns and vocabulary. Never write a sentence that you cannot speak with ease, even if the phrasing and vocabulary are abstract and formal. If you do use slang in an informal essay, don't call attention to it by putting the word or phrase in quotation marks.

485

EXERCISES

1. Write down slang words and phrases that you associate with a particular group like rock musicians or football fans. Be ready to discuss how wide or restricted in use you believe these words and phrases are.

2. What images and feelings do the following words convey to you?

   a. glitzy   **d.** nerdy
   b. sleazy   **e.** wimpy
   c. smarmy

30d   Jargon

1   Uses of technical words

Jargon is the special, technical vocabulary of a profession or craft. Auto mechanics talk a special jargon (or *argot*); so do astronauts, football players, chemists, and even thieves. Jargon has important uses in general and technical writing. An article on "micromechanical devices," in a magazine directed to scientists and general readers, contains these sentences:

> The etch rate of a doping-dependent etchant (a category that overlaps the categories of isotropic and anisotropic etchants) depends on the type of dopant atoms and their concentration. The isotropic etchant HNA is doping-dependent in some mixture ratios; it etches heavily doped silicon much faster than it etches lightly doped silicon.
> —James B. Angell, Stephen C. Terry, and Phillip W. Barth, "Silicon Micromechanical Devices," *Scientific American*, April 1983

The authors carefully define the special term "doping-dependent etchant." Once defined, it forms a special language—a sequence of technical terms with their own grammatical forms (*dope, doping, doped*). Technical writing sometimes resembles a shorthand whose conciseness and concreteness are virtues in scientific and other kinds of specialized writing.

2 Misuses of technical words

Can the technical ideas just discussed be stated in plain English, without using technical language?

This is the question you must answer in deciding whether to write in a technical or nontechnical style. As the preceding passage shows, jargon permits you to write a verbal shorthand, often with a considerable saving of words. Writing in a nontechnical style to a general audience requires more explanation and definition of terms. Probably most members of a general audience would be unable to grasp this definition of micromechanical devices in the same article:

> Silicon is a semiconductor, one of the elements that lie between the metals and the nonmetals in the periodic table of the elements.

Those unfamiliar with chemical terms would need to be told what a semiconductor is. No further definition would be needed, however, for specialists in the field.

Like slang, jargon can confuse readers, particularly when it is used out of its field. Some types of jargon are more likely to confuse readers. Most sports jargon is familiar enough not to cause confusion, unlike the jargon of technical fields like computer programming. Richard Reinhold cites the jargon or "computerese" of people who work with computers, including the words and phrases "bandwidth," "windowing," "I'm interrupt driven," "He's a read-only memory," "He's pushing things on the stack." Reinhold illustrates how jargon comes into use outside its field: a computer engineer uses the phrase "core dumped," meaning to empty the computer of its memory, to describe how she made complaints to her employer:

> She might have added that the experience was a "gating event," that is, a crucial turning point, again taken from computerese. A gate on a silicon microprocessor chip is a key element in controlling its logic.
>
> —Richard Reinhold, "Computer People Are Creating a Valley of Babble in California," *New York Times*, February 19, 1984

The word *jargon* also refers to a string of vague words and unclear metaphors that makes writing clumsy and unintelligible:

> "Realization has grown that the curriculum or the experiences of learners change and improve only as those who are most directly

involved examine their goals, improve their understandings and increase their skill in performing the tasks necessary to reach newly defined goals. This places the focus upon teacher, lay citizen and learner as partners in curricular improvement and as the individuals who must change, if there is to be curricular change."

Cited in Stuart Chase, The Power of Words

Notice that the second sentence repeats the first, using some of the same abstract words (*curriculum, change, improve*). The term *curriculum*, defined as "the experiences of learners," seems to depart from its usual meaning of course of study. We expect the second sentence to state a new idea; it does not. The metaphor *places the focus upon* increases the confusion.

In general discourse, many technical terms become clumsy jargon. Both the general reader and the specialist probably would struggle with the meaning of the preceding passage. Technical jargon can also confuse discussion of serious issues by disguising the facts. A critic of jargon cites this deceptive use of the word *environment:*

> In the jargon of the traffic planning industry, what an *environmental* area really means is a device for channeling motor traffic out of your street into someone else's, if possible three or four blocks away.

—Philip Howard, Weasel Words

It is important, then, not to introduce technical terms into a general discussion unnecessarily. Watch out for technical jargon that is meaningful only to the technicians or workers who use it, and reserve your use of technical jargon for discussions of technical subjects. Watch out also for clumsy, unintelligible jargon. It sounds pretentious to say that you are "accessing a loan" when you mean you are borrowing money. When you discover that you have misused jargon in this way, recast the statement in the simplest language possible.

EXERCISES

1. Rewrite the statements cited by Stuart Chase on page 489, clarifying the terms or using different ones. Use the fewest words possible.
2. Compile a short list of technical terms in a game or sport you play. Then write a brief account of an aspect of the game or sport, clarifying these terms for a beginner.

30e Avoiding sexist language

People have long been sensitive to the effect of derogatory words that generate contempt toward ethnic and racial minorities. But until recently most have ignored subtler kinds of discrimination and unfairness toward women in the use of descriptive terms and masculine pronouns that stereotype women or exclude them from the discussion. With increased sensitivity to discrimination against women, use of the generic *he* and *him* to refer to both men and women is decreasing. Neutral terms are gradually replacing sexist ones.

Many publishing houses, governmental agencies, and other groups and writers now substitute neutral titles for occupations traditionally identified with men or women: *clergy* for *clergyman, flight attendant* for *stewardess.* Terms like *authoress, poetess,* and *waitress* that make special identifications of women are quickly disappearing; the terms *author, poet,* and *waiter* refer increasingly to men and women. Some people substitute *person* in all words compounded with *man,* but this practice has not been universally accepted for use with multisyllabic words like *congressperson.* Here are some of the nonsexist substitutes that are gaining wide acceptance:

Sexist Terms	Nonsexist Alternatives
businessman	business executive, manager
caveman	cave dweller
chairman	chair, chairperson
cleaning lady	domestic, household worker
committeeman	committee member
fireman	fire fighter
foreman	supervisor
housewife	homemaker
layman	ordinary person, nonspecialist, layperson
mailman	letter carrier, mail carrier
man, mankind	humankind, humanity, human beings, people
man-made	manufactured, synthetic, artificial
middle man	contact, broker
policeman	police officer

Sexist Terms	Nonsexist Alternatives
salesman	salesperson
statesman	diplomat
waitress	waiter, server
workmen, working man	workers, worker

Recasting your sentences to avoid using masculine pronouns exclusively and unfairly is sometimes more difficult than finding a neutral substitute for a sexist noun (see 10b). A common solution is to use dual pronouns:

Each senator departed for *his or her* district.

Many writers reject this solution because continuous repetition of *his or her* and other dual pronoun combinations becomes monotonous, distracting the reader from the content of the paragraph or essay. The most common solution to this problem is to pluralize the subject:

Singular	Plural
Each student stated *his* reason for enrolling in the course.	The students stated *their* reasons for enrolling in the course.
Everyone over eighteen has the right to cast *his* vote.	Those over eighteen have the right to cast *their* vote.
Don't make fun of a person if you want *his* friendship.	Don't make fun of people if you want *their* friendship.

An alternative solution is to change the masculine pronoun to a neutral determiner:

Each student stated a reason for enrolling in the course.
Everyone over eighteen has the right to cast a vote.
Don't make fun of a person if you want to keep a friendship.

Omitting the pronoun altogether is often possible. Compare the following sentences:

The researcher must *check his facts* repeatedly.	The researcher must *check facts* repeatedly.

Finally, the passive voice is sometimes workable when the omission of a pronoun or the use of a neutral determiner is awkward or impossible:

He must take special care in recording facts.	*Special care must be taken* in recording facts.

Alleen Pace Nilsen points out that good writers can be fair to the two sexes by following these two principles:

They use inclusive language so as not to ignore one sex or imply that all members of particular groups belong to the same sex. Even when groups are predominantly made up of members of one sex, they are careful to leave the door open for participation by individuals of the other sex.

They treat people as individuals rather than ascribing to them characteristics based on sex-role stereotyping. When writing about males and females engaged in similar activities, they treat their subjects equally.

—"Using Language That Is Fair to Both Sexes"

Summary

30a   Make your ideas concrete by naming things that embody them:

Abstract
Scientific achievement often has a price.

Concrete
Many pesticides that increase crop production at the same time pollute water and air.

30b   Be as specific as your discussion requires:

General
I pounded the nail with a hammer.

Specific
I pounded the nail with a small-headed claw hammer.

30c   Use slang sparingly in informal writing, and omit it in general and formal discourse.

30d   Use technical jargon only in technical discussions, and avoid vague words and unclear metaphors that make writing clumsy and unintelligible.

30e   Avoid sexist language. Use nouns and pronouns so that they do not stereotype men or women or exclude either sex from the discussion.

31

Using Figurative Language

Figurative language or figures of speech depart from the literal meanings of words in unusual or striking ways. This quality of figurative language is valuable in making descriptions more vivid and in highlighting ideas. Used properly, figurative language can enliven ideas and evoke emotion. Misused, it can distract readers by making a statement difficult to understand or by calling attention to itself. This chapter discusses the effective and ineffective uses of metaphor, simile, personification, hyperbole, and other common figures of speech.

31a Using metaphors and other figures of speech

1 Metaphor, simile, personification

A **metaphor** is a figure of speech that talks about one thing as if it were something else. For example, the literal meaning of the word *cosmetic* is a product that improves the look of the skin. We use the same word figuratively in referring to "cosmetic statements" designed to make an explanation or a policy look better than it is. Thus, the phrase *cosmetic statements* is a metaphor.

When used in writing, metaphors and other figures of speech serve to make ideas more vivid and concrete and to evoke emotions by calling comparisons to mind. You often use metaphors in speaking that name the thing talked about and the vehicle that provides the comparison:

> dead of night
> family of nations
> dogs of war

The words *dead, family,* and *dogs* are the vehicles that provide the comparisons in metaphors. Other kinds of metaphor, however, do not name or specify the vehicle of comparison:

> He began to walk back along the tracks, for less than a mile away, he knew, where the stream boiled over the lip of a dam, there was a bridge.
>
> —Thomas Wolfe, *The Web and the Rock*

This sentence contains an implicit comparison between a fast-moving stream and a liquid boiling in a container. The author names the thing he is describing—the stream—but only implies the vehicle of the metaphor—the boiling liquid.

Some metaphors require the reader to guess the thing being described as well as the thing or vehicle used to describe it. The following example compares scientific research to a journey—the vehicle of the metaphor. However, neither the thing described nor the vehicle used to describe it is explicitly named:

> We sought, instead, an adventurous existence amidst the crater lands and ice fields of self–generated ideas. Clambering onward, we have slowly made our way out of a maze of isolated peaks into the level plains of science.
>
> —Loren Eiseley, *The Unexpected Universe*

Notice the explicit metaphors in these sentences, including the phrase *maze of isolated peaks.*

Eiseley's sentences show that metaphor develops from analogy. Charles Rembar introduces a discussion of the role of the lawyer through comparison of the courtroom with a battlefield: "The litigating lawyer is a mercenary, one of the few remaining examples of the hired combatant." Rembar develops his comparison using metaphor:

> The need for combativeness arises from the fact that our legal system is an adversary system, the hypothesis being that contention *forces out* the truth. This presupposes partisanship and bias; since the *partisans* are opposed, the *thrashing* and *wrangling* sends the facts to the surface.
>
> —*The End of Obscenity* (emphasis added)

Rembar *extends* the analogy between the lawyer and the mercenary and therefore the metaphor. Both are hostile; their hostility has the approval of society; both act by exact rules.

A **simile** is even closer to analogy in that it stresses the likeness between two things. However, a simile always uses the word *like* or *as* to announce the likeness of things:

> The covers once prized apart would never close; those books once open stayed open and lay on their backs helplessly fluttering their leaves *like* a turned-over June bug. They were as light *as* a matchbox.
>
> —Eudora Welty, "A Sweet Devouring" (emphasis added)

Unlike metaphor, simile always *names* both elements of the comparison. In the preceding passage, Welty wants us to imagine the open book and the turned-over bug and then the matchbox to which the two are compared.

Personification gives human or animate qualities to inanimate things so that they seem to possess life:

> The sun had risen, and the sky above the houses wore an air of extraordinary beauty, simplicity and peace.
>
> —Virginia Woolf, *The Years*
>
> North Richmond Street, being blind, was a quiet street except at the hour when the Christian Brothers' School set the boys free. An uninhabited house of two storeys stood at the blind end, detached from its neighbors in a square ground. The other houses of the street, conscious of decent lives within them, gazed at one another with brown imperturbable faces.
>
> —James Joyce, "Araby"

Woolf personifies the sky as a beautiful woman, then she develops the implied comparison. Joyce personifies the Dublin houses as people satisfied with their own dull lives and aware but uninterested in the world about them. Like Woolf and Joyce, you can appeal to the reader's emotions through personification. Images of human and animate life awaken the imagination.

2 Uses of figurative language

You will find metaphor, simile, and personification highly useful in making descriptive statements vivid and intense:

> Autumn comes to the sea with a fresh blaze of phosphorescence, when every wave crest is aflame. Here and there the whole surface may glow with *sheets of cold fire, while below schools of fish pour through the water like molten metal.*
> —Rachel Carson, *The Sea around Us* (emphasis added)

Carson uses metaphor in referring to the flaming wave crests and "sheets of cold fire" and simile in comparing schools of fish to molten metal. These metaphors help us see the "fresh blaze of phosphorescence."

To use metaphor effectively, you must maintain the central impression or idea of your sentence or paragraph. You can do this best by keeping your metaphors brief and condensed, as Carson does in giving an instant impression of the ocean. Although you notice the metaphors in her sentences, they do not blur the central impression. Like Carson, you can use metaphor in exposition to convey your central ideas more vividly. Carson uses metaphorical description to explain that organisms in the water cause the ocean to shine; the metaphors make her description and central impression more vivid.

Carson is writing to a general audience about a scientific topic. So is the author of the following description of the interior of the atom:

> Under a microscope the material of the rock is revealed to be a tangle of interlocking crystals. An electron microscope can uncover the individual atoms, spaced out in a regular array with large gaps in between. Probing into the atoms themselves, we find that they are almost entirely empty space. The tiny nucleus occupies a mere trillionth (10^{-12}) of the atom's volume. The rest is populated by a *cloud* of neither-here-nor-there *ephemeral* electrons, *pinpricks* of solidity whirling about in *oceans* of *void*.
> —Paul Davies, *Superforce* (emphasis added)

Figurative language is appropriate in explaining scientific ideas to the general reader. However, figurative language is uncommon in scientific or technical exposition that aims at exact definition and analysis. In your science courses, your instructors may ask you to write examination answers and papers in a literal style, free of metaphor and other figures of speech.

You will find figurative language particularly useful in persuasive writing that appeals to the reader's emotions. Rachel Carson uses simile and metaphor in asking her readers to imagine the effects of powerful insecticides on wildlife:

> Who has made the decision that sets in motion these chains of poisonings, this ever-widening wave of death that spreads out, like ripples when a pebble is dropped into a still pond? Who has placed in one pan of the scales the leaves that might have been eaten by the beetles and in the other the pitiful heaps of many-hued feathers, the lifeless remains of the birds that fell before the unselective bludgeon of insecticidal poisons? Who has decided— who has the *right* to decide—for the countless legions of people who were not consulted that the supreme value is a world without insects, even though it be also a sterile world ungraced by the curving wing of a bird in flight?
> —*Silent Spring*

Figurative language will help to make your writing more vivid and to stir the imagination of your reader. (Section 36c discusses the fairness of such appeals to emotion made through figures of speech.)

3 Dead and stale metaphors

When metaphors are overused and absorbed into everyday language, they lose their power to evoke images and feelings. In the paragraph on the atom quoted on page 495, you probably did not picture the images intended to be conveyed by the words and phrases *tangle, interlocked, spaced out, gaps,* and *probing.* We refer to such metaphors as *dead* or *submerged:*

> Economics is a science—some would say a non-science—of metaphors. Growth, inflation, depression are terms that have been around for so long that they have become what the language experts call dead metaphors—dead in the sense that they have been severed from their original biological, physical or psychological roots.
> —Leonard Silk, " 'Soft Landing': Metaphor for Now,"
> *New York Times,* July 21, 1989

Dead metaphors form a large group of the familiar phrases we depend on in speaking and writing. By contrast with dead or submerged metaphors, **stale metaphors** weaken writing. These are metaphors that you have heard or seen in print so often that they have lost their flavor and originality.

At worst, stale metaphors suggest thoughtlessness or insincerity. Here are a few common ones:

Stale Metaphors

down-to-earth personality	breezy style of talk
air of confidence	sidesplitting joke
swollen ego	red-hot temper
apple pie order	last-ditch stand
killing glance	hot potato

Many of your sentences will contain some dead metaphors. Avoiding them is not only extremely difficult but also unnecessary, for it would be at the cost of an easy style that moves from idea to idea without strain. Stale metaphors, however, should be avoided in writing. You can rid your writing of stale metaphors by using instead exact details that help readers see the subject or imagine the situation you are describing.

4 Mixed metaphor

A **mixed metaphor** presents conflicting images that blur the idea and usually seem ludicrous:

> The critic dug his own grave with his acid tongue.

The meaning of this sentence becomes absurd when you try to imagine or visualize what the critic is doing. Try to visualize the metaphors contained in the following statements:

Mixed Metaphors

This city has a barrel of problems and nobody to tackle them honestly.

People squawk about how bad the streets are but sit on their hands when the time comes to fix them.

For those who seek truth in a jungle of madness, life is one big slap in the face.

A farfetched or exaggerated metaphor can also obscure the central idea of a sentence, as in this confusing statement made by a political candidate:

> A beachhead of opportunity and growth lies ahead for Americans who seize the future with their own heart, spirit, and open hands.

The word *beachhead* refers to a section of coastal land taken and defended in a war by an invading army. The metaphor is farfetched because the speaker does not mean to introduce images of war. The word *seize* creates more ambiguity, and the words *heart* and *spirit* mean the same thing. The concluding metaphor *open hands* makes the statement even more confusing because it conflicts with the image suggested in the earlier hackneyed phrase *seize the future.*

The colorful language of some news reporting and press releases depends on a rapid succession of metaphors that sometimes create the same effect as mixed metaphor:

> She is the rural neophyte waiting in a subway, a free spirit drinking Greek wine in the moonlight, an organic Earth Mother dispensing fresh bread and herb tea, and the reticent feminist who by trial and error has charted the male as well as the female ego.
> —*Time Magazine*, December 16, 1974 (describing the singer
> Joni Mitchell; quoted by Nora Ephron,
> "How to Write a Newsmagazine Cover Story")

This statement would probably hold the attention of most readers for only a short time before it became hard to follow. Readers look for relief in plain statements and simple images. Writing that calls too much attention to colorful language quickly becomes tiring to read.

5 Hyperbole and other figurative language

In expressive, referential, persuasive, and literary discourse, we most often use metaphor, simile, and personification to convey emotional attitudes and to make ideas vivid. However, there are several other common figures of speech that are also useful in writing.

Hyperbole. **Hyperbole** is deliberate exaggeration, often used humorously. Woody Allen uses hyperbole to satirize course descriptions in college bulletins, in this instance a course in rapid reading:

> This course will increase reading speed a little each day until the end of the term, by which time the student will be requested to read *The Brothers Karamazov* in fifteen minutes.
> —"Spring Bulletin"

The exaggeration highlights the preposterous claims of college bulletins and similar advertisements.

Understatement. The opposite of hyperbole is **understatement,** or saying less than what one means or what the occasion warrants:

> Banks are not incomprehensible. Bankers understand them—at least some do, somewhat, some of the time. But the rest of us have to take it on faith that the banking system works swimmingly.
> —George F. Will, "The Take-for-Granted Quotient"

Will means that banks are incomprehensible, even to bankers. Understatement is effective in forcing the reader to consider what has been left unsaid and to consider the consequences of what the discussion merely hints at.

Irony. An **ironic statement** says something contrary to what we expect the speaker or writer to say:

> The virtue of a college degree is that it shuts off the asking of certain kinds of questions, some of them embarrassing. It is a certificate of safety, both to the holder and to the nation in general.
> H. L. Mencken, "The Boon of Culture"

We expect Mencken to say that the virtue of a college degree is that it encourages questions, not that it shuts them off. Mencken might have spoken this sentence with a smile, an acknowledgment of the surprise that the statement produces.

An ironic statement sometimes implies the opposite of what the words actually say. Mark Twain uses irony in this way in the "notice" that opens his *Adventures of Huckleberry Finn:*

> Persons attempting to find a motive in this narrative will be prosecuted; persons attempting to find a moral in it will be banished; persons attempting to find a plot in it will be shot.

Sarcasm is a more extreme form of irony that is usually intended to ridicule or mock:

> We are waiting for the long-promised invasion. So are the fishes.
> —Winston S. Churchill (on the threat of German invasion of the British Isles in World War II)

Satirists depend on sarcasm. Sinclair Lewis uses sarcasm in humorously satirizing an industrious public health director:

> Now Almus Pickerbaugh had published scientific papers— often. He had published them in the *Midwest Medical Quarterly,*

of which he was one of fourteen editors. He had discovered the germ of epilepsy and the germ of cancer—two entirely different germs of cancer. Usually it took him a fortnight to make the discovery, write the report, and have it accepted. Martin lacked this admirable facility.

> —*Arrowsmith*

Paradox. **Paradox** states a seeming contradiction or puzzle, something that awaits explanation:

> The ringing of a telephone is always louder in an empty house.
> —Joyce Carol Oates, "I Was in Love"
> To oppose something is to maintain it.
> —Ursula K. Le Guin, *The Left Hand of Darkness*

Often presented as an epigram or pithy truth, paradox heightens our awareness of a situation or problem that demands solution—for example, the paradox that homelessness increases in periods of economic prosperity.

Synecdoche. **Synecdoche** uses a member of a class to represent the whole class, as in the expression *meat and potatoes* in reference to food or in the following reference to the Hollywood star system:

> The star system undoubtedly is the most original invention of the movies—in a synecdochal sense, it contains and *is* the movies.
> —Milton Klonsky, "Along the Midway of Mass Culture"

Part of an object may also represent the whole. In the following statement, the color of a house stands for the whole house:

> Our house stood apart. A gaudy yellow in a row of white bungalows.
> —Richard Rodriguez, *Hunger of Memory*

Like metaphors, synecdoches can sharpen ideas and impressions.

Metonymy. Closely related to synecdoche, **metonymy** names something through a quality or thing associated with it:

> The White House announced a new report dealing with unemployment in textiles and steel.

The terms *White House, textiles,* and *steel* stand for presidential administration and the textile and steel industries.

500

Synecdoche and metonymy are abbreviated ways of speaking and writing, a valuable saving of words in discourse.

Oxymoron. An **oxymoron** is a special kind of metaphor that unites conflicting images or ideas in a single phrase:

> I have no relish for the country; it is a kind of healthy grave.
> —Sydney Smith

The following statement joins opposites to state a paradox:

> The lightness of living without the weight of a past is a heavy burden; producing that burden is an oppressor's tactic.
> —George F. Will, "Cracking the Ice," *Newsweek*, June 19, 1988

The following procedures will help to make your use of figurative language more effective:

- In revising a draft, test your metaphors and other figures of speech for clarity, consistency, and effectiveness. Watch for figurative language that blurs an idea or distracts attention from the central idea.
- If the figure of speech makes the passage so vivid that you notice only it, take the advice of the eighteenth-century writer Samuel Johnson:

  > An old tutor of a college said to one of his pupils: Read over your compositions, and wherever you meet with a passage which you think is particularly fine, strike it out.
  > —James Boswell, *Life of Dr. Johnson* [quoting Dr. Johnson]

- Never use the same metaphor, simile, personification, or other figure of speech more than once in the same essay without good reason. In repeating a figure of speech, you may be depending on a cliché (see 31b), stale metaphor, or popular expression that you use regularly in speaking and writing. In this instance, try restating the idea without the help of figurative language. Or, in restating the idea, you may think of a new and apt metaphor to replace the stale one.

EXERCISES

1. Are the metaphors in the following statement from the *Congressional Record* effective or ineffective? Why?

   > With at least $263 billion already obligated to be spent by Congress over the next 40 years on public housing, we have dug a deep trench by obviously biting off more than we could chew.

501

2. Add similes, metaphors, personifications, or other figures of speech to the following sentences to make the ideas they convey more vivid:
   a. The plane had trouble rising from the ground.
   b. Failure needs our help.
   c. Friendships take time to develop.
   d. The skier moved clumsily down the slope.
   e. Listening to rock is different from listening to country music.
3. Paraphrase one of the following passages by changing the similes, metaphors, personifications, and other figures of speech into literal statements. What is gained or lost in clarity of expression in making these changes?
   a. Americans don't like plain talk anymore. Nowadays they like fat talk. Show them a lean, plain word that cuts to the bone and watch them lard it with thick greasy syllables front and back until it wheezes and gasps for breath as it comes lumbering down upon some poor threadbare sentence like a sack of iron on a swayback horse.

   —Russell Baker, "American Fat"
   b. My daddy's face is a study. Winter moves into it and presides there. His eyes become a cliff of snow threatening to avalanche; his eyebrows bend like black limbs of leafless trees. His skin takes on the pale, cheerless yellow of winter sun; for a jaw he has the edges of a snowbound field dotted with stubble; his high forehead is the frozen sweep of the Erie, hiding currents of gelid thoughts that eddy in darkness.

   —Toni Morrison, *The Bluest Eye* ■

31b Clichés

A **cliché** is a trite, overused expression that blurs the central idea of a sentence and that should be avoided in writing. Familiar expressions and phrases become clichés when they substitute for thought. Thus, the cliché creates the impression of insincerity or thoughtlessness by expressing ideas or feelings with the ease of a valentine verse or birthday message.

Stale metaphors are clichés, though not all clichés contain metaphor. The following stale metaphors have become clichés:

Common Clichés to Avoid

chip off the old block	luck of the Irish
nutty as a fruit cake	Numero Uno
staff of life	Mr. Nice Guy
mean as a junkyard dog	Miss Personality
cool as a cucumber	cheap as dirt
hot as blazes	right as rain
apple of her eye	lull after the storm
American as apple pie	clean as a whistle

Popular expressions and quotations often become clichés through constant repetition:

Not if I were the last person on earth!
It's the effort that counts.
All's well that ends well.
He snatched victory out of the jaws of defeat.

Rapid writing such as freewriting sometimes produces clichés and other careless expressions. These may appear even in later drafts, following revision. You may also tend to use clichés mistakenly when you want to make your writing more colorful and exciting. You can avoid clichés and stale metaphors by watching for them at all stages of the writing process.

EXERCISES

1. Examine some advertisements for a particular product—an automobile, a laundry detergent, a brand of lipstick, face cream, or hair oil—to determine the extent to which these ads depend on clichés or pat phrases. Be ready to discuss the effectiveness of advertising language.

2. Martin Plissner gives these examples of clichés in politics:

   The underdogs were uniformly "dogged" or "undaunted" in their endeavors, taking their "uphill campaigns" from one "last ditch stand" to another, struggling to "get a foothold" before their contributions "dried up," "grasping at straws" as they faced the prospect of being "written off."
   —"The Power of Babble"

What are some of the current pat phrases or clichés used in recent political campaigns?

31c Euphemisms

Euphemism is an inoffensive or pleasing substitute for some act or condition that we prefer not to name directly. Here is a list of some familiar euphemisms and the reality they describe:

Euphemism	Named Directly
passed away, left us	died
deceased, departed	dead person
disadvantaged neighborhood	slum
senior citizen, gold ager	old person
reformatory	prison
short wait	two hours
happy	drunk, on dope
nervous breakdown	mental collapse
executive assistant	secretary
low achiever	poor student

The motive for euphemism is often to avoid giving pain. Euphemisms such as *passed away* and *deceased* soften the harshness of words like *died* or *dead* when consoling someone. But euphemism, in disguising a reality that is difficult to face, may mislead the listener or reader with ambiguous terms. Asked by a friend to judge a piece of writing, you may call it "striking" or "exceptional" to avoid saying that you don't like it. You have equivocated to retain a friend, a dishonest but understandable motive (see 37a). You can, however, state your opinions honestly and directly by adopting a friendly tone and suggesting improvements.

Euphemism is sometimes vicious, as in the use in wartime of the word *pacify* or *waste* to avoid saying *kill* (e.g., "We pacified the village"). In "Politics and the English Language," George Orwell cites the use of the euphemism *justifiable severity* to avoid naming the act of *torture*. Euphemism is vicious when its purpose is to lie or disguise an ugly act or idea. Clear thinking does not guarantee clear writing, but your writing cannot be clear or direct unless your thinking is. Usually, though, euphemism becomes a habit when the writer is unwilling to state facts simply and accurately or to give things their proper names. Orwell states: "But if thought corrupts language, language can also corrupt thought." Orwell gives the following excellent advice: "This invasion of one's mind by ready–made phrases . . . can only be prevented if one is constantly on guard against them."

Rhymed words

Rhymed words are frequently used in poetry and descriptive writing. The following descriptive passage uses rhymed words and heavily rhythmic sentences to convey intense emotion:

> The circus train had stopped in the heart of the country, for what reason he did not know. He could hear the languid and intermittent breathing of the engine, the strangeness of men's voices in the dark, the casual stamp of the horses in their cars, and all around him the attentive and vital silence of the earth.
> —Thomas Wolfe, *The Web and the Rock*

Sometimes the vowels of adjacent words rhyme:

vital, silence

Sometimes consonants and vowels echo in words in the same passage:

engine, strangeness, stopped, heart

In ordinary exposition, a string of rhyming vowels or alliterated words (words opening with the same consonantal sounds) can be distracting or annoying:

I see no *mean* bet*ween* the extr*eme* viewpoints presented.

Two or more repeated consonants in words close to one another can be equally distracting:

*R*eally *r*eliable *r*eading tests assist the *r*eading teacher at all grade levels.

To revise annoying sentences of this kind, find substitutes for the rhyming words:

Reliable tests of reading ability help teachers at all grade levels.

EXERCISE

Revise the following sentences to eliminate misused and mixed metaphors, clichés, euphemisms, and rhymed words:

1. The sanitary engineer was emptying the receptacle full of discarded food and paper.
2. His response was off target and missed my point.
3. The thunder of her words sank upon the audience.
4. My high-flying kite seemed bright in the sunlight.
5. The speaker then hammered home his point, taking a dig at his opponent as he did so.
6. He is Mr. Right for the job.
7. Exam week almost put me in the booby hatch but now everything is hunky-dory.
8. The trailer truck is stuck in the mud.
9. His performance of the role of Hamlet was greeted by the audience with a not altogether approving sound.
10. Deaf to the shouts from the gallery, the actor pretended not to hear the names he was being called.
11. We wrestled with what to do about inflation, then punched at each other's solutions.
12. The play is not exactly a barrel of laughs.
13. The candidate's lack of sympathy with the proposal was apparent in the not too favorable comments he made to the press.
14. Nobody knows, I suppose, how many oppose the school's closing.
15. Living in the fast track, he was flying high and fast. ∎

Summary

31a Use figurative language to make ideas vivid and concrete.

Use simile, metaphor, and personification to evoke feeling through comparison (**31a 1**).

Farfetched metaphors create confusion and ambiguity (**31a 2**):

> A beachhead of opportunity and growth lies ahead for Americans who seize the future with their own heart, spirit, and open hands.

Stale metaphors suggest thoughtlessness or insincerity (**31a 3**):

> Though he walks with an air of confidence, he has a down-to-earth personality.

Mixed metaphors can be ludicrous and confusing (**31a 4**):

> The critic dug his own grave with his acid tongue.

31b Clichés are trite, overused expressions that blur the central image or idea.

> I feel right as rain and cool as a cucumber.

31c Don't use euphemisms or inoffensive, pleasing statements to equivocate or disguise the facts.

> Many golden-agers live in disadvantaged neighborhoods.

31d In ordinary exposition, avoid rhymed syllables that call attention to themselves.

Awkward	**Improved**
*R*eally *r*eliable *r*eading tests assist the *r*eading teacher at all grade levels.	Reliable tests of reading ability help teachers at all grade levels.

Using the Dictionary

32

The dictionary is indispensable in speaking and writing. The dictionary not only gives the current meanings of words but also describes their origins and pronunciation. It also provides information on scientific and technical terms, rare and obsolete words, synonyms and antonyms, biographical and geographical names, abbreviations, and symbols. A dictionary, then, is essential in writing college papers and reports. In the course of revising and editing, you will use the dictionary frequently to check the spellings and to verify the meanings of words. In typing your papers, you will need a dictionary to determine the correct hyphenation of words that fall at the end of a typed line.

These uses of the dictionary are the focus of this chapter. Also discussed are historical and specialized dictionaries which you will have occasion to use in your college courses. (The use of specialized dictionaries in research is covered in Chapter 39.)

508

32a Abridged and unabridged dictionaries

Your college dictionary describes the current usage of words. It lists not only the most common words but also uncommon and obsolete words that you may come across in your reading. Standard **abridged** or condensed dictionaries include the following:

> *American Heritage Dictionary of the English Language,* Second College Edition (1982)
> *The Random House College Dictionary,* Revised Edition (1984)
> *Webster's Ninth New Collegiate Dictionary* (1987)
> *Webster's New World Dictionary of the American Language,* Third College Edition (1988)

To use a standard college dictionary effectively, you should become familiar with its frontmatter and backmatter. The frontmatter always includes an explanation of how definitions are arranged and the philosophy governing usage. Many dictionaries also include a history of the English language and short essays on various topics relating to language and vocabulary. *American Heritage Dictionary,* for example, supplements its history of English with articles on English dialects, grammar, spelling, and pronunciation. The backmatter of most college dictionaries also differs. *Webster's Ninth New Collegiate* includes a brief handbook of style. *American Heritage* includes an appendix of roots in English and other Indo-European languages. Separate listings of foreign words and phrases, abbreviations, scientific and technical terms, biographical and geographical names, and colleges and universities also appear as part of the backmatter in many college dictionaries, including *Webster's Ninth New Collegiate Dictionary.*

The arrangement of definitions also varies among dictionaries. *Webster's Ninth New Collegiate Dictionary* and *Webster's New World* list definitions in chronological order; *American Heritage* and *Random House* list them in the order of currency and frequent use. Information on usage varies in nature and quantity. In short articles following the definition, *American Heritage* summarizes the opinions of a panel of "recognized leaders" on usage of words like *ain't.* Other dictionaries give information on usage in separate articles or include it in the definition. *Webster's New World* gives extensive information on idiomatic expressions (e.g., *quite a few*).

Unabridged dictionaries give highly detailed definitions and usually more complete information on a range of topics, including the origin or etymology of words. Standard unabridged dictionaries include the following:

> *Oxford English Dictionary* (16 volumes, with supplements)
> *Webster's Third New International Dictionary*
> *The Random House Dictionary of the English Language*, Second Edition

The *Oxford English Dictionary* (called the *OED*), is universal in its coverage of English words. It is also available in a two-volume, small-print edition (accompanied by a magnifying glass) and is conveniently abridged in *The Oxford Universal Dictionary*. Your college library may have *Webster's Third* and other single-volume, unabridged dictionaries available in its reference rooms. The *OED* also is usually shelved in the reference section of the library.

Finding information in the dictionary

Your college dictionary is an indispensable tool. You will use it to check for the exact meaning of words, misspellings, syllable breaks, and special symbols. You will also find your dictionary useful in other ways as you become familiar with its contents and organization.

The dictionary provides a wide range of information about a word in the main listing (see the accompanying example for the word *average* from *Webster's New World Dictionary*). In particular, the dictionary describes these features of a word:

- **Syllabication,** or the division of syllables in a word, is shown in the boldface listing of the word and is usually indicated by periods or hyphens (e.g., *av·er·age*). Syllabication is important in pronouncing the word or in hyphenating it at the end of a typed line.
- **Pronunciation** of the word in the phonetic alphabet. The phonetic alphabet, with examples, usually appears in the inside front or back cover of a dictionary and at the bottom of pages.

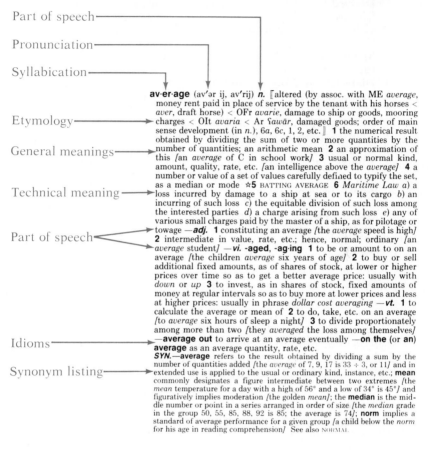

Part of speech

Pronunciation

Syllabication

Etymology

General meanings

Technical meaning

Part of speech

Idioms

Synonym listing

av·er·age (av'ər ij, av'rij) **n.** ⟦altered (by assoc. with ME *average*, money rent paid in place of service by the tenant with his horses < *aver*, draft horse) < OFr *avarie*, damage to ship or goods, mooring charges < OIt *avaria* < Ar ʕawār, damaged goods; order of main sense development (in *n.*), 6a, 6c, 1, 2, etc. ⟧ **1** the numerical result obtained by dividing the sum of two or more quantities by the number of quantities; an arithmetic mean **2** an approximation of this ⟦an *average* of C in school work⟧ **3** usual or normal kind, amount, quality, rate, etc. ⟦an intelligence above the *average*⟧ **4** a number or value of a set of values carefully defined to typify the set, as a median or mode ☆**5** BATTING AVERAGE **6** *Maritime Law a)* a loss incurred by damage to a ship at sea or to its cargo *b)* an incurring of such loss *c)* the equitable division of such loss among the interested parties *d)* a charge arising from such loss *e)* any of various small charges paid by the master of a ship, as for pilotage or towage —**adj.** **1** constituting an average ⟦the *average* speed is high⟧ **2** intermediate in value, rate, etc.; hence, normal; ordinary ⟦an *average* student⟧ —**vi.** **-aged, -ag·ing 1** to be or amount to on an average ⟦the children *average* six years of age⟧ **2** to buy or sell additional fixed amounts, as of shares of stock, at lower or higher prices over time so as to get a better average price: usually with *down* or *up* **3** to invest, as in shares of stock, fixed amounts of money at regular intervals so as to buy more at lower prices and less at higher prices: usually in phrase *dollar cost averaging* —**vt.** **1** to calculate the average or mean of **2** to do, take, etc. on an average ⟦to *average* six hours of sleep a night⟧ **3** to divide proportionately among more than two ⟦they *averaged* the loss among themselves⟧ —**average out** to arrive at an average eventually —**on the** (or **an**) **average** as an average quantity, rate, etc.
SYN.—**average** refers to the result obtained by dividing a sum by the number of quantities added ⟦the *average* of 7, 9, 17 is 33 ÷ 3, or 11⟧ and in extended use is applied to the usual or ordinary kind, instance, etc.; **mean** commonly designates a figure intermediate between two extremes ⟦the *mean* temperature for a day with a high of 56° and a low of 34° is 45°⟧ and figuratively implies moderation ⟦the golden *mean*⟧; the **median** is the middle number or point in a series arranged in order of size ⟦the *median* grade in the group 50, 55, 85, 88, 92 is 85; the average is 74⟧; **norm** implies a standard of average performance for a given group ⟦a child below the *norm* for his age in reading comprehension⟧ See also NORMAL

Sample dictionary listing for the word *average*.

- **Part of speech,** usually abbreviated (e.g., *n.* for *noun* and *adj.* for *adjective*). Checking for the part of speech of a word is essential in finding the definition you need.
- **Etymology,** or the origin of the word.
- **Current meanings** of a word, including rare and archaic forms and meanings (*madding* as a rare form of *maddening*, *feeble* and *infirm* as archaic meanings of *silly*).
- **Technical meanings** and **field labels** (the meaning of *average* in marine law).
- **Inflected forms** of the word (*averaged, averaging*).

- **Derived forms,** or forms of the word taking prefixes and suffixes (*collapsible* and *collapsibility*).
- **Colloquial expressions** (*cool* in the expression "cool one's heels").
- **Slang** (*cool* in the sense of desirable or fashionable, as in "cool car").
- **Dialectal meanings,** or meanings peculiar to a region ("bid" in the sense of invite, as in "bid them to the house").
- **Obsolete meanings,** found in writings of earlier periods (*nice* in the sense of foolish, as in "a nice way of talking").
- **Abbreviations** (*C.* and *Cong.* as abbreviations of *Congress* and *Congressional*).
- **Idioms,** or standard popular phrases that depart from usual grammatical patterns ("average out" and "on the average").
- **Usage,** or preferred and unpreferred meanings and forms of the word (see 32f).
- **Synonyms** and **antonyms,** or words with similar and opposite meanings (see 32e).

Denotative and connotative definitions

Dictionaries usually give information on two essential kinds of meaning, denotative and connotative. A **denotative definition** identifies a thing, like the color *yellow,* by singling it out from other things like it and stating its characteristics:

> a color whose hue resembles that of ripe lemons or sunflowers or is that of the portion of the spectrum lying between green and orange.
>
> —*Webster's Ninth New College Dictionary*

Webster's Ninth also gives other denotations of *yellow* and defines related words: *yellow bile, yellow-dog contract, yellow dwarf.*

A **connotative definition,** by contrast, states the ideas, feelings, attitudes, and auras of meaning commonly associated with a word. The word *yellow* connotes cowardice; *red,* anger; *blue,* sadness or melancholy. The dictionary occasionally includes denotations and connotations special to a class of people or a region. The word *ghetto,* referring originally to a walled area of a European city where Jews were once confined, today denotes an urban district in which any minority population is forced to live because of racial, religious, or economic discrimination. The word generally connotes poverty, misery, and injustice.

You will have occasion to give denotative and connotative definitions in your writing (see 6c). Distinguishing the denotation of a word from its connotations is a good way to clarify a potentially confusing word. If the word is a familiar one, the context or surrounding sentences usually clarify its familiar meaning. But the context may not clarify a special meaning you want to convey. In expository writing, you cannot depend on context to clarify abstract or technical words, particularly in discussing a theory or describing a process. Where possible, work the definition into the discussion, as the author of the following passage does in defining business jargon:

> Meanwhile, not only does a different voice come from each company when it does speak, but many different voices from within the same company. The language of external pronouncements is not the same as the language of internal communication. It is a little like the old practice of using Latin for formal occasions and the local patois for daily intercourse. Today, in business as in government, bureaucracy has invented a third language, a jargon of its own, for its procedural and transactional documents.
> —Louis B. Lundborg, "The Voices of Business"

EXERCISES

1. What help does your dictionary give you in pronouncing the following words?
a.	present (noun)	**f.**	notoriety
b.	present (verb)	**g.**	wholly
c.	Aristophanes	**h.**	analysis
d.	immunity	**i.**	Worcester (Massachusetts)
e.	ravioli	**j.**	Reykjavik (Iceland)

2. Assume you are describing an orange to a child who has never seen or tasted one and wants to know what it is. If you begin with the classification or genus *fruit,* how many specific differences must you give in your definition? What if you begin with the genus *citrus fruits?* What class would you choose in defining the word to a child?

3. What associations can you make with the orange to help the child better understand what it is? How many of these are personal to you, and how many do you think are associations of most people?

4. Examine the dictionary definitions for the following uses of the word *football.* How broad is the genus to which each definition is fitted? Can you think of a broader genus or a

513

more limited one with which the definition might have begun?

a. American game
b. British game
c. object
d. anything kicked around

5. What help does the dictionary give you in trying to discover the denotative and connotative meanings of the phrase *political football*?

6. What do the following idioms mean? Does the dictionary specify their level of usage?

a. come at	**e.** from hand to hand
b. come in for	**f.** from hand to mouth
c. come around	**g.** hand down
d. rave about	**h.** shove off

7. Under what field (technical) entries do you find explanations of the following in your dictionary?

a. the symbol "F" for function
b. *vessel*, as a canal for the conducting of water
c. *bar*, as a part of a horse's hoof
d. *bar*, as a horizontal line on a shield
e. *close*, as a characteristic of vowels

32d Etymology

Etymology refers to the origin of a word, often helpful in understanding its current meanings. The dictionary gives the etymology of a word in parentheses or brackets toward the beginning or at the end of the definition. In our example of the *Webster's New World Dictionary* definition of *average*, the etymology appears in brackets toward the beginning of the definition (see page 511). The dictionary tells us that the English word *average* is probably derived from the French word *avarie* or the Italian word *avaria*, both derived from an Arabic word referring to damaged goods and mooring charges. The etymology also traces the development *average* as an English word in marine law, namely as the term for the damage to goods in a ship at sea, for the equal division of charges paid to owners of the goods, and for the charge itself. The dictionary uses these meanings to shed light on general meanings of *average*, listed before the special meanings of the word in marine law.

The original meaning of a word may not be the same as the current meaning. The word *silly*, from the Old English word *saelig*, originally had several meanings, among them blessed, prosperous, happy, and innocent. In time, innocent qualities came to be confused with simple or foolish qualities. Today, *silly* chiefly means foolish (as in "a silly remark"). Although we no longer use *silly* to mean innocent or happy, the original meaning of the word sheds light on its present connotations: a silly mood sometimes means a happy one.

You will find other useful information in special dictionaries and books on etymology. These include the following:

William Morris and Mary Morris, eds., *Dictionary of Word and Phrase Origins* (1971)
Oxford Dictionary of English Etymology (1966)
Eric Partridge, *Origins: A Short Etymological Dictionary of Modern English* (1966)

EXERCISE

What information does your dictionary give on the origins of the following words? Is this information of help in understanding the current use of each word?

1. barbecue
2. college
3. daisy
4. disciple, discipline (field of knowledge)
5. Greenland
6. grudge
7. stooge
8. stool pigeon
9. superficial
10. ventriloquist

32e Synonyms and antonyms

Synonyms are words with the same or similar meanings. **Antonyms** are words with opposite meanings. The amount of information given by dictionaries on synonyms and antonyms varies. Most desk dictionaries include synonym listings for some words.

Synonym listings compare the meanings of similar or related words like *average, mean,* and *median* (see page 511). The listing appears following the definition or that of a similar word. A cross-reference ("*Syn.* see *average*") directs you to the listing. Words with multiple meanings may appear in several listings; the word *average,* for example, also appears in the synonym listings for *normal, regular,* and other related words.

Synonym listings are an invaluable part of a dictionary. If the dictionary fails to provide a meaning you are seeking, you may find it in the synonym listing. The more you consult synonym listings (in your college dictionary or a special dictionary of synonyms), the sharper your sense of the nuances and precise meanings of words will become.

Webster's New World Dictionary gives the antonyms *abnormal* and *unusual* at the end of the synonym listing for *normal.* Special dictionaries like *Webster's Dictionary of Synonyms* give additional information. *Webster's* lists the synonyms of the word *normal* as *regular, typical,* and *natural.* It also cites closely related or analogous terms (such as *ordinary, common,* and *usual*) and discusses *normal* in special articles on some of these analogous terms.

A **thesaurus** lists but does not discuss various synonyms of words. The thesaurus is useful in recalling a word by looking up words related to it. (See the list in 32f of special dictionaries of etymology, slang, and other kinds of words.)

EXERCISES

1. Use the synonym listings or definitions in your dictionary to state the exact difference in meaning between the following words:
   a. example, pattern
   b. faker, imposter
   c. lavish, extravagant
   d. peculiar, strange
   e. standard, archetype
2. Where do the synonyms of *convoke* appear in your dictionary?
3. What synonym of *hateful* would you use to describe something disgusting or offensive?
4. Under what circumstances would you refer to something as an *enigma* rather than as a *mystery*?
5. What are the antonyms of the words *firm* and *impel*? ∎

You often want to know what meanings of a word are appropriate and inappropriate in various writing situations. Can a word you use informally also be used in formal writing? The amount of discussion of doubtful words like *ain't* and *irregardless* varies from dictionary to dictionary.

Your dictionary sometimes gives the background or exact range of meanings of a word needed to understand its use in a particular passage. *Webster's New World Dictionary* states that in physics the word *oscillate* means to "vary between maximum and minimum values." To use a word exactly, you must sometimes know its meanings in various contexts. *Horizon* has special meanings in astronomy and geology. Dictionaries usually distinguish these contexts by field entries. Thus the *New World Dictionary* defines *horizon* as "the line where the sky seems to meet the earth." This is the *visible* or *apparent horizon.* Under the field entry *astronomy,* the dictionary gives the additional definition of *sensible horizon* to distinguish this technical use of the word from its general use:

> the plane extending at right angles to the direction of gravity from the eye of the observer to the celestial sphere.

Dictionaries usually indicate what function words or prepositions are used with certain verbs. A lawyer is *admitted to* the bar; we are *admitted* to a place. The occasional idiom *admit of* is used to mean "warrant," as in the following sentence:

> Her statements will not admit of any other interpretation.

Special dictionaries and other special reference works give additional help with idioms and other matters of usage. Here is a partial list:

Jacques Barzun, *Simple and Direct* (1976)
H. W. Fowler, *Dictionary of Modern English Usage,* 2nd ed., edited by Ernest Gowers (1965)
H. L. Mencken, *The American Language,* 4th ed. (1980)
Margaret Nicholson, *Dictionary of American-English Usage* (1957)
Eric Partridge, *Dictionary of Slang and Unconventional English* (1970)

Harold Wentworth and Stuart Berg Flexner, eds., *Dictionary of American Slang* (1975)

In addition, special reference guides to ethnic, social, and regional dialects are available in your library. In reading a novel by I. B. Singer or Saul Bellow, you may need a translation of a Yiddish word or a listing of its connotations and nuances. You can find this information in Leo Rosten's *The Joys of Yiddish* (1968), a compendium in dictionary form of Yiddish terms and the occasions of their use, with illustrations from Jewish humor and literature of words like *shlemiel, shlimazl,* and *nebech.*

The reference section of your college library contains specialized dictionaries that you will find useful in your course work and in research. These dictionaries and encyclopedias define the jargon or technical language of different professions and disciplines, such as business, economics, law, medicine, and philosophy. (See 39e for a partial listing of specialized dictionaries.)

Here are some final suggestions on how to use your college dictionary effectively:

- Keep your dictionary nearby during all stages of the writing process. In revising your papers, look up words that do not express your exact meaning or that you may have used incorrectly. Your instructor may identify some of these in commenting on a draft of the paper. Since you probably use these words frequently, keep a log of them, noting their exact meanings.

- When you check the meaning of a word in the dictionary, look at the words just above and just below the definition as well. These definitions may contain related meanings. For example, if you are seeking the meaning of *integer,* a term in mathematics, you will find additional information in the definitions of *integral* and *integral calculus.*

- If you sense that you haven't chosen the right word, circle it or make a checkmark in the margin of your draft. Then use the synonym listings in your dictionary or thesaurus to find the right word.

EXERCISES

1. Compare the discussion of *ain't* in two of the college dictionaries listed in 32a. Do the dictionaries give the same advice on usage of the word? Is the word considered substandard by both dictionaries?

2. What information does your college dictionary give on the use of the following words in standard English:
   a. hip (adjective)
   b. irregardless
   c. lush (noun)
   d. nohow
   e. that (relative pronoun)
3. What does your dictionary tell you about the current use of the following words and phrases? Are they described as archaic or obsolete, slang or colloquial?
   a. crummy
   b. come a cropper
   c. fetching (adjective)
   d. tope
   e. binge

32g Historical dictionaries

Historical dictionaries trace the current and obsolete meanings of English words, from their earliest appearance in documents to their present usage. You will find historical dictionaries essential in investigating the meanings of unfamiliar words, particularly those used in books and articles written before the twentieth century. The *Oxford English Dictionary* (generally called the *OED*), is universal in its coverage of English words in Great Britain, the United States, and other English-speaking countries. The *Dictionary of American English* and *Dictionary of Americanisms* give the same thorough coverage of American English.

Historical dictionaries can help you in reading a work containing obsolete or special words. *Oliver Twist*, Dickens's novel about early nineteenth-century London crime, contains the words *cribs* ("hideouts"), *beaks* ("police magistrates"), *lagging* ("the sentence of transport to a penal colony"), and *fogle*. Some of these words are listed in dictionaries of current usage. But to understand the now obsolete word *fogle* as well as what "fogle hunters" did, you would need to consult the *Oxford English Dictionary* (see the accompanying figure). The word *fogle* was a slang word for silk handkerchief. Thus a "fogle hunter"—the term Dickens uses to describe juvenile thieves—was a thief who stole valuable handkerchiefs.

519

Usage

Pronunciation

Definition

Citations

Combined forms

Citations

fogle ('fəʊg(ə)l). ~*slang*. A handkerchief or neckerchief, usually of silk.
　1811 *Lexicon Balatron.*, *Fogle*, a silk handkerchief. **1834** W. H. AINSWORTH *Rookwood* III. v, Fogles and fawnies soon went their way. **1840** BARHAM *Ingol. Leg.*, *Tragedy* vii, The 'fogle' that caused all this breeze.
　b. *Comb.*, as **fogle-hunter**, a pick-pocket; **fogle-drawing**, **-hunting** *vbl. sbs.*, picking pockets.
　1823 *Grose's Dict. Vulg. Tongue* (ed. Egan), *Fogle Hunter*, a pickpocket. *Cant.* **1823** 'JON BEE' *Slang* s.v. *Fogle*, 'He's out a fogle-hunting.' Sometimes 'tis said .. 'fogle-drawing.' **1838** DICKENS *O. Twist* xi, A young fogle-hunter.

Sample entry from a historical dictionary.

Historical dictionaries are also particularly useful in tracing the changing meanings of words over time. In nineteenth-century literature, for example, *virus* refers to a poisonous substance—not to the specific agent of the common cold, measles, AIDS, or other viral disease identified in the twentieth-century meaning of *virus*.

EXERCISES

1. According to the *Oxford English Dictionary* or the shorter *Oxford Universal Dictionary,* what meanings of the following words are either obsolete or limited to England or the British Isles?
   a. heifer
   b. hedge
   c. journey
   d. kindle
   e. manifest (noun)
2. Use the *Oxford English Dictionary, Dictionary of American English,* or *Dictionary of Americanisms* to answer the following questions:
   a. What is the origin of the word *handicap*? Do we still use the word in its original sense?
   b. What is an obsolete use of the word *hog*? Is the word ever used to describe animals other than swine?
   c. In what sports is the word *slog* a special term?
   d. What is the origin of the word *vermin*? Is the word still used in its original sense? Does it have special meanings in English-speaking countries other than Great Britain?

520

e. What is the earliest recorded use of the word *gelatin?* To what extent has its meaning changed?

f. What meanings of *suffrage* are rare or obsolete?

g. What is the origin of the word *Eskimo?* Does it describe North American inhabitants only? ■

Summary

32a Consult an unabridged dictionary when your abridged college dictionary does not contain the information you need about a word.

32b Use your dictionary to check current meanings and other information about words.

32c Distinguish denotative from connotative meanings of words.

32d The etymology or original meaning of a word sometimes helps to explain its current meaning.

32e Use the synonym listings in your dictionary to determine which of several closely related words fits your intended meaning.

32f The dictionary explains word usage in various fields, defines idiomatic phrases, and gives information on technical and dialectal words, jargon, slang, and other matters of usage.

32g Use a historical dictionary to find the meaning of an obsolete or archaic word.

Building a Vocabulary

33

The wider your vocabulary, the greater the stock of words available to you in writing. To a great extent, your vocabulary builds in proportion to what you hear and read. But you can build it further through knowledge of the nature and origin of words, particularly how words form from various roots and how prefixes and suffixes function.

33a | Using prefixes and suffixes

A **prefix** is a sound attached to the beginning of a word, changing its form. A **suffix** is a sound attached to the end of a word for the same purpose. Prefixes and suffixes increase the word stock of a language by adapting words to a wide range of uses.

1 Word roots

Words are created from **roots,** or units of sound that form meaningful base words. Some words are formed from one root, whereas two or more roots combine to form other words. Words like *act* and *love* are called **free roots** because they can stand alone as words. Most English roots (*child, move*) are of this type. English also has a small number of **bound roots** that cannot stand alone as words. These include *-ceive* and *-tain*, from which numerous words are formed (*deceive, receive, detain, retain*). **Affixes** attach to free and bound roots to form other words (*actable, action, react, reaction, reactionary, unactable*).

The dictionary sometimes lists word roots or the base forms of words in its etymology, or tracing of word origins (see 32d). In taking note of the base word, you may be reminded of other words that sound like the word you are looking up in the dictionary. The root meaning of a word can help you understand the meaning of similar but unfamiliar words that you come across in your reading.

Here are some proven ways by which you can discover and retain the meanings of words and build your vocabulary:

- If you do not have a dictionary at hand while reading, make a note of unfamiliar words and the pages on which they appear. Look up their meanings later on when you have access to a dictionary.
- Although guessing at the meaning of a word is sometimes sufficient, it is best to look up the word in the dictionary and read the definition carefully. Also take note of any synonyms (words with the same or almost the same meaning) or antonyms (words with opposite meanings) that the dictionary lists in the definition (see 32e).
- Keep a log of the words you look up in the dictionary perhaps noting related meanings and forms as well. You will find these notations of benefit in reading a textbook or collateral reading assigned in a course.
- If the book you are reading contains a special glossary of terms, consult it as often as necessary and make a note of special terms.
- Make your own index of key terms as you read, noting the pages on which they appear. Also make cross-references to related terms. This will not only help to build your vocabulary but will also deepen your understanding of the subject and discipline.

2 Prefixes

You will increase your vocabulary considerably by becoming familiar with common **affixes,** sounds attached to the beginning or end of a word. Prefixes do not change the base or root, the part of the word that remains unchanged when you add an affix. Some prefixes have more than one meaning. The following is a partial list of prefixes and meanings:

Prefix	Example	Meaning
ab-	abduct	from
abs-	abstract (summarize from)	from
ad-	adjoin	to, toward
ante-	anteroom	before
anti-	antidote	against
be-	befriend	furnish with
	beset	around
bi-	bilingual	two
bio-	biology	life
co-, com-	cooperate, complement	together with
con-	conformist	with
contra-	contradict	against
counter-	counterargue	against
de-	decline	down
dia-	diagonal	across
dis-	disjoin	separation
	dissatisfy	fail
dys-	dysfunction	bad
en-	engrave	in
epi-	epidemic	all over
ex-	expell	from, out of
extra-	extracurricular	outside of
for-	forget	put away
fore-	foreground	in front
hyper-	hyperactive	excessive
hypo-	hypodermic	beneath
	hypothermia	lacking in
il- (before *l*)	illogical	not
im-	immodest	not
	immerse	in
in-	incorrect	not
	inflow	in
inter-	intervene	between
intra-	intracity	within
intro-	introduce	within, into
ir- (before *r*)	irreligious	not
meta-	metaphor	beyond
mis-	mistake	wrong
non-	nonfunctioning	not
ob-	obstacle	against
	object	to
para-	parallel	beside

Prefix	Example	Meaning
per-	perfect	entirely
	pertain	through
peri-	perimeter	around
post-	postgame	after
pre-	pregame	before
pro-	prophet	ahead of
pur-	purpose	for
re-	regain	again
semi-	semifinal	half, part
sub-	submerge	under
super-	supercargo	over, above
syl- (before *-l*)	syllogism	with
sym- (before *m, b, p*)	symmetry, symbol, sympathy	with
syn-	synthesis	with
sys-	system	with
trans-	transact	across
tri-	triple	three
ultra-	ultramodern	extreme
un-	untrue	not
under-	underwear	beneath
uni-	uniform	one
with-	withdraw	away
	withstand	against

EXERCISE

Use your dictionary to determine how the prefix and root join to form meaning in the following words:

1. contravene
2. dysentery
3. disinfectant
4. extrapolate
5. subordinate
6. synergy
7. transliteration
8. universal
9. periscope
10. propagate
11. transfigure
12. synopsis
13. hyperbole
14. irreversible
15. intravenous
16. misdirection
17. remission
18. correlative
19. intervene
20. unnatural

3 Suffixes

You will also build your vocabulary by becoming familiar with common **suffixes.** Unlike prefixes, some suffixes change the base word (e.g., when the suffix *-cy* is added to the word *pres-*

ident it becomes *presidency*). Notice also that many suffixes have different meanings with different words. You will find a full listing of meanings in the dictionary definitions of suffixes. Here is a partial list of suffixes and meanings:

Suffix	Example	Meaning
-able	eatable, sizeable, agreeable	capable or worthy of, possessing qualities of, inclined to
-age	postage	cost of
	marriage	act of
-ance	vigilance	state of
-ant	accountant	person, thing
-ar	stellar	like
-ary	supplementary	connecting to
-ate	dehydrate	cause of
	vaccinate	treat
	directorate	function, agent
-cy	bankruptcy	condition
	presidency	office
-ence	excellence	quality, state
-ery	bakery	place of
	surgery	art, profession
	slavery	condition
-ful	hopeful	full of
	helpful	ability, tendency
	armful	quantity
-ible	collectible	variant of *-able;* used with words derived from Latin
-ic	comic	like
-ical	comical	like
-ice	justice	condition
-ise, -ize	realise, galvanize	make into
-ish	Irish	belonging to
-ism	alcoholism	condition
	theism, Catholicism	theory, religion
	criticism	activity, process
-ive	creative	characteristic of
-less	witless	without
-like	catlike	resembling
-logy	biology, geology	names of sciences
	anthology, trilogy	collections
-ly	motherly, quickly, weekly	having the qualities of, in a particular way, at a particular time
-ment	argument	act of
	bewilderment	state of

Suffix	Example	Meaning
-mony	matrimony	state of
-ness	richness	condition
-ory	laboratory	place of
-ous	obvious	characteristic of
-some	loathsome	tending to
	chromosome	body
-ulent	opulent	full of
-ulous	ridiculous	full of
-ure	exposure	act, state
-ward	westward	direction
-ways	sideways	direction
-wise	likewise	direction, manner
-y	happy	characterized by
	victory	state, condition

EXERCISE

Change the following words by adding the appropriate suffixes. Be ready to state how the suffix changes the meaning of each word.

1. flex
2. harm
3. fool
4. memory
5. left
6. fraud
7. clock
8. jealous
9. envious
10. sense

33b	Reading and vocabulary

There is no substitute for reading in building an active vocabulary. Through reading you learn how words are used in current discourse. Of course, your main purpose in reading is not to build your vocabulary but to concentrate on what the writer is saying. But as you read you often pause to guess the meanings of unfamiliar words or to look them up in the dictionary—and it is these activities that help you the most in building a vocabulary.

Although the dictionary supplies the general meaning of a word or term, it often does not distinguish the special meanings or connotations that the word takes on in certain situations, such as political and other debates (see 32c). In some instances, a term may be so new that it isn't listed in the dictionary. Usually you can determine the special meanings of a new word from the context or surrounding statements. Consider, for example, the italicized words in the following passage on the events in Eastern Europe and Central America in 1989:

> Perhaps the end of 1989 is at last the answer to 1789, whose *bicentennial* the French celebrated so *flamboyantly* last summer. In his book on the French revolution, *Citizens,* Simon Schama stressed the dangers. A reviewer noted his suggestion that the ensuing "bestialities touched on some fundamental flaw within the revolutionary ideal itself—that there is, inescapably, in the very process of *liberation* a *paradox* of *violation.*"
>
> It is a flaw inherent in violence and the arrogance of supposing there is a ready-made formula for the good society, one that can be imported or imposed. In addition, the revolutionary French had the misfortune of facing an angry, armed *coterie* of European monarchs determined to stifle their "community of free citizens."
>
> —Flora Lewis, "Tale of Two Dictators," *New York Times,*
> January 3, 1990 (emphasis added)

If you did not know the meaning of *bicentennial,* the references to 1789 and 1989 perhaps told you that a bicentennial is a two-hundred-year anniversary. The prefix *bi-* (meaning "two") is an additional help in interpreting the word. You may also have guessed that *paradox* means contradiction and *coterie* means group of people, and you probably guessed the meaning of *liberation* and *violence* from their context. But context does not always supply the full or accurate meaning of a word. Looking up *paradox* and *coterie* in a dictionary would give you more precise meanings and add to your understanding of the passage. It is essential, then, to look up unfamiliar words in reading for information as well as for the pleasure of ideas.

Summary

33a Build your vocabulary by becoming familiar with the meanings of common prefixes and suffixes and how they are added to word roots to form words.

33b As you read, look up the meanings of unfamiliar words in the dictionary and keep a log of them.

PART EIGHT

SOUND REASONING

Inductive
Reasoning

34

Argument uses evidence to prove a thesis. Examples of argumentative writing include newspaper editorials, letters to the editor, advertisements, political addresses, petitions, and other oral and written communication that ask readers or listeners to support a particular issue. You use argument in writing of your own that gives reasons for supporting or rejecting a proposal or for taking action on an issue. The evidence for your own arguments and those of others comes from a wide range of sources, including personal experience and observation, beliefs, and widely accepted ideas. The basic sources for researching such evidence include historical documents, statistical and opinion surveys, and laboratory experiments.

Persuasion is the counterpart of argument. A letter to the editor or an argumentative essay seeks to persuade a particular audience. In writing such a letter or essay, you take account of the attitudes and concerns of your readers, and you appeal to their reason and feelings. You also seek to win their trust by showing that you are informed on the subject and are honest and fair in arguing your case.

To argue a point and to persuade your readers most effectively, you will use inductive and deductive reasoning and you will explain the nature of the evidence you present—our focus in Chapters 34 and 35 of Part Eight. Chapter 36 discusses the organization of persuasive essays and the types of appeals you can make in them. In Chapter 37, you will learn how to avoid fallacious reasoning and appeals to emotion that can weaken arguments and make them less persuasive. We begin by considering inductive reasoning—the process of generalizing from experience, observation, and other evidence of the senses.

34a The nature of inductive reasoning

1 Common inductive arguments

An **inductive argument** is a generalization based on experience and observation. You are reasoning inductively when, on the basis of a series of expressway tie-ups, you decide to take an alternate route to school or work. Your decision is based on what happened to you the day before and during the past month. In making your decision, you consider these and other facts, make comparisons with other routes, and analyze the causes of the delays. Your reasoning is based on evidence derived from your personal observations and experience.

Here is an inductive argument that reasons from everyday facts and observations:

> I hear that computers are indispensable household management tools. I must run a very simple household, because all my important documents, checks and receipts of the past five years are filed in three-quarters of a shoe box. At that rate, I should need about five shoe boxes in my lifetime. Five shoe boxes take up less space than the average computer. Shoe boxes also cost less and don't use electricity. In case of fire, flood or theft, either system is useless, so, all things considered, I don't see the advantages of having a computer when it comes to organizing receipts, warranties and records of payment.
> —Katherine Gale DaCosta, "Anticomputerism,"
> *New York Times*, August 27, 1984

DaCosta concludes that a computer is of no advantage to her in managing a household and probably won't be of any advantage in the future. Her evidence is drawn entirely from her personal experience and observations.

531

Inductive reasoning also draws on other sources based on the senses. These include eyewitness testimony, extended comparison or analogy, laboratory experiments, field studies, opinion surveys, statistical studies, and library research. Inductive reasoning plays an important role in scientific and other investigations as well as in everyday experience. Your college courses will acquaint you with these sources and give you opportunities to work with them.

Types of Evidence in Inductive Arguments
Personal experience and observation
Testimonials, or other eyewitness accounts
Well-established facts
Laboratory experiments
Field studies
Statistical surveys
Library research
Analogy
Causal analysis

2 Limiting the conclusion

Inductive arguments state probable conclusions and make limited predictions. DaCosta does not conclude in the preceding passage that computers are of no use to anyone else or that they are dispensable household-management tools. These conclusions would have been broader than her evidence allows.

How you limit or qualify your conclusion depends on the nature of the evidence you present. Sometimes the evidence presented is so strong that the conclusion has a high degree of probability. But even evidence of this kind is subject to challenge. For example, many scientists today accept the earth's rapid warming in coming years as a near certainty because, in their view, the accumulated evidence strongly supports this conclusion. But note that other evidence collected by the National Aeronautics and Space Administration leads other scientists to hold their judgment. Inductive arguments cannot claim absolute certainty for several reasons:

▪ Predictions are never absolute certainties. No amount of evidence can prove with certainty that the earth will continue to warm rapidly. Not even the prediction that the sun will rise in the morning is absolutely certain. Your experiences driving to work make it probable you will experience more traffic delays, but they do not prove that delays will occur. Thus, you can increase the probability of your conclusion through other inductive evidence, but your prediction remains a probability.

■ You can never guarantee that you possess all relevant facts. For example, you may be unaware that road construction is ending on a highway where tie-ups have been frequent. In assembling evidence, you make the decision at some point to make an "inductive leap" from the facts you have collected to generalization or conclusion. Later you may discover that you made this leap too early. In your everyday experience, you continually revise judgments and conclusions in light of new evidence.

■ Evidence from the senses may be deficient. Eyes and ears often deceive. Like early astronomers who observed the heavens without the aid of telescopes, you may lack the instruments needed to see the world as it really is. Scientists cannot be sure that existing instruments, even highly precise ones like the electron microscope, are adequate.

However, inductive arguments can make a certain generalization on the basis of a "perfect induction" or limited sample. For example, you can say with certainty that all drivers on your block have good driving records (none have received a traffic citation or have had a traffic accident) because you can verify these facts. However, you could not predict the records of drivers on the next block on the basis of this evidence alone. You would need other evidence to make a judgment of this kind.

EXERCISES

1. What information would you need to decide whether your neighbors who drive are typical of most drivers in your town or city?
2. What facts about your neighbors would be irrelevant in determining whether they are typical?
3. What could you predict about the driving habits of people in your town or city on the basis of this sample? ■

34b Sampling

Your inductive argument will be of worth to your reader if it contains **accurate evidence.** To show that facts are accurate, you may appeal to common experience or cite authorities on the subject. A good inductive argument also generalizes from **typical evidence,** not from exceptional experiences or circumstances. It also makes **limited predictions** and draws **limited inferences** or conclusions from the specific facts and experiences presented, not from unspecified ones. All generalizations depend on a **representative sample,** or members of a class or group considered typical of all members. Statistical studies are often based on representative samples. Deriving an accurate statistical sample depends on complex methods that are beyond the scope of this discussion. However, we should consider ways of making samples accurate and fair.

The sample should be typical of the class. Consider the following generalization:

> If teenagers in my high school are typical, teenage drivers are as good as any on the road.

The speaker recognizes that the teenage drivers in the sample must be typical of teenage drivers everywhere if the conclusion is to merit consideration. The teenagers are typical if they show the same variations in age, driving education and experience, and any other traits characteristic of the broader group they are said to typify. Were you to object that these teenagers are not typical because their high school is in a rural area, the speaker would have to prove that driving in rural areas is typical of driving everywhere. If driving in rural areas is not typical in all respects, the generalization would have to be qualified to take account of exceptions.

The sample should be broad enough to give significant information. Assume that the speaker generalizes further and says that, in comparison to teenagers, elderly people are unreliable drivers. The sample must include enough people or things to represent the class covered by the generalization. In testing this statement, you would want to know whether the speaker has observed elderly drivers in various places and circumstances. A sample based on a limited group, even one selected randomly—for example, elderly people driving on a Sunday afternoon in April, on a lightly traveled street—is of little worth. On the same principle, in statements about "one out of two" drivers or smokers or toothpaste users, you would want to know the total number of people sampled. Only two people need be interviewed to create such a statistic.

The sample should be based on usual, not unusual circumstances. The sample will be unrepresentative if it limits itself to people or things observed in unusual circumstances. A sample based on elderly people driving on icy streets in January does not support a generalization that presumably covers driving in all kinds of weather at all times of the year. It also tells us nothing about the elderly. Probably everyone at times has trouble driving on icy streets.

The generalization or conclusion cannot be broader than the evidence warrants. As noted above, the conclusion must be properly limited. The sample just cited may support the generalization that some elderly people do not drive well on icy streets, a statement better qualified than the original statement cited. But the sample does not support the generalization that elderly people are worse drivers than younger or middle-aged people in the same circumstances. Notice also that a reliable sample does not allow you to draw conclusions about the driving habits of any single driver in the class, nor about *all* drivers.

The wording of the argument must be clear. Unless the terms of your argument are exact, your readers may not know what group of people the sample includes and what broader group of people it represents. The phrase *elderly people*, for example, is vague. The sample may refer to people fifty years of age or older or to people in their seventies or eighties, and the generalization it supports may refer to an equally vague group. Terms like *yuppie* and *senior citizen* are based on social attitudes that often bias the sample and the conclusion drawn.

All relevant facts must be considered in interpreting evidence. Suppose that you are comparing the traffic fatalities that occurred in 1979 and 1989. You notice a decline for drivers in your state and the same proportional decline in the number of drunk drivers arrested—a decline you attribute to the recent change in laws governing drunk driving. The statistical correlation might be significant if the decline occurred in all age groups. It would be less significant if the decline occurred only in some groups, though the statistical correlation does provide *some* evidence that the change in law has reduced traffic fatalities. Other evidence is needed to strengthen this argument. And other facts that might account for the decline

535

deserve consideration, such as increased enforcement of speeding laws in the intervening years.

EXERCISES

1. What evidence would you need to prove that people who drive on the right-hand side of the highway (as drivers do in the United States) are better drivers than those who drive on the left-hand side (as drivers do in Great Britain)?

2. What evidence might pet owners present to prove that their pets "understand" what the owners are saying to them? What would you accept as reliable evidence that the pets understand English?

3. An advertisement for a "nutritive sweetener" includes the following statement:

> An amount equal in sweetness to one teaspoon of sugar contains just one-tenth of one calorie. So it can reduce the number of empty calories in some foods as much as 95 percent.

Is the advertisement saying that the 95-percent reduction is related to one teaspoon of sugar? And what is the meaning of the word *reduce*? Does it mean that the sweetener removes anything from the food? Exactly what does the sweetener do? ∎

34c | Using analogy

1 The nature of analogy

Arguments from analogy are inductive because they are based on observation and experience. **Analogy** is a point-by-point comparison between different things that share important similarities. Analogy is often used to illustrate an idea or to prove a point (see 6g). In scientific investigation, analogy often provides hypotheses that researchers test by other methods.

In arguing for the exploration of outer space, Carl Sagan compares humans, confined to earth in their quest of knowledge, to linguists, confined on an island:

> A fundamental area of common interest is the problem of perspective. The exploration of space permits us to see our planet and ourselves in a new light. *We are like linguists on an isolated island where only one language is spoken.* We can construct gen-

eral theories of language, but we have only one example to examine. It is unlikely that our understanding of language will have
the generality that a mature science of human linguistics
requires.
—"Space Exploration: The Scientific Interest" (emphasis added)

Sagan then extends his analogy to scientists working under a
similar restriction:

*There are many branches of science where our knowledge is
similarly provincial and parochial, restricted to a single example
among a vast multitude of possible cases.* Only by examining the
range of cases available elsewhere can a broad and general science be devised.
—"Space Exploration: The Scientific Interest" (emphasis added)

Sagan underscores the similarities in his analogy: What is true
of linguists must be true of all humans, including scientists.

2 The limits of analogy

The limits of an analogy should be made clear to the reader.
You may want to state these limits directly as well as the extent
to which the analogy supports your generalization. Sagan does
not say that access to extraterrestrial knowledge will solve the
problems of earth. He says only that wider knowledge would
allow us to see earth from a new perspective. He has limited
his analogy.

You can test your analogy by asking whether the differences between the things being compared are significant
enough to weaken the conclusion. It is important to identify
important differences and to show that they do not weaken
the argument. In Sagan's analogy, linguists are asking specific
questions about a single area of knowledge; human beings are
different in that they ask a wide range of questions. But this
difference does not weaken Sagan's conclusion. Linguists and
humans would both profit from a wider body of "examples."

Remember that no argument from analogy can be stronger
than its underlying assumptions or facts. All of these need to
be evaluated by appealing to experience. For example, Des-
mond Morris argues by analogy that humans resemble other
primates in their craving of sweets:

As the natural food of primates becomes riper and more suitable
for consumption, it usually becomes sweeter, and monkeys and
apes have a strong reaction to anything that is strongly endowed

with this taste. Like other primates, we find it hard to resist "sweets."

—The Naked Ape

But note this qualification in the introduction to Morris's book:

Because of the size of the task, it will be necessary to oversimplify in some manner. The way I shall do this is largely to ignore the detailed ramifications of technology and verbalization, and concentrate instead on those aspects of our lives that have obvious counterparts in other species: such activities as feeding, grooming, sleeping, fighting, mating and care of the young.

—The Naked Ape

Morris seems to consider "verbalization" an insignificant difference. But is it insignificant?

You can test his statement by referring to your own experience. Do words influence your own preference for sweets? What influence does advertising have on your like or dislike of certain foods? And is there any contrary evidence, such as people who don't like sweets? In developing your own analogy, you need to ask similar questions. These questions will be effective if the points of similarity and difference in your analogy are clear in your mind.

Analogy by itself seldom provides enough evidence to support a strong conclusion. For this reason, analogy is best used with other evidence, perhaps personal experience and observation. Morris supports his argument from analogy in noting that humans have "sweet shops" but not "sour shops" and like to end their meal with something sweet. In inductive arguments, the more varied the evidence, the stronger the conclusion.

EXERCISES

1. What arguments by analogy does the writer of the following passage on hostage taking reject, and why? What analogy does she use in arguing this rejection?

> I am always struck by a couple of particularly bad formulations that are used in these episodes. One holds that the hostages are "being treated well," so long as they get some food and soap and are not being physically beaten. It reminds me of that old standby about how the woman had been raped "but not harmed" by her assailant. The absence of a bash to the face in neither case constitutes absence of harm or good treatment. By the very act

of their capture our hostages are being brutally mistreated.

The other especially unfortunate formulation is that which holds that we are in a "war" with terrorism. But war, with its rules and its purposes and its causes, for all its irrationality and evil, is exactly what we are not in. And to say we are is to do several things. It is to elevate these grubby criminal acts to a status they don't deserve; it is to cast, at least indirectly, all Americans as enemy civilians or belligerents and thus fair game; and it is to misdescribe the nature of the assault itself. Soldiers may behave thuggishly, but there is a difference between soldiers and thugs. And there is a difference too between being a prisoner of war and being a hostage hauled off a plane.

—Meg Greenfield, "Accepting the Unacceptable,"
Newsweek, July 1, 1985

2. In several trial paragraphs, develop an argument from analogy of your own. State the points of similarity relevant to your conclusion. Then defend your analogy by showing that the differences between the things you are comparing do not weaken the conclusion. Be sure to limit your conclusions to what the analogy shows.

3. Write an additional paragraph for your argument that uses personal experience and observations to support your conclusion. Then organize all of the paragraphs you've written into an argumentative essay. ■

34d	Using causal analysis

In reasoning about causes and effects, you do the same as in arguing from analogy: you make predictions. If you observe the cause of an event in the present, you expect to find the same cause in the future and you argue that a similar event in the past had the same cause. This is called **causal analysis** (6i).

1 Arguing from causes

The word *cause* has different meanings. Assume that you recently witnessed a traffic accident "caused" by a drunk driver. Is the "cause" of the accident the amount of alcohol in the blood? Or is the "cause" a celebration or a frustrating experience that led the driver to drink heavily?

In looking for causes, you are looking for two types:

- **Immediate causes** (in this case, intoxication and the decision to drive while intoxicated).
- **Remote causes** (the social and psychological conditions or circumstances that encourage drunk driving).

Causal analysis may center on immediate causes or on remote causes or both. Considering the immediate cause of traffic accidents involving drunk drivers, you discuss measures to take drunk drivers off the road. Considering remote causes, you discuss effective ways of reducing alcoholism.

The word *cause* also refers to two possible conditions:

- The **necessary conditions** that must be present when an event occurs.
- The **sufficient conditions** in whose presence the event must occur.

These conditions are often the subject of investigation in tracing an immediate cause. Thus, to prove that a person is intoxicated, the investigator must find alcohol in the blood. Alcohol is a *necessary condition* of intoxication, and evidence of a minimum amount of alcohol in the blood is legally *sufficient* to prove that a driver is intoxicated.

2 Arguing from effects

Causal arguments often trace effects to a probable cause. The following paragraph traces the effects of marathon talks on collective bargaining:

> Marathon talks are a relatively new development in labor negotiations. As the representatives of employer and union pound along, gasping out proposals about wage differentials and grievance procedures, and accusing each other of not engaging in genuine collective bargaining, the virtue of marathon talks becomes clear. It is that the parties quickly tire of the pace and, rather than go on running, come to an agreement. Even if they keep going, an artfully placed last ditch is provided for them to fall into, and these last-ditch talks avert, as last-ditch talks will, a costly walkout. It is a more effective and healthier method than the one so often recommended by irate citizens, locking them in a room until they come up with a contract.
> —Edwin Newman, *Strictly Speaking*

Newman uses these effects to argue that marathon talking is "more effective and healthier" than forcing negotiators to stay in a room until they reach agreement.

☑

Checklist: Inductive Reasoning

1. Are my facts accurate, typical, relevant, and sufficient to make my point?
2. Are my samples broad enough, representative, and clear in wording? Have I sampled people or things in typical rather than special or unusual circumstances?
3. In arguing from analogy, have I stated the similarities clearly and noted the differences and limits of the analogy?
4. Have I clarified the sense in which I analyze causes?

Arguments from effects usually combine with arguments from causes and sometimes with statistical arguments.

The following guidelines will help you develop effective causal arguments:

- Clarify the kind of cause you are identifying. Explain, for example, that you are referring to an immediately preceding event or to one in the past. You need not use the technical names to identify them if the discussion clarifies them sufficiently.
- Limit your conclusion properly. You can point to a necessary condition of good driving—proper driver training—without claiming that everyone who takes a driving course will be a good driver.
- If possible, support your causal analysis with observations, testimonials, and other inductive evidence. The more varied the evidence you present for an inductive generalization, the stronger the proof.

EXERCISES

1. Distinguish the immediate and remote causes of an exam you recently passed or an argument you engaged in recently.
2. Oncogenes are genes associated with tumors. The following paragraph discusses the role of oncogenes in cancer. What does the author mean by the words *necessary* and *sufficient*? Does he state or imply that oncogenes do not act alone in creating tumors?

> The creation of a single oncogene may be *necessary* for the genesis of a tumor, but it is far from being *suffi-*

541

cient. Tumorigenesis is a multistep process. The evolution of a line of tumor cells seems to depend, at the very least, on the accumulation of mutations altering a number of genes, among them oncogenes. The altered genes then function in concert to create full-fledged malignant growth.
—Robert A. Weinberg, "Finding the Anti-Oncogene," *Scientific American,* September 1988 (emphasis added) ■

34e Using inductive evidence

In writing an argumentative essay, you discuss issues within a frame of shared knowledge and assumptions. A letter to the editor addresses a particular issue, defined and argued in previous editorials and letters. The background and inductive evidence you provide and the appeals you make to your readers depend on current discussion and debate. In the course of your letter, you may present several kinds of inductive evidence—personal experience and observation, analogy, causal analysis, and the like. How you organize this evidence depends on the occasion and the audience you are addressing.

In college work, you also work within a frame of knowledge and assumptions. In each field or discipline, you acquire a body of facts and assumptions shared by specialists. You also acquire knowledge of methods and standards by which experiments and research are conducted. When you perform experiments, make observations, do surveys, and collect facts in library research, you work with different kinds of fact and different assumptions. Reports and papers in chemistry and other sciences support their conclusions with measurements. Papers in English, history, and philosophy depend on other standards and methods of evaluation. In writing a report or term paper, you are learning to gather reliable evidence, sort and weigh it, and use it to support or defend a conclusion or thesis.

Each field or discipline makes different use of inductive evidence. You will rely most on your personal experience and observation for evidence in papers written for humanities and social science courses. Causal analysis in the humanities is less formal than in other fields. For example, papers in chemistry and physics often call for exact analysis of necessary and sufficient conditions. Your analysis of conditions may be less exact and technical in an English or a history paper. Analogy plays an important role in argumentative papers in the humanities and social sciences. It is important also in reasoning in the sciences. Statistical sampling plays a role in most disciplines; it is an essential method of research in sociology, political science, and other social sciences.

Chapters 43 and 44 discuss the special requirements of writing in the humanities, social sciences, and sciences. Section 36b discusses ways of organizing inductive arguments.

Summary

34a Inductive reasoning.

Generalize from typical evidence, not from exceptional experiences and circumstances (34a 1).

Make the evidence in inductive arguments pertinent to the conclusion (34a 1).

Limit your conclusion to what the evidence shows, and qualify it carefully (34a 2).

34b In using a sample of people or things, define the sample carefully, making it representative of the class discussed and broad enough to be significant, and basing it on typical, not unusual, circumstances.

34c Analogy.

When using analogy as proof, be sure that the differences between the things analogized don't weaken the argument (34c 1).

State the limits of the analogy (34c 2).

34d Causal analysis.

In developing a causal argument, clarify the sense in which you use the word *cause* (34d 1).

Combine arguments from effects with arguments from cause and with other inductive arguments where appropriate (34d 2).

34e Use the inductive evidence and methods of research appropriate to a field of study.

Deductive Reasoning

35

□

□

Deductive reasoning is the process of drawing inferences or conclusions from statements assumed to be true. In deductive reasoning, you show that one truth or generalization necessarily leads to another through a process of correct reasoning. The premises are thus evidence for the conclusion. The word *deduct* has retained its original Latin meaning of "lead away." This chapter describes some basic methods of deduction that are useful in argumentative writing.

35a | The nature of deductive reasoning

1 Deductive versus inductive reasoning

When you reason *inductively*, you generalize from particulars of experience. When you look to see what **inferences** necessarily follow from generalizations, you are reasoning deductively:

Since all reptiles are cold-blooded, and all snakes are reptiles, all snakes must be cold-blooded.

Since all eligible voters are citizens, and all farmers in the county are eligible voters, all farmers in the county are citizens.

In drawing necessary inferences from generalizations based on repeated observations and personal experience, deductive reasoning is the counterpart of inductive reasoning.

However, deductive reasoning extends further. You use deductive reasoning when you draw conclusions from beliefs, assumptions, and widely accepted truths. You draw them also from established scientific laws and mathematical axioms and postulates. You come across deductive reasoning often in your reading, as in the following passage on education:

> Society is to be improved not by forcing a program of social reform down its throat, through the schools or otherwise, but by the improvement of the individuals who compose it. As Plato said, "Governments reflect human nature. States are not made out of stone or wood, but out of the characters of their citizens: these turn the scale and draw everything after them." The individual is the heart of society.
>
> —Robert M. Hutchins, "The Basis of Education"

Hutchins makes an inference about the purpose of education from an idea that he considers true without qualification: the purpose of education is to improve people, for "the individual is the heart of society." Hutchins would hold this definition to be true even if no such society or system of education had ever existed. Deductive reasoning uses statements of this kind as evidence for its conclusions.

2 Premises and conclusions

In deductive reasoning, inferences follow necessarily from **premises,** or statements assumed to be true. A popular example is the syllogism proving Socrates is mortal. If it is true that all humans are mortal, and it is also true that Socrates is a human, it *must* follow that Socrates is mortal. The conclusion (*Socrates is mortal*) is a necessary inference from the premises that form the evidence (*All humans are mortal; Socrates is a human*).

The conclusions reached in inductive arguments have a degree of probability and cannot claim absolute certainty (see 34a). A deductive argument makes a claim to certainty, but in

545

a special sense. If the process of reasoning in a deductive argument is correct, we say that the inferences follow necessarily from the premises. Thus, many writers claim certainty because they assume that their premises are true without qualification. Their deductive arguments rest solely on a statement of the premises and the inferences they make from them; they present no support or backing. One good example is the opening sentence of the Declaration of Independence: "We hold these truths to be self-evident."

Yet not all deductive arguments reason from premises thought by the authors to be "self-evident" or true without qualification. When the premises take the form of inductive generalizations contingent upon human experience, writers usually defend or justify them by telling us where their premises come from and what evidence supports them. They also explain and defend the standards used to judge the evidence. This kind of explanation and defense is common in addressing the general reader; explanation and defense are, however, often absent when writers address colleagues and workers in the same field, people who share their ideas. The philosopher Stephen Toulmin points out that each discipline—law, medicine, engineering, history, mathematics—defines its own evidence and standards and each is therefore a "field of argument."[1] Arguments are in this sense "field–dependent."

Types of Evidence in Deductive Arguments
Inductive generalizations
Beliefs
Assumptions
Widely accepted truths
Scientific laws
Axioms
Postulates

35b | Formal deductive arguments

1 The process of inference

A deductive argument is called a **syllogism** when it is presented formally, as in the examples that follow. There are many kinds of deductive arguments and syllogisms, most of which

[1]*The Uses of Argument* (Cambridge, England: Cambridge UP, 1958), pp. 14–17.

can be broadly characterized as unconditional (categorical) or conditional (hypothetical). Among the various types of **unconditional** or **categorical** arguments is a relatively simple kind of syllogism that contains **affirmative premises,** which state or affirm that a class contains a property or quality of some kind:

Major premise:	All eligible voters are citizens.
Minor premise:	All farmers in the county are eligible voters.
Conclusion:	Therefore, all farmers in the county are citizens.

Here is the formula of the argument:

$$A = B$$
$$C = A$$
$$C = B$$

This unqualified or categorical argument is valid in its reasoning; thus, we call it a **valid argument.** The word *valid* means only that the process of reasoning from premises to conclusion is correct. This process of reasoning begins with a **major premise,** a proposition or statement that you hold to be true. To this statement you fit a **minor premise,** a second and more limited generalization than the first. You then draw an inference or conclusion from these two statements. To test the validity of such an argument, you place one class into another to determine whether the conclusion follows directly and necessarily from the major and minor premises:

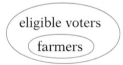

eligible voters

farmers

The test shows that what is true of the class (*eligible voters*) is true of all members contained in the class (*farmers*). Thus, the conclusion follows logically from the premises.

Some categorical syllogisms contain **universal premises** that make statements about all members of a class, as in the preceding example. Other syllogisms contain both a universal premise and a **particular premise** that refers to only some members of the class:

Universal premise:	*All* eligible voters are citizens.
Particular premise:	*Some* farmers in the county are eligible voters.
Conclusion:	Therefore, *some* farmers in the county are citizens.

547

Valid syllogisms can also contain one **negative premise.** The following is also a valid argument:

> No eligible voters in the county are high taxpayers.
> All farmers in the county are eligible voters.
> No farmers in the county are high taxpayers.

In contrast to categorical or unconditional syllogisms, **conditional** or **hypothetical** syllogisms reason from a possible or hypothetical situation and its consequence. In the following valid hypothetical argument, the minor premise affirms the antecedent statement:

> If the water contains lead [*antecedent*], then it is unsafe to drink [*consequent*].
> The water contains lead.
> Therefore, the water is unsafe to drink.

Another type of valid hypothetical argument denies the consequent and the conclusion denies the antecedent:

> If the water is from the well, then it is safe to drink.
> The water is not safe to drink.
> Therefore, the water is not from the well.

In yet another type of conditional syllogism, called **disjunctive,** you reason about alternative propositions. Here is a valid disjunctive argument:

> Either the ship reached port or the ship sank.
> The ship did not reach port.
> Therefore, the ship sank.

2 Sound reasoning

To many people, the word *valid* means true (as in "a valid point"). But validity and truth are not the same thing. An argument may be valid in its reasoning and yet reach a false conclusion because one or both of its premises are false, as in the following statement:

> Elderly people are unsteady drivers because they are infirm.

Here is the complete argument, stated as a syllogism to test its premises and process of inference:

> *Major premise:* All infirm people are unsteady drivers.
> *Minor premise:* All elderly people are infirm people.
> *Conclusion:* Therefore, all elderly people are unsteady drivers.

A **sound argument** is true in its premises and valid in its reasoning. The process of reasoning is correct in a sound argument. What is true of all infirm people must be true of elderly people. But is it true that all infirm people are unsteady drivers? And is it true that all elderly people are physically infirm? You probably agree that at least one of these premises is false. Admittedly, some elderly people are infirm, but not all of them are infirm. Thus, the minor premise generalizes falsely. And the major premise is vague. Some physical infirmities do not affect driving ability. Although the process of reasoning is correct, the argument is unsound. Like many similar statements and assumptions, this argument is based on a popular but false and harmful stereotype.

3 Undistributed middle term

There are various processes of reasoning that can make an argument invalid. Invalid arguments frequently contain an **undistributed middle term.** The **middle term** of a syllogism is the term that appears in both the major and minor premises but not in the conclusion. In the following invalid argument, the middle term is *reptiles:*

Invalid

Major premise:	All snakes are reptiles.
Minor premise:	All alligators are reptiles.
Conclusion:	Therefore, all alligators are snakes.

In a valid argument, one of the premises refers to *all* of the members of the middle term; that is, the term is **distributed.** In the preceding argument, the middle term *reptile* is undistributed in either premise. The conclusion connects alligators and snakes on the basis of their inclusion in the class *reptiles*. But neither premise refers to the whole class of reptiles or sum of its divisions. The premises indicate only that the class of reptiles *contains* snakes and alligators. Snakes and alligators may, and in fact do, belong to separate divisions of the class. Thus, the argument is invalid because the premises provide no evidence for the conclusion.

4 Other features of invalid arguments

Although the validity of deductive arguments is sometimes difficult to assess, you can watch for certain errors in reasoning

549

that signal problems. A valid deductive argument must conform to the following guidelines. If it breaks one or more of these rules, it is considered invalid.

The terms of the argument must have the same meaning in the premises and conclusion. Consider the following invalid argument:

Invalid

Major premise:	Unsteady people are bad drivers.
Minor premise:	Unemployed people are unsteady people.
Conclusion:	Therefore, unemployed people are bad drivers.

The term *unsteady* has more than one meaning in this argument. In the major premise, it means physically infirm; in the minor premise it means without a livelihood. The unsteady people cited in the premises belong to different classes—the class of the infirm and the class of the unemployed. Thus, no inference can be drawn from these premises.

If one of the premises is negative, the conclusion must also be negative. The following valid argument draws a negative conclusion from the premises:

Valid

Major premise:	Careful drivers are alert people.
Minor premise:	No drunks are careful drivers.
Conclusion:	Therefore, no drunks are alert people.

Notice that the premises do not warrant the inference that drunks would necessarily be alert if sober.

If both premises are negative, no conclusion is possible. The following argument is invalid because it draws a positive conclusion drawn from negative premises:

Invalid

Major premise:	No drunks are careful drivers.
Minor premise:	No alert people are drunks.
Conclusion:	Therefore, alert people are careful drivers.

The two negative premises do not provide evidence for the conclusion, for they say nothing positive about careful drivers or alert people. The conclusion makes a positive statement about the two classes on information other than that given in the premises.

A conditional or hypothetical syllogism is invalid if it affirms the consequent or denies the antecedent (see page 548). Consider the following example:

Invalid

Major premise:	If I pass the exam with at least an 85 [*antecedent*], I earn an "A" [*consequent*].
Minor premise:	I earned an "A."
Conclusion:	Therefore, I passed the exam with at least an 85.

The argument is invalid because the minor premise affirms the consequent (*I earn an "A"*), not the antecedent. The conditional statement (*If I pass . . .*) does not say that passing the exam with at least an 85 is the *only* way to earn an "A"; high grades on quizzes and term papers might be another way of earning an "A." Yet the conclusion implies that there is only one way to earn an "A." The conclusion obviously goes beyond what the conditional premise says or implies.

The following conditional argument is invalid because the minor premise denies the antecedent:

Major premise:	If I pass the exam with at least an 85, I earn an "A."
Minor premise:	I did not pass the exam with at least an 85.
Conclusion:	Therefore, I did not earn an "A."

Again, the conclusion goes beyond what the conditional premise says.

5 Enthymemic argument

Most deductive arguments are not stated formally as syllogisms. In your own arguments, you probably imply one of the premises or even the conclusion, usually because the premise or conclusion is so obvious that it need not be stated explicitly. George F. Will states in his essay "Bearbaiting and Boxing": "Good government and the good life depend on good values and passions, and some entertainments are inimical to these." He need not add that some entertainments are inimical to good government and the good life.

Consider this version of the syllogism presented earlier:

Since unalert people are bad drivers, and drunks are unalert people, drunks are bad drivers.

Here are alternative ways of stating this same argument:

Major premise implied:	Since drunks are unalert people, they are bad drivers.
Major premise:	Unalert people are bad drivers.
Minor premise implied:	Drunks are bad drivers because unalert people are.
Minor premise:	Drunks are unalert people.
Conclusion implied:	Unalert people are bad drivers, and drunks are unalert people.
Conclusion:	Drunks are bad drivers.

Arguments of this kind, called **enthymemes,** are the chief form of argument in debate and in persuasive writing. Most of your deductive arguments probably occur in this form. Since most deductive reasoning is enthymemic, discovering the missing premise or conclusion is essential in rebutting an argument in debate. You may wish to rebut your opponent by identifying an implied or hidden premise and showing it to be false. Your opponent may, in turn, challenge a hidden premise in your argument.

The situation is more complex in persuasive writing. In contrast to a debate, your audience is not present as you draft a persuasive argument. To make your essay effective, you need to follow certain guidelines.

Clarify your premises and conclusion. The persuasiveness of your essay may depend on your clarifying your premises or conclusion for your reader. Although you may think that the premises are too obvious to require statement or defense, your readers may not find them obvious at all. Thus, to make your essay persuasive, you must anticipate how your readers will interpret your premises and conclusion.

Identify each inference in the draft you are revising. In drafting a persuasive essay, you may not be aware of inferences you have made. A good way to identify them is to mark sentences that look like inferences. Look for words like *so, thus, then,* and *therefore* that usually introduce inferences and conclusions. Then look to see whether these sentences draw conclusions from the evidence presented and draw them properly. Remember that true statements can lead to false conclusions, false statements to true ones. Don't assume that your conclusion must be true because your premises are true. Testing the validity of the inference or conclusion is usually difficult because of the many valid and invalid forms of deductive argument. But you may be able to catch one or more of the few simple errors described earlier in the chapter.

Defend the premises of your argument. Your evidence may consist of assumptions, truths, or unquestioned facts that you believe require no defense or supporting evidence. This kind of argument is likely to convince readers who already share your assumptions or beliefs, but it will not convince those who have different beliefs. There are few truths as universal as "All humans are mortal." In most cases, you should defend your assumptions and beliefs and explain why you hold them. This is always necessary when your evidence consists of facts, gen-

Checklist: Deductive Arguments

1. What is the origin of my premises? Do I hold them as given or "self-evident" truths that require no explanation or defense? Or are they generalizations based on well-tested observation and personal experience?
2. Is my argument sound? Are my premises true or well-established, and is the process of reasoning from my premises to my conclusion valid?
3. Will my audience understand my premises? If not, what explanation can I give them to make my argument understandable?
4. Will my audience accept these premises as sufficient evidence for the conclusions I draw from them? If not, what defense can I make of them?
5. Need I state my argument fully? If I leave one of the premises or the conclusion of my argument unstated, will my reader be able to complete the argument and test my reasoning?

eralizations drawn from everyday experience, and other evidence of the senses. (Chapter 36 further examines the role of argument in persuasive writing and the organization of persuasive essays.)

 35c

Analysis of a deductive argument: Richard Moran, "To Improve Prison Conditions, We Must First Improve Slums"

In the following essay by Richard Moran, the author draws an inference from a basic assumption or idea and then defends it. The idea is that of "less eligibility," stated by the dramatist and social critic George Bernard Shaw in 1920. A prison must be wretched, Shaw says, because "if the prison does not underbid the slum in human misery, the slum will empty and the prison will fill." Moran draws the conclusion that the indignities suffered in American prisons today arise from this assumption:

> This principle of "less eligibility" still guides our thinking about punishment and our approach to the conditions of confinement. (paragraph 4)

No other assumption can explain these conditions and Moran does not suggest another, though he states that "to much of the public the conditions at these and other prisons must be shocking and unacceptable" (paragraph 6). The conclusion Moran reaches is an immediate inference from this assumption: "The only way to improve conditions in prison is to improve conditions in the slums" (paragraph 9).

The fact that so many people are shocked by prison conditions is evidence for Moran of the principle. If it were not for the idea of "less eligibility," the prison system and society as a whole would have no reason to subject prisoners to indignities like those suffered in Oklahoma and West Virginia. "To those who believe that life in prison must always be worse than life on the outside, these conditions seem just about right," Moran states in paragraph 6. In this way Moran explains his assumption and defends it.

TO IMPROVE PRISON CONDITIONS, WE MUST FIRST IMPROVE SLUMS
Richard Moran

1   Last week, watching news from the prison takeover in West Virginia, our attention again was drawn to the problems that breed violence in our nation's prisons. Overcrowding, idleness and despair are contributing factors, but the crisis cannot be understood adequately without knowledge of the place of prisons in society. And for this we need a historical perspective.

2   In attempting to explain the deplorable conditions in English prisons, George Bernard Shaw wrote in 1920 that the living conditions of the poor were "so wretched that it would be impossible to conduct a prison humanely without making the lot of the criminal more eligible (desirable) than that of many free citizens. If the prison does not underbid the slum in human misery, the slum will empty and the prison will fill."

3   Shaw was merely restating the principle of "less eligibility," which was first formulated in the 17th century. In its basic form, the principle maintains that the conditions in prison must always be worse than the standard of living of the poorest members of society. Otherwise people would commit crimes in order to get into prison.

4   This principle of "less eligibility" still guides our thinking about punishment and our approach to the conditions of confinement. As such, it can help us understand the recent riot at the Oklahoma State Prison, where inmates allege that prison administrators have evidenced a deliberate indifference to the physical and psychological needs of inmates: that inmates are forced to wear degrading striped uniforms, eat rancid food and remain idle all day. The lack of jobs at the prison has left most inmates with no way of earning spending money or "good time" credit. These conditions, it is charged, violate a prisoner's constitutional right to protection against cruel and unusual punishment.

5   In West Virginia, the rioting inmates complained that their cells were unheated in winter and suffocatingly hot in summer, that they seldom had hot meals and were denied the "right" to wear a beard or mustache.

6   To those who believe that life in prison must always be worse than life on the outside, these conditions seem just about right. But to much of the public the conditions at these and other prisons must be shocking and unacceptable.

7   Nevertheless, prison administrators are really not to blame, for they are in a no-win situation. If prisons provide a modest but comfortable standard of living—with adequate food, shelter and health care—if they provide adequate recreational and educational facilities as well as vocational training—things that most of the poor do not have—they will be accused of coddling criminals. And if they do not have a credible deterrent to misbehavior in the prison, such as solitary confinement or short-term withdrawal of food, how can they hope to manage the inmate population?

8   All of this is not an excuse for conditions at our prisons; there are no excuses—but there are explanations. And the principle of "less eligibility" is an explanation. It helps us understand why efforts to reform the punishment of criminals are limited by the living conditions of the lowest social class. It explains why reform efforts, however humanitarian and well-meaning, can never go beyond this restriction.

9   The only way to improve conditions in prison is to improve conditions in the slums. There is no other way.

EXERCISE

Is the principle of "less eligibility" a convincing explanation of the deplorable prison conditions that Moran discusses? Why, or why not? If you disagree with Moran's point, what other explanation can you suggest? Do you think that the people who believe in a harsh prison life also condone the cruel treatment of prisoners? Explain. ■

35d | Fields of argument

1 Claim, grounds, warrant, backing

We noted earlier the philosopher Stephen Toulmin's point that arguments vary from one field of knowledge to another—that they are "field-dependent." What is accepted as reliable evidence in one **field of argument** may not be accepted in other fields. Lawyers, scientists, philosophers, and literary scholars have their own methods of research and standards by which they judge arguments.

Toulmin suggests a highly useful way of analyzing arguments. Instead of talking about premises and conclusion, Toulmin uses other terms that clarify their role in arguments on specific topics. Whatever the field, an argument makes a **claim,** presents **grounds** for the claim, possibly presents a **warrant** in experience or law for the grounds, and possibly **backs** the warrant with additional proof and **qualifies** the conclusion.

Claim:	The thesis, conclusion, or the point at issue in the argument.
Grounds:	The evidence presented to support the claim.
Warrants:	Statutes, scientific laws, and the like that justify use of the evidence to prove the claim.
Backing:	Support for the warrant, or proof that the statute exists or that the scientific law is well established and accepted.
Qualifier:	States the limits of the conclusion through words like *some* and *most*; notes exceptions.

In this way Toulmin clarifies the nature of premises and the evidence presented in their defense in the many kinds of argument.

Let's assume that medical researchers make the claim that vaccination for measles can probably eliminate this viral disease worldwide. Their argument takes the following form:

Claim:	Mass inoculation can probably eliminate measles worldwide.
Grounds:	Mass inoculation reduced the incidence of measles in the United States. Mass inoculation seems to have eliminated smallpox—another viral disease. The opportunity to contract measles and smallpox grows smaller as the number of infected people decreases.
Warrants:	Anyone immunized for measles probably cannot transmit the disease. The incidence of an infectious disease decreases as the number of infected people grows smaller. Epidemics depend on dense contact between infected people.
Backing:	Experimental evidence and experience with patients strongly support these medical theories.
Qualifiers:	Words and phrases like *probably* and *strongly support.*

If challenged, these researchers might give other warrants like the following:

> Modes of transmission and immunization are the same for people worldwide.
> The measles virus is probably the same in all countries.

This is, in fact, the argument that was made in 1972 by specialists in infectious diseases on the basis of knowledge and assumptions about viral diseases current at the time:

> Optimists have pointed out that if, as seems almost certain, any person immunized against measles cannot subsequently become a source of measles infection for others, measles could in principle be eradicated from the world by general immunization. Even if only 90 per cent of children were immunized this would probably ensure that measles would fail to spread. Measles seems to be caused by exactly the same virus everywhere in the world, and if this holds true, ten years of universal vaccination might get rid of it completely.
> —Sir MacFarlane Burnet and David O. White,
> *Natural History of Infectious Disease*, 4th ed.

If Burnet and White were writing about measles in 1989 instead of 1972, they would probably present current facts about the disease as grounds for their claim. For example, they might cite statistics reported by the Centers for Disease Control in Atlanta, Georgia—specifically, that only 5,600 cases of measles were reported in the United States (in twenty-three states) in the first five months of 1989, versus the 500,000 cases in 1963, the year inoculation began with a live virus vaccine. These statistics show a sharp decline.

New research and theories about viral infection would provide new or additional warrants. But researchers continue to disagree about the nature and control of viral diseases, in part because of experience with AIDS in the 1980s. Burnet and White would no doubt take account of these disagreements and rival theories in backing new warrants and making new claims.

2 Organizing arguments

In presenting claim, grounds, warrants, and backing, you are asking the following questions:

Claim:	What claim am I making? What am I asking my audience to believe? What conclusion or inference does my evidence support?
Grounds:	What facts support my claim?
Warrants:	What assumptions, theories, laws, or other established truths suggest that my facts support my claim?
Backing:	Why should we trust these assumptions or theories? What proof exists for them? What shows that they are recognized and accepted?

You will find these questions useful in testing your whole argument. Its effectiveness depends on how accurately and thoroughly you clarify the facts and justify your use of them to support your claim. Its effectiveness also depends on the order in which you present claim, grounds, and warrants. For example, you may decide to begin with the grounds of your argument and their warrants and build to your claim. Decisions on organization depend on what your audience knows and believes about the subject. (Chapter 36 discusses ways of organizing persuasive essays.)

EXERCISES

1. Answer the following questions about Richard Moran's essay on page 555:
   a. On what grounds does Moran make the claim that prison conditions will not improve until slums improve? What appeals to experience does he make?
   b. Does Moran state or imply a warrant in citing the general attitude toward poverty in analyzing the general attitude toward prison life? Explain.
2. Answer these questions about a magazine advertisement for an over-the-counter cold remedy or a similar product:
   a. What claim does the advertisement make for the product? How specific is the claim?
   b. On what grounds does the advertisement support this claim?
   c. Does the advertisement state or imply a warrant for citing these grounds in support of its claim? Explain.
   d. What kind of backing might be cited for the warrant or any other warrant you can think of? Does the advertisement back its warrant, if any? ∎

Summary

35a Deductive reasoning.

Your argument will be sound if you reason correctly from premises that are true (**35a 2**):

> If all reptiles are cold-blooded, and all snakes are reptiles, then all snakes must be cold-blooded.

35b Formal deductive arguments.

Your argument will be invalid if the middle term is not distributed in one of the premises (**35b 3**):

> **Invalid**
> All snakes are reptiles.
> All alligators are reptiles.
> Therefore, all alligators are snakes.

Your argument will also be invalid if a term has different meanings in each of the premises, contains a negative premise and a positive conclusion, or draws a conclusion from two negative premises (**35b 4**).

You can present your argument as an enthymeme if the missing premise or conclusion is clear to the reader (**35b 5**):

> Drunks are bad drivers because they are unsteady behind the wheel.

35d In making a claim, give the evidence or grounds for it, then your warrant for using the evidence to support the claim. Back your warrant by showing that it is recognized and accepted within the field of argument.

The Persuasive Essay

36

□

□

Persuasion is the counterpart of argument which reasons from evidence to conclusions; for your goal in writing an argument is to convince your readers to accept it. In earlier chapters, we considered the appeal to reason. But this is only one of several appeals you can make to your readers. You may also appeal to their feelings, perhaps to arouse their concern about an issue and convince them to take some action. You may also appeal to your readers' character, trust, and respect. Readers will not be convinced by your argument if you do not persuade them that your presentation is sincere, honest, and fair.

This chapter discusses the relationships between persuasion and argument and suggests ways of making these appeals to reason, emotion, and character as effective as possible in an essay.

561

36a   Persuasion and audience

1   Uses of the persuasive argument

In **persuasive arguments,** you urge the audience to recognize that an issue exists, to feel concern about it, and perhaps to take action. In your argument, you may be defending a course of action, making a proposal, or urging acceptance of a policy. For example, you might use a deductive argument to demonstrate the inherent worth of a proposal (as Brenda Wahler does in her essay on comparable worth later in the chapter) and you might use an inductive argument to show its probable benefits. Like Richard Moran does in his essay on prison life in Chapter 35 (page 555), you might show that experience and observation contradict a mistaken idea, and you might use a deductive argument to explore a contrary idea. You might also use an inductive argument in challenging a mistaken assumption or belief, as William Raspberry does in challenging the idea that ethnic groups have special innate abilities:

> In one sense, what I am talking about is the importance of developing positive ethnic traditions. Maybe Jews have an innate talent for communication; maybe the Chinese are born with a gift for mathematical reasoning; maybe blacks are naturally blessed with athletic grace. I doubt it. What is at work, I suspect, is the assumption, inculcat   early in their lives, that this is a thing our people do well.
> —William Raspberry, "Black—By Definition"

2   Gauging the audience

In planning a persuasive essay, you want to gauge or appraise your audience. Your presentation of the argument must depend on their knowledge of the subject and their interests. The questions you ask about your audience are the same questions you ask in planning an expository essay, with the difference that you are also concerned with ideas and attitudes (see 1b). The shape and content of your argument will become clear as you gauge the interests and attitudes of your readers. The strategies of argument and the focus you choose must depend in large part on whether your audience is a general or a special one (see 1b).

In writing arguments for a **general audience,** you must take account of a wide range of personal opinions, beliefs, and knowledge of the subject. Since many in your audience won't accept your premises, you must explain what your premises mean and why you hold them if you hope to be persuasive. In writing for a **special audience,** however, you probably know much more about your readers' opinions and concerns, and you may not have to explain as much.

A persuasive essay is much like a debate in which you defend your beliefs and opinions to a specific opponent. In an oral debate, the give and take of ideas forces you and your opponent to state your individual beliefs and opinions fully and to give grounds for holding them. In making your defense, you are responding to specific arguments and objections. And having your opponent present gives you an opportunity to re-state your ideas and perhaps marshal additional evidence in refutation. Each of you may give warrants for the grounds you have presented as well as backing for these warrants (see 35d).

In written debate or argument, however, your audience is not present to question and raise objections. You must, there-fore, anticipate the questions and objections that your readers will raise. The more informed you are about your audience and the questions they will raise, the more successful your argument will be. If you begin to write without sufficient prep-aration, you are not likely to convince your audience of your thesis.

3 Focusing the argument

In a debate, the opponents may be in agreement on certain points at issue in the argument. For example, in debating whether smoking should be prohibited in public places, you and your opponent may agree that the **point-at-issue** is the risk to health. However, the point-at-issue may actually be-come the focus of the argument. If you argue that the risk to health is paramount, your opponent may acknowledge that a risk exists but insist that the point-at-issue is one of the indi-vidual's right to smoke.

For example, in an essay on smoking in public places, the head of a company defends a ban on smoking at the company office:

> According to a congressional study, the cost to the economy aver-ages $65 billion annually in increased medical bills, premature death and time lost from work. And as a major participant in the

field of health-care financing, we have an obligation to prove that, if properly conceived, a smoke-free working environment is attainable.

—Ian M. Rolland, "A Burning Issue on the Job and Off,"
Newsweek, January 13, 1986

An assistant law school dean disagrees that the point-at-issue is the risk to health. He argues that the issue is rather discrimination against the smoker:

Employers ought not to be able to impose their concepts of morality, or health, on employees on pain of loss of a job or on denial of the opportunity to compete. No employers ought to have the power to decide what we do in private.

—Bernard J. Dushman, "A Burning Issue on the Job and Off,"
Newsweek, January 13, 1986

Although each writer argues a different point, each takes account of other arguments. Rolland rejects the charge of intrusion into the lives of employees:

We are not trying to dictate personal lifestyles. We encourage our employees to stop smoking altogether, but they cannot smoke on the job.

Dushman cites instances where banning extends beyond the workplace, intruding on individual rights:

It doesn't matter if the employees do not smoke during working hours or if they limit their smoking to the privacy of their homes. If they smoke at all, they won't be hired.

Needless detail and discussion blur an argument. Your own argument will be clear if you define the point-at-issue early in the paper and focus on that point throughout your discussion. Narrowing the focus in this way generates interest in the subject and holds the readers' attention. The more prominent and focused your argument is, the more persuasive your essay will be.

 Appealing to reason

You are **appealing to reason** by making your argument logical and by taking account of what your readers know and believe about your subject. This estimate determines the order in which you present your evidence.

1 Organizing deductive arguments

Although formal deductive arguments and syllogisms proceed from major and minor premises to inference or conclusion (see 35b), in a persuasive essay you can present these elements in any order you wish. The following argument draws a conclusion about the education best suited to American society from a premise that states what that society needs to make progress:

> All these considerations suggest the true character of education; it is the life-long process of growth—physical, mental, moral, aesthetic. It is not primarily training, though training is part of it. Central are the stimulation and the discipline of the individual. This does not require every individual to be a scholar. The wisdom of the world is not confined to the learned; often it is found in the perceptive experience of those whose schooling has not carried them into "higher education." Their shrewd insights on public as well as private matters are part of the historical record of progress.
>
> **Minor premise**   There is no such thing as "mass education." Every use of the phrase is a denial of a vital reality; education is a wholly individual process. The life of the mind—despite all pressures to invade it—remains a private life. It occurs in each person uniquely. We do democracy no service in seeking to inhibit thought—free, wide-ranging, hazardous.
>
> **Major premise**   **Conclusion**   The American system is built upon the thesis that conformity is not the way to progress. Without independence of mind there is no freedom for the individual. Therefore education should never over-accent "adjustment." Whenever that emphasis is dominant, it is a deliberate effort to defeat the infinite variety that enriches society and the world.
>
> —Henry M. Wriston,
> "The Challenge of Being Free"

Wriston's whole essay consists of a chain of propositions that form a series of connected arguments. The basic argument of these three paragraphs can be summarized informally:

Major Premise:	A system that promotes independent thought is one that best allows American society to progress.
Minor Premise:	An educational system that develops the individual and doesn't overemphasize social adjustment is one that promotes independent thought.
Conclusion:	Such a system is one that best allows American society to progress.

Wriston does not present the argument in this order, as the marginal annotations show. Instead, he leads from his minor premise to his major one by defending the idea that "the stimulation and the discipline of the individual" is basic to the "true character of education." Wriston begins with this point probably because many readers believe that social adjustment and vocational training are the chief ends of education and therefore need to be informed, and perhaps persuaded, that education must serve the individual. Wriston, in fact, argues earlier in the same essay that democracy is workable only when "the individual as a physical, intellectual and moral integer is put at the center." Wriston reinforces his defense of his minor premise by stressing, in a later paragraph, that when vocational training is primary, other important needs are undervalued:

> The educative process should never be distorted by the nation's "need" for scientists, or engineers, or doctors, or any other specific profession or skill. Whenever counseling and curriculum stress vocation primarily, they underestimate needs just as vital, though not statistically conspicuous.

Wriston might have begun with his major premise and proceeded to his minor premise and conclusion, or he might have begun with his conclusion and then stated his premises.

The knowledge and beliefs of your readers are decisive. In choosing a pattern or organization for your own deductive argument, you should consider which pattern makes your discussion more understandable and convincing. Usually, your premises need illustration and backing, for statements that you consider true may not seem true to some of your readers (35a). Like Wriston, you may wish to begin with the premise that requires most explanation or defense. Or you may begin with your conclusion (or claim) and proceed to your premises and your explanation of them (or to warrants and backing). Your readers will want to know what these statements mean and why you hold them. Specific facts will increase their understanding and help to persuade them.

2 Organizing inductive arguments

An inductive argument generalizes from particulars of experience—observation, experimentation, analogy, statistical evidence, or causal analysis (34a–e). As with deductive essays, the persuasiveness of an inductive essay depends not only on the worth of the argument but also on its organization. To make your inductive argument convincing, you might begin with experiences or observations that you believe will be of most interest to your readers. You then might proceed to other evidence that supports your thesis and conclude with your most decisive or controversial evidence. As with a deductive essay, you might introduce the thesis of an inductive essay early in the discussion or, if it is a controversial thesis, build up to its introduction later in the paper.

To be persuasive, your inductive essay should appeal to the experience of your readers. The writer of the following passage makes such an appeal in arguing that "women are expected to play a passive role while men play an active one":

> One indication of women's passive role is the fact that they are often identified as something to eat. What's more passive than a plate of food? Last spring I saw an announcement advertising the Indiana University English Department picnic. It read "Good Food! Delicious Women!" The publicity committee was probably jumped on by local feminists, but it's nothing new to look on women as "delectable morsels." Even women compliment each other with: "You look good enough to eat," or "You have a peaches and cream complexion." Modern slang constantly comes up with new terms, but some of the old standbys for women are *cute tomato, dish, peach, sharp cookie, cheese cake, honey, sugar,* and *sweetie-pie.* A man may occasionally be addressed as *honey* or described as a *hunk of meat,* but certainly men are not laid out on a buffet and labeled as women are.
>
> —Alleen Pace Nilsen, "Sexism in English"

Pace writes to an audience familiar with the usage she describes, and she builds the paragraph to evidence she considers most convincing. If she had instead written to an audience unfamiliar with this usage, she might have organized the paragraph in a different way.

Note that most arguments use both inductive and deductive reasoning. Some begin by making generalizations about personal experiences and observations, then make necessary inferences from these generalizations. Both kinds of reasoning can be decisive in developing the thesis.

Checklist: Organizing the Persuasive Essay

1. To what type of audience am I addressing my argument—a special or general one? How much does my audience know about my subject? Do my readers have similar or different opinions on the issue? Do they agree on the point-at-issue in the controversy?
2. Is the nature of my evidence clear? Is the weight given it in my argument clear?
3. Does my evidence support my thesis? Have I limited my thesis to what my evidence shows?
4. In my deductive argument, have I explained, defended, and illustrated my premises? Are my inferences clear?
5. What kind of organization will best persuade my audience? Should I present my thesis early in the essay or build up to its introduction later on?
6. Have I defined the point-at-issue and focused on it throughout the essay?

---

3 Placing the thesis

You should **place the thesis** of your argument where you think it will be most effective. In oral debates, the thesis is almost always stated toward the start. The same is true of written arguments on the pros and cons of an issue. Traditionally, the thesis of persuasive essays follows the introduction and statement of the facts of the case. Arguments in support of the thesis and the refutation of opposing arguments usually follow (see 36d). The conclusion of the essay may restate the thesis in light of the supporting arguments and the refutation of opposing views.

Newspaper and magazine editorials often begin with a statement of the thesis, consistent with the practice of putting important facts and ideas at the beginning of a news story or article. In a persuasive essay, however, opening with the thesis can seem abrupt and awkward. Placing the thesis later in the essay has the advantage of preparing an indifferent or a disagreeable audience for a controversial idea.

36c Appealing to emotion and character

An effective argument appeals fairly to the readers' emotions and character. You **appeal to emotion** in showing how the issue affects your readers' lives. You **appeal to character** in showing your audience that you have presented the facts and treated your opponents honestly and fairly. One of your goals is to arouse your readers' concerns and feelings. Another is to win their trust.

To make your appeals to emotion and character effective, you must first assess your audience. This includes being attentive to their interests and concerns and taking account of the knowledge and assumptions you share with them. You want your readers to see that you are interested in them and that your purpose is to convince them. More importantly, you want to convey your interest in and knowledge of the subject. You cannot expect to gain the interest of your readers if you don't make it clear why the topic interests you.

1 Appeal to your readers' values and concerns. You need not name these values or concerns directly in appealing to emotion. They will be apparent in how you begin your essay and focus on the issue. The following writer begins an essay on homelessness by focusing on facts that should concern the reader:

> Meet the Garage People of Los Angeles. Out West in the land of freeways, they live in hutches meant for cars. The Couch People of South Carolina are not video-prone Yuppies: by night they occupy the sofas of their friends, by day they hit the streets. From New York to Chicago and on to Seattle, a sad, transcontinental horde is taking shape. Bench people snooze in public parks. Beyond the mission soup kitchen, Box people crawl into hovels of

cardboard. On warmer ground lie the People of the Grate. "We are watching a Darwinian struggle for housing," says Robert Hayes, a sympathizer in New York. "And the weak are losing."

> —Tom Mathews, "What Can Be Done?", *Newsweek*,
> March 21, 1988

In his essay, Mathews does not speak to his readers directly about their values or concerns. He instead makes indirect references like the following:

> The strain should disturb everyone. But right now most people seem to prefer fighting over ideological and economic purity to collaborating on a common attack.
> —"What Can Be Done?"

2 Begin with a statistical fact or other information that arouses concern.   A startling statistic can help to make the reader aware of a situation that deserves attention:

> What are housewives if not working women? According to a recent study, the average housewife works 99.6 hours a week at a variety of jobs (purchasing agent, cook, cleaner, economist, chauffeur, etc.) for which the combined hourly pay scales would have earned her an annual salary of $17,351.88 in the 1978 job market.
> —Casey Miller and Kate Swift, "Women and Work"

3 Use images that appeal to the imagination.   Images arouse emotions. They help the reader imagine the world of the homeless in Mathews's essay. Appealing to reason through images that are supported by facts is a fair way of arguing; it permits readers to make their own judgments on the basis of the facts. Images supported by facts also appeal to character. By presenting facts without exaggeration or distortion, the writer gains the reader's trust. Appeals to reason, emotion, and character join in this way.

36d

Analysis of a persuasive essay:
Brenda Wahler, "Let's Enact
Comparable Worth"

You will have occasion to write persuasive essays that make a case for or against a policy or proposal and that answer or refute opponents. This section describes and analyzes a model student essay on an issue of current interest.

Persuasive arguments often follow an organization derived from forensic rhetoric, or spoken arguments in criminal law. Prosecutors and defense lawyers often use this pattern:

- *Introduction* to the issue.
- *Statement of the facts or background* (called the *narration*).
- *Statement of the thesis,* or position to be taken on the issue, and an outline of the argument (*division of proofs*).
- *Arguments supporting the thesis* (called the *confirmation*).
- *Answers to objections* (called the *refutation*).
- *Conclusion,* or review of the confirming arguments and final appeal to the reader's good sense and judgment.

In a persuasive essay, these parts may be combined or presented in an order different from that shown. For example, the facts of the case might be presented as part of the supporting arguments, and the refutation might precede or be combined with the confirmation. Some persuasive essays depend entirely on supporting arguments and do not answer objections.

Following is a description of each of these parts of a persuasive essay, with comments on how they are used in the accompanying model paper on comparable worth by Brenda Wahler.

Introduction
The **introduction** to a persuasive essay will be most effective if you state the issue as concisely as possible. Your essay will not be persuasive unless the reader understands why the issue is worth arguing. When the issue is a long-standing and complex one, the introduction may require more than a few sentences or a paragraph. The introduction should show that the issue affects the reader.

Paragraphs 1–3 Brenda Wahler introduces her argument through an *example:* the disparity in wages of a female secretary and a male traffic attendant working at the same university. Wahler shows that their pay is inequitable. She concludes her introductory *comparison* by asking why American women earn on the average considerably less than American men. In asking this question, Wahler appeals to her readers' sense of fairness and justice.

Narration
The audience must know the facts of your case if you hope to be convincing. As in legal indictments and defenses, the background of the case may be extensive. If the issue is a familiar one, the background often serves as a reminder of the chief facts. Although you can present the **narration** as a unit, you may wish to supply pertinent facts in the introduction and later parts of the essay.

LET'S ENACT COMPARABLE WORTH

Brenda Wahler

Intro-
duction

1   "Sandra" works as a Secretary III at a large university. To get her job, she needed a high school diploma and two years prior experience. She must manage a small office, supervise other clerical employees, order supplies, and keep books in addition to regular clerical duties such as typing and taking shorthand. There are two male and 328 female Secretary III's at the University (Remick 11).

2   "Jack" is a Traffic Guide at the same university. He needed a valid driver's license to get his job. He collects parking fees and directs visitors to parking areas and offices. Seventy-five percent of the Traffic Guides at the university are male (Remick 11).

3   Jack earns a higher salary than Sandra. They work for the same employer and are represented by the same union. Why is it that Sandra, with a job requiring more education, more experience, and more responsibility than Jack's job, earns less than Jack? Why is it that, on a nationwide average, women earn only 63 cents to every dollar earned by men (Beck 22)?

Narra-
tion

4   One reason for the disparity in earnings is that many jobs are, for all practical purposes, segregated by sex. While there is no _legal_ barrier to women or men who wish to enter nontraditional occupations, the fact remains that whether from intentional

573

Thesis Statement

In written arguments that debate pros and cons, the **thesis** often follows the introduction or the narration. Wherever it appears, the thesis must be prominent. Placed early in the essay, it directs your readers through the argument. You may wish to **outline** your argument following your thesis statement as part of your introduction.

Paragraphs 4–5   Wahler presents the background of the issue in her opening paragraphs (paragraphs 4 and 5) as well as later in the essay. Her introductory comparison contains an example of current disparities in the pay of men and women. In paragraph 5, she describes the current situation, quoting a public official on comparable worth. In later paragraphs, Wahler briefly mentions changing patterns of male and female employment in America. Wahler uses her narration in paragraph 4 to lead into the statement of her thesis in paragraph 5: "Comparable worth is a solution to the problem."

Her outline, or division of proofs, follows. Wahler will show that comparable worth has been carefully planned, is "workable," and is fair and equitable. Wahler wins the readers' confidence in showing that she is fully informed on the issue by referring to reliable sources.

Confirmation

Your **confirmation,** or arguments in support of the thesis, may be organized in the manner of inductive, deductive, and mixed arguments. See the discussion of possible arrangements in 35d and 36b.

Paragraphs 6–15   Wahler begins her confirmation in paragraph 6 by proving that comparable worth is tested and uncomplicated. She calls attention to "point factor job evaluation systems" used in business, government, and other fields. This demonstration that comparable worth has been "well thought out" leads to the point-at-issue:

discrimination, conscious and unconscious
social pressure, or any other cause, many
individuals work in jobs dominated by one
sex or the other. When this tendency is combined with the historical pattern of paying
women less than men, the result is the current situation where jobs held mostly by
women tend to pay less than jobs held predominantly by men.

Thesis 5   Comparable worth is a solution to the
problem. In spite of U.S. Commission on
Civil Rights chair Clarence Pendleton, Jr.'s
remark that comparable worth is the "looni-

Division est idea since 'Loony Tunes'" (Pendleton
of proofs 382), comparable worth is in fact a well
thought out, workable idea. In essence, it
attempts to compare unlike jobs in an impartial manner in order to free wage guidelines
of discriminatory features. Different jobs
are broken down into common factors such as
education level needed for the job, responsibility required, physical effort needed,
dangers and hazards, and other conditions or
requirements. Points are assigned to each
factor, and by comparing the results from
various jobs, the relative value of each job
is indicated.

Confir- 6   The reader may think the above method
mation of comparing unlike jobs is an untested and
extremely complicated idea. This is not the
case. Corporate America, the government, and
other institutions have used systems such as
this--called point factor job evaluation
systems--for nearly fifty years (Remick 2;

```
The real question is this: Given evidence that jobs
held predominantly by women tend to pay less than they
are worth, shall the situation be changed, and if so,
how?
```

Wahler interrupts her confirmation to answer five objections raised to comparable worth (paragraphs 7–15). Following this refutation, she returns to her supporting arguments. Since the confirmation contains stronger arguments than the refutation, the reader may forget what these arguments are. Wahler finds a solution in breaking her confirmation so that the refutation leads into her strongest confirming arguments.

Refutation
Refutation, or answer to objections, often follows the confirmation or defense of the thesis. Sometimes the two are combined. The advantage of placing the refutation late in the essay is that answers are in the reader's mind at the end. The order of ideas is important both in the confirmation and refutation. You may choose to begin with the less significant arguments or objection and proceed to the most important. Or, you might begin with an objection of most interest or concern to the audience and proceed to one of less interest or concern.

Paragraphs 7–15 Wahler states and answers five objections to comparable worth.

First objection (paragraph 7) Supporters of comparable worth exaggerate the problem. Actually, no problem really exists. Women leave work because of marriage and children and as a result lose seniority.
Rebuttal Wahler argues that studies show the opposite. Wahler partially restates her thesis in rebuttal:

```
In other words, there is a substantial disparity in
wages that cannot be explained except by the common de-
nominator of women holding many of the lower-paying
jobs.
```

Bergmann). Businesses and government have long needed to compare jobs in terms of their relative values, whether comparing janitors to chauffers or comparing the governor of a state to the chair of the board of a major corporation. The question is not if unlike jobs can be compared. They can and they are. The real question is this: Given evidence that jobs held predominantly by women tend to pay less than they are worth, shall the situation be changed, and if so, how?

Point-at-issue

Refuta-tion

7   Those who feel that there is no reason to change the situation, and thus oppose comparable worth, make several criticisms. First, they deny that there is a problem. They try to explain away differences in pay by saying that women are more likely to leave work to care for children or to follow a spouse in a job transfer, thus hurting their seniority. Critics also suggest that women tend to be less skilled and less educated, and so are employed in more low-paying jobs than are many men. But studies disprove this assertion. In a study done at a large university with a nonacademic support staff of over six thousand people, jobs where more than 70 percent of the personnel were one sex or the other were singled out and compared. When these "sex segregated" jobs were compared (with factors such as seniority and education level compensated for), there was a 20 percent gap between the wages paid in "men's" occupations and those paid in "women's" occupations (Remick 10).

First objection

Second objection (paragraph 8)   Women's jobs are not as important as men's jobs.
Rebuttal   Wahler argues that the decline in wages occurred because women were traditionally paid less than men, not because the work declined in importance.

Third objection (paragraphs 9–11)   Women have "questionable value in the work force."
Rebuttal   Wahler states a number of facts and statistics. She answers the related objection that the disparity in wages can be solved by women entering "high-paying 'nontraditional' occupations," those usually filled by men. She points out that not enough of these jobs exist and attacks the implication that the jobs women do perform are of less value. She is here identifying and rebutting the underlying logic of the argument against comparable worth.

In other words, there is a substantial disparity in wages that cannot be explained except by the common denominator of women holding many of the lower-paying jobs.

Second 8
objection
The next criticism is that jobs held mostly by women are simply not worth as much. This is a very common reason given for the low wages of these jobs. But a very effective rebuttal to this was given in the New York Times of June 3, 1985. It was pointed out that secretarial work was once a field dominated by men, particularly before the turn of the century, and had been considered work with upward mobility, good status, and good pay. All of these benefits have declined in real terms, and this decline parallels the shift from male to female dominance in this area of work. The same thing has happened in the garment trade, in teaching, and in other areas where women have come to dominate jobs that were once considered "men's work" (Miller).

Third 9
objection
Another argument is heard. Not only can differences in pay be explained away, opponents declare, but in fact women themselves are of questionable value in the work force. The reasoning was once given that women were only going to work until they married, or were working merely for a little extra "mad money." But for most women, this is not the case. Even the still-heard argument that the work force is dominated by upper-middle-class women who primarily need "psychic gratification" (Picus) does not hold up. Women work for need as well as for a sense

579

Fourth objection (paragraphs 12–14)   Comparable worth is costly and has a "potential high cost and negative effect on the economy." Wahler argues that, where comparable worth has been adopted, costs have been reasonable. She then corrects several misconceptions and misstatements of fact.

of self-worth. The reality is that in 1950,
70 percent of American households were
headed by men who were the sole supporters
of their family; by 1984, the figure had
plummeted to less than 15 percent (Rosenberg
337).

10   Women are in the work force today because they must be. Some are sole supporters
of a family: divorced women, single parents,
widows. Others have a spouse who is disabled
or unemployed. And even in a more traditional two-adult household, two incomes are
increasingly necessary in order to simply
make ends meet.

11   Therefore, it is clear that women are a
vital part of the work force and are here to
stay. It is also clear that it makes no
sense to downgrade the value of a job simply
because it is normally held by women. It
must furthermore be noted that it would be
impossible to solve the problem by expecting
all working women to enter high-paying "nontraditional" occupations. First, there are
simply not enough openings to accommodate
such a large influx of workers, and second,
the jobs held by many women are valuable.
The world would be a much less satisfactory
place if there were no secretaries, nurses,
lab technicians, elementary school teachers,
or housekeepers.

Fourth 12   Now it is time to deal with the criti-
objection cism that comparable worth is unworkable due
to its potential high cost and negative effect on the economy. Opponents cite predictions of 9.7 percent inflation and tremen-

Rebuttal (paragraphs 12–14)   Wahler uses statistical evidence to correct an important mistatement of fact. Focusing on Clarence H. Pendleton, Jr.'s assertion that comparative worth will cost each state $6.4 billion annually, Wahler cites the cost to Minnesota of $4 million over a four-year period and the cost to Los Angeles of $12 million in a settlement with municipal workers. The state of Washington provides even more decisive evidence: an out-of-court settlement covering approximately 35,000 workers will cost $103 million. Wahler then reminds the reader of her thesis, first introduced in paragraph 5: costs for comparable worth have been reasonable for states and municipalities. Wahler then proceeds to her fifth and final objection.

dous unemployment (Pendleton 384). But in
nations such as Australia, where 30 percent
raises were given in traditional women's occupations to bring about pay equity, no such
dire circumstances arose (Bergmann). Not
only does it appear that the economy can
handle comparable worth pay adjustments, but
also the cost is not as great as critics
like to claim. In the state of Minnesota,
where comparable worth in the public sector
was implemented by legislation, it cost the
state about $11 million a year for four
years. This affected eight thousand workers
and amounted to about 4 percent of the
state's salary budget ("Pay Equity"). The
facts are in stark contrast to Mr. Pendleton's assertion that comparable worth could
cost $6.4 <u>billion</u> per state per year on into
the indefinite future (Pendleton 382)! In
the city of Los Angeles, comparable worth
for municipal workers was achieved through
collective bargaining and will cost the city
a total of $12 million ("Pay Equity"). Simi-
lar relatively reasonable costs have been
true for many of the states that have implemented comparable worth as well as for municipalities such as Colorado Springs, San
Francisco, San Jose, and Spokane (Miller).

13   Another misconception based on the potential for very high costs is that comparable worth must be implemented due to litiga-
tion settlements involving back pay. The
lawsuit of the American Federation of State,
County and Municipal Employees against the

Fifth objection (paragraph 15)   Supply and demand should determine wages.
Rebuttal   Most nurses are female; most lawyers are male. Nurses are in demand but wages have not risen; lawyers are not in demand but their wages have risen.

state of Washington was anticipated by some
to cost as much as a billion dollars if back
pay was awarded for the twelve years it took
to settle the dispute. But the case was settled out of court without back pay, and will
cost $103 million. Considering the settle-
ment will affect some 35,000 workers, the
amount is not as large as it may seem ("Montana's Comp."). If past history is a reliable indicator, the great majority of comparable worth disputes will be settled by
legislation, collective bargaining, or policy decisions--not lawsuits.

14   Another source of misinformation comes
from the fact that billions of dollars are
spent each year on regular pay increases for
workers. Some of the misleading statistics
on the cost of comparable worth come from
studies that include <u>scheduled</u> pay increases
along with the figures for pay equity increases.

Fifth ob- 15   Finally, there is the question of the
jection   impact on the so-called free market. The argument is that wages should be set by supply
and demand, prevailing market conditions,
and so on (Hackett 336). The problem is that
there is no market that is not already influenced by government policy, taxation policy, union agreements, traditional biases
(including sexism), and a host of other factors. In fact, even the "law" of supply and
demand has limits. One can see that in the
field of nursing, for example, where wages
have <u>not</u> in fact risen to the degree necessary to respond to a shortage of qualified

Confirmation **(continued)**

Paragraph 16   Wahler restates her thesis and supports it with three points: (a) comparable worth entails an objective comparison of jobs and values; (b) not all women's jobs will increase in wages; and (c) some men's jobs that are undervalued will also increase.

Paragraph 17   Wahler argues that comparable worth is workable and can be implemented through legislation, negotiation, company policy, union action, and merit pay. She cites AT&T and other corporate success with comparable worth.

nurses. Likewise, in spite of a glut of lawyers that is observable in some areas, lawyers' fees have not shown signs of being
lowered in substantial amounts. It seems
that there are already many factors influ-
encing wages above and beyond the "free
market."

Return
to con-
firma-
tion
16   With comparable worth, different jobs
can be compared on a more objective basis,
eliminating sex, race, and other unfair criteria so that a more truly accurate evaluation is applied to the value of a job. Not
all "women's" jobs may see an increase in
pay, and some "men's" jobs that have also
been traditionally undervalued may see
raises. As mentioned earlier, the procedures
for bringing about equity in wages by comparing unlike jobs have long been in use and
are workable.

17   Comparable worth can be implemented in
several ways. In government, it can be
achieved through legislation, union negotiations, or through executive policy decision
making. In the private sector, unions again
can effectively act to bring about pay equity. Management in the private sector can
also choose to implement comparable worth
for a number of reasons, among them the potential for higher productivity by workers
who have increased morale based on full recognition of the value of the work they do.
Large corporations such as AT&T have already
implemented the policy of comparable worth
and are pleased with the results.

Paragraph 18   Wahler gives facts and the testimony of an economist in support of comparable worth. She uses these facts and testimony as the *grounds* of her argument (see 35d). Her *warrant* for citing these grounds is her statement that "it is moral and just to correct past inequities." Wahler also presents an enthymemic argument (see 35b): if it is "moral and just to correct past inequities," then comparable worth is moral and just.

Paragraph 19   Through the example of Colorado Springs, Colorado, Wahler makes the implicit point that comparable worth is not an untried or radical proposal favored only by women.

Conclusion

The **conclusion** is the place to restate your thesis, review the confirming arguments and the refutation, and make a final appeal to the reader. The length of the conclusion depends on how many ideas you want or need to review.

18   Barbara Bergmann points out, "Nobody's pay need go down. Nor will budgets or profits be wiped out" (112). Existing law prohibits lowering wages for the purpose of achieving pay equity (BNA 116-19). When budgets allow it, comparable worth is implemented along with and in addition to regular salary increases. In areas of budget constraints, comparable worth can still be brought about by making adjustments in pay increases that have already been budgeted for. Although some individuals may be unhappy to see smaller than usual pay increases for a few years, it is not a permanent condition. Furthermore, it is moral and just to correct past inequities, especially when workers in all jobs ultimately benefit from the improved working conditions that can come about from higher morale, lower turnover, and better productivity.

19   A case in point is the city of Colorado Springs, Colorado. Comparable worth has been implemented for municipal workers in that city, and the mayor, a conservative male Republican, has answered criticism in just this fashion: "We did something fair and just, and in return we got ourselves great employee morale, lower turnover, and higher productivity. Isn't that what the private sector is always looking for?" (Picus 5).

Conclu- 20   It can be said that comparable worth is
sion   a promising and logical answer to the problem of the traditional undervaluing of jobs held predominantly by women. It is becoming policy across the country in both liberal

589

Paragraph 20   Wahler restates her thesis and then appeals to conservatives and liberals to take action. She makes a final appeal to end "all discrimination against women in the workplace."

Wahler appeals to reason through a well-constructed and carefully organized argument. She appeals to emotion in making an indirect appeal to her readers' sense of fairness. Throughout the essay she stresses that comparable worth is designed to end discrimination in wages. Wahler appeals to character in showing her readers that she is in command of facts; she also states opposing ideas fully and answers them seriously. Readers opposing comparable worth may be encouraged by her honesty to consider her argument. Appeals to reason, emotion, and character combine effectively in Wahler's essay.

and conservative enclaves. It is a valuable
system worthy of bipartisan support. The
time has come to take this step toward ending once and for all discrimination against
women in the workplace.

WORKS CITED

Beck, Melinda, Gloria Borger, and Diane Weathers.
    "Women's Work--And Wages." Newsweek 9 July 1984:
    22-23.

Bergmann, Barbara R. "Pay Equity--How to Argue Back."
    Ms. Nov. 1985: 112.

Bureau of National Affairs, Inc. The Comparable Worth
    Issue: A BNA Special Report. Washington, DC: BNA
    Books, 1981.

Hackett, Clifford. "Better from a Distance." Commonweal
    31 May 1985: 336+.

Miller, Joyce D. Letter. New York Times 3 June 1982: A18.

"Montana's Comparable Worth Different Than
    Washington's." Bozeman Daily Chronicle 19 Aug.
    1986: 4.

"Pay Equity for Jobs Held by Women: How States and
    Cities Put It into Practice." Christian Science
    Monitor 19 June 1985: 4.

Pendleton, Clarence M., Jr. "Comparable Worth Is Not
    Pay Equity: Loony Tunes and the Tooth Fairy."
    Vital Speeches of the Day 1 Apr. 1985: 382-384.

Picus, Joy. "Comparable Worth Concept Will Prevail."
    Editorial. Los Angeles Times 18 Sept. 1985, sec. 2:5.

Remick, Helen. "Beyond Equal Pay for Equal Work:
    Comparable Worth in the State of Washington."
    Wellesley College, Center for Research on Women,
    May 1978.

Rosenberg, Jan. "Judging on the Merits." Commonweal 31
    May 1985:337-340.

EXERCISES

1. Make notes on the discussion of a current issue, policy, or proposal in recent newspaper and magazine columns, editorials, and letters to the editor. After classifying the evidence you find (e.g., as particulars of experience, analogy, causal analysis, sampling, or given truths), write an essay that summarizes what you consider important arguments for and against the policy or proposal. In organizing your essay, consider the outline of parts given on page 571. Rearrange the parts of your argument in a way that will be most persuasive to the audience you have in mind.

2. First analyze the following argument by Menninger to discover what kind of evidence the author presents for the conclusion. Then write an essay stating the extent of your agreement or disagreement with Menninger. Be careful to clarify the kind of evidence you present for your conclusion.

> Although most of us *say* we deplore cruelty and destructiveness, we are partially deceiving ourselves. We disown violence, ascribing the love of it to other people. But the facts speak for themselves. We do love violence, all of us, and we all feel secretly guilty for it, which is another clue to public resistance to crime-control reform.
>
> —Karl Menninger, "The Crime of Punishment" ∎

Summary

36a   Persuasion and audience.

Consider the nature of your audience in organizing the arguments in your persuasive essay (36a 1–2).

State the point-at-issue and focus on this point throughout your essay (36a 3).

36b   Appealing to reason and organizing the essay.

In writing a deductive argument, choose the most effective organization for your premises and conclusion (36b 1).

In writing an inductive argument, present your evidence in the order that will best convince your audience (36b 2).

In a mixed argument, join deductive and inductive arguments in a way suited to the purpose of the essay and the audience (36b 2).

Introduce your thesis early in the essay unless you have reason to build up to its introduction later on (**36b 3**).

36c To persuade your audience to accept your argument, appeal to their reason and feelings and earn their trust by arguing honestly and fairly.

36d Organize your essay with an introduction, statement of the facts, thesis statement and outline, confirmation or presentation of ideas in support of your thesis, refutation, and conclusion.

In your introduction, state the issue of the essay concisely.

Give the background of the issue, your thesis or proposition, and your outline of the argument toward the beginning of the essay.

Organize your confirming arguments carefully, distinguishing the kinds of argument and evidence.

In your refutation, state and answer objections to your argument honestly and fairly.

In the conclusion, you may restate the thesis, review the confirming arguments and your refutation, and make a final appeal to your readers.

Fallacies in Reasoning 37

□

Errors in reasoning, called **fallacies,** weaken arguments through faulty inferences and unfair appeals to emotion. Fallacies of relevance falsely claim to provide sufficient evidence for the conclusion; fallacies of causation make false inferences about causes and effects; and fallacies of emotion make singular and misleading appeals to emotion. In this chapter, we focus on the many types of fallacies that fall into these three broad classes and discuss ways of avoiding them in your arguments.

You need to be alert to fallacious reasoning in arguments that you read and those of your own writing. Fallacies undermine the credibility of any argument by suggesting to readers that the writer is seeking to manipulate them. Credibility is undermined further when the argument lacks reason or evidence. Sometimes writers and speakers appear to be arguing when in fact they are only voicing their opinions without concern for proper evidence or reasoning. Arguments such as this express nothing more than strong emotion, and the people who write or speak them probably have no wish to conciliate or reach agreement with their opponents. Indeed, many who engage in political campaigns and in debates over capital punishment, abortion, and nuclear disarmament treat their opponents as enemies.

Reason and emotion are not independent faculties. Arguments that appeal to reason usually also appeal to emotion; the ideas that you argue about are usually ones that you care about strongly. It is possible to argue logically and fairly, at the same time showing that you care about the issue. Thus, you can make your arguments effective by avoiding fallacies in your writing.

37a | Fallacies of relevance

Fallacies of relevance occur when the writer claims to provide sufficient evidence for the conclusion but that evidence is in fact insufficient or irrelevant to the argument. There are many different types of fallacies of relevance.

1 Circular definition and reasoning

A **circular definition** uses the term it is seeking to define and thereby provides insufficient information:

> *Militarism* is the idealizing of the *military* caste and the belief that this caste should rule the country.

The word *military* makes this definition circular because it is a form of the word being defined and therefore adds no real meaning to the definition of *militarism*. The phrase *military caste* is also ambiguous: it is not clear whether *caste* refers to members of the armed forces or to those who favor military rule.

Circular definition sometimes occurs because the speaker or writer wants to disguise a belief or to avoid the real point or issue. Note that the term *militarism* may refer to military dictatorship or to military discipline as the ideal of conduct for citizens of a country. It can also refer to the policy that war is the best means to settle disputes between nations. Broad and ambiguous terms are sometimes used by dishonest writers to equivocate or mislead the reader.

595

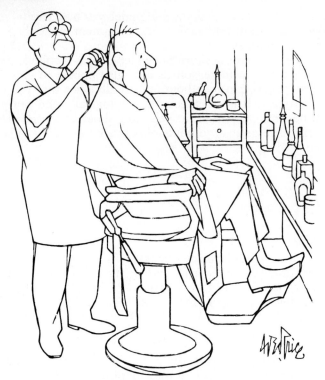

*"There's so much in what you say that I wonder if
I might have thirty minutes or so to digest it."*

Drawing by Geo. Price; © 1983 The New Yorker Magazine, Inc.

Like circular definition, **circular argument** (or **circular reasoning**) gives insufficient evidence for a proposition by restating it in different words and disguising it as evidence:

> *Militarism is a failed* "ism" because use of the *military has failed* as a political policy in the twentieth century.

The second part of this sentence simply restates the first part without giving any evidence in support of the argument.

Circular arguments are particularly hard to spot when metaphor substitutes for literal restatement of the proposition:

> Militarism is a failed "ism" because the "man on horseback" is a failed idea.

The phrase *man on horseback*, a metaphor for military dictator, has essentially the same meaning as *militarism*, and the words *ism* and *idea* also mean the same thing. The sentence does not explain *why* the idea of the "man on horseback" failed.

2 Begging the question

Instead of arguing a question or issue, some writers and speakers **beg the question** by assuming that the idea they are trying to prove is a given truth:

> Isn't your statement obviously biased?

The word *obviously* shows that the speaker believes the statement is biased but provides no evidence to prove that this is true. The following question also begs the question:

> Aren't dirty movies pornographic?

Note that the question is not begged if the opponents have previously agreed on what is pornographic and are judging a particular film by this definition. The question is begged only if the point-at-issue in the debate is the definition of pornography itself (see 36a). The field of argument (see 35d) here establishes a standard of fair and logical debate.

Thus, recognizing this type of fallacy is not difficult when a political candidate refers to his "jackass opponent." But the fallacy is more difficult to recognize when the adjective occupies a less prominent or emphatic position in the statement. Many people who pretend to argue the question actually beg it through loaded words and statements.

In writing your own persuasive essays, you should watch for repetitive words and statements that make your definitions and statements circular and for words and phrases that beg the question you are asking. You should watch also for strong adjectives like *abhorrent* and *barbaric* and adverbs like *obviously* (as in "the obviously barbaric practice of smoking on airplanes") that inappropriately characterize the question or statement. If in doubt, rephrase the question or statement without using adjectives or adverbs.

3 Complex question

A **complex question** forces the listener or reader to answer an *implied* question in the course of answering another. For example, assume you are asked the following question during a debate on building a nuclear power plant in your area:

> Are you in favor of building nuclear power plants near cities, promoting industry and putting people to work?

If you answer no to this question, you have been forced into saying that you oppose industry and the jobs that such a plant will create. The fair way to reason is to ask one question at a time:

> Are you in favor of building nuclear power plants? If so, do you favor building them close to large cities?

The question of industry and jobs probably belongs to another argument. Note again that the question is a fair one if the debaters have reached agreement on the prior question.

4 Hasty generalization

A **hasty generalization** draws conclusions on the basis of unusual or insufficient evidence. Consider again this statement from Chapter 34:

> Elderly people are unsteady drivers.

If you base the statement on your observations of elderly people driving on icy streets, you have leaped to a conclusion without sufficient evidence. Before you can make a fair generalization, you must observe elderly people driving under all types of weather conditions. The same faulty reasoning is the basis of these hasty generalizations:

> Redheads have hot tempers.
> Great Danes have human qualities.

Stereotypes arise from hasty generalizations of this kind:

> Albert Einstein was Jewish; Jews, therefore, must be good in science.
> Michael Jordan is black; blacks, therefore, must be good athletes.

But most stereotypes describe negative qualities:

> Women reporters are rude and aggressive.
> Californians are faddish.

The person making these statements ignores the numerous exceptions or explains them through special circumstances ("she's not yet rude or aggressive because she started reporting last week," "he's not yet faddish because he's lived in Los Angeles a short time"). Once a stereotype is fixed in the mind, it is always possible to find someone who fits the image. Instead of presenting real evidence, the person presents the stereotype as a belief or given truth.

It is important to note that a generalization is unproven if an exception to it cannot be explained. The statement that "the exception proves the rule" does not mean that every rule has an exception; rather, it means that the *apparent* exception or difficult case tells the researcher whether the rule indeed applies to all instances. If the generalization or rule cannot explain the exception, it is not a rule at all. Although scientists formulate theories and stipulate definitions on the basis of incomplete or uncertain evidence, at some point in their investigation they make the decision to take the "inductive leap" and generalize their findings. However, a scientific law must be modified or reformulated if it cannot explain contradictory evidence that appears. Scientists may, however, disagree on whether the evidence constitutes an exception.

Note that the words *maybe, perhaps,* and *possibly* often disguise a hasty generalization to which there are obvious or proven exceptions:

> Great Danes *perhaps* understand words, though not all of them respond to statements they hear.

In your own persuasive essay, you should test your generalizations to be sure that you have given them sufficient support and have not generalized from unusual evidence. When you apply a generalization or a rule to a particular situation, you should verify that the situation is not exceptional. It may not be immediately obvious that the situation is an exception. (See 34a for a more detailed discussion of adequate generalization.)

5 Fallacy of the single case

The **fallacy of the single case,** or "the lonely fact," as David Hackett Fischer refers to it, generalizes on the basis of a single sample that is too small to be representative of the class it attempts to describe. For example, one unhappy experience with a teacher tells you nothing about teachers in general. You cannot make fair judgments about all members of a profession or age or ethnic group on the basis of a single observation or encounter. This type of fallacy often results in stereotypes.

6 Accident

Accident is the fallacy of applying a general truth, law, or regulation to an exceptional or unusual circumstance. We occasionally hear of a law enforced in situations so exceptional or accidental that legislators did not think of excluding it in writing the law. Or the exception was too obvious to be stated. For example, a law forbidding jaywalking obviously excludes intersections under construction. It would be fallacious to reason that a jaywalker had broken the law in this circumstance.

Debates on medical ethics often focus on whether a principle of conduct is in all circumstances applicable. For instance, the debaters might agree that doctors should give patients the facts about their illnesses, but they may disagree on whether the principle applies only to patients able to survive the bad news. In this instance, what is fallacious reasoning depends on recognized exceptions to the law or ethical maxim in the particular field of argument. Note that the standards of one field may conflict with those of another. Lawyers may contest in court the decision of a doctor to withhold information from an "exceptional" patient. In your own essays, note the special standards, laws, or ethical maxims that support your reasoning about a situation or your selection of an instance or example.

7 False analogy

An analogy gives weight to an argument if the similarities between the things being compared are relevant to the conclusion, if the conclusion is drawn from these similarities, and if the differences do not weaken the conclusion (see 34c). A **false analogy** fails to meet one or more of the requirements of an analogy.

Consider the following argument:

> Recruits become soldiers through constant drill and obedience to superiors. Wars could not be fought and won otherwise. Similarly, children become soldiers in the war against ignorance through drill and obedience to their teachers. The war against ignorance could not be won otherwise.

To test the analogy in this argument, you should ask whether differences in age between children and recruits and differences in the aims of military training and education weaken the conclusion. The phrase *obedience to superiors* is crucial. An appeal to experience is indispensable in judging analogies. Do children really learn by following orders, or do they learn by playing an active role, perhaps by questioning and challenging authority? If the latter is the case, the analogy is false.

False analogies are not always so obvious, particularly when they depend on a metaphor that implies a comparison (see 31a). The following statement uses several metaphors in this way:

> Vandalism will continue as long as *Pollyanna* teachers insist on *coddling* the *savages* who are tearing up our schools.

The sexist word *Pollyanna* implies comparison with a sentimental and overly optimistic little girl; the word *coddling* implies that the students, are like infants; and *savages* implies the stereotype of tribal people. In reading the statement, you may be unaware of the false analogies implied by these words, though their intent is clear. Metaphors like these can be insidious in argument when they attempt to shape emotional attitudes.

You may not be aware that your argument contains false analogies. You should watch for words and phrases like *similarly* and *by contrast* that signal comparisons and for metaphorical statements that can mark false analogies. It is important to test each analogy carefully, making sure that you do not make false comparisons between things and that the differences between the things analogized do not weaken the argument.

8 Equivocation

To **equivocate** means to use deliberately ambiguous words to deceive. The word *exceptional*, for example, can mean either excellent in quality or poor in quality. The statement that a performance is "exceptionally interesting" means either the performance was excellent or it was poor: we cannot tell which. The word *unsteady* means physically infirm; it can also mean intoxicated and indecisive. So the campaign statement that a candidate will not give "steady" leadership equivocates by not stating the disqualifications.

601

These are obvious examples. Equivocation is hard to avoid when we want to soften statements through euphemism (see 31c) or disguise our feelings or opinions. The language of diplomacy easily falls into equivocation. Politicians resort to it in promising to give an issue "the attention it deserves." Even though they may mean that the issue will be given no attention at all, they don't say this. When diplomats fail to reach agreement or when they exchange angry words, they report their meeting as "serious and useful." Language that equivocates also begs the question.

At times, loosely defined or indefinite terms create **unintentional ambiguity.** You may not realize that you have used an ambiguous term until a reader or opponent in a debate calls your attention to it. Sometimes ambiguity exists without either you or your opponent recognizing it. This situation occurs with popular terms so wide and loose that they serve everyone in the debate. The term *irresponsible* is an example. In a debate over governmental spending, one person may consider an increase in welfare payments irresponsible, whereas the other person may consider an increase in weapons spending irresponsible. But both persons agree on the need for "responsible government." Such broad agreement may relieve conflict, but it does not conciliate. Indeed, conciliation is probably not the intention of either speaker.

In writing a persuasive essay, you will find your dictionary indispensable in deciding whether key words in your argument are ambiguous or equivocal. If in doubt about the possible meanings of a word, consult the synonym listing in your dictionary.

9 False dilemma

A **false dilemma** presents only two alternative solutions to a problem and ignores all other alternatives. The words *either/ or* often mark a false dilemma in argument:

> *Either* we drill for oil wherever necessary—even in national forests—*or* we run out of energy by the end of the century.

This statement asks you to reach a conclusion on the basis of incomplete grounds or evidence. The statement deliberately neglects to mention alternative energy sources such as solar energy so as not to draw your attention to them. One way to show this dilemma is false is to mention several alternative energy sources (solar energy, thermal energy). Another way to refute the dilemma is to show that one or both of the proposed alternatives are false. In showing that they are false, you are not proving that another alternative exists. Nor are you required to do so.

Fair arguments identify all serious possibilities and proposals and weigh them. In developing a fair argument, you need to identify the proposed alternatives and then give reasons why some of them are not feasible. This identification is the job of refutation in pro and con arguments (see 36d). In identifying nonfeasible alternatives, you also gain the advantage of anticipating the possible objections to your own argument.

10 Irrelevant conclusion

An **irrelevant conclusion** fails to address the point-at-issue in an argument and instead affirms another unrelated or irrelevant idea. What is irrelevant, though, depends on the specific issue in the debate.

Consider, for example, a debate over college parking lots: Should the lots, particularly those close to classroom buildings, be open to students and faculty alike? A debater in favor of separate parking lots argues that the college has an obligation to provide sufficient parking space for its faculty and students. A debater opposed to separate parking lots argues that the college should introduce bus service on campus. Although both propositions may be worth debating in their own right, they are irrelevant to the point-at-issue.

To state an irrelevant conclusion is to win assent not for the specific proposition but rather for an idea or conclusion that the writer knows is not controversial. Such diversions often explain sudden shifts in subject or point of view or are used to divert the audience's attention away from the point-at-issue.

11 Argument from ignorance

An **argument from ignorance** reasons incorrectly that a proposition is true simply because it has not been disproved. For example, those who claim that earth is being visited regularly by UFOs often argue that no proof *against* UFOs exists. Such reasoning is also basic to the theories that the government is concealing proof of UFOs to prevent national panic or to gain a military advantage. Those arguing often attempt to shift the burden of proof for or against the proposition to their opponents.

An argument from ignorance is difficult to combat in debate when one party to the argument accuses another of hiding the truth or of being part of a conspiracy. Because conspiracies depend on secrecy, the person accused cannot always provide evidence of innocence. In these instances, the accuser may attempt to shift the burden of proof to the accused, in this instance proof of innocence. As with the other fallacies dis-

---

Checklist: Fallacies of Relevance

1. In defining a word, have I made my definition circular by using a form of the word? Have I reasoned in a circular way by restating in different words a proposition I am trying to prove?
2. Have I begged the question under debate by assuming as true what I am trying to prove?
3. In asking a question, have I forced my reader to answer "yes" or "no" to a question that is not under discussion?
4. Have I generalized on the basis of insufficient evidence or from a single inadequate example?
5. Have I generalized on the basis of exceptional circumstances that require special consideration?
6. In arguing by analogy, are the points of similarity relevant to my conclusion? Are there significant differences between the things analogized that weaken the analogy?
7. Have I equivocated in my argument by using vague or ambiguous words?
8. Have I forced my reader to choose between two alternatives when more than two exist?
9. Have I failed to address the point-at-issue in an argument and instead argued an irrelevant point?
10. Have I argued falsely that an idea must be true because no one has disproved it?

cussed in this chapter, it is easy to argue from ignorance in attempting to prove something for which no evidence exists.

37b | Fallacies of causation

Fallacies of causation wrongly identify or simplify causes and effects. These fallacies are among the most common in argument.

1 *Post hoc* fallacy

The ***post hoc* fallacy** assumes that one event is the cause of another event on the sole basis that the first happens before the second. For example, if the stock market crashes following a record heat wave, then the heat wave must have caused the crash. The name of this fallacy is short for the Latin *post hoc, ergo propter hoc,* meaning "after this, therefore because of this."

Causal analysis looks for other conditions that contributed to the event. Scientists know enough about some physical events like snowfalls and even earthquakes to point to a number of conditions necessary to cause them to happen. But scientists cannot say that a heavy snowfall or earthquake will always occur when these conditions are present (see 34d). Analysis of stock prices has a lower degree of probability because the range of possible conditions is wider and human acts play a role. Temporal relationship, the basis of the *post hoc* fallacy, is only one necessary condition among many in the analysis of an event. It is never the cause.

Stereotypes and prejudices can arise from *post hoc* fallacies. For instance, if the crime rate rises at the same time large numbers of immigrants enter a city, some people may point to the immigrants as the cause of the rise in crime, ignoring other possible causes or conditions such as a lack of jobs. Notice that a decrease in the crime rate probably would not be credited to these same immigrants.

2 Fallacy of reduction

The **fallacy of reduction,** related to the "fallacy of the single case" (37a), singles out one cause without considering other

605

possible causes. A variety of causes produces a fall in stock prices or a disastrous oil spill or the bombing of an embassy or the rise or fall in the rate of inflation. But politicians often believe it is advantageous in debate to reduce events to a single cause, perhaps to the act of a single person. Thinking in a reductive way is merely a way of looking for easy solutions to complex problems.

In writing your own arguments, you may want to single out a particular cause or effect to discuss it in depth and focus the readers' attention. But it is important also to tell your readers that other causes exist that are outside the scope of your discussion. When you do cite several contributing causes, don't make the serious mistake of discussing them as if they were equally significant. Your decision to attend college was undoubtedly shaped by a number of causes, not all of them of the same importance. In discussing causes, then, be sure to weigh them and to indicate their relative importance.

Statements of cause and effect are sometimes hard to spot in argument. Words like *because, since, so, then,* and *therefore* often identify them. After identifying these statements in your writing, you should check them for the faults described in this section.

37c Fallacious appeals to emotion

Fallacies of emotion are often hidden in adjectives and adverbs that color your statements. Your language need not be emotionally neutral for your argument to be fair and objective, but appeals to emotion should have the support of reason.

1 *Argumentum ad hominem*

Argumentum ad hominem, in Latin the "argument to the man," attacks the proposer of an idea or policy to avoid dealing with the idea or policy directly:

> What kind of Neanderthal would want to open federal lands to oil exploration? No one except a dummy blind to the consequences.

The person making this attack "poisons the well," for discussion of the issue becomes impossible once motives are attacked. The purpose of the statement is obviously to make the character of the proposer the issue. Of course, character may be a legitimate issue in a political campaign. It is not the issue in a debate over oil leases.

An argument is also *ad hominem* if it appeals to the special interest or situation of the listener or reader. The person trying to win approval for oil drilling on federal lands is engaging in *ad hominem* argument in referring to or hinting at the profits to be made by drillers and oil company stockholders in the audience.

We would not be discussing this fallacy if name-calling and appeals to special interests were not effective in debate. They are effective because they confirm the beliefs of people who agree with the attacker and dispose bystanders to the argument to join the winning side. Clearly the attack is on reason itself. The gain in *ad hominem* arguments may be short-lived, however, once the emotional attack is forgotten and the audience realizes that the issue still remains to be solved.

Your own arguments will be effective if you examine the proposal on its merits, without attacking your opponent's character or suggesting bad motives. Diverting attention from the proposal suggests that you are doubtful of its merits.

2 *Argumentum ad populum*

Argumentum ad populum —in Latin an "argument to the people"—is an appeal to popular feeling or social, racial, sexist, or religious prejudice. In stating qualifications for political office, a candidate may refer to having been born in the area or may pay tribute to a widely admired local citizen or politician. Negative appeals are possible, too. The candidate may hint at family connections that dispose the audience against the opposing candidate, perhaps referring to the opponent's enormous wealth or to a parent who made a "fortune in oil."

Appeals to patriotic feeling are proper when they do not substitute for serious argument over public issues. No public address is without appeal to the interests and loyalties of the audience, but these appeals must be open and fair. And they must not substitute for serious discussion or introduce irrelevant evidence.

3 Appeal to force

An **appeal to force** is a threat, open or veiled. Open threats are often designed to make rational discussion impossible, as in Adolf Hitler's statement to the Austrian chancellor in 1938, threatening to use his storm troopers and Nazi supporters in Austria to take over the country:

> Listen, you don't really think you can move a single stone in Austria without my hearing about it the next day, do you? . . . I have only to give an order, and in one single night all your ridiculous defense mechanisms will be blown to bits. You don't seriously believe that you can stop me for half an hour, do you? . . . I would very much like to save Austria from such a fate, because such an action would mean blood. After the Army, my S.A. and Austrian Legion would move in, and nobody can stop their just revenge—not even I.
>   —William L. Shirer, *The Rise and Fall of the Third Reich*

Veiled threats are more subtle than open ones, particularly when they appeal to self-interest. "Those who are not with us are against us," the speaker or writer implies in suggesting that our support for another candidate would be a dangerous act. Once the threat of force enters a debate, the issue is seldom decided on the basis of reason.

4 Linking

Linking occurs when you connect a revered person (such as Thomas Jefferson or Helen Keller) with an issue without stating why that person would approve or disapprove of the connection. We find this appeal frequently in advertising and politics.

If the opinion of the revered person is pertinent to the issue, then the link is legitimate. The opinions of former presidents and other officials are pertinent in a discussion of American involvement in Central America or the Middle East. If these opinions are left unexplained or constitute the only evidence for the conclusion, they are considered fallacious.

Supporting your statements with references to revered men and women of the past may give your readers the impression that your argument is weak. Appeals to force and authority can create the same impression.

5 Appeal to authority

An **appeal to authority** asks us to agree with a position on the basis of an expert—perhaps a respected historian or scientist—whose knowledge of the issue is presumably superior to ours. An appeal to authority is fallacious when it constitutes the only evidence for the conclusion.

It is common in literary discussions to refer to literary authorities, scholars and critics who have written extensively about William Shakespeare or T. S. Eliot or Emily Dickinson. Scholars and critics may provide us with reliable facts necessary in interpreting plays and poems; however, their opinions cannot be taken as the sole evidence for the meaning of a play or poem, at least not without presenting their evidence and explaining why it is worth citing. In writing essays for a course in literature, you may cite a writer on the subject in *support* of your interpretation. But the citation should not be your sole evidence. The major interpretation of the work should be your own.

The same guideline applies for essays written in other courses. You will need to cite the facts provided by historians and political and social scientists. But their interpretations of these facts cannot and should not substitute for your own analysis and discussion. (See 40a on the use of primary and secondary evidence in documented papers.)

EXERCISE

Identify one or more fallacies in each of the following statements. Then write what you consider a fair statement of each argument or proposal.

1. Teddy Roosevelt, a great outdoorsman and conservationist, would have supported my proposal to drill for oil in Yellowstone.
2. We must drill for oil on federal lands because people are not conserving enough gas.
3. Do you support the idea that America can go on squandering natural resources without paying a higher price for fuel later on?
4. New sources must be found because we need new supplies of fuel.
5. We need to oppose the landgrabbers and special interests supporting this bill to drill on federal lands.

6. Are you in favor of guaranteeing the future of your children by supporting research in solar energy?
7. Either we find new fuels, or we all start walking to work.
8. Why do we need to drill on federal lands? We need to find new sources of energy. And abundant sources exist on federal lands.
9. Exploitation means letting people exploit natural resources for their personal gain without regard to the public interest.
10. The unanimous vote on the bill in the recent session of Congress shows that the American people—man, woman, and child—support this stand.
11. If schools continue to harbor vandals and delinquents, they should be run as zoos are.
12. The diplomatic corps is good training for an advertising agency.

Summary

37a   Fallacies of relevance.

Don't make your definition circular by using the term you are defining (37a 1):

Circular Definition
Militarism is the idealizing of the *military* caste and the belief that this caste should rule the country.

A circular argument gives insufficient evidence for a proposition by restating it in different words (37a 1):

Circular Reasoning
Militarism is a failed "ism" *because the military has failed* as a political policy in the twentieth century.

Don't beg the question by assuming as true the idea you are proving (37a 2):

Unfair
Isn't that movie obviously pornographic?

Don't use complex questions that force a person to answer an implied question in answering the question asked (37a 3):

Complex Question
Do you favor building nuclear plants that put people to work?

Don't use hasty generalizations that reason on the sole basis of untypical or exceptional evidence **(37a 4)**:

Hasty Generalization
Redheads have hot tempers.

Don't generalize from a single case or apply a principle or regulation to an exceptional instance **(37a 5–6)**.

Watch for false analogies in which the similarities are not pertinent to the conclusion and the differences weaken the conclusion **(37a 7)**.

Avoid ambiguous words that make statements equivocal **(37a 8)**:

Equivocation
The performance is *exceptionally* interesting.

Don't force the reader to choose between two alternatives or solutions when other alternatives exist **(37a 9)**:

False Dilemma
Either we drill for oil in national forests, or we run out of energy by the end of the century.

In arguing a point, give reasons that address the issue under discussion, not reasons that support another **(37a 10)**.

Don't assume that something is true because it has not been disproved **(37a 11)**:

Argument from Ignorance
UFOs have visited earth because no one has shown they haven't.

37b Fallacies of causation.

Don't assume that one event is the cause of another merely because the first one happens before the second **(37b 1)**:

***Post hoc* Fallacy**
The stock market crashed following a record heat wave; the heat wave must have caused the crash.

Consider other possible causes of an event instead of attributing it to a single cause **(37b 2)**.

37c Fallacious appeals to emotion.

Attack the reasoning of an opponent, not the opponent's character or motives **(37c 1)**:

Argumentum ad hominem
What kind of Neanderthal would open federal lands to oil exploration?

Don't appeal to popular feeling or prejudice to win your argument **(37c 2)**.

Don't use appeals to force—open or veiled threats—designed to make reasoned argument impossible **(37c 3)**.

Don't link a revered person with an issue without saying why the person would approve or disapprove the connection **(37c 4)**:

Vague
Thomas Jefferson would have supported oil exploration on federal lands.

Don't ask your reader to agree with a view or position merely because you refer to or quote an authority **(37c 5)**.

PART NINE

THE
RESEARCH
PAPER

Planning the Research Paper 38

Part Nine focuses on the research paper, one of the most important kinds of writing you will do in college and later. In this chapter, we concentrate on how to find a subject and locate source materials in the college library. The remaining chapters in Part Nine describe how to evaluate source materials, how to integrate them into the paper, and how to document sources using MLA, APA, and CBE styles of documentation. Chapter 42 contains a sample research paper that illustrates methods of research and MLA parenthetical documentation.

38a | The nature of research

When you conduct **research**, you gather information about a subject to analyze a problem or argue a thesis. The information you gather comes from a wide range of sources, including systematic observation, experimentation, interviews, government documents, articles, books, and letters. In the course of investigation, you evaluate and interpret the evidence gathered and perhaps test earlier findings and theories in light of it. Scientific research today is usually a collaboration of specialists who combine their knowledge and experience in investigating a problem. In your science courses, you may have an opportunity to collaborate with other students in investigating a problem. Usually, though, college research is on an assigned topic that you work on independently.

The **research** or **documented paper** has an important place in every field of study. Many of your college courses will require research papers, each having a different purpose and approach and using special source materials. For example, a research paper on tranquilizing drugs would vary in these ways in different courses of study:

- In a paper for a psychology course, you might investigate the use of tranquilizing drugs to treat mental disorders. To compare the action of the drugs with other therapies, you would draw on articles and books by psychologists, biochemists, and others in the field who deal with mental disorders and come to some conclusions. Your research may also include interviews and a statistical study.

- In a paper for a sociology course, you might investigate the social effects of common tranquilizers. To document these effects, you would compare published reports of case workers and psychotherapists. You might also interview a drug counselor at a local clinic.

- In a paper for a chemistry course, you might investigate recent advances in tranquilizing drugs. You might report on important chemical experiments that test the reliability of the drugs.

- In a paper for an English or philosophy course, you might examine ethical arguments for and against the use of tranquilizing drugs in treating troubled children.

Researchers in every field value accuracy, precision, and original thought. But the same researchers work with different evidence and collect, evaluate, and present it in different ways. The research papers that you write in some of your college courses will acquaint you with the evidence used in the particular field and the uses made of it. Each paper will require you to ask different questions and use different methods of research. However, the process of choosing a subject, limiting it, defining the purpose of your investigation, and searching for source materials is generally the same in all fields. Although the process of finding source materials is somewhat different from the possible invention techniques described in section 2d, you will have the opportunity to engage in brainstorming, clustering, and similar activities while writing research papers. You will also need to write several drafts of your research paper and revise and edit them.

38b Choosing a topic

1 General guidelines

In your college courses, a topic may be assigned for research or you may choose the topic with the advice of your instructor. Your research will be most effective if you take the time to do the following preliminary activities.

Clarify the purpose of your research. Whether your topic is assigned or one of your own choosing, you need to determine your purpose in writing: Is it to inform your readers about the subject, to verify the information about the subject, or to use this information to argue a point?

Define your audience and gauge its knowledge of the subject. If you are writing to a general audience unfamiliar with the subject, you will need to gather details on the background of the subject and of technical matters needed to understand the ideas you are presenting. This information will also be of use in reminding readers familiar with the subject of important background and technical details. Special readers in a particular field probably will expect additional technical evidence. You will want to collect sufficient information to serve any needs that arise in the course of drafting the paper.

Choose a topic and source materials that fit the assignment. The purpose of research assignments in introductory college courses is to acquaint you with the methods of research and source materials used in various fields. Your instructors do not expect you to make the advanced contribution to knowledge expected in a thesis or dissertation. Rather, they want you to choose a topic appropriate to the field, develop a limited thesis, and support it with appropriate source materials. If in doubt, discuss your choice of topic and possible source materials with your instructor before beginning your research.

Choose a topic of interest to you. A research paper presents an opportunity to investigate a topic that interests you strongly. The more the topic engages your interest, the more effective your research and paper will be.

Have a clear idea of the materials to be used. Determine whether your instructor wants you to use only **primary sources**—eyewitness accounts and writings by participants in an event—or to supplement them with **secondary sources**, which evaluate and interpret primary sources.

Limit the scope of your research. The scope of your research paper depends on the assignment and on the availability of source materials. At some point in planning your paper, though, you want to limit the scope of your research. If your topic is too broad, your research may require a vast number of sources impossible to evaluate and interpret in the time you have to complete the assignment. This limitation will continue in the course of drafting and revising the paper, as you discover points that you wish to develop in depth or new ideas suggested by your material.

Choose materials that you can work with. Technical subjects may call for a knowledge of technical terms and ideas. Scan your source material to be certain that you understand the subject and are able to discuss it knowledgeably.

Be objective in your selection of materials. In doing research for an argumentative paper, for instance, look for materials that support a range of views on the subject, not just a single view or your own view. Research gives you an opportunity to consider all the facts of a case. Persuasive writing is most effective when you consider other views and objections and prepare to answer them.

Plan your research. Because the process of research is often complex, you will find it helpful to work with a schedule that details the target date for completion of each step, such as when you will search for materials and when you will write the paper. This schedule will also help you to decide whether you have time to search elsewhere for source materials not available in your college library.

Checklist: First Steps in Research

1. Define the purpose of the research project.
2. Define the audience for your paper and gauge its knowledge of the subject.
3. Make a preliminary search for materials.
4. Limit the topic.
5. Compile a bibliography of source materials.
6. Collect and evaluate these materials.
7. Develop a working thesis.
8. Make out a tentative schedule.

2 A topic suggested by reading

If you are asked to choose a topic for a research paper, one may be suggested by the reading you do in the course. George Bernard Shaw's play *The Doctor's Dilemma* (1904) suggested several research topics to a researcher we will call Mary Smith—assigned a research paper in a course in the literature of medicine. In the play and the preface he wrote to it later, Shaw satirizes doctors who charge high fees for removing nonexistent organs, misapply the discoveries of medical science, and protect themselves from public exposure. Although most of the doctors in the play respect science, they are ignorant of it. Shaw admits in his preface that there are a "few intelligent doctors who point out rightly that all treatments are experiments on the patient."

Mary began her search for a topic by considering some questions that arose while discussing the play in class:

How true a picture of nineteenth-century and early
    twentieth-century doctors does Shaw give in the
    play?

How much did doctors in the nineteenth century know
    about the causes of disease?

Shaw says in the preface that doctoring "is not
    even the art of keeping people in health...."

Doctoring is "the art of curing illnesses." How
did doctors try to cure illnesses? Were they concerned about preventing illness?

It occurred to Mary that she might investigate Shaw's suggestion that the best doctors in his time relied on practical experience rather than on instruments and questionable scientific
theory. If nineteenth-century accounts of medical practice
were available, she might be able to test Shaw's idea with firsthand evidence. Finding out how nineteenth-century doctors
treated illness might incidentally provide insight into some aspect of present-day medicine.

Mary had a general topic and a particular audience in
mind—her classmates and instructor. Mary's topic was a broad
one. She still had to narrow her focus and define the aim or
purpose of her study with greater exactness. A preliminary
search of the library might suggest a possible limitation. She
would also have to read the source materials she found to
narrow her topic further.

 A preliminary search

Mary Smith began her search for a topic at her college
library. Like Mary, once you select a topic for research, you
want to be sure that your college library contains adequate
source materials. To be adequate, these materials should be
diverse in approach toward the subject. If an event you want
to investigate is a recent one, your library may not have sufficient materials for you to work with; and your investigation
is not likely to be rewarding if you have available only a few
recent newspaper and magazine articles. The library also may
not have materials on highly specialized topics. If your college
library has an interlibrary loan service, you may be able to
borrow materials from other libraries (see 39f). However, you
need to be sure you have enough time to secure materials
through an interlibrary loan.

Your preliminary search for source materials should begin
with the subject catalog or on-line catalog, periodical indexes,
specialized bibliographies, and other reference books in your
college library (see 39a–f). You will find guides to reference

sources, like Eugene P. Sheehy's *Guide to Reference Books*, of particular value. During this preliminary search, you have the opportunity to limit and refine your topic.

Mary found that her college library contained several general reference works on nineteenth-century medicine and two general studies of nineteenth-century disease epidemics. A nearby medical library contained books by nineteenth-century doctors on epidemic diseases as well as some nineteenth-century medical journals. All of these sources would be useful in Mary's study of nineteenth-century medical practices.

Checklist: Sources Listing Available Materials

1. *Library of Congress Subject Headings*
2. Subject catalogs, on cards or on-line
3. Guides to reference books
4. Periodical indexes
5. Specialized bibliographies

 38d Limiting the topic

How broad or narrow should your initial topic and search for source materials be?

You may want to broaden the topic or instead limit your original topic as you discover new materials and a new focus. It is often advantageous to begin your search with a broad subject and narrow it gradually. A broad investigation acquaints you with the background of the subject and suggests numerous topics for investigation, some perhaps more promising than the topics you originally had in mind. Further reading may still suggest other topics or a revision of the one you are working with.

The extent to which you limit a topic depends on the purpose of your investigation. Failure to define purpose often leads to wasted effort in finding a suitable subject. For example, if your purpose is to find the facts of a case and thereby illuminate current debate, you may spend needless time searching for materials that express opinions but present no facts. Of course, both your purpose and limited topic may change in the course of searching for and then reading source materials. But you should have a purpose in mind at each stage of your search.

With a limited topic and a specific purpose in mind, you are ready to consider ways of searching for relevant source materials. The more exactly Mary Smith defined her purpose, the easier it was for her to select a topic and search for source materials. Reviewing the topics discussed in class and jotting down other questions and topics in the course of further reading proved indispensable to Mary. She decided to use Shaw's play *The Doctor's Dilemma* as the springboard for an investigation of nineteenth-century medicine—specifically, the assumptions that doctors made about disease in treating patients. Mary decided that she would use Shaw's play to introduce the topic and to focus on the thinking and behavior of nineteenth-century doctors.

Mary Smith's preliminary search and reading suggested to her that investigating nineteenth-century medical practice was a broad undertaking requiring information on a wide range of topics. But she found that the topic could be limited in various ways:

Broad Focus	Narrow Focus
Nineteenth-century medical practice	Medical practice during epidemics
Cholera	Cholera epidemics in England and the United States, 1832-1860
Theories of disease	Theories of cholera
Implications for medicine	Implications for nineteenth-century medical practice

On the basis of her search, Mary narrowed the broad topic *nineteenth-century medical treatment* to the more specific and manageable topic *treatment of cholera in England and the United States from 1832 to 1860.* Information on cholera epidemics would serve as background, providing a basis for understanding the medical treatment in the nineteenth century and possibly today.

Treatment of cholera in England and America during a specific period of time was a good choice for a research paper for the following reasons:

- An investigation of medical treatment in the nineteenth century would require a representative sample of medical accounts describing the treatment of a specific disease (see 34b).
- Reputable studies of the history of cholera in England and the United States as well as firsthand accounts of scientists and medical doctors are available.
- The availability of reliable secondary sources on the topic would help in interpreting the writings of doctors and observers.
- A study of medical views in epidemic years would be broad enough to support a generalization about nineteenth-century medical practice.

In choosing her topic, Mary knew that her findings would not be conclusive. At best she could hope to reach a limited understanding of the thinking of the nineteenth-century doctor, and she might also be able to make a qualified judgment about Shaw's view of the doctor. A study reaching broader conclusions and judgments was beyond what the assignment called for. It also required special competence in interpreting medical evidence.

Consider the relevance of the source materials you collect in light of one or more tentative topics and the purpose of your research. The worth of the materials you gather for a research paper depends on the purpose you have in mind. Some of the source materials you collect may contain important background that may prove decisive in changing your readers' opinions. Some may prove interesting in their own right but will have no direct bearing on your topic. However, these materials may encourage you to reconsider your topic and purpose. The materials themselves may surprise you, suggesting a topic you could not have formulated at the start of your research. This source of information might be the focus of an even more limited topic, one of even greater importance and interest to you. Thus, it is essential to have your purpose in mind as you proceed from stage to stage, even if you later redefine it or change the focus of your investigation.

EXERCISES

1. Suggest several possible ways to limit one of the following topics in light of a specific purpose—for example, to give information, to analyze a problem, or to argue a thesis:
   a. television news
   b. the reporting of national elections
   c. the influence of political commentators
   d. television news and newspaper or magazine reporting
   e. the image of politicians on television and in movies
2. List several topics for investigation suggested by a novel or play you have recently read or seen performed. Be ready to discuss possible uses to which this investigation might be put and how you would proceed with the investigation in the beginning stages.
3. Investigate the source materials available for a paper on the nuclear power accident at Three Mile Island near Harrisburg, Pennsylvania, in April of 1979, or the accident at Chernobyl in the Soviet Union on April 25, 1986. What source materials are listed in your library's catalog, indexes, and other reference works?

Summary

38a Choose a research strategy that will help you gather information about a subject.

38b Clarify the purpose of your research and have a clear idea of the source materials to be used.
Choose a topic and source materials that fit the assignment.

38c Conduct a preliminary search for source materials.

38d Limit your topic in light of the available materials.

Finding Source Materials

39

Following your preliminary search and initial limiting of topic, you are ready to compile a **working bibliography** of articles and books pertinent to your subject. The best place to begin is the reference area of your college library, which contains a card or on-line catalog and various reference books that will guide you to the source material available on your topic. This can be an unnecessarily time-consuming job if you are unfamiliar with the resources of the library and how to use them. In this chapter, then, we focus on how to use the library catalog, indexes, abstracts, bibliographies, and other reference works to gather sources for your working bibliography. You should also consult your college librarian for information on the library's collection and the resources available for doing research.

39a | Using the library catalog

The library catalog contains information on the books available in the library. If your library uses a **card catalog**, you will probably find separate catalogs for subject, author, and title. If your library uses an **on-line catalog** (see 39a 4), you will find separate terminals for author and title and for subject searches. To compile a working bibliography for a research paper, it is usually best to begin with the **subject catalog**.

1 Library of Congress subject headings

What headings will you find books listed under in the subject catalog?

Most subject catalogs classify the library's book holdings by headings listed in *Library of Congress Subject Headings (LCSH)*, a set of reference books usually available in the reference or catalog area of the library. *LCSH* is an invaluable tool in finding source materials. A search of the subject catalog under LC headings will not only tell you what books the library contains on your subject but will also suggest other headings under which books on your subject may be classified. The accompanying figure is an excerpt from *LCSH* that shows the subject headings related to Mary Smith's topic *cholera*. Notice the general heading *Cholera, Asiatic* (the heading that Mary searched under) and the LC classification letters under which books on Asiatic cholera are shelved in the library. The break-

Sample LCSH entry.

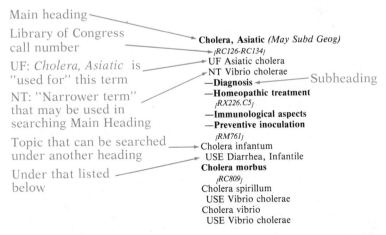

Main heading

Library of Congress
call number

UF: *Cholera, Asiatic* is
"used for" this term

NT: "Narrower term"
that may be used in
searching Main Heading

Topic that can be searched
under another heading

Under that listed
below

Cholera, Asiatic *(May Subd Geog)*
  [RC126-RC134]
UF Asiatic cholera
NT Vibrio cholerae
  —**Diagnosis** ◄——— Subheading
  —**Homeopathic treatment**
    [RX226.C5]
  —**Immunological aspects**
  —**Preventive inoculation**
    [RM761]
Cholera infantum
  USE Diarrhea, Infantile
Cholera morbus
  [RC809]
Cholera spirillum
  USE Vibrio cholerae
Cholera vibrio
  USE Vibrio cholerae

625

down of topics lists the general classification numbers for special studies of cholera as a disease. Although *LCSH* does not list specific book titles, its general classification numbers are helpful in searching the library stacks.

Scan other columns of *Library of Congress Subject Headings* for other pertinent headings. And do the same in searching the card or on-line catalog. You probably will find valuable materials listed under several classifications.

2 Recording information

From the catalog card or on-line catalog screen, you can learn whether a book suits your needs, or you may discover that you excluded a book that is pertinent to your research.

In collecting source materials for her paper, Mary Smith found catalog cards on two specific studies of cholera and one general study of social behavior in the college library (see the accompanying figure). The first two cards give information about author, book title, publisher, date and place of publication, LC and Dewey Decimal call numbers, and a physical description of the books. The card for Margaret Pelling's *Cholera, Fever and English Medicine, 1825–1865* gives additional information about the content of the book and the series in which it is published. The **tracings**—a list of general headings near the bottom of the card under which the book is also filed in the catalog—give even more information about the contents of Pelling's book. The third card illustrates a listing of a book by title rather than by author or editor.

When you find titles pertinent to your research topic in the library card or on-line catalog, you need to record certain information about the books and make other related searches in the catalog before organizing your working bibliography.

Record the complete call number of a book. You will need the **call number** of a book to request it or to look for it in the library stacks. It is important to take the time to record this number accurately, so you won't have to spend needless time searching the library catalog later on. In addition to the call number, record any information pertaining to the location of the material in special collections of the library.

Record the author, title, and publication data. Take the time now to record accurately the author's name, the book title and subtitle, the publisher, and the place and date of publi-

Sample cards from a library catalog.

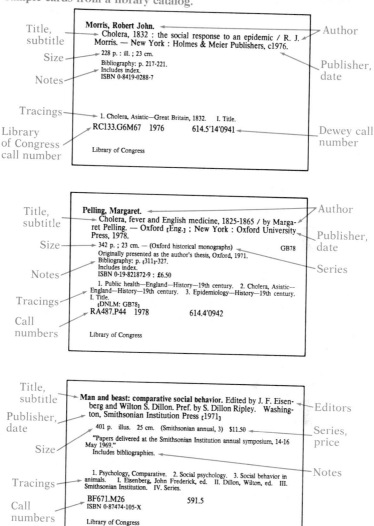

Title, subtitle
Size
Notes
Tracings
Library of Congress call number

Morris, Robert John.
Cholera, 1832 : the social response to an epidemic / R. J. Morris. — New York : Holmes & Meier Publishers, c1976.
228 p. : ill. ; 23 cm.
Bibliography: p. 217-221.
Includes index.
ISBN 0-8419-0288-7

1. Cholera, Asiatic—Great Britain, 1832.   I. Title.
RC133.G6M67   1976   614.5′14′0941

Library of Congress

Author
Publisher, date
Dewey call number

Title, subtitle
Size
Notes
Tracings
Call numbers

Pelling, Margaret.
Cholera, fever and English medicine, 1825-1865 / by Margaret Pelling. — Oxford ₍Eng.₎ ; New York : Oxford University Press, 1978.
342 p. ; 23 cm. — (Oxford historical monographs)   GB78
Originally presented as the author's thesis, Oxford, 1971.
Bibliography: p. ₍311₎-327.
Includes index.
ISBN 0-19-821872-9 : £6.50
1. Public health—England—History—19th century.   2. Cholera, Asiatic—England—History—19th century.   3. Epidemiology—History—19th century. I. Title.
₍DNLM: GB78₎
RA487.P44   1978   614.4′0942

Library of Congress

Author
Publisher, date
Series

Title, subtitle
Publisher, date
Size
Tracings
Call numbers

Man and beast: comparative social behavior. Edited by J. F. Eisenberg and Wilton S. Dillon. Pref. by S. Dillon Ripley.   Washington, Smithsonian Institution Press ₍1971₎
401 p.   illus.   25 cm.   (Smithsonian annual, 3) $11.50
"Papers delivered at the Smithsonian Institution annual symposium, 14-16 May 1969."
Includes bibliographies.
1. Psychology, Comparative.   2. Social psychology.   3. Social behavior in animals.   I. Eisenberg, John Frederick, ed.   II. Dillon, Wilton, ed.   III. Smithsonian Institution.   IV. Series.
BF671.M26   591.5
ISBN 0-87474-105-X

Library of Congress

Editors
Series, price
Notes

cation. Also make a note of any other information on the card that may help you locate other related source material. Always check this recorded information for accuracy, as this will save valuable time later on when you compile a list of the sources used in the paper.

627

Make a note of other subject headings and classification numbers that turn up in your search. Books on the same subject are often classified under various headings and have different call numbers. Also take note of the tracings (see the sample cards), which direct you to other subject headings in the library catalog.

Make a thorough search of the catalog. Since books are listed under different headings in the subject catalog, you may miss important titles if you limit your search to one heading. The subject catalog also does not list all books by the same author under a single topical heading. Thus, it is often useful to consult the author and title catalog for additional books by an author on the same or a related topic.

Consult the author and title catalog. After you complete your search of the subject catalog, use the author and title catalog to find additional books by a particular author or to find books by an author who you know has written on the subject. For example, if your subject is capital punishment and you know that Norman Mailer wrote an article on that topic for a weekly magazine, you could consult the author and title catalog to see if it lists any books by Mailer on capital punishment. In this case, you may find a card for *The Executioner's Song*, Mailer's book on Gary Gilmore, who was executed in Utah in 1978.

Remember that you can learn much about a book from the catalog card, including whether the book is on the topic you are investigating. For example, Vine DeLoria's book *Custer Died for Our Sins* is not a study of General Custer or the Battle of Little Big Horn as its title suggests; rather, as the catalog card will tell you, it is a collection of essays on Indian rights. Although Carl Sagan's *Broca's Brain* contains an essay on the nineteenth-century French surgeon, the catalog card for the book will tell you that it is actually a collection of essays on modern science and pseudo-science.

Organize your bibliography. As you search the library catalog, you should record the titles in an order that will be useful to you when you look for the books in the library stacks and later when you organize your final list of sources. Classify your sources by subject or author if you are working with a limited number of writers. Classify them by type of publication if you are using a variety of books, articles, government documents, and the like (see 39b–f).

If a book listed in the library catalog is not in the stacks, put a hold on it at the circulation desk; if the book is on extended loan, the circulation librarian may be able to recall it in time for your paper. If a book you need is not in the library collection, your reference librarian may be able to secure a copy through an interlibrary loan (see 39f).

3 Using library classifications

Knowing the details of the library classification system will speed your search for source materials relevant to your topic. Many nonacademic libraries use the older **Dewey Decimal** classification of books. However, most academic libraries use the **Library of Congress** classification system and sometimes have a separate collection of older books classified under Dewey Decimal. Dewey Decimal uses numbers beginning with three digits (000 to 999) to classify books by subject and by genre or literary type (essays, novels, poetry, plays). Library of Congress classifies works by subject, period, and author, as well as by genre. The LC call number contains a single or multiple letter followed by a number. Books are divided into these general classes:

Library of Congress Classifications

A	General Works
B	Philosophy, Religion
C	Auxiliary Sciences of History
D	History and Topography (except America)
E–F	American History
G	Geography, Anthropology
H	Social Sciences
J	Political Science
K	Law
L	Education
M	Music
N	Fine Arts
P	Language and Literature
Q	Science
R	Medicine
S	Agriculture, Plant and Animal Industry
T	Technology
U	Military Science
V	Naval Science
Z	Bibliography and Library Science

For example, the Library of Congress system classifies literary works by period and region (English literature under the PR classification, American literature under the PS) and subclassifies them by author—first works by the author, then biographical and critical studies. Shakespeare's plays and biographies and critical studies of Shakespeare are classified with other literary works published in sixteenth- and early seventeenth-century England. The Library of Congress also classifies books by genre. You may find English and American works of fiction combined under the PZ classification and broadly divided by period and author. Some libraries classify all writings by the same author under the same general call number. For example, your library may shelve novels of Virginia Woolf under the PZ classification, with other novels of the same period, or with other writings of Woolf and books about her under the PR classification. Knowing these classifications can help in searching the library stacks for other books without having to return to the catalog.

4   Using the on-line catalog

An **on-line catalog** is a computerized listing of the books available in the library and provides the same information as that in card catalogs. Public terminals located at various places in the library give access to the on-line catalog. Some terminals have attached printers that provide printouts of catalog entries. Some libraries have special terminals that provide subject searches and printouts of author and subject bibliographies, a great help when you are searching for materials for research papers. In addition, the library may provide a terminal that tells you whether a book is on the shelf or on loan; you may even be able to use the terminal to reserve the book through the circulation department. The reference desk can make a copy of the on-line description on request. The on-line catalog may also display a map of the library that shows you the physical location where a book is shelved. In some libraries, the on-line catalog is accessible through home computer and telephone hookup.

EXERCISES

1. Record the information that your library card or on-line catalog gives on the contents of one of the following books:
   a. John Updike, *Hugging the Shore*

b. John Gardner, *Grendel*
c. Annie Dillard, *Pilgrim at Tinker Creek*
d. Aleksandr Solzhenitsyn, *The Gulag Archipelago*
e. James Watson, *The Double Helix*
2. What does the LC call number tell you about the book?

39b Using indexes

In addition to books, many research papers require that you consult journal and newspaper articles and other sources of information on a topic. To find articles on your topic, you need to consult general and specialized indexes. An **index** lists articles and other source materials, usually by author and title. Some indexes also provide lengthy descriptions of the materials they list. Major indexes are usually kept in the reference section of the library.

Mary Smith searched for articles on cholera in the *Readers' Guide to Periodical Literature*. She also consulted the *Humanities Index* and the *Social Sciences Index*, companion indexes to the *Readers' Guide* that use the same format. (The figure on page 632 shows a recent entry in the *Social Sciences Index*.) In addition, Mary found special indexes to nineteenth-century periodicals useful, such as *Poole's Index to Periodical Literature, 1801–1907* and *Palmer's Index to the [London] Times*, both of which list articles on cholera. The indexes to *Lancet*, a leading nineteenth-century medical journal still in publication, provided her with firsthand accounts of cholera epidemics by doctors and surgeons.

1 Indexes to general periodicals

You will find **general periodical indexes** most helpful in finding articles on your topic. These indexes include the following:

Readers' Guide to Periodical Literature [1900–present]. A major index to more than 150 periodicals of general interest like *Atlantic Monthly* and *Harper's Magazine.*
Humanities Index [1974–present]. Author and subject index to specialized periodicals in English and other modern languages, classics, philosophy, and linguistics. Supersedes the *Social Sci-*

Sample entry from *Social Sciences Index*.

Main heading ──────▶ **Diseases**—Causes—*cont.*
The "Disease-prone personality": a meta-analytic view of the construct. H. S. Friedman and S. Booth-Kewley. bibl *Am Psychol* 42:539–55 Je '87; Discussion. 43:749–51 S '88
The evolution of mycobacterial disease in human populations: a reevaluation [Amerindians] G. A. Clark and others. bibl *Curr Anthropol* 28:45–51 F '87; Discussion. 28:51–62 F '87; 29:315–16 Ap '88

Title of article ─── Health and disease: what can medicine do for philosophy?

Author ─────────▶ J. G. Scadding. *J Med Ethics* 14:118–24 S '88
Hookworm and pellagra: exemplary diseases in the new South. S. J. Kunitz. bibl *J Health Soc Behav* 29:139–48

Journal ─────── Je '88
An ill nature. J. Berlfein. *Psychol Today* 22:16 Mr '88

Volume ─────── In time of plague: the history and social consequences of lethal epidemic disease [symposium] *Soc Res* 55:323–528 Aut '88

Pages ───── Migration and morbidity: implications for geographical studies of disease. G. Bentham. *Soc Sci Med* 26

Month and year ─── no1:49–54 '88
Pluralistic etiological systems in their social context: a Brazilian case study. N. Ngokwey. *Soc Sci Med* 26 no8:793–802 '88
Psychological and behavioral factors in dermatitis. E. Doherty. bibl *Psychol Rep* 61:727–32 D '87
Stress and coping in relation to health and disease [symposium]; ed. by Lowrens J. Menges. *Soc Sci Med* 26 no3:277–392 '88
Traditional thought and modern Western surgery. P Katz and F. R. Kirkland. *Soc Sci Med* 26 no12:1175–81 '88

Subheading ──────────────▶ **Classification**
HIV infection and AIDS: definition and classification of disease. M. L. Smiley. *Death Stud* 12 no5–6:399–415 '88

Diagnosis
See Diagnosis
Environmental aspects
See Environmentally induced diseases
Geographical distribution
See Geography, Medical
Prevention
A framework for assessing productivity loss from schistosomiasis. C. Wiemer. bibl *J Hum Resour* 23:320–41 Summ '88
Impact and costs of varicella prevention in a university hospital. D. J. Weber and others. *Am J Public Health* 78:19–23 Ja '88
Psychosomatic aspects
See Medicine, Psychosomatic

Heading under which topic is listed in *SSI*

ences and Humanities Index [1965–1974] and the *International Index* [1907–1965].

Social Sciences and Humanities Index [1965–1974]. Supersedes the *International Index to Periodicals* [1907–1965]. Since 1974, published separately as the *Social Sciences Index* and the *Humanities Index.*

International Index to Periodicals [1907–1965]. Index to specialized periodicals in special fields. Superseded by *Social Sciences and Humanities Index* [1965–1974].

Magazine Index [1976–present]. Subject index to periodicals; on microfilm. Indexes over twice as many periodicals as the *Readers' Guide* and cumulates for five years.

Popular Periodicals Index [1973–present]. Lists articles in popular periodicals that are not listed in other indexes.

Poole's Index to Periodical Literature [1802–1907]. Subject index to articles published in major British and American periodicals during the nineteenth and early twentieth centuries. No author or title index.

Ulrich's International Periodical Directory [1932–present]. Subject classification of periodicals. Particularly valuable in locating periodicals in specific fields of research.

2 Newspaper indexes

Newspaper indexes sometimes list events chronologically, under general topics, as in the *New York Times Index* listing for cholera in the figure on page 634. The following indexes are the most useful in locating source material in major newspapers:

The [London] Times Index [1973–present]. Continues the *Index to the [London] Times* [1906–1972]. See also *Palmer's Index to the Times* [1790–June 1941], an author and subject index to the British newspaper of record.

National Newspaper Index [1979–present]. Index to articles from major newspapers like the *Los Angeles Times, New York Times, Wall Street Journal, Washington Post,* and others. Microfilm.

Newsbank [1970–present]. Indexes articles from over one hundred city and regional newspapers. Microfiche.

New York Times Index [1913–present]. Author and subject index to articles published in this major newspaper. Indispensable to the study of past and current events in the United States and the world. See also *Prior Series,* 1851–1912, in different cumulations and arrangements.

Wall Street Journal Index [1958–present]. Published monthly.

Sample entry from the *New York Times Index.*

CHOLERA

Short (length) ——————— Ethiopian authorities say they are testing for cholera at famine refugee camp in Harbu (S), Ja 24,I,9:5

Red Cross reports cholera has killed 1,000 people in Somalia and as many as 300,000 others risk contracting disease; some dead include Ethiopian refugees who fled to Somalia from drought-stricken homeland (S), Ap 6,I,4:6

Cholera epidemic in Somalia camp for Ethiopian refugees reportedly has claimed over 1,500 lives and spread to four other camps (S), Ap 10,I,7:4

Summary of news story ——————— Officials of French doctors' group Doctors Without Borders say they have successfully contained outbreak of cholera at Ethiopian famine relief camp in Korem; aid workers say announcement is likely to stir controversy because Government has long denied presence of cholera in country; there are no reliable figures on how many deaths have resulted; Dr Brigitte Vasset says about 20% of those infected--fewer than 250 people--have died over last six weeks (M), My 16,I,3:4

Medium (length) ———————

Date and issue of *Times* (May 16, Sect. 1, p. 3, col. 4) ——————— Western relief workers and diplomats say that disease believed to be cholera has broken out in two more Ethiopian famine relief centers, although Ethiopian Government denies that cholera exists in Ethiopia; cholera is highly contagious, and countries that belong to World Health Organization are obliged to report any outbreaks (M), My 19,I,9:1

Cholera again breaks out among famine refugees in northwestern Somalia and is spreading to refugee camps in other districts (S), Je 27,I,5:1

Medical authorities in Addis Ababa, Ethiopia, say cholera appears to be spreading in city; similar reports also come from Sudan; one doctor estimates there are 300 new cases daily in Addis Ababa; Government has denied existence of cholera in country, saying cases really are 'acute diarrhea' (S), Ag 2,I,2:3

Cholera, thought to have been under control in Sudan, reportedly has reached epidemic proportions in some areas; Sudanese Government refuses to confirm existence of disease and refugee officials insist on calling it 'severe, acute gastro-enteritis' (S), Ag 2,I,2:4

Ten new cases of cholera are diagnosed in Kuwait, bringing total number of cases to 20; officials claim earlier cases originated abroad (S), Ag 18,I,4:4

Cholera has spread across Sudan and Ethiopia, reaching important urban centers whose slums are likely to make disease difficult to contain; governments continue to deny disease's existence; map; photo (M), Ag 18,IV,5:1

3 Specialized indexes

The following **specialized indexes** are valuable resources of information on field-specific publications:

Applied Science and Technology Index [1958–present]. Included in *Industrial Arts Index* [1913–1957].

Art Index [1929–present].

Biography Index [1947–present].

Book Review Digest [1905–present]. Includes extracts from book reviews. Invaluable for judging the reliability of books.

British Humanities Index [1962–present]. Indexes articles on arts and politics in British periodicals.

Business Periodicals Index [1958–present]. Included in *Industrial Arts Index* [1913–1957].

Congressional Record [1873–present]. Earlier years are covered under other titles. Frequent indexes, often bound separately.

Cumulated Index Medicus [1960–present]. Annual cumulations of monthly issues. Earlier indexes published under various titles: *Index Medicus* [1879–1899, 1903–1927]; *Quarterly Cumulative Index Medicus* [1927–1956]; *Current List of Medical Literature* [1941–1959]. Author and subject index in medicine and related fields, including pertinent articles and books in the humanities and social sciences. Sometimes available for computer search at medical libraries through Medline, National Library of Medicine.

Dramatic Index [1909–1949]. Index to articles on authors, plays, and performances in the inclusive dates.

Education Index [1929–present].

Essay and General Literature Index [1900–present]. Index to essays and articles published in book-length collections. The first volume covers 1900 to 1934. Cumulated supplements in addition to semiannual and annual cumulations. Indispensable in locating materials not listed in the card catalog or general indexes.

General Sciences Index [1978–present].

Granger's Index to Poetry, 8th Edition [1904–present]. Indexes poems published in more than five hundred anthologies. Current edition omits some of the titles in earlier editions.

Index to Publications of the United States Congress [1970–present]. Abstracts of House and Senate committee hearings, documents, reports, and other congressional publications. Valuable index of subjects and names. Four- and five-year cumulative indexes.

Music Index [1949–present].

Philosopher's Index [1967–present].

Psychological Abstracts [1927–present]. Published monthly and in cumulations. Continuation of *Psychological Index* [1894–1935], which was published annually.

Vertical File Index [1935–present]. Index to pamphlets from various sources.

In using periodical indexes, consult the guide to abbreviations at the beginning of each volume. When you find articles pertinent to your topic, record the volume number, date of issue, and page numbers for each one. You will need this information to find the articles in bound volumes or on microfilm, or to request copies of them.

Sheehy's *Guide to Reference Books* (see 39e) is a special guide that directs the reader to other specialized indexes and reference books like the following:

Afro-American Poetry and Drama, 1760–1975
American Indian Index [1953–1968]
Chicano Periodical Index [1967–1978]
Index to Literature on the American Indian [1970–present]

4 Abstracts

An **abstract** is a short summary of an article or a book. Many journals print abstracts in the table of contents of an issue or immediately preceding the text of the article. Abstracts are also collected in special indexes in certain fields. The information in abstracts can tell you if a book or article is pertinent to the topic you are researching. Following are important volume-length series of abstracts in the humanities, social sciences, and natural and physical sciences:

Abstracts of English Studies   *Economics Abstracts*
Biological Abstracts   *Historical Abstracts*
Chemical Abstracts   *Physics Abstracts*
Communications Abstracts   *Research in Education*
Dissertation Abstracts   *Psychological Abstracts*
Dissertation Abstracts International   *Science Abstracts*
  [since 1969]   *Sociological Abstracts*
Ecology Abstracts   *Women Studies Abstracts*

Abstracts are also available through data-base searches of bibliographies (see 39f). Mary Smith found useful the abstracts that a data-base search produced on her topic (see the figure on page 649). These summaries save considerable time in determining whether the content of an article is useful. However, if the abstract fails to give you enough information, you should consult the actual article to determine its relevance to your topic.

39c Using bibliographies

A **bibliography** is a listing of articles and books in a particular field. Some bibliographies list articles and books by particular authors or periods. Bibliographies often contain annotations or descriptive and evaluative notes. The bibliographies that appear at the end of scholarly books, monographs, and general studies of a subject are particularly valuable in research.

In the subject catalog of the medical library, Mary Smith found listings for contemporary treatises on cholera and special book-length studies or monographs that supplement the studies of cholera she found in the college library. Through the bibliographies in Pelling, Morris, and other books, she located firsthand accounts of cholera, written at the time of cholera epidemics in England.

Your library's reference collection may contain specialized bibliographies on your topic. These are listed in the subject catalog. Also useful are the bibliographies in books—sometimes at the end of chapters, sometimes at the end of the book—and those in magazine and journal articles, directing you to essential materials in a field. *Scientific American,* for example, includes a useful listing of articles and books on every topic covered in an issue.

Many scholarly journals publish annual bibliographies or special bibliographies in issues devoted to particular writers. In the special bibliographies in journals on nineteenth-century English literature, Mary Smith found a listing of articles on writers like Charles Dickens who wrote about poverty and disease in nineteenth-century England. The following bibliographies are among the most important in the field of English:

Modern Humanities Research Association, *Annual Bibliography of English Language and Literature* [1920–present].

Bibliographic Index [1937–present]. Lists special bibliographies contained in books like Jonathan Miller's *The Body in Question,* a study of physiology that contains a valuable listing of books on the history and philosophy of science, physiology, perception, and the "sociology of healing."

Literary History of the United States, volume 2, 4th edition, revised (1974). First published in 1948.

MLA International Bibliography of Books and Articles on the Modern Languages and Literatures [1921–present].

New Cambridge Bibliography of English Literature [1969–1977].

English Association, *The Year's Work in English Studies* [1919–present].

Checklist: Looking for Source Materials

1. Look for topical headings in *Library of Congress Subject Headings.*
2. Use the *LCSH* headings to search the subject catalog.
3. Make notes of other topical headings you find in your search.
4. Consult the author and title catalog for additional listings.
5. Consult periodical indexes for pertinent articles as well as specialized indexes, bibliographies, and other reference works for additional listings.
6. Look through the catalog or file of government documents.

39d Government documents

Government documents are usually shelved under the Library of Congress Z classification, often in a separate room of the library. Here you will find the *Congressional Record* as well as numerous reports and bulletins published by various government departments and agencies. Here you will also find documents published by state governments. The number of publications of the United States government is vast, and you may need the help of a librarian to find them. Your library probably has a separate card or on-line catalog for government publications.

Following is a partial list of guides to U.S. government documents:

Catalog of Government Publications in the Research Libraries, 40 vols. (1972).
Guide to U.S. Government Publications [1973–present].
Index to Publications of the United States Congress [1970– present].

Monthly Catalog of United States Government Publications [1895–present].

William P. Leidy, *A Popular Guide to Government Publications,* 4th edition (1976).

Public Affairs Information Service [1915–present]. Subject index to government publications including books and periodicals.

Sally Wynkoop, *Subject Guide to Government Reference Books* (1972).

The following are useful guides to foreign government documents:

Bibliographic Guide to Government Publications: Foreign [1975–present].

United Nations Documents Index [1950–present].

39e Using reference books

Reference books can direct you to still other source materials and help you in evaluating and interpreting them. Some of these reference books are guides to using other reference books in various fields; others contain information on general and special topics in dictionary form. You will find these books in the reference section of your library.

Checklist: Reference Books

1. Guides to reference books
2. Indexes to periodicals
3. Bibliographies
4. Abstracts
5. Encyclopedias
6. Dictionaries of the English language
7. Dictionaries on special topics
8. Biographical dictionaries
9. Yearbooks and almanacs

1 Guides to reference books

Your library may have a separate catalog for the reference books in its collection. These books are usually listed by subject only. In addition, reference books are shelved under different classifications: encyclopedias are often shelved at the beginning of the collection, and reference books on specialized topics follow. Take a few minutes to walk through the reference stacks and familiarize yourself with this arrangement. Notice that *Library of Congress Subject Headings* provides the general LC classification number for reference books in special fields. If necessary, ask a reference librarian for help in finding the reference books you need.

Eugene P. Sheehy's *Guide to Reference Books,* 10th edition (1986), is the basic reference guide to standard reference books in every field. The number of major reference books has increased so rapidly in recent years that you will need to consult guides like Sheehy's to find reference books and lists of source materials in fields like English literature, history, and medicine. Other valuable guides to reference books include the following:

> Arthur J. Walford, ed., *Guide to Reference Material,* 4th edition (1980–1982).
> *The IMS . . . Ayer Directory of Publications* [1983–present]. A continuation of *Ayer Directory of Publications* [1880–1982; incorporating earlier Ayer directories under other titles].
> Richard D. Altick and Andrew Wright, *Selective Bibliography for the study of English and American Literature,* 6th edition (1979). A listing of special bibliographies, indexes, and reference works.
> Theodore Besterman, *World Bibliography of Bibliographies,* 4th edition (1965–1966).
> Alice F. Toomey, *A World Bibliography of Bibliographies,* 1964–1974 (1977; a continuation of Besterman).

The following books discuss how to use reference guides:

> Jean Key Gates, *Guide to the Use of Libraries and Information Sources,* 6th edition (1988).
> William Katz, *Your Library: A Reference Guide,* 2nd edition (1984).

2 General encyclopedias

An **encyclopedia** lists articles in dictionary form and provides detailed information on a wide range of subjects, usually for the general reader. When you use an encyclopedia, consult the most recent edition on the shelf. However, your library may hold earlier editions that you will find useful. Older editions are valuable in searching for biographical and historical information omitted or covered only briefly in current reference books. Since information is quickly outdated, encyclopedias and other reference materials must be used with caution. Whenever possible, verify in other sources the factual information taken from encyclopedias and other reference books. Verification is particularly necessary with scientific details and theories.

Following is a partial list of useful encyclopedias:

Chambers's Encyclopaedia, new revised edition
Collier's Encyclopedia
Encyclopedia Americana
Encyclopedia of Black America
Encyclopedia Canadiana
Jewish Encyclopedia
New Columbia Encyclopedia, 4th edition
New Encyclopaedia Britannica, 15th edition. Supersedes the *Encyclopaedia Britannica,* still of use from the 9th edition (1902–1903) to the 14th edition (1929) and subsequent unnumbered revisions. The 11th edition contains highly regarded essays in the humanities. The 15th edition includes the *Micropaedia,* containing general information in short reference articles, and the *Macropaedia,* containing longer articles on special subjects.

Some of the preceding encyclopedia publishers also publish yearbooks (see 39e 4).

3 Biographical guides

Biographical guides provide information about people's lives and achievements. To locate articles and biographical sketches, consult the *Biography Index* (1947–present). Your college library may also contain *Biography Master Index,* a microfiche listing of articles in dictionaries, newspaper obituaries, and other sources. The *New York Times Obituaries Index* [1868–1978] directs you to death notices published in the *Times.* Annual volumes of the *New York Times Index* must be searched (under the heading "Deaths") for obituaries of people who have died since 1978.

Consult current editions of *Who's Who, International Who's Who,* and *Who's Who in America* (and regional volumes in the

641

same series) on living people. If your source suggests that the person you seek information on is no longer living, consult the encyclopedias listed in the preceding section and the following basic biographical sources (and supplements if any):

American Men and Women of Science, 15th edition
American Men and Women of Science: Social and Behavioral Sciences, 13th edition
Contemporary Authors
Current Biography
Dictionary of American Biography
Dictionary of National Biography [British]
International Who's Who
New York Times Biographical Service
New York Times Obituaries Index
Webster's Biographical Dictionary
Who's Who [mainly British]
Who's Who in America

4 Yearbooks and almanacs

Since most **yearbooks** and **almanacs** appear annually, the most recent edition should be consulted. The following are valuable sources of current facts:

Americana Annual [1923–present]
Britannica Book of the Year [1938–present]
Facts on File [1940–present]
Information Please Almanac [1947–present]
[London] Times Atlas of the World
New York Times Atlas of the World
State and Metropolitan Area Databook [1979–present]
Statesman's Year-Book [1864–present]
Statistical Abstract of the United States [1878–present]
[United Nations] *Statistical Yearbook* [1949–present]
United States Government Manual [1935–present]
Vital Statistics of the United States [1937–present]
World Almanac and Book of Facts [1868–present]
World Tables, 3rd edition
Year Book of World Affairs [1947–present]

5 Special dictionaries, encyclopedias, handbooks, and manuals

The following special dictionaries and other reference books contain detailed and technical information on specific topics in various fields:

Business
Glenn G. Munn, *Encyclopedia of Banking and Finance*, 8th edition (1983)
Irvin Graham, *Encyclopedia of Advertising*, 2nd edition (1969)
Encyclopedia of Management, 3rd edition, ed. Carl Heyel (1982)
Handbook of Modern Marketing, 2nd edition, ed. Victor P. Buell (1986)

Economics
American Dictionary of Economics (1983)
Encyclopedia of Economics (1981)
The McGraw-Hill Dictionary of Modern Economics, 3rd edition (1983)
Donald Moffat, *Economics Dictionary*, 2nd edition (1983)

Education, Psychology, Sociology
Carter V. Good, *Dictionary of Education*, 3rd edition (1973)
Encyclopedia of Education (1971)
Hans J. Eysenck, *Encyclopedia of Psychology*, 2nd edition (1979)
International Encyclopedia of the Social Sciences (1968–1980)
New Dictionary of the Social Sciences, ed. G. Duncan Mitchell (1979)

Engineering
Bill Gunston, *Jane's Aerospace Dictionary* (1980)
Aviation and Space Dictionary, 7th edition (1989)
Leonard C. Urquhart, *Civil Engineering Handbook*, 4th edition (1959)
Byron D. Tapley, *Handbook of Engineering Fundamentals*, 4th edition (1989)
Encyclopedia of Computer Science and Technology, ed. Jack Belzer et al. (1975–1980)
Encyclopedia of Chemistry, 4th edition, ed. Douglas Considine (1984)
Encyclopedia of Energy Technology (1983)
Perry's Chemical Engineer's Handbook, 6th edition (1984)
Thesaurus of Engineering and Scientific Terms, revised edition (1967)

Fine Arts
Anatole Chujoy and P. W. Manchester, *The Dance Encyclopedia*, revised edition (1967)
Leslie D. Stroebel and Hollis N. Todd, *Dictionary of Contemporary Photography* (1974)
Encyclopedia of Painting, ed. Bernard S. Myers (1979)

643

Encyclopedia of World Art (1959–1983)
Willi Apel, *Harvard Dictionary of Music,* 2nd revised edition
(1969)
Oscar Thompson and N. Slonimsky, *International Cyclopedia of
Music and Musicians,* 11th edition (1985)
New Grove Dictionary of Music and Musicians, ed. Stanley Sadie
(1980)
Oxford Companion to Art, ed. Harold Osborne (1970)
Oxford Companion to Music, 10th edition, ed. Percy A. Scholes
(1970)
Michael Kennedy, *Oxford Dictionary of Music* (1985)
Oxford Companion to the Theatre, 4th edition, ed. Phyllis Hartnoll
(1983)

Geography
Columbia Lippincott Gazetteer of the World (1962)
Encyclopaedia Britannica World Atlas International (1969)
National Geographic Atlas of the World, 5th edition (1981)
The Times Atlas of the World, 2nd edition (1983)

History
Cambridge Ancient History (1970–1984; under revision)
Cambridge History of Latin America (1985–1986)
Cambridge Medieval History (1966–67)
Encyclopedia of American History, 6th edition, ed. Richard B.
Morris (1982)
New Illustrated Encyclopedia of World History, 5th edition, ed.
William L. Langer (1975)
Harvard Guide to American History, ed. Frank Freidel and Rich-
ard K. Showman (1974)
New Cambridge Modern History (1957–1980)

Literature and Linguistics
Bartlett's Familiar Quotations, 15th edition (1980)
Cassell's Encyclopedia of World Literature, revised edition (1973)
C. Hugh Holman and William Harmon, *A Handbook to Literature,*
5th edition (1980)
Harvard Guide to Contemporary American Writing, ed. Daniel
Hoffman (1982)
Albert C. Baugh and Thomas Cable, *A History of the English Lan-
guage,* 3rd edition (1978)
Oxford Companion to American Literature, 5th edition, ed. James
D. Hart (1983)
Oxford Companion to English Literature, 5th edition, ed. Margaret
Drabble (1987)
Oxford Dictionary of Quotations, 3rd edition (1979)

The Reader's Adviser, 13th edition (1988)
R. H. Robins, *General Linguistics,* 4th edition (1989)
William Rose Benét, *The Reader's Encyclopedia,* 2nd edition (1965)
Reader's Encyclopedia of Shakespeare, ed. Oscar J. Campbell and Edward G. Quinn (1966)

Mythology
Funk and Wagnall's Standard Dictionary of Folklore, Mythology, and Legend (1973)
Larousse World Mythology (1989)
Oxford Classical Dictionary, 2nd edition (1970)

Natural and Physical Sciences
Peter Gray, *Encyclopedia of the Biological Sciences,* 2nd edition (1970)
Encyclopedia of Physics (1981)
McGraw-Hill Encyclopedia of Science and Technology, 5th edition (1982)
McGraw-Hill Encyclopedia of Ocean and Atmospheric Sciences (1979)
George Sarton, *Introduction to the History of Science* (1927–75)
Van Nostrand Reinhold Encyclopedia of Chemistry, 4th edition (1984)
Van Nostrand's Scientific Encyclopedia, 7th edition (1988)

Philosophy
James O. Urmson, *The Concise Encyclopedia of Western Philosophy and Philosophers,* 2nd edition (1975)
Encyclopedia of Philosophy (1967)

Political Science
Jack C. Plano and Milton Greenberg, *The American Political Dictionary,* 8th edition (1989)
Book of the States (1935–present)
Foreign Affairs Bibliography (1933–1976)
Fred I. Greenstein and Nelson W. Polsby, *Handbook of Political Science* (1975)
Political Handbook of the World (1975–present)

Popular Culture
International Television Almanac (1956–present)
Oxford Companion to Film, ed. Liz-Anne Bawden (1976)
World Encyclopedia of the Film, ed. Tim Cawkwell and John Milton Smith (1972)

Religion

Anchor Bible (1964–in progress)

Dictionary of the Bible, ed. F. C. Grant and H. H. Rowley (1963)

Dictionary of the Bible, ed. James Hastings (1898–1904)

Encyclopaedia Biblica (1950–82)

Encyclopaedia Judaica (1972)

Encyclopaedia of Islam (1954–83)

Oxford Dictionary of the Christian Church, 2nd edition, ed. F. L. Cross and E. A. Livingston (1974)

Encyclopedia of Religion and Ethics, ed. James Hastings (1908–27)

The Interpreter's Dictionary of the Bible (1962, 1976)

New Catholic Encyclopedia (1967–79)

A Reader's Guide to the Great Religions, 2nd edition, ed. Charles J. Adams (1977)

Richard C. White, *The Vocabulary of the Church* (1960)

EXERCISES

1. Consult a copy of Sheehy's *Guide to Reference Books* in your library. How is the book organized? What information is given about each entry? Of what general value is this information in doing research?
2. What reference books does Sheehy recommend for research on the following topics?
   a. federal regulation of television
   b. U.S. House of Representatives
   c. Battle of Gettysburg
   d. F. Scott Fitzgerald's novels
3. What uses does the *Ayer Directory of Newspapers and Periodicals* have in research on the 1988 presidential election?
4. What indexes and special dictionaries would you use to locate sources on the following topics?
   a. articles published before 1960 on Emily Dickinson's poems
   b. the birth of the Solidarity Union in Poland
   c. U.S. Supreme Court decisions on capital punishment in the 1970s
   d. laser technology
   e. William Faulkner's education
5. What yearbooks, almanacs, and biographical dictionaries would give you information on the following topics? What is that information?
   a. Pulitzer Prize for Fiction in 1980
   b. the early career of Carl Sandburg

   c. the population of New York City in 1980

   d. the writings of Helen Keller

   e. the political career of Franklin Delano Roosevelt

6. What information does your library card or on-line catalog give you about the subjects of the following books?

   a. Frederick Lewis Allen, *Only Yesterday*

   b. Samuel Butler, *Erewhon*

   c. Rachel Carson, *Silent Spring*

   d. Joan Didion, *Salvador*

   e. Edward Jay Epstein, *Inquest*

7. Use the full resources of your library reference section to answer the following questions. To locate particular books, consult Eugene P. Sheehy, *Guide to Reference Books* and other guides to reference books listed in 39e.

   a. What reference works contain a biography of Associate Supreme Court Justice Sandra Day O'Connor?

   b. Where can you find the complete text of the U.S. Supreme Court *Miranda* decision? What justice of the court wrote the decision? Was the decision unanimous? What two books contain discussions of the *Miranda* decision? Who is Miranda and why was his conviction appealed to the Supreme Court?

   c. What is the meaning and origin of the phrase *ad astra per aspera*?

   d. What do panhandlers and thieves mean by the word *gull*?

   e. Who was Sojourner Truth, and in what American city did she deliver a famous speech?

   f. What is the source of the title *Far From the Madding Crowd*, a novel by Thomas Hardy? What is the name of its heroine?

   g. What is KPA an abbreviation for?

   h. What reference books list lines of poetry by subject?

   i. Which is the oldest of the New Testament Gospels?

   j. Who won the Nobel Prize for Literature in 1970? How many of his writings had been published in his native country prior to 1970? How many have been published there since 1970?

   k. What is the origin of the term *Legionnaires' disease*? Is the disease bacterial or viral?

   l. How does the word *malaria* reflect early theories of its origin before the twentieth century?

   m. How is a concerto grosso different from a symphony?

   n. What is the present population of the United States?

   o. What federal department administers the Coast Guard? ∎

39f | Data-base searches and other resources

Your college library may have available other resources for research. These include data-base searches, interlibrary loans, and special collections of published books and unpublished documents.

1 Data-base searches

A **data base** is an index of books, articles, and other source materials that is stored electronically. The data base is searched through *key words* that the reference librarian uses to conduct the search, usually in your presence.

The search is conducted through the Lockheed DIALOG Information Retrieval Service and other services that provide special bibliographies, abstracts of articles, and copies of documents for a fee. To do a data-base search, you need to make an appointment with a reference librarian, who will ask you to describe your research project and to suggest key terms. The headings found in *Library of Congress Subject Headings* and the library catalogs you consulted early in your research will be helpful in suggesting key terms. In most libraries, the person requesting a search pays a fee based on the length of the search. Your reference librarian will give you information on the cost and other details of a search.

The figure on page 649 shows part of the data-base search conducted for Mary Smith through Lockheed DIALOG. Notice that each item retrieved gives full bibliographical information about the source and usually an abstract of the article or book, both useful in deciding whether to search the library for it or request a loan. The first of the items retrieved helped Mary evaluate Margaret Pelling's study of cholera in England, a book in her college library. The second item gave Mary an understanding of the effects of the disease on the poor. Both abstracts were sufficient to judge the usefulness of these books.

The more than three hundred data bases that can be searched include the following:

> BIOSIS, or *Biological Abstracts and Biosearch Index* (a major source of articles in the biological sciences)

BOOK REVIEW INDEX
CHEMICAL ABSTRACTS
CONGRESSIONAL RECORD ABSTRACTS
DISSERTATION ABSTRACTS (abstracts of doctoral dissertations)
ENERGYLINE (energy uses and government policy)
ENVIROLINE (environmental issues and government policy)
ERIC (Educational Resources Information Center, National Institute of Education; a wide range of source materials in education and other fields)
LEXIS (law)
MEDLINE (*Index Medicus*)
MLA BIBLIOGRAPHY (books and articles in English and other humanities)
NATIONAL TECHNICAL INFORMATION SERVICE
NATIONAL NEWSPAPER INDEX
PAIS INTERNATIONAL (public affairs)
PSYCHOLOGICAL ABSTRACTS
SCISEARCH (source materials in the sciences, 1974–present)
SOCIAL SCISEARCH (source materials in the social sciences)
SOCIOLOGICAL ABSTRACTS

Sample item from a data-base search.

```
1088081    35A-09162
MEDICINE AND COMMUNITY IN VICTORIAN BRITAIN.
 Rosenberg, Charles E
 J. of Interdisciplinary Hist. 1981 11(4): 677-684.
NOTE: 3 notes.
DOCUMENT TYPE: ARTICLE
ABSTRACT: Reviews the following books: John M.  Eyler's Victorian Social
 Medicine: The Ideas and Methods of William Farr  (1979) and Margaret
 Pelling's Cholera, Fever and English Medicine, 1825-1865  (1978).  These
 books, which could be considered medical histories written for the
 layman, analyze the interest in medicine and health in 19th-century
 Victorian England. (C. R. Gunter, Jr. )
DESCRIPTORS: Great Britain ; Medicine -(review article) ; 19c ; Eyler,
 John M ; Pelling, Margaret
HISTORICAL PERIOD: 1800H
 HISTORICAL PERIOD (Starting): 19c
 HISTORICAL PERIOD (Ending):   19c

 c1990, ABC-Clio, Inc.
```

2 Interlibrary loans and special collections

Your reference librarian may be able to secure source materials unavailable in the library through an **interlibrary loan**.

However, an interlibrary loan usually takes a week or longer, so you want to request the materials early enough to use them in your paper.

Rare books and unpublished documents are usually stored in **special collections**. You will probably need permission from the library to consult these materials. Special restrictions often govern their inspection, mainly because they are in fragile condition.

Some of the source materials you are seeking may be stored on **microfilm** and **microfiche**. The library has special machines available for reading materials in these forms and making photocopies. Most libraries have copying machines available and will inform you about copyright restrictions in making copies. In addition, your library may have a separate **audiovisual** section containing sound recordings, videocassettes, and machines for listening and viewing these materials. These collections are often listed in a special catalog.

Summary

39a Use *Library of Congress Subject Headings* as well as the headings in the card or on-line catalog to find source materials in the library.

Search the subject catalog under headings appropriate to your topic (**39a 1**).

Search the author and title catalog for additional titles (**39a 1**).

Record complete information about the book, including the call number and other information that will help you locate other source material (**39a 2**).

Become familiar with the classification system used by your library as well as how to use it to search for books (**39a 3**).

39b Locate articles, essays, pamphlets, abstracts, and other source materials in general and specialized periodical indexes.

39c Use specialized bibliographies to locate other valuable source material.

39d Search for government documents in special card and on-line catalogs.

39e Use reference books like encyclopedias, dictionaries, and biographical guides to locate additional source materials and to evaluate and interpret your sources.

39f Use a data-base search to supplement your research as well as interlibrary loans and special collections as needed.

Working with 40
Sources

□

Once you have collected adequate source materials for the topic you are researching, you need to sort them into groups, evaluate them, and choose those that you find most reliable and relevant to your investigation. These sources should then be grouped in some useful order; for example, one source may provide the background necessary to understanding another. You should also jot down a preliminary outline or sequence of topics for your research paper, as this will help you organize your source material. In the evaluation of sources, some need only be scanned to find material of use in your research; others need to be read carefully. With these jobs completed, you are ready to take notes on your sources. These notes will take the form of summary, paraphrase, or direct quotation. This chapter describes how to work with and take notes on the source materials collected for the research paper.

40a Primary and secondary sources

Primary sources include eyewitness accounts, reports of participants, interviews, and other writings associated directly with an event. In literary studies, primary evidence includes letters, journals, diaries, autobiographical writings, essays, and even works of poetry and fiction that reflect the conditions of a particular age. In the sciences and social sciences, primary sources include field observations, laboratory experiments, interviews, surveys of opinion, and other inductive evidence. **Secondary sources** interpret and evaluate primary sources. These may appear in articles, books, theses, dissertations, and other documents written after and about the event.

Both primary and secondary sources provide evidence essential to your research. Primary evidence is the subject of your investigation; secondary sources help you verify that your primary sources are reliable. Secondary sources also help you interpret particular facts and statements and determine their accuracy by providing the *context* of ideas that surround statements and facts in source materials of any period. They give the necessary backgrounds.

Secondary sources are necessary because primary evidence is often in dispute; even those trained to make careful observations and record them accurately often disagree on methods of investigation and results. For example, primary evidence studied by trained experts who investigated the murder of President John F. Kennedy in 1963 remains the subject of intense controversy. At the time of the event, eyewitnesses disagreed about what they saw; trained experts continue to disagree about what a film of the shooting and a sound recording of the event prove. Secondary sources are essential to interpreting primary evidence. It would be impossible to analyze this primary evidence about Kennedy's assassination without the help of specialists in ballistics and forensic medicine. But primary and secondary sources both need verification; neither may be reliable in whole or in part.

40b   Evaluating sources

In using a primary source, you want to verify that you have the complete document or complete testimony of an eyewitness and that it contains reliable evidence. The inclusion of a book in your college library and the imprint of a university press are not sufficient guarantees of reliability. You should check the preface or introduction for details about the author and the nature of the documents or testimony contained in the book. You can also scan a few paragraphs of the introductory and concluding chapters and of a chapter pertinent to your research topic, so to get a good idea of the point of view and technical level of the work. The reliability of the source can be verified by reading reviews of it, usually listed or summarized in the *Book Review Digest* (see 39b), as well as discussions of the work in other reference sources. Citation indexes like *Science Citation Index* will tell you how many times an article has been cited by other researchers. The citation allows you to find out what has been said about the work. Citation indexes are available in the arts and humanities, social sciences, and some other fields.

Secondary sources need the same verification, particularly when you are investigating a controversial issue like the Kennedy murder. Again, prefatory material may give some indication of the qualifications of an author; so may the sources cited in footnotes or listed at the end of book. The publishing data of a secondary source is important. If the library contains several editions of a secondary source, always use the latest edition. A book on physics published in the 1920s is not a reliable source on atomic theory, but note that scientific writings from the early twentieth century may contain ideas of interest and value today. Particularly in using an older book in the sciences, you need to confirm statements of fact.

Verifying the reliability of sources is seldom an easy process, as two experienced historians note:

> It may seem more difficult to know when to be skeptical about small details in genuine documents than to doubt a legend or anecdote that sounds too pat to be true, but Verification may be as laborious in the one case as in the other.
> —Jacques Barzun and Henry F. Graff, *The Modern Researcher*

The assumptions, reasoning, and interpretation of evidence in sources need to be examined closely. Observations, facts, statistics, and even studies conducted by specialists over several years are subject to different interpretations. In reading your sources, you need to look for differences in approach and emphasis. Also watch for ideas and assumptions that may guide an author's interpretation of evidence; one writer may be interested in the social implications of an event, another in the psychological implications. As you read, watch for special biases or unsupported statements of opinion. These signs indicate that the source may be unreliable.

You will find a log valuable for recording leads to other sources suggested by your reading and for ideas and details that may be of use later. In evaluating source materials for your research paper, make note of assumptions, details that reveal a point of view or special interpretation, biases, and unsupported opinions. You may even wish to comment on these in your paper.

Checklist: Ways to Evaluate a Source

1. Examine the contents of a work, including its table of contents, index, prefatory material, notes, and bibliography.
2. Scan the introductory and concluding chapters as well as the chapters most relevant to your topic.
3. Compare reviews of the book.
4. Watch for discussion of the book or article in sources already verified.
5. Look for a listing or recommendation of the source in reference books and other guides in the field.
6. Look for facts, statistics, and other supporting evidence.
7. Watch for biases and unsupported statements of opinion and interpretation as you read.

EXERCISES

1. What primary and secondary sources does your college library contain on one of the following topics?

   a. the legislative career of Abraham Lincoln
   b. Winston S. Churchill's leadership of Great Britain during
      World War II
   c. Thomas Jefferson's views on slavery
   d. Teapot Dome
   e. the Senate career of Gerald R. Ford
2. What kind of secondary sources would you look for to show
   that the following documents are genuine?
   a. a letter written by Thomas Jefferson that states his moral
      opposition to slavery
   b. a letter written by Abraham Lincoln that describes the
      writing of the Gettysburg Address
   c. an eyewitness report of the Battle of Gettysburg
   d. a signed confession by someone claiming to have partic-
      ipated in the killing of Abraham Lincoln
   e. a story about a nineteenth-century Missouri river town,
      claimed to be the work of Mark Twain

40c | Taking notes

   Having sorted and evaluated your sources, you are ready
to take notes on the ideas and details that will form your research paper. You begin by scanning your sources to find material relevant to your topic. You then read this material carefully and record information about it. It is important to take
careful notes; you don't want to have to return to your original
sources to check for accuracy later on. Further, careless notes
are often the sources of misinterpretation, misquotation, false
attribution, plagiarism, and other faults of research papers.

1 Writing effective notes

Reliable notes contain information that will be useful to you
a week, a month, or even years later. Reliable notes convey the
context of words, phrases, and sentences you have summarized, paraphrased, or quoted. In reading an article or book,
you absorb its **context**—that is, the relationship of ideas and
details, the point of view of the author, and the nuances or
special accents and meanings of words and phrases. Outside
this context, your notes—whether quotations, paraphrases, or
interpretive statements of your own—become meaningless.

For this reason, you must strive to convey in your notes the context of the source concisely and informatively. Your notes will not be useful if you must return to the source to explain an entry or to check the accuracy of your details, quotations, and paraphrases. Thus, in addition to conveying the context of a source, your notes should clearly indicate whether the information recorded is paraphrased or quoted directly.

Index cards are a convenient means of taking notes, but you may prefer to use a notebook or a laptop computer. You also may choose to photocopy some of the source material you find in your search of the library. Photocopies are convenient in checking your final paper for accuracy, but they are not a substitute for careful note-taking. Copying pages will not help you to think in depth about the subject. In taking notes, you digest the meaning of your sources, an essential part of the

"And just which of your remarks did I take out of context?"

Drawing by Joe Mirachi; © 1985 by The New Yorker Magazine, Inc.

research process that doesn't occur in marking up a photocopied page.

Mary Smith began her reading and note-taking with John Snow's *On the Mode of Communication of Cholera*, a primary source that her secondary sources referred to frequently. Published in 1854, Snow's work was indispensable to Mary's investigation. Following is the original Snow passage that she found especially important.

> There were a few cases of cholera in the neighbourhood of Broad Street, Golden Square, in the latter part of August; and the so-called outbreak, which commenced in the night between the 31st August and the 1st September, was, as in all similar instances only a violent increase of the malady. As soon as I became acquainted with the situation and extent of this irruption of cholera, I suspected some contamination of the water of the much-frequented street-pump in Broad Street, near the end of Cambridge Street; but on examining the water, on the evening of the 3rd September, I found so little impurity in it of an organic nature, that I hesitated to come to a conclusion. Further inquiry, however, showed me that there was no other circumstance or agent common to the circumscribed locality in which this sudden increase of cholera occurred, and not extending beyond it, except the water of the above mentioned pump. I found, moreover, that the water varied, during the next two days, in the amount of organic impurity, visible to the naked eye, on close inspection, in the form of small white, flocculent particles; and I concluded that, at the commencement of the outbreak, it might possibly have been still more impure. I requested permission, therefore, to take a list, at the General Register Office, of the deaths from cholera, registered during the week ending 2nd September, in the sub-districts of Golden Square, Berwick Street, and St. Ann's, Soho, which was kindly granted. Eighty-nine deaths from cholera were registered, during the week, in the three sub-districts. Of these, only six occurred in the four first days of the week; four occurred on Thursday, the 31st August; and the remaining seventy-nine on Friday and Saturday. I considered, therefore, that the outbreak commenced on the Thursday; and I made inquiry, in detail, respecting the eighty-three deaths registered as having taken place during the last three days of the week.
>
> —John Snow, from *On the Mode of Communication of Cholera* (1854)

Mary wrote the accompanying bibliography card on John Snow's work and the note card on the passage. A **bibliography card**, containing complete information about a source, is used to compile the list of sources, appearing at the end of the paper under the heading "Works Cited." A **note card**, containing summary, paraphrase, and direct quotation of source material, is used in the text of the paper. Combining the two types of information would make cards (or equivalent notes) difficult to use.

Bibliography card.

John Snow, *On the Mode of Communication of Cholera*, 1854.
In Source Book of Medical History, ed.
Logan Clendening, 468-73
New York: Dover, 1960
Originally published 1942
New York: Henry Schuman

Note card.

Snow, *Communication*   *Source Book*, 469
studied outbreak of cholera Aug. 31-Sept. 1854 in Soho, London
Snow refers to "irruption of cholera"
"I suspected some contamination of the water of the much-
frequented street-pump in Broad Street..."
says he found "so little impurity in it of an organic
nature, that I hesitated to come to a conclusion."
so Snow knew the disease was cholera.
important phrase "no other circumstance or agent"
he is isolating the cause   looking for the one thing
present in the outbreak.
"there was no other circumstance or agent common to
the circumscribed locality"
Note "organic nature"- important, but what does Snow mean?

Mary's bibliography card tells us that she found Snow's work in a 1960 reprint of the first edition: *Source Book of Medical History*, edited by Logan Clendening. She gives this information in her paper as well, in the list of works cited. Mary's note card gives the author and title of the work in shortened form. It also provides enough information to understand what Snow is saying about the outbreak of cholera, including where and on what days the outbreak occurred. Mary also quotes important phrases that reveal Snow's reasoning about the contaminated water supply. By quoting part of the statement that "I found so little impurity in it of an organic nature, that I hesitated to come to a conclusion," and the statement that he found "no other circumstance or agent common to the circumscribed locality," Mary shows the exact language used by a nineteenth-century scientist in tracing causes. Snow was looking for the conditions of the outbreak—the time period, the place, the source—as well as the carrier. All are important to Mary's investigation. The cause of the outbreak, his analysis shows, was not a simple one. Snow was eliminating other possible causes of the disease in considering the street-pump. Mary quotes other statements in other notes that show Snow was reasoning cautiously and was prepared to qualify his findings. Following these details she notes the importance of the phrase "organic nature." Facts do not become evidence until they are interpreted. She will need to interpret this and other key phrases in her paper.

To be certain that nothing important in the original sentence was lost in her reduction, Mary might have quoted the entire sentence concerning the common agent. However, only key details and statements need to be recorded if the context of the statement is clear.

Your own note cards will be effective if you observe the following guidelines:

- Write on one side of the card only to avoid missing information recorded, when you later use the note card.
- Use note cards (or a notebook) to record information about the content of a source. Record the complete publication data on a separate bibliography card.
- Use complete sentences when preparing note cards. In quoting phrases from a source, incorporate them into complete sentences and explain the context of each phrase you quote (as Mary does in the note card shown on page 659). Notes written in incomplete sentences or unconnected phrases may be vague and unclear

later on when you return to your note cards in drafting the paper.

- Be specific in noting the ideas and details of a passage, and include examples that clarify the passage.
- Proofread each note card as you complete it to avoid having to return to the source later on to correct a mistake or to clarify a faulty paraphrase or summary.
- Make each note card stand alone as a source of information. Don't record several bits of unrelated information on a single note card. Instead, devote a single card to the quotation, paraphrase, or summary of a passage. If a passage contains so much information that it requires a second note card, connect that card clearly to the first, repeating details about the source.
- On each bibliography card, record for books the author's name, title and subtitle, publisher, site, publication date, and the inclusive page numbers on which the passage appears (see Mary's bibliography card on page 659). For articles, record the author's name and article title, the full name of the journal, newspaper, or magazine, volume number and year, page numbers, and any special information about a particular issue or section.
- No matter how many note cards you write for a particular source, be sure that every note card contains at least the author's last name, a short title of the work, and a page number. Don't use numbers to link your note cards to your bibliography cards, for you may misnumber one or more of the cards. The author's last name and the shortened title included on your note cards serve this function.
- Write your notes as clearly and neatly as possible. Scribbled notes that can't be deciphered a day or a week after you write them will be of little use in drafting the paper.

2 Direct quotation, paraphrase, and summary

Your note cards should contain a mix of direct quotation, paraphrase, and summary. A **direct quotation** reproduces the exact words of an author and is enclosed in quotation marks. A **paraphrase** gives the ideas of a passage in the order they appear in the original source but in your own words. A **summary** gives the gist or main points of a passage in your own words but not necessarily in the same order. Consider these examples:

Direct Quotation

"As soon as I became acquainted with the situation and extent of this irruption of cholera, I suspected some

contamination of the water of the much-frequented
street-pump in Broad Street, near the end of evening of
the 3rd September, I found so little impurity in it of
an organic nature, that I hesitated to come to a conclusion. Further inquiry, however, showed me that there
was no other circumstance or agent common to the circumscribed locality in which this sudden increase of
cholera occurred, and not extending beyond it, except
the water of the above mentioned pump." (John Snow, <u>On
the Mode of Communication of Cholera</u> [1854]; Logan
Clendening, ed. <u>Source Book of Medical History</u> [New
York: Dover, 1960], p. 469.)

Paraphrase

Snow states that, first testing water from the Broad
Street street-pump, he did not find enough organic impurity to conclude that the pump was responsible for
the rise in cholera in the neighborhood. In investigating the outbreak further, Snow could not find any other
possible condition or source in the area except the
street-pump.

Summary

Though Snow hesitated to draw a conclusion from the organic material found in water from the Broad Street
street-pump, he later concluded that nothing else in
the area could explain the rise in cholera.

You should use direct quotation, paraphrase, and summary in your notes but for specific purposes. A summary is
sufficient when the reasoning and specific details of a passage
are unimportant to your topic or point. Paraphrase is sufficient
when specific reasoning and details are important. Direct quotation is desirable when paraphrase or summary cannot convey the sense or meaning that you want to record. Quotations
should not be random or aimless. You should quote only what
you cannot put into your own words without a substantial loss

of meaning. For example, you might want to quote some or all of a passage that would lose its special accent and eloquent force if you paraphrased it. Or you might want to quote key phrases or those that would lose significant meaning in summary or paraphrase. If you want to convey an essential idea through a key phrase, incorporate it into your sentence and enclose the phrase in quotation marks, as Mary Smith does in this sentence from an early draft of her paper:

> Snow concluded that "no other circumstance or agent" was present in the neighborhood when the outbreak of cholera occurred.

Do the same in quoting a whole sentence from the passage:

> Snow concluded that "the water varied, during the next two days, in the amount of organic impurity, visible to the naked eye, on close inspection, in the form of small white, flocculent particles...."

Your use of quotation, paraphrase, and summary will be effective if you follow these guidelines:

- Use paraphrase or summary to record ideas that lose nothing in translation. Paraphrase is desirable when it is important to present the ideas of a passage in the order they occur. If order is unimportant, then summary is desirable. Through paraphrase and summary you will gain an understanding and mastery of your sources that direct quotation cannot provide.
- When you quote a phrase, always make a note about its context. That is, explain the author's use of the phrase. If you quote out of context, you risk changing the author's intended meaning and thereby may mislead your readers. You will need information about the context when you quote or refer to the phrase or the example in the paper.
- Quote only those phrases or sentences that would lose meaning in paraphrase or summary (see 40c 2). State in the note card or notebook page whether your note on the passage is paraphrase or summary.
- Try not to quote too much. The key phrases you quote won't gain emphasis if you use quotation excessively in your paper. Think of a quotation as a kind of illustration or example, not as a substitute for your description of an author's idea. The quotation

should be only a part of your total explanation or argument. If your notes consist of a string of direct quotations, you may later have to return to your original sources to digest the ideas fully.

■ In taking notes on a passage, be careful not to include your own interpretation or opinion. If you mix interpretation and opinion with paraphrase and summary, you will have trouble distinguishing them when you draft the paper. Record your opinions and interpretations separately, perhaps in a list of some sort, or on the bottom of your note cards, labeling them clearly.

3 Ellipsis in quoted material

In taking notes, you will have frequent occasion to omit nonessential words and phrases from quoted material. An **ellipsis**—three spaced periods or ellipsis points (see 26c)—is used to show the omission of words and phrases from a passage. The ellipsis also marks the omission of one or more sentences from a quoted passage. When you omit words, phrases, or sentences from a quotation, though, what remains must be grammatically complete. In addition, the omission must not change the author's meaning.

In quoting from John Snow's work, Mary Smith used the ellipsis in the following ways to show her omissions of words and phrases not essential to her discussion:

Omission of Nonessential Clause and Phrase

Original	Reduced
The keeper of a coffee-shop in the neighbourhood, which was frequented by mechanics, and where the pump-water was supplied at dinner time, informed me (on 6th September) that she was already aware of nine of her customers who were dead.	"The keeper of a coffee-shop in the neighbourhood ... where the pump-water was supplied at dinner time, informed me ... that she was already aware of nine of her customers who were dead."

Omission of Nonessential Phrase

Original	Reduced
The pump was frequented much more than is usual, even for a London pump in a populous neighbourhood.	"The pump was frequented much more than is usual...."

664

Note that, in the second example, the ellipsis follows the sentence period.

Nothing must be omitted from a quotation that is essential to its intended meaning. In the following sentence, for example, omitting the italicized opening or closing phrase would alter the meaning:

> *With regard to the deaths occurring in the locality belonging to the pump,* there were sixty-one instances in which I was informed that the deceased persons used to drink the pump-water from Broad Street, *either constantly or occasionally.*

The opening phrase must be included in the quotation because it specifies where the deaths occurred; the closing phrase must be included because it notes that all of the victims had drunk the water. The fact that some had drunk the water "occasionally" suggests that the polluted water was deadly.

You should show all omissions at the beginning and at the end of quotations in your notes. However, in the final paper you may choose not to show these omissions when you use partial quotations. In this case, ellipsis points are necessary to mark an omission at the beginning or end of a sentence only when you want to point out to the reader that the rest of the original sentence is important but not essential to its meaning or to your discussion.

4 Making additions to quoted material

You may occasionally come across a probable error in a source, perhaps a misspelling or mistaken choice of word. If the word is an obvious misprint, correct it in your note without calling attention to the error. However, the misspelling may be the deliberate choice of the author and not a printer's error; that is, the author may also have chosen the word in question. In these circumstances, add the word *sic* in brackets to show that the error is not your own. *Sic* means "just as I found it":

```
Smith states, "The two are alien [sic] in their
thinking."
```

The writer probably meant *alike*, but *alien* does fit the context and it may be the author's word.

If necessary, add explanatory information to a quotation

in brackets to distinguish your words from the original author's:

Smith states, "They parted as friends and colleagues on September 6 [1982]."

If you underline or italicize words in a quoted passage for emphasis, state this fact in parentheses following the quotation:

Orwell's choice of words and similes is significant: "The inflated style is itself a kind of <u>euphemism</u>. A mass of Latin words falls upon the facts like <u>soft snow</u>, blurring the outlines and covering up all the details" (emphasis added).

(See 25d and 26d on other uses of brackets and italics.)

Checklist: Omissions and Additions in Quoted Material

1. Omit words, phrases, and sentences from quoted material that are not essential to your discussion. Although parts of passages may be omitted, what remains must be grammatically complete.
2. Use three spaced periods—the ellipsis—to indicate omissions from a quotation.
3. If the omission occurs at the end of a sentence, put the three spaced periods after the period that ends the sentence.
4. Add your own explanatory comments to a quotation in brackets. If you underline parts of the quotation for emphasis, indicate this in parentheses after the closing quotation mark.

EXERCISES

1. Write a note card that records the essential facts and ideas of the following passage. Quote at least one important phrase as well.

> In many ways homeless people have become "resident strangers," people who have lost their roles within society, along with their homes. Evidence for this can be found in the generic term, "homeless": an undifferentiated form rather than mothers, children, fathers, sons, and daughters whose misfortunes and society's failures have led them to the streets, the welfare hotels, or the shelters. The label serves to obscure their heterogeneity. By depersonalizing them, the impact of their plight is blunted; we distance them from our own lives and fail to address the serious and complex social problems that have produced them in the numbers we see today. It is critical that the psychological, economic, and political dimensions of homelessness be understood and that the distorted, romantic, and inaccurate images of homeless life be disabused.
> —Leanne G. Rivlin, "A New Look at the Homeless"

2. Write a paraphrase of the preceding paragraph, retaining only the essential ideas. Then write a brief summary.
3. What phrases or sentences would you quote rather than paraphrase in discussing this passage in a paper?

 40d A note on plagiarism

Plagiarism is the use of another writer's words and ideas as if they were your own. Intentional plagiarism is a dishonest act that can have severe consequences. Copyright law protects authors from plagiarism and colleges usually penalize students who intentionally plagiarize.

Some plagiarism is accidental. It can arise from carelessness in note-taking, particularly when the note-taker is not paying attention to quoted words. When paraphrasing a passage in the paper, the writer may include phrases, clauses, and whole sentences and forget to enclose them in quotation marks. All direct quotation, paraphrase, and summary, however, need to be acknowledged and fully cited. The plagiarism in the following example is especially glaring since almost an entire passage is reproduced without quotation marks or adequate crediting of the source:

Source

Sylvester Graham was right, of course. His fear that commercially baked, and adulterated, white bread portended a sweeping displacement of natural foods by artificial products has been realized to a disturbing degree in the twentieth century.
—James C. Whorton, *Crusaders for Fitness: The History of American Health Reformers* (Princeton, N.J.: Princeton UP, 1982, p. 331)

Plagiarism

```
American health reformers were right in fearing that
commercially baked, and adulterated, white bread por-
tended a sweeping displacement of natural foods by ar-
tificial products. One of these reformers was Sylvester
Graham, inventor of the Graham cracker.
```

A common and unintentional plagiarism occurs with short phrases that the writer forgets to enclose in quotation marks on the note card and later in the paper:

Plagiarism

```
The adulteration of food happened to a disturbing de-
gree in the twentieth century.
```

The words *to a disturbing degree in the twentieth century* are Whorton's, not those of the writer, who should have spotted these accidental borrowings in using the quoted material. An instructor reading the paper probably would assume the plagiarism is intentional.

You should take special care not to incorporate ideas from a source in your paper without proper acknowledgment. Whorton's statement that health reformers like Graham predicted the adulteration of food should be acknowledged even if Whorton is not quoted. However, *common knowledge* need not be quoted or acknowledged in the text. It is common knowledge, for example, that Sylvester Graham invented the Graham cracker. The reader should be in no doubt about the source of an idea or an uncommon fact. Listing the source in

Checklist: Avoiding Plagiarism

1. Take notes carefully and proofread as you write them.
2. Don't use ideas, details, or examples from your sources in your notes or paper without proper acknowledgment.
3. Don't quote from your sources without enclosing all quoted material in quotation marks—both on your note cards and in the paper.
4. Acknowledge the sources of all paraphrased and summarized material.
5. Don't acknowledge common facts. Do acknowledge unusual statements of fact or theories in your source.
6. The listing of a source in the bibliography or "Works Cited" is not adequate acknowledgment of an idea or example used in the paper. Acknowledge the source directly in the text.

the bibliography or "Works Cited" section of the paper is not adequate acknowledgment; you should cite the source directly in the text.

Careful note-taking can help you to avoid unintentional plagiarism. You should proofread each of your note cards to be certain that quotation marks enclose all quoted material. Most errors occur with paraphrase and summary. A careful check is essential when you are taking notes and again when you are preparing the final paper to ensure that phrases and ideas from your sources are not incorporated into your own sentences without quotation marks or proper credit.

40e Using research notes

Writing a research paper is in many ways similar to writing the personal essay and expository paper discussed in Chapters 1–4. The difference is in the use of source material in drafting the paper and later in revising it. Let us look at the process of using research notes in the planning and writing of the research paper.

1 Sorting and outlining

In preparing to draft your paper, you may find some or all of the invention techniques described in Chapter 2 useful (see 2d). For example, sorting your evidence and using a topic outline may reveal connections and relationships in the material you have collected.

Writing a topic outline may help you to work out an idea that covers the topics you worked with in your notes. But consider your outline a tentative plan only. In the course of researching further and drafting and revising, you may decide to change the order of ideas or their relative weight; you may discover alternative ways to use the evidence recorded in your notes. A quotation or idea you have paraphrased may give better support to another point.

Having written her notes, Mary Smith sorted them in groups and looked for possible connections and related ideas. In grouping the note cards, she formed several clusters, including the following:

```
Chadwick    diet          definitions
Budd        terror        miasmas
Snow        debauchery    polluted water and food
            drunkenness   vibrio cholerae
```

A number of possible ideas and hypotheses occurred to Mary in the course of sorting details and thinking about their implications. She jotted down these ideas as she proceeded, for several might serve as the thesis of her paper. One particular detail caught Mary's attention—women in England and America were identified as carriers in nineteenth-century cholera epidemics. After considering its possible implications, she decided to add the idea to the second cluster even though she was uncertain about the connection.

One question particularly interested Mary: Why were women particularly identified as carriers of the disease? She introduced this idea into an outline of the main topics she had been working with:

TOPIC OUTLINE

Introduction: Shaw's view of doctors

I. History and nature of cholera
   A. Definition of cholera
      1. Early nineteenth-century definition
      2. The definition today
   B. Theories of cholera up to 1860
      1. Localist theory
      2. Contagionist theory
   C. Early nineteenth-century theorists
      1. Edwin Chadwick
      2. William Budd
      3. John Snow

II. Nineteenth-century social attitudes and medical theories
   A. Social attitudes
      1. General public
      2. Doctors and surgeons
   B. Medical theories
      1. Diet
      2. Terror
      3. Drunkenness and debauchery
      4. Women as carriers

2   Formulating a working thesis

With your tentative outline and research notes close at hand, you are ready to formulate a **working thesis**—a hypothesis about or explanation of the evidence collected. As you engage in further research and thought, you will have several more opportunities to refine your thesis. You should be prepared to qualify your working thesis if you find that your evidence does not support it completely.

Writing an outline helped Mary formulate a working thesis, one that she would revise at a later stage in drafting her paper:

```
The treatment of cholera suggests that Shaw's picture
of doctors is not entirely imagined.
```

The following procedures will help you formulate a work-able thesis:

- As you take notes on your sources and sort your evidence, jot down ideas as they occur to you, distinguishing your interpretations and opinions from those in your sources. It is important to jot ideas down right away, for you will have the opportunity to refine them later on.
- Use these ideas to formulate a working thesis that interprets your evidence. Your working thesis should be the outcome of your reading and thoughts about the topic. Don't try to mold your evidence to fit an opinion you hold or are determined to defend; your evidence must make its own points for you.
- Work out a plan, perhaps a topic outline, that incorporates the main points covered in your notes. Use the outline, as a tentative plan and as a means to test your working thesis.
- Be prepared to revise your thesis in drafting your paper. It isn't until you actually begin writing that you discover all you want to say.

3 Drafting the paper

Your research notes are central to the drafting of your paper. Before writing your first draft, read your note cards and other notations to remind yourself of the details and ideas in your source materials. The more familiar you are with these materials, the more smoothly ideas and details will fall into place as you write. Your evidence may suggest many other ideas and perhaps further revision of your working thesis. Jotting these down as they occur to you is valuable. One of these ideas may even suggest research at another time on another subject.

Mary Smith's topic outline was a preliminary trying out of her ideas. The first draft of a paper is also a trying out of ideas—a thinking through of the evidence and ideas of the paper. Like Mary, you should give considerable thought to the evidence, but the act of stating these ideas probably will suggest connections and possibilities that didn't occur to you at the start of your investigation. Changes in focus, emphasis, and subject often occur throughout the stages of prewriting, writing, and later revision.

You may wish to write a first draft of the paper quickly with occasional reference to your ideas and notes to distinguish your ideas from those in your sources. At this point in writing the paper, your main concern is with how your argument holds together, not how it reads. Consult your notes before you begin to write the draft, but be sure that the words you use are your own. You should avoid copying your notes directly into the draft. Putting ideas into your own words is a way of making sure that you understand them.

You may have to make several starts until the paper begins to take shape. If a new arrangement of ideas occurs to you in the course of writing, you should ignore your outline and not interrupt the draft to revise it.

Checklist: Drafting and Revising the Paper

1. Put the ideas of your paper in your own words in a trial draft, consulting your outline and notes if necessary as you write.
2. Don't interrupt the writing of the draft to check your sources. Make notes of ideas and details to check later.
3. Keep your notes close at hand in writing your second draft. Rephrase your ideas, incorporating direct quotation, paraphrase, and summary from your notes.
4. Ignore your outline if a new idea or better arrangement of ideas occurs to you. Don't interrupt your writing to revise the outline.
5. Discuss your evidence and connect it to your working thesis.
6. Don't force unnecessary ideas and details into the discussion. You are not obligated to use all of the information on your note cards.
7. Document and properly punctuate all direct quotations, paraphrases, and summaries.
8. In revising the paper, read the paper through to see that the ideas and supporting evidence develop your thesis.
9. Rework the argument and, if necessary, support it with new evidence and reformulate your thesis.

In your second draft, you want to integrate your notes into the discussion, making sure that they support your argument. Identify each source you refer to in the second draft, and be careful to keep the quotations, paraphrases, and summaries you distinguished in your notes distinct in the paper as well. It is usually at this point that plagiarism accidentally occurs.

Aim for economy of explanation and illustration in your writing. You have probably collected more material in your research than you need to develop your final thesis. Nevertheless, you won't know exactly how much of this material you will need until after you draft the paper and have your final thesis and organization of ideas in mind.

4   Revising the paper

In the course of revising her first and second drafts, Mary Smith developed some of her ideas with additional evidence; other ideas were discarded. She also jotted down ideas suggested by the evidence she was discussing. One of these ideas she chose to present as her thesis.

In revising your own draft, look for points that need development through additional details and facts. As new possibilities arise, you may do further reading and note-taking. Problems in interpretation often appear for the first time in the course of using an idea from your source material. You may discover that interpretation of a passage depends on missing facts you did not think of investigating when you first paraphrased or quoted a passage. For example, the missing facts may have to do with special meanings that require a historical dictionary, such as checking a word like *virus*, common in nineteenth-century medical literature. You may need to find new facts that explain a procedure that seemed clear when you wrote the note card but is not clear when you try to explain it in the paper.

Look also for points that you have overdeveloped. If you tried to use all of the material you gathered for the paper, you may have to delete sentences or even whole paragraphs. Few writers like to cut ideas and details from their writing, particularly ideas and details gathered with difficulty. You will probably need to cut more from the draft than you need to add.

In revising your research paper, read to get a sense of the whole argument and the way your evidence supports your ideas. Ask yourself whether the evidence directly supports the point. The ideas of the paper should work together to support the thesis you have formulated. If they do not, you may need to rethink your argument and state a new thesis. Remember also that the evidence you gathered gives *some* support to your thesis. You will need to phrase your thesis carefully so that you do not claim more than your evidence allows.

As you revise, you will notice sentences that need rephrasing and paragraphs that need reorganization. You will give these features close attention now and later on when you edit the paper. In preparing the final draft, Mary edited it, giving close attention to her spelling, grammar, and punctuation, and proofread it a final time. Mary's final paper appears in Chapter 42. For details on the mechanics of the paper see Chapter 47.

Summary

40a Use primary sources—eyewitness accounts, letters, and documents by participants in an event—to verify other sources. Use secondary sources—discussions of eyewitness accounts and other primary evidence—to authenticate and interpret your primary sources.

40b Evaluate the reliability of your sources by examining their content, reading reviews of them, and watching for unsupported statements of opinion.

40c Your notes should record the details and context of a source in a form that will be useful to you when you are ready to draft your paper.

Use complete sentences and give complete information about each source in your notes **(40c 1)**.

Quote your sources accurately and avoid mixing quotation with paraphrase or summary **(40c 2)**.

Use paraphrase or summary to record the sense of the original passage. Use direct quotation when the wording is highly significant or when its special meaning would be lost in paraphrase **(40c 2)**.

Use ellipsis points to mark omissions of nonessential words, phrases, and sentences from quotations **(40c 3)**.

If you add explanatory information and comments to a quotation, enclose them in brackets **(40c 4)**.

40d Don't use the words or ideas of another writer in your notes or paper without proper acknowledgment. Acknowledge all quotation, paraphrase, and summary of your sources. Proofread your notes to avoid unintentional plagiarism.

40e Integrate your notes into the paper as you draft it.

Sorting evidence and writing a topic outline will help you in organizing your paper **(40e 1)**.

A working thesis will help you in thinking out your ideas **(40e 2)**.

Revise your thesis and organization as needed in the course of drafting and revising the paper **(40e 3–4)**.

Documenting the Research Paper

41

The research paper requires that you document the sources you use completely and accurately. The purpose of **documentation** is to help the reader verify the information contained in an essay or article. Documentation also serves to give proper credit to the authors whose ideas and details you use in the paper and to alert your reader to what is borrowed. In documenting a source, you provide the specific information your reader needs to locate it, including the author, title, publisher, date, edition, and volume and page numbers. Further, this information is presented in a special way.

Although all disciplines require documentation of sources, each has its own requirements for formatting the documentation. This chapter describes three current methods of documentation that you will be asked to use in papers written for different courses. **MLA-style** documentation is recommended by the Modern Language Association for use in the humanities, **APA-style** is recommended by the American Psychological Association for use in the social sciences, and **CBE-style** is recommended by the Council of Biology Editors for use in the biological sciences.

41a MLA parenthetical documentation

In 1984, the Modern Language Association (MLA) recommended parenthetical documentation for use in the humanities, a method that had long been in use in the social and natural sciences. Textual citations appear in *parentheses* rather than in raised note numbers. **MLA parenthetical documentation**, now in wide use in the humanities, is the preferred alternative to endnote and footnote documentation (see 41b) and other methods still in use. This section describes how to document your sources according to the format set forth in the *MLA Handbook for Writers of Research Papers*, 3rd edition (New York: MLA, 1988).

1 Preparing the list of works cited

A completed research paper includes a list of sources or **works cited**. This list appears at the end of the paper and is titled "Works Cited." In preparing the entries for your list of works cited, observe the following guidelines:

- Start "Works Cited" on a separate page. Double-space the entries. Begin each entry flush left and indent subsequent lines of the same entry five spaces.
- Give the author's last name first. Copy the author's name from the title page of the work, not from the catalog card or other reference tool. If only the initial letter of the author's first name appears there, you may include the full name if you need to avoid confusion with another author with the same last name and initial. In this case, add the omitted letters of the first name in brackets:

  Smith, J[ohn].

  You can find the names of most authors in biographical dictionaries and the *Biography Index* (39e).
- Underline the title and subtitle of a book. Put the title of an article in quotation marks; underline the title of the journal or other periodical. Use a colon to separate the subtitle from the title.
- If you are using an edition of a book other than the first, give the date of publication of the new edition, not the original date of publication. Give the edition number (except for first editions) and the series exactly as they appear on the title or copyright page of the original book.

- If the book has an editor or translator, give this information after the title and edition number.
- Give the city of publication, the publisher's name, and the year in parentheses. Include the state (Cambridge, MA) or country (Harmondsworth, Eng.) of publication only when you need to distinguish the city from another city of the same name or to identify an unfamiliar place. If the title page lists more than one city of publication, give only the first city listed there. If two publishers are listed, give both with their respective cities.
- Use abbreviated forms of publishers' names, omitting words like *Company, Corp., Inc., Press,* and *Publishers.* For example, *Macmillan* is sufficient for identifying *Macmillan Publishing Company, Harper* for *Harper & Row,* and *Norton* for *W. W. Norton.* For university presses, abbreviate the words *University* and *Press* as follows:

```
Princeton UP

U of Michigan P

State U of New York P
```

- Give volume numbers of books in arabic numerals even if the title page of a book shows a roman numeral. (See the sample entries on page 683 for multivolume works published in the same year and in different years.)
- Use the abbreviation *Vol.* for volume, but omit *p.* and *pp.* in page references. Use *Vol.* only with books as shown below.
- Separate the title of the article from the journal title with a period, followed by the volume number in arabic numerals, the year of publication (in parentheses), and the inclusive page numbers, following a colon. Add the number of the issue (4.3) if each issue is numbered independently.

Following are model MLA-style entries for a book and a journal article:

MLA-style book entry.

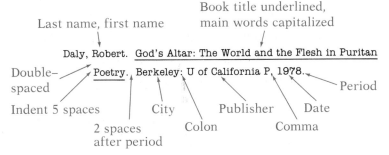

679

MLA-style journal entry.

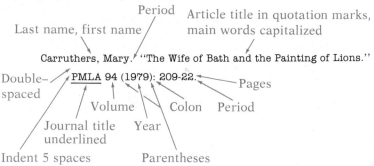

Period

Last name, first name

Article title in quotation marks, main words capitalized

Carruthers, Mary. "The Wife of Bath and the Painting of Lions."

Double-spaced

PMLA 94 (1979): 209-22.

Pages

Volume   Colon   Period

Journal title
underlined

Year

Indent 5 spaces   Parentheses

Checklist: Guide to Works Cited Sample Entries

Books
1. Book: single author
2. Book: two or three authors
3. Book: more than three authors
4. Book: one or more editors
5. Multivolume work published in the same year
6. Multivolume work published in different years
7. Book in a series
8. Published proceedings
9. Translation
10. Multiple publishers
11. Corporate author
12. Anonymous book
13. Republished book
14. Book published before 1900
15. Play, poem, story, chapter, or essay in an anthology or collection
16. Book with an uncertain publication date
17. Preface, introduction, foreword, afterword, or notes
18. Government publication
19. Pamphlet
20. Published letters

21. Encyclopedia or reference article
22. Unpublished and published dissertation

Periodicals
23. Journal article
24. Newspaper or magazine article
25. Editorial, letter to the editor
26. Abstract
27. Review

Other Sources
28. Musical composition, recording, work of art
29. Film or videotape
30. Television or radio program
31. Interview
32. Lecture or address
33. Legal reference

Following is a list of sample entries for the MLA "Works Cited." The checklist above identifies each entry. For additional entries, see *MLA Handbook for Writers of Research Papers*, 3rd edition (1988).

Sample MLA-Style Works Cited Entries

Books
Works cited entries for books must give enough information for readers to locate a particular volume and edition. The entries that follow show how to do so.

1. *Book: single author*
   In the following listing, three hyphens and a period mark the second book by Lewis Thomas:

   Thomas, Elizabeth Marshall. The Harmless People. New

   York: Knopf, 1959.

   Thomas, Lewis. The Medusa and the Snail. New York:

   Viking, 1979.

   ---. The Youngest Science: Notes of a Medicine-

   Watcher. New York: Viking, 1983.

In citing a later edition of a work, give information about the editor (if different from the author) and the edition following the title:

Hopkins, Gerard Manley. <u>The Poems of Gerard Manley</u>
<u>Hopkins</u>. Ed. W. H. Gardner. 3rd ed. New York:
Oxford UP. 1948.

Notice that *editor* and *edition* are both abbreviated *ed.*

2. *Book: two or three authors*

Gedo, John E., and Arnold Goldberg. <u>Models of the</u>
<u>Mind: A Psychoanalytic Theory</u>. Chicago: U of
Chicago P, 1973.

Stockwell, Robert P., Paul Schachter, and Barbara Hall
Partee. <u>The Major Syntactic Structures of</u>
<u>English</u>. New York: Holt, 1973.

3. *Book: more than three authors*
If the book has more than three authors, you can list the first given on the title page, followed by *et al.*:

Quirk, Randolph, et al. <u>A Grammar of Contemporary</u>
<u>English</u>. New York: Seminar, 1972.

List the authors in full if you have reason to identify them:

Quirk, Randolph, Sidney Greenbaum, Geoffrey Leech, and
Jan Svartvik. <u>A Grammar of Contemporary English</u>.
New York: Seminar, 1972.

4. *Book: one or more editors*
The name of an editor of a collection of essays or papers opens the entry:

Tompkins, Jane P., ed. <u>Reader-Response Criticism: From</u>
<u>Formalism to Post-Structuralism</u>. Baltimore: Johns
Hopkins UP, 1980.

The editor's name ordinarily follows the title of a work by another author. Use the abbreviation *ed.* for editor:

Orwell, George. <u>The Orwell Reader: Fiction, Essays,</u>
<u>and Reportage</u>. Ed. Richard H. Rovere. New York:
Harcourt, 1956.

If your citation is to the introduction, foreword, notes, or other contribution of the editor, give the editor's name, followed by *ed.*, the particular section written by the editor, and then the title of the work (see also entry 17). The author's name follows as shown:

Rovere, Richard H., ed. Introduction. <u>The Orwell</u>
<u>Reader: Fiction, Essays, and Reportage</u>. By George
Orwell. New York: Harcourt, 1956. xvi–xvii.

5. *Multivolume work published in the same year*
If a work consists of more than one volume, give the volume number and the total number of volumes in arabic numerals. Follow the style of the first entry if you used all volumes of a multivolume work. If you used only a particular volume, name it specifically as in the second entry shown here.

Johnson, Edgar. <u>Charles Dickens: His Tragedy and</u>
<u>Triumph</u>. 2 vols. New York: Simon, 1952.
Shaw, Bernard. <u>The Doctor's Dilemma</u>. Vol. 1 of
<u>Complete Plays with Prefaces</u>. 4 vols. New York:
Dodd, 1963.

6. *Multivolume work published in different years*
Include the volume number, the total number of volumes, and the inclusive years of publication as follows:

Durant, Will. <u>The Renaissance</u>. New York: Simon, 1953.
Vol. 5 of <u>The Story of Civilization</u>. 11 vols.
1935-75.

7. *Book in a series*
   Put the name of the series after the book title. Use the abbreviation *ser.* if the word *series* is part of the name:

   Ehrman, Madeline E. The Meanings of the Modals in

   Present Day American English. Janua Linguarum,

   Ser. Practica 45. The Hague: Mouton, 1966.

8. *Published proceedings*
   The title of a paper delivered at a conference and published in a collection appears in quotation marks. The title of the book-length collection of the papers delivered at the proceedings of a conference is underlined.

   Chomsky, Noam. "The Logical Basis of Linguistic

   Theory." Proceedings of the Ninth International

   Congress of Linguistics. Ed. Horace G. Lunt. The

   Hague: Mouton, 1964. 914-78.

9. *Translation*

   Solzhenitsyn, Aleksandr I. The Gulag Archipelago 1918-

   1956: An Experiment in Literary Investigation

   I-II. Trans. Thomas P. Whitney. New York: Harper,

   1973.

   Note that the given name *Aleksandr* appears on the title page. Some books of Solzhenitsyn spell the name *Alexander*.

10. *Multiple publishers*
    List multiple publishers that appear on the title page:

    Schoenbaum, S. Shakespeare's Lives. Oxford: Clarendon;

    New York: Oxford UP, 1970.

    If the title page gives more than one city for a single publisher, cite the first city only. Note that the title page of *Shakespeare's Lives* abbreviates Schoenbaum's given name.

11. *Corporate author*
If the author named on the title page of a book is a corporation, agency, or institution rather than an individual, give the corporate name in the author position:

American Red Cross. First Aid and Personal Safety. 2nd
ed. New York: Doubleday, 1979.

12. *Anonymous book*
Begin an entry for an anonymous book—one that gives no author on the title page—with the title:

The Famous Victories of Henry the Fifth. London:
Thomas Crede, 1898.

13. *Republished book*
The original date of a republished book follows the title:

Baldwin, James. Notes of a Native Son. 1955. New York:
Bantam, 1968.

Add information about the introduction or other editorial matter added to the republished version after the original data of publication:

Hardy, Thomas. Jude the Obscure. 1896. Introd. C. H.
Sisson. Harmondsworth, Eng.: Penguin, 1978.

14. *Book published before 1900*
For a book published before 1900, you may omit the publisher's name:

Brigham, A. A Treatise on Epidemic Cholera. Hartford,
1832.

15. *Play, poem, story, chapter, or essay in an anthology or collection*
Give complete information about the anthology as well as the inclusive page numbers of the specific work within it:

Browning, Robert. "Fra Lippo Lippi." Victorian Poetry
and Poetics. Ed. Walter E. Houghton and G. Robert
Stange. 2nd ed. Boston: Houghton, 1968. 209-14.

If you are citing an essay or article that has been republished in a collection, give the details of the earlier publication and *rpt.* for "reprinted in" when appropriate:

> Kiparsky, Paul. "Stress, Syntax and Meter." Language
> 51 (1975): 576-616. Rpt. in Essays in Modern
> Stylistics. Ed. Donald C. Freeman. London:
> Methuen, 1981. 225-72.

16. *Book with an uncertain publication date*
In the following entry, the probable date of publication appears in brackets to show that it does not appear in the book:

> Marchand, Hans. The Categories and Types of Present-
> Day English Word-Formation. Alabama Linguistic
> and Philological Ser. 13. Tuscaloosa: U of
> Alabama P [1967?].

If the date of publication or the place or the name of the publisher is not given in the book and you cannot supply them from another source, use the abbreviation *n.p.* (no place; no publisher) and *n.d.* (no date). If the book is unpaginated, use the abbreviation *N. pag.*:

> N.p.: World Publications, 1956. 210-250.
>
> New York: n.p., 1956. 210-250.
>
> New York: World Publications, n.d. 210-250.
>
> New York: World Publications, 1956. N. pag.

17. *Preface, introduction, foreword, afterword, or notes*
If your reference is to the author or editor of an introduction or other interpretive material, cite this author or editor first, then the work and the author. The inclusive page numbers follow the publisher and date:

> Schorer, Mark. Afterword. Main Street. By Sinclair
> Lewis. New York: Signet-NAL, 1961. 433-39.

18. *Government publication*

> United States. Bureau of the Census. <u>Poverty in the</u>
>   <u>United States: 1987</u>. Current Population Reports,
>   Ser. P-60, No. 163. Washington: GPO, 1989.

19. *Pamphlet*
Treat a pamphlet like a book. If a pamphlet has no author,
begin the entry with the title.

> <u>Volkswriter 4 and Your Printer: Technical Information</u>.
>   Monterey, CA: Lifetree Software, 1989.

20. *Published letters*

> Woolf, Virginia. "To Quentin Bell." 17 Feb. 1930.
>   Letter 2145 in <u>The Letters of Virginia Woolf</u>. Ed.
>   Nigel Nicolson and Joanne Trautmann. Vol. 5. New
>   York: Harcourt, 1979. 141-42.

21. *Encyclopedia or reference article*
Begin the entry with the author if the encyclopedia article
is signed. If initials follow the article, look up the name of the
author in the list of contributors, usually in the first or final
volume. If the article is unsigned, begin with the title. Include
the edition of the encyclopedia but not the editor or publisher:

> Bernays, Paul. "David Hilbert." <u>Encyclopedia of</u>
>   <u>Philosophy</u>. 1967.
> "Slavery." <u>Encyclopedia of Black America</u>. 1981.

22. *Unpublished and published dissertation*
The title of an unpublished dissertation appears in quotation marks. Note the two spaces before and after the descriptive
abbreviation *Diss.*:

> Tang, Ho Yin. "The Enigma of Hog Cholera:
>   Controversies, Cause, and Control,
>   1833-1917." Diss. U of Minnesota, 1986.

A published dissertation is cited as a book, with additional information on the university and year of completion:

```
Rosenbaum, Peter S. The Grammar of English Predicate
     Complement Constructions. Diss. M.I.T., 1965.
     Research Monograph 47. Cambridge: M.I.T. Press,
     1967.
```

Periodicals

Works cited entries for articles published in periodicals must also give enough information for readers to locate particular volumes and issues. Most scholarly journals number pages consecutively through a single volume, but some number pages by issue. Most magazines (like *Newsweek* and *Time*) number pages by issue; others (like *Consumer Reports*) number pages by volume.

23. *Journal article*

The following entry is for a journal that numbers its pages continuously throughout a volume:

```
Knowles, John H. "The Responsibility of the
     Individual." Daedalus 106 (1977): 57-80.
```

For a journal that numbers each issue separately, the issue number and the volume number are separated by a period:

```
Spangler, Lynn C. "A Historical Overview of Female
     Friendships on Prime-Time Television." Journal of
     Popular Culture 22.4 (1989): 13-23.
```

24. *Newspaper or magazine article*

If a magazine is published weekly or biweekly, give the day, month, and year:

```
Moore, Kathleen Dean. "When Mercy Weakens Justice."
     New York Times 10 Aug. 1989: A23.
```

If a magazine is published monthly, give the month and year:

```
Koretz, Jane F., and George H. Handelman. "How the
    Human Eye Focuses." Scientific American July
    1988: 92-99.
```

If a magazine article is numbered continuously, give the inclusive page numbers, as shown in the citation of the *Scientific American* article. If the page numbering is discontinuous, indicate the first page only and add "+" to show that the pages following are discontinuous:

```
Ackerman, Diane. "Bats." New Yorker. 29 Feb. 1988:
    37+.
```

Omit the volume number in citing articles from newspapers, magazines, and journals.

25. *Editorial, letter to the editor*

```
"Greening the Cabinet." Editorial. New York Times
    25 Jan. 1990, sec. A: 22.
De Vriest, Simon J. Letter. Newsweek 29 Jan. 1990: 20.
```

26. *Abstract*
  You will find dissertation abstracts in *Dissertation Abstracts (DA)* and after 1969 in *Dissertations Abstracts International (DAI)*, published now in three series, shown as A, B, or C after the dissertation number:

```
Tang, Ho Yin. "The Enigma of Hog Cholera:
    Controversies, Cause, and Control, 1833-1917."
    DAI 47 (1987): 3172A. U of Minnesota.
```

27. *Review*
  If a review of a published work, film, play, or musical or theatrical performance is signed and titled, open the citation with the author of the review:

```
Leithauser, Brad. "Enfevered." Rev. of Coleridge:
    Early Visions, by Richard Holmes. New Yorker
    2 July 1990: 68-73.
```

If a review is titled but unsigned, open the citation with the title of the review:

```
"Rhythm and Scansion." Rev. of The Musical Basis of
     Verse, by J. C. Dabney. Times Literary Supplement
     22 Aug. 1902: 251.
```

If a review is untitled and unsigned, open the citation with the title of the work reviewed:

```
Rev. of Sara Coleridge: Her Life and Essays, by
     Bradford Keyes Mudge. New Yorker 19 Feb. 1990:
     112.
```

Other Sources
Papers in the fine arts and other fields often refer to audiovisual source materials. You should list as much information as your reader needs to find the source material.

28. *Musical composition, recording, work of art*
Don't underline works identified by form (e.g., symphony, concerto, suite). Underline titles of works, including those in which the word *symphony* or *concerto* is part of the title:

```
Brahms, Johannes. Symphony No. 1 in C minor, op. 68.
     Cond. Loren Maazel. Cleveland Orch. London, CS
     7007, 1976.
Tchaikovsky, Peter I. A Manfred Symphony, op. 58.
     Cond. Andre Previn. London Symphony Orch. Angel,
     37018, 1974.
Turner, William. The Shipwreck. Tate Gallery. London.
```

29. *Film or videotape*

```
Hamlet. Dir. Laurence Olivier. With Laurence Olivier,
     Eileen Herlie, Jean Simmons, and Basil Sydney.
     Rank, 1948.
Life in Camelot: The Kennedy Years. Videocassette.
     Prod. Peter W. Kunhardt. HBO Video, 1988. 55 min.
```

30. *Television or radio program*

> <u>The Bombing of Pan Am 103</u>. Frontline. PBS. WNET, New
> York. 23 Jan. 1990.

31. *Interview*

> Smith, John. Personal interview. 18 May 1984.

32. *Lecture or address*

> McCawley, James D. "Can You Count Pluses and Minuses
> before You Can Count?" Third Annual Midwest
> Regional Conference of the Chicago Linguistic
> Society. Chicago, 6 May 1967.

33. *Legal reference*
The following reference to a court opinion gives the name of the case, the source of the opinion in the *Federal Supplement*, the court in which the opinion was delivered (New York District Court), and the year:

> Goodis v. United Artists Television. 278 Fed. Supp.
> 122. NY Dist. Ct. 1968.

Your works cited entries should appear as an alphabetized list. Some papers contain other kinds of bibliographies, for example, an annotated list of recommended readings on the topic of the paper. In bibliographies of this kind, the list of titles can be divided by topic or some other category, for example:

- By nature of the source (primary sources, secondary sources).
- By topic (e.g., measles, smallpox, yellow fever in a paper on viruses).
- By period (eighteenth century, nineteenth century, and so on).
- By authors (Emily Brontë, Charles Dickens, George Eliot).
- By genre (poems, plays, novels, essays).

See the *MLA Handbook*, 3rd edition, for other rules and sample entries. See also the entries in the sample paper using MLA style in Chapter 42.

2 Citing sources in the text

In MLA parenthetical documentation, citations enclosed in parentheses in the text refer the reader to the list of works cited at the end of the paper.

Sample parenthetical citations

Reference to author and page
A textual reference or citation always follows a direct quotation, paraphrase, or summary, in as concise a form as possible. For a direct quotation, always include the page number:

```
The Kalahari Desert is "a vast sweep of dry bush des-
ert," in the words of one visitor to South-West Africa
(Thomas 3).
```

The parenthetical citation is to the book by Elizabeth Marshall Thomas listed in the sample entries on page 681.

Reference to page number
If you give the author's name in the text, you need only give the page number in the citation:

```
Elizabeth Marshall Thomas describes the "palmful of
little white beads" that a woman in the Kalahari Desert
uses to treat gangrene (233).
```

Reference to two or more works of an author
When you cite two or more works by the same writer, use shortened titles to distinguish them:

```
In his essay "Medical Lessons from History," Lewis
Thomas states that the nineteenth-century doctor "could
be depended on to explain things, to relieve anxieties,
and to be on hand" (Medusa 135). Thomas's father was
such a doctor, as he shows in The Youngest Science
(1-11).
```

The citations in this example are to the Lewis Thomas books listed in the sample entries on page 681.

Reference to more than one work

If your list includes two or more of an author's works, and you do not name the author in the text, cite the author and the work as follows:

```
Today people hear so much illness that they "believe
that they are fundamentally fragile, always on the
verge of mortal disease" (Thomas, Medusa 39).
```

Note that the parenthetical reference follows the closing quotation mark and precedes the period of the sentence.

Reference to authors with the same last name

In citing works by writers with the same last name in the same paper, give the full name in the text:

```
Lewis Thomas suggests that people are healthier than
they realize (Medusa 39).
```

Reference to a multivolume work

In citing a passage in a multivolume work, include the volume number. The following citation is to a two-volume book on the life of Charles Dickens (see item 5 in the list of sample entries):

```
Johnson states that Dickens was "fiercely sure that all
achievement is possible" (1: 132).
```

If you do not include the author's name in the text, put it in the citation:

```
One biographer states that Dickens was "fiercely sure
that all achievement is possible" (Johnson 1: 132).
```

Reference to an encyclopedia or reference article

When you cite an article in an encyclopedia or other reference book, give the author or the title of the article only:

```
David Hilbert asked questions that created modern math-
ematics (Bernays).
```

693

Volume and page numbers are omitted when the reference work is in dictionary form, as in the *Encyclopedia of Philosophy*, to which the preceding citation is made (see item 21 in the list of sample entries).

Reference to a scholarly article
Cite journal articles in the same way you cite books. Give the page number only, if the author's name appears in the text.

3 MLA abbreviations

Abbreviations save space in typing papers. MLA recommends the following abbreviations in parenthetical citations and the list of works cited.

app. [appendix]
assn. [association]
c. [c. 1546: *circa* or "about" 1546]
ch., chs. [chapter, chapters]
comp. [compiler]
diss. [dissertation]
ed. [edition, editor, edited by]
et al. [Latin *et alii*: and others]
fig. [figure]
illus. [illustrator, illustration]
inc. [incorporated; including]
introd. [introduction]
ms., mss. [manuscript, manuscripts]
n.d. [no date of publication given]
no. [number]
n.p. [no place of publication given, no publisher]
n. pag. [no pagination]
pseud. [pseudonym]
rept. [reprint]
rev. [revised, revised by]
sec. [section]
trans. [translator]
U [university]
UP [university press]
vol., vols. [volume, volumes]

The following months are abbreviated as follows:

Jan., Feb., Mar., Apr., Aug., Sept., Oct., Nov., Dec.

Note that May, June, and July are never abbreviated. MLA also uses postal abbreviations for states.

4 Explanatory notes

Explanatory facts and parenthetical comments that you want to add to a paper should appear at the foot of the page or as numbered endnotes at the end of the paper. Raised numbers are inserted in the text where most appropriate to alert the reader to the notes. Explanatory notes should help the reader understand the source material and your interpretation of it. For example, you might discuss the reliability of a source you are quoting or explain why the evidence presented came to the attention of researchers only recently.

Explanatory notes should be brief statements of only a few lines that are directly relevant to the subject but that would interrupt your discussion if placed in the text. They should not be extended essays that occupy half the page. If you find that you are writing a lengthy note, the content may be important enough to belong in the main text of the paper. Resist the temptation to put into notes all remaining material that you could not use in the paper.

41b MLA endnotes and footnotes

The standard format for documentation before 1984 was the **MLA endnote/footnote** method. This style is still used by many writers in the humanities, and you may be asked to use it rather than MLA parenthetical documentation. Basically, the same information found in parenthentical documentation is in endnotes or footnotes, but in different formats. Familiarity with endnotes and footnotes will also help you in working with source materials that contain them.

1 Using endnotes or footnotes

Endnotes and footnotes follow the same format but appear in different places in the paper. **Footnotes** appear at the bottom of the page, two double-spaces (or four lines) below the text and are single-spaced. In research papers, **endnotes** are used more often than footnotes. They appear in a numbered list at the end of the paper under the heading "Notes" and are double-spaced. The heading is centered one inch below the top of the page and the endnotes begin one double-space below. Indent the first line of each endnote or footnote five spaces from the left margin; successive lines are flush with the left margin. (See the model notes that follow.)

Indicate an endnote and footnote in the text with a raised number (^{1}) immediately following the last word of the sentence:

> Daly states that the world of the American Puritan was symbolic: "Things meant."^{1}

Occasionally, the note number may appear within a sentence, such as after an author's name or book title. But wherever the note number appears in the sentence, the same raised number *begins* the endnote or footnote.

The endnote/footnote system sometimes requires a separate list of references under the heading "Bibliography," which follows the list of endnotes. If your instructor wants you to provide a bibliography, follow the format shown on pages 681–91 for the list of works cited. Bibliographies save the reader from having to hunt through the endnotes or footnotes for citations. Your instructor may not require a bibliography in a short research paper.

If you use endnotes or footnotes, you may add explanatory facts or comments to the notes or present these in separate notes. All notes are numbered consecutively, whether they are citation or explanatory notes.

2 Note form and logic

In writing endnotes or footnotes, observe the following examples and guidelines:

MLA-style note for a book.

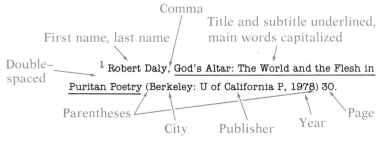

MLA-style note for a journal article.

Comma

First name, last name

Article title in quotation marks,
main words capitalized

Double-
spaced

[2] Mary Carruthers, "The Wife of Bath and the Painting of
Lions," PMLA 94 (1979): 214.

Comma   Volume   Colon   Period

Journal title   Year
underlined

Page

Parentheses

Sample MLA-Style Notes

Following are sample notes illustrating MLA footnote and endnote style. For additional examples see *MLA Handbook for
Writers of Research Papers*, 3rd edition, pp. 183–200.

Books

1. *Book: single author*

[1] Elizabeth Thomas Marshall, The Harmless People
(New York: Knopf, 1959) 233.

2. *Book: two or three authors*

[1] Robert P. Stockwell, Paul Schachter, and
Barbara Hall Partee, The Major Syntactic Structures of
English (New York: Holt, 1973) 45.

3. *Book: one or more editors*

[1] George Orwell, The Orwell Reader: Fiction,
Essays, and Reportage, ed. Richard H. Rovere (New
York: Harcourt, 1956) 167.

[2] Richard H. Rovere, ed., The Orwell Reader:
Fiction, Essays, and Reportage, by George Orwell (New
York: Harcourt, 1956) xvii.

4. *Multivolume work published in the same year*

   [1] Edgar Johnson, <u>Charles Dickens: His Tragedy and Triumph</u>, vol. 1 (New York: Simon, 1952) 457-58.

   [2] Bernard Shaw, <u>The Doctor's Dilemma, Complete Plays with Prefaces</u>, vol. 1 (New York: Dodd, 1963) 87.

5. *Multivolume work published in different years*

   [1] Will Durant, <u>The Renaissance</u> (New York: Simon, 1953) 42, vol. 5 of <u>The Story of Civilization</u>, 1935-75.

6. *Book in series*

   [1] Madeline E. Ehrman, <u>The Meanings of the Modals in Present Day American English</u>, Janua Linguarum, Ser. Practica 45 (The Hague: Mouton, 1966) 45.

   [1] Thomas Hardy, <u>Jude the Obscure</u>, introd. C. H. Sisson (1896; Harmondsworth, Eng.: Penguin, 1978) 7.

7. *Play, poem, story, chapter, or essay in an anthology or collection*

   [1] Robert Browning, "Fra Lippo Lippi," <u>Victorian Poetry and Poetics</u>, ed. Walter E. Houghton and G. Robert Stange, 2nd ed. (Boston: Houghton, 1968) 210.

   [2] Paul Kiparsky, "Stress, Syntax and Meter," <u>Language</u> 51 (1975): 576-616; rpt. in <u>Essays in Modern Stylistics</u>, ed. Donald C. Freeman (London: Methuen, 1981) 227.

8. *Preface, introduction, foreword, afterword, or notes*

   [1] Mark Schorer, afterword, <u>Main Street</u>, by Sinclair Lewis (New York: Signet-NAL, 1961) 435.

9. *Government publication*

> [1] United States, Bureau of the Census, Poverty in the United States, Current Population Reports, Ser. P-60, No. 163 (Washington: GPO, 1989) 47-48.

10. *Letters*

> [1] Virginia Woolf, "To Quentin Bell," 17 Feb. 1930, letter 2145 of The Letters of Virginia Woolf, ed. Nigel Nicolson and Joanne Trautmann, vol. 5 (New York: Harcourt, 1979) 141.

11. *Encyclopedia or reference article*

> [1] Paul Bernays, "David Hilbert," Encyclopedia of Philosophy, 1967.
> [2] "Slavery," Encyclopedia of Black America, 1981.

Periodicals
12. *Journal article*

> [1] John H. Knowles, "The Responsibility of the Individual," Daedalus 106 (1977): 58. [continuous pagination]
> [2] Lynn C. Spangler, "A Historical Overview of Female Friendships on Prime-Time Television," Journal of Popular Culture 22.4 (1989): 15-16. [pagination by issue]

13. *Newspaper or magazine article*

> [1] Kathleen Dean Moore, "When Mercy Weakens Justice," New York Times 10 Aug. 1989: A23.
> [2] Diane Ackerman, "Bats," New Yorker 29 Feb. 1988: 38.

14. *Editorial, letter to the editor*

> [1] "Greening the Cabinet," editorial, <u>New York
> Times</u>, 25 Jan. 1990, sec. A: 22.
> [2] Simon J. De Vries, letter, <u>Newsweek</u> 29 Jan.
> 1990: 20.

3 Successive references

In successive references, use a shortened form for subsequent references to a source fully cited in an earlier note. Successive references no longer require Latin abbreviations (*ibid.*, for the work cited in the preceding note; *op. cit.* for the work cited in an earlier note; *loc. cit.* for the place cited).

MLA Handbook recommends that subsequent references contain only the author's last name and a page reference. If you cite different works by the same author, include shortened titles as well:

> [1] Lewis Thomas, <u>The Medusa and the Snail: More
> Notes of a Biology Watcher</u> (New York: Viking, 1979) 40.
> [2] Lewis Thomas, <u>The Youngest Science: Notes of a
> Medicine-Watcher</u> (New York: Viking, 1983) 134-35.
> [3] Thomas, <u>Medusa</u> 42.
> [4] Thomas, <u>Youngest Science</u> 136.

If you refer to different writers with the same last name (e.g., Elizabeth Marshall Thomas and Lewis Thomas) in successive notes, refer to their books by shortened titles as well:

> [1] Elizabeth Marshall Thomas, <u>The Harmless People</u>
> (New York: Knopf, 1959) 42.
> [2] Thomas 86.
> [3] Lewis Thomas, <u>The Youngest Science: Notes of a
> Medicine-Watcher</u> (New York: Viking, 1983) 134-35.
> [4] Lewis Thomas, <u>The Medusa and the Snail: More
> Notes of a Biology Watcher</u> (New York: Viking, 1979) 40.

700

⁵ Thomas, <u>Medusa</u> 49.

⁶ Thomas, <u>Youngest</u> 78.

 ## APA parenthetical documentation

In research papers for psychology courses and other social sciences, you will most often use **APA parenthetical documentation**, recommended by the American Psychological Association in its *Publication Manual*, 3rd edition (Washington, DC: APA, 1983).

1 Preparing the list of references

As in MLA parenthetical documentation, references in APA documentation appear in parentheses in the text and a list of sources appears on a separate page immediately following the text of the paper. Use the following format for the APA references list:

- List the sources referred to in the paper under the heading "References," centered one inch below the top of the page. Do not underline or place the heading in quotation marks. Double-space the list, beginning each entry at the left margin, and indenting three spaces for the second or turn line of an entry.
- Begin each entry with the names of all authors and editors, using initials for first and middle names. Invert each author's or editor's name and initials, separating two or more names with commas and using an ampersand (&) in place of the word *and*. If the persons cited edited the book, give this information immediately following the names as follows:

Tomkins, S. S., & Izard, C. E. (Eds.) (1965).

- Place the year of publication in parentheses following the author's name, as shown above. Then list the source. If a source is a book, capitalize only the first word of the title and the subtitle and all proper nouns. Underline the title and subtitle. If the book is an edition, add this information in parentheses (2nd ed.) following the title. Conclude the entry with the city and location if needed for identification (e.g., Oxford, OH) and the name of the publisher in short form (usually the first word of the name is sufficient). Give the full name of a university press.

- If a source is a magazine journal article, list the article first, then the publication. Do not underline the title of the article or place it in quotation marks; underline the journal title. Capitalize only the first word of the article, but capitalize the key words of the journal title. Follow the journal title with its volume number, in arabic numerals, and the inclusive pages. See the examples below for spacing and punctuation of the entries.
- Arrange the references list alphabetically by last name and by title if a source has no author or editor. Drop the words *A*, *An*, and *The* in listing. Arrange works by the same author, or groups of authors, chronologically from the earliest to the most recent publication, using lower case letters to distinguish those published in the same year:

      1977a, 1977b, 1977c, and so on

APA-style book entry.

Date in parentheses

2 spaces

Last name, first initial(s)

Title and subtitle underlined; capitalize only the first words or proper nouns

Bettelheim, B. (1977). The uses of enchantment: The meaning and importance of fairy tales. New York: Knopf.

Double-spaced

Indent 3 spaces

2 spaces   City   Colon   Publisher

Period

APA-style journal entry.

Date

Last name, initial(s)

Article title—no quotation marks; only first word and proper nouns are capitalized

Period

Journal title underlined

Ruse, M. (1975). Charles Darwin and artificial selection. Journal of the History of Ideas, 36, 339-350.

Pages

Period

Double-spaced

Indent 3 spaces

Volume number underlined

Commas

Sample APA-Style References

Book: Single Author

Fenichel, O. (1945). The psychoanalytic theory of
neurosis. New York: Norton.

Book: Two or More Authors

Gedo, J. E., & Goldberg, A. (1973). Models of the mind:
A psychoanalytic theory. Chicago: University of
Chicago Press.

Edited Book

Tomkins, S. S., & Izard, C. E. (Eds.). (1965). Affect,
cognition, and personality: Empirical studies. New
York: Springer.

Revised Edition

Arendt, H. (1966). The origins of totalitarianism (rev.
ed.). New York: Harcourt.

Book without a Named Author or Editor

The Price Waterhouse personal tax adviser. (1988). New
York: Bantam.

Article or Chapter in a Multivolume Work

Freud, S. (1959). Inhibitions, symptoms, and anxiety.
In J. Strachey (Ed. and Trans.), The standard
edition of the complete psychological works of
Sigmund Freud: Vol. 20 (pp. 77-175). London:
Hogarth. (Original work published in 1926)

Article or Essay in an Anthology

Ackerknecht, E. H. (1977). Paleopathology. In D. Landry
(Ed.), Culture, disease, and healing: Studies in
medical anthropology (pp. 72-77). New York:
Macmillan.

Government Document

Internal Revenue Service. (1989). Your federal income
tax (Publication 17). Washington, DC: U.S.
Government Printing Office.

Journal Article, Two to Five Authors:
Continuous Pagination

Berger, P., Hamburg, P., & Hamburg, D. (1977). Mental
health: Progress and problems. Daedalus, 106,
261-276.

Journal Article, Six or More Authors:
Continuous Pagination

Ironson, G. H., Gellman, M. D., Spitzer, S. B., Llabre,
M. M., Pasin, R. D., Weidler, D. J., & Schneiderman,
N. (1989). Predicting home and work blood pressure
measurements from resting baselines and laboratory
reactivity in black and white Americans.
Psychophysiology, 26, 174-184.

Journal Article: Pagination by Issue

Jahoda, M. (1988). Economic recession and mental
health: Some conceptual issues. Journal of Social
Issues, 44(4), 13-23.

Journal Article: Corporate Author

American Psychological Association. (1986). Guidelines
for ethical conduct in the care and use of animals.
Journal of the Experimental Analysis of Behavior,
45, 127-132.

Magazine Article

Cole, D. (1989, June). The entrepreneurial self.
Psychology Today, pp. 60-63.

[Notice the abbreviation *pp.* with magazine and newspaper articles but not with journal articles.]

Newspaper Article, Discontinuous Pages

```
McFadden, R. D. (1990, April 23). Millions join battle
    for a beloved planet. New York Times, pp. A1, B12.
```

Interview

```
Paris Review. (1963). [Interview with Ralph Ellison].
    Writers at work: Second series. New York: Viking.
```

Book Review

```
Bridgeman, B. (1987, January 16). Psychology and
    neuroscience [Review of Dialogues in cognitive
    neuroscience]. Science, 235, 373-374.
```

Computer Software

```
Cindex 4.0: Software for professional indexers (1989).
    [Computer program]. Rochester, NY: Indexing
    Research.
```

For other entries not shown here, see the APA *Publication Manual*. For a sample paper using APA documentation, see 44c.

2 Citing sources in the text

The APA recommends the following guidelines in preparing parenthetical citations for the text:

- Cite all information taken from sources, including direct quotation, summary, paraphrase, or general citation to the whole work. Place the citation in parentheses following the last word of the sentence and before the period. Include the last name of the author, the date of the source, and the inclusive page numbers as follows:

```
In psychoanalytic theory "the patient misunderstands
the present in terms of the past" (Fenichel, 1945,
p. 29).
```

If you mention the author in the text, include only the year and the page in parentheses:

```
Fenichel (1945) states that in psychoanalytic theory
"the patient misunderstands the present in terms of the
past" (p. 29).
```

Use the abbreviations *p.* and *pp.* with page numbers. Also use *chap.* for *chapter* and *vol.* for *volume*.

- If your source has two authors, use an ampersand (Gedo & Goldberg) in your parenthetical reference, but use *and* (Gedo and Goldberg) if authors' names are not given parenthetically.
- List all authors in the list of references regardless of number. In the text, however, give only up to five authors in the first parenthetical citation; in subsequent citations name the first one only and follow this with "et al." If the publication has six or more authors, give the surname of the first author and "et al." in the first as well as subsequent citations. Remember that the date of publication follows authors' names at each citation:

```
(Tomkins & Izard, 1985)
(Jones et al., 1986)
```

- If you identify a source by title rather than author in your list of references, cite the title in short form in parentheses:

```
(Guidelines for Research, p. 51)
```

- Omit page numbers if you are referring to the content of a book or article as a whole:

```
(Guidelines for Research, 1982)
```

- Put graphs and tables at appropriate places in the text or in appendices following the list of references.

3 Explanatory notes

You may add notes to the paper that explain points in the text and that cannot be incorporated without interrupting the discussion awkwardly. These notes should be brief and significant in content. Present these notes in a double-spaced and numbered list, following the text of your paper. As in MLA documentation, references to notes are marked by raised numbers in the text and in the list (see 41b). List the notes under the heading "Footnotes," centered at the top of the page (do not underline or place the heading in quotation marks). The first line of each note is indented five spaces.

(See section 44c for a sample paper using APA-style documentation.)

 CBE documentation

Papers in the biological sciences most often use **CBE parenthetical documentation**, recommended by the Council of Biology Editors in its *CBE Style Manual*, 5th edition (Bethesda, MD: CBE, 1983). As in APA documentation, you make parenthetical citations to a list of sources at the end of the paper, under a suitable heading like "Literature Cited" or "References."

The *CBE Style Manual* describes several kinds of citation systems. In the common *name-year system*, the name and year of publication appear in parentheses (Mayr 1982) and refer to an alphabetized list of authors at the end of the paper. As in APA style, works by the same author are listed chronologically (from earliest to most recent publication) and works published in the same year are distinguished by lowercase letters (1944a, 1944b). Some journals also include page references (Mayr 1982, p. 78–80).

In CBE style, only the first word of a title (not subtitle) is capitalized. Some scientific journals abbreviate journal titles; some do not. CBE recommends that, if abbreviations are used, they follow those in the *International List of Title Word Abbreviations*, in the reference section of your library. However, single-word titles like *Science* are unabbreviated. Note that the name of the publisher is given in full. Use the following models in listing multiple authors and punctuating entries.

The *CBE Style Manual* makes no general recommendation on the inclusion of specific page references for books and periodicals. Ask your instructor for details of an entry if specific page references are required.

Following are model entries for a book and an article:

CBE-style book entry.

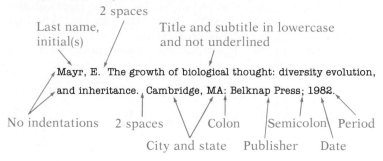

CBE-style journal entry.

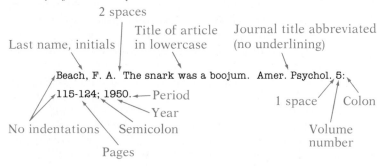

Sample CBE-Style References

Following are sample entries for the CBE list of references:

Book: Single Author

Fenichel, O. The psychoanalytic theory of neurosis.
New York: W. W. Norton Co.; 1945.

Book: Two or More Authors

Gedo, J. E.; Goldberg. A. Models of the mind: a
psychoanalytic theory. Chicago: University of Chicago
Press; 1973.

Edited Book

Landy, D., editor. Culture, disease, and healing: studies in medical anthropology. New York: Macmillan Publishing Co.; 1977.

Corporate Author

National Research Council. Report of the committee on maternal and child health research. Washington, DC: National Academy of Sciences; 1976.

Journal Article

Khoury, G.; Gruss, P. Enhancer elements. Cell. 33:313-314; 1983.

Mayr, E. The birds of Timor and Sumba. Bull. Amer. Mus. Nat. Hist. 82:127-194; 1944a. [continuous pagination]

Mayr, E. Wallace's line in the light of recent zoogeographic studies. Quart. Rev. Biol. 29: 1-14; 1944b.

Miller, A.; Mintzer, I. Global warning: no nuclear quick fix. Bull. of the Atomic Scientists (June):46(5):30-34; 1990. [discontinuous pagination]

Newspaper article

Brooke, J. Ancient find, but how ancient? New York Times. 1990 April 17; Sect. C:1 (col. 1), 10 (col. 1).

For other CBE-style entries not shown here, see the *CBE Style Manual*. For a sample paper using CBE documentation, see 44d.

For other documentation styles in the sciences and social sciences, see the following guides:

Handbook for Authors of Papers in American Chemical Society Publications. Washington, DC: American Chemical Society, 1978.

A Manual for Authors of Mathematical Papers. 7th ed. Providence: American Mathematical Society, 1980.

Style Manual for Guidance in the Preparation of Papers. 3rd ed. New York: American Institute of Physics, 1978.

Summary

41a Sample entries for the list of works cited in MLA parenthetical documentation:

```
Daly, Robert. God's Altar: The World and the Flesh
     in Puritan Poetry. Berkeley: U of California
     P, 1978.
Carruthers, Mary. "The Wife of Bath and the
     Painting of Lions." PMLA 94 (1979): 209-22.
     [continuous pagination]
Spangler, Lynn C. "A Historical Overview of Female
     Friendships on Prime-Time Television." Journal
     of Popular Culture 22.4 (1989): 13-23.
     [pagination by issue]
Moore, Kathleen Dean. "When Mercy Weakens Justice."
     New York Times 10 Aug. 1989: A23.
```

41b Sample entries for MLA-style endnotes and footnotes:

```
     1 Robert Daly, God's Altar: The World and the
Flesh in Puritan Poetry (Berkeley: U of California
P, 1978) 30.
     2 Mary Carruthers, "The Wife of Bath and the
Painting of Lions," PMLA 94 (1979): 214.
[continuous pagination]
```

41c Sample entries for the APA-style references list:

```
Bettelheim, B. (1977). The uses of enchantment: The
     meaning and importance of fairy tales. New York:
     Knopf.
Ruse, M. (1975). Charles Darwin and artificial
     selection. Journal of the History of Ideas, 36,
     339-350. [continuous pagination]
```

Tomkins, S. S., & Izard, C. E. (Eds.). (1965).
Affect, cognition, and personality: Empirical
studies. New York: Springer.

Ackerknecht, E. H. (1977). Paleopathology. In D.
Landry (Ed.), Culture, disease, and healing:
Studies in medical anthropology (pp. 72-77). New
York: Macmillan.

41d Sample entries for the CBE-style references list:

Mayr, E. The growth of biological thought:
diversity, evolution, and inheritance. Cambridge,
MA: Belknap Press, 1982.

Gedo, J. E.; Goldberg, A. Models of the mind: a
psychoanalytic theory. Chicago: University of
Chicago Press; 1973.

Beach, F. A. The snark was a boojum. Amer. Psychol.
5:115-124; 1950. [continuous pagination]

A Sample
Research Paper

42

In this chapter, we examine Mary Smith's research paper on nineteenth-century medical theories of cholera, which is reprinted on the following pages. Mary's paper illustrates some of the methods you can put to use in your research papers. For example, it uses MLA-style parenthetical documentation, with textual citations that correspond to a list of works cited that appears at the end. The paper also uses explanatory notes to introduce information that Mary found in her sources but that would have interrupted her discussion if she had included it in the text. Mary used a wide range of primary and secondary sources in her research, as is indicated by her list of works cited. To support some of the ideas she found in secondary studies of cholera, Mary cites primary sources like books written during the nineteenth-century cholera epidemics in England and America. These primary sources, interpreted in light of special studies of the disease, produced interesting discoveries about nineteenth-century medical theory and answered one of the questions that originally led Mary to her research topic.

Mary's research paper is accompanied by detailed comments that appear on the pages opposite her text. These comments point out important aspects of the paper, such as its organization, use of source materials, and other features of research papers discussed in the earlier chapters of Part Nine.

713

Format of the paper

The *MLA Handbook* recommends formatting the first page of the paper by typing your last name, the name of your instructor, class, and date one inch below the top of the page, double-spaced and flush with the left margin. Center the title of your paper on the next line. Capitalize key words and do not underline or put the title in quotation marks. On all pages of the paper, type your last name and the page number flush with the right margin, a half-inch below the top. Leave margins of one inch on the two sides of the page and at the top and bottom. Use double-space throughout the paper.

Paragraphs 1–5: Introduction

The *introduction* to a paper (see 38d) usually states the central topic and introduces the thesis. Mary Smith uses her introduction to state a question and to introduce her thesis.

Paragraph 1   The quotations in paragraph 1 generate interest in the topic. Mary quotes key statements that show Shaw's feelings about the medical profession.

Quotations that require less than four typed lines are run into the text. In her opening paragraphs, Mary runs her short quotations into the text.

Mary uses ellipsis points to show that words have been omitted from Shaw's original sentence.

Paragraph 2   Mary narrows her subject to medical ignorance and misuse of science. She excludes details on Shaw's experiences with doctors because extraneous details would divert attention from the central topic.

The parenthetical citations in this paragraph give the page number of Shaw's preface, cited fully at the end of the paper in Works Cited. Shaw's name is not included in the citations because he is mentioned in the paragraph.

Paragraph 3   Mary implies the topic of her paper by summarizing the questions raised by Shaw's statements.

Mary Smith

Professor Jones

Humanities 201

10 December 1990

The Medical View of Cholera: 1832-67

1   In the preface to his 1904 play <u>The Doctor's</u>
<u>Dilemma</u>, George Bernard Shaw attacks medicine in his
time as a "murderous absurdity" (1). "The tragedy of
illness at present," he states, "is that it delivers
you helplessly into the hands of a profession which you
deeply mistrust" (2). The causes of mistrust include
cruelties in the name of knowledge, the lack of honor
and conscience, and pandering to the desires of their
patients: "What they [doctors] commonly mistake for
these is sentimentality and an intense dread of doing
anything that everybody else does not do, or omitting
to do anything that everybody else does" (3).

2   Shaw attacks most vigorously the ignorance of doctors and misuse of science. The doctor, he states,
often "draws disastrous conclusions from his clinical
experience because he has no conception of scientific
method ..." (18). But Shaw is not here making a case
for scientific medicine, for he believed in good diet,
sanitation, and other means of preventing disease, not
in the new therapies of medical science like vaccination. "Doctoring is an art, not a science," he states.
"Doctoring is not even the art of keeping people in
health ... it is the art of curing illnesses" (18).

3   Shaw's statements raise important questions for
readers of his preface and play. Do his views accu-

Paragraph 4 Summarizing the approach to be taken and the evidence to be presented in the paper gives the reader a map to follow and an indication of purpose. The opening sentence introduces the thesis, stated partially in paragraph 5 and stated fully in paragraphs 21 and 23. Mary builds up to her thesis, a useful technique when the thesis is controversial or difficult to explain without full details.

Notice Mary's succinct statement of important facts. Mary does not give a reference because these facts are common knowledge.

Paragraph 5 The reader needs to know why the evidence to be presented warrants the conclusion. Mary justifies her reasons for examining Shaw's ideas in light of cholera epidemics in Great Britain and the United States: scientific understanding of the disease advanced in the nineteenth century, yet social attitudes continued to influence discussion. She thus explains why her evidence will warrant the conclusion she reaches. (See 35d on warrants in reasoning.) The paragraph ends with a partial statement of the thesis.

Facts need interpretation. In stating a key fact about the 1832 epidemic, Mary explains why doctors needed social explanations. Mary adds other relevant facts from her sources.

716

rately reflect medical practice in the nineteenth century, the period referred to in the preface? Were doctors influenced more by social attitudes than by
medical science?

4   A partial answer can be given through how English
and American doctors in the nineteenth century reasoned
about and treated disease--in particular, a disease new
to most of them. Cholera first appeared in Great Britain in 1832, following outbreaks in other European
countries; the epidemic spread quickly to the United
States. Numerous nineteenth-century medical reports and
books describe the medical response. Many English doctors had observed and treated this disease in Asiatic
countries, particularly in India, but most doctors in
England and America were treating the disease for the
first time.

5   Cholera is a good test of Shaw's ideas because
scientific understanding of the disease increased in
the nineteenth century; doctors and scientists discovered first its means of transmission, then its bacterial origin. Social attitudes stand out in discussions
of the disease: some English and Americans identified
cholera with the Asiatic poor and apparently believed
that white people seldom contracted it. In 1832, however, many white people did contract cholera--a fact
that required a social explanation. The effects of
cholera on English towns was devastating in epidemic
years. In the 1853 cholera epidemic in the northern
town of Newcastle-upon-Tyne with a population of
90,000, records show that more than 1500 people died
(Callcott 167). The total number of deaths in England

Paragraphs 6–12: Statement of Background
The *narration* or statement of background (see 36d) presents the reader with the facts needed to understand the discussion.

Paragraph 6   Mary begins the main body of her paper by defining the term *cholera*, then briefly tracing the history of the disease. In defining the word, she gives its etymology. Mary is providing important facts needed by the general reader.

Paragraph 7   Details of the disease prepare the reader for the popular medical opinion that cholera was a disease of the poor (paragraph 8). Notice the economical presentation of facts and the citation of sources.

Smith 3

and Wales in the same year was 11,000 (Callcott, 176).
For this reason doctors theorized about the disease in
numerous articles and books published in England and
the United States in 1832 and later years. These publications clearly support Shaw's view that doctors were
influenced by social attitudes in their theory of cholera and reports on patients.

6   The etymology of the word <u>cholera</u> tells much about
nineteenth-century theories and social attitudes toward
the disease. The word derives from the Greek for bile--
the ancient Greek term for the disease referring to
bilious diarrhea. In ancient times, cholera was also
identified with other serious gastrointestinal infec-
tions and also appendicitis and ptomaine poisoning
(Pollitzer 14-15). Cholera was also the name for a
milder disease called "British" or "European" cholera
or "summer diarrhea." Today, the word describes viru-
lent Asiatic cholera, caused by bacteria identified by
the German bacteriologist Robert Koch in 1883; it was
Asiatic cholera that struck England in 1832 (Barau and
Burrows 10).

7   Localizing in the small intestines, cholera starts
with violent diarrhea and sometimes vomiting. The so-
called rice-water diarrhea that follows is watery and
contains mucus. The final stages of the disease show
severe dehydration and shrivelling and discoloration of
the skin, loss of potassium and electrolyte, and weak
pulse and rapid heartbeat (Pierce 1598-1600). Medical
scientists in the later nineteenth century divided
sharply on the effects of the disease on the intestinal
lining. Scientists today have isolated most of the con-

Paragraph 8   Mary uses her opening sentences to keep her topic—social attitudes—before the reader. She also focuses on details that explain why doctors thought cholera was a racial or ethnic disease.

Mary will document this and other assumptions later in the paper (paragraphs 16–18) and use them as decisive evidence for her thesis, stated fully in paragraph 21.

Paragraph 9   Mary uses her background for a double purpose: she informs the reader of the facts and uses these facts to build her ar-

ditions that produce cholera. A recent medical observer states: "The disease appears to cause virtually no organ or system damage which cannot be explained by the water and electrolyte imbalance resulting from the severe dehydration" (Phillips 70).

8   Because cholera originated in Asia and struck the poor hardest, it was called by one medical observer in England "the poor man's disease," a common view expressed in newspapers and medical reports in 1832 (Morris 85). Ironically, this opinion seems to be correct, for many well-nourished people survive the cholera bacterium or vibrio without showing symptoms; malnourished people are more susceptible (Morris 15). Thus many Europeans in the East survived cholera epidemics as did many Asiatics, though British officials worried about the toll of cholera among soldiers stationed in British India, where from ten to fifteen million Indian people died of the disease between 1815 and 1865, according to one estimate one-sixteenth of the population in the 1817-21 epidemic (Arnold 120). It is not surprising, then, that in the early nineteenth century many doctors thought of cholera as a racial or ethnic disease and, as in ancient times, defined the disease through its symptoms and chiefly through its discharges. In his study of the 1832 cholera epidemic in England, Morris quotes the <u>London Times</u> (13 February 1832): "The real causes of the disease are poverty, bad living, insufficient clothing, dirty streets and dwellings, united with occasional excess" (85).

9   The popular "localist" theory of cholera in nineteenth-century England connected the disease further

gument that "localist" theory associated stenches with poor districts, thereby strengthening social explanations.

The first citation gives the date of issue only since the sentence mentions the *Times*. Margaret Pelling's name is excluded from the second citation because the source is clearly her book.

Paragraph 10   A persuasive argument depends on closely reasoned evidence. The concise statement of Budd's and Snow's findings allows the reader to consider important evidence. Mary quotes Snow at length because his findings were decisive and they show that scientific evidence existed as early as 1854. The second quotation from Snow shows that some investigators did reason about disease without reference to social attitudes. This quotation is indented because it requires more than four typed lines; it is indented ten spaces from the left margin.

with gases and miasmas rising from filth in poor districts. In 1832, the <u>London Times</u> reported complaints
of stench coming from privies and butcher markets in
East London, people referring to the stench as "pesti-
lential vapour" (23 July 1832). In her study of cholera
in nineteenth-century England, Margaret Pelling states
that many English people believed "all smell is disease" (59). Pelling quotes a surgeon testifying before
a sanitary commission in 1831: "I have not the slight-
est doubt that in <u>certain constitutions</u> of the atmosphere there is nothing so likely to produce disease"
(59; emphasis added). "Localists" like the social re-
former Sir Edwin Chadwick recommended sanitation as a
preventive of epidemics, even though he was ignorant of
the real cause (229-39). Sanitation reform, led by
prominent members of the clergy and other nonmedical
people, in fact anticipated the scientific findings of
medical "contagionists" at work in the 1850s (Kerr
672-76).

10   The rival "contagionist" theory was that cholera
is water-borne as well as air-borne. In 1849, a Bristol
doctor, William Budd, concluded from rice-water discharges examined under the microscope that cholera is
transmitted by "fungoid" microscopic animals (qtd. in
Pelling 170). Budd credited the water-borne theory to
John Snow, who in the same year argued that cholera
spreads through "morbid matter" passing from a patient
through discharges. These pollute food and water and
pass in this way to other patients (qtd. in Pelling
160, 204). In 1854, Snow published his proof that a
cholera outbreak in the Soho section of London could be

Paragraph 11 A new topic justifies a separate paragraph. In this short paragraph, Mary briefly summarizes the localist response to Snow.

Paragraphs 12–20: Confirmation
or Supporting Arguments

The *confirmation* or arguments in support of the thesis usually follow the presentation of background facts (36d). Since Mary is not refuting another interpretation of the same facts, she presents supporting arguments only.

Paragraph 12 In her opening sentence Mary summarizes her point in paragraphs 10–11 that new ways of thinking about disease were replacing old ones. The concluding sentence and the *Times* quotation introduce arguments that support Mary's thesis that social prejudice influenced doctors. The first of these arguments is that doctors looked to the diet of the poor as a cause of cholera. Mary begins with this least significant but important point.

traced to a much-used street pump. Hearing of the outbreak, he suspected that the water was contaminated:
"on examining the water, on the evening of the 3rd September, I found so little impurity in it of an organic
nature, that I hesitated to come to a conclusion"
(469). But further investigation led Snow to conclude
that cholera had to be water-borne:

> Further inquiry, however, showed me that
> there was no other circumstance or agent com-
> mon to the circumscribed locality in which
> this sudden increase of cholera occurred, and
> not extending beyond it, except the water of
> the above mentioned pump. (469)

11   Localists responded to Snow by arguing that the
water had been contaminated by air-borne poisons: the
agent that could change organic matter into poison in
the air could do so in the water as well (Pelling 222).
Opinion on the matter was divided for many years afterward.

12   Scientific reasoning and new theories of causation
were replacing old ways of thinking about the disease,
as Budd and Snow show. Doctors were increasingly held
in disrepute, as sanitarians gained influence. James
Stansfeld, first president of the Local Government
Board, a merging of public health and Poor Law administration through parliamentary acts in 1871 and 1872,
stated that the goals of sanitary protection were
"cleanliness and purity," and added that "they did not
want medical men to effect that" (Novak 453). Medical
reports published from 1832 to 1867 and later show that
social prejudice influenced many doctors and observers

Paragraph 12   Mary indents a long quotation from the *Medical Gazette* because it requires more than four typed lines. Quotations of fewer than four typed lines are run into the text and, unlike indented quotations, appear in quotation marks.

Paragraph 13   Important evidence deserves emphasis. Mary's two-sentence paragraph interprets the *Times* quotation from the *Medical Gazette*. Mary sets off the paragraph to stress an important point. The assumption that the poor eat vegetables raw led the writer of the *Gazette* to miss an important cause of infection.

Paragraph 14   Paraphrase is sufficient when the order of details and explanation is significant but not the exact wording. Mary quotes Brigham's 1832 treatise because the wording is significant; she might have paraphrased or quoted Chapman if she believed the passage gave added insight into medical thinking.

as they searched for evidence in the living conditions
of the poor. For example, many held to the view that
the diet of the poor was a major cause of cholera. The
London Times reprinted this statement from the Medical
Gazette:

> In all the countries which cholera has vis-
> ited, the most fatal irruptions have been
> among those whose diet is at once impover-
> ished and stimulated; nor is it possible to
> conceive anything possessed of these charac-
> teristics more strongly than salads, or other
> raw vegetables, and half-ripe fruits, quali-
> fied with copious libations of adulterated
> gin. Of how many among our poorer brethren do
> these constitute a part at least, and often a
> very large part, of their daily subsistence.
> (14 July 1832)

13   Ironically, the possible uncleanliness of the food
(and water) is not considered in this statement, even
though the writer stresses that vegetables are eaten
raw and washed down with abundant amounts of gin.

14   The writer possibly misses the point because of
concern with the character of the poor. The Medical
Gazette explicitly associates the poor with gin-
drinking. The poor suffer other weaknesses of character. Fear makes the poor susceptible to cholera, several writers note. An 1832 treatise on cholera states:
"Both fear and the cholera drive the blood from the ex-
terior upon the heart, arrest or derange the secre-
tions, hinder assimilation, and of course produce in-

Paragraph 15   Key phrases need a context and interpretation. Mary quotes a key phrase from the *Medical Gazette*—linking the evidence on diet to new evidence on drunkenness. The extended quotation singles out the "low Irish," further evidence of how stereotypes governed medical thinking. Both quotations supply the context of the statements. Further, Mary interprets the evidence for the reader ("It is one step from this kind of reasoning"). She does not link quotations without interpretation.

Paragraph 16   A persuasive essay arranges evidence in a clear order. Mary discusses the proposed causes in the order of importance to her thesis, not necessarily in the order of importance to medical authorities. The influence of social attitudes is most apparent in statements of the day on sexual debauchery.

The reader discovers the relative importance of the evidence by how much is quoted and discussed. Mary quotes Chapman at length because he provides decisive evidence for her thesis.

Smith 8

digestion, and disorder of the stomach and bowels"
(Brigham 352).

15   The _Times_ article shows that another cause associated with the poor is drunkenness. The _Medical Gazette_
refers to "copious libations of adulterated gin" (_London Times_ 14 July 1832). An 1866 treatise refers to
predisposing effects of "nervous stimulants" (Chapman
172). An American writer, Dudley Atkins, quotes from
the Special Medical Council of New York City: "In regard to intemperance, it is now universally known, that
Cholera has a most peculiar affinity for the system of
a drunkard; so much so, that it is a very rare thing
for the intemperate to escape--generally speaking, it
is almost as rare for the temperate and uniformly prudent to be attacked" (qtd. in Atkins 66). It is one
step from this kind of reasoning to the identification
of a class of people most disposed to the disease. In
his sketch of cholera in New York City in 1832, Atkins
states:

> As a class of people, the low Irish [in New
> York City] suffered most, being exceedingly
> dirty in their habits, much addicted to intemperance, and crowded together in the worst
> portions of the city, both as regards the
> kind of houses and the quarter in which they
> resided. (Atkins 15)

16   People disposed to sexual debauchery are also susceptible, some doctors thought. Atkins states in the
same sketch: "Venereal excesses, and debauchery in general, exposed in many cases to very sudden and fatal
attacks. In truth there is perhaps no more common cause

Paragraph 16   Mary quotes key phrases like "solar heat" and "special aptitude," instead of paraphrasing them, because Chapman attaches special meanings to them. Mary is underscoring racial assumptions.

Paragraph 17   Mary builds to even more convincing evidence—the attitude toward female prostitutes and the recommendation of the Oxford Board of Health. She quotes a key portion of this very telling recommendation.

of a sudden and rapidly fatal attack, especially if
preceded by a neglected diarrhoea, than a midnight de-
bauch" (Atkins 18). Asiatics were thought to be particularly susceptible. John Chapman, writing in 1866, suggests that "solar heat" creates a "special aptitude"
for cholera, refers to debauchery as a "predisposing
cause," and draws this racial conclusion about the
Asiatic origin of the disease: "As Asiatic races are
peculiarly prone to sexual intemperance, it is not unlikely that this is one of the causes of the frightful
destructiveness of the disease amongst them, and especially in India" (170).

17   Consistent with this view, some doctors also assumed women were not only susceptible to cholera but
were possible carriers. Prostitutes are the obvious
target of suspicion in a book published in 1832: "The
comparative exemption enjoyed by females, has been entirely lost to them by a dissolute mode of life. Women
of this class have been among the foremost sufferers
from Cholera" (Bell and Condie 49). This belief probably explains why in 1832 the Oxford Board of Health
recommended the reformation of prostitutes as a preventive measure:

>   It appears to this Board of great importance
>   viewing the matter in its lower instead of
>   its higher affinities and entertaining it
>   simply as a sanitary and precautionary
>   measure that it would be conducive to public
>   health and safety under the present calamity
>   of cholerous sickness to effect some amelio-
>   ration in the habits of the common prosti-

Paragraph 18 Mary again presents her interpretation of an important statement in a separate paragraph to highlight them. She calls attention to the key words *natural* and *spiritual*.

Paragraph 19 Mary's parenthetical citation refers to Robert J. Morris's discussion on pages 133–39 of his book of moral views and their influence on medical opinion. Instead of quoting an example from Morris, she gives an example from a different source she came upon in her research and then quotes a contemporary statement that strongly supports her thesis.

Smith 10

tute--their homes and homesteads, the locali-
ties of their residences, their destitute as
well as their debased condition, and generally in their natural and statistical as well
as their spiritual and eternal relations.
(qtd. in Morris 199)

18   The statement of the Oxford Board of Health implies that prostitutes' surroundings and their "destitute as well as their debased condition" made them contagious. This assumption is also plain in the words
<u>natural</u> and <u>spiritual</u> in the final sentence.

19   The poor, Asiatics, women--these classes are the
most susceptible to the disease, in the stated views of
nineteenth-century medical authorities and observers.
Clearly, moral views influenced public attitudes; the
suffering of the poor, many believed, was the will of
God--a just punishment for their sins (Morris 133-39).
Moral views, too, influenced medical theory. Cholera
could not be a contagious disease wrote John Lizars in
his 1848 treatise on cholera:

Had the public, therefore, in place of being
terrified with the bugbear contagion, been
warned, by the same authorities, of this un-
disputed fact, that Cholera is epidemic--that
it had been cast upon us by the inscrutable
workings of Divine Providence, which no human
power can avert; and that no man could tell
who would be affected or who would escape,
the same precautions as to health, temper-
ance, cleanliness, and attention to the wants

Paragraph 20   In a long essay, the reader needs a reminder of the thesis and the evidence presented. Having stated her thesis partially and presented her evidence, Mary is ready to conclude her paper. She summarizes the evidence presented in paragraphs 13–19: social attitudes continued to influence medical thought in face of mounting scientific evidence.

Paragraph 21–23: Conclusion
Mary uses her conclusion to state her thesis fully and to draw further inferences from her evidence.

Paragraph 21   Returning to key quotations is an effective way of reminding the reader of the topic and fully stating the thesis. Mary returns here to the opening discussion of Shaw, quoting the key statement first quoted in paragraph 1. She then states her thesis fully in the concluding sentence.

Paragraph 22   Authoritative opinions give some support to an argument. Mary quotes an authoritative opinion in support of her thesis. To make her argument even more persuasive, she presents new evidence from her sources to support it.

Paragraph 23   In her concluding paragraph, Mary restates her thesis and the central argument of the essay. In her concluding statement

and comforts of the poor, would have been observed. (67)

20   These opinions existed in face of mounting evidence that cholera had a necessary and demonstrable
physical cause. As we have seen, some doctors and scientists like William Budd and John Snow were looking
for evidence that proved a direct link between contaminated water and the outbreak of cholera, though they
probably did not dismiss diet, alcohol, and environment
as possible contributing causes.

21   The medical statements and theories quoted do not
prove conclusively that Shaw is correct that doctors in
his time had no more honor or conscience than other
people, nor that they had "an intense dread of doing
anything that everybody else does not do, or omitting
to do anything that everybody else does" (3). But the
statements do show that Shaw had a basis for stating
that doctors were not different from ordinary people.
The evidence shows that social attitudes strongly influenced medical theory in the nineteenth century.

22   The evidence also gives support to Shaw's belief
that many doctors did not reason as scientists. Morris
confirms this idea in his study of the literature on
cholera:

            The men who wrote the cholera literature of
            1832 did not talk in terms of a scientific
            community, indeed they preferred the more
            gentlemanly term natural philosopher to that
            of a scientist. (178)

23   The nineteenth-century treatises on cholera
clearly reflect social attitudes of the age. Social at-

on Shaw, she returns to a question raised by her reading of *The Doctor's Dilemma*: Does Shaw's characterization of doctors as ignorant of science and conventional in their thinking about disease have a basis in fact? Mary states that it does, then briefly refers to Shaw's explanation for the ignorance of the medical profession and its distrust of science. Her final quotation from the preface invites the reader to consider an important question: how much does distrust of "exceptional" people influence social attitudes and popular reasoning on important issues in any age? Mary does not explore this question—here perhaps is a topic for another paper. Instead, she uses her concluding sentence to remind the reader of her thesis.

titudes more than scientific theory provide the explanation for the causes of the disease and the susceptibility of certain classes of people. Shaw's statements in the preface to <u>The Doctor's Dilemma</u> thus have a basis in fact. Many doctors were ignorant of science, reasoning instead from social assumptions about disease in poor people and women. The evidence shows that social and moral attitudes strongly influenced medical theory. Shaw suggests a reason: the general public is suspicious of the exceptional person, not the average physician, who shares their routine assumptions and prejudices: "If you would see public dislike surging up in a moment against an individual, you must watch one who does something unusual, no matter how sensible it may be" (43). John Snow's career and the slow acceptance of his findings support Shaw's view. The ignorance of doctors and mistrust of science was in fact slow to change.

Works Cited
Mary's "Works Cited" list uses the format and model entries described in 41a. Note that the heading "Works Cited" appears one inch below the top of the page. The entries that follow are one inch from each side of the page and from the bottom. The second or turn lines of entries are indented five spaces.

Mary underlines book titles and gives only the city and date in citing books published before 1900. In citing books published after 1900, Mary shortens the name of the publisher ("Holmes" for "Holmes and Meier Publishers," "Dodd" for "Dodd, Mead and Company," "Oxford UP" for "Oxford University Press," and so on).

In citing periodicals, the name of the article appears in quotation marks; the name of the periodical is underlined. The volume number and year of publication (in parentheses) follow in arabic numerals. A colon separates this information from the inclusive pages of the article.

Smith 13

Works Cited

Arnold, David. "Cholera and Colonialism in British
India." Past and Present 113 (1986): 118-51.

Atkins, Dudley, ed. Reports of Hospital Physicians and
Other Documents in Relation to the Epidemic of
Cholera of 1832. New York, 1832.

Barau, Dhiman, and William Burrows, eds. Cholera.
Philadelphia: Saunders, 1974.

Bell, John, and D. Francis Condie. Epidemic Cholera.
Philadelphia, 1832.

Brigham, A. A Treatise on Epidemic Cholera. Hartford,
1832.

Callcott, Maureen. "The Challenge of Cholera: Last Epidemic at Newcastle upon Tyne." Northern History 20
(1984): 167-86.

Chadwick, Edwin. The Health of Nations. 1867. 2 vols.
London: Dawsons, 1965.

Chapman, John. Diarrhoea and Cholera. 2nd ed. London,
1866.

Kerr, Barbara. "Henry Moule and Cholera in Dorset:
Nineteenth-Century Sanitary Reform." History Today
28 (1978): 672-80.

Lizars, John. Substance of the Investigations Regarding
Cholera Asphyxia. Edinburgh, 1848.

[London] Times. 14 July 1832.

---. 23 July 1832.

Morris, Robert John. Cholera 1832: The Social Responses
to an Epidemic. New York: Holmes, 1976.

Novak, Steven J. "Professionalism and Bureaucracy:
English Doctors and Victorian Public Health Admin-

istration." <u>Journal of Social History</u> 6 (1973):
440-62.

Pelling, Margaret. <u>Cholera, Fever and English Medicine:
1825-1865</u>. London: Oxford UP, 1978.

Phillips, Robert Allan. "Asiatic Cholera." <u>Annual Review of Medicine</u> 19 (1968): 69-80.

Pierce, Nathaniel F. "Cholera." <u>Textbook of Medicine</u>.
17th ed. Ed. James E. Wyngaarden and Lloyd H.
Smith, Jr. Philadelphia: Saunders, 1985.

Pollitzer, R. <u>Cholera</u>. Geneva: World Health Organization, 1959.

Shaw, Bernard. <u>The Doctor's Dilemma</u>. Vol 1. of <u>Complete
Plays with Prefaces</u>. 4 vols. New York: Dodd, 1963.

Snow, John. <u>On the Mode of Communication of Cholera</u>.
1854. Rpt. in <u>Source Book of Medical History</u>. Ed.
Logan Clendening. New York: Dover, 1960; New York:
Schuman, 1942. 468-73.

EXERCISE

1. Read the passage from John Snow's *On the Mode of Communication of Cholera* on page 658. What point is Snow making in stating that "the water varied . . . in the amount of organic impurity, visible to the naked eye"?

2. Would Mary have strengthened her discussion of Snow in paragraphs 10 and 11 by noting this statement? Or is the statement not relevant to her discussion?

3. Mary does not give a full account of nineteenth-century cholera epidemics in England and the United States. Would discussion of mortality rates, similarities and differences in treatment of the disease, or other topics have strengthened her paper? Or would it have been irrelevant?

4. Mary introduces her discussion of nineteenth-century medical practice through Shaw's views on doctors. If Mary decided to revise the paper and focus instead on Shaw's views, what information about Shaw would she need to add? What paragraphs on cholera might she retain for the purpose of illustration? What paragraphs or sections would be nonessential or irrelevant?

5. At the end of her paper, Mary quotes Shaw's statement on public distrust of original thinkers and doers. How do her findings on the medical view of cholera support this statement? Where would you look for evidence of present-day attitudes toward doctors and medical practice?

PART TEN

WRITING IN SEVERAL FIELDS

Writing in the Humanities 43

You are likely to encounter many different kinds of writing situations in your college courses and later in your career. For an English course, for example, you may be asked to write an analysis of a novel, short story, or poem. For a course in psychology or sociology, you may be asked to write a term paper or report on a topic in the field. Your writing in chemistry and physics courses is likely to include detailed reports of laboratory experiments. In addition, you will encounter other types of writing later on, such as job application letters and the resume. Good writing is expected in all fields. The papers you write in English, psychology, sociology, chemistry, and physics should all exhibit the same qualities of good writing described in Parts One through Eight of this book. However, as you become familiar with the styles of discourses in various fields of study, you will discover that vocabularies and writing styles differ in some ways. The more writing you do in college, the more you will become proficient in these various styles.

The different conventions for writing, researching, and documentation in the humanities, social sciences, and natural and applied sciences are our focus in Chapters 43 and 44 of

744

Part Ten. In Chapters 45 and 46, we turn to the standards of other types of writing—course and reading notes, exam answers, and business writing. We begin in this chapter with the special requirements of writing in the humanities.

43a Vocabulary and writing style

The **humanities** traditionally include ancient and modern languages, English, literature, history, philosophy, art, music, drama, and religion. Some areas of the humanities overlap in other fields; for instance, history is often treated as a social science. The term *humanities* broadly refers to the study of human language, thought, and art, but this definition does not clearly set the humanities apart from other fields like anthropology that also study human culture.

One decisive difference between the humanities and all other fields of study is in the use of language. You will find in your humanities courses a greater use of "emotive" language. The novelist or poet uses "emotive" language to imagine and describe things in nature and society that the social or natural scientist, and the philosopher and the historian too, would describe in precise, emotionally neutral language. This is why a paper that uses imagistic and metaphorical language is appropriate for a writing course but would be unacceptable for a course in biology or electrical engineering. Your courses in different fields will introduce you to the special vocabularies and writing styles. Although the vocabularies and writing styles of all disciplines have much in common, they are also very different. The words are part of a frame of discourse—of shared assumptions, definitions, ways of looking and describing people. In writing as a humanist or sociologist, for example, you use words with multiple meanings and references known to those in the field.

Sentence style in the humanities is no different from that in other fields. Papers in the humanities are usually formal in sentence structure and diction (see 29b). Like writers in other disciplines, writers on literature, philosophy, and history use abstract words in discussing abstract ideas:

But metaphor is not merely a matter of language. It is a matter of conceptual structure. And conceptual structure is not merely a matter of the intellect—it involves all the natural dimensions of our experience, including aspects of our sense experiences: color, shape, texture, sound, etc.

—George Lakoff and Mark Johnson, *Metaphors We Live By*

However, references to the writer's feelings and responses are more common because papers in literature courses often focus on the writer's experience with and interpretation of a literary work. The resources of language are also wider in expressive and literary writing. The writer of fiction re-creates an event or experience by using concrete words, similes, metaphors, and other figurative language (see 31a). So does the essayist— and so may you in a paper for an English course, in conveying your ideas and impressions of a literary work.

Following are some suggestions on how to become familiar with the writing style and vocabulary common in the humanities as well as how to use them to your advantage in writing papers:

- In reading texts and critical essays in the humanities, take note of the writing style, perhaps the mix of abstract ideas and specific details, or the mix of formal terms with concrete words (see 30a–b), or the shape of sentences and paragraphs.
- Keep a log of unfamiliar terms that you come across in your reading and that your instructor uses in class. Also note special uses of familiar terms like *metaphor* and compare these uses with the dictionary meanings of these words. Consult special glossaries and dictionaries (see 39e), and make notes on special definitions and examples.
- But don't use a technical word unless your discussion requires it. For example, the term *protagonist* is appropriate in a technical discussion; the equivalent terms *hero* and *heroine* are appropriate in a general discussion of a play. Always be sure that you know the meaning of a technical word so you don't use it incorrectly. Avoid using technical words to make your paper sound authoritative, as you risk sounding pompous instead. In the following example, the writer misuses the word *introspection*:

    Kant engaged in a thorough introspection of the ratiocinative process.

It is always best to express an idea simply and clearly:

    Kant examined the process of thinking.

(For additional discussion of informal and formal styles of writing, see 1c and 29b.)

43b Papers in the humanities

The major types of writing in the humanities include personal essays, book reviews, and various types of analyses of literary and historical works. Let us review these types briefly.

1 The personal essay

The **personal essay** is often autobiographical. In writing a personal essay, you describe experiences and convey your personal views of people, places, events, and ideas, as Glenn Grube does in his essay about his visit to the Department of Motor Vehicles in section 4d. In an informal essay, you may also give your thoughts and feelings at the moment of writing. The word *essay*—derived from a Latin word meaning "to weigh"—occasionally suggests this kind of monetary flight of mind or exploration. "I add, but I do not correct," the sixteenth-century French essayist Montaigne wrote about his early personal essays, some of which resemble the journal entries discussed in section 2b. For Montaigne and many essayists today, essay writing is an act of continuous self-discovery: "I desire to be seen in my simple, natural, and everyday dress, without artifice or constraint; for it is myself I portray."

Personal essays, expressive in intent, have different purposes and thus have different kinds of focus and organization. No two essayists write about the same opinions or attitudes or write from the same point of view. These differences explain why personal essays, or indeed essays of any kind, are never written according to a single pattern. You can write personal essays on any topics that capture your imagination and interest and in a variety of patterns. Because the range of topics and patterns is so wide, finding the proper focus is often difficult. The British essayist Virginia Woolf warns that too broad a focus may invite us to write so generally that our personal thoughts and feelings are not conveyed to the reader:

> If men and women must write, let them leave the great mysteries of art and literature unassailed; if they told us frankly not of the books that we can all read and the pictures which hang for us all to see, but of that single book to which they alone have the key and of that solitary picture whose face is shrouded to all but

747

one gaze—if they would write of themselves—such writing would
have its own permanent value.

— "The Decay of Essay-Writing"

2   Book review

A **book review** may analyze an aspect of a work in depth or
may give readers enough information about a work of literature or philosophy to decide whether it is worth reading. The
review may include any of the following information about the
work:

- A general outline of the opening pages without telling the whole
  story.
- An explanation of biographical, historical, or other backgrounds
  relevant to the work.
- A structural or thematic analysis of the work.
- A description of the major characters and any subordinate
  characters that make the book worth reading.
- A comparative evaluation of the work with others by the same
  author or by authors of similar books.
- A brief, often subjective evaluation of the work that points to
  aspects of it that are particularly interesting.

3   Structural analysis

Writing in the humanities often involves the **structural analysis** of a literary, musical, artistic, or philosophical work, or
of historical documents. A common writing assignment in
English courses is to analyze one or more features of a literary
work, including character, plot, narrative devices, setting, imagery, symbolism, tone, and rhythm. For example, in a paper
on Shakespeare's plays, you might trace the development of a
Shakespearean character or comment on the metaphor of a
Shakespearean speech or show how the action in one of the
plays builds up to a climax. In a short paper or essay examination, the assignment may be limited to one or two features
of the work. In a longer paper, however, you may be required
to analyze several features and relate these to the overall thematic structure. Following are some useful questions to consider while analyzing the major aspects of a literary work.

Character.   **Character** refers to the sum of qualities that
you discover about the various persons portrayed in a play,

story, or novel. These qualities motivate the action. To make an effective character analysis, consider these questions:

- How simple or complex is the character? Do you find a single quality of character or several, perhaps contradictory qualities that make the character seem "round" rather than "flat"?
- Does the character develop or change through the story, or does the character stay the same?
- Does the character show self-awareness—usually a mark of the developing "round" character?
- Do subordinate characters shed light on one or more of the central characters by making qualities of the central character stand out?

Plot. **Plot** refers to the interrelated or entangled events or action in a literary work. To analyze plot, ask these questions:

- What happens in the work, and how can you explain what happens? For example, is the plot the outcome of what the characters do and say? Or do chance events shape the action?
- How complicated or tangled is the plot? What explains the complications or entanglements?

Narrative devices. There are many different types of **narrative devices** that writers use for specific purposes. Plays often have subordinate characters whose main job is to give the audience important facts about the major characters and action. Stories and novels all contain **narrators**; some narrators are identified and others are unnamed voices who tell the story. Plays like Thornton Wilder's *Our Town* use special narrators who stand apart from and observe the action. To analyze the narrative devices of a work, consider these questions:

- Is the narrator a central character in the work? Or is the narrator an onlooker?
- Is the narrator identified by name? Is the narrator in full possession of the facts of the story? Or does the narrator seem unaware of certain facts, as a very young narrator of events in the adult world must be?
- Does the narrator speak for the author of the work, or do you sense a separation between the values of the author and the values of the narrator?

Setting. Every work of literature has a **setting**, a place where the action occurs. To analyze the importance of setting

749

in a work, ask these questions:

- How important is the backdrop or setting to understanding the plot and characters?
- How does the author make readers aware of the setting?
- Could the action have occurred anywhere or only in the particular setting of the work?

Imagery. **Images** are sensory pictures or impressions conveyed in descriptive passages and statements of characters. To analyze an author's use of imagery, consider these questions:

- Does the author develop the theme of the work through recurrent images; that is, through pictures, sounds, or other sensory impressions?
- Does the author use visual or another type of imagery more than other kinds?
- Does the author seek, like the novelist Joseph Conrad, through "the power of the written word, to make you hear, to make you feel . . . to make you *see*"?

Symbolism. A literary **symbol** is a character or object that conveys an idea central to the work. Examples of symbols used in this way include the white whale in *Moby Dick* and the letter "A" in *The Scarlet Letter*. To analyze an author's use of symbolism, first determine how and at what point in the work you became aware of the image and its purpose, and then how the symbol is developed in the remainder of the work.

Tone. The **tone** of a literary work is the particular attitude toward the characters, action, or setting conveyed by the narrative voice. To discover and analyze the tone of a work, consider whether the narration is ironic, sarcastic, joyous, sorrowful, or indifferent, as well as whether the tone changes in the course of the work.

Rhythm. **Rhythm** refers to the pattern of sounds in a dramatic speech, a poem, or a prose passage. To analyze an author's use of rhythm, consider these questions:

- What is the meter of the passage or poem?
- Where does the author break the regular meter to give unexpected emphasis to a syllable or word?
- What repeated phrase or clause patterns give a prose passage a pronounced rhythm?
- What does the rhythm contribute to the tone of the passage or the work?

4 Thematic analysis

In a **thematic analysis**, you discuss the themes or ideas of a literary work, specifically how the author introduces and dramatizes them and what the author intends to say in the work. Its focus is on the implied or stated thesis, much like the "morals" of parables and fables. Thematic analysis is often combined with analysis of character, plot, and setting. The same questions may be asked about a philosophical work that dramatizes a character and incident, as in many of Plato's dialogues. The following questions are helpful in thematic analysis:

- What does the title of the work suggest about the nature and thematic concerns of the work?
- Does the author state a theme at the beginning of the work, as Shakespeare does in the prologue to *Romeo and Juliet* in referring to "star-crossed lovers" and "parents' strife"?
- Does the narrator of the work speak for the author of the work? Do one or more characters in a story, novel, play, or poem speak for the author? (For example, does Socrates in the *Apology* speak for Plato, the author of the dialogue?)
- Does the author depend on the plot to reveal the theme of the work or to express a central idea?
- Does the author reveal a theme or central idea through the setting, as Mark Twain does in his picture of Mississippi River towns in *Life on the Mississippi* and *Huckleberry Finn*?
- Does the theme or central idea unfold as the work proceeds? Or does the author state the idea at the beginning and then develop it?
- Does the author want only to give readers a picture of life? Or does the author also want readers to think about an issue in a new way or take action to correct an injustice?

5 Rhetorical analysis

The various aspects of a literary work may also be interpreted through **rhetorical analysis**. According to the rhetorician Kenneth Burke, a dramatic event in a movie, play, poem, short story, or novel may be analyzed systematically by inquiring about these five main aspects: the *act*, the *agent* or person performing the act, the means or *agency* used, the place or *scene*, and the intent or *purpose*:

Act	Action or plot
Agent	Central character or series of characters responsible for what happens

Agency   Language through which the reader discovers the
          nature of the characters and plot
Scene   Setting of the action
Purpose   Motives of the characters

For example, in analyzing Mark Antony's oration at the funeral of Julius Caesar, in Shakespeare's play, you would give attention to the following:

Act   Antony's arousing the Romans to vengeance in de-
         scribing Caesar's life and death
Agent   Antony
Agency   Language through which Antony arouses the
         crowd
Scene   Caesar's funeral in Rome
Purpose   Antony's plan to avenge the murder of Caesar

Checklist: Questions for Rhetorical Analysis of a Literary Work

1. What happened?
2. Who performed the act?
3. How was it performed?
4. When and where was it performed?
5. Why was it performed?

The literary critic Susan R. Horton* suggests that systematic interpretation may proceed up "the interpretive ladder" by considering the work in relation to the writer, then in relation to the reader, to other works of literature, to communication in general, and finally to the culture. The interpreter is asking the following questions:

- What do *biographical, psychological,* and *historical* studies reveal about the work?
- What does a *structural analysis* and a *thematic analysis*, including analysis of the narrative structure, reveal?
- What is the *literary genre* of the work? Is it a fairy tale, melodrama, moral fable, comedy, tragedy, or satire? How does the work resemble others in the same genre? How is it different?

*Interpreting Interpreting (Baltimore: John Hopkins UP, 1979), pp. 69–71.

- What are its *linguistic features* or special qualities of language? How is it like other forms of communication or "speech acts"? How is it different?
- What is the *cultural significance* of the work? What does it tell about the society and age in which the work is set? (For example, what does *Huckleberry Finn* reveal about slavery in nineteenth-century America and its effect on owners and slaves in the years before the Civil War?)

6 Analysis of a historical work

Analysis of a philosophical work is usually thematic, as in an analysis of the assumptions and reasoning of the Declaration of Independence. Following Horton's interpretive ladder, you might investigate the biographical and historical backgrounds of the work like the origin of Jefferson's ideas about revolution and the composition of the Declaration. You then might compare it to other manifestoes, analyze its emotive and philosophical language, and comment on its continuing influence.

Burke's method of systematic analysis is useful in writing critical papers in a history course. The following passage is an account of the proclamation of the Declaration of Independence, in Philadelphia, on July 8, 1776, by the Local Committee of Safety. Malone is explaining what part the author of the Declaration, Thomas Jefferson, took in the proclamation and later in the signing of the document:

Agent	Jefferson must have been present but he was not in the spotlight; nobody announced that he was
Agency	the author of this paper or led him forward upon
Scene	the stage to take a bow. Cheers mounted to the sky;
Act	battalions paraded on the Common; and the bells rang all day and most of the night. This was in cele-
Purpose	bration not of a document but of an event. The tie with the Mother Country had been cut and Congress

as a body was responsible for that dangerous and fateful action. Not until July 19 did Congress order that the Declaration be engrossed on parchment and signed by the members. Jefferson himself could not have affixed his own name until August 2. The names of the delegates were well known, but the signatures themselves were not made public until the following January and Jefferson's was one of many, even then.

—Dumas Malone, *Jefferson the Virginian*

You might make use of Burke's terms in asking what the agency, or signing of the Declaration on July 19 and later, reveals about Thomas Jefferson, the agent of the Declaration. At the beginning of the paragraph and in the succeeding, Malone asks what the scene in Philadelphia reveals about Jefferson (the agent):

Agent	This is another way of saying that his chief fame
Scene	from the Declaration lay in the future. As he poked around the shops of Philadelphia bystanders may have pointed him out as an influential delegate, but they did not hail him as the author and he probably
Agency	would not have wanted them to. At the moment, in fact, his pride in authorship was slight, for he believed that Congress had manhandled his composition and marred its strength. He cared little for general applause but he wanted to guard his own literary reputation among the select. He made copies of his own draft as it had emerged from the committee, and sent these to some of his friends; they could compare it with the final version and judge whether it was better or worse for the critics.

—Jefferson the Virginian

43c Research papers
       in the humanities

Chapters 41 and 42 describe MLA parenthetical documentation and other styles used in the humanities. Research papers in the humanities contain no standard formal divisions, in contrast to research papers in the sciences (see 44c and 44d). You may, however, divide a short paper into self-contained sections by typing an additional double space between them. As an alternative, you can give these sections numbers or numbers and headings (e.g., *1 The Writing of the Declaration*), omitting extra space below the section heading. Numbers (with or without a period) and headings appear flush with the left margin of the paper.

A research paper should contain an introduction, body, and conclusion. However, these parts should not be separated or labeled as such. Your **introduction** ordinarily contains a statement of the problem to be dealt with in the paper, background and review of criticism or previous research that your research clarifies or corrects, and a statement of the thesis. The **body** of the paper contains your main evidence, or if your paper is a persuasive argument, a confirmation or presentation of supporting arguments and a refutation of counter arguments. The **conclusion** usually restates the thesis and sometimes recommends further research on the subject. These are essentially the parts of Brenda Wahler's paper on comparative worth (in section 36d) and Mary Smith's paper on the medical theories of cholera (in Chapter 42).

Checklist: Organizing the Humanities Research Paper

Introduction
> Statement of purpose
> Background of the topic
> Review of criticism
> Statement of the thesis
> Brief outline of the main discussion or argument

Body
> Main evidence in support of the thesis
> Response to or refutation of other writers on the subject

Conclusion
> Brief review of main evidence
> Restatement of the thesis
> List of works cited or references

 43d A sample literary analysis: Glenn Grube, "Pain and Death in Emily Dickinson's Poetry"

The following student paper on Emily Dickinson illustrates one type of literary analysis you may be asked to write in a course in literature. Glenn Grube analyzes three poems by Dickinson to show that the same theme is explored in each of them but in different ways. The complexity of Dickinson's attitude toward herself and toward her work emerges through Glenn's comparison of the poems.

Structural and thematic analysis work together in Glenn's paper, as the marginal comments show. Glenn points to uses of slant rhyme, words with approximate rather than exact rhyme, and words with a sometimes irregular meter to suggest what he describes in his introduction as "a division . . . in thought and feeling" in Dickinson. Glenn builds his analysis to a summary statement of this division. He thus introduces his thesis early in the paper and restates it in his conclusion. The body of the paper consists of his systematic analysis and interpretation. Notice how Glenn reminds the reader of his thesis as his analysis progresses.

The three poems of Emily Dickinson, reprinted in full, are double-spaced, with an additional space to mark stanza breaks. Glenn used Thomas H. Johnson's edition of the poems, which reproduces Dickinson's original capitalization and punctuation, not an edition that regularizes these features. Notice that the three poems are typed as blocks and indented 10 spaces from the left margin, consistent MLA-style documentation. In his concluding paragraph, Glenn incorporates a short quotation into the text, marking the line break with a slash (see 25e).

Grube 1

Pain and Death in Emily Dickinson's Poetry
by Glenn Grube

Statement
of subject

A common theme in Emily Dickinson's poetry is pain. Dickinson writes often and
diversely on the subject, especially on the
mental anguish associated with the life of a

Limitation solitary poet. Two of Dickinson's poems that
present opposing views of the benefits of
pain suggest a division that she knows well
in thought and feeling. The first poem glo-
rifies pain as the one truth of being, the
"look of Agony" that cannot be evaded:

> I like a look of Agony,
> Because I know it's true--
> Men do not sham Convulsion,
> Nor simulate, a Throe--
>
> The Eyes glaze once--and that is
>   Death--
> Impossible to feign
> The Beads upon the Forehead
> By homely Anguish strung.

Thematic
analysis

Dickinson is saying that pain is one certain
truth of life, and death is another, "impossible to feign." The anguish of living prepares for the agony of death.

Compari-
son

Dickinson's second poem is more ambiguous in its attitude toward pain. At first it
embraces grief as familiar and comforting.
The pain is described as the result of
power. The grief of failure is shown as

superior to the pain brought on by success:

> I can wade Grief--
> Whole Pools of it--
> I'm used to that--
> But the least push of Joy
> Breaks up my feet--
> And I tip--drunken--
> Let no Pebble--smile--
> 'Twas the new Liquor--
> That was all!

> Power is only Pain--
> Stranded, thro' Discipline,
> Till Weights--will hang--
> Give Balm--to Giants--
> And they'll wilt, like Men--
> Give Himmaleh--
> They'll Carry--Him!

These two poems go together superbly as an example of the contradictions embraced by Dickinson and her poetry. Since they were written so close in time, probably in 1861, and yet are so different, they exhibit con-

Thematic analysis tradictory attitudes and feelings that mark Dickinson's poetry at this and perhaps other periods in her life. Dickinson's poetry is full of irony and contradiction. Pain is truth, she writes, but she does not want

New theme success because of its pain. One of her constant themes is that to evade success is to shun truth. Even in her most private compo-

sitions, Dickinson returns to this theme.
The "least push of Joy" leads to the lies
that she tells herself.

Pain is true, death is the inevitable
conclusion of life, success can bring pain,
and grief is comfortable. These two poems
say all this, and yet the poet still fears
pain and death and desires success and hap-

Structural analysis

piness. What she knows intellectually is
different from what she feels in her heart.
Her poetry melds idea and feeling through
subtle, complex metaphors, the "weights" of

Metaphor analyzed

success that "hang" and eventually "wilt."
She wants pain and failure because they impel her to write. What she actually wants is
happiness and success.

Meter related to theme

Dickinson's contradictory attitudes toward issues like pain is one possible reason
for her use of slant rhyme. The quickly
changing attitudes in these poems show ambivalence and emotional vacillation. This
ambivalence is enhanced by the irregular meter and half or slant rhyme in the following
concluding verses of another poem:

> The eagle of his Nest
> No easier divest--
> And gain the Sky
> Than mayest Thou--
>
> Except Thyself may be
> Thine Enemy--

Grube 4

Captivity is Consciousness--

So's Liberty.

Meter and
rhyme

The irregular meter (the rhyming of <u>be</u>
with unstressed syllables in <u>enemy</u> and <u>lib-</u>
<u>erty</u>) and rhyme scheme (the closely rhymed
(<u>eagle</u> and <u>easier</u>) in this poem help to make
its point.

Ideas keep changing and truth is not
absolute for Dickinson. Here both captivity
and liberty engender consciousness. This
paradox is similar to the similarly paradox-

Thesis

ical treatment of pain in the earlier poems;
Dickinson is not sure what she means or what
she wants. In the previous poems rhyme is
almost nonexistent. A few half-rhymes (<u>true</u>

Structural
and the-
matic anal-
yses

and <u>throe</u>, <u>pain</u> and <u>discipline</u>) suggest the
structure of a fully rhymed poem, but these
border on free verse. They go where Dickinson takes them, which is in two opposite directions at the same time. The lines "Except
Thyself may be/Thine Enemy" sum up what
Dickinson says and how she says it. She
would like to be the eagle but she cannot
soar. She writes that she does not want the
joy, but joy is what she wants. Pain is true
and should be worn proudly like a necklace,
but Dickinson cannot escape from her fear of

Restate-
ment of
thesis

pain and death. Her contradictory attitudes
toward pain and joy, failure and success,
are shown in the poem.

760

Summary

43a Use concrete words, similes, metaphors, and other figurative language to convey your ideas and impressions in papers written for humanities courses.

43b Use a consistent form of analysis.

In writing a personal essay, describe your personal experiences and convey your personal views of people, places, events, and ideas **(43b 1)**.

In writing a book review, outline the work, give relevant background information, analyze key episodes and characters, compare the work to others like it, and point to aspects of it that you found particularly interesting **(43b 2)**.

In a structural analysis, deal with character, plot, narrative devices, setting, and other features pertinent to your ideas about the work **(43b 3)**.

In a thematic analysis, discuss how the author introduces and dramatizes major themes or ideas **(43b 4)**.

In rhetorical analysis, interpret a work by showing the relationships among the action or plot, the central characters, the language of the work, and the setting **(43b 5)**.

In a historical analysis, use the same systematic approach to interpret a historical event **(43b 6)**.

43c Use the standard format for organizing research papers in the humanities.

Writing in the Social Sciences, Natural Sciences, and Applied Sciences

44

□

□

The social sciences, natural sciences, and applied sciences have their own writing requirements. In the **social sciences**, including sociology, psychology, and political science, scientific methods are used to study human behavior and institutions. In the **natural sciences**, such as biology, chemistry, geography, and physics, scientific methods are used to study the physical world. **Applied sciences** like mechanical and electrical engineering use scientific methods to find practical uses for facts discovered about the physical world. Papers in these fields are different from papers in the humanities in their focus on experimental methods, data, and results.

44a | The stages of scientific investigation

The social sciences and natural and applied sciences use **empirical evidence** based on systematic observation and experimentation. They also frequently use quantitative tests and measurements in interpreting data; statistical correlations shown in tables and graphs often make these results available to the reader. The same general process of investigation is used in history, linguistics, and other humanities that work with empirical evidence. But each field in the humanities and the sciences has its own body of facts, assumptions, methods and tools of research, goals, standards, and special ways of evaluating research. You will become familiar with these methods, goals, and standards in your college courses.

Scientific investigation sometimes begins with an unexpected observation, such as when an astronomer sees a strange object in a telescopic scan of the night sky. But contrary to the view that research begins without expectations or preparation, researchers usually begin with knowledge and assumptions, methods and procedures, and a set of definitions or technical vocabulary shared with other researchers in the same field. Thus the astronomer who makes a sighting is prepared by knowledge and previous experience to recognize an unfamiliar object and to form a **hypothesis** or possible explanation of it. Hypotheses also originate in reading about the experiments and observations of other researchers. Experiments and observations usually leave some questions unanswered and suggest possible new research on the subject.

Checklist: Stages in Scientific Investigation

1. Identify a problem for research, perhaps by observation or reading published research.
2. Formulate a hypothesis or tentative explanation.
3. Devise methods or procedures to test the hypothesis, including experiments, systematic observations, and measurements.
4. Collect and analyze data.
5. Interpret the results.
6. Formulate additional hypotheses, methods, and procedures if needed.
7. Publish data and results in a form that allows other researchers to test the results.

Research requires preparation. Deciding on a general method and devising experiments is a major step in the research process. Another major step is the investigation, followed by the interpretation of the results and subsequent reporting of the research in scholarly journals and at meetings and conferences. The process of investigation is one you will follow in the laboratory and the field; through lab experiments and field observations you will gain a detailed knowledge of the stages of scientific investigation.

44b Writing in the sciences

Like the humanities, the sciences value precision in the statement of ideas, exactness in the reporting of observation and experimentation, conciseness, sound reasoning, effective organization, and clear, orderly exposition. The more exact the wording of a statement, the more valuable the statement is to other researchers. Following are some of the qualities you should aim for in writing in your science courses.

Exactness of detail and terms. Readers of scientific papers and reports expect exact details and wording of ideas, for the aim of scientific writing is to describe the procedures and results of research so precisely that other researchers can verify it by repeating the steps. In your own field and lab reports, statements should be as precise as you can make them. In preparing to write your reports, you need to check the meaning and usage of technical terms. Your instructors will look for the technical meanings of terms in your examinations and course papers, and they will expect you to use these terms appropriately and exactly.

Objectivity. The kind of writing you will do in courses in the sciences is different from the writing in humanities courses in its greater objectivity and abstractness. Essayists who write about the world of nature often give us their impressions of what they see. Usually they want to communicate an experience by evoking its qualities through imagery and metaphor. Scientific reports do not necessarily make the world of nature present to us as we read. Where a paper for an English course may draw on personal impressions and personal value judgments, a paper for a sociology or biology course will exclude these. The absence of a subjective point of view marks most writing in the sciences. For scientists seek to free their writing of personal bias and opinion.

Because scientific writing aims at objectivity, scientific papers and reports contain fewer personal references (*I saw, I felt at that moment*) than do literary essays. In your own reports and papers, watch for sentences that begin with *I*. If you make a needless personal reference, recast the sentence to focus instead on the activity or discovery. When a science writer makes a personal reference, it is usually to pinpoint the time and place of the experiment or observation and usually not to express personal expectations or feelings. An exception is the popular essay on a scientific topic, addressed to a general audience.

Scientific writing uses the passive voice often, because it is useful in emphasizing the act and not the actor (see 12e). In your own science papers, use the passive voice to focus on a procedure or result, but use it with care. If you use the passive voice in every sentence, your paper or report may sound wordy and awkward.

Thoroughness.   Scientific writing is thorough. A scientific report describes every step of an experiment and all relevant details, including measurements made at each stage. It also takes note of failures or exceptional results and any ambiguous findings. To be objective, a scientific report gives all evidence fair consideration, even evidence that seems to limit or qualify the results. The report usually concludes by stating the degree of probability of the results and exploring the implications of the experiment. Thoroughness is essential if other researchers are to duplicate the experiment and test the results. The researcher indeed often recommends new avenues of investigation.

44c   Papers in the social sciences

The social sciences study people in their social setting or environment and usually make predictions on the basis of this study. Because human behavior is complex and therefore difficult to study, sociologists, psychologists, and other social scientists state the precise behavior and social conditions under study and limit their conclusions carefully. Whereas the novelist or playwright is free to invent and imagine human beings and their society, social scientists restrict themselves to what they can see, compare, and measure. Even "common sense" beliefs require verification.

In your social science courses, you will learn to use field observation, interview, questionnaire, survey, case history, and other research techniques in reports and papers. The following section and conclusion of a paper on why victims don't report crimes illustrate many of the features of papers in the social sciences. Drawing on a range of sources, the authors use case history, survey, statistical analysis, and other empirical evidence to define a problem and to give a qualified answer to it. The section on fear reprinted here is one of five sections that provide evidence in the whole paper. As you read this passage, note the marginal descriptions of some of the techniques that you can put to use in your reports and papers. Notice that the authors verify points that may seem obvious to the general reader but nevertheless require proof.

Fear*

Interpretation of evidence drawn from various sources

On the emotional level, victimization produces fear and anxiety, particularly about one's own safety and security. The experience is often sudden and uncontrollable, and sometimes physically injurious. Such an unpredictable event makes a person feel violated or vulnerable (Barkas, 1978). Extreme fear may immobilize a victim, making an activity like reporting impossible. If the person does not find some way to exert control over the trauma, it will lead to depression and helplessness (Abramson & Martin, 1981; Janoff-Bulman, 1979).

By trying to avoid the pain of fear, victims may also avoid making contact with any person or group (such as the police) that could conjure up these feelings or create another fear-eliciting situation. Common sense would tell us that being exposed to a criminal act is indeed fear arousing. (See Greenberg & Ruback, 1982). Empirical support for this proposition is extensive.

*From Robert F. Kidd and Ellen F. Chayet. "Why Do Victims Fail to Report? The Psychology of Criminal Victimization," *Journal of Social Issues* 40 (1984): 41–42, 48–49.

Detailed
report of
a single
source

In one study, Veronen, Kilpatrick, and Resick (1979; also Kilpatrick, Resick, & Veronen, 1981) examined the anxiety and fear reactions of 25 rape victims immediately after and 2–3 hours after the rape occurred. Their analysis suggests that victims experienced profound psychological and physiological symptoms. Victims reported experiencing shaking or trembling (96%), pain (68%), tight muscles (68%), headaches (60%), and other physiological correlates of extreme distress. During the post-rape period, victims said that they also experienced worry (96%), exhaustion (96%), restlessness (88%), fright (88%), and terror (80%). The investigators concluded that the "rape victim experiences significant fear and anxiety as a result of the sexual assault. These fears begin immediately and may continue for months or even years. It is our theoretical position that rape-related fears may be so severe that treatment is required" (p. 149).

Focus on
an extreme
example of
victimiza-
tion

Rape, however, represents an extreme instance of criminal victimization, inasmuch as the violence of the crime is inherently fear producing. All violent crimes are fear evoking. For instance, a study of robbery victims (Cohen, 1974), of whom two thirds had also been physically assaulted, identified a pervasive state of anxiety following the event. A general paranoia and manifestations of somatized anxiety, such as sleeplessness and inability to eat, were noted. Such fear had significantly altered victims' life activities.

Statistical
evidence
drawn
from a
study of
several
crimes

A survey of 274 victims of major crimes (assault, burglary, and robbery) in New York City stressed that the primary reaction to the experience was psychological (Friedman, Bischoff, Davis, & Person, 1982). Three quarters of the individuals surveyed reported extreme emotional reactions, ranging from nervousness and anxiety to anger. Sixty percent felt significantly less safe following victimization. Nearly half reported a fear of being victimized again.

Related
question
suggested
by study

How much fear, though, is aroused in victims of lesser, nonviolent offenses? We could not find any data that pertained specifically to this question. Perhaps the notion of victim fear is so well documented by common sense, or "so obvious" to citizens and scientists alike that it does not require empirical evidence. It is reasonable to speculate that criminal victimization at any level produces some fear.

Conclusion

In deciding whether to report a crime, victims are confronted with two options. Neither is totally satisfactory. We have argued that those who report later learn that contacting the police is a costly, time-consuming activity, often leaving the victims feeling helpless and fearful. Such expectations appear to contribute to other victims' unwillingness to make their suffering known to the police. Such feelings of fear and helplessness probably reflect systematic problems in the criminal justice community.

Admittedly, much of the data referred to in this article were collected for other purposes and involved methods that do not easily render the findings amenable to psychological analysis. Crime survey statistics that deal with people's reasons for not reporting have been subjected to criticisms by psychologists (e.g., Greenberg, Wilson, & Mills, 1982); these statistics represent aggregate data and offer little information about the responses of individuals. The findings of surveys are descriptive rather than analytic. The questions in the surveys do not try to elucidate the reasons behind nonreporting. It is difficult, therefore, to draw clear psychological conclusions from such survey data.

Nevertheless, such surveys do provide important data—nearly the only national data on the experiences of victims. As long as their shortcomings are acknowledged, their findings are adequate for formulating theory about the topic. Existing evidence points repeatedly to the conclusion that crime victims consider their situation rationally. Although they may misperceive how much control they themselves might have exercised over their initial experience, they do not exaggerate the abilities of the authorities. To the contrary, for classes of crimes including rape, victims tend to view the police as a potential source of further victimization. They may therefore see their report of a crime as futile, or, at worst, as a costly and depersonalizing ordeal.

The parallel between the impotence of victims and the impotence they attribute to authorities deserves further study. Is this agreement coincidental? Or do victims project their own powerlessness onto authorities? Could it be that recent attribution theories have overemphasized victims' irrational and self-protective processes? Crime victims' abilities to see their own and the police's powerlessness accurately may be more adaptive than either assuaging their fear or accentuating their personal control.

References in APA-style documentation

References

Abramson, L. Y., & Martin D. J. (1981). Depression and the causal inference process. In J. Harvey, W. Ickes, & R. Kidd (Eds.), *New directions in attribution research* (Vol. 3, pp. 117–168). Hillsdale, NJ: Lawrence Erlbaum Associates.

Barkas, J. L. (1978). *Victims.* New York: Scribner's.

Cohen, Y. (1974). Crisis intervention and the victim of robbery. In I. Drapkin & E. Viano (Eds.), *Victimology: A new focus* (Vol. 3, pp. 17–28). Lexington, MA: D. C. Heath.

Friedman, K., Bischoff, H., Davis, R., & Person, A. (1982). *Victims and helpers: Reactions to crime.* Washington, DC: National Institute of Justice.

Greenberg, M. S., & Ruback, R. B. (1982). *Social psychology of the criminal justice system.* Monterey, CA: Brooks/Cole.

Greenberg, M. S., Wilson, C. E., & Mills, M. K. (1982). Victim decision-making: An experimental approach. In V. Konecni & E. Ebbesen (Eds.), *The criminal justice system: A social-psychological analysis* (pp. 73–94). San Francisco, CA: Freeman.

Janoff-Bulman, R. (1979). Characterological versus behavioral self-blame: Inquiries into depression and rape. *Journal of Personality and Social Psychology, 37,* 1798–1809.

Kilpatrick, D. G., Resick, P., & Veronen, L. (1981). Effects of a rape experience: A longitudinal study. *Journal of Social Issues, 37*(4), 105–122.

Veronen, L. J., Kilpatrick, D. G., & Resick, P. A. (1979). Treating fear and anxiety in rape victims: Implications for the criminal justice system. In W. Parsonage (Ed.), *Perspectives on victimology* (pp. 148–159). Beverly Hills, CA: Sage.

1   Case studies

In a sociology or psychology course, you may be asked to write a **case study** of a person, a family, or other social group. Usually the purpose of an assigned case study is to give you practice working with a particular social theory and the research techniques that apply to a limited sample.

Case studies use samples to make predictions about the broader class of people represented (see 34b). For example, you might be asked in a sociology course to write a case study of a group of children playing at recess in a school where you are doing student teaching. In doing so, you would name the school and the exact day on which you observed the children, identify the children by age and gender, and give details of what you observed, including perhaps a description of games ordinarily played by children attending the school. Your conclusions would draw on theories of behavior you studied in the course. In assigning a case study, your instructor will probably discuss how to interpret your observations and to format the study.

A case study usually contains the following details:

- Day, time, and place of study
- Activity observed
- Person or group by age and gender
- Background or history of the person or group
- Other characteristics important to the study
- What you saw and heard
- Interpretation and general conclusions
- Recommendations for further research

In writing a case study or using case studies as a secondary source in your research, keep the following guidelines in mind:

- Avoid mixing observations with background or conclusions.
- Make your details exact. In reporting the conclusions reached in your source, be as specific as you can about the psychological or social theory applied to the case, and identify the technical terms used in your source.
- State these conclusions in your own words, and avoid incorporating unfamiliar or unusual terms into your discussion.

2 Surveys and statistical studies

Surveys play an essential role in determining political attitudes and preferences, in marketing products, and in engaging in other activities that depend on an assessment of public attitudes and behavior. Scientific samples and statistical analyses are the subjects of technical courses, in which you will be given specific formats to follow in presenting graphs and statistical tables.

In your research paper, you may have occasion to refer to graphs and tables in your sources. Reproduce these exactly as you find them, credit your sources, and interpret the data with care. Remember that, as in other kinds of inductive reasoning, surveys predict only what a group of people *may* do or think, not what any single person may. In no instance do surveys predict what an individual or group *will* do (see 34b).

3 Interviews

In courses that ask you to gather opinions on an issue, **interviews** are the research method of choice. In your research paper, interviews may support other kinds of evidence. Here are some suggestions for conducting interviews:

You should choose to interview a person who can make a valuable contribution to your investigation, perhaps an eyewitness to an important event, a person with special knowledge, or the author of an article or book you are using in your investigation. These people may help you interpret a puzzling piece of evidence.

In arranging the interview, you should have a specific purpose in mind and know what use you intend to make of the information you will receive. You should also tell your informant how long you expect the interview to last and what equipment you will be bringing (e.g., a tape recorder).

In preparing for the interview, you should write out the questions you intend to ask. However, in conducting the interview, it is best not to read the questions to your informant or refer to them frequently. If other questions occur to you in the course of the interview, you should jot them down and return to them later in the interview.

It is sometimes advantageous to begin with factual questions that let the informant identify ideas and interests of concern. Once you have identified the ideas and interests of your informant, you should ask specific questions that elicit details and let the informant introduce other ideas and concerns. It is essential to be clear whether you are asking for a fact or an opinion—the difference is an important one. It is also essential to avoid interrupting answers with questions on other topics or with your own experiences or opinions.

Watch for answers that show emotion. These may reveal a particular bias or unusual point of view that you will need to consider in evaluating the whole interview. Also give the person time to develop an answer. Often the initial response is less reliable or useful than side comments made by the informant. Memory often comes alive as events are recalled and details are corrected. At the conclusion of the interview, read aloud the notes you have taken to give the informant an opportunity to correct statements and answers. If you conduct the interview using a tape recorder, play back portions and, if necessary, ask for clarification and additional details.

If possible, interview several people. Reports of traffic accidents show that participants and bystanders, standing and sitting in different places, see and interpret events differently. Where possible verify the information through other primary and secondary evidence (see 34a, 40 a–b), and keep a careful record of discrepancies and contradictions you notice in published accounts of the event and the testimony given in the interviews.

Finally, bring the equipment you need for the interview. Avoid borrowing paper and pencil from the person being interviewed. If you bring a tape recorder, ask permission to use it, and have the recorder ready for use.

4 Questionnaires

Questionnaires are another common way of gathering information in the social sciences. The following suggestions may help you to ask questions that encourage clear and informative answers:

- Always state your purpose at the outset of asking questions and explain what you intend to do with the results.
- As in an interview, have a clear purpose in mind. It may help to write down the information you are are seeking through the questionnaire.
- As in an interview, ask questions in an order that will best elicit the information you want.
- Ask specific questions that invite specific responses. Leave space on the questionnaire for additional responses and comments on the questions.
- Check for repetitious questions. Watch for similar words that rephrase the same idea. Note, however, that many questionnaires deliberately repeat questions in different words to discover ambiguous or contradictory attitudes.
- Don't phrase a question so to suggest its answer. For example, avoid beginning a question with phrases like "Isn't it true that. . . ."

■ Don't ask a complex question (37a) that forces the person to agree to or concede a position on an issue—"Is solar energy less desirable than nuclear power?" In answering this question, the informant is being forced to concede that nuclear power is desirable (see "complex question" in 37a). First ask whether the person considers nuclear power desirable, then ask about solar energy.

5 Abstracts

An **abstract** is a summary of an article or chapter of a book, giving a brief statement of the content and sometimes summarizing methods and results. An abstract is not a paraphrase (see 40c), and it contains no quotations and no additional commentary or interpretation. The following abstract of the Kidd and Chayet article on why victims do not report crimes summarizes the main argument and conclusions. Unlike the shorter abstract on page 788, this abstract refers to the kind of reasoning employed in the study.

> This article reviews emotional and cognitive reactions to criminal victimization. It draws connections between the contents of these reactions and victims' reluctance to report the crime to authorities. Since between one half and two thirds of all crimes are not so reported, understanding these connections is critical. We argue that nonreporting is the result of three factors acting singly or in concert: (a) victim fear, (b) feelings of helplessness and the perceived powerlessness of police, and (c) the threat of further victimization from authorities. We believe victims react in relatively rational ways. Despite the apparent loss of control and the strong fear engendered by the experience, the victimization does not lead people to report it to authorities. Instead, reporting to police is often realistically viewed by victims as ineffective and potentially costly.
> —Robert F. Kidd and Ellen F. Chayet, "Why Do Victims Fail to Report? The Psychology of Criminal Victimization," *Journal of Social Issues* 40 (1984):39.

Abstracts have many uses. They give the reader a quick look at the chief content or argument of an article or chapter, and they provide a record for use in later research. Researchers often read abstracts of articles in a particular field to define a problem for investigation and find out what research has been conducted. Abstracts in many of the social sciences are available through on-line data bases, usually for a fee (see 39f).

6 The research paper

The research paper in the social sciences uses some or all of the methods discussed in this section. The standard documentation format is the APA parenthetical style described in section 41c. The APA recommends that research papers contain the following sections as needed:

- A self-explanatory *title* that states the central topic of the paper.
- An *abstract* of 75 to 100 words that states the purpose, thesis, sources, and implications of the study.
- An *introduction*, unlabeled, that defines the problem to be dealt with in the paper and describes the research methods to be used. The introduction includes the background of the study, a brief review of previous research on the subject, and a statement of how the present study connects to earlier research.
- A section titled *Method*, a description of the techniques or methods of research, in sufficient detail to permit other researchers to test the methods and conclusions of the study. Subsections are labeled *subjects*, *apparatus* or *materials*, and *procedure*.
- A section titled *Results* that states the main findings and gives a detailed report of the evidence, including data that does not support the initial hypothesis.
- A section titled *Discussion* that states how the research supports the thesis and clarifies and adds to previous research. The researcher states the limits of the study, acknowledging results that do not support the thesis or conclusion. If this section is short, it may be combined with the previous section under the heading *Results and Discussion*.
- *Multiple Experiments*, or a description of separate experiments used in research, with a brief discussion of the results of each.
- *References*, following the APA formats given in 41c.
- *Appendices*, or additional graphs, tables, and discussion of material in the study that would interrupt the text inappropriately but may be needed by some readers.

Not all of these sections (or labels) appear in all articles in social science journals or in all papers written for courses in the social sciences. For example, Sheila Woody's research paper in the following section does not contain these formal divisions, though it illustrates many of them. Ask your instructor about what to include. [For a more detailed description of the contents of a research paper, see *Publication Manual of the American Psychological Association*, 3rd edition (Washington, DC: APA, 1983), pp. 22–29.]

Checklist: Organizing the Social Sciences Research Paper

Abstract
Introduction
    Statement of background
    Method
    Subjects
    Apparatus or materials
    Procedure
Results
Discussion
Multiple experiments
References
Appendix

7 Research paper using APA parenthetical documentation: Sheila Roxanne Woody, "Ethics of Nonhuman Animal Experimentation"

The following is part of a student research paper on the ethics of animal experimentation that draws on a wide range of published research in the social sciences. (The outline that Sheila Woody included with the paper has been omitted here.) The paper uses the documentation method of the American Psychological Association (APA) to cite sources (see 38d). However, Sheila uses her own observations in combination with published research to argue her thesis. Her research paper is actually a persuasive argument, as the marginal comments point out.

Sheila uses empirical evidence to argue that guidelines are needed to eliminate repetitiveness and cruelty in animal experimentation. This idea is Sheila's main *thesis*. She states at the outset that she is not opposed to all research using animals; her argument is limited to those features of animal research in urgent need of reform. In particular, she refutes a key argument of proponents of animal research: moral objections to animal research are misplaced because, unlike humans, animals are not moral beings. Sheila attacks the assumption underlying this view—that animals lack intellect.

Notice that Sheila's argument follows the traditional organization described in Chapter 36 on the persuasive essay. Her paper opens with an *introduction* and brief statement of the *background* of the controversy. Sheila then limits her topic to a specific issue and states her primary thesis. Her argument against animal research is followed by a detailed refutation, a summary, and a list of references. Sources are cited parenthetically by author's last name or short title, date, and page number. In APA-style documentation, quotations shorter than 40 words are incorporated in the text, as shown on page 780; quotations longer than 40 words are typed as a block, 5 spaces from the left margin. Sheila documents facts and ideas taken from her sources, as well as direct quotations.

Ethics of
1

Ethics of Nonhuman Animal Experimentation   Title,
Sheila Roxanne Woody   author,
University of Georgia   name of
   school
   centered

Psychology   Additional
Dr. Stuart Katz   information
October 20, 1987   centered

Introduction: Brief description of animal research in the United States and United Kingdom

Accurate statistics are not available concerning the actual number of animals used in American laboratories each year for research and experimentation because researchers are not compelled to report these figures. However, based on the number of published studies each year, as well as comparison with official reports from the United Kingdom, estimates of the number of living animals used yearly in American laboratories range between 20 million and 125 million (Ryder, 1975, p. 35).

Statement of topic

The ethical issue of animal rights in laboratory experiments has become an increasingly controversial topic in the last ten years. Experimenters resent what they see as intrusion into their decisions about research, and animal welfare activists often deny the value of any experimentation. An evaluation that takes into account the legitimate concerns of both sides could form a base for establishing guidelines concerning nonhuman animal welfare while still promoting the pursuit of worthwhile research.

Thesis: Guidelines are needed for non-human animal research.

Questioning the morality of using nonhuman animals in laboratories is not merely an academic exercise. Numerous examples can be cited of experiments that are unnecessary, cruel, or repetitious.

Secondary thesis: Studies based on animal research achieve little useful information.

Some studies may appear on the surface to be worthwhile, but they may accomplish very little in real terms. This is frequently true when a researcher attempts to extrapolate from animal research to humans, particularly with hereditary diseases. For example, methods can be devised to create ulcers or epilepsy in animals. While the symptoms and behaviors of these induced disorders closely resemble those of the natural disorders in humans, the origins are different in crucial respects:

Background: Description of animal research

> They [gastric and duodenal ulcers] never occur naturally in animals, and they are hard to reproduce experimentally. They have been so produced, but usually by methods of gross damage that have no relation to any possible causative factor in man; moreover, these experimental ulcers are superficial and heal rapidly and bear little resemblance to the indurated chronic ulcers we see in our patients. ("Reactions to," 1954, p. 1195)

Key example

Indent all paragraphs 5 spaces from the left margin. Indent block quotations 10 spaces.

Second key example

There are many examples of nonessential research. Some of the studies are undertaken to reach conclusions that common sense could have reached. For example, Professor P. L.

Broadhurst reports that psychologists have blinded rats, then deafened them, and finally eliminated olfaction to find out how rats learn in a maze. It is no wonder that "it was found that rats deprived in this way showed very little ability to learn" (Ryder, 1976, pp. 35–36).

Development of secondary thesis: Animal research is repetitious.

Other studies are costly repetitions. The National Institute of Health underwrote a 30-year study of sleep deprivation costing $51,000. In this study, animals were forced to run for 23 hours, rest an hour, then run for 23 more hours. During the hour of rest, a gun was shot off to disturb the weary animals. The experiment was a repetition of others performed in 1927, 1929, and 1946 (Morse, 1968, p. 29).

Examples

Animal research is cruel.

Many studies seem unnecessarily cruel. The University of Michigan conducted an experiment in which cats were repeatedly struck on the head by a pneumatic hammer. Although the cats were given a relaxant to reduce their motor activity and facilitate their handling, they were still conscious when struck, and none of them received anesthesia. All of the cats suffered severe brain concussions, as anticipated (Morse, 1968, p. 29). Similar experiments have been conducted at other major universities with other species.

Statement of major argument in favor of animal research: Animals are beyond our "moral concern."

Various reasons were given for these studies. Broadhurst's could shed light on learning theory. The repeated sleep-deprivation experiments could improve statistical controls and physiological measurements of the earlier studies. Information about the course of severe concussions was gained in the last study. However, the issue at hand is not only the practical value of the studies but also the cost in animal suffering.

Refutation of argument: Analysis of the basic assumption that animals are beyond "moral concern" because they lack intellect

One justification for such abuses is many scientists' opinion that animals do not fall within the bounds of moral concern. Laws protect human subjects, but even without laws, researchers would consider trauma studies, drug-addiction studies, and so on to be unethical if human subjects were required. What is the basis for the double standard? The major distinction seems to be the level of intellect. We assume that human beings are capable of abstract thought and rationalization and that other animals are not.

Further analysis of assumption: Basis of view that animals lack intellect

Many writers and researchers maintain that because language users (humans) are assumed to be able to form concepts, any being unable to use human language must lack that ability. Theories of language that are based on the heritability of linguistic roles,

Ethics of

6

such as Noam Chomsky's theory of universal
grammar, would rule that any communication
among animals could not be considered "language" unless it followed these presumed ge-
netic grammatical rules found in human languages of all cultures (Chomsky, 1959,
pp. 26–58). If human language is viewed as
the central trait proving that a being has
intelligence, then no other animal could
possibly have it.

*Further
analysis:*
Conse-
quence of
view—vivi-
section

On such a basis was vivisection justi-
fied when it was first practiced. For example, in the thirteenth century Saint Thomas
Aquinas wrote:

> Dumb animals and plants are devoid
> of the life of reason whereby to
> set themselves in motion; they are
> moved, as it were, by another, by
> a kind of natural impulse, a sign
> of which is that they are natu-
> rally enslaved and accommodated to
> the uses of others. (1976, p. 57)

*Continued
refutation:*
Argument
of propo-
nents is
contradic-
tory and
unsup-
ported.

The irony of using language as a test
is that while nonhuman animals are considered to be similar to humans for the convenience of research, they are considered to be
completely separate for moral purposes. In
addition, use of the language test as a basis for a moral decision does not exempt all
humans from painful experiences. Infants,

Ethics of

7

comatose persons, autistic persons, and the
severely mentally retarded could ethically
be used if language alone were a valid criterion, since they cannot speak to demonstrate their intelligence.

Continued
refutation:
Appeal to
experience

Furthermore, an animal's inability to
say what it is aware of does not determine
the range of its awareness. When Spot sees
his owner take out his leash and responds by
running in a circle, wagging his tail, and
looking what can only be described as ex-
cited, is it not reasonable that Spot has an
expectation of being taken for a run in the
fresh air? Spot has not demonstrated a so-
phisticated refinement of thought complete
with an extemporaneous discourse on his expectations, yet his actions lead a reasonable person to believe that he knows what is
about to happen. Of course, granting that
animals have a modicum of intelligence does
not imply that they are capable of a full
range of abstract thoughts. However, as
Charles Darwin notes:

Appeal to
observa-
tion—testi-
mony of
Charles
Darwin

> how little can the hard-worked
> wife of an Australian savage, who
> uses very few abstract words and
> cannot count above four, exert her
> self-consciousness or reflect on
> the nature of her own existence.
> (1976, p. 77)

*Summary
of refuta-
tion*

  Since language is simply a tool for expressing meaning, rather than the meaning
itself, the best way to judge the intelligence of a being is to evaluate its behavior
in the whole context of its natural environment. Human language indicates the cognitive
abilities of humans, but other animals, such
as chimpanzees, also indicate intelligence
with communication complex enough and spontaneous enough to be called language. Although chimpanzees do not have the abstract
conceptualization behind their communication, often humans, as Wittgenstein notes,
do not use these "higher" thought processes
while speaking (1965, p. 9).

Ethics of

9

References

First line
of entry
flush with
left mar-
gin, three-
spaced in-
dentation
for turn
lines

Last name
and initial

Initial and
last name
when cit-
ing collec-
tion of an-
thology

Publication
date fol-
lowing
author.

Title in
lower case
except for
proper
nouns

Aquinas, St. T. (1976). Differences between rational and other creatures. In T. Regan & P. Singer (Eds.), Animal rights and human obligations (pp. 33–47). Englewood Cliffs, NJ: Prentice-Hall.

Chomsky, N. (1959). A review of B. F. Skinner's Verbal behavior. Language, 35, 26–58.

Darwin, C. (1976). Comparison of the mental powers of man and the lower animals. In T. Regan & P. Singer (Eds.), Animal rights and human obligations (pp. 72–81). Englewood Cliffs, NJ: Prentice-Hall.

Dewsbury, D. (1978). Comparative animal behavior. New York: McGraw-Hill.

Fox, M. (1980). Returning to Eden. New York: Viking.

Griffin, D. (1976) The question of animal awareness. New York: Rockefeller University Press.

Kummer, H. (1971). Primate societies. Arlington Heights, MA: AHM Publishing.

Midgley, M. (1984). Animals and why they matter. Athens, GA: University of Georgia Press.

Morse, M. (1968). Ordeal of the animals. Englewood Cliffs, NJ: Prentice-Hall.

Reactions to stress. (1954, May 22). British Medical Journal 1, 1195–96.

Regan, T. (1983). The case for animal

Publisher's
full name

rights. Berkeley: University of California Press.

Ryder, R. (1975). Victims of science. London: Davis-Poynter.

Ryder, R. (1976). Experiments on animals. In
T. Regan & P. Singer (Eds.), Animal
rights and human obligations (pp. 72–81).
Englewood Cliffs, NJ: Prentice-Hall.

Wittgenstein, L. (1965). The blue and brown
books. New York, Harper & Row.

44d Papers in the natural and applied sciences

The natural and applied sciences also have their own special vocabularies and methods of research. In the laboratory and in the field, you will gain experience with the same process of investigation described in section 44a. This process determines the form of the reports and papers you will be asked to write in your science courses. Some formats and types of papers are the same, and some are different. Following is a brief description of the major types of writing particular to the natural and applied sciences.

1 Research log

The **research log** is a detailed record of each step in an experiment or observation and the findings of each step. A log plays an essential role in performing experiments, for you will use the log in writing a report of the experiment. A log is also indispensable in discussing your research with your instructor and classmates.

No researcher relies on memory to make observations or perform experiments. In a research log, you should write down a measurement or a chemical reaction at the moment you make the finding—not a day or an hour or even five minutes later. You should also describe exactly every detail of the experiment or observation—the instruments used, the insect observed, the particular animal injected. The research log must be clear to you and other researchers so that it can be consulted later on.

2 Abstracts

As in a report or paper in the social sciences, an **abstract**—a summary of essential ideas and details—usually precedes the main text of a scientific paper. A scientific abstract has the same structure and function as the abstract in the social sciences (see 44c). The following abstract introduces a scientific report published in a leading journal:

Abstract

On the basis of the fact that the youngest neutron stars such as the Crab pulsar and the Vela pulsar emit strong gamma-ray radiation, it is suggested that a few gamma-ray sources may be identified with young compact sources formed in the events of guest stars. Two such sources, 2CG 353+16 and 2CG 254+01, are identified with guest stars observed in the 14th century B.C. and A.D. 1230, respectively.

—Zhen-Ru Wang, "Two Gamma-Ray Sources and Ancient Guest Stars," *Science,* 20 March 1987

Notice the concision of the abstract. Another astronomer reading this abstract discovers what observations the author made and what conclusion the author reached.

3 Field and laboratory reports

A **field report** gives a detailed account of observations made outside the laboratory. A **laboratory report** traces an experiment from its opening to its final steps. Your field and laboratory reports should include the following information:

- The purpose of the observation or experiment.
- The date, place, and duration of the observation.
- The instruments used and procedures followed.
- The steps and process, and the exact details of each.
- The evidence, including an analysis of its causes and effects and a discussion of its implications.
- Conclusions and suggestions for additional observations or further research.

4 The scientific paper

The **scientific paper** is usually an extended report of research in the field or laboratory that includes a review of previous research. It also usually combines various kinds of analysis in discussing the evidence studied. The scientific paper in the natural and applied sciences usually includes the following parts:

- *Title*, stating the subject of the paper and sometimes the major procedure followed.
- *Abstract* or summary of the report, describing what the report does or summarizing its contents.

- *Introduction,* stating the problem studied in the report or the hypothesis being tested.
- *Review of the literature,* a review of previous research that summarizes and evaluates its assumptions, methods, and results.
- *Materials and methods,* describing the instruments and procedures employed.
- *Results,* stating the specific findings without interpretation or discussion.
- *Discussion* of the original problem or hypothesis in light of the findings.
- *Conclusion* that relates the findings to previous research, draws theoretical conclusions, and makes proposals for additional research and testing of old and new hypotheses.
- *References,* listing the sources cited in the paper.
- *Appendices,* containing additional graphs, tables, and other supporting evidence.

Scientific papers make extensive use of headings and sub-headings for easy access to their contents. Scientific papers lack the linear patterns of narratives and many papers in the humanities, for scientists reading a report must be able to find specific material without having to read the whole report. And, as Owen T. Su's paper on molecular structure shows (see page 791), scientific reports are written for special audiences familiar with the terminology and the procedures described.

As in papers written for social science courses, the requirements for the reporting of data and results also vary in the natural and applied sciences. Each science has special standards of evaluating evidence and reporting it, usually stated in your laboratory or field manual. Your instructor will also comment on these standards and guidelines throughout the course and will probably specify a particular format for lab reports and research papers. The following style manuals contain guidelines for papers in chemistry, mathematics, and physics:

American Chemical Society, *Handbook for Authors of Papers in American Chemical Society Publications* (Washington: American Chemical Society, 1978).

American Mathematical Society, *A Manual for Authors of Mathematical Papers,* 8th edition (Providence, R.I.: American Mathematical Society, 1984).

American Institute of Physics, *Style Manual for Guidance in Preparation of Papers,* 3rd edition (New York: American Institute of Physics, 1978).

☑

> **Checklist: Organizing the Scientific Research Paper**
>
> 1. Title
> 2. Abstract
> 3. Introduction
> 4. Review of previous research
> 5. Methods and materials
> 6. Results
> 7. Discussion
> 8. Conclusion
> 9. References
> 10. Appendices

5 A sample research paper: Owen T. Su, "Regulation of Gene Expression: The Role of Long Terminal Repeats"

Following are the last three paragraphs of the introduction to a student paper in biology. In these paragraphs, Owen T. Su reviews previous research on "long terminal repeats" or LTRs, defined in the opening sentence of the paper as "regions of DNA which are constructed in the host cell after retroviral infection." DNA is a nucleic acid located in the nuclei of cells and responsible for hereditary characteristics. RNA is a nucleic acid that controls cellular activities. The HIV-1 virus is a retrovirus implicated in Acquired Immune Deficiency Syndrome (AIDS). Owen's paper is not, however, about AIDS, but about how the DNA and RNA molecules replicate or reproduce themselves and then terminate this process.

Owen is writing to an audience of specialists and thus assumes that they are familiar with technical terms like *tat gene* and *footprinting* and with procedures used by researchers. In his review of research, Owen discusses the significance of other findings and defines a problem for new research.

Owen uses the documentation style recommended by the Council of Biology in its *CBE Style Manual,* 5th edition (Bethesda, MD: CBE, 1983) and discussed in section 41d of the *Handbook.* Only the references corresponding to the citations in the text are included here.

Su 1

Regulation of Gene Expression:

The Role of Long Terminal Repeats

by Owen T. Su

Concluding
paragraphs
of intro-
duction

The LTR of HIV-1 has recently been shown to contain a region that, when transcribed into RNA, can form a hairpin (Feng and Holland, 1988). The *tat* gene product appears to interact specifically with the sequence $^{+30}$ CUGGG $^{+34}$. If the hairpin, as predicted by Watson-Crick base pairing, does form, the pentanucleotide resides in the loop of the hairpin. Interaction of the *tat* gene product with this RNA structure would imply some posttranscriptional role of the trans-activating factor. What role this may be is, at this moment, unknown.

LTR regulation is at present a popular technique for determining the transforming capability of gene products. Much of the work involving LTRs after 1985 involves placing different genes under LTR and SV40 promotor control, even though the mechanism of these promotors is as yet unknown.

The techniques used to study LTR regulation of transcription have mainly searched for transcriptional controls provided by the LTR. Deletion/insertion/substitution manipulations of LTR DNA, footprinting, mRNA production assays, gene control via LTRs, and sequencing have all yielded information re-

Su 2

garding the critical regions for LTR regulation. They have not, however, elucidated the
mechanisms through which these regions exert
their regulatory properties. The enhancer
characteristics are also poorly understood.
That these sequences can act from either a
5' or 3' is particularly interesting. It has
been speculated that they can offer a bidi-
rectional entry site for RNA polymerase II
or one of its subunits (Khoury and Gruss,
1983). More secondary structural analysis
needs to be performed on these regions.

References

Feng, S., Holland, E. HIV-1 TAT Transactiva-
tion Requires the Loop Sequence Within Tar.
Nature 334, 165–167; 1988.
Khoury, G., Gruss, P. Enhancer Elements.
Cell 33, 313–314; 1983.

Summary

44a The steps of scientific investigation include forming a hypothesis, choosing a method of investigation and specific procedures, using these procedures to collect data, interpreting the results of the investigation, formulating a new or modified hypothesis, recommending further research if appropriate, and publishing the details of the research.

44b Learn the writing style and special vocabulary appropriate to each field in the social sciences and natural and applied sciences, and strive for exactness of detail, objectivity, and thoroughness in your writing.

44c Papers in the social sciences deal with social topics that can be observed, compared, and measured.

In using case studies as a secondary source in your research, avoid mixing observations with background or conclusions, be as specific as you can about the psychological or social theory applied to the case, and identify the technical terms used in your source **(44c 1)**.

In using surveys and statistical studies in your research, reproduce them exactly as you find them and interpret them with care **(44c 2)**.

In conducting an interview, ask specific questions that elicit details and let the informant introduce other ideas and concerns **(44c 3)**.

In writing questionnaires, ask specific questions that invite specific responses and avoid asking a complex question **(44c 4)**.

In writing an abstract, summarize the general argument and perhaps the methods of research used **(44c 5)**.

Use the standard formats for documenting and organizing research papers in the social sciences **(44c 6)**.

44d In papers in the natural and applied sciences, use the research log, abstract, field and laboratory reports, and the basic components of a scientific paper.

Course Notes and Examination Answers

45

□

□

In this chapter, we turn to other types of writing assignments—course notes and examination answers. Gaining knowledge is an important goal in your college courses. But learning how to retain that knowledge and communicate it effectively are equally important ones. To achieve these goals, you need to know how to take effective lecture and reading notes that will be of permanent use. You also need to know how to write effective exam answers.

45a | Lecture notes

Note-taking plays an important role in the preparation and writing of a research paper, as we learned in Chapter 40. But note-taking serves many other purposes. You will need to take accurate notes on your course lectures and on the textbook and supplementary reading you do—all situations that require different skills. Your notes will not be useful to you if they are not accurate and effective.

1 Ineffective notes

Consider the sample notes shown below, taken during an introductory lecture on viruses in a biology course. How useful will these notes be to the student at the time of a quiz or an exam?

The student will find these notes of little use. Although the notes give the gist of the instructor's explanation, they will be confusing to the writer later on; they fail to distinguish between the words, phrases, and sentences of the instructor and those of the class. The words *configuration, symmetry,* and *capsomere* are probably the instructor's; uncertain about their meaning, the note-taker recorded these words without paraphrasing or defining them in the context of the lecture. The note-taker often uses indentations to show the relationship between ideas—a common but ineffective practice, because indentations do not substitute for specific connecting phrases. These notes would be useful in preparing for a quiz or an exam only if they were rewritten in the writer's own words and in complete sentences, without depending on indentation. They would also need to cover the topics of the lecture more thoroughly (e.g., the old definition of *virus,* mentioned in the lecture, is not explained in the notes).

The notation on "Burnet"—mentioned by the instructor— is a reminder that the course text contains a detailed discus-

Ineffective lecture notes.

> *Types of infectious agents*
>
> *viruses*
>
>> *acellular in structure, chemical composition or replication*
>>
>> *DNA or RNA core—two types of viruses old definition and new*
>>
>> *protein coat around nucleic acid some viruses have additional coat from host tissue*
>>
>> *viruses also classified by symmetry (see <u>Burnet</u>)*
>>
>> *capsomeres (?) specific configuration*

sion of viruses. Here is a pertinent passage in the text that the student should consult to fill in gaps and define key terms:

> The new approaches have changed the whole outlook on viruses. Even the definition of a virus nowadays is quite different from the old one, which stated that a virus was a microorganism capable of multiplying only within living cells. The present approach is to define a virus as a structure composed of a protein coat surrounding a nucleic acid molecule, either RNA or DNA, which is capable of replication only within living cells. A virus is not an organism; it has no metabolism and is wholly dependent for its reproduction on mechanisms provided by its host cell.
> —Sir Macfarlane Burnet and David O. White, *Natural History of Infectious Diseases*, 4th ed.
> (Cambridge, Eng.: Cambridge UP, 1972), p. 53.

Burnet and White's description of viruses clarifies details in the notes by connecting various bits of information, including the old and new definition of *virus*. The student would have to consult other reference books to clarify and possibly correct these notes.

2 Effective notes

While taking notes on an article or a book, you can proceed at your own pace, pausing to digest a difficult idea or example or returning to important passages to correct a note. Taking notes on a lecture, however, is quite different. Consider the skills needed in taking notes on a lecture. Here you depend on the spoken word, though your instructor may write important words and phrases on the board. You also depend on your ability to record important words and phrases correctly and to write them down without losing the thread of the ongoing discussion. For example, a lecturer refers to the "Houghton Mifflin edition" of Ralph Waldo Emerson, and a listener writes down "hot muffins," putting a large question mark beside the doubtful phrase. Mistakes of this sort are easy to make. If the listener does not check the phrase following the lecture, the mistake may turn up in a course paper or an examination answer.

Learning how to write accurate, useful, and effective lecture notes comes with practice. You will take effective lecture notes if you follow these guidelines:

- Write in complete phrases or sentences, not in single words. What is clear at the time you write down a word probably won't be clear a week later or even later the same day. If the rapidity of the lecture prevents you from writing in complete sentences, rewrite the notes in sentences as soon as possible after the lecture.

- Include connecting words, phrases, and sentences *(thus, therefore, as a result, these form a process)* that show the relationship between ideas and details. Your notes should have the continuity of a well-organized exposition or argument.
- If in doubt about a proper name, term, detail, or idea, put a question mark in the margin and check your textbook or a reference book for proper spelling or explanatory details. Don't take time in class to look up the name or phrase in your text or a dictionary you may have with you. If necessary, ask your instructor later for clarification if you cannot find a reference.
- Write marginal notes on questions or ideas suggested to you by the lecture, and do so at the moment they occur to you. For you may forget them as the lecture progresses and as other ideas capture your attention.
- In class or soon afterward, record the pertinent pages of your textbook or other sources assigned on the topic, particularly those mentioned by your instructor during the lecture.

EXERCISES

1. Rewrite the notes on viruses in complete sentences, adding explanatory details on RNA and DNA from an unabridged dictionary or a desk encyclopedia or other reference work.
2. Write a summary of the preceding section (45a) without looking back at it. Then check the summary with the text to test the accuracy of your memory and note-taking. ■

45b Reading notes

1 Ineffective notes

Many students take careful notes during lectures but neglect to take effective notes on their reading, preferring instead to underline and write marginal comments in their texts. Although these are useful techniques, they do not substitute for careful note-taking. Reading notes are as important as lecture notes in retaining knowledge and communicating that knowledge effectively.

Ineffective reading notes.

kwashiorkor
contrast with marasmus

occurs in conditions of extreme social disruption

term from Ghanaian (Ghana?)
means "second-child disease"
children weaned too soon because mother is pregnant or
has had second baby
belief that weaned child is jealous and causes disease
put on standard diet of starchy food
relieves hunger but lacks protein needed for growth

Consider the sample notes shown above, taken on a passage in a textbook for a health sciences course. The word *kwashiorkor* refers to a nutritional disease in evidence today in famine- and war-stricken parts of Africa. Here is the original passage summarized in the notes:

> Marasmus is apt to occur under conditions of extreme social disruption: profound cultural change, famine, drought, war, or epidemics. On the other hand, it is appallingly common that the deficiency disease kwashiorkor, a Ghanaian word meaning "second-child disease," is found primarily in children who consume insufficient protein for their growth and maintenance needs. This happens particularly to children who have been weaned, generally because another child has arrived or is on the way (which is why some Ghanaian mothers believe the disease is caused by jealousy). The weanling is then shifted to a diet considered appropriate in his culture. Distressingly often, this is a starchy pap based on yams, taro, corn, rice, barley gruel, or any one of the culturally designated diets in which calorie intake is sufficient to satisfy hunger but insufficient to meet the critical protein requirements demanded by the growth phase of the child.
> —Corinne Shear Wood, *Human Sickness and Health*
> (Mountain View, CA: Mayfield, 1979), p. 73

How accurate are these reading notes, and how useful will they be to the student later on?

First, the notes fail to distinguish between direct quotations and paraphrases. If the writer later wanted to use the information in the notes in a paper or report, the notes would not indicate which phrases should appear in quotation marks. Careless note-taking is thus a common cause of unintentional plagiarism (see 40d).

Second, the words and phrases in the notes are not likely to be meaningful to the writer later on because they are not explained in the original context of the text. For example, the notes don't make clear that the disease being discussed is kwashiorkor and not marasmus, another nutritional disease defined by the author earlier in the chapter:

> When a daily diet is chronically deficient in both calories and protein, there ensues a syndrome called marasmus, from the Greek word meaning "to waste away."
> —Corinne Shear Wood, *Human Sickness and Health*, p. 69

The phrases recorded stand without clear reference. It is marasmus that occurs during famine and other periods of disaster. Kwashiorkor may occur during these periods, but Wood states that kwashiorkor occurs at all times—a point lost in the notes. Asked on an exam to distinguish the two kinds of disease, the writer is likely to confuse them or state the difference imprecisely.

2 Effective notes

To make sure that your reading notes are accurate and of use later on, write in complete sentences, in summary or paraphrase—quote only those phrases or sentences that cannot be put into your own words without loss of special nuance or emphasis. Be careful also to record full information about the source, including author, complete title, publisher, and date of publication at the beginning of an entry. Subsequent notes from the same source may be identified in short form, as in the following note that paraphrases Wood's definition of *kwashiorkor:*

Effective Reading Notes

Marasmus, a nutritional disease caused by calorie and
protein deficiency, strikes during periods of famine
and other disaster (p. 69). Kwashiorkor, or "second-
child disease" in Ghanaian, is a nutritional disease
that occurs when children are weaned early; the mother
may be pregnant or may have borne another child. The
weaned child is fed a diet able to relieve hunger but

short on protein needed for growth (Corinne Shear Wood,
Human Sickness, p. 73).

Notice that the writer of these notes returns to the earlier definition of marasmus, incorporates it as an extension of the
paraphrase, and includes a page reference to the definition.
With a technical passage, be as specific as you can even at the
risk of wordiness. The more familiar you are with the subject,
the more concise your summary and paraphrase will be.

You may find it helpful to outline a passage instead of
summarizing or paraphrasing it. Here is brief topic outline of
Wood's definition of *kwashiorkor:*

Characteristics of kwashiorkor
A. Differences from marasmus
   1. Protein deficiency vs. caloric and protein de-
      ficiency in marasmus
   2. Occurs at all times vs. most frequent occur-
      rence of marasmus in times of disaster
B. Causes
   1. Weaning of child because of "second-child"
      syndrome
      a. Pregnancy of mother
      b. Arrival of another baby
   2. Stunted growth resulting from protein-poor diet

An outline has the attraction of conciseness for some writers,
but notice again the danger of haphazard arrangement of
words and phrases.

Here are some additional suggestions for taking useful
reading notes:

- To write successful notes, think out the ideas and then write them
  down in summary or in paraphrase. A *summary* is a concise
  statement in your own words of the main ideas of a piece of
  writing; a *paraphrase* is a sentence-for-sentence summary in your
  own words (see 40c). Neither summary nor paraphrase interprets
  or comments on the ideas of the work. As in notes written for
  research papers, distinguish carefully between summary and
  paraphrase.

▪ Jot down your ideas about the work and mark them clearly as your own; these will be of value in reviewing your notes and in defining topics for research and for papers.

The purpose of note-taking is the same whether you're taking notes in the classroom, the library, or at your desk—accurate statements, exact wording, and precise documentation are essential if the notes are to be useful to you later. Notes made up of unconnected words and phrases will be difficult if not impossible to understand once you have forgotten their context.

Checklist: Effective Course Notes

1. Use complete phrases and sentences when taking notes.
2. Clarify the relationships among ideas by using connecting words, phrases, and sentences.
3. Verify unfamiliar words and phrases in your text or another reference book, or ask your instructor to explain them. Do not leave unfamiliar terms unexplained in your notes.
4. Record your own comments and ideas suggested to you by the lecture or reading as they occur to you. Clearly label them as your own.
5. Clearly identify direct quotations, paraphrases, and summaries of other sources in your notes.
6. Add cross-references to your text and other sources that may be useful later on. Record accurate information about texts and other sources.

45c Examination answers

1 Ineffective answers

Consider the following question and answer for an exam in a health sciences course:

Question

How would you distinguish by sight a first-degree burn from a second-degree burn?

Answer

First-degree burns sometimes seem more serious than second-degree ones because they can hurt more. Sunburns are a good example. Both can be soaked in cold water, then dressed. The blisters in second-degree burns shouldn't be broken. A doctor or nurse can tell the difference right away and will know how to treat the burn. Third-degree burns are the most serious; the burn area looks white or ashy. Most of the skin has been destroyed. Unlike the first-degree and second-degree burn, third-degree burns should not be soaked in cold water because this will cause shock.

The answer does not address the original question of how to distinguish a first-degree from a second-degree burn by sight. The answer has no central point or focus; instead, the details are presented haphazardly, in the order they occur to the writer. The writer probably remembers the differences between third-degree and second-degree burns but not those between second-degree and first-degree ones, which usually hurt less. Lacking a central point, the answer is diffuse.

A unified examination answer considers a single characteristic fully instead of jumping from one to another. In a well-focused, coherent answer, the details support a central point and transitional words connect the details.

2 Effective answers

Although you need exact knowledge of the subject to write a successful examination answer, knowing the facts is no guarantee of success. You also need to organize your details carefully, addressing the question directly and omitting details not pertinent to it.

Here are some suggestions for organizing and developing effective examination answers:

- Know exactly how much time you have to write the answers, and work with this time limit in mind. An excellent answer to one question may have less weight if you are left with insufficient time to answer the other questions of the exam.
- Read each exam question carefully. You will lose valuable time if you discover in the course of writing that you misunderstood the question and must rewrite the answer. A useful check is to restate the question in stating the answer.
- Organize your answers carefully, writing complete, carefully constructed sentences and unified paragraphs that center on a single idea. Begin with your central idea and develop it with exact details, or build up to the idea through an accumulation of detail. Avoid a haphazard assembly of facts and ideas. The structure of your answer should be obvious to your instructor.
- Use transitional words and phrases to make your answers coherent. Omit side comments and irrelevant details.
- Address the question directly and stay with the question. Don't stray to another point or a side issue.
- Show that you have thought about the question by avoiding pat phrases and clichés. Avoid unloading miscellaneous facts memorized from your notes and reading. State the essential details, and state them exactly even though they are familiar ones. The purpose of the exam is to test the exactness of your knowledge.
- Don't assume that details speak for themselves. Having stated the facts, you need to interpret them. Show how facts connect and what they imply. A mere assemblage of facts and details tells your instructor nothing.
- Don't state your ideas in general terms. Give supporting details to be sure that all of your statements are well supported.
- Reserve time to proofread for sentence structure and spelling and to check your answers for accuracy. It is easy to confuse names and details when writing under pressure.

The following answers also address the earlier question on first- and second-degree burns:

Question
How would you distinguish by sight a first-degree burn from a second-degree burn?

Answer 1
```
A first-degree burn is red or discolored, slightly
swollen, and painful. A second-degree burn is also red,
sometimes spotted or blotched, usually blistered and
```

more swollen, and wet in appearance. It also has pene-
trated deeper into the surface and takes longer to heal
than a first-degree burn.

Answer 2

First-degree burns are superficial burns caused by
staying out in the sun too long or touching hot things.
They have the usual characteristics of a bad sunburn.
First-degree burns may hurt less than second-degree
burns, which usually are deeper and more severe.
Second-degree burns take longer to heal than first-
degree burns.

Which do you think is the better answer?

Answer 1 distinguishes carefully between the signs shared
by the two kinds of burn (redness and swelling) and the differences between these signs (in second-degree burns the spotting and blotching of the skin). Answer 1 also pinpoints additional signs in second-degree burns, such as blistering and
greater penetration of the skin. The difference in healing is
stated at the end of the answer, an appropriate place since this
sign would be noticed last.

In comparing second-degree and first-degree burns, an-

Checklist: Effective Exam Answers

1. Use specific details and well-supported ideas to answer exam questions.
2. Avoid reference to irrelevant details or side comments.
3. Write your answers in complete, well-constructed
   sentences and unified paragraphs.
4. Proofread your answers for errors in spelling and
   grammar.
5. Work at a pace that is appropriate to the amount
   of time you have to complete the exam.

swer 2 only alludes to their characteristics and does not discuss their appearance. The writer probably assumes that the instructor knows the facts about the kinds of burns. But the question is asking about these facts, so they cannot be omitted no matter how obvious they may seem. Answer 1, then, is the stronger answer.

3 Interpretation and judgment

Many exam questions ask for your interpretation of facts. In answering a question that calls for interpretation or judgment, you should discuss the facts in the appropriate context. Consider the following answer to this question about one of Hamlet's soliloquies in the Shakespearean play:

Question
What does Hamlet's soliloquy beginning "To be, or not to be" show about his state of mind and the revenge he is pursuing against Claudius, the murderer of Hamlet's father?

Ineffective Answer

In his soliloquy, Hamlet asks if it is better to live or die. He wonders if it is better to suffer the "slings and arrows of outrageous fortune" (one of Shakespeare's most famous lines) or do something to end them. He says life is so painful that many people would kill themselves if they weren't afraid of what would happen to them after committing suicide. Hamlet realizes that "conscience does make cowards of us all" (another famous line in the play). These thoughts show what is on Hamlet's mind long before the players perform "The Murder of Gonzago." Hamlet expects to unmask Claudius through this "play within a play." So we know Hamlet is pursuing the revenge in arranging the play, but the soliloquy tells us what his feelings are about its success.

To explain the feelings and thoughts that Hamlet is expressing in the play, the writer must refer to the events that led to his soliloquy. The writer must also state whether Hamlet is expressing these feelings and thoughts for the first time in the play. The preceding answer does not give this information; instead it attempts to answer the question by merely summarizing Hamlet's speech and adding irrelevant comments on two of the lines. The writer assumes that a detailed account of Hamlet's thoughts on suicide will serve to define the character's state of mind and show how actively he is pursuing the revenge. The concluding sentences do state that Hamlet is pursuing revenge, but they are not connected to the soliloquy. A summary of facts says nothing meaningful unless the writer connects and interprets them.

Facts must be interpreted to have meaning. A recitation of the events in Shakespeare's plays reveals nothing about Hamlet as a person, about the meaning of his actions, or about the attitude or feelings that Shakespeare wishes the audience to hold about Hamlet.

Summary

45a Take lecture notes that will be useful later on.

Write course notes in phrases or complete sentences **(45a 1)**.

Ineffective notes mix words, phrases, and sentences haphazardly, without showing the relationship among ideas **(45a 2)**.

45b Take reading notes that clarify the context of the author's ideas.

Accuracy and full documentation are essential **(45b 1)**.

Effective notes distinguish between paraphrase and direct quotation and fully document the source **(45b 2)**.

45c Answer exam questions concisely and with an interpretation of facts.

Effective examination answers address the questions directly and state the details exactly **(45c 1–2)**.

Ineffective answers substitute summary for interpretation **(45c 3)**.

Business Writing

When you set out to begin your full-time career, one of your first tasks will be to write a letter applying for a job. With this letter you will include a resume that summarizes your background and qualifications for the job. Once you are on the job, you will engage in yet other kinds of writing–business letters, memorandums, recommendations, proposals, and defenses of policies and actions taken. Outside of the office, you will also have occasion to write personal requests for service, letters of response, and letters of complaint. In this chapter, we turn to the conventions that govern these various kinds of writing situations.

46a Writing for business

Letters of application, business letters, memorandums, and other types of **business writing** have conventional formats that give readers easy access to information. Effective business writing is clear, concise, and direct, and it gauges its audience in selecting and organizing details.

1 General guidelines

Your own business letters will be effective if you observe the following guidelines:

- State your purpose in the first paragraph so that your reader does not have to hunt for it in the letter.
- Avoid crowding several pieces of information or several requests into a single paragraph.
- Emphasize the reader as much as the writer, especially in the opening and closing paragraphs.
- Be direct but polite in making your request or in responding to the recipient of the letter. If you are giving this person a positive answer, it is a good idea to state that fact early in the letter. If instead you are refusing a request, you should identify positive features of the proposal in addition to stating the reasons for the refusal.
- Make your letter positive in tone, even if you are refusing a request. When you must refuse, suggest an alternative solution or other action that your reader may take, and avoid lecturing the reader about past mistakes or steps that should have been taken. Make your critical comments brief and specific.
- Address the subject of your letter as directly as possible. Avoid indirect statements and appeals. The writer of the following sentences avoids making direct statements for fear of sounding rude or angry but ends up sounding uncertain and timid:

  Indirect Statements
  I wonder if I may apply for the position you advertised . . .
  If I may be permitted to introduce myself . . .
  Knowing how busy you are at this time of year, I apologize for bothering you about a matter as small as . . .
  Please write me whenever you find the time . . .

- Don't issue commands or make threats, as these make conciliation difficult or impossible:

  Unnecessary Threats
  Let me know immediately whether I meet your qualifications for the job . . .
  I am writing you before I hire a lawyer to file suit against Connecticut Motor Sales . . .
  I demand an answer by return mail . . .

808

- Avoid sandwiched criticism (e.g., "Your proposal is fantastic, but ..."). Your reader will not be fooled by insincere praise that cushions bad news.
- Keep your sentences pointed, simple, and clear by avoiding unnecessary words and phrases. Your reader should not have to read a sentence twice to discover your meaning:

> **Wordy and Unclear**
> If I may have a few moments of your time, I should like to review my qualifications for the position that you advertised in the issue of the *Hartford Courant* dated ...
> Having now reviewed my academic background, I turn to my work experience, which I trust meets your qualifications for the position you advertised ...
> With respect to the matter of the warranty that expired the week before the trouble I described commenced ...

- Maintain a formal tone in all business correspondence. Avoid a chatty or familiar tone, even if the person you are addressing is a friend:

> **Too Informal**
> I've probably gone on too long about myself ...
> I get a kick out of working with computers ...

- Include the details and information relevant to your correspondence. Exclude irrelevant personal references or details and unnecessary information:

> **Irrelevant Details**
> I will be available for an interview, except for the last week in March, at which time my family and I will be taking a long-awaited vacation in the "Big Apple" ...
> Patsy Murphy, who worked in your company several years ago, is a good friend of mine and sends her regards ...

- Avoid overusing the passive voice. For example, the statement "Refusal is mandatory because the applicant did not give full details" is cold and may even seem like a threat. Instead, say something like "We need additional details about the accident to make a decision about your claim."

2 Format

In typing a letter of application or business letter, observe these guidelines on **format**:

- Single-space the body of the letter and double-space between paragraphs with or without indentation. Align the left margin of your home address and the date with the left margin of the complimentary close and signature. (See the sample letter on page 813.)

- Following the complimentary close, skip four spaces and type your name directly below it. Sign your full name in ink.
- Type *Copy* or *cc.* in the lower left-hand corner of the letter to note that others have received a copy of it. If you include a resume or other document with the letter, type *Enc.* or *Enclosure* in the lower left-hand corner to indicate that other items are enclosed. (See the sample letter on page 814.)
- Verify names and spelling. Call the school or company or consult a directory.
- On the envelope, center the name of the recipient and the address in block form. Type your name and address in the upper left-hand corner. (See the sample envelope on page 815.)
- Use a good-quality bond paper for your correspondence; do not use erasable paper. If you type your letter, use a fresh, black-colored ribbon. If you write the letter with a word processor, use a letter-quality printer. (Some dot-matrix printers approach letter quality.)
- Proofread the letter and envelope carefully.
- Keep copies of all letters you send.

Letters of application and business letters use three standard formats. In the **full block** format, all elements of the letter are aligned at the left margin. Business letters written on company letterhead usually follow the full block format. The **modified block** and **indented** formats are common in letters without letterheads, such as job application letters. The basic characteristics of each format are as follows:

Full Block
1. All elements of the letter—the date, the name and address of the recipient, the complimentary close, and the signature—are aligned at the left margin.
2. Paragraphs are separated by two lines of space and the first line of each paragraph is not indented.

Modified Block (see page 813)
1. The address of the sender, the date, the complimentary close, and the signature are all indented so that they position toward the right margin of the letter.
2. The inside address and salutation are aligned with the left margin of the letter.
3. Paragraphs are separated by two lines of space and are not indented.

Indented (see page 814)
1. The address of the sender, the date, the complimentary close, and the signature are indented like in the modified block form, toward the right margin of the letter.
2. The inside address and salutation are aligned with the left margin.
3. Paragraphs are separated by two lines of space and each paragraph begins with an indentation of at least five spaces.

Some business writers use a less common method called **full block simplified format**. In this format, the salutation and complimentary close are omitted. A heading typed in capital letters and stating the subject of the letter replaces the salutation:

```
REQUEST FOR ENGINE REPLACEMENT
```

This heading appears flush with the left margin, as shown here. The signature of the writer appears in place of the complimentary close; it is followed by the typed name and any further identification.

3 Salutations and complimentary closes

Salutations are conventional in business letters and other correspondence. Address a company officer or governmental or school official as *Mr.* or *Ms.*, and use titles like *Dr.* and *President* where appropriate. You should avoid the general salutations *Dear Sirs* and *Gentlemen* because these exclude women. Using a given name is acceptable only if you know the person well and you are addressing that person only. The given name is inappropriate in writing a letter that will be read by others.

Complimentary closes are also standard in business letters and other types of correspondence. Depending on your writing situation, you may use a formal complimentary close like *Sincerely* or *Cordially,* or a less formal one like *Regards* or *Best Wishes.* Avoid flowery and pretentious salutations and complimentary closes like these:

My dear Mr. Roberts
Humbly yours
With all due respect
Most gratefully
I remain yours very truly

Finally, sign your letter with your complete name. Don't give your first name only or a nickname (e.g., *"Butch" Abernathy, Bob,* or *Janie*).

4 Letters of application

An effective **letter of application** states essential facts in a concise style; it conveys your interest in the job and states your qualifications briefly but effectively. To be concise, the letter should not sound curt or blunt or familiar in tone.

The accompanying sample letter meets these requirements. The writer conveys his interest in the job and summarizes his qualifications and background in a formal tone. The letter is written in the modified block format. Follow these guidelines in writing your own job application letters:

- Address a specific officer of the company by name. For example, don't address the envelope to the company president or open the letter with "Dear Company President" or "Dear Personnel Director."
- State the purpose of your letter concisely and directly in the first paragraph. State your interest in the job.
- In your middle paragraphs, focus on your qualifications for the job. Don't give a complete description of your work experience or educational background, as this is the function of your resume (see 46b). Rather, focus on those qualifications that best illustrate your ability to do the job.
- In stressing your qualifications, however, don't overstate your abilities or conceal important information.
- In the last paragraph of your letter, express a willingness to cooperate and to keep the communication going.
- Use an appropriate salutation and closing phrase.
- Always include a resume with a job application letter. The resume details your work experience, educational history, and other pertinent information. The resume also allows you to focus in your letter on your most important qualifications for the job.
- Enclose your letter and resume in a properly addressed envelope. Follow the format discussed on page 810 and shown in the accompanying sample envelope.

5 Business letters

An effective **business letter** states essential facts in a concise style. The sample letter on page 814 is written in the indented format.

Sample Job Application Letter—Modified Block Format

Return address, date centered

1150 South Ledge Road
Hartford, CT 06120
May 1, 1990

One space

Ms. Kathleen Peters
President, Health Care Systems, Inc.
400 Harbor Road
New Haven, CT 06510

Inside address

One space

Dear Ms. Peters:] *Salutation*

One space

Please consider me for the opening in biomedical engineering at Health Care Systems, advertised in the <u>Hartford Courant</u>
on April 26. My work experience, educational background, and
interests meet the qualifications listed in your advertisement.
Dr. William Lesser, a consultant with Health Care Systems, told
me of the advances your company has made in image-processing
equipment and encouraged me to apply.

Double space

My work experience fits me for this position. I have worked as
an associate designer at New Era Machines, Inc., in Farmington,
Connecticut, mainly in designing machinery used in monitoring
cardiac patients. At New Era I also helped to design software
for image-processing and other medical equipment. Experience
with computer equipment adds to my qualifications. I repaired
personal computers at Eagle Computers, Inc., in Enfield,
Connecticut.

Double space

In these jobs I developed the skills essential in biomedical
engineering. Though my qualifications fit me for work with
medical equipment and with software, my chief goal is to work in
image processing. I am applying for the position at Health Care
Systems because your company is a leader in this field.

Double space

North Central University Placement Office will send my
credentials upon your request. I am available for an interview
at your convenience. In the meantime, I look forward to hearing
from you and to discussing employment at your company.

One space

Sincerely,

Signature block
Four spaces

Robert Goldsmith

Robert Goldsmith

Enclosure

Sample Business Letter—Indented Format

Centered
address
and date

1150 South Ledge Road
Hartford, CT 06120
May 15, 1990

Mr. Arthur Bailey
President, Connecticut Motor Sales
1740 North Cole Street
Hartford, CT 06150

Dear Mr. Bailey:

5-space in-
dentation
     Connecticut Motor Sales has a reputation for standing behind its automobiles. For that reason I am requesting your help with the 1986 model all-terrain vehicle I bought in June 1989. Even though my new-car warranty expired one week before the transmission failed, I request that Connecticut Motor Sales replace the engine and repair the transmission at its own expense.

    The enclosed copies of receipts show that your service department worked on the transmission three times in the first four months after purchase and several more times before the warranty expired. This service record suggests the transmission was defective at the time I bought the car. The Consumer Protection Office informs me that other owners have filed similar complaints with the manufacturer.

    Your service manager told me he cannot make repairs at the expense of Connecticut Motor Sales without your authorization. I am including a copy of the service record during the warranty period. Please let me hear from you within a few days. You can also reach me at home in the evening. The number is 555-0018.

Sincerely,

Jane Goldsmith

Jane Goldsmith

cc.
Enc.

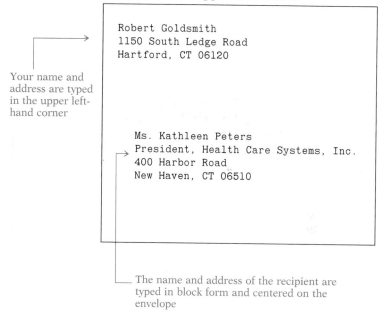

**Sample Envelope for a Job
Application Letter**

```
Robert Goldsmith
1150 South Ledge Road
Hartford, CT 06120




        Ms. Kathleen Peters
        President, Health Care Systems, Inc.
        400 Harbor Road
        New Haven, CT 06510
```

Your name and
address are typed
in the upper left-
hand corner

The name and address of the recipient are
typed in block form and centered on the
envelope

Keep the following points in mind when writing requests or responses, letters of complaint, and memorandums:

- State your request or complaint in the opening paragraph. Don't begin with a lengthy review of the problem or situation, and don't build to your point through a mass of details.
- Provide the details your reader needs in the middle paragraphs.
- Be clear about what the person addressed should do. Don't expect the reader to make inferences from a history of the problem or details only.
- Avoid indirect requests like "It would be helpful if. . . ." If you want the person to provide a solution or remedy, be direct in your request without being rude. Focus on what should be done, not on old wrongs and bad motives. Show your willingness to see another point of view and conciliate.
- Extend your appreciation to the reader for considering your request.

Sample Memorandum

CONNECTICUT MOTOR SALES

MEMORANDUM

June 12, 1990

To: Sales, Front Office, Car Maintenance

From: Arthur Bailey

Subject: 1985-1986 All-terrain vehicles, V-8 engine 205

We have received several letters and calls from owners asking for repairs and replacement of faulty transmissions on 1985 and 1986 all-terrain vehicles.

The manufacturer warrants us to make repairs without cost, if in the judgment of the service manager the transmission is repairable. We are warranted to replace transmissions only upon the district supervisor's approval.

If you receive a call from an owner, please take down the name and number and full details of the complaint. Make no promises. We will respond by letter.

AB:mr

6 Memorandums

A **memo** usually addresses a single issue or problem or makes a single request, sometimes in one or two paragraphs, sometimes in several pages. As in other business correspondence, essential facts are highlighted.

The point of the memorandum is stated in the opening paragraph or opening heading. Since the memorandum is designed to be read quickly, the request may be outlined or listed in words and phrases.

The accompanying sample memorandum illustrates the standard memo format.

46b The resume

An effective **resume** gives a prospective employer a detailed summary of your qualifications in an accessible form, clearly and concisely. A resume omits unessential facts, but optional details about your personal interests and activities— for example, volunteer work and hobbies—can also be included in brief form.

There are two ways to organize a resume:

- *Chronologically*—by time, for example beginning with recent work experience and proceeding to educational experience in the past.
- *Emphatically*—beginning with the most important and proceeding to the least important details.

The advantage of a chronological organization is that it emphasizes recent work or educational experience. The advantage of the emphatic type is that it highlights your qualifications for the job you are seeking.

Since the reader of your resume must be able to find essential facts quickly, prominent headings (in capitals or italics) divide the various parts of the resume. In the accompanying sample resume, these headings are centered; the alternative is to position them in list form in the left margin. Always give the most recent facts first under each heading.

Sample Resume

Robert Goldsmith
1150 South Ledge Road
Hartford, CT 06120
Phone (203) 555-0018

Objective

Position as a biomedical engineer, with specialization
in image processing and computer applications in
health-care equipment.

Work Experience

September 1982-present: Biomedical Engineer, New Era
Machines, Inc., Farmington, Connecticut 06035:
  Worked with a team of engineers in designing
  monitoring equipment for cardiac units.
  Wrote software with biomedical applications.
September 1978-July 1981: Service Department, Eagle
Computer Company, Enfield, Connecticut:
  Repaired computers and printers.

Education

1977-82: North Central University. Graduated cum laude,
B.S. in Electrical Engineering, June 1981; M.S. in
Electrical Engineering, June 1981.
Minors: Marketing, Computer Programming (FORTRAN,
PASCAL, other computer languages)
Overall grade point average: 3.7.
Average in major: 3.5.
Graduated from Simsbury High School, Simsbury,
Connecticut, 1977.

Achievements and Interests

Engineering Honor Society, North Central University,
1980-82.
Engineering scholarship, North Central University,
1977-81.
Member of a Hartford area computer club.

References

References furnished upon request.

Your resume should include details on the following information:

- *Personal data*—Your name, home address, and telephone number; other addresses and phone numbers where a prospective employer can reach you. You need not identify your race, gender, religion, or age.
- *Career objectives*—A brief statement of your short- and long-term goals; in particular, the kind of job you are seeking.
- *Work experience*—Full-time jobs you have held, beginning with the most recent. Give a brief description of each job, emphasizing skills acquired and other qualifications.
- *Other experience*—Part-time or summer jobs that add to your qualifications. However, don't list part-time jobs that are irrelevant to the job you are now seeking.
- *Educational experience*—Give the name of the university you attended, the inclusive dates, and your major and minor subjects. Also give your overall grade point average and the average in your major if it is high.
- *Professional organizations and special honors*—List memberships in organizations in your field as well as prizes and professional honors you received. Don't mention prizes won in local contests and organizations that have no bearing on your qualifications.
- *Activities and interests*—List any special activities and interests that bear on your qualifications. You may also wish to list hobbies and service activities. List offices held in clubs if these have bearing.
- *References*—Note that references are available on request. You may wish to include the name and address of your college placement office that holds your dossier.

Summary

46a In all business correspondence, state your purpose concisely and directly, giving pertinent facts only.

Put important information early in the letter, avoid crowding several pieces of information into a single paragraph, and make your letter positive in tone (**46a 1**).

Use standard formats in writing business letters and letters of application (**46a 2**).

Use conventional salutations and complimentary closes (**46a 3**).

In writing a letter of application, stress positive qualifications without overstating them or concealing important information (46a 4).

Make your business letter specific and direct (46a 5).

Address a single issue or problem in a memorandum, and highlight important facts (46a 6).

46b Organize your resume chronologically or emphatically.

In your resume, give your personal history clearly and concisely, and omit nonessential details.

PART ELEVEN

PREPARING THE MANUSCRIPT

Mechanics of 47
the Paper

□

In this chapter, we turn to the **mechanics** of preparing the final draft of a paper for submission—the actual typing of the paper and the materials used, and the process of proofreading and making final corrections. Most disciplines have their own requirements for formatting the typewritten paper, just as they do for documenting sources (see Chapter 41). The format described in this chapter is based on the *MLA Handbook for Writers of Research Papers,* 3rd edition, for papers in the humanities. For papers in the social sciences and the natural and applied sciences, refer to the style manuals listed in sections 41c and 41b. Consult your instructor if you are in doubt about which format to follow.

47a General practices

1 Paper and writing materials

Type your final draft on white, twenty-pound bond paper of 8-½ × 11 inches in size. Sixteen-pound paper doesn't take erasures well, and "erasable" paper is undesirable because it smudges easily and can't be corrected in ink. Onion skin is suitable only for carbon copies. Type on one side of the page only, using a fresh, black ribbon. To prevent smudged letters, clean your typewriter keys occasionally.

If your instructor says that a handwritten paper is acceptable, use good-quality ruled paper without holes in the left-hand margin. However, don't use narrowly ruled paper, as this will make it difficult for both you and your instructor to read and correct. Also avoid using colored or "erasable" paper or sheets torn from a spiral notebook. Write as neatly as possible on only one side of a page and in blue or black ink.

If you write your paper on a word processor, use the same kind of paper as in typing. Although some dot-matrix printers approach typed pages in quality of printing, most produce indistinct typefaces that are difficult to read. Letter-quality and laser printers, however, produce better results and are acceptable for college and business papers.

2 Line spacing

Double-space all elements of a typed paper—the text, indented quotations of prose and poetry, the list of works cited or references, and so on. If you are writing the paper by hand, avoid using paper with narrow spacing. Don't add extra space between paragraphs in typed or handwritten papers.

Occasionally, a final word or phrase of a paragraph ends at the top of the page. To avoid these "orphans" or "widows," shorten the previous page by a line, carrying the final line of the paragraph to the top of the next page. Some word-processing programs have a provision for avoiding orphaned words.

3 Margins and titles

Leave one-inch margins at the left and right of the page as well as at the top and bottom. Although word processors permit you to "justify" the right-hand margin—that is, align it evenly—justification is usually undesirable because it makes the spacing between letters and words uneven. Don't justify the right margin unless your word processor allows proportional spacing. A ragged right margin is the common practice.

In the upper left-hand corner of the first page of your paper, list your name, your instructor's name, the title of the course, and the date. Double space this list and position it one inch from the top of the page. Center the title of your paper below this list, double spacing between them. Also double-space between the title and the first line of the text (see page 715). Don't put a period after the title and don't underline it or put it in quotation marks. Capitalize the first letter of all words in the title except articles, prepositions, and conjunctions, unless these are the first or last words:

```
Between the Woods and the Water
```

If your instructor requests a separate title page, center the title and your name (on separate lines) in the middle of the page. You may list the other information, double-spaced and centered lower on the page.

4 Indentation

Indent the beginning of each paragraph five spaces from the left-hand margin. Set off quotations of more than four typed lines in block form, indenting them ten spaces from the left margin as follows:

```
In her preface to John Keats: The Making of a
Poet, Aileen Ward states the purpose of her book:
          The profound and delighted and ultimately
          tragic insight into human life which Keats
          communicated so immediately and directly in
          his letters was something he learned only
          slowly to express in his poetry as he re-
          shaped his poetic medium to convey it.
          Slowly--that is, in three years of the most
          concentrated effort in our literature. My
          account of his life, therefore, is concerned
          primarily with the development of his char-
          acter as a poet--that audacious act of self-
          creation which he described in connection
          with the writing of Endymion. (ix-x)
```

Do not indent quotations of less than five typed lines; rather, incorporate them into your text and enclose them in quotation marks:

> In her <u>John Keats: The Making of a Poet</u>, Aileen
> Ward states that the three years in which Keats created
> his final style is "the most concentrated effort in our
> literature" (x).

If you quote several paragraphs, indent the block quotation ten spaces and the beginning of each new paragraph five spaces. (See 26b and 40c for additional guidelines on using quotations.)

5 Italics and quotation marks

To show italics in typed papers, underline the word, phrase, or sentence. Use italics to emphasize a word or phrase or to single out a word that you are discussing as a word (e.g., "The word *cheese* is derived from the Latin word *cāseus*.") Use quotation marks to enclose quoted words, phrases, and sentences of no more than four typed lines. (See 26b and 26d for additional guidelines on italics and quotation marks.)

6 Page numbering

In the upper right-hand corner of each page, including the first, type your last name and the page number in a single line. Position it a half-inch from the top of the page and align it with the right-hand margin as accurately as possible (see page 715).

7 Word spacing, word breaks, and special symbols

Space once after commas, colons, and semicolons; space twice after periods, question marks, and exclamation points.

Distinguish between the hyphen and the dash by typing two hypens (--) to create the dash (—). If your typewriter does not print brackets or other symbols, leave enough space between words to write them in by hand.

825

In typing, it is often necessary to break words that do not fit at the end of a typed line. In these instances, divide words at the syllable break. Use your dictionary to check the syllabication of a word when in doubt. Do not break one-syllable words. Also, do not break words such that one part of the divided word contains a single letter or only the last two letters of the word. The following word breaks are incorrect:

Incorrect	Correct
a- bout	gov- ernor
deal- t	hard- wood
happen- ed	indus- try
step-fath- er	spon- taneous

In addition, avoid breaking words that fall at the end of the first or last line of text on a typed page. Never begin a new line with a punctuation mark or a final bracket, final parenthesis mark, or other symbol. If your word-processing program has automatic hyphenation, check to be sure that the word breaks are correct.

8 Corrections

Mark a correction neatly above the typed line, using a caret if you are making an addition:

Dickens

I have a book by⌃ on the shelf.

Words and short phrases may be added above the typed lines. However, if more extensive additions are required or if the paper is excessively marked with corrections, you should retype pages of it as needed.

Other types of handwritten corrections are made as follows:

Transposition of letters

I have a book on the ⟋h⟍elf.

Transposition of words

I have a ⟋red⟍large⟍book on the shelf.

Spacing between letters

```
I have a large book on the shelf.
```

Closing letters

```
I have a lar ge book on the shelf.
```

Dropping a letter and closing a word

```
I have a large book on the shelf.
```

Erase and type over a misspelled or incorrect word, or use white correction fluid to cover and type in the correction. If the page contains numerous corrections, it is best to retype it.

47b Proofreading

Proofread your final draft with care. Look for mistakes in content and mechanics, including misstatements, misspellings, sentence fragments, run-on sentences, misused commas and semicolons, and missing or misused punctuation. Careful writers usually proofread a paper more than once, sometimes looking for grammatical errors the first time and for misspelled words and punctuation errors the second time. Spelling checks and grammar checks in word-processing programs are useful, but they are not a substitute for your own careful proofreading.

Probably no advice is so necessary yet often ignored, for the prospect of rewriting or retyping a page is not a pleasant one. Proofreading is nevertheless a job that you must do with care. Though all of us quickly spot errors and misprints in the writing of others, we often have trouble spotting our own. In proofreading, try to look at the words as words but at the same time don't lose track of the content. Often the best proofreading is done at least a day after writing the final draft.

Finally, always make a duplicate copy of your paper before submitting it to your instructor.

Writing with a Word Processor

48

The word processor is quickly replacing the typewriter as the preferred mechanical writing device. Perhaps the chief advantage of the word processor is the ease with which papers may be revised and edited, tasks that require considerable rewriting by hand and retyping on a conventional typewriter. The word processor saves time by allowing you to make corrections and move words, sentences, and paragraphs from one part of an essay to another without recopying. Some word processing programs allow you to save deleted sentences and paragraphs for possible restoration or use in a later draft. Special word-processing programs can even assist you in inventing ideas and organizing them. Special programs also ease the job of creating tables of contents, bibliographies, footnotes, endnotes, and indexes. In this chapter, we turn to some of the ways that a word processor can assist you at various stages of writing a paper.

48a Using a word processor at various stages of writing

1 Planning

Since a word processor operates with considerable versatility and speed, it is useful for the techniques of invention described in Chapter 2. Words and phrases can be typed on the screen as quickly as they come to mind and just as quickly moved or erased. Ease of operation makes the word processor particularly useful in freewriting. Outlining is also easy to do because of the ability of the word processor to move blocks of words. Special outlining programs can assist you in experimenting with different arrangements. These programs expand and format the outline at several levels as you think of ideas and add them.

2 Drafting and revising

A word processor allows you to write a first draft quickly, without losing an idea or a detail that may occur to you in the course of writing. In addition, drafts can be saved under different file names in case you want to refer to them in a later draft. Some word-processing programs provide a "window" that shows a list or part of another document in a corner of the screen. This feature is useful in comparing sentences and paragraphs from various drafts of the paper.

The ease with which words and sentences can be corrected or deleted on the screen makes the word processor especially useful in revising papers. Words, sentences, and paragraphs can also be moved to other places through function keys or commands. Other capabilities of the word processor that worked for you in drafting your paper can work just as well in revising it. You can again retrieve an earlier draft for comparison with your present one and take advantage of a window. In addition to revising on-screen, you can make prints of your drafts and revise them by hand, away from the computer. You should always do this with a final draft, for sentences and paragraphs often seem different on paper. Once you have made revisions on paper, and you are satisfied with them, you can transfer them to your word-processing file.

3 Editing and proofreading

The word processor also makes it easier to make final corrections in grammar, punctuation, and spelling. For example, you can use the search command to replace a misspelled word with the correct spelling in other parts of the paper.

Many word processor programs perform grammar and spelling checks, but these should only supplement your own careful check of grammar and spelling. There is no substitute for your own attentive revision, editing, and proofreading of your final draft. Machines have limitations; grammar and spelling checks work with only a limited number of words and patterns. The word processor cannot phrase ideas or arrange them in sentences and paragraphs that convey your train of thought. Word processors do not think.

48b Operating a word processor

1 Functions

Various other functions of word processors make writing less time consuming. Remember that these functions do not work in quite the same way in all programs, so be sure to familiarize yourself with your program manual. A list of useful functions that you are likely to encounter follows.

Format.   In typing a paper on a word processor, you must remember what **formats** you want to use. In some programs, margins, tabs, line lengths, page lengths, and indentations are stored in formats that you create while writing on screen. In the course of writing, for example, you can change from the format you are using for your paragraphs to a format that indents a block quotation. In addition, the word processor allows you to highlight ideas not only with standard underlining (or italics) but also with **boldface**. Your manual contains specific instructions on these essential functions.

Deletion.   As noted earlier, the ease with which you can **delete** letters, words, phrases, and whole lines with a word processor lets you focus your attention on what you want to say. You need not pause (as you must in typing) to erase or strike over a word or phrase. But give changes the same careful thought as you give in typing or writing by hand.

Block move. The **block move** capability eases the process of moving whole sentences and paragraphs to other parts of the paper, indispensable in drafting, revising, and editing. Most programs allow you to move columns as well—important in papers containing tables and columns of figures.

Copy block and column. In the course of writing, you may wish to see whether a sentence, paragraph, or column of figures would be more appropriate in another part of the paper. The **copy block** capability allows you to do so. Unlike block moves, the text or column that you have copied remains in its original place. After you decide which block is in the right place, you can use block delete to remove the extra copy.

Inserting a document. In revising and editing a paper, you may wish to **insert** a file or a portion of a file or perhaps an earlier draft into another. This capability is especially useful for building the bibliography for your paper.

Note file. In the course of writing, you may want to save sentences that do not fit the document in its present state but that you might reintroduce or append to the essay as a note. Many programs have a provision to store sentences or paragraphs you delete in a separate note file for use at a later time. This provision is especially useful in rephrasing and restating ideas.

Search command. The **search command** feature allows you to search for a particular word that appears several times in your paper and replace it with another. For example, if you wanted to replace the word *satirical* with the word *humorous* throughout your paper, the program would locate each occurrence of *satirical*, make the replacement, and reformat the text. In using this facility, you must be sure that you want the word replaced in all sentences. Make sure that you replace only whole words and not strips of characters within longer words.

Your word-processing manual contains information on other functions that you will find useful in drafting, revising, and editing your papers.

2 Do's and don'ts

The word processor is a valuable writing tool, but it cannot write for you. To use a word processor to best advantage, follow these guidelines:

Study your word-processing manual carefully, and use the on-screen tutorials that come with your word-processing program. It may take practice to give the correct command or use function keys to your best advantage.

Don't work with your original system and program disks. At the time you set up your word-processing program, you will make copies of the operating system disk and program disks. Store the original disks in the pockets provided in the manual and use your copies. It is essential to use copies of your working disks in case the originals are damaged.

Give each file a name that describes its contents. If your essay is stored in a series of files, use the same file name and add a numeral to distinguish them—for example, *AIDS1*, *AIDS2*, *AIDS3*. Your word-processing program will have special instructions on naming files.

Keep a log of file names. In a log of file names, write a brief description of the contents of each file. This log is indispensable in calling up files at a later time.

Save your drafts under different file names. You may wish to get advice on more than one draft of your paper, and you may later decide to use an earlier draft in part or as a whole. Record these special file names in your log.

Don't press buttons in a hurry. Take your time in editing the text, particularly when learning to use a program that assigns functions to special keys. If you are in too much of a hurry, you may press an "erase" or "delete" button instead of the button that reformats the paragraph or make a similar mistake. Keep in mind what jobs your function keys perform. If a reference card accompanies the program, keep it close at hand.

Save your document frequently in the course of creating and editing. A safe practice is to save each screen as you draft or revise a paper. Don't wait to save until you reach the end of a session at the computer; if a power failure occurs or you accidentally turn off the computer, you will lose your recent work.

Use your backup system.   A reliable backup system is essential in word processing. Your program gives you the option of saving the previous version of your document on the same floppy disk or on your hard disk. If you lose the file you are working on, you will able to return to the previous version and pick up the revision or editing at that point. Always keep formatted disks in reserve.

Use the program utilities.   Utilities in the word processing program make it possible to format blank disks, copy disks, erase a file, change a file name, create a file directory, and perform many other jobs. You will find a full description of these utilities in the manual that accompanies your system disk.

Check your margins, tabs, indentations, and spacing.   Before printing a document, you may wish to reformat a paragraph or page. Your program will be able to reformat the entire document format by format, without requiring you to change margins or tabs paragraph by paragraph. This time-saving operation is called *global reformatting*. Before you print a file, proofread the document and check your page layouts. Your printer manual will give you additional help in producing readable pages.

Don't start the page with an "orphan" or a "widow."   An "orphan" is the closing word of a sentence, a "widow" the closing few words of a paragraph that stand alone at the top of a page. Shorten the previous page by one line so that at least a full line of the paragraph on the previous page appears at the top of the next page.

Proofread the paper version of your work after you have printed it.   It is easy to miss mistakes on screen. If you use a spell-checking utility, check again for misspellings when you print your files. The program dictionary holds only a limited number of words and cannot check most proper names.

Some word-processing programs are designed for writers with considerable experience and facility; others are better suited to those with little or no previous experience with word processing. In selecting a program, be sure that it fits your needs and has such necessary capabilities as automatic formatting, automatic hyphenation, and a backup system that automatically saves the previous version of your file.

The word processor is a valuable tool, but it cannot write your paper for you; it is not a substitute for your imagination or powers of thought. It can, however, speed up and ease the process of capturing ideas and working with them on screen and on paper. There may be times, however, when you may prefer to work with pen and paper or with the typewriter. Or you may decide that you write best in these traditional ways.

GLOSSARY OF COMMON USAGE

□

This glossary lists words and phrases commonly misused by writers and describes their proper usage. These words and phrases are often misused because they are similar in pronunciation or spelling or because their usage is appropriate in one level of writing but inappropriate in another.

The following abbreviations are used to identify parts of speech: verb (v.), adjective (adj.), adverb (adv.), preposition (prep.), conjunction (conj.), noun (n.). The term *colloquial* is used to refer to conversational or spoken English; that is, everyday expressions that may be inappropriate in general and formal writing (see 29b). The label *nonstandard* refers to words and phrases not considered *standard English*. Finally, the word *jargon* describes clumsy or repetitive words and phrases that make sentences difficult to read (see 30d).

a, an *A* is used before words beginning with a consonant, *an* before words that are written or sounded with a vowel (*a horror film, an hour ago*).

accept, except *Accept* (v.) means "to receive" or "approve of something." *Except* (v.) means "to leave out" or "exclude something." *Except* (prep.) means "other than"; it is used most often as a preposition:

> I accepted his explanation.
> No one except Mary came.

adapt, adopt   *Adapt* (v.) means "to change something" or "to serve a new use":

> She adapted the play for children.

Adopt (v.) means "to make one's own" or "to take control":

> We adopted a stray dog.

advice, advise   *Advice* is the noun:

> She gave me advice.

Advise is the verb:

> I advised her to take the course.

affect, effect   The noun *affect* refers to an influence or controlling state. The noun *effect* refers to a resulting state:

> The experiment measures the affect of nervous impulses.
> She is testing the effect of barbiturates on sleep.

The verb *affect* means "to influence":

> Hot weather affects his mood.

The verb *effect* is the formal (and often stilted) way of saying "to cause" or "to bring about."

> The new tax law is intended to effect a change in attitude.

aggravate, irritate   To *aggravate* (v.) is to make worse something already unpleasant:

> The shooting aggravated the tension.

In formal writing, avoid using *aggravate* to mean "irritate" or "annoy" (as in *The sarcastic remark aggravated me*).

agree to, agree with   *Agree to* (v.) means "to consent":

> I agree to meet with her.

Agree with (v.) means "to be in harmony with":

> I agree with your thinking on the matter.

ain't   The word *ain't* is nonstandard in written English for *am not, is not, has not, have not.*

all ready, already   *All ready* (pron. and adj.) means "fully prepared":

> I am all ready to go.

Already (adv.) means "previously" or "by now":

> The plane has already landed.
> He should have already departed.

all right   The usual spelling for the adjective meaning "pleasing," "safe," or "acceptable."

all together, altogether   *All together* (pron. and adj.) means "to be as one":

> The family is all together.

Altogether (adv.) means "entirely":

> I am altogether in agreement.

allusion, illusion   An *allusion* (n.) is an indirect reference:

> She made an allusion to the accident in asking if anyone was hurt.

An *illusion* (n.) is a deceptive appearance:

> He gives the illusion of being smart.

See also *refer, allude*.

almost, most   *Almost* (adv.) means "nearly":

> He almost succeeded.

Most (n.) means "the greater part":

> Most who enroll do succeed.

Most is used in informal speech to mean "almost":

> **Colloquial**   I see her most every night.

Use *almost* in general and formal English:

> I see her almost every night.

among, between   In formal English, *among* (prep.) refers to more than two:

> What is a little disagreement among friends?

Between (prep.) refers to two people or things, including one thing and a group:

G-3

There is no disagreement between John and his friends.

amount, number *Amount* (n.) is used with noncountable things:

The amount of sand in the box . . .

Number (n.) is used with countable things:

The number of plants in the garden . . .

and/or *And/or* (conj.) is inappropriate except in business writing. Write out the *and* and the *or*:

John and Mary are coming, or perhaps only John.

and which, but which *And which* and *but which* are nonstandard usage. *And* and *but* should not be used with a relative clause:

Nonstandard She ate the broccoli, but which she dislikes.
Standard She ate the broccoli, which she dislikes.

anxious, eager *Anxious* (adj.) means "to be fearful" or "to be worried." The word is a weak substitute for *eager* (adj.):

Ambiguous He is anxious to talk to you.
Clear He is eager to talk to you.

any one, anyone *Any one* is used to single out one person or thing out of several:

Choose any one book but don't take them all.

Anyone (pron.) refers to an unspecified person or thing:

Anyone can run a computer who makes the effort.

anyways, anywheres Use *anyway, anywhere.*

apt, liable, likely *Apt* (adj.) means "tends":

He is apt to complain if he gets the chance.

Liable (adj.) means "legally obligated" or "at risk":

She is liable to the rental agency for the damage to the car.
He is liable to get pneumonia if his cold persists.

Apt is used informally to mean "liable," with the added meaning of "likely":

Your car is apt to be towed if you park it there.

G-4

Likely, sometimes used as a synonym of *liable,* better expresses the idea of probability:

Ambiguous	She is liable to get a promotion if she stays with the company.
Clear	She is likely to receive a promotion if she stays with the company.

as The word *as* is a confusing substitute for *because* or *while*:

Confusing	As we are leaving, we need to lock the door.
Improved	Because we are leaving, we need to lock the door.

As is also a nonstandard substitute for *who* or *whether*:

Nonstandard	She is the woman as told me the address.
Standard	She is the woman who told me the address.

For standard usage, see *as, like.*

as, like Both words function as prepositions—*as* expresses exact resemblance, *like* expresses similarity:

He served as a marine.
He looks like a marine.

As (conj.) introduces full clauses:

As the guide said, the water was too polluted to drink.

Like is acceptable in sentences such as the following one:

He looks like his father [he looks like his father looks].

as, than In comparisons, pronouns that follow the conjunctions *as* and *than* take the subject or object case form depending on whether they are the subject or object of the governing verb:

She is as young as I [am young].
She is older than I [am older].

She praises him as much as [she praises] me.
She praises him more than [she praises] me.

as to *As to* is a weak substitute for *about* or *concerning*:

Awkward	I asked as to his grades.
Improved	I asked about his grades.

awhile, a while *Awhile* means "for a certain time" and is used adverbially:

G-5

Sit awhile!

A while singles out the time:

She won't be back for a while.

bad, badly   Verbs of sense (*feel, smell, taste*) like *to be* verbs take adjectives as complements:

I feel so bad.

In general English, *badly* means "imperfectly" or "in a bad way":

He drives badly.

being that   *Being that* is colloquial for *because*:

Colloquial   We'll stay home being that you're sick.
General and formal   We'll stay home because you're sick.

beside, besides   *Beside* (prep.) means "next to":

The chair is beside the bed.

Besides (prep.) means "in addition":

Who's coming besides you?

between, among   See *among, between*.

bring, take   You *bring* something toward a person or place, and you *take* something away:

I'll bring a cake to the party.
Please take the cake out of the oven.

but that   The phrase *but that* is considered jargon; it adds nothing to a sentence:

Wordy   I don't question but that you're right.
Improved   I don't question that you're right.

See also *can't help but*.

can, may   *May* (v.) is standard in asking permission:

May I leave when the speaker finishes?

Can (v.) expresses the ability to perform an act:

Can I get to the airport by bus?

can't help but   The word *but* is redundant in this phrase. Compare the following:

Wordy I can't help but cry that he left.
Improved I can't help crying that he left.

censor, censure *Censor* (v.) means "to cut out" or "forbid publication of material considered objectionable":

The government censored most of the document before releasing it.

Censure (v.) means "to condemn" or "reprimand officially":

The Senate voted to censure the conduct of one of its members.

center around Avoid the redundant *center around*. The standard expression is *center on*:

The course centers on foreign policy in the 1980s.

complement, compliment To *complement* (v.) is "to complete" or "to form part of" or "to add":

The crew complemented the ship.

To *compliment* (v.) is "to praise":

The captain complimented the crew.

conscience, conscious *Conscience* (n.) refers to the power of distinguishing right from wrong. *Conscious* (adj.) describes the state of awareness or wakefulness:

He is conscious of his mistake.
His conscience told him not to cash the check.

contact Substitute "talk to" or "write" for the colloquial *contact* (v.):

Colloquial He contacted the police about the accident.
General He talked to the police about the accident.

continual, continuous *Continual* (adj.) means "intermittent" or "recurrent":

There were continual interruptions from the spectators.

Continuous (adj.) means "ongoing, without interruption":

There was continuous noise in the room.

could of, should of, would of Often confused with the standard verbs *could have, should have, would have, could've, should've would've*:

Nonstandard You should of come to the review session.
Standard You should have come to the review session.

data *Data* (n.) is commonly used for the singular and plural. In formal writing, use *data* in the plural.

different from, different than Use *different from* with a noun phrase in formal writing to note a difference:

New York is different from Los Angeles.

Different than is a colloquial substitute:

New York is different than Los Angeles.

differ from, differ with *Differ from* is to be unlike or dissimilar (*As a city Boston differs from New York*). *Differ with* is to be in disagreement (*I differ with that opinion of New York*).

disinterested, uninterested A *disinterested* observer of an event is impartial or has no desire to gain from the outcome:

He showed he was disinterested when he refused to take sides in the debate.

An *uninterested* observer is indifferent or unconcerned:

He showed he was uninterested when he left the hall and did not return.

don't *Don't* is the contraction of *do not*, not *does not* (doesn't).

due to Idiomatic after the verb *is*:

The rise in prices is due to the drought.

The phrase *due to* is awkward when used with other verbs:

Awkward The rise in prices happened due to the drought.
Improved The drought caused prices to rise.

effect, affect See *affect, effect*.

either, each *Either* (adj.) usually means one or the other. *Each* (adj.) means one of several:

Inexact Hydrants are on either side of the street.
Improved Hydrants are on each side of the street.

enthused Colloquial for "be enthusiastic," preferred by many in formal writing:

She was enthusiastic about going.

equally as good A redundant expression:

Redundant The two proposals are equally as good.
Improved The two proposals are equally good.

etc. *Etc.* means "and the rest" and "so forth." *And etc.* is redundant. In formal writing, use *and so on* or *and so forth* instead.

ever The word *ever* is redundant in the following sentence:

Redundant There is never a breeze ever.
Improved There is never a breeze.

except, accept See *accept, except.*

explicit, implicit *Explicit* (adj.) means "outright" or "direct":

His instructions were explicit.

Implicit (adj.) means "suggested" or "indirect":

His warning was implicit.

farther, further *Farther* (adv.) is used to refer to distance:

How much farther is Chicago from St. Louis?

Further (adv.) also refers to distance. *Further* (adj.) is used to mean "additional" in referring to things other than distance, such as knowledge and time:

She gave us further knowledge about the city.
We need further time to finish the job.

feasible, probable *Feasible* (adj.) means "can be done," *not* "probable":

Inexact It is feasible he will come.
Exact Spanning the river is feasible.

fewer, less *Fewer* (adj.) is used with count nouns:

fewer pages, fewer pencils, fewer glasses, fewer calories

Less (adj.) is used with noncount or mass nouns:

less water, less grass

finalize Jargon for "came to," "reached," and "completed":

Jargon We finalized the report in time for the meeting.
Improved We completed the report in time for the meeting.

first, firstly   *First* (*second, third,* and so on) is the preferred form.

first, last   See *former, latter.*

formally, formerly   *Formally* (adv.) refers to structure or conventional behavior. *Formerly* (adv.) refers to action in the past:

> Your letter is formally correct but still unclear.
> She was formerly vice president of the company.

former, latter   *Former* (adj.) refers to the first of two things mentioned; *latter* (adj.) refers to the second:

> I do well in chemistry and biology, but I like the former and dislike the latter.

With a series of three or more, use *first* and *last*:

> I do well in chemistry, physics, biology, but I like the first and dislike the last.

gets to   The colloquial expression *gets to* is used to mean "become." Use the latter word in written English:

Informal	Driving to work soon gets to be a nuisance.
General and formal	Driving to work soon becomes a nuisance.

good, well   *Good* is the adjective; *well* is the adverb:

Incorrect	The cake tastes well.
Correct	The cake tastes good.

The statement *I feel well* means "to feel in good health." The statement *I feel good* means "to be in good spirits."

good and   Colloquial for *very*. Use *very* in written English.

hang, hung   Objects are *hung,* people are *hanged.* The phrase *hung jury* means "deadlocked."

hardly   *Hardly* (adv.) is redundant when used with other negative words:

Nonstandard	She has not hardly spoken a word.
Standard	She has hardly spoken a word.

hisself   Nonstandard for *himself.*

hopefully   *Hopefully* means "with hope":

We watched the approaching ship hopefully.

Hopefully is a colloquial substitute for *We hoped*. *Hopefully* makes the following sentence awkward because it seems to modify *war*:

Awkward   The war hopefully will end.
Exact   We hope the war will end.

if, whether   *If* (conj.) is colloquial for *whether* (or *whether not*) in considering alternatives:

I asked if he wanted to go hiking or stay home.

Use *whether* in formal English:

I asked whether he wanted to go hiking or stay home.

illusion   See *allusion, illusion*.

imply, infer   *Imply* (v.) means "to hint" or "to suggest something":

She implied by her sarcasm that he was acting foolish.

Infer (v.) means "to draw a conclusion from a statement":

I inferred from her sarcasm that she thought the same of me.

in, into   *In* (prep.) refers to a general location:

The office is in the building.

Into (prep.) specifies the act of motion:

She met him going into the building.

individual, person   Although widely used instead of *person*, (n.) the word *individual* (n.) can be ambiguous:

He is not the individual I thought he was.

This sentence can mean either of the following:

I mistook him for someone else.
He is a conformist.

The word *person* is preferable unless you want to single out a person from a group:

She stands out as an individual.

infer   See *imply, infer*.

inside of, outside of   See *outside of, inside of*.

G-11

irregardless   A redundant word. Use *regardless* instead.

irritate   See *aggravate, irritate.*

is when, is where, is because   These expressions introduce awkward and inexact predicates:

Nonstandard	The picnic is when you eat outdoors.
Standard	You eat outdoors on picnics.
Nonstandard	A concerto is where one or more solo instruments play with an orchestra.
Standard	A concerto is a musical composition for one or more solo instruments and orchestra.
Nonstandard	The quarantine is because of citrus canker.
Standard	The orchard has been quarantined because of citrus canker.

See also *faulty predication* (section 19c) and *mixed constructions* (19a).

item   *Item* (n.) refers to each single article in a list:

We identified each item on the list.

The word also has the colloquial meaning of "thing" or "matter":

Informal	The committee has another item to consider.
Formal	The committee has another proposal to consider.

its, it's   *Its* is the possessive form of *it:*

the tail of the dog, its tail

It's is the contraction of *it is:*

It's snowing.

kind of, sort of   These expressions are used with *this* and *that* in the singular and with *these* and *those* in the plural:

this kind of food, that sort of fish
these kinds of vegetables, those sorts of cars

lay, lie   *Lay* means "to put" or "to place something." In the active voice, this transitive verb always takes an object that receives the action. In the passive voice, this receiver becomes the subject:

Active Voice	**Passive Voice**
I lay the book on the table.	The book is laid on the table.
I laid the book on the table.	The book was laid on the table.
I have laid the book on the table in the past.	The book had been laid on the table.

Lie means "to be situated" or "reclined" and does not take an object:

Akron lies south of Cleveland.
I lie down to sleep. [*present tense*]
I lay down to nap. [*past tense*]
I have lain awake since these headaches began.

leave, let   *Leave* (v.) means "to go away," *let* (v.) means "to permit":

Leave the room!
Let him explain!

liable   See *apt, liable, likely.*

like   See *as, like.*

literally   In general and formal English, *literally* (adv.) means "exactly" or "actually":

We interpreted her words literally.

The colloquial use of *literally* to mean "truly" is inappropriate in formal writing:

Colloquial	She was literally dumbfounded.
General and formal	She was truly dumbfounded.

loose, lose   These words are easily confused. *Loose* (adj.) means "free" or "unconfined":

The dog is running loose.
The bolt is loose.

Loose (v.) expresses the same meanings:

He loosed the dog in the field.

Lose (v.) means "to mislay" or "to give up control":

I lose my way every time I drive to Lansing.

may   See *can, may.*

maybe, may be   *Maybe* (adv.) means "perhaps." *May be* is the verb phrase:

> Maybe I will go to the beach today.
> I may be going to the beach today.

media   *Media* is a plural word that takes a plural verb (*The media are present*), even when it is used as a collective noun.

most   See *almost, most.*

myself, himself, herself, yourself   These reflexive pronouns are used to call attention to the subject as actor:

> She fixed the wiring herself.

They substitute colloquially for *me, him, her, your*:

> No one can repair it but myself.

Using the pronoun *me* (or equivalent pronouns—see 8b) instead of *myself* prevents the sentence from sounding awkward:

> No one can repair it but me.

Avoid using reflexive pronouns with prepositions:

> **Nonstandard**   She is going with himself to the concert.
> **Standard**   She is going with him to the concert.

never   The colloquial use of *never* (adv.) can be ambiguous:

> **Ambiguous**   He never knew it could be so warm in January.
> **Improved**   He did not know it could be so warm in January.

See also *ever.*

nohow, nowheres   Nonstandard forms of *in no way* and *nowhere.*

not unlikely   *Likely* is sufficient:

> It is likely he will come.

number   See *amount, number.*

of, have   The words *of* and *have* are sometimes confused in writing because they sound alike. Do not use *of* after verbs that take *have*:

> **Nonstandard**   I should of asked permission to leave work early.
> **Standard**   I should have asked permission to leave work early.

of which, whose   *Whose* indicates possession and usually refers to people and animate things. It also substitutes for *of which*:

>**Standard**   That's the book whose cover I tore.
>**Improved**   I tore the cover of that book.

See also *who's, whose.*

off, of   The words *off* (adv.) and *of* (prep.) are easily confused. Compare the following:

>I tore the cover off.
>I tore the cover of the book.

off of   *Of* is redundant in this phrase:

>**Redundant**   He tore the address label off of the cover.
>**Improved**   He tore the address label off the cover.

on account of   Jargon that makes a sentence wordy:

>**Wordy**   I am going on account of what happened.
>**Improved**   I am going because of what happened.

onto, on to   *Onto* (prep.) means "to a place on." *On to* joins an adverb (attached to a verb like *turned*) to a preposition (introducing a phrase like *to the highway*):

>The sculptor put the statue onto the pedestal.
>The car turned on to the highway from the side street.

outside of, inside of   *Of* is redundant in these colloquial expressions:

>**Colloquial**   The car is parked outside of the house.
>**General and formal**   The car is parked outside the house.

owing to the fact that   A wordy and awkward expression; substitute the word *because.*

party, person   *Party* (n.) is a pretentious substitute for *person*:

>**Pretentious**   She is the party I described to you.
>**Improved**   She is the person I described to you.

person   See *individual, person.*

phenomena, phenomenon (n.)   Use the singular *phenomenon* to describe a single occurrence; *phenomena* is the plural form:

>**Nonstandard**   Political apathy is a phenomena today.
>**Standard**   Political apathy is a phenomenon today.

plenty   *Plenty* (n.) is used in standard English with the sense of "quite enough" or "more than enough":

> We have plenty of food.

It is used adverbially instead of *very* or *quite*:

> We are plenty tired.

pretty   Colloquial for *rather, somewhat,* and *very*:

> **Informal**   She is pretty tired.
> **General and formal**   She is rather tired.
>
> **Informal**   She is pretty angry.
> **General and formal**   She is furious.

previous to   Jargon that makes a sentence wordy:

> **Wordy**   He went to the park previous to her.
> **Improved**   He went to the park before she did.

principal, principle   *Principal* (adj.) means "main" or "leading":

> The drought is the principal cause of the rise in prices.

The noun form has the same meaning:

> She is a school principal.

Principle (n.) means "rule" or "maxim":

> The first principle of good driving is common sense.

Principle is not used as an adjective:

> **Incorrect**   Drought is a principle cause of famine.
> **Correct**   Drought is a principal cause of famine.

proceed   This word is often mistaken as a synonym of *went*. *Proceed* (v.) means "to advance" or "to continue after a momentary stop":

> **Pretentious**   He proceeded to the park.
> **Improved**   He went to the park.

raise, rise   *Raise* (v.) means "to lift something"; in the active voice, it takes a direct object that receives the action:

> I raised the window.

Rise (v.) means "to go up" or "to get up" and does not take an object:

> I rise at six o'clock every morning.

real, really *Real* is colloquial for *really* (as in *a real fine movie*). *Really* is the preferred form in general and formal writing:

> This is a really fine book.

reason is because A colloquial expression that makes a sentence wordy and awkward:

Awkward	The reason for inflation is because interest rates dropped.
Improved	The reason for the inflation is that interest rates dropped.
	The drop in interest rates caused inflation.

refer, allude *Refer* (v.) means "to call attention to something directly":

> The writer refers to Lincoln's statement on "government of the people, by the people, and for the people."

Allude (v.) means "to call attention indirectly":

> The writer alludes to Lincoln's famous statement on government.

regarding Jargon like *regarding, in regard to,* and *in respect to* have simple equivalents:

Wordy	Regarding your request for an extension of time, you can have it.
Improved	You can have the extension of time you requested.
Wordy	I am writing in respect to the matter stated in your letter.
Improved	I am writing in answer to your letter.

rise See *raise, rise*.

set, sit In the active voice, *set* (v.) takes an object that receives the action:

> I set the book on the table.

In the passive voice, the receiver becomes the subject:

Nonstandard	The book was sat on the table.
Standard	The book was set on the table.

Sit does not take an object in the active voice:

Nonstandard	I set on the chair.
Standard	I sit down. I am sitting on the chair.

shall, will *Will* (v.) is now standard in all three persons; *shall* is reserved for particularly emphatic statements:

We will solve the problem if we work together.
We shall conquer!

Shall is also required in questions asking for consent or agreement:

Shall we begin?

similar as   The standard phrase is *similar to*:

Nonstandard   She is similar in belief as her sister.
Standard   She is similar in belief to her sister.

supposed to   The standard form is *supposed to*, not *suppose to*.

sure, surely   *Sure* is the colloquial form:

Colloquial   That is sure not what he said.
General and formal   That is surely not what he said.

sure and, sure of   These colloquial expressions are inappropriate in formal writing:

Colloquial   Be sure and finish by noon.
General and formal   Be sure to finish by noon.

Sure of can make a statement ambiguous:

Ambiguous   She is sure of coming.
Clear and informal   We are sure that she is coming.
Formal   We are certain she will come.

than, as   See *as, than.*

than, then   *Than,* the conjunction used in comparisons, should not be confused with *then,* the adverb used to indicate progression:

Incorrect   This summer is hotter then last summer.
Correct   This summer is hotter than last summer.

Incorrect   I went to the bank and than to the library.
Correct   I went to the bank and then to the library.

than what   Wordy for *than.* Compare the following:

Wordy   It is simpler than what you think.
Improved   It is simpler than you think.

that, which   See *which, that.*

their, there, they're   *Their* is the possessive form of *they*:

They sold their books.

There is an adverb indicating place or an expletive without meaning that completes a sentence:

Adverb   Put the book there.
Expletive   There are three books on the table.

They're is the contracted form of *they are.*

theirselves   Nonstandard for *themselves.*

this here   *This here* is an intensifier in certain dialects (as in *This here car*). It is nonstandard in formal English.

thusly   Nonstandard for *thus.*

through, throughout   *Through* means "by way of." *Throughout* means "in every part of":

Confusing   He discusses the causes of the war through the book.
Clear   He discusses the causes of the war throughout the book.

to, too   *To* is the preposition:

I am going to the store.

Too is the adverb meaning "also":

Are you coming, too?

type of   The phrase *type of* can make a sentence wordy:

Wordy   Science fiction is the type of fiction I like.
Improved   I like science fiction.

Use *type of* in distinguishing kinds:

Science fiction is an important type of fiction.

used to   The correct form is *used to,* not *use to.*

very   Use *very* (adv.) sparingly as an intensifier. Try to use a stronger adjective:

Weak   He is very tired.
Improved   He is exhausted.

want to   Colloquial for *should*:

Informal   You want to read this editorial.
General   You should read this editorial.

G-19

well   See *good, well.*

where, that   The colloquial use of *where* instead of *that* is inappropriate in writing:

> **Nonstandard**   I read where Alice won the race.
> **Standard**   I read that Alice won the race.

where at   *At* is redundant in this expression:

> **Redundant**   Do you know where Des Moines is at?
> **Improved**   Do you know where Des Moines is?

which, that   *Which* and *that* are relative pronouns used to refer to things and less commonly to people, usually groups of people. *Which* is used to introduce a nonrestrictive clause that adds information to a sentence and is set off with commas. *That* is used to introduce a restrictive clause that is not set off with commas:

> The battleship that arrived yesterday will remain in port a week.
> The *Iowa,* which docked yesterday, will be in port a week.

The *which* clause gives additional information about the ship; the *that* clause identifies the ship. (See 11c.)

who, whom   In formal usage, the pronoun *who* (and *whoever*) is used in subject positions, *whom* (and *whomever*) in object positions:

> He is the person who called.
> Give the book to whoever calls.
> He is the person whom you called.
> Give the book to whomever you want.

In informal and often general English, *who* usually replaces *whom* when the object function is not obvious:

> Who did you give the book to?

At all levels of speech and writing, *whom* is required immediately after a preposition except when *who* or *whoever* is the subject in a clause:

> To whom am I speaking?
> Give the book to whoever answers the door.

See section 11c.

who's, whose   *Who's* is a contraction of *who is* (as in *Who's coming?*). *Whose* is the possessive form of *who* (as in *Whose house is that?*).

G-20

GLOSSARY OF GRAMMATICAL □

□

The following glossary will help you to understand terms used in analyzing sentences throughout the text. Cross-references are provided to discussion of these terms.

absolute phrase A phrase modifying the whole sentence and consisting of a noun and modifier, usually a present or past participle:

> The water being polluted, the officials sealed the well.

Also called a *noun absolute.* (See sections 7b, 8a 4, 16b 5.)

active voice See *voice.*

adjectival A word, phrase, or clause that serves as an adjective. (See 7c 4.)

adjective A word that describes or modifies a noun, pronoun, or other nominal. (See 8c.)

adjective clause See *dependent clause.*

adjective complement An adjective that describes the subject of the clause (following a linking verb) or the object ("We found the explanation *convincing*"). See also *linking verb; complement.* (See 8c.)

adverb   A word or phrase that modifies or describes a verb (ran *quickly*), an adjective (*intensely* hot), another adverb (*very* quickly), or a whole clause (*Fortunately*, the storm caused little damage.) (See 9d.)

adverb clause   See *dependent clause.*

adverbial   A word, phrase, or clause that serves as an adverb. (See 7c 5.)

antecedent   An earlier word or phrase referred to by a pronoun in the sentence:

> She described the *accident* and how *it* happened.

antithesis   The balancing of contrasting phrases or clauses in a sentence (see 14c):

> We observe today not a victory of party but a celebration of freedom—symbolizing an end as well as a beginning—signifying renewal as well as change.
>
>   —President John F. Kennedy

See also *balance.*

appositive   A word or phrase that names or defines the word or phrase that usually precedes it:

> The man in the yard, *an official of the Health Department,* declared the water safe for drinking.

(See 8a 4.)

article   One class of words *a, an,* and *the* that describe nouns. See also *determiner.* (See 8a 3.)

aspect   The use of verb auxiliaries to show that the action is ongoing or show when it began or ended. *Progressive verbs* (*I am laughing, I was laughing*) express the event as ongoing in the present or in the past. *Perfect verbs* show the event or action as beginning in the past and continuing into the present (present perfect: *I have laughed*), or beginning and ending in the past (past perfect: *I had laughed*). The traditional future perfect (*I will have laughed*) shows the action beginning and ending in the future. See also *Auxiliary; future tense; tense.* (See 9b 3.)

auxiliary Auxiliary verbs (*have, be, do*) combine with the present or past participle to form verb phrases (*is writing, has written*). The modal auxiliaries (*shall, should, will, would, can, could, may, might, must, ought,* and so on) combine with the simple base or infinitive verb (*to write*) to express intent, will, possibility, obligation, need, and other ideas (*must write*). See also *infinitive; verb.* (See 9b 1–2.)

balance The use of strict parallelism in phrases and clauses throughout a sentence (see 14c):

> Over and over again they [the Greeks] emphasize the brevity and the failure of all human endeavor, the swift passing of all that is beautiful and joyful.
> —Edith Hamilton

See also *antithesis.*

case The form of a noun or pronoun that shows its grammatical function in the sentence. English has three cases— *nominative* or *subjective, possessive,* and *objective.* Nouns have the same form in the nominative and objective cases. Nouns form the possessive by adding -*'s* or an apostrophe only. Pronouns have different forms in all three cases. (See 8a 1 and 8b 1.)

clause Words that form a subject and a predicate. A clause may stand alone as a sentence or help to form a sentence or modify a sentence element. See also *independent clause; dependent clause.* (See 7c.)

collective noun See *noun.*

comma splice The misuse of the comma to join independent clauses without a coordinating conjunction:

> I grow tomatoes, I never eat them because they upset me.

(See 17a.)

common noun See *noun.*

complement A word or phrase that forms the predicate. A *subjective complement* ("That book is a *dictionary,*" "Lemons taste *sour*") is the equivalent of or the modifier of the subject following a *to be* verb, a verb of sense, or a form of *become, seem, appear,* and *remain.* An *objective complement* ("I consider the book *a masterpiece,*" "I consider the proposal *brilliant*") completes the direct object (if a nominal) or describes it (if an adjectival). (See 7b and 7c.)

complex sentence A sentence containing an independent clause and one or more dependent clauses (see 7d):

> I grow tomatoes although I never eat them.
> Although I never eat them, I grow tomatoes [that are] sometimes as big as oranges.

compound sentence Two or more independent clauses and their word or phrasal modifiers, joined by coordinating conjunctions:

> The book with the torn cover is an English dictionary, and the book with the red cover is a French dictionary.

(See 7d.)

compound-complex sentence Two or more independent clauses joined by one or more dependent clauses:

> I grow tomatoes although I never eat them, but I eat all the lettuce and radishes that I also grow.

(See 7d.)

conjunction A broad class of words that connect other words, phrases (*bread and butter*), or clauses of equal rank. *Coordinating conjunctions* (*and, but, yet, for, so, or, nor*) connect clauses often of the same weight (*I grow tomatoes but I can't eat them*). *Subordinating conjunctions* (*since, when, although, while,* and the like) join dependent or subordinate clauses to independent or main ones (*Although I grow tomatoes, I don't pick them myself*). *Correlative conjunctions* (*both ... and, either ... or, neither ... nor, not only ... but also, on the one hand ... on the other hand*) join complementary ideas. (See 9e 2, 10a 10.)

conjunctive adverb An adverbial modifier that follows the semicolon in joined independent clauses:

> I grow tomatoes; *however,* I never eat them.

(See 9d, 23a 2.)

coordinating conjunction See *conjunction.*

correlative conjunction See *conjunction.*

count noun See *noun.*

cumulative sentence   A sentence that begins with the core idea and adds explanatory or amplifying details or afterthoughts:

> The storm broke suddenly, sending people scurrying for cover.

Sometimes called a *loose sentence.* (See 13a 1.)

dangling modifier   An unclear modifier that has no explicit word in the sentence to modify:

> **Ambiguous**   Driving down the highway, a bear was seen.
> **Clear**   Driving down the highway, we saw a bear.

(See 20e.)

dependent clause   A clause that serves as a sentence constituent or as a modifier and therefore cannot stand alone as a sentence. Dependent clauses serve as nominals (*noun clause*), adjectivals (*adjective clause*), and adverbials (*adverb clause*). (See 7b.)

determiner   A word that gives information about the noun in a sentence. Determiners include articles, demonstrative pronouns, possessive pronouns, and other nominals. See also *article; nominal; pronoun.* (See 8a 3.)

direct object   A sentence constituent that completes a transitive verb by naming the action performed:

> The coach gave *instructions.*

(See 7b.)

elliptical sentence   A sentence shortened to a phrase. Also a sentence with understood omissions:

> She is a better driver than I [am a driver].
> [She is] a woman before her time.

(See 15a.)

expletive   "Empty" or "dummy" words that open a sentence when the subject is delayed to a later position for emphasis. (See 9e 3.)

fragment   A detached phrase, clause, or appositive that is an incomplete statement:

> who was driving down the highway
> without a reason for failing

(See 16b.)

G-25

function word A word that substitutes for inflections in expressing grammatical meaning (e.g., *of* substitutes for *-'s* in possessives: *the man's hat, the hat of the man*).

fused sentence A sentence in which independent clauses run together without punctuation:

> Don't forget to fill the tank you don't have enough gas to reach Cleveland.

(See 17b.)

future tense English has no future tense. Unlike the present and past tenses, which use inflections (*-s, -ed*) to form certain words, futurity in English is expressed through auxiliaries (*shall, will*) attached to the base infinitive (*will go*) or to a second auxiliary and participle (*will be going, will have gone*). It is traditional to speak of these forms as the future tense. See also *tense*. (See 9a 2.)

gerund A verb form ending in *-ing* (*running, laughing*) that serves as subject, object, or complement. (See 9c.)

imperative mood See *mood*.

indefinite pronoun See *pronoun*.

independent clause An independent clause can stand alone as a complete sentence:

> The men from the Health Department tested the water.

(See 7c 2.)

indicative mood See *mood*.

indirect object In a sentence containing a transitive verb, the indirect object is the first of two objects receiving the action:

> The coach gave *the team* instructions.

(See 7b.)

infinitive The base form of the verb (*walk, play*) without indication of tense, number, or person. In its base form, the infinitive combines with auxiliaries to form verb phrases. In its verbal form (*to walk, to play*), the infinitive can serve as a noun ("I want to walk, not *ride*"), an adjective ("I have reason *to walk*"), or an adverb ("I am going downtown *to shop*"). See also *verb*. (See 9a, 9b 1, and 9d.)

inflection Change in the form of a word to show its grammatical meaning (*man, men, man's, men's; laughs, laughed*). See also *verb*.

interjection A word or phrase that expresses strong emotion (*Oh!; How absurd!*). (See 9f.)

interrogative pronoun See *pronoun*.

intransitive verb See *transitive verb*.

linking verb Any form of the *to be* verb, verbs of sense (sight, smell, taste, sound, touch), and the verbs *become, seem, appear, remain*, and others. Linking verbs take subjective complements or adjective complements that show equality or equivalence:

> I am a healthy person. [*subject complement*]
> I am healthy. [*adjective complement*]
> I feel better. [*adjective complement.*]
> The food tastes good. [*adjective complement*]

See also *verb*. (See 9b 1.)

loose sentence See *cumulative sentence*.

main clause See *independent clause*.

mass noun See *noun*.

mid-branching sentence A sentence that begins with the main clause and interrupts it with explanatory details:

> For anxiety, *as we have come to use it to describe our characteristic state of mind,* can be contrasted with the active fear of hunger, loss, violence, and death.
> —Margaret Mead (emphasis added)

(See 13a 3.)

modal auxiliary See *auxiliary*.

mood The feature of the verb that expresses the intent of the speaker. Verbs in the *indicative mood* state facts (*I am going*); verbs in the *subjunctive mood* express a wish or possibility (*If I were going*); verbs in the *imperative mood* give commands (*Go!*). (See 9a 4.)

nominal A word, phrase, or clause that serves as a noun in a sentence. (See 7c 3.)

nonrestrictive modifier A phrase or clause set off by commas that adds nonessential information to a sentence and that may be omitted without a significant change in meaning:

> The Health Department officials, *who did extensive tests of our water,* declared the water unsafe for drinking. [*adjectival clause*]
> *Speaking to the audience from the stage,* the official declared the water unsafe for drinking. [*adjectival phrase*]
> *When she rose to speak,* the second official explained why the water was unsafe. [*adverbial clause*]

See also *restrictive modifier.* (See 7c 2 and 22a.)

noun A word that names or points to a person, place, event, or object. Nouns change in form to show number and possession (*girl, girls, girl's, girls'*). *Common nouns* point to classes of people or objects (*girls, mountains*). *Proper nouns* point to specific people or objects (*Elizabeth, Mount Hood*). *Collective nouns* are singular in form and refer to a group (*class, crowd, regiment*). *Count nouns* refer to things that can be counted and have singular and plural forms (*girl, girls*). *Mass nouns* refer to things that cannot be counted and therefore have no plural forms (*health, grease, tennis*). (See 8a.)

noun absolute See *absolute phrase.*

noun clause See *dependent clause.*

noun phrase A simple noun (*men*) or a noun with its modifiers (*the men from the Health Department*) that forms the subject, object, or complement in a clause. (See 8a 1.)

objective complement See *complement.*

parallelism Words, phrases, or clauses that are similar in grammatical form and that perform the same function in the sentence:

> On my vacation I'm going *to hike, to swim,* and *to climb.*

(See 14a.)

participle The base verb combined with *-ing* (*present participle*) or *-ed* and other endings (*past participle*) to form adjectivals (*the flooding river; the flooded bank*) or to form a verb phrase (*was flooding*). (See also *aspect; tense.*) (See 9b and 9c.)

passive voice See *voice.*

past tense See *tense.*

perfect aspect See *aspect.*

periodic sentence   A sentence that builds to the core idea through modifying phrases or clauses:

> Water is a universal symbol. Tamed and trickling out of the tap, softened and fluoridated, warmed in the boiler by fires burning million-year-old oil, it is still not quite a commodity.
> —Elizabeth Janeway

(See 13a 2.)

personal pronoun   See *pronoun.*

phrase   A combination of words lacking subject and predicate that functions as subject, predicate, modifier, or other unit in the sentence. See also *noun phrase; prepositional phrase; verb phrase.* (See 7b.)

predicate   That part of the sentence that makes a statement about the subject. (See 7b and 7c.)

predicate adjective   An adjective that follows one of the forms of *be* or another linking verb like *become, taste,* and *smell:*

> The water is *muddy.*
> After a storm the water becomes *calm.*
> The water smells *foul.*

See also *complement.* (See 7b and 7c.)

predicate nominative   A nominal that serves as a subjective complement. See also *complement.*

preposition   A word or phrase (*of, to, beyond,* and *instead of*) that combines with a noun or pronoun to modify another part of the clause. (See 9e.)

prepositional phrase   A preposition and its object (*to the west; of the boat; beyond the horizon*). (See 9e.)

present tense   See *tense.*

progressive aspect   See *aspect.*

pronoun   Words that replace nouns and have separate forms to distinguish their use as subject, object, or possessive (*I, my, mine, me, we, our, them*) and to distinguish gender (*he, she, it*) and number (*he, she, it, they*). *Personal pronouns* identify people or things. *Relative pronouns* (*who, whoever, which, whichever, that*) introduce certain dependent clauses. *Interrogative pronouns* (*who, what, which*) begin questions. *Indefinite pronouns* (*some, everybody*) do not specify particular persons or objects. *Reflexive pronouns* refer to the noun or pronoun acting as the subject (*I myself*) or show that the subject and object of the clause are the same (*I washed myself*). The *reciprocal pronouns each other* and *one another* express mutual relationship. (See 8b.)

proper noun   See *noun.*

reflexive pronoun   See *pronoun.*

relative pronoun   See *pronoun.*

restrictive modifier   A phrase or clause that gives essential information:

> The men *who drank the water* are from the Health Department. [*adjectival clause*]
> *Drinking the water,* they noticed a slightly bitter taste. [*participial phrase*]
> They found increased pollution *when they tested the water downstream.* [*adverbial clause*]

See also *nonrestrictive modifier.* (See 7c 2 and 22a.)

sentence   A statement, a question, a command, a request, or an exclamation containing subject and predicate and making a complete statement. (See 7a, 7b, and 7c.)

simple sentence   A single independent clause and its word or phrasal modifiers:

> The green book has a torn cover.

(See 7d.)

squinting modifier   A modifier misplaced between two words, both of which it seems to modify:

> People who watch television *rarely* read much.

(See 20b.)

subject   The topic of a sentence about which something is usually predicated or declared. (See 7b.)

subjective complement   See *complement.*

subjunctive mood   See *mood.*

subordinate clause   See *dependent clause.*

subordinating conjunction   See *conjunction.*

tense   The feature of the verb that shows the time of the action. Verbs in the *present tense* and *past tense* show, respectively, that the action is occurring at the time the speaker is talking or occurred in the past or began then. See also *aspect; future tense; verb.* (See 9a 2 and 9b 3.)

transitive verb   In the active voice, *transitive verbs* take direct objects that receive the action (*The dog bit the man*). In the passive voice, this object becomes the subject of the sentence (*The man was bitten by the dog*). *Intransitive verbs* (*I ran*) do not require objects but may take complements (*I ran into the house*). See also *verb.* (See 9a 1.)

verb   Words that help to make statements or predications about nouns or pronouns. *Main* or *finite verbs* (*walk, see, eat, go*) show the present tense sometimes through inflections or word endings (*she walks*), sometimes without inflection (*I walk*). *Regular verbs* add *-d* or *-ed* to form the past tense. *Irregular verbs* change the base word or finite verb to show present tense, past tense, present participle, or past participle (*lie, lay, lying, lain*). See also *transitive verb; linking verb.* (See 9a.)

verb phrase   Primary auxiliaries (forms of *have* and *be*) and modal auxiliaries (*must, should, will,* and so on) combine with the present or past participle to create verb phrases (*have run, must have run, must have been running, will have been running*). Modal auxiliaries combine with the base or infinitive form (*must run, should run, will run*). See also *auxiliary.* (See 9b.)

voice   The feature of the verb that indicates whether the subject is performing or receiving the action. In the *active voice,* the subject performs the action of the verb (*The ball struck the net*). In the *passive voice,* the subject is the receiver of the verb (*The net was struck by the ball*). (See 9a 3 and 18a 7.)

ACKNOWLEDGMENTS

Glenn Grube. "Mild Protest at the DMV." Reprinted by permission.

Patricia Skovran. Annotations on Glenn Grube, "Mild Protest at the DMV." Reprinted by permission.

Webster's New World Dictionary Third College Edition, © 1988. Sample dictionary listings for the words *average* and *horizon* used by permission of the publisher, New World Dictionaries, a division of Simon & Schuster Inc., New York.

Oxford English Dictionary, Second Edition, Oxford University Press, Oxford, England, 1989. Sample dictionary listings for the words *fogle* and *fogle-drawing* used by permission.

Webster's Ninth New Collegiate Dictionary © 1990 by Merriam-Webster Inc., publisher of the Merriam-Webster dictionaries. Sample dictionary listing for the word *yellow* used by permission.

Richard Moran. "Slums Need to Be Improved First, Then Prisons." *Los Angeles Times,* January 7, 1986. Reprinted by permission of the author.

Brenda Wahler. "Let's Enact Comparable Worth." Reprinted by permission.

Library of Congress Subject Headings, 12th edition. Washington, DC: Library of Congress, 1988. Vol. 1, p. 737. Sample LCSH entry.

Social Sciences Index, vol. 15, April 1988–March 1989, The H. W. Wilson Company, New York. Sample entry reprinted by permission.

New York Times Index, vol. 73. Copyright © 1985 by The New York Times Company. Sample entry reprinted by permission.

Historical Abstracts data-base, Dialog file 39, © 1990, ABC-CL10, Inc. Sample item reprinted by permission of Dialog Information Services, Inc., and ABC-CL10, Inc.

Glenn Grube. "Pain and Death in Emily Dickinson's Poetry." Reprinted by permission.

Emily Dickinson. Poems 241, 252, and 384 (portion). From *The Complete Poems of Emily Dickinson,* edited by Thomas H. Johnson. Copyright by Little, Brown and Company, Publishers. Reprinted courtesy of the publisher.

Sheila Roxanne Woody. "Ethics of Nonhuman Animal Experimentation." Reprinted by permission.

Acknowledgments

Owen T. Su. "Regulation of Gene Expression: The Role of Long Terminal Repeats." Reprinted by permission.

Robert F. Kidd and Ellen F. Chayet. "Why Do Victims Fail to Report? The Psychology of Criminal Victimization," *Journal of Social Issues* 40 (1984): 41–42, 48–49. Published by the Society for the Psychological Study of Social Issues, Ann Arbor, MI. Reprinted by permission.

INDEX

Index

Index

Index

Parts of speech (*Continued*)
see also Adjective; Adverb; Articles; Conjunction; Determiners; Noun; Preposition; Pronoun; Verb
party, person, G15
Passive voice, defined, G31
  misuses, 245–46
  uses, 233, 246
  see also Voice
past, passed, 451
Past participle, 174
Past perfect and progressive tense and aspect, 183–84, G22, G31
  and sequence of tenses, 320–22
Past tense, 176, G31
  and sequence of tenses, 320–22
Pentad (Kenneth Burke), in literary analysis, 751–54
Perfect aspect, of verbs, 183–84, G28
Period
  with abbreviations, 436–37
  with indirect question, 362
  with statement of fact, 362
  with unemphatic request or command, 362
Periodic sentence, 251–54, G29
person, individual, G15
person, party, G15
Person shifts in, 315–16
Personal essay, 747–48
  see also Essay
Personal names
  abbreviations, 436–37
  capitalization, 432–33
Personal pronoun, 165, 214–18, G29
Personification, 494–96
Persuasion, defined, 530, 561–62
  appeal to character, 569–70
  appeal to emotion, 569–70
  appeal to reason, 564–68
Persuasive essay, defined, 3, 8–9
  audience, 562–63
  focus, 563–64
  organization
    deductive, 565–66
    inductive, 567–68
  parts of essay, 571
    conclusion, 571, 588
    confirmation, 571, 574, 584
    introduction, 571, 572
    narration, 571, 572

    refutation, 571, 576
    thesis statement, 571, 574–75
  see also Essay
phenomena, phenomenon, G15
Phrase, defined, 153–55, G29
  function in sentence, 153–54
  misplaced, 344–45
  see also Absolute phrase; Noun phrase; Prepositional phrase; Verb: verb phrase
Phrase reduction, 278–79
  see also Clause reduction
Pitch of voice. *See* Intonation
Place names
  abbreviations, 438
  capitalization, 433
  plurals, 456
Plagiarism, 667–69
Planning the paper, 47–59, 72–75
  with a word processor, 829
plenty, G16
Plot, in literary analysis, 749
Plurals
  foreign words, 457
  letters of alphabet, 401–402
  nouns, 161–62, 456
  place names, 456
  pronouns, 166–67, 214
  verbs, 176
Poetry
  punctuation in quoting, 414
  punctuation of titles, 426
Point-at-issue, in persuasive argument, 563–64
Poole's Index to Periodical Literature, 633
Popular Periodicals Index, 633
Possessive case, defined, 166, G23
  noun, 160
  pronoun, 166–67, 216
  see also Apostrophe; Possessive noun
Possessive noun, as antecedent, 216
Possessive pronouns, defined, 163, G29
  and ambiguity, 216
  see also Apostrophe
Post hoc fallacy, 605
Precising definition, 127–28
Predicate, of sentence, defined, 149–50, G29
  expanding the predicate, 236–37
  faulty predication, 337–38

I-16

Index

Index